Labor Markets and Economic Development

As developing and transition economies enter the next phase of reforms, labor market issues increasingly come to the fore. With the increased competition from globalization, the discussion is shifting to the need for greater labor market flexibility, appropriate labor market regulation, and the creation of "good" jobs. Moreover, the greater actual and perceived insecurity in labor markets has generated a new agenda on how to structure safety nets. The older questions about the nature and links between the formal and informal labor markets reappear with new dimensions and significance. In addition, it is clear that an accurate understanding of how labor markets function is essential if we are to analyze alternative policy proposals in the wake of these concerns.

With this background, Cornell University and the International Policy Center at the Gerald R. Ford School of Public Policy of the University of Michigan hosted a major international conference—"Labor Markets in Developing and Transition Economies: Emerging Policy and Analytical Issues" in May 2007, at the Ford School in Ann Arbor, Michigan. This book presents theoretical, empirical, and policy chapters, most of which consist of revised lectures that were presented at the conference. The volume is divided into four key sections: (I) Employment, Poverty, and Labor Market Dynamics, (II) Formality, Informality, and Labor Market Regulation, (III) Trade and Labor, and (IV) Human Capital, Productivity, and Gender.

Bringing together the latest research from leading labor economists, this book will be of interest to research and postgraduate students of labor, development, and transition economics, as well as to policy analysts and NGOs.

Ravi Kanbur is T. H. Lee Professor of World Affairs, International Professor of Applied Economics and Management, and Professor of Economics at Cornell University

Jan Svejnar is Director of the International Policy Center at the Gerald R. Ford School of Public Policy, the Everett E. Berg Professor of Business Administration, and Professor of Economics and Public Policy at the University of Michigan.

Routledge Studies in Development Economics

1 **Economic Development in the Middle East**
Rodney Wilson

2 **Monetary and Financial Policies in Developing Countries**
Growth and stabilization
Akhtar Hossain and Anis Chowdhury

3 **New Directions in Development Economics**
Growth, environmental concerns and government in the 1990s
Edited by Mats Lundahl and Benno J. Ndulu

4 **Financial Liberalization and Investment**
Kanhaya L. Gupta and Robert Lensink

5 **Liberalization in the Developing World**
Institutional and economic changes in Latin America, Africa and Asia
Edited by Alex E. Fernández Jilberto and André Mommen

6 **Financial Development and Economic Growth**
Theory and experiences from developing countries
Edited by Niels Hermes and Robert Lensink

7 **The South African Economy**
Macroeconomic prospects for the medium term
Finn Tarp and Peter Brixen

8 **Public Sector Pay and Adjustment**
Lessons from five countries
Edited by Christopher Colclough

9 **Europe and Economic Reform in Africa**
Structural adjustment and economic diplomacy
Obed O. Mailafia

10 **Post-apartheid Southern Africa**
Economic challenges and policies for the future
Edited by Lennart Petersson

11 **Financial Integration and Development**
Liberalization and reform in sub-Saharan Africa
Ernest Aryeetey and Machiko Nissanke

12 **Regionalization and Globalization in the Modern World Economy**
Perspectives on the Third World and transitional economies
Edited by Alex E. Fernández Jilberto and André Mommen

13 The African Economy
Policy, institutions and the future
Steve Kayizzi-Mugerwa

14 Recovery from Armed Conflict in Developing Countries
Edited by Geoff Harris

15 Small Enterprises and Economic Development
The dynamics of micro and small enterprises
Carl Liedholm and Donald C. Mead

16 The World Bank
New agendas in a changing world
Michelle Miller-Adams

17 Development Policy in the Twenty-First Century
Beyond the post-Washington consensus
Edited by Ben Fine, Costas Lapavitsas and Jonathan Pincus

18 State-Owned Enterprises in the Middle East and North Africa
Privatization, performance and reform
Edited by Merih Celasun

19 Finance and Competitiveness in Developing Countries
Edited by José María Fanelli and Rohinton Medhora

20 Contemporary Issues in Development Economics
Edited by B.N. Ghosh

21 Mexico Beyond NAFTA
Edited by Martín Puchet Anyul and Lionello F. Punzo

22 Economies in Transition
A guide to China, Cuba, Mongolia, North Korea and Vietnam at the turn of the twenty-first century
Ian Jeffries

23 Population, Economic Growth and Agriculture in Less Developed Countries
Nadia Cuffaro

24 From Crisis to Growth in Africa?
Edited by Mats Lundal

25 The Macroeconomics of Monetary Union
An analysis of the CFA franc zone
David Fielding

26 Endogenous Development
Networking, innovation, institutions and cities
Antonio Vasquez-Barquero

27 Labour Relations in Development
Edited by Alex E. Fernández Jilberto and Marieke Riethof

28 Globalization, Marginalization and Development
Edited by S. Mansoob Murshed

29 Programme Aid and Development
Beyond conditionality
Howard White and Geske Dijkstra

30 Competitiveness Strategy in Developing Countries
A manual for policy analysis
Edited by Ganeshan Wignaraja

31 The African Manufacturing Firm
An analysis based on firm surveys in sub-Saharan Africa
Dipak Mazumdar and Ata Mazaheri

32 Trade Policy, Growth and Poverty in Asian Developing Countries
Edited by Kishor Sharma

33 International Competitiveness, Investment and Finance
A case study of India
Edited by A. Ganesh Kumar, Kunal Sen and Rajendra R. Vaidya

34 The Pattern of Aid Giving
The impact of good governance on
development assistance
Eric Neumayer

**35 New International Poverty
Reduction Strategies**
*Edited by Jean-Pierre Cling,
Mireille Razafindrakoto and
François Roubaud*

36 Targeting Development
Critical perspectives on the
Millennium Development Goals
*Edited by Richard Black
and Howard White*

**37 Essays on Balance of Payments
Constrained Growth**
Theory and evidence
*Edited by J.S.L. McCombie and
A.P. Thirlwall*

**38 The Private Sector After
Communism**
New entrepreneurial firms in
transition economies
*Jan Winiecki, Vladimir Benacek and
Mihaly Laki*

**39 Information Technology
and Development**
A new paradigm for delivering the
internet to rural areas in developing
countries
Jeffrey James

40 The Economics of Palestine
Economic policy and institutional
reform for a viable Palestine state
*Edited by David Cobham and
Nu'man Kanafani*

41 Development Dilemmas
The methods and political ethics of
growth policy
Melvin Ayogu and Don Ross

**42 Rural Livelihoods and Poverty
Reduction Policies**
*Edited by Frank Ellis and
H. Ade Freeman*

**43 Beyond Market-Driven
Development**
Drawing on the experience of Asia
and Latin America
*Edited by Makoto Noguchi and
Costas Lapavitsas*

**44 The Political Economy of
Reform Failure**
*Edited by Mats Lundahl and
Michael L. Wyzan*

**45 Overcoming Inequality in Latin
America**
Issues and challenges for the
twenty-first century
*Edited by Ricardo Gottschalk and
Patricia Justino*

**46 Trade, Growth and Inequality in
the Era of Globalization**
*Edited by Kishor Sharma and
Oliver Morrissey*

47 Microfinance
Perils and prospects
Edited by Jude L. Fernando

**48 The IMF, World Bank and
Policy Reform**
*Edited by Alberto Paloni and
Maurizio Zanardi*

49 Managing Development
Globalization, economic
restructuring and social policy
Edited by Junji Nakagawa

50 Who Gains from Free Trade?
Export-led growth, inequality and
poverty in Latin America
*Edited by Rob Vos, Enrique Ganuza,
Samuel Morley, and
Sherman Robinson*

51 **Evolution of Markets and Institutions**
A study of an emerging economy
Murali Patibandla

52 **The New Famines**
Why famines exist in an era of globalization
Edited by Stephen Devereux

53 **Development Ethics at work**
Explorations—1960–2002
Denis Goulet

54 **Law Reform in Developing and Transitional States**
Edited by Tim Lindsey

55 **The Asymmetries of Globalization**
Edited by Pan A. Yotopoulos and Donato Romano

56 **Ideas, Policies and Economic Development in the Americas**
Edited by Esteban Pérez-Caldentey and Matias Vernengo

57 **European Union Trade Politics and Development**
Everything but arms unravelled
Edited by Gerrit Faber and Jan Orbie

58 **Membership Based Organizations of the Poor**
Edited by Martha Chen, Renana Jhabvala, Ravi Kanbur and Carol Richards

59 **The Politics of Aid Selectivity**
Good governance criteria in World Bank, U.S. and Dutch Development Assistance
Wil Hout

60 **Economic Development, Education and Transnational Corporations**
Mark Hanson

61 **Achieving Economic Development in the Era of Globalization**
Shalendra Sharma

62 **Sustainable Development and Free Trade**
Shawkat Alam

63 **The Impact of International Debt Relief**
Geske Dijkstra

64 **Europe's Troubled Region**
Economic development, institutional reform and social welfare in the Western Balkans
William Bartlett

65 **Work, Female Empowerment and Economic Development**
Sara Horrell, Hazel Johnson and Paul Mosley

66 **The Chronically Poor in Rural Bangladesh**
Livelihood constraints and capabilities
Pk. Md. Motiur Rahman, Noriatsu Matsui and Yukio Ikemoto

67 **Public-Private Partnerships in Health Care in India**
Lessons for developing countries
A. Venkat Raman and James Warner Björkman

68 **Rural Poverty and Income Dynamics in Asia and Africa**
Edited by Keijiro Otsuka, Jonna P. Estudillo and Yasuyuki Sawada

69 **Microfinance: A Reader**
David Hulme and Thankom Arun

70 **AID and International NGOs**
Dirk-Jan Koch

71 Development Macroeconomics
Essays in memory of Anita Ghatak
*Edited by Subrata Ghatak and
Paul Levine*

**72 Taxation in a Low
Income Economy**
The case of Mozambique
Channing Arndt and Finn Tarp

**73 Labor Markets and Economic
Development**
*Edited by Ravi Kanbur and
Jan Svejnar*

Labor Markets and Economic Development

Edited by Ravi Kanbur and Jan Svejnar

Routledge
Taylor & Francis Group

LONDON AND NEW YORK

First published 2009
by Routledge
2 Park Square, Milton Park, Abingdon, Oxon OX14 4RN

Simultaneously published in the USA and Canada
by Routledge
711 Third Avenue, New York, NY 10017

*Routledge is an imprint of the Taylor & Francis Group,
an informa business*

© 2009 selection and editorial matter; Ravi Kanbur and Jan Svejnar;
individual chapters; the contributors

Typeset in Times New Roman by
RefineCatch Limited, Bungay, Suffolk

First issued in paperback in 2013

British Library Cataloguing in Publication Data
A catalogue record for this book is available from the British Library

Library of Congress Cataloging-in-Publication Data
    Labour markets and economic development / edited by Ravi Kanbur
and Jan Svejnar.
        p. cm.
    Revisions of papers presented at the conference held in Ann Arbor,
Mich. in May 2007.
    Includes bibliographical references and index.
    1. Labor market—Congresses.   Economic development—
Congresses. 3. Wages—Congresses.   I. Kanbur, Ravi.   II. Svejnar,
Jan.
    HD5701.3.L328 2009
    331.1—dc22
                                                            2008036735

ISBN13: 978–0–415–74357–0 (pbk)
ISBN13: 978–0–415–77741–4 (hbk)
ISBN13: 978–0–203–88169–9 (pbk)

Contents

Acknowledgements   xii
List of tables   xiii
List of figures   xxi
List of contributors   xxv

1 **Overview**   1
RAVI KANBUR AND JAN SVEJNAR

PART I
Employment, poverty, and labor market dynamics   13

2 **Does employment generation really matter for poverty reduction?**   15
CATALINA GUTIERREZ, PIERELLA PACI, CARLO ORECCHIA, AND PIETER SERNEELS

3 **Employment elasticity in organized manufacturing in India**   40
DIPAK MAZUMDAR AND SANDIP SARKAR

4 **Wage determination and wage inequality inside a Russian firm in late transition: evidence from personnel data, 1997–2002**   62
THOMAS DOHMEN, HARTMUT LEHMANN, AND MARK E. SCHAFFER

5 **Education and youth unemployment in South Africa**   90
DAVID LAM, MURRAY LEIBBRANDT, AND CECIL MLATSHENI

6 **Analysis of attrition patterns in the Turkish Household Labor Force Survey, 2000–2002**   110
İNSAN TUNALI

x   *Contents*

PART II

Formality, informality, and labor market regulation   137

7   Monopsonistic competition in formal and
    informal labor markets   139
    TED TO

8   Entrepreneurial entry in a developing economy   157
    JOHN BENNETT AND SAUL ESTRIN

9   Multiple-job-holding in Tanzania   176
    THEIS THEISEN

10 Regulation of entry, informality, and policy
    complementarities   197
    MARIANO BOSCH

11 Can social programs reduce productivity and
    growth? A hypothesis for Mexico   218
    SANTIAGO LEVY

12 Minimum wages in Kenya   236
    MABEL ANDALÓN AND CARMEN PAGÉS

13 Labor market flexibility: insurance versus
    efficiency and the Indian experience   269
    ERROL D'SOUZA

14 Labor productivity growth, informal wage, and
    capital mobility: a general equilibrium analysis   286
    SUGATA MARJIT AND SAIBAL KAR

PART III

Trade and labor   299

15 Trade and labor standards: new empirical evidence   301
    YIAGADEESEN SAMY AND VIVEK H. DEHEJIA

16 Do foreign-owned firms pay more? Evidence from
    the Indonesian manufacturing sector   319
    ANN E. HARRISON AND JASON SCORSE

17 Gender inequality in the labor market during
economic transition: changes in India's manufacturing sector 341
NIDHIYA MENON AND YANA VAN DER MEULEN RODGERS

PART IV
Human capital, productivity, and gender 365

18 Multidimensional human capital, wages, and
endogenous employment status in Ghana 367
NIELS-HUGO BLUNCH

19 Wage convergence and inequality after unification:
(East) Germany in transition 387
JOHANNES GERNANDT AND FRIEDHELM PFEIFFER

20 Child work and schooling costs in rural Northern India 405
GAUTAM HAZARIKA AND ARJUN SINGH BEDI

21 Glass ceilings, sticky floors, or sticky doors?
A quantile regression approach to exploring gender wage gaps
in Sri Lanka 426
DILENI GUNEWARDENA, DARSHI ABEYRATHNA,
AMALIE ELLAGALA, KAMANI RAJAKARUNA, AND
SHOBANA RAJENDRAN

22 Skills, training, and enterprise performance: survey
evidence from transition countries in Central and Eastern Europe 449
JOE EMANUELE COLOMBANO AND LIBOR KRKOSKA

23 Exploring gender wage "discrimination" in South
Africa, 1995–2004: a quantile regression approach 468
MIRACLE NTULI

24 The determinants of female labor supply in Belarus 496
FRANCESCO PASTORE AND ALINA VERASHCHAGINA

25 Islands through the glass ceiling? Evidence of
gender wage gaps in Madagascar and Mauritius 521
CHRISTOPHE J. NORDMAN AND FRANÇOIS-CHARLES WOLFF

Index 545

Acknowledgements

The Editors would like to acknowledge the financial support of Cornell University, the International Policy Center at the Gerald R. Ford School of Public Policy of the University of Michigan, and the International Development Research Centre (IDRC). Sue Snyder at Cornell and Faith Vlcek at Michigan provided excellent administrative support without which the conference and the volume would not have happened.

Tables

2.1	Sample description	22
2.2	Percent change in headcount ratio and aggregate growth	27
2.3	Poverty changes and the employment/productivity intensity of growth	28
2.4	Poverty changes and sectoral employment/ productivity intensity	28
2.5	Poverty changes and the sectoral employment intensity of growth	29
2.6	Poverty changes and the sectoral productivity intensity of growth	30
2.7	Instrumental variable regression. Changes in poverty and the sectoral employment/productivity intensity of growth	33
2.A1	List of countries and spells	36
2.A2	Other countries in the sample that have some outlier observations	38
2.A3	Correlation between measures of employment and productivity-intensive growth	39
3.1	Growth rate of value added and employment elasticity	42
3.2	Proportionate growth rates of selected variables for four periods	49
3.3	The relative importance of the wage–employment trade-off and the DRER effect	53
3.4	Proportionate growth rates for the public and the private sectors, 1986/7–1994/5	54
3.5	Classification of industries by technology level and exposure to trade, 1991	55
3.6	Trends in selected variables by industry groups 1986/7–1996/7	56
4.1	Composition of workforce (in %), 1997–2002	68
4.2	Hiring and separation rates (in %), 1997–2002	69
4.3	Hiring and separation and turnover rates (in %) in sample of industrial firms in the region, 1998–2001	70

4.4   Determinants of wages, 1997   72
4.5   Shares of monthly compensation components   73
4.6   Transition probabilities between quintiles of real
       wages in 1997 and 2002 (in %); all continuous employees   76
4.7   Real wage growth, 1997–2002   77
4.8   Real wage growth 1997–2002 by employee category   80
4.9   Differences between ages in firm and average wages
       in sample of industrial firms in the region in 1997 rubles,
       1998–2002   81
4.10   Evolution of earnings inequality measured by Gini
       coefficients   83
4.11   Gini decomposition by income source   84
4.12   Contributions of source incomes on inequality   85
4.13   General Entropy Index (GEI) and its decomposition
       into within and between parts   85
5.1   Population percentages of youth aged 14–22, Cape Town
       versus the rest of South Africa   93
5.2   Levels of education of 14–22-year-olds, Cape Town,
       and the rest of South Africa   93
5.3   Employment status of 15–22-year-old youth in
       Cape Town and the rest of South Africa, 2001 census   94
5.4   Percentage enrolled and grade attainment, Cape Area Panel
       Study wave 1, 2002   97
5.5   Percentage currently working, worked in last 12 months,
       and ever worked, Cape Area Panel Study wave 1, 2002   100
5.6   Descriptive statistics for variables in probit regressions,
       CAPS respondents out of school 0–48 months, 2002–2006   105
5.7   Probit regressions for working in months after
       leaving school, Cape area panel study   106
6.1   Summary statistics on the working samples (initial
       visit). Household heads, age 20–54   117
6.2   FGM tests of the null hypothesis that attrition is
       ignorable versus not: Signs (p-values) from the probit
       estimates for model 5 reported in Tables 6.A3–6.A5   120
6.3   Attrition patterns as of 3, 12, and 15 months,
       households with 20–54-year-old heads. Qualitative results
       from the probit estimates for model 5 reported in
       Tables 6.A3–6.A5   121
6.4   BGLW Tests of the null hypothesis that attrition is
       ignorable versus not: Signs (p-values) from the probit
       estimates for model II reported in Tables 6.A6–6.A7   123
6.A1   Rotation plan of the HLFS 2000–2 and the observation
       plan of the present study   128
6.A2   Risk sets and proportion of attritors [$p(A) = 1$] by *observation
       unit*, attrition type [A(m)] and survey round   129

6.A3 Probit estimates of attrition at 3 months,
   households with 20–54-year-old heads. Dependent variable:
   $A(3) = 1$ if attritor, $= 0$ else   130

6.A4 Probit estimates of attrition at 12 months, households
   with 20–54-year-old heads. Dependent variable:
   $A(12) = 1$ if attritor, $= 0$ else   131

6.A5 Probit estimates of attrition at 15 months,
   households with 20–54-year-old heads. Dependent variable:
   $A(15) = 1$ if attritor, $= 0$ else   132

6.A6 Probit estimates of the 1st visit participation outcome,
   20–54 year-old household heads. Dependent variable:
   LFP $= 1$ if participant, $= 0$ if not   133

6.A7 Probit estimates of the first visit unemployment outcome,
   20–54-year-old household heads. Dependent variable:
   unemp $= 1$ if participant, $= 0$ if not (conditional on LFP $=1$)   135

8.1   Profits at $t = 2$ when A informal at $t = 1$ ($\beta = 1$; $\rho > 0$)   169

9.1   Definitions and descriptive statistics of variables in
   the participation functions   186

9.2   Definitions and descriptive statistics of variables in
   the earnings function. Sub-sample of formal private sector
   workers, $n = 58$ 187

9.3   Estimation results for the earnings function   187

9.4   Estimation results for structural-form logit model   189

9.5   Estimated income and wage coefficients when different
   (groups of) taste shifters are left out of the participation
   equation   191

9.A1 Sample means by sector for correlates in the multinomial
   logit model for sector allocation of workers   195

9.A2 Estimation results for multinomial logit model   196

10.1   Comparison between FLP and base-line model   211

10.2   Increase in start-up costs   212

11.1   Mexico's labor force, 2006 (thousands of workers)   219

11.2   INEGI versus IMSS registries of workers and firms, 2003   228

11.3   Social programs and the profitability of investment options   230

12.1   Gazetted monthly basic minimum wages for
   agricultural industry, 1997–2004, Kenyan shillings   240

12.2   Gazetted monthly basic minimum wages for non-
   agricultural industry in urban areas excluding housing allowance
   (general order), 1998–2000 and 2002–2004, Kenyan shillings   241

12.3   Descriptive statistics   245

12.4   Minimum wage indicators: fraction below, fraction at
   MW, fraction affected, and Kaitz index   247

12.5   Minimum wage indicators by gender   248

12.6   Minimum wage indicators by education level   249

12.7   Minimum wage indicators by age   250

12.8   Minimum wage indicators by location   251
12.9   Minimum wages relative to the median for all
        salaried workers 1998/9   253
12.10   Effect of minimum wages on wages. Dependent
        variable: Natural logarithm of real wages   258
12.11   Structure of employment and minimum to median
        wage ratio for each occupation–location pair   263
12.12   Structure of employment and ratio of minimum to
        median wage (Median wage for all salaried employees)   264
13.1   Estimated effect of various factors on log registered
        manufacturing output per capita   274
13.2   Efficiency wages when firms and workers are
        opportunistic   281
14.A1   State-wise skill concentration rank in India   295
14.A2   State-wise real GVA/worker, real fixed assets and real
        wage (informal)   297
15.1   Estimated coefficients for equation (3)—developing
        countries (1990–2001)   309
15.2   Labor standards and trade openness—developing
        countries (1990–2001)   310
15.3   Child labor and openness to trade (developing
        countries 1990–2001)—OLS and IV estimates   312
16.1   Summary statistics 1990   323
16.2   Summary statistics 1999   324
16.3   Dependent variable: log average wage of unskilled
        workers (1990–9)   327
16.4   Dependent variable: log average wages of skilled
        workers (1990–9)   328
16.5   Dependent variable: log average wages of unskilled
        workers (1995–7)   329
16.6   Dependent variable: log average wages of unskilled
        workers (1995–7)   330
16.7   Dependent variable: log average wages of skilled
        workers (1995–7)   331
16.8   Dependent variable: log average wages of skilled
        workers (1995–7)   332
16.9   Dependent variable: log average wage of unskilled
        workers (only firms with changes in foreign ownership
        1995–7)   334
16.10   Dependent variable: log average wages of skilled
        workers (only firms with changes in foreign ownership
        1995–7)   335
16.11   Dependent variable: log average wage of unskilled
        workers (1995–7) (reduced sample: only textile, apparel,
        and footwear industries)   336

16.12 Dependent variable: log average wage of skilled
      workers (1995–7) (reduced sample: only textile, apparel, and
      footwear industries)   337
17.1 Employment structure in India by gender, 1983–2004 (in %)   346
17.2 Female–male wage ratios in India's manufacturing
      sector, 1983–2004 (in %)   346
17.3 Mean female position in the male residual wage
      distribution, 1983–2004 (in %)   348
17.4 Residual wage dispersion for men, 1983–2004 (in log
      points)   349
17.5 Oaxaca–Blinder decomposition of male–female
      wage gap (in log points)   352
17.6 Annual rates of change in the male–female wage gap
      (in %)   353
17.7 Test of male–female residual wage gaps and trade
      competition (in log points; standard errors in
      parentheses)   357
17.A1 Descriptive and regression analyses: variables and
      data sources   360
17.A2 Concordance between ISIC revision 2, NIC 1970,
      and NIC 1998 codes   361
17.A3 Means and standard deviations for wage earners in
      manufacturing, 1983–2004   362
17.A4 Coefficient estimates from male wage regressions
      (in log points; standard errors in parentheses)   363
18.1 Marginal effects for education and literacy and
      numeracy from employment status equation   375
18.2 Marginal effects for education and literacy and
      numeracy from wage equation   377
18.A1 Descriptive statistics for employment status from
      estimation samples (employment status equations)   385
18.A2 Descriptive statistics for wages, education, and
      literacy and numeracy (wage equations)   385
19.1 Mean real gross hourly wages (€) in the four samples   391
19.2 Descriptive statistics of socio-economic
      characteristics, 1992 and 2005   394
19.3 Wage convergence and wage inequality: East German
      workers, West German workers, and West German statistical
      twins   398
19.4 Wage convergence in the groups of migrants and
      commuters   399
19.5 Composition, price and residual effects, 1994–2005   402
20.1 Work participation rates (per cent) of
      10–14-year-old children in rural Uttar Pradesh and
      Bihar, 1997–8   413

20.2	School enrollment rates (per cent) of 10–14-year-old children in rural Uttar Pradesh and Bihar, 1997–8	413
20.3	Full sample descriptive statistics	414
20.4	Determinants of work probit marginal effects	416
20.5	Determinants of school enrollment probit marginal effects	418
20.6	Select multinomial logit estimates and marginal effects	419
20.7	Determinants of extra-household and intra-household work probit marginal effects	421
20.8	Determinants of economic and domestic work probit marginal effects	423
21.1	Raw and estimated wage gaps, 1996/7 and 2003/4	432
21.2	Raw wage gaps as % of male gap, 1996/97 & 2003/04	433
21.3	Unexplained gaps as a % of the wage gap	441
21.4	Summary of results, sticky floors and glass ceilings	444
22.1	Correlation between human capital measures	453
22.2	Extent of training by firm ownership, size, and location	455
22.3	Training by firm type and human capital	457
22.4	Skill perception by firm type and human capital	459
22.5	Relationship between sales growth, enterprise training and human capital	461
22.6	Relationship between employment growth, enterprise training and country-level human capital	463
23.1	Descriptive statistics for African employees by gender (1995, 1999, and 2004)	476
23.2a	Quantile regressions for African men and women's log real wages (1995)	480
23.2b	Quantile regressions for African men and women's log real wages (1999)	483
23.2c	Quantile regressions for African men and women's log real wages (2004)	486
23.3	Gender gaps (observed and counterfactual) 1995, 1999, and 2004	490
24.1	Maximum likelihood estimates for the selectivity corrected female wage equation. The role of household characteristics	504
24.2	Maximum likelihood estimates for the selectivity corrected female wage equation. The role of the household's income	507
24.3	Maximum likelihood estimates for the selectivity corrected female wage equation. The role of regional characteristics	508
24.4	Structural female labor force participation model as based on Table 24.1	510

24.5	Structural female labor force participation model as based on Table 24.2	511
24.6	Wage elasticity of labor supply for different groups of women	512
24.A1	Definition of variables	517
24.A2	Descriptive statistics	519
25.1	Descriptive statistics of the workers	526
25.2	Descriptive statistics of the firms	528
25.3	Linear regressions of the log hourly wage rate	531
25.4	Decomposition analysis of the factors contributing to the log wage (in %)	534
25.5	Decomposition of the gender wage gap using OLS and fixed effects regression	535
25.6	Quantile regressions of the log hourly wage rate	538
25.7	Quantile decomposition of the gender wage gap	540

Figures

2.1	Empirical link between the components of per capita GDP, growth, and changes in poverty. Developing countries 1980–2002	23
2.2	Correlation of changes in poverty and in value added per capita with changes in output per worker for three sectors	25
2.3	Correlation of changes in poverty and in value added per capita with employment growth for three sectors	26
3.1	Employment and real GVA (1974–5 to 2004–5)	41
3.2	Wage–efficiency relationship	46
3.3	General equilibrium	47
4.1	Profitability (profit/sales in %)	65
4.2	Real monthly wage in thousand 1997 rubles	65
4.3	Real wage distributions in 1997	67
4.4	Distribution of basic real wage in rubles—all employees	71
4.5	Distribution of total real compensation in rubles—all employees	74
4.6	Real wage distributions in 2002	75
4.7	Real wage growth, 1997–2002	76
5.1	Transitions from school to work CAPS respondents age 23–25, 2005	98
5.2	Work and job search by months since left school. Males out of school at least 36 months	102
5.3	Work and job search by months since left school. Females out of school at least 36 months	104
7.1	Equilibrium number of employers	149
9.1	Consumer choice	179
9.2	Probability of participation in the informal sector as a function of virtual income	190
10.1	No formal sector	201
10.2	Formal and informal sectors	202
10.3	No informal sector	202
10.4	Equilibrium	208
10.5	Increase in start-up costs	209

10.6	Effects of start-up costs and monitoring of the size of the informal sector	213
10.7	Effects of start-up costs and monitoring on the unemployment rate	213
10.8	Effects of start-up cost and unemployment benefits on the size of the informal sector	214
10.9	Effects of start-up costs and unemployment benefits on the unemployment rate	214
11.1	Social security with a formal and an informal sector	222
11.2	The labor market with social security and social protection	224
12.1	Evolution of minimum wage, GDP per capita, and average wage in real terms	243
12.2	Ratio of minimum to average wage	243
12.3	Minimum wage level (relative to median wage for salaried population) and percentage of non-compliance by occupation–location pairs	254
12.4	Minimum wages in agricultural industry. Formal sector 1998/9: distribution of wages and minimum wages	255
12.5	Minimum wages in agricultural industry. Informal sector 1998/9: distribution of wages and minimum wages	255
12.6	Minimum wages in general order (urban areas). Formal sector 1998/9: distribution of wages and minimum wages	256
12.7	Minimum wages in general order. Informal sector 1998/9: distribution of wages and minimum wages	257
12.8	Minimum wage and structure of employment	261
13.1	Formal and informal contracts in registered firms	278
14.1	Determination of wage and rental rate	289
A15.1	Child labor and trade openness: developing countries (1990–2001)	315
A15.2	Civil liberties and trade openness: developing countries (1990–2001)	315
16.1	Non-compliance with the minimum wage laws 1990–1999	322
16.2	Real minimum wage in rupiahs (1990–1999)	322
16.3	Average real wages paid to unskilled workers in rupiahs (1990–1999)	323
16.4	Average real wages paid to skilled workers in rupiahs (1990–1999)	323
17.1	Trade ratios and female/male wage ratios, 1980–2004	345
19.1	GDP and unemployment in East Germany and migration to the West, 1991–2005	389
19.2	Wage convergence between 1992 and 2005: East Germans, migrants, and commuters compared to West Germans	392
19.3	Wage distributions for four groups of workers and selected years	393

19.4	Wage convergence of East German workers with their West German statistical twins between 2000 and 2005	399
19.5	The evolution of wage distributions for East and West German workers	401
21.1	Kernel density functions, pooled sample 1996/7 and 2003/4	434
21.2	Kernel density functions, public and private sectors, 1996/7 and 2003/4	435
21.3	Gender wage gap due to differences in coefficients, part time, occupation and industry dummies excluded, 1996/7	436
21.4	Gender wage gap due to differences in coefficients, part time, occupation and industry dummies excluded, 2003/4	437
21.5	Gender wage gap due to differences in coefficients, part time, occupation, and industry dummies included, 1996/7	438
21.6	Gender wage gap due to differences in coefficients, part time, occupation and industry dummies included, 2003/2004	439
23.1	Real wages for Africans by gender (1995–2005)	469
23.2	Sample delimitation process	475
23.3	Distribution of real wages for Africans by gender	478
24.1	Cross-country differences in attitudes towards the role of men and women in the household	499
24.2	Wage elasticity of labor supply by deciles of the log hourly wage distribution	513
25.1	The gender gap in Mauritius and Madagascar Islands	529

Contributors

Darshi Abeyrathna, B.A. (Peradeniya) is a Health Management Assistant at the Ministry of Health, Sri Lanka and M.A. Candidate in Economics at the University of Peradeniya, Sri Lanka.

Mabel Andalón is a Ph.D. student in the Department of Policy Analysis and Management at Cornell University. Her research fields include labor economics, health economics, and development economics. She is a Research Affiliate at IZA.

Arjun Singh Bedi is Professor in the Economics of Development Group at the Institute of Social Studies in The Hague. He has held positions at the University of Bonn and Columbia University. He holds degrees from St Stephen's College, Delhi University, and Tulane University, New Orleans.

John Bennett is Professor of Economics and Director of the Centre for Economic Development and Institutions, Brunel University. He was formerly at the University of Wales, Cardiff and Swansea, and has held visiting positions at Washington University (St Louis) and Queen's University at Kingston, Ontario. He has degrees from Cambridge and Sussex.

Niels-Hugo Blunch is Assistant Professor of Economics at Washington and Lee University and Research Fellow at IZA (Institute for the Study of Labor). He has been a consultant to the United Nations (UNICEF) and the World Bank and holds degrees from University of Aarhus, University of Southampton, and The George Washington University.

Mariano Bosch is an assistant professor at University of Alicante. He holds a Ph.D. from the London School of Economics. He has served as a consultant for the World Bank and the Inter American Development Bank.

Joe Emanuele Colombano is currently with the European Bank for Reconstruction and Development in London. Joe came to the EBRD after a five-year experience at the World Bank in Washington DC, where he worked on Eastern Europe and Central Asia. Joe graduated from Harvard University.

Vivek H. Dehejia is Associate Professor of Economics at Carleton University in Ottawa, Canada, and Research Fellow of CESifo in Munich, Germany. He holds a Ph.D. from Columbia University in New York. He has published in numerous scientific journals, and spoken and lectured widely around the world. Dehejia's research centres on debates around globalization and currency regimes, and on economic applications of choice theory.

Thomas Dohmen is Director of the Research Centre for Education and the Labour Market (ROA) and Professor of Education and the Labour Market in the Department of Economics and Business Administration of Maastricht University. He holds Masters Degrees in Economics from the University of Warwick (England) and Maastricht University and a doctoral degree from Maastricht University. He was formerly employed at IZA in Bonn.

Errol D'Souza is Professor of Economics at the Indian Institute of Management, Ahmedabad. He served earlier at the University of Mumbai as the Industrial Finance Corporation of India Chair Professor and is an alumnus of the Jawaharlal Nehru University.

Amalie Ellagala, B.A. (Peradeniya) is an M.A. Candidate at the Postgraduate Institute of Agriculture, University of Peradeniya, Sri Lanka.

Saul Estrin is Professor in the Managerial Economics and Strategy Group of the Department of Management at the London School of Economics. He was formerly the Addeco Professor of Business and Society at London Business School and research director of its Centre for New and Emerging Markets. He was educated at Cambridge and Sussex Universities and has worked as consultant for various multilateral agencies including the World Bank, EBRD and United Nations.

Johannes Gernandt studied economics at the University of Mannheim. In 2005 he joined the labour and human resources management department at the ZEW. His research centres on labour market issues such as wage inequality, entry wages, migration, and education.

Dileni Gunewardena, Ph.D. (American), B.A. (Peradeniya) is a Senior Lecturer in Economics at the University of Peradeniya, and Associate, Centre for Poverty Analysis, Sri Lanka. Her areas of research include the analysis of gender and ethnic wage differentials, poverty and inequality, and child malnutrition in Sri Lanka.

Catalina Gutierrez is a consultant for the Poverty Reduction and Development Effectiveness Group at World Bank. She has also worked at the Colombian Central Bank, at Fedesarrollo Research Center and as adviser for the Bogota Council. She holds a Masters and B.A in Economics from Universidad de los Andes (Colombia) and a Ph.D. from New York University.

Ann E. Harrison is a Professor of Agricultural and Resource Economics at the

University of California, Berkeley and a Research Associate at the National Bureau of Economic Research. Previously she taught at Columbia and Harvard University. She was also in the Young Professional Program at the World Bank. She holds degrees from the University of California, Berkeley, the University of Paris, and Princeton University.

Gautam Hazarika is at the School of Business of the University of Texas at Brownsville. He is jointly a Research Fellow at the Institute for the Study of Labor (IZA), Bonn. He holds degrees from Delhi University and the University of Rochester.

Ravi Kanbur is T. H. Lee Professor of World Affairs, International Professor of Applied Economics and Management, and Professor of Economics at Cornell University. He has served on the staff of the World Bank, including as the Chief Economist for Africa. He holds degrees from Cambridge and from Oxford.

Saibal Kar is a Fellow (Associate Professor) at the Centre for Studies in Social Sciences, Calcutta, India and a Humboldt Fellow at HWWI, Hamburg, Germany. He has held visiting positions at WIDER, Helsinki, University of East Anglia, UK, and Santa Fe Institute, USA. He holds degrees from Universities of Calcutta and Northern Illinois.

Libor Krkoska is currently the Head of the EBRD Resident Office in Moldova. He joined the EBRD in 1997 and worked for more than ten years in the Office of the Chief Economist in the EBRD headquarters in London, including as a senior economist for Russia. Libor holds a Ph.D. in Economics from CERGE in Prague, including a stay at the University of Pennsylvania as a Fulbright Scholar.

David Lam is Professor of Economics and Research Professor in the Population Studies Center at the University of Michigan. He received his Ph.D. in Economics from the University of California, Berkeley. He has been a visiting professor in the School of Economics at the University of Cape Town.

Hartmut Lehmann is Professor of Economic Policy at the University of Bologna and Director of the Program "Labor Markets in Emerging and Transition Economies" at IZA, Bonn. He has been a consultant to the OECD and to the World Bank. He holds degrees from the University of California, Berkeley and the London School of Economics.

Murray Leibbrandt is Professor of Economics and the Director of the Southern Africa Labour and Development Research Unit in the School of Economics at the University of Cape Town. Currently he holds the National Research Foundation Research Chair in Poverty and Inequality Research. He received his Ph.D. in Economics at the University of Notre Dame.

Santiago Levy is Vice President for Sectors at the InterAmerican Development

Bank. He has served on the Mexican government as President of the Competition Commisssion, Deputy Minister of Finance and Director General of Social Security. He holds degrees from Boston University.

Sugata Marjit is the Director and Reserve Bank of India Professor of Industrial Economics at the Centre for Studies in Social Sciences, Calcutta, India. He has held Visiting Positions at the Universities of Bonn, Cornell, Erasmus (Rotterdam), Munich, Nottingham, Rochester, Sydney and the IMF. He was educated at Presidency College, Calcutta and Universities of Calcutta and Rochester.

Dipak Mazumdar has been associated as a researcher with the University of Toronto since his retirement from the World Bank in 1994. During this period he has continued his active research interests in development which he had pursued at the World Bank. This has resulted in two major books *The African Manufacturing Firm* and *Globalization, Labor Markets and Inequality in India*, both published in recent years by Routledge. Before joining the World Bank Dr Mazumdar taught Economics for ten years at the London School for Economics.

Nidhiya Menon is Assistant Professor in the Department of Economics and the International Business School at Brandeis University. Her research interests lie in development economics, applied microeconomics and labor. She has held past positions at the World Bank, the Grameen Bank, and the International Labor Office. She has a BA from Mount Holyoke College and a Ph.D. in economics from Brown.

Cecil Mlatsheni is a lecturer in the School of Economics and a research associate of the Southern Africa Labour and Development Research Unit at the University of Cape Town. He is busy with a Ph.D. dissertation in which he addresses the problem of youth unemployment in South Africa.

Christophe J. Nordman is an IRD (French Institute of Research for Development) Research Fellow, assigned to DIAL in Paris, an IRD research unit on development economics, France. He is also Associate Research Fellow of SKOPE at the University of Oxford. He received a Ph.D. in Economics from University of Paris I Panthéon-Sorbonne in 2002.

Miracle Ntuli is a Lecturer in the School of Economics and Business Sciences and a Research Associate of the African Microeconomic Research Unit at the University of the Witwatersrand. She did her PhD at the University of Cape Town under the supervision of A/Professor Martin Wittenberg.

Carlo Orecchia holds degrees in Economics from the University of Rome "La Sapienza" and "Tor Vergata" and is currently a Ph.D. candidate. He was part of the World Bank Internship Program in 2007 and is a consultant for ISAE (Institute for Studies and Economic Analyses) in Rome.

Pierella Paci is a lead economist in the Poverty Reduction and Development Effectiveness Group at the World Bank. Before joining the World Bank she was a Professor in Economics at the University of Sussex (UK) and City University (London). She holds degrees in Economics from the University of Rome (Italy) and the Universities of York and Manchester (UK).

Carmen Pagés is Principal Research Economist at the Research Department of the Inter-American Development Bank. She has also served at the World Bank where she developed the work for Kenya. She holds a M.A. degree from the University Autonoma of Barcelona, and a Ph.D. in Economics from Boston University.

Francesco Pastore is Assistant Professor at Seconda Università di Napoli and a research fellow of IZA Bonn. He obtained his Ph.D. in Economics at the University of Sussex, UK. He has acted as a consultant for the International Labour Office and the United Nations Development Program.

Friedhelm Pfeiffer is senior researcher at the Centre for European Economic Research (ZEW Mannheim) and lecturer at the University of Mannheim. His research areas include the economics and psychology of skill formation over the life cycle and the inequality of human capital.

Kamani Rajakaruna, B.A. (Peradeniya) is a Research Officer at the Department of Inland Revenue, Sri Lanka and M.A. Candidate, Postgraduate Institute of Agriculture at the University of Peradeniya, Sri Lanka.

Shobana Rajendran, M.Phil, M.A. B.A. (Peradeniya) is a Senior Lecturer in Economics at the University of Peradeniya, Sri Lanka. Her areas of research include Gender, Labour and Human Rights.

Yana van der Meulen Rodgers is Associate Professor of Women's and Gender Studies at Rutgers University. Her research and teaching focus on feminist economics, child well-being, and development economics. She consults with the World Bank and the United Nations, and has a B.A. from Cornell and a Ph.D. in Economics from Harvard.

Yiagadeesen Samy is an Assistant Professor at the Norman Paterson School of International Affairs, Carleton University in Ottawa, Canada. He holds a Ph.D. in Economics from the University of Ottawa and his current research interests include trade and labour standards, foreign direct investment, aid and debt relief, and the determinants of state fragility. Some of his recent publications have appeared in *Canadian Foreign Policy* and *Foreign Policy Analysis*.

Sandip Sarkar is a Senior Research Fellow at the Institute of Human Development in Delhi—a research institute created under the auspices of the Indian Society of Labor Economics. He has been associated with several research projects on the Indian economy and was co-author of *Globalization, Labor Markets and Inequality in India* (Routledge 2008). He is currently working on a further research project with Dipak Mazumdar following up on some issues identified in the book.

Mark E. Schaffer is Director, Center for Economic Reform and Transformation and Professor of Economics at Heriot-Watt University, and Research Fellow at Centre for Economic Policy Research (London), the William Davidson Institute at the University of Michigan, and the Institute for the Study of Labor (Bonn). He holds degrees from Harvard, Stanford, and the London School of Economics.

Jason Scorse is Assistant Professor of International Policy Studies at the Monterey Institute. He holds degrees from UC-Berkeley.

Pieter Serneels is a Lecturer in Development Economics at the University of East Anglia. He has served on the staff of the World Bank and the International Labor Organization, and has held positions at the Universities of Oxford and Copenhagen. He holds degrees in Economics from Warwick and Oxford.

Jan Svejnar is the Everett E. Berg Professor of Business Administration and Professor of Economics and Public Policy at the University of Michigan He is also Director of the International Policy Center at the University of Michigan Gerald R. Ford School of Public Policy and Chairman of the Executive and Supervisory Committee of CERGE-EI in Prague. He holds degrees from Cornell and Princeton.

Theis Theisen is Associate Professor at the University of Agder, Norway. He has previously held positions at The Norwegian Ministry of Finance, and served as a member of the board of directors of various private companies. He was educated at the University of Oslo.

Ted To is a research economist at the US Bureau of Labor Statistics. He has previously worked at the Center for Economic Research in the Netherlands, the US International Trade Commission and the Universities of St Andrews and Warwick in the UK.

Insan Tunali is an Associate Professor of Economics at Koc University, located in Istanbul. He earned his Ph.D. at the University of Wisconsin and served as a faculty member at Cornell and Tulane Universities before moving to Turkey.

Alina Verashchagina is a Ph.D. Candidate in Economics at the University of Siena, Italy.

François-Charles Wolff is Professor at the Institut d'Economie et de Management at the University of Nantes, France. He is also Associate Researcher at the Direction des Recherches sur le Vieillissement, Caisse Nationale d'Assurance Vieillesse, and at the Institut National des Études Démographiques, Paris. He received a Ph.D. in Economics from University of Nantes in 1998 and is Agrégé des Universités since 2004.

1 Overview*

Ravi Kanbur and Jan Svejnar

As developing and transition economies enter the next phase of reforms, labor market issues increasingly come to the fore. With the increased competition from globalization, the discussion is shifting to the need for greater labor market flexibility, appropriate labor market regulation, and the creation of "good" jobs. Moreover, the greater actual and perceived insecurity in labor markets has generated a new agenda on how to structure safety nets. The older questions about the nature and links between the formal and informal labor markets reappear with new dimensions and significance. In addition, it is clear that an accurate understanding of how labor markets function is essential if we are to analyze alternative policy proposals in the wake of these concerns.

With this background, Cornell University and the International Policy Center at the Gerald R. Ford School of Public Policy of the University of Michigan hosted a major international conference—"Labor Markets in Developing and Transition Economies: Emerging Policy and Analytical Issues"—on May 25–7, 2007, at the Ford School in Ann Arbor, Michigan. The authors served as organizers of the conference, as well as editors of the present volume. This book presents theoretical, empirical, and policy chapters, most of which consist of revised papers that were presented at the conference. This overview provides the reader with a brief sketch of the arguments and findings of the chapters. The volume is divided into four parts: (I) Employment, Poverty, and Labor Market Dynamics, (II) Formality, Informality, and Labor Market Regulation, (III) Trade and Labor, and (IV) Human Capital, Productivity, and Gender.

Part I of the book focuses on labor market dynamics, including issues of employment growth and poverty, multiple job holding, race discrimination, biases introduced by attrition in labor force surveys, labor productivity growth and capital mobility, and the role of internal versus external labor markets in wage determination. The findings in this part of the volume suggest that policy makers ought to focus on: the interplay between principal sectors (e.g. agriculture and non-agriculture) when addressing the interplay of growth, employment, productivity, and poverty; the effects of rising wages and shifts in producer and consumer prices (the domestic real exchange rate) on employment; the relationship between the nature of the retirement system and informality as informal work appears to serve as a direct substitute for a pension system; the racial/ethnic component to the young people's success in finding work, and the extent to which quality of schooling differs across racial/ethnic groups. Finally, since micro data are increasingly used to inform policy, the findings in this part of the book strongly suggest that attention be paid to issues such as attrition in labor force and household surveys since, in the absence of careful treatment of these issues, the resulting estimates of policy effects may be biased.

Gutierrez, Paci, Orecchia, and Serneels note that many studies have detected a positive association between overall economic growth and poverty alleviation and that a new consensus is emerging that an important transmission channel between growth and poverty is the impact of growth on the employment opportunities of the poor. They point out that these stylized facts have led analysts and policy makers to focus on "jobless growth" as a major challenge in the struggle to ensure that poor benefit from economic growth. They also stress that in many developing countries poverty is not associated with unemployment but with low returns to labor in existing activities. This leads the authors to examine what types of aggregate and sectoral productivity and employment growth result in greater or lesser poverty reduction. They use 1980–2004 data on 106 short growth spells in 39 developing countries to perform a series of regressions assessing and decomposing the link between poverty and growth at the aggregate and sectoral levels. Using their decomposition methodology, the authors support the basic hypothesis that growth is associated with a reduction in poverty and they find that in the aggregate, employment-intensive growth does not matter for poverty any more than productivity-intensive growth. At the sector level, however, the authors demonstrate that employment-intensive growth in the secondary sector is associated with poverty reduction, while in agriculture it is associated with poverty increase. Productivity-intensive growth in agriculture has a positive correlation with poverty reduction, but his phenomenon may also reflect a movement of people out of agriculture. The results imply that policy makers ought to move beyond aggregate figures and correlations and focus instead on the sectoral aspects of growth, employment, productivity, and poverty.

Dipak Mazumdar and Sandip Sarkar focus on the dynamic relationship between growth and employment in India. In particular, they examine the determinants of relationship between overall employment and output growth—the "employment elasticity"—in the formal (organized) sector of Indian industrial firms before, during and after the reform of the Indian labor market. The authors show that this employment elasticity has varied dramatically across different policy periods, ranging from +0.99 in 1974–1980 to −1.39 in 1996–2001. They then examine the elasticity of employment with respect to (i) producer and consumer prices (the domestic real exchange rate), (ii) value added, and (iii) wages. They find that the most important variables affecting the overall employment elasticity are the wage-employment trade-off and the "price effect," with the latter being at least partly exogenous. The authors discuss how these findings are consistent with capital and labor being treated as quasi-fixed factors by firms and what the implications are for the dynamics of factor markets in different sectors of the economy.

Thomas Dohmen, Hartmut Lehmann, and Mark Schaffer use unique personnel data to analyze wage determination and wage inequality inside a Russian firm during 1997–2002. The authors test the competing hypotheses that wages are determined by (a) institutional factors related to industrial relations and an internal labor market, or (b) interplay of conditions in local labor markets, labor market institutions and optimization. They find that local labor market conditions have a strong impact on wage-setting at the firm level and that remuneration is not determined by formal internal rules and a stable institutionalized structure of wages. In times of high labor turn-over, the managers are willing to pay higher than average real wages to attract and retain workers. In addition, real wages fall substantially for employees who initially earned the highest rents. Overall, the authors show that market forces influence the wage policies of the firm and that considerations for a stable internal labor market are of less concern.

David Lam, Murray Leibbrandt, and Cecil Mlatsheni use a newly collected longitudinal youth data set, the Cape Area Panel Study, to examine the role of education in youth employment and unemployment. The authors start by providing data on the transitions from schooling to employment and unemployment, and note that after leaving the educational system, young people have difficulty making the transition from school to work. Moreover, whites are much more successful in attaining work than coloured South Africans who are in turn more successful than Africans. Racial differences are noticeable even before the young people finish school, with white and coloured youth being more likely to work during the years they are enrolled in school. The authors then model transitions to the work force using a probit model and find that schooling as well as ability, proxied by the literacy and numeracy exam, increase the probability of employment, as does being in good health and completing secondary education. The results clearly display a racial component to success in finding work and since the literacy and numeracy exams may also reflect quality of schooling, they raise the question of whether quality of schooling differs across the racial groups.

Insan Tunali examines attrition patterns in the Turkish Household Labor Force Survey (HLFS) from 2000 to 2002. Attrition is an important issue in that if it is related to labor force status of individuals, it may result in biases in labor market indicators. Using 12 rounds of quarterly household level data from the survey, Tunali finds that household attrition is likely to be affected by the labor market status of the head of household. In order to test for non-ignorable attrition, Tunali follows the model of Fitzgerald (1998) and performs the FGM and BGLW tests on a probit model in which the probability of attrition is dependent upon the labor force status of the household head, household characteristics, and the survey round. The model is estimated for every attrition interval (3, 12, 15 months) and Tunali finds that the probability of attrition is 8% in three months, 18.3% in 12 months, and 24.7% in 15 months. Based on these findings, Tunali suggests that indicators on transition dynamics be included among the information published on the basis of the HLFS.

The studies in Part II of the book examine issues of formality and informality of employment in the context of different market structures and regulations. In recent years, there has been an active debate about the extent and nature of the informal sector, but the debate has not resulted in a generally accepted definition or understanding of informality. Existing evidence suggests that tax and social security contributions, as well as government regulatory activities, are among the main causes of the existence of informal economy. Researchers hence usually take informality to imply non-participation or only partial participation of firms and workers in the tax and social security system, and their non-compliance or only partial compliance with regulatory requirements. For expositional clarity, it is useful to distinguish between two types of informal sector. The first type is a "fallback" sector in which individuals and firms end up as a result of not being able to survive in the formal sector. These firms and individuals could be market entrants that have not yet acquired the capabilities needed to compete in the formal sector, or they may be former participants in the formal sector that have not succeeded there. They are "rationed" into the fallback, informal sector by not being able to survive in the formal sector. They have low productivity and low wages, but are able to survive productively in the regulation- and tax-free informal sector. The second type of informal sector is an "optimizing" sector, which the participants select by choice because it gives them higher utility (combination of risk-adjusted income plus leisure). They move to the informal sector in response to disincentives associated with being in the formal sector. In this case, employers and/or employees are not rationed, but respond to incentives to avoid paying taxes and conforming to regulations. The reality is obviously a mixture of the two phenomena and the challenge for research and policy is to understand and determine the extent of each of them.

Ted To contributes to our understanding of informality by developing a theoretical model that provides a new explanation of the empirically observed phenomena that workers (a) often choose to work in the informal sector even if formal sector jobs are available to them at higher wages than jobs in the informal sector, and (b) willingly move between the two sectors in either direction. To's explanation consists of the formal and informal labor markets operating in the framework of oligopsony or monopolistic competition. He notes that the traditional competitive Harris–Todaro framework cannot be reconciled with workers locating voluntarily in the informal sector unless the formal and informal labor markets are fully integrated. In the competitive setting, full integration in turn implies equalization of the formal and informal sector wage rates, which is not corroborated by the evidence. To shows that oligopsony and monopsonistic competition models yield predictions that are consistent with the observed evidence and lend themselves to policy work. To also points to interesting areas for future research. One is to combine the oligopsony/monopolistic competition framework with that of Harris–Todaro to account for involuntary unemployment and/or location in the informal sector. Another is to account for wage spillovers across the sectors as a function of marginal products of labor varying with the number of establishments or total unemployment in each sector.

John Bennett and Saul Estrin link the issue of formality and informality with entrepreneurship. They develop a basic two-firm, two-period model of a developing economy with firm entry into industries that had previously not existed within the country. The profitability of introducing the technology for a new industry is uncertain. The model divides formal and informal firms by size and, as such, a profitable industry would prove more profitable in formality than informality. In the model, entrepreneurs use the informal market to test industry profitability, and, in some cases, the industry would never be established without the existence of the informal sector. Thus, the model implies that the informal sector may play an essential role in the growth of industries in a developing economy. They also consider how credit constraints may affect the pattern of entry.

Theis Theisen uses Tanzanian data to ascertain what determines whether individuals who work in the formal sector also participate in the informal labor market. This is the first estimation of a structural form participation function of multiple job-holding in developing countries. Theisen uses data gathered from 247 workers in five towns and 45 formal sector firms; these workers were asked questions regarding home production, underemployment, and informal work. Theisen performs four regressions: first, he estimates a structural-form multinomial logit model describing the allocation of workers in the formal sector; second, he estimates an earnings function for private sector formal workers; third, the estimated private sector earnings are used to estimate a "virtual wage rate" for all persons; and, finally, he estimates two different logit models to determine the decision to hold an informal sector job. The results indicate that income and the presence of children inversely affect participation in the informal sector, while informal sector participation is positively related to age and being female. The finding that income, being male, and the presence of small children have a negative effect on participation in a secondary job is similar to findings in the United States, while the positive effect of age is opposite to the US findings. Theisen argues that the differential effect of age in Tanzania and the USA is probably attributable to the superior retirement system in advanced economies such as in the USA. In particular, his explanation that informal work serves as a substitute for a pension system in Tanzania is plausible; while in the West, older workers retire from their second job as they age, Theisen's results indicate that older Tanzanians will take on a second job in their old age.

Mariano Bosch tackles the issue of formality versus informality in the context of a labor market search model, in which individuals decide whether to become workers or entrepreneurs on the basis of their managerial ability and the start-up costs associated with being in the formal sector. Formal entrepreneurs get to employ more productive workers but also face start up-costs (regulation). The informal sector entrepreneurs avoid these costs but work with a worse technology. Workers direct their search toward the formal or informal sector. More regulation expands the informal economy, but the effect on unemployment is unclear—the formal sector destroys jobs but also creates opportunities for both entrepreneurs and workers to shift into the informal sector. The net effect on unemployment depends on policy parameters such as the level of unemployment benefits, and attitudes and policies toward informality.

Santiago Levy uses institutional information, theoretical modeling, and data from Mexico to demonstrate that Mexican social programs are a source of informality and may lower growth and productivity by distorting the choices of firms and workers. The programs do so by segmenting the labor market through taxation of formal salaried workers and subsidies for informal and non-salary workers. Levy develops a model with salaried, self-employed, and non-salaried firm labor; firms may choose to be formal or informal. Formal firms, however, are required to pay social security benefits even though workers in both sectors receive social benefits. As a result, productivity is lowered and investment decisions are distorted. Levy argues that, in order to correct for these inefficiencies, Mexican social programs—and by implication similar programs in other countries—ought to be redesigned to ensure that formal and informal workers enjoy equal benefits and that the benefits are paid for with the same source of revenue.

Mabel Andalón and Carmen Pagés examine the performance of the minimum wage legislation in Kenya. The authors select coverage and enforcement, as well as the effect on wages and employment, as the criteria of performance of the minimum wage system. They use Kenya's 1998/9 Integrated Labor Force Survey, containing 11,040 households and 52,016 individuals, to find that the minimum wage was more strongly enforced and had stronger effects in non-agriculture than agriculture. Minimum wages are found to have a positive effect on the wages of women and low-educated workers in non-agricultural activities in urban areas, but not in agricultural activities. Furthermore, they resulted in a lower proportion of workers in formal employment. The authors suggest that the apparent non-compliance is a result of either the complexity of the minimum wage system, outdated job-wage classifications, or minimum wages being too high.

Errol D'Souza examines the trade-off between insurance and efficiency associated with job security regulations in India. He notes that while workers consider the trade-off between shirking and working, employers consider the trade-off between honoring a contract and terminating employment. D'Souza examines theoretical and empirical evidence related to the effect of job security regulation on the efficiency of the Indian labor market and concludes that although increased job security does increase rigidity in the labor market, it also allows workers to be insured efficiently in a manner which would not occur in an unregulated labor market. Employment protection may result in workers investing in a job and employers honoring contracts, but the challenge is how to achieve this without the "protection becoming protectionist."

Sugata Marjit and Saibal Kar note that recent growth experience in India suggests that an important role is played by a skill-based service sector and productivity improvement rather than a rise in physical capital accumulation. In order to provide an understanding of this phenomenon, the authors develop a general equilibrium model dealing with labor productivity growth, informal wages, and capital mobility. The model has three sectors: one for skilled formal workers, one for unskilled formal workers, and a third one for unskilled informal workers. The goal of the analysis is to consider the role of an increase in the productivity of labor in the formal sector on the wage rate in the informal sector. The model predicts that in the short run improved productivity of skilled workers decreases informal sector wages, but that the effect is nil in the long run if capital is perfectly mobile across sectors. It also predicts that an increase in the productivity of unskilled workers in the formal sector may increase informal sector wages in the short run, but not in the long run, depending upon capital mobility. Finally, secular productivity growth in the informal sector may result in a lower wage of informal sector workers if capital mobility is restricted between the formal and informal sectors but not when there is full capital mobility. The analysis shows that capital mobility plays a crucial part and that measures such as further development of the financial sector may have a beneficial effect not only on the formal sector but on the informal sector as well.

Part III of the book examines the interplay of trade and labor issues. The chapters respond to the substantial general interest in this area, with key issues being whether labor regulation makes a country disadvantaged in trade, whether trade openness erodes labor standards, whether foreign firms pay higher wages than domestic firms, and whether trade reforms affect different groups of workers differently.

Yiagadeesen Samy and Vivek Dehejia start by presenting a review of the literature on the relationship between labor standards and trade. The authors then estimate a simple econometric model, using data from the ILOLEX database and other sources, with the log of manufacturing exports as a percentage of total GDP determined by the ratio of population to land, by literacy, and by labor standards. They find weak support for the notion that nations with lower labor standards hold an advantage in trade and no evidence that openness in trade encourages a worsening of labor standards. The authors suggest that future research focus on efficient methods to include labor standard codes in trade agreements.

Ann Harrison and Jason Scorse examine whether foreign firms pay higher wages than domestic firms. This is a widely debated issue, since foreign firms appear to pay higher wages, but they also seem to use "higher quality" workers. Harrison and Scorse use firm-level data collected by the Indonesian government for the period 1990–9. Unlike other studies that control for heterogeneity of workers only at an aggregate level of "skilled" versus "unskilled," Harrison and Scorse are able to control for detailed worker characteristics, thus making their results more credible. They find that the wage premium for unskilled workers is relatively low, in the range of 5% to 10%, once education and gender are controlled for. However, a relatively high wage premium of 20% to 30% persists for skilled workers even after controlling for these factors. This evidence suggests that foreign-owned firms do pay a wage premium, especially for skilled employees.

Nidhiya Menon and Yana van der Meulen Rodgers use household-level data from India's National Sample Survey Organization covering 1987–2004 to examine the effect of Indian trade reform of the early 1990s on women's relative wages. Indeed, despite a relative improvement in women's educational attainment, the mean gender wage ratio in manufacturing remained constant at about 49% between 1987 and 2004. The authors perform two decomposition exercises. The first decomposes the wage differential into the explained wage gap (a function of measured gender productivity differences) and the unexplained gap. The second decomposition allocates the gender wage gap to the gap due to observed worker characteristics, changes from market returns, and the unexplained gap. The authors find compelling evidence that unmeasured gender-related factors have become more important and have offset female gains due to education and observed productivity characteristics over the time period. Furthermore, industry-level analysis suggests that competitive forces from trade in concentrated industries are a plausible explanation for the increasing residual wage differential between men and women. These results support theories of bargaining power and wage setting, and they suggest that the introduction of anti-poverty programs directed towards Indian women could prove beneficial.

Papers in part IV analyze issues related to various forms of human capital, wages, productivity, and gender. These studies suggest that there are various alternative ways to invest in productive human capital—human capital at the country-level is positively associated with firm-level performance, heterogeneity of firm characteristics accounts for a part of the gender wage gap—and that despite integrative reforms wage differentials persist across gender and regional dimensions.

Niels-Hugo Blunch uses data from the Ghana Living Standards Survey to consider the role of alternative ways to acquire skills—primarily skills gained through adult literacy programs, technical and vocational training, and higher education. Blunch estimates employment by a multinomial logit model in which probability of employment is affected by formal education, adult literacy program participation, literacy, numeracy, parental employment status, and basic control variables. Next, a conditional wage equation is estimated in which the log of the wage depends on a "vector of selection terms" from the previous regression, formal education, and basic control variables. The author finds that basic cognitive skills such as literacy and numeracy tend to increase employment. Furthermore, the results indicate that those who were involved in adult literacy programs are more likely to be employed and, in particular, self-employed. These results suggest that it is important to differentiate the role of different forms of human capital and for policy makers to consider improvements to adult education alongside primary education.

Johannes Gernandt and Friedhelm Pfeiffer examine the changes in wages and wage inequality in Germany, following the unification of East and West Germany. The analysis is particularly interesting because the equalization of wages and living standards in the two parts of the country has been one of the main political goals of the German government. The authors use the German Socio-Economic Panel to compare the data of three groups of workers—defined as stayers, migrants, and commuters to West Germany, all of whom lived in East Germany in 1989—with groups of West German "statistical twins." The authors find that after 15 years of transition wages did not converge for the largest group of workers—those who still work in East Germany. However, wage convergence has been fully achieved for migrants and almost achieved for commuters. Furthermore, wage inequality in East Germany converged to that of West Germany. The two labor markets hence still exhibit difference in the level of wages, but not in the degree of intra-regional wage inequality.

Gautum Hazarika and Arjun Bedi examine the issue of child work and schooling. Using data from the Survey of Living Conditions and the World Bank's Living Standards Measurement Survey, the authors consider the impact of schooling costs in the Indian provinces of Uttar Pradesh and Bihar on the propensity of children to attend school and work. Hazarikia and Bedia estimate two models: one on the decision of a child to work given schooling costs and other correlates, and one on the decision to attend school based on similar variables. The authors' results indicate that increased schooling costs encourage additional child labor and discourage school attendance. Moreover, they find a similar magnitude for each effect, indicating that the activities are strong substitutes for one another. The results therefore suggest that education intervention programs, designed to improve accessibility, should be effective in the two states.

Dileni Gunewardena, Darshi Abeyrathna, Amalie Ellagala, Kamani Rajakaruna, and Shobana Rajendran use Sri Lanka's Quarterly Labor Force Surveys to examine the changes in the private and public gender wage gaps in Sri Lanka from 1996 to 2004. The author utilizes a quantile regression approach, using the Blinder–Oaxaca and Machado–Mata decompositions. The results indicate that although the unconditional public sector wage gap favours women, the conditional wage gap in the public sector favours males, when controlling for part-time status, occupation, and industry. This suggests that women are underpaid relative to men and further analysis indicates that the extent of underpayment is greater at the bottom of the wage distribution.

Finally, the authors find evidence that is consistent with women selecting into "better paying" occupations. While women in these occupations are paid less than their male counterparts, they are paid better than women in other occupations and industries. Thus, the paper implies that Sri Lanka is still faced with gender inequality and points to possible areas where one could target public policy.

Joe Colombano and Libor Krkoska examine the relationship between firm-level training, country-level skills, and enterprise performance in transition economies. The authors use the Business Environment and Economic Performance Survey (BEEPS) data from the European Bank for Reconstruction and Development (EBRD) and the World Bank, as well as IEA data on academic competence and OECD data on functional competence. They find that academic and functional competence is positively associated with sales growth at the firm level. They also find that firms are more likely to conduct training programs in countries where the workforce is better skilled, controlling for enterprise and country characteristics—a finding that implies that firm-level training further enlarges the skill gap across countries. Finally, increased firm-level training is found to be positively related to sales growth. These results suggest that a country's human capital endowment is positively related to firm performance and that the higher amount of firm-level training in human capital rich countries enlarges the gap between the human capital poor and rich countries.

Miracle Ntuli examines the nature of gender wage discrimination in South Africa during the 1995–2004 period. Applying a quantile regression and counterfactual decomposition approaches to data from the 2004 Labor Force Survey and the 1995 and 1999 October Household Surveys, Ntuli considers whether a "glass ceiling" (gender gap is wider at the top than at the bottom of the wage distribution) or a "sticky floor" (gender gap is wider at the bottom than at the top of the wage distribution) is present in the South African formal labor market and whether the gender wage gap has changed over time. Ntuli finds that, contrary to expectations, the gender wage gap has, in fact, increased over the decade. She also finds evidence for the presence of a sticky floor in the general labor market. Ntuli suggests that the government ensure compliance with anti-discrimination policies enacted over the decade and attempt to counteract the cultural subordination of women in order to reverse the trend.

Francesco Pastore and Alina Verashchagina note that while in many transition economies the gender pay gap has remained the same in the presence of (and possibly because of the) falling female employment rates, in Belarus the gender pay gap has increased while women's activity rate has been unchanged in the country's unusually slow transition. The authors use data from the Belarusian Household Survey in 1996 and 2001 to explain the stable participation of women and the rising gender wage gap in Belarus. They estimate a selectivity corrected wage function to compute an expected wage offer for women, followed by a probit equation for structural female labor supply with the computed wage included as a regressor. The results indicate that proxies for the opportunity cost of working, such as the presence of young children or senior household members, do decrease participation but are not concentrated in any particular group of women. The elasticity of female participation to wages is found to be low. Women in low-income households have significantly below-average participation rates, which the authors highlight as a potential poverty trap. Finally, the authors find that there has been a tendency for women to shift towards low-wage jobs and that female labor force participation has remained high. This suggests that women are likely being forced to work as a result of poverty rather than choice.

Christophe Nordman and François-Charles Wolff examine the gender wage gaps in Madagascar and Mauritius. Using matched employer–employee data collected in 2005, the authors focus on the role of firm characteristics and job segregation across firms as potential factors to explain the gender wage gap and the possible presence of a glass ceiling. The authors find that the two economies differ in that the magnitude of the adjusted gender wage gap is almost insignificant in Madagascar and high in Mauritius. However, accounting for firm heterogeneity is important on both islands and they highlight gender segregation across firms—the existence of high-paying firms for men and low-paying firms for women. Finally, the authors find no compelling evidence of a glass-ceiling phenomenon in either island. The study shows that there is heterogeneity in Africa with respect to the situation of women in the labor market and that firm heterogeneity is an important factor that has not been detected without matched employer–employee data.

Overall, the theoretical and empirical studies assembled in the present volume contribute in a number of ways to the understanding of key labor market phenomena in developing and transition economies. Most importantly, they demonstrate the renewed vigor of analytical policy-oriented research in labor markets and development; they provide important policy lessons and identify key areas for future research and debate.

Note

* We would like to thank Robert Gillezeau for valuable research assistance.

Part I

Employment, poverty, and labor market dynamics

2 Does employment generation really matter for poverty reduction?[*]

Catalina Gutierrez, Pierella Paci, Carlo Orecchia, and Pieter Serneels

Introduction

Extensive evidence exists that, although growth explains a large part of poverty changes, there is a wide disparity in the poverty impact of different growth patterns[1] and the volume of literature on the factors that explain these differences is growing.[2] Consensus also emerging is that an important transmission channel between growth and poverty reduction is its impact on the employment opportunities for the poor.[3] Thus, policy makers have become increasingly concerned with "jobless growth" as a major obstacle for the poor benefiting from the recent positive trends in growth worldwide.

However, in many low-income countries, poverty is not associated with lack of employment (or unemployed) but with the low returns to labor in existing activities. Thus, policies should focus more on ways of raising the income of the "working poor", than on raising employment rates. The related policy question then is whether the incomes of the low-paid are more effectively raised by a growth pattern that favors the sectors of the economy in which they mostly work or by a pattern that expands employment opportunities in the sectors where they do not, so as to encourage shifts away from low-pay sectors into areas where returns to labor are higher.

Despite the clear importance of these questions for the effective formulation of inclusive growth strategies, the understanding of the mechanisms through which this channel operates remains until now rather limited and this leads to a lack of evidence-based policy making in this area. The purpose of this paper is to deepen an understanding of this by empirically evaluating the correlation between different aggregate and sectoral employment/productivity profiles of the associated poverty changes.

The paper is structured as follows: section 1 presents a brief review of the theoretical and empirical evidence on the link between poverty and growth patterns. Section 2 discusses the methodology and data. Section 3 illustrates the stylized facts on the correlation between the growth patterns and poverty. Section 4 analyzes the effects of growth patterns on poverty and discusses and tests causality issues, and Section 5 presents the paper's conclusions.

Conceptual framework: why would the sectoral growth pattern or its employment profile matter for poverty?

Among the growing literature on the study of which factors explain the effectiveness of growth in reducing poverty, an important set of papers has concentrated on the sectoral growth pattern. For example, Loayza and Raddatz (2006) find that growth in unskilled intensive sectors contributed to changes in poverty. Ravallion and Datt (2002) link sectoral value-added growth to poverty changes in India, and find that growth in agriculture helped to reduce poverty while growth in manufacturing did not. Satchi and Temple (2006) show how dualism may play an important role in how the growth pattern translates into rises in employment and wages, and that while growth in agriculture potentially raises poverty, urban growth reduces poverty. Other policy-oriented research has reached similar conclusions. For example, the World Bank (2005) studied 11 countries and found evidence that access to non-farm rural employment and informal urban employment helped the poor to benefit from the growth process. It also found that in three of the 14 countries studied, pro-poor growth was associated with more labor-intensive growth.[4] In a related analysis, Islam (2004) uses a cross-country sample of developing countries to find out whether the employment intensity of growth in manufacturing contributes to explaining poverty reduction; and Prasada Rao et al. (2004) analyze the effects of output per worker. Neither finds robust relationships. More recently, a study by Kakwani, Neri, and Son (2006) decomposes the sources of pro-poor growth in a case study for Brazil. The authors find that productivity was the major labor income source of pro-poor growth, while the role of employment growth was small. The role of productivity growth in agriculture on poverty has also been the focus of much work. The results from Computable General Equilibrium (CGE) literature suggest that factor market assumptions and agricultural trade are crucial in determining the poverty reducing impact of agricultural productivity (Coxhead and Warr 1995; Fane and Warr 2002). In an empirical paper, Datt and Ravallion (1998) find that productivity growth in India decreased poverty.

The empirical evidence from country case studies discussed above appears to point to the fact that the sectoral growth pattern and its employment and productivity profile matter for poverty alleviation. This fact should come as no surprise because the poor and the non-poor own factors in different proportions; as long as different growth patterns affect factor demands and factor returns differently, their poverty impact is likely to differ. It is less clear from the evidence whether productivity or employment growth are at the core of reductions in poverty, or which are the sectors in which growth has more impact. Nor is it clear whether general patterns hold across many countries, as most of the studies are country specific.

With some notable exceptions (Satchi and Temple 2006; Loayza and Raddatz 2006), the available theoretical models yield little insight into these issues. In a simple competitive supply and demand framework, with no frictions or barriers to mobility, the economy is always at "full employment," and so there is no scope for "employment (rate) intensive growth," but the sectoral pattern of growth would still matter: growth in a sector would raise the demand for labor and would raise wages everywhere uniformly, but the amount of upward pressure exerted on wages would depend on the amount of labor the growing sector is demanding, in other words on its relative labor intensity. Under perfect mobility and factor price equalization, growth in sectors such as agriculture (which is mostly labor-intensive in developing countries) would achieve a greater reduction of poverty than, for example, growth in high-tech manufacturing or utilities, which are less labor-intensive.[5]

In models with friction and barriers to mobility, or in models of labor market segmentation, there is space for employment-intensive growth—that is, growth that is accompanied by increases in the employment rate. The theoretical literature on labor markets in developing countries stresses the duality and segmentation of these labor markets. At the core of this model is the idea that there is a "bad jobs sector" and a "good jobs sector." In the good jobs sector, returns to labor are higher. In the bad jobs sector, returns to labor are low, so households that earn a living in the bad jobs sector are more likely to be poorer than the rest. Jobs in the good jobs sectors are rationed because wages are institutionally set above the competitive market clearing level. There may be minimum wages, unions may bargain for higher wages, firms may set "efficiency wages" and so on. On top of the limited mobility created by the above market clearing wages, there may be geographic, ethnic, and educational barriers to mobility. This rationing implies that workers queue for "good jobs" while unemployed or employed in the bad jobs sector.

Under such models the sectoral pattern of growth may have a crucial role in alleviating poverty. For example, if there are extensive barriers to mobility between sectors so that factor returns do not equate across sectors, then growth in the sectors in which the poor are found may be more effective at moving people out of poverty than growth in the sectors to which the poor have limited mobility. If there are no extensive barriers to mobility, then growth in the good jobs sectors may be more effective in pulling people into the higher earning sectors and out of poverty. On the other hand, the distribution of the poor between the unemployment state and the bad jobs sector will determine whether cutting unemployment or moving people out of the bad jobs sector will have a greater impact on poverty.

A thorough modeling of these links is beyond the scope of this paper. Instead, we hope that by highlighting the empirical correlations between growth patterns and poverty for many countries we can provide some input into the debate on how employment generation and productivity growth affect poverty in the short run. It is important to emphasize that, although the evidence provided here seems to suggest plausible causality from the pattern of growth to poverty changes, we do not pretend to assert unequivocal causality, but rather, highlight the coincidence of phenomena that might have a causal interpretation. Whether a causal interpretation can be given will depend largely on the theoretical model that one believes underlies the observed relationships.

Methodology and data

Profiling growth: a Shapley decomposition approach

The first task in understanding how the sectoral growth patterns and their employment and productivity profile affect poverty is to find a suitable methodology to profile growth. Ideally, the methodology should be able to provide some measures of how employment-intensive or productivity-intensive a growth process is, and how this intensity is distributed across sectors of economic activity.

A simple way of understanding how growth is associated with increases in productivity and employment at the aggregate level and by sectors is to perform a simple decomposition of per capita GDP growth in three components: productivity changes, employment rate changes, and demographic changes. In doing so, it should be noted that per capita GDP, $Y/N = y$ can be expressed as:

$$\frac{Y}{N} = \frac{Y}{E}\frac{E}{A}\frac{A}{N} \tag{1}$$

or

$$y = \omega * e * a$$

where Y is value added, E is employment, A is the population of working age, and N is the total population. The ratio $\omega = Y/E$ corresponds to output per worker, $e = E/A$ corresponds to the share of the working-age population employed, and $a = A/N$ corresponds to the share of the population of working age.

The decomposition can be easily extended to multiple sectors:

$$\frac{Y}{N} = \left(\sum_s \frac{Y_s}{E_s}\frac{E_s}{A}\right)\frac{A}{N} \tag{2}$$

or equivalently

$$y = \left(\sum_s \omega_s * e_s\right) * a$$

where the sub-index s stands for the sector of economic activity.

We use a Shapley decomposition to decompose growth in changes in the aggregates ω, e, and a; and changes in the vectors of sectoral labor productivities (ω_1, ω_2, . . ., ω_s) and employment levels (e_1, e_2, . . ., e_s). This approach is based on the marginal effect on the value of a variable/indicator, of sequentially eliminating the change in each of the contributory factors. It assigns to each factor the average of its marginal contribution in all possible elimination sequences (Shorrocks 1999). For example, in equation (1), the amount of growth attributed to changes in output per worker (ω) is the growth in per capita value added under the hypothetical scenario in which employment rates (e) and the share of the working-age population (a) had remained constant but output per worker had changed as observed. The difference between the resulting hypothetical growth and the observed growth is defined as the contribution of changes in output per worker to per capita value-added growth.[6]

Shapley decompositions have the advantage of being additive. In other words, let, $\bar{\omega}$, $\bar{e}$ and $\bar{a}$ be the marginal contribution of each component to the observed change in per capita value added, obtained through the Shapley decomposition, then:

$$\bar{\omega} + \bar{e} + \bar{a} = \frac{\Delta y}{y}.$$

In a similar way decomposing equation (2) would yield:

$$\sum_s \bar{\omega}_s + \sum_s \bar{e}_s + \bar{a} = \frac{\Delta y}{y}.$$

In this case $\bar{e}$ would be the amount of growth that can be linked to changes in the employment rate as measured by the ratio between total employment and the working-age population. Although employment rates as defined by the ILO measure the population that "participates" in the labor market that is employed, throughout this paper the term "employment rate" will refer to employment as a fraction of the working-age population.[7] Increases in employment rates would thus reflect both increases in participation and movements of people out of unemployment and into employment.

The term $\bar{\omega}$ will capture changes in output per worker, but its interpretation is not so straightforward. Increases in output per worker can come from three different sources: (i) increases in the capital/labor ratio; (ii) increases in total factor productivity (TFP); and (iii) relocation of jobs from bad jobs sectors (low productivity) to good jobs sectors (high productivity). It should be noted that it may also capture cyclical behavior of output: firms operating in economic downturns may have underutilized capital; when the demand rises again, it will be reflected as a rise in output per worker. Throughout this paper we will refer to output per worker as productivity, on the understanding that it is measuring average output per worker and captures all of the above-mentioned factors.

The component $\bar{a}$ reflects changes in the demographic structure of the population. For example, despite rises in labor productivity and employment, countries with a rapidly rising young population may see a decline in per capita income if the employment and productivity growth is not sufficient to counter the growing dependency ratio.

To differentiate sectoral employment/productivity intensity from aggregate intensities, we will use sub-indexes. The term $\bar{e}_s$ will denote the amount of growth that can be linked to changes in the share of employment of sector *s*. The term $\bar{\omega}_s$ will denote the amount of growth that can be linked to productivity changes in sector *s*.

Using the methodology described above, a growth episode can be profiled in two different ways by the vectors $(\bar{\omega}, \bar{e}, \bar{a})$ and $(\bar{\omega}_1, \bar{\omega}_2, \ldots, \bar{\omega}_S; \bar{e}_1, \bar{e}_2, \ldots, \bar{e}_S; \bar{a})$. The first vector would profile growth according to aggregate productivity, employment, and demographic changes. The second vector would profile growth according to changes in sectoral productivity, in sectoral employment shares, and in aggregate demographic changes.

For our purposes, the value of $\bar{e}$ is a better measure of the employment-intensity of growth than the employment elasticity of output because (i) it relates the number of jobs generated, *relative* to the working-age population, and (ii) it combines both the effects of the employment (rate) elasticity of growth and the amount of growth, thus looking at the amount of jobs generated (for the same elasticity higher growth would generate more jobs).[8]

Exploring the link between the sectoral growth pattern, its productivity and employment intensity, and its poverty reducing impact

Once growth has been profiled, the second step is to link the profile of growth with poverty changes. To do so, we regress each of the components that profile growth against percent changes in poverty. This would be the equivalent of regressing percent changes in poverty against aggregate growth, which is the route followed by the poverty-growth literature.[9] In this case, however, we have decomposed aggregate growth into different terms. To analyze whether poverty changes are correlated with the aggregate employment and productivity profile, we can estimate the following equation:

$$\frac{\Delta P}{P} = \beta_0 + \beta_1 \bar{e} + \beta_2 \bar{\omega} + \beta_3 \bar{a} \tag{3}$$

if movements out of non-employment and into employment reduce poverty, then we would expect the coefficient of $\bar{e}$ to be significantly and negatively correlated with changes in headcount poverty *P*. On the other hand if the income of the poor rises because they change from low productivity jobs to high productivity jobs, or because their earnings are positively correlated with TFP or the capital/labor ratio, then the coefficient on $\overline{\omega}$ should be significantly and negatively correlated with changes in poverty. If increases in the fraction of the working population reduce poverty, then the coefficient on $\overline{a}$ should be significant and negative. Note that if $\beta_1 = \beta_2 = \beta_3$, then equation (3) would boil down to $\Delta P / P = \beta_0 + \beta_1(\Delta y / y)$, and what would matter would be overall growth rather than its profile.

Finally, to estimate whether the sectoral productivity and employment profile of growth is correlated with changes in poverty, we would estimate:

$$\frac{\Delta P}{P} = \beta_0 + \sum\nolimits_{s=1}^{S} \beta_s \overline{e}_s + \sum\nolimits_{s=1}^{S} \gamma_s \overline{\omega}_s + \delta\overline{a} \tag{4}$$

Interpretation of the coefficients is straightforward. As all variables are in percentage changes, the coefficients are the (partial) elasticity of poverty with respect to our measure of employment-intensive growth or productivity-intensive growth. Because of the way the decomposition is performed, β_s will indicate the percentage change in the headcount poverty ratio that is likely to accompany a 1% increase in our employment-intensive measure in sector s. Analogously, the coefficient γ_s will indicate the percentage change in the headcount poverty ratio for a 1% growth in our measure of productivity-intensive growth in sector s.

The data

We use data on total and sectoral GDP, poverty, population, and employment. The analysis covers the period between 1980 and 2004, and uses a sample of 39 developing countries, and 106 growth spells.[10] By "growth spells" we refer to a particular growth episode in a given country. The length and number of spells depend on data availability, and will vary from country to country. A growth spell is constructed as the change in value added per capita in two consecutive periods.

Data on aggregate GDP come from the World Bank's World Development Indicators. To construct sectoral GDP we use data from the UN National Accounts, which give the share of GDP by sector. UN data on National Accounts has value added disaggregated into seven sectors (ISCS-revision 3 definitions): agriculture, hunting, forestry and fishing; mining and utilities; manufacturing; construction; wholesale, retail, restaurant and hotels; transport, storage and communications; and other activities. Data on population comes from the UN population division. Data on poverty comes from the World Bank Poverty Database. Finally, data on employment come from the ILO-KILM database. Despite its wealth of information, KILM has some limitations for comparability across countries and within countries across time. However, the KILM database does provide the necessary information to control for differences in measurement and coverage between and within countries. In addition, the coverage for sub-Saharan Africa is low, so that we tried to supplement the ILO data with other sources for this region.[11] Care is taken so that sectoral employment classification from the ILO is consistent with the sectoral aggregation of the UN National Accounts

Each observation in our sample is a short-run "growth spell" constructed for each country as the percentage change in value added per capita (VA) between *two consecutive comparable points in time*. For each VA growth spell the corresponding changes (for the exact same years) in employment to labor force ratios (E/A) by sectors, value added per worker (Y/E) by sectors, and ratio of labor force to total population (A/N) are constructed. To link the profile of growth to poverty, the corresponding changes in the poverty head-count ratio are constructed. Care is taken to ensure that the spells are comparable in time by taking into consideration that, within a spell, the poverty is defined using the same welfare indicator (income or consumption) and employment series are comparable. The average duration of the growth spells is 2.2 years and the longest spell is 8 years.

Table 2.1 describes the sample. Despite the low coverage of sub-Saharan Africa and the Middle East and North Africa, we are able to capture 15% of all low-income countries.

Results: what do the stylized facts say?

Figure 2.1 presents stylized facts on the empirical link between growth and changes in poverty in all countries for which data were available. Each data

Table 2.1 Sample description

Countries grouped by region and income level	Number of countries in the region	Number of countries in the sample	% of countries in the sample
By region			
Sub-Saharan Africa	48	4	8.3
East Asia and the Pacific	24	5	20.8
Europe and Central Asia	27	9	33.3
Latin America and the Caribbean	31	17	54.8
Middle East and North Africa	14	1	7.1
South Asia	8	3	37.5
Total	152	39	24.3
By income level			
Low income	53	8	15.0
Lower middle income	58	20	34.5
Upper middle income	41	11	26.8
Total	152	39	24.3

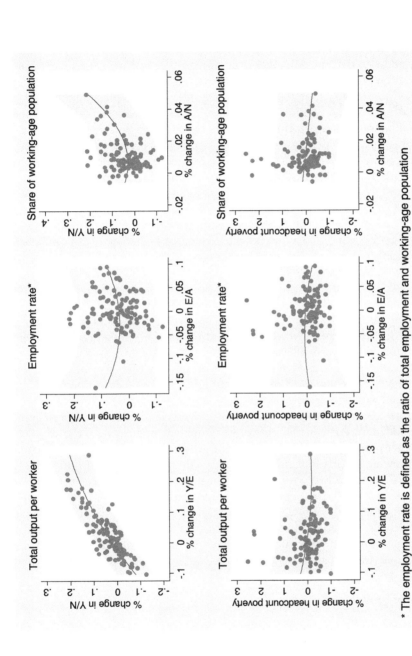

Figure 2.1 Empirical link between the components of per capita GDP, growth, and changes in poverty. Developing countries 1980–2002.

* The employment rate is defined as the ratio of total employment and working-age population

point in the figure corresponds to a specific growth spell in a country. The first row of plots in Figure 2.1 illustrates the correlation between *per capita value added* and percentage changes in productivity (first plot), employment rates (second plot), and the share of population of working age (third plot). The strong positive correlation between changes in productivity and per capita value added stands out. Changes in employment as well in as the share of the population of working age are also positively correlated with increases in per capita value added, but their confidence intervals are substantially wider, suggesting that the relation is less strong. The second row of plots in the figure illustrates how percentage changes in *headcount poverty* correlate with the same three components. All of these components appear to be negatively correlated with poverty, although the correlations appear to be small and the confidence intervals large. The positive correlation is perhaps not surprising: higher value added per worker can translate into higher labor income either through higher wages or through higher profits from self-employment, and thus it can alleviate poverty. Higher employment rates would imply more people working and thus more people earning. A higher share of population of working age means that each working-age member has fewer people to support on his/her income.

Figure 2.2 illustrates how changes in poverty and value added per capita are correlated with changes in sectoral value added per worker. A simple look at the figure suggests that there may be important differences. For example, growth in output per worker in agriculture and services appears strongly correlated with poverty alleviation, while productivity growth in manufacturing does not seem to have a clear effect on poverty (first row of plots). On the other hand, changes in productivity in all sectors seem to be positively associated with aggregate growth.

Figure 2.3 illustrates how changes in poverty and changes in per capita value added are correlated with sectoral employment growth. There are clear differences among sectors. Employment growth in agriculture is associated with growing poverty, but employment growth in manufacturing and services seems to be associated with decreases in poverty. The relationship between changes in overall per capita value added and employment rates in the different sectors also differ. Increases in employment in agriculture appear negatively correlated with overall growth, while the opposite holds true for manufacturing and construction, suggesting important differential effects between agriculture and non-agriculture.

Results: growth and poverty

Not all growths are equal for poverty

We proceed to analyze whether growth patterns matter for poverty changes using the headcount poverty ratio as a dependent variable.[12] We first analyze the relationship between poverty changes and the aggregate employment/

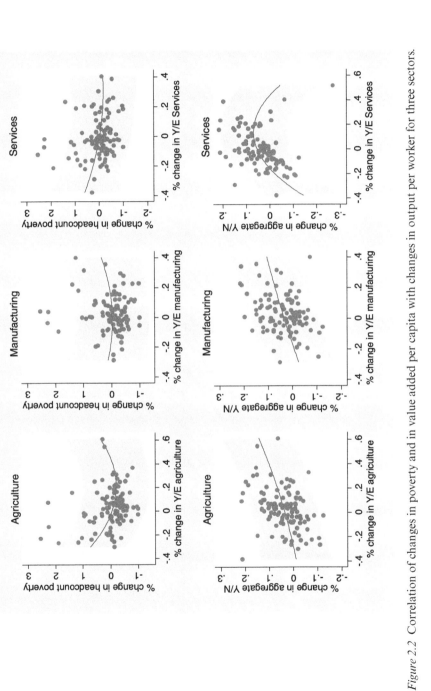

Figure 2.2 Correlation of changes in poverty and in value added per capita with changes in output per worker for three sectors.

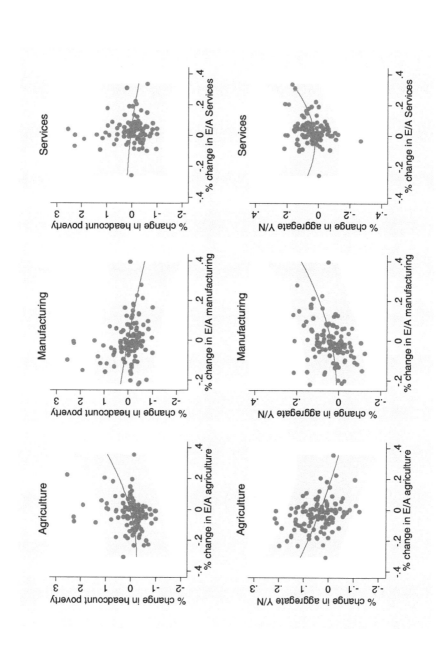

Figure 2.3 Correlation of changes in poverty and in value added per capita with employment growth for three sectors.

productivity profile of growth (equation (3)) and then whether the sectoral employment and productivity profile matters for poverty reduction (equation (4)). For each equation we estimate several models. Model (1) is the benchmark estimation, with no controls. Model (2) controls for changes in inequality, for the initial levels of inequality, GDP, poverty levels, and for their interactions.[13] Only the parsimonious specification with changes in inequality (measured by the Gini coefficient of mean survey income) is reported as this is the only significant correlation. Model (3) estimates a separate regression for non-LAC countries, to test whether results are driven by the large number of LAC countries in our sample. Finally, Model (4) uses only the positive growth spells. All errors are clustered by country and outliers excluded from the sample.

Table 2.2 illustrates the emerging correlation between aggregate growth in per capita value added and poverty reduction. Our results suggest that a 1% growth of per capita value added reduces poverty headcount ratios by around 4%.

Table 2.3 shows the correlation between poverty changes and the aggregate employment and productivity profile of growth (equation (3)). Both the aggregate productivity intensity of growth and the aggregate employment intensity are correlated with poverty reduction and a test for the equality of the coefficients cannot be rejected in any of the models estimated. However, the significance level of the coefficient for employment is lower, suggesting productivity-intensive growth to be more robustly correlated with poverty reduction.

Table 2.4 illustrates the results of estimating equation (4) which quantifies the sectoral employment and productivity intensity of growth on poverty. As mentioned previously, $\bar{e}_s$ reflects how much of the observed aggregate growth (measured as percentage change in value added per worker) can be linked to increases in employment in sector s, and $\bar{\omega}_s$ corresponds to the amount of growth that can be linked to changes in productivity in sector s. We perform the estimation for seven and three sector disaggregations but only report the estimation for the latter as we cannot reject equality of coefficients across

Table 2.2 Percent change in headcount ratio and aggregate growth

	(1) Benchmark	(2) Controls	(3) Non-LAC	(4) Positive growth
Change in Y/N (%)	−3.616***	−3.650***	−4.848***	−3.280***
	(−3.95)	(−4.19)	(−3.39)	(−3.87)
Change in Gini (%)		2.562***	2.375***	1.729***
		(2.82)	(3.03)	(3.33)
Constant	0.151*	0.158*	0.310*	0.130
	(1.79)	(1.92)	(1.75)	(1.41)
Observations	104	104	41	73
Adjusted *R*-squared	0.139	0.241	0.283	0.215

Table 2.3 Poverty changes and the employment/productivity intensity of growth

	(1) Benchmark	(2) Controls	(3) Non-LAC	(4) Positive growth
Share of population of working age A/N	−2.895 (−0.59)	−2.287 (−0.48)	−8.124 (−1.29)	1.395 (0.29)
Value added per worker Y/E	−3.612*** (−3.95)	−3.686*** (−4.26)	−4.391** (−2.76)	−3.828*** (−3.35)
Employment rate E/A	−4.604** (−2.59)	−4.783** (−2.64)	−6.905** (−2.36)	−3.413** (−2.47)
Change in Gini (%)		2.586*** (2.84)	2.341*** (3.26)	1.719*** (3.42)
Constant	0.144 (1.37)	0.146 (1.45)	0.302* (1.76)	0.102 (1.04)
Observations	104	104	41	73
Adjusted *R*-squared	0.127	0.233	0.270	0.207

Table 2.4 Poverty changes and sectoral employment/productivity intensity

	(1) Benchmark	(2) Controls	(3) Non-LAC	(4) Positive growth
Employment-intensive growth in agriculture (primary sector)	2.003 (0.37)	3.393 (0.68)	−0.428 (−0.04)	4.780 (1.41)
Employment-intensive growth in secondary sector	−6.578*** (−4.60)	5.487*** (−3.89)	5.987*** (−3.16)	4.845*** (−4.78)
Employment-intensive growth in tertiary sector	−2.887 (−1.17)	−4.529* (−1.87)	−7.414* (−2.02)	−2.250 (−1.53)
Productivity-intensive growth in agriculture (primary sector)	−4.504 (−1.17)	−3.344 (−0.95)	−5.345 (−0.81)	−3.325 (−1.15)
Productivity-intensive growth in secondary sector	−1.753 (−1.16)	−1.287 (−1.00)	1.507 (0.43)	1.523 (1.09)
Productivity-intensive growth in tertiary sector	−0.621 (−0.52)	−1.651 (−1.62)	−2.843 (−1.44)	−1.804 (−1.29)
Change in Gini (%)		2.893*** (3.24)	2.869*** (5.05)	2.211*** (4.98)
Constant	0.0778 (1.10)	0.121 (1.66)	0.173 (1.06)	0.0400 (0.58)
Observations	98	98	37	68
Adjusted *R*-squared	0.140	0.275	0.311	0.420

sub-sectors in the seven-sector case. In general, employment-intensive growth in the secondary and tertiary sectors is negatively correlated with poverty reduction while employment-intensive growth in agriculture is uncorrelated with poverty. This correlation is robust for the secondary sector and for tertiary in non-lack countries but in Latin American and Caribbean (LAC) countries, employment growth in the tertiary sector is positively correlated with poverty. However, there is substantial heterogeneity across sub-sectors with commerce and services driving the positive effect.[14] Sectoral productivity-intensive growth, however, does not seem to be robustly correlated with poverty reduction.

Our measures of employment-intensive and productivity-intensive growth are negatively correlated, within sectors. Although this is to be expected because of decreasing marginal productivity, the magnitude of the correlation is particularly high for the agricultural sector (see Annex). A possible explanation is that in the short run the measurement of output is less accurate than the measurement of employment—a factor that can be particularly important in the case of agriculture and services because of the implicit difficulty in measuring non-marketable output. By including productivity and employment jointly, we might be unable to disentangle their effects. We explore this issue by regressing poverty changes against our measures of employment and productivity separately (Tables 2.5 and 2.6).

The main difference in the results with those of Table 2.4, is that productivity-intensive growth in agriculture is robustly correlated with poverty reduction, and employment-intensive growth in agriculture is robustly correlated with poverty increases. It is therefore difficult to determine whether they are capturing different phenomena or the same phenomena. An alternative explanation is related to traditional sector dualism, where output in

Table 2.5 Poverty changes and the sectoral employment intensity of growth

	(1) Benchmark	*(2)* Controls	*(4)* Non-LAC	*(5)* Positive growth
Employment-intensive growth in agriculture	8.014*** (3.32)	8.900*** (4.01)	6.467* (1.95)	8.859*** (4.31)
Employment-intensive growth in secondary sector	−6.141*** (−4.86)	.705*** (−4.48)	−7.159*** (−4.41)	.999*** (−5.34)
Employment-intensive growth in tertiary sector	−2.404 (−1.28)	−3.111 (−1.60)	−5.324* (−1.84)	−0.863 (−0.62)
Change in Gini (%)		2.848*** (3.31)	2.702*** (4.10)	2.179*** (4.52)
Constant	0.0693 (1.05)	0.0966 (1.44)	0.120 (1.16)	0.0107 (0.19)
Observations	98	98	37	68
Adjusted *R*-squared	0.143	0.276	0.333	0.415

Table 2.6 Poverty changes and the sectoral productivity intensity of growth

	(1) Benchmark	(2) Controls	(4) Non-LAC	(5) Positive growth
Productivity-intensive growth in agriculture	−7.227*** (−3.00)	−7.131*** (−3.45)	−9.452** (−2.64)	−7.112*** (−3.88)
Productivity-intensive growth in secondary sector	0.596 (0.33)	0.813 (0.53)	3.624 (0.90)	5.081** (2.69)
Productivity-intensive growth in tertiary sector	−0.726 (−0.72)	−1.149 (−1.17)	−0.643 (−0.29)	−1.324 (−0.97)
Change in Gini (%)		2.810*** (3.34)	2.783*** (3.99)	2.003*** (3.67)
Constant	0.0277 (0.43)	0.0412 (0.64)	0.0458 (0.31)	−0.0894 (−1.36)
Observations	98	98	37	68
Adjusted *R*-squared	0.045	0.174	0.185	0.317

agriculture is fixed and earnings in this sector are equal to average output per worker. Therefore, employment-intensive growth in agriculture would be equivalent to the negative of productivity-intensive growth in the sector, and productivity growth in agriculture might be reflecting outflows of workers from agriculture. In addition, productivity-intensive growth in the secondary sector is positively correlated with poverty when the sample is reduced to positive growth periods. Thus, in this sample there is some evidence for the hypothesis that jobless manufacturing growth might increase poverty. The sample is concentrated among LAC countries, and it might in fact be capturing the increases in productivity in the regions during the 1990s, (mostly due to within-firm efficiency increases), a period during which the region saw very modest changes in poverty.

In summary, we find that aggregate employment and productivity-intensive growth have a similar effect on poverty reduction. However, the sectoral employment and productivity profile of growth has heterogeneous effects depending on the sector. We find that employment-intensive growth in agriculture is correlated with rising poverty while employment-intensive growth in the secondary sector is correlated with reductions in poverty. On the other hand, productivity-intensive growth in agriculture is correlated with poverty reductions while productivity-intensive growth in the secondary and tertiary sectors has an ambiguous relation with poverty. The effects of the agricultural profile of growth are difficult to disentangle, as employment and productivity changes are strongly correlated. The evidence also shows that there is some heterogeneity among countries, with LAC countries showing a different behavior from the rest. The correlation between growth profiles and poverty reduction also shows asymmetries between positive and negative growth spells.

The size of these effects is important: a 1% employment-intensive growth in agriculture is associated with a rise in the headcount poverty by around 6.5% (the headcount poverty goes from 45% to 48%). A 1% employment-intensive growth in manufacturing decreases poverty by 5–7%. Productivity-intensive growth in agriculture reduces poverty by 4–9%. Finally, it is worth highlighting that increasing inequality has a non-negligible contribution to poverty reduction. For our sample of short-run growth spells an increase in the Gini coefficient of 1%, increases head-count poverty by around 2–3%.

Exploring causality

Beyond stylized facts, it is hard to disentangle the causality from the growth patterns to poverty changes due to the difficulty of finding adequate instruments for the employment and productivity intensity of growth. However, this paper goes some way towards addressing this issue using the Instrumental Variables (IV) Technique. We explored a number of possible instruments for the causality between aggregate growth patterns and poverty but were unable to identify suitable candidates for which data was available. Thus, we settled for the results of section 4.1 as merely suggestive of the existing correlation.

In focusing on the effect of sectoral employment and productivity changes on poverty, the paper focuses on testing whether employment changes in the secondary sector and productivity changes in agriculture are indeed causally related to poverty reduction. Reverse causality may result from urban crisis increasing poverty and prompting workers to move to agriculture as a safety net. This inflow of workers into agriculture may then reduce productivity in the sector, as well as reducing the share of employment in services and manufacturing. Thus employment reductions in manufacturing and productivity reductions in agriculture may both be a response to rising poverty in urban areas induced by exogenous shocks. However, this would result in employment in urban sectors—i.e. manufacturing and services—being negatively correlated with agricultural employment, and this is contrary to the evidence from the sample which suggests that employment changes in manufacturing are positively correlated with those in agriculture (see Annex). This suggests that an exogenous force is pulling employment in both sectors at the same time. Nevertheless, it is worth considering the non-exogeneity of the sectoral pattern of growth using IV.

To calculate for employment intensive growth in manufacturing we use the average minimum wage in the 5-year period immediately prior to the growth spell being considered. Minimum wages should affect supply and demand decisions to the formal sector, which is overwhelmingly concentrated in the secondary sector and in manufacturing; but because they are computed as the average prior to the growth spell there is no reason to believe they should affect subsequent changes in poverty. We also use the share of workers in agriculture at the beginning of the spell, which should be an indicator of the amount of "surplus labor" available to the manufacturing sector to grow without pushing up wages. We use initial levels of poverty to proxy for the generosity of safety nets/social protection. To instrument for productivity intensive growth in agriculture we use several measures of education of the population at the beginning of the spell.[15] The final specification uses the share of population with secondary education. We could reject the null hypothesis that the instruments were weak at a 5% confidence level, with a relative OLS bias of 5% using the Stock and Yogo test.[16] The *J*-statistic for the test that the instruments were exogenous could not reject the null of exogeneity; thus, at least from a statistical point of view, our instruments are "good" and uncorrelated with the error term. Table 2.7 summarizes the instrumented results as well as the first-stage regression diagnostics. The instrumental variable results support causality from the pattern of growth to poverty reduction, with the effects being much larger than those suggested by un-instrumented regressions.

Conclusions

In this paper we analyzed the relationship between poverty and the employment and productivity profile of growth, both at the aggregate level and by sectors.

We decomposed per capita value-added growth among labor market components (employment, productivity, and demographic changes) and empirically analyzed how each component affects poverty.

We complement the existing literature in several ways. First, we go beyond the sectoral pattern of growth or its overall employment intensity and we analyze the role of sectoral productivity and employment intensity in poverty alleviation. Second, we use a decomposition methodology to construct a measure of employment-intensive growth and an analogous measure of productivity-intensive growth. We believe this measure addresses some conceptual and empirical weaknesses of the more commonly used measure: the employment elasticity of growth. Third, our study includes a larger percentage of countries than previous studies.

We find that the sectoral growth pattern and the employment/productivity profile vary significantly among countries. In the aggregate, the employment intensity of growth does not seem to matter for poverty any more than the productivity intensity; but the sectoral pattern of employment generation and productivity growth is important. The results appear to suggest that employment-intensive growth in the secondary sector alleviates poverty. By contrast, more employment-intensive growth in agriculture tends to be correlated with increases in poverty while productivity-intensive growth in agriculture has a significant correlation with poverty reduction, although both measures are highly correlated so that it is difficult to assess whether productivity increases in agriculture are different from "moving workers out of agriculture."

The results imply that focusing on the overall employment elasticity of

Table 2.7 Instrumental variable regression. Changes in poverty and the sectoral employment/productivity intensity of growth

	Coefficient	Robust standard error	z	P > z	95% Confidence Interval	
Agricultural productivity intensive growth	−11.01	5.77	−1.91	0.06	−22.31	0.29
Secondary sector employment intensive growth	−6.84	3.23	−2.12	0.03	−13.17	−0.51
Changes in the Gini coefficient	4.42	2.03	2.17	0.03	0.44	8.41
Constant	0.10	0.09	1.17	0.24	−0.07	0.28

Number of clusters = 15
Number of obs. = 39
Centered $R2$ = 0.3775
Un-centered $R2$ = 0.3781

Hansen J statistic (overidentification test of all instruments): 1.048
Chi-sq(2)
P-value = 0.59202

Summary results for first-stage regressions:

	Stock and Yogo tests for weakness of instruments				
	Shea				Critical value for 5% maximum bias
Variable	*Partial R2*	*Partial R2*	*F(4,9)*	*F(2,5)*	*P-value*
Agricultural productivity intensive growth	0.3626	0.4488	23.79	11.04	0.0001
Secondary sector employment intensive growth	0.3245	0.4016	18.09	11.04	0.0002
NB: first-stage *F*-state cluster-robust					

growth may not be an effective way to increase the poverty impact of growth. It is important for policy makers to move beyond the aggregate figure of growth and its impact on employment and to place greater focus on the sectoral distribution of growth and its employment and productivity profile.

Notes

*   We would like to thank the participants at the Cornell-Michigan Conference on "Labor Markets in Transition and Developing Economies: Emerging Policy and

Analytical Issues" May 24–6, 2007; at the "Second IZA/World Bank Conference on Employment and Development," June 8–9, 2007; and at the "Poverty Impact Analysis, Monitoring and Evaluation" Brown Bag Lunch Series; for helpful comments. We would also like to thank Jonathan Temple, Ravi Kanbur, Jeemol Unni, Jeff Dayton-Johnson, Germano Mwabu, and Duncan Campbell for comments and advice. All errors and omissions are solely ours. The views expressed here are those of the authors and do not necessarily represent the views of the institution for which they work.

 1 For cross-country evidence of the link between poverty and growth, see Besley and Burgess (2004), Bourguignon (2002), Dollar and Kraay (2002), Kraay (2006), López (2004) and Ravallion (2005); for cross-regional and time series, see Ravallion and Chen (2004) and Ravallion and Datt (2002); for micro analysis, see Bibi (2005), Contreras (2001), and Menezes-Filho and Vasconcellos (2004).
 2 See, for example, Dollar and Kraay (2002), Kraay (2006), Ravallion (2005), Ravallion (2005), Ravallion and Datt (2002), Loayza and Raddatz (2006), and Bourguignon (2002).
 3 This point has been made before by Agenor (2004), Satchi and Temple (2006), and Rama and Artecona (2002).
 4 These three countries were Indonesia, Vietnam, and Tunisia.
 5 See Loayza and Raddatz (2006) for a model that deals with this mechanism.
 6 Gutierrez, C., Paci, P., Orecchia, C., and Serneels, P., (2007). Does Employment Generation Really Matter for Poverty Reduction? (Annex). World Bank Policy Research Working Paper No. 4442, Washington DC. See http://www.worldbank.org/employment for details on the decomposition.
 7 In developing countries measuring participation is often extremely difficult as much of the labor exchange takes place outside the labor market and for household consumption. Thus the working-age population is a better measure of available labor supply than the number of those participating actively in the labor market.
 8 In addition, empirically, arriving at consistent estimates of partial elasticity of employment with respect to growth at the aggregate level is often difficult (Hamermesh 1986, 1993); and cross-country data is often limited.
 9 It should be noted that most of the poverty-growth literature uses changes in mean survey income as a measure for growth. Instead, we are concerned with growth in per capita value added.
10 The Annex lists the growth spells.
11 In particular we include data on employment based on calculations from microdata for three African: Senegal (World Bank 2007a); Ghana (World Bank 2007b); and Madagascar (World Bank 2007c).
12 We report only one poverty measure as, in our sample, changes in poverty depth are strongly correlated with changes in headcount poverty.
13 The correlation between poverty and changes in distribution is well known (Bourguignon 2002). Inequality may also affect the pattern of growth. Higher levels of inequality may promote pro-capital or pro-labor policies or anti-agricultural bias (see Loayza and Raddatz 2006). Initial levels of inequality and of mean income, as well as the interaction of both, were also included but were found to be insignificant.
14 Results available upon request.
15 Source of minimum wage data is: Sulla Scarpetta and Pierre (mimeo). Data on education comes from UNESCO.
16 If we accept weak instruments and only a 5% relative bias of IV, compared to un-instrumented OLS regression, our instruments are correlated with our explanatory variable and our model is identified with a 5% significance level. With more than one potentially endogenous repressor the first-stage F-statistic is not a good measure of how good the instruments are (see Stock and Yogo 2002).

References

Agénor, P.-R. (2004) "The Macroeconomics of Poverty Reduction." Discussion Paper Series No 043, September 2004. Centre for Growth and Business Cycle Research, Economics, University of Manchester, Manchester, M13 9PL, UK.

Besley, T. and R. Burgess (2004) "Can Labor Regulation Hinder Economic Performance? Evidence from India." *Quarterly Journal of Economics* 119 (1): 91–132.

Bibi, S. (2005) "When Is Economic Growth Pro-Poor? Evidence from Tunisia." Cahier de recherche/Working Paper 05–22, CIRPEE.

Bourguignon, F. (2002) "The Growth Elasticity of Poverty Reduction: Explaining heterogeneity across countries and time periods." DELTA Working Papers No. 2002–3.

Contreras, D. (2001) "Economic Growth and Poverty Reduction by Region: Chile 1990–96," *Development Policy Review*, 19(3): 291–302.

Coxhead, I. and P. G. Warr (1995) "Does Technical Progress in Agriculture Alleviate Poverty? A Philippine case study." *Australian Journal of Agricultural Economics* 39(1): 25–54.

Datt, G. and M. Ravallion (1998) "Farm Productivity and Rural Poverty in India." *Journal of Development Studies* 24(4): 62–85.

Dollar, D. and A. Kraay (2002) "Growth Is Good for the Poor." *Journal of Economic Growth* 7(3): 195–225.

Fane, G. and P. Warr (2002) "How Economic Growth Reduces Poverty." WIDER Discussion Paper No. 2002/19, United Nations University Centre 53–70, Jingumae 5-chome, Shibuya-ku, Tokyo, Japan.

Hamermesh, D. (1986) "The Demand for Labor in the Long Run." *Handbook of Labor Economics*, edited by O. Ashenfelter and R. Layard, I: 429–71. Amsterdam, Netherlands: Elsevier Science Publisher.

Hamermesh, D. (1993) *Labor Demand*. Princeton, NJ: Princeton University Press.

Islam, R. (2004) "The Nexus of Economic Growth, Employment and Poverty Reduction: An empirical analysis." Issues in Employment and Poverty Discussion Paper 14, January 2004. Geneva: International Labour Office.

Kakwani, N., M. Neri, and H. H. Son (2006) "Linkages between Pro-poor Growth, Social Programmes and Labour Market: The Recent Brazilian Experience." Working paper No. 26, Brazil: UNDP International Poverty Center.

Kraay, A. (2006) "When Is Growth Pro-poor? Evidence from a Panel of Countries." *Journal of Development Economics* 80(1): 198–227.

Loayza, N. and C. Raddatz (2006) "The Composition of Growth Matters for Poverty Alleviation." Mimeo, Washington, DC: World Bank.

Lopez, J. H. (2004) "Pro-Growth, Pro-Poor: Is there a tradeoff?" Policy Research Paper No. 3378. Washington, DC: World Bank.

Menezes-Filho, N. and L. Vasconcellos (2004) "Operationalizing Pro-Poor Growth: A country study for Brazil." Background Paper in the Operationalizing Pro-Poor Growth Program Series by Agence Française pour le Développement, Bundesministerium für Wirtschaftlieche Zusammenarbeit. Washington DC: UK Department for International Development and The World Bank.

Prasada R., D. S. Colleli, J. Timothy, and M. Alauddin (2004) "Agricultural Productivity Growth and Poverty in Developing Countries, 1970–2000." Employment Strategy Papers No. 2004/9, Employment Trends Department, Geneva: ILO.

Rama, M. and R. Artecona (2002) "A Database for Labor Market Indicators Across Countries." Mimeo, Washington, DC: World Bank, June 2002.

Ravallion, M. (2005) "Inequality Is Good for the Poor." Policy Research Working Paper 3377. Washington DC.: World Bank.

—— and G. Datt (2002) "Why Has Economic Growth Been More Pro-Poor in Some States of India than Others?" *Journal of Development Economics* 381–400.

—— and S. Chen (2004) "China's (Uneven) Progress Against Poverty." Policy Research Paper No. 3408, Washington, DC: World Bank.

Satchi, M. and J. Temple (2006) *Growth and Labor Markets in Developing Countries.* Department of Economics, University of Bristol Discussion Papers, Bristol, UK.

Shorrocks, A. F. (1999) "Decomposition Procedures for Distributional Analysis: A unified framework based on the Shapley value." Mimeo, University of Essex, UK.

Stock, J. H. and M. Yogo (2002) "Testing for Weak Instruments in IV linear Regression." Technical Working Paper 284 NBER.

Sulla, S. and P. "A Database for Labor Market Regulations and Institutions Across Countries." Mimeo, World Bank, unpublished.

World Bank (2005) "Pro-Poor Growth in the 1990's: Lessons and Insights from 14 Countries." Agence Française pour le Développement, Bundesministerium für Wirtschaftlieche Zusammenarbeit, UK. Department for International Development and The World Bank, Washington DC.

World Bank (2007a) "A la Recherche de l'Emploi—Le Chemin vers la Prospérité—Senegal." Country Economic Memorandum, Washington DC: World Bank.

World Bank (2007b) "The Role of Employment and Earnings for Shared Growth: The Case of Ghana." Mimeo, Washington DC: World Bank.

World Bank (2007c) "The Role of Employment and Earnings for Shared Growth: The Case of Madagascar." Mimeo, Washington DC.: World Bank.

Annex: Sample and descriptive statistics

Table 2.A1 List of countries and spells

Country	Spell	Region	Income Level
Argentina	96–8	Latin America and Caribbean	Upper middle
Argentina	98–01	Latin America and Caribbean	Upper middle
Azerbaijan	01–2	Europe and Central Asia	Lower middle
Bangladesh	83–5	South Asia	Low
Bolivia	97–9	Latin America and Caribbean	Lower middle
Brazil	02–3	Latin America and Caribbean	Lower middle
Brazil	81–4	Latin America and Caribbean	Lower middle
Brazil	84–5	Latin America and Caribbean	Lower middle
Brazil	85–7	Latin America and Caribbean	Lower middle
Brazil	87–9	Latin America and Caribbean	Lower middle
Brazil	89–90	Latin America and Caribbean	Lower middle
Brazil	92–3	Latin America and Caribbean	Lower middle
Brazil	93–5	Latin America and Caribbean	Lower middle
Brazil	95–6	Latin America and Caribbean	Lower middle
Brazil	96–7	Latin America and Caribbean	Lower middle
Brazil	97–8	Latin America and Caribbean	Lower middle
Brazil	98–9	Latin America and Caribbean	Lower middle
Brazil	99–01	Latin America and Caribbean	Lower middle
Chile	87–9	Latin America and Caribbean	Upper middle
Chile	89–90	Latin America and Caribbean	Upper middle

Chile	90–2	Latin America and Caribbean	Upper middle
Chile	92–4	Latin America and Caribbean	Upper middle
Chile	96–8	Latin America and Caribbean	Upper middle
Chile	98–00	Latin America and Caribbean	Upper middle
Colombia	88–9	Latin America and Caribbean	Lower middle
Colombia	91–5	Latin America and Caribbean	Lower middle
Colombia	95–6	Latin America and Caribbean	Lower middle
Colombia	96–98	Latin America and Caribbean	Lower middle
Colombia	98–9	Latin America and Caribbean	Lower middle
Colombia	99–00	Latin America and Caribbean	Lower middle
Costa Rica	90–3	Latin America and Caribbean	Upper middle
Costa Rica	93–6	Latin America and Caribbean	Upper middle
Costa Rica	96–7	Latin America and Caribbean	Upper middle
Costa Rica	97–8	Latin America and Caribbean	Upper middle
Croatia	00–1	Europe and Central Asia	Upper middle
Croatia	98–9	Europe and Central Asia	Upper middle
Croatia	99–00	Europe and Central Asia	Upper middle
Dominican Republic	92–6	Latin America and Caribbean	Lower middle
Ecuador	94–8	Latin America and Caribbean	Lower middle
Egypt	90–5	Middle East and North Africa	Lower middle
Egypt	95–9	Middle East and North Africa	Lower middle
El Salvador	96–7	Latin America and Caribbean	Lower middle
Georgia	00–1	Europe and Central Asia	Lower middle
Georgia	01–2	Europe and Central Asia	Lower middle
Georgia	02–3	Europe and Central Asia	Lower middle
Georgia	98–9	Europe and Central Asia	Lower middle
Georgia	99–00	Europe and Central Asia	Lower middle
Honduras	96–8	Latin America and Caribbean	Lower middle
Honduras	98–9	Latin America and Caribbean	Lower middle
Indonesia	93–6	East Asia and Pacific	Lower middle
Indonesia	96–8	East Asia and Pacific	Lower middle
Indonesia	98–9	East Asia and Pacific	Lower middle
Jamaica	92–3	Latin America and Caribbean	Lower middle
Jamaica	93–6	Latin America and Caribbean	Lower middle
Jamaica	96–9	Latin America and Caribbean	Lower middle
Jamaica	99–00	Latin America and Caribbean	Lower middle
Kazakhstan	02–3	Europe and Central Asia	Lower middle
Malaysia	84–7	East Asia and Pacific	Upper middle
Malaysia	87–9	East Asia and Pacific	Upper middle
Malaysia	89–92	East Asia and Pacific	Upper middle
Malaysia	95–7	East Asia and Pacific	Upper middle
Mexico	00–2	Latin America and Caribbean	Upper middle
Mexico	96–8	Latin America and Caribbean	Upper middle
Mexico	98–00	Latin America and Caribbean	Upper middle
Mongolia	95–8	East Asia and Pacific	Low
Nicaragua	93–8	Latin America and Caribbean	Lower middle
Nicaragua	98–01	Latin America and Caribbean	Lower middle
Pakistan	90–2	South Asia	Low
Pakistan	92–6	South Asia	Low
Panama	00–1	Latin America and Caribbean	Upper middle
Panama	01–2	Latin America and Caribbean	Upper middle
Panama	91–5	Latin America and Caribbean	Upper middle
Panama	95–6	Latin America and Caribbean	Upper middle
Panama	96–00	Latin America and Caribbean	Upper middle

(*Continued overleaf*)

Table 2.A1 Continued

Country	Spell	Region	Income Level
Peru	00–1	Latin America and Caribbean	Lower middle
Peru	96–00	Latin America and Caribbean	Lower middle
Republic of Moldova	01–2	Europe and Central Asia	Lower middle
Republic of Moldova	02–3	Europe and Central Asia	Lower middle
Republic of Moldova	99–01	Europe and Central Asia	Lower middle
Romania	02–3	Europe and Central Asia	Upper middle
Romania	98–00	Europe and Central Asia	Upper middle
Senegal	91–4	Sub-Saharan Africa	Low
Senegal	94–01	Sub-Saharan Africa	Low
TFYR Macedonia	02–3	Europe and Central Asia	Lower middle
Thailand	98–9	East Asia and Pacific	Lower middle
Thailand	99–00	East Asia and Pacific	Lower middle
Trinidad and Tobago	88–92	Latin America and Caribbean	Upper middle
Turkey	00–2	Europe and Central Asia	Upper middle
Turkey	02–3	Europe and Central Asia	Upper middle
Turkey	94–00	Europe and Central Asia	Upper middle
Venezuela	81–7	Latin America and Caribbean	Upper middle
Venezuela	87–9	Latin America and Caribbean	Upper middle
Venezuela	89–93	Latin America and Caribbean	Upper middle
Venezuela	93–5	Latin America and Caribbean	Upper middle
Venezuela	95–6	Latin America and Caribbean	Upper middle
Venezuela	96–7	Latin America and Caribbean	Upper middle
Venezuela	97–8	Latin America and Caribbean	Upper middle
Venezuela	98–00	Latin America and Caribbean	Upper middle
Vietnam	02–4	East Asia and Pacific	Low
Vietnam	98–02	East Asia and Pacific	Low
Zambia	96–8	Sub-Saharan Africa	Low

Table 2.A2 Other countries in the sample that have some outlier observations

Country	Spell	Region	Income level
Argentina	01–2	Latin America and Caribbean	Upper middle
Brazil	01–2	Latin America and Caribbean	Lower middle
Bulgaria	97–01	Europe and Central Asia	Lower middle
Bulgaria	89–97	Europe and Central Asia	Lower middle
Colombia	80–8	Latin America and Caribbean	Lower middle
El Salvador	95–6	Latin America and Caribbean	Lower middle
Ghana	91–8	Sub-Saharan Africa	Low
Honduras	90–2	Latin America and Caribbean	Lower middle
Kazakhstan	01–2	Europe and Central Asia	Lower middle
Madagascar	99–01	Sub-Saharan Africa	Low
Malaysia	92–5	East Asia and Pacific	Upper middle
Mongolia	95–8	East Asia and Pacific	Low
Peru	90–6	Latin America and Caribbean	Lower middle
Sri Lanka	85–90	South Asia	Lower middle
Thailand	96–8	East Asia and Pacific	Lower middle

Table 2.A3 Correlation between measures of employment and productivity-intensive growth

	Employment-intensive growth			Productivity-intensive growth		
	Agriculture	Secondary sector	Tertiary sector	Agriculture	Secondary sector	Tertiary sector
Employment-intensive growth Agriculture	1					
Employment-intensive growth Secondary sector	0.5247	1				
Employment-intensive growth Tertiary sector	0.7629	0.6417	1			
Agriculture productivity-intensive growth	−0.9064	−0.5305	−0.7173	1		
Secondary sector Productivity-intensive growth	−0.5159	−0.4914	−0.4957	0.4275	1	
Tertiary sector Productivity-intensive growth	−0.6672	−0.3713	−0.7685	0.5468	0.4080	1

3 Employment elasticity in organized manufacturing in India*

Dipak Mazumdar and Sandip Sarkar

The problem of low employment elasticity in manufacturing—that is, the feeling that employment growth has been lagging seriously behind output growth—has been a serious issue in development economics since the 1960s, when concerns about the employment problem in third-world countries began to be discussed (see, for example, Morawetz 1974). It has been a particularly important matter of concern in India, which has had a dismal record on employment generation in "organized (formal) manufacturing in recent years. The concern is a serious one for two basic reasons: first, formal manufacturing has been traditionally expected to take the lead in the generation of new productive employment and to have large multiplier effects on the other sectors; and second, because of the huge labor productivity differential between the organized and the unorganized sectors, wage levels are at a much lower level in informal manufacturing, and so the dependence on the latter for manufacturing growth does not do much for raising living standards at the lower part of the distribution.

In this paper we undertake a systematic analysis of the determinants of employment elasticity in Indian formal manufacturing based on the unit-level data available from the *Annual Survey of Industry* (ASI) conducted by the Central Statistical Office of the Government of India. The paper is set out as follows. In Section 1 we give an overview of the behavior over time in employment elasticity in this sector over the last four decades. We are able to classify the entire period into four completed and one ongoing sub-periods which reveal a cyclical pattern of the value of employment elasticity. The political economy of the four completed periods are explained. Section 2 sets out the outline of the decomposition model, used elsewhere by Mazumdar (2003), which seeks to break down the different factors affecting the growth rate of employment given the growth rate of output (value added in constant prices). This section also goes beyond the earlier paper in setting out a model of the equilibrium of the firm which illuminates the economic process behind the decomposition model. The three factors shaping the value of employment elasticity are (i) the trend in the share of wages; (ii) the wage–employment trade-off; and (iii) the movement in the domestic real exchange rate (DRER) or the ratio of the producer price index to the consumer price index. While the third is more a product of macro-economic factors, the first two are primarily labor market variables. The mechanics underlying the movements in the three variables are explained. The results of the empirical application of the decomposition model are spelled out in Section 3 for the various periods distinguished. They show the relative importance of the three factors over the cycles. In Section 4 we turn to some analysis with disaggregated sectors of formal manufacturing. In particular we discuss the experiences of the public and private sectors of formal manufacturing as well as those of different sub-groups of industry, distinguished by the dual criteria of exposure to world markets and the level of technology. Section 5 summarizes some of the more important results.

1 Classifying the periods of manufacturing growth in terms of employment elasticity

The organized manufacturing sector in India has grown at different rates in different periods of its development in the last 30 years. At the same time employment elasticity—the rate of growth of employment relative to output growth—has also varied enormously over these phases of growth. Figure 3.1 plots the volume of employment against the real value added in manufacturing (at constant prices) in logarithmic scale, so that the slope of the curve gives an idea of the changing value of employment elasticity in different periods.

We are able to distinguish between five periods in terms of distinct breaks in the value of employment elasticity (i) 1974–80 when employment elasticity had a high positive value of 0.99; (ii) the 1980–6 period of "jobless growth" when employment elasticity actually turned negative (with an average value of –0.16); (iii) the reform period of 1986–96, which saw a recovery of the

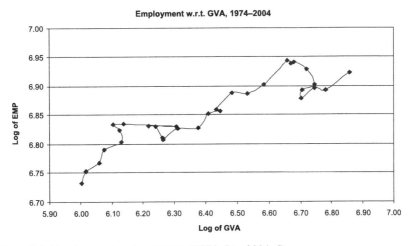

Figure 3.1 Employment and real GVA (1974–5 to 2004–5).

employment elasticity to positive values (increasing to 0.33), although significantly lower than the value attained in the first period; (iv) the post-reform period of recession,1996–2001; and (v) the current boom which is still ongoing. These periods also witnessed widely differing growth rates of value added. The data are given in Table 3.1.

The latest figure we have from the ASI is for the year 2004–5. The number of years covered for the last period is too few to give us reliable estimates of trends. We can only talk about the likely developments for this last period—which is still ongoing. Further comments on period V are therefore mostly consigned to the endnotes. The discussion in the text concentrates on the first four periods of Table 3.1.

It transpires that the periods distinguished above are reasonably separate in terms of the politics of Indian economic policy. The beginning of the 1980s has been identified by some researchers as having an "attitudinal shift" towards private business on the part of the government (Rodrik and Subramanaian 2004). "The change was inaugurated with the return of a much-chastened Indira Gandhi to political power in the 1980s after a three-year rule by the Janata Party . . . But the attitudinal change was grounded primarily in political calculation, and not in a desire to enhance the efficiency of the economic regime" (ibid, 15). The motivation has been ascribed to Indira Gandhi's desire to undercut one prong of the support of the Janata Party coming from organized business groups. "This shift had more to do with currying favor with existing business interests (essentially large, politically influential firms in the formal manufacturing sector) than with liberalizing the system" (ibid). Rodrik and Subramanain had identified in a more detailed way the significant increase in growth rate—of organized manufacturing in particular—evident in the data of Figure 3.1. They also pointed out that when the industrial firms were operating so far below the production possibility frontier small changes in government policy—even of the "attitudinal shift" kind could—bring about a substantial response.

Indira Gandhi herself was not able to go through with much of a substantial reform program even if she had planned to do so. After her assassination, it was left to Rajiv Gandhi to start on some pieces of substantive reform. It is customary to date the coming of reforms from 1991. This is because

Table 3.1 Growth rate of value added and employment elasticity

Period	Value added growth	Employment elasticity
I 1974–80	3.99	0.99
II 1980–6	6.21	−0.17
III 1986–96	10.65	0.33
IV 1996–2001	1.75	−1.39
V 2001–2004	12.54	0.28

Note: The years reported in column 1 are the first of two successive half-year periods; for example, 1974 is an abbreviation for 1974–5.

liberalization on the external and trade accounts were only then seriously addressed as part of the package agreed with the IMF after the serious balance of payments crisis of 1991. However, as indicated above, the reform process had started earlier in a substantive way. The decade spanning the period stretching from the mid-1980s to the mid-1990s could be regarded legitimately as the reform period. This was the period that saw an upsurge of business optimism in the organized manufacturing sector, leading not only to a still higher growth rate of output, but also, as we shall see, a large lift in the investment ratio as manufacturing firms sought to build up their capacity. The overhang of the excess capacity of the controlled era of low efficiency had presumably been run down by the surge in output growth, starting at the beginning of the 1980s.

Period IV in the table has seen a post-reform recession. The windfall gains forming the initial liberalization of the economy had been realized, and the manufacturing sector had to adjust to the more difficult problems of market growth in a competitive environment. The reform process itself might have slowed down as policy makers and the various interest groups started to grapple with the thorny issues of continuing on the reform path.

The turnaround in Indian manufacturing came in 2000–1 and is still continuing. The record for Period V is incomplete, but it is clear that there has been a significant recovery in output growth and along with it, the value of employment elasticity.

2 The determinants of employment elasticity: a conceptual framework

This section discusses the conceptual framework for analyzing the significant factors determining employment elasticity which has been used for the analysis of the Indian data. It will hopefully identify the quantitative importance of some of the critical variables which have affected the growth of employment in Indian manufacturing, and the way they have varied over the four periods distinguished in the last section. The empirical results are presented in the next section following a discussion of the analytical framework.

Employment growth in manufacturing is obviously limited by the rate of growth of output or value added; but given the growth rate of output, there are three important elements determining the value of employment elasticity:

i the trend in the share of wages, i.e. the rate of growth of the wage bill relative to value added in current prices facing the producer (a);

ii the relative rates of increase in the producer and consumer price indices (DRER)—which determines the value of the wage bill for the workers in terms of the prices facing them;

iii the trade-off between employment increase and real wage increase.

The process is shown in the following box:

> **Output Growth $\Rightarrow$ Wage bill growth $\Rightarrow$ DRER $\Rightarrow$ Wage bill growth $\Rightarrow$ Emp-Wage Tradeoff**
>
> *(producer prices) a (producer prices) P_p/P_c (consumer prices)*

We can use an algebraic decomposition, explained elsewhere (Mazumdar 2003) to quantify the different elements:

$$\dot{L} = a\dot{v} + [a\dot{P}_p - \dot{P}_c] - \dot{w} \tag{1}$$

where w is the real wage (average earnings per worker); v is value added (in constant producer prices); L is employment; P_p is the index of producer prices, P_c is the index of consumer prices; and a is a technological and behavioral parameter which is assumed to remain constant over the period under consideration. A variable written with a dot on top (˙) represents the *proportionate* rate of change of the variable concerned.

The equation for employment elasticity can be derived from (1), and reads as follows:

$$\dot{L}/\dot{v} = a + [a\dot{P}_p - \dot{P}_c]/\dot{v} - \dot{w}/\dot{v} \tag{1a}$$

where a defines the rate of growth of the wage bill relative to the growth rate of output and hence determines the trend of the share of wages over the time-period being considered. The relative movements of the producer price and the consumer price indices, DRER, translates the wage bill growth into real terms (in terms of consumer prices).

The first term of equation (1) can be considered to be the "output effect" on employment growth, and the second term (within square brackets) the "price-effect." The negative relationship between $\dot{w}$ and $\dot{L}$ clearly shows the wage–employment trade-off, i.e. the way the growing wage bill cake is divided between wage increase and employment increase.

If the firm has no external source of finance, and can neither accumulate nor draw down financial reserves, then it must balance its books at every stage, and equation (1) is an identity. No firm can be expected to behave in this way. Generally, it would have a means of external borrowing, but in order not to face bankruptcy, it will aim at achieving a target gearing ratio. This target has to be reached, not on a day-to-day basis, but over a period of time—usually determined by its accounting period of consequence. Equation (1) then becomes a condition of equilibrium of the firm which enables it to maintain a stable gearing ratio over time. The model then has to be completed by a theory of the equilibrium of the firm in which the interconnected variables would force the firm towards this equilibrium.

The model of the firm and its equilibrium

We have assumed that one of the key determinants of employment elasticity—the DRER—is an exogenously determined variable. Prices of both producer goods and consumer goods are given to the firm. The other two, the share of wages and the wage–employment trade-off, are both labor market variables. They are separate decisions, shaped by different groups of considerations.

We postulate that (i) the decision about the share of wages is tied to the decision about the investment ratio that the firm seeks to attain over the period of its forthcoming business plan. (ii) The wage–employment trade-off, on the other hand, is a decision about where the firm chooses to locate itself on the wage–efficiency function facing each worker.

(i) There is a long tradition in economics that has worked with the idea that firms finance investment principally from the internal surpluses generated by the firm. Even though we have external financing, the need to achieve the target gearing ratio effectively makes internal sources the principal source of investment. Thus, the share of profits in value added is the crucial variable here. In fact it can be postulated that it is the investment rate which determines the share of profits (and hence wages).[1]

This does not mean that firms are able to fix their investment arbitrarily so that any share of wages will do. For any investment rate there is a determined level of the wage bill corresponding to the wage share. The firm must make sure that this level of the wage bill is sufficient to elicit the supply of labor needed to work with the investment achieved.

(ii) There is, however, another point of decision-making involved in the firm. The supply of work (in efficiency units) is a function of two variables: the number of workers and the supply of efficiency units per worker. The latter is positively related to the wage rate.[2]

For the profit-maximizing firm, for a given wage bill, the optimum labor supply will be achieved where the marginal cost of hiring an extra body of workers is exactly equal to the marginal cost of increasing the same number of labor units by increasing the wage rate of the existing workforce. The firm will generally not locate itself on this "least cost" point even if it is able to identify it a priori. It will be subject to institutional pressures from the state, labor organization and the employers' perception of significant institutional pressure.[3] If, for example, the power of "insiders" in the workforce is strong, employers might be induced to locate on a higher point of the wage–efficiency curve with a high wage per man and a high rate of supply of efficiency units. A similar situation might arise if job security laws make employers wary of the cost of employing a large body of workers which might be difficult to lay off. On the other hand, state and/or union political pressure might force firms to inflate the number of privileged workers employed in the formal sector firms (which we are considering) leading to the firm locating itself to a point to the left of the "optimum" (most profitable) point on the wage–efficiency function.

The two decisions about the share of wages (influenced by the desired investment ratio) and the wage per man offered (influenced by the firm's position on the wage–employment function) have to be consistent with each other, and the consistency is imposed by the production function facing the firm.

It should be clear that the decisions taken by the firm discussed above are decisions about the coming planning period and hence will be critically influenced by *expectations*. However, we can illustrate the mechanics of the equilibrium to which the firm tends by considering a static model at a point of time. Figure 3.2 illustrates the decision about the location of the firm in the wage–efficiency space (which determines the wage–employment trade-off in our dynamic decomposition). L^* is the level of efficiency unit per worker (corresponding to the wage W^* per worker) at which the wage cost per efficiency unit is minimized—if the supply of labor to the individual firm is perfectly elastic at the going wage. In a pseudo-monopsonistic labor market in which the individual firm operates with its own body of selected and "attached" workers, the firm will generally be faced with an upward sloping supply curve of labor to itself. Thus, the optimum least-cost point for the firm is to locate itself at wage W with a supply of efficiency units of L (given by the point of tangency of the marginal cost of hiring extra workers within the wage–efficiency curve). In general the firm is not able to operate at this least-cost point because of institutional pressure from either the state and labor organizations, or its own perceptions about the cost of employing quasi-fixed labor. Thus, the position of the firm on the wage–efficiency curve will be generally either to the right or the left of the least-cost point given by the W-L configuration. The wage-cost per efficiency unit per work could in either case be higher than the lowest cost. Figure 3.3 shows how this decision has to be consistent with the decision about the investment ratio (and hence the share of profits).

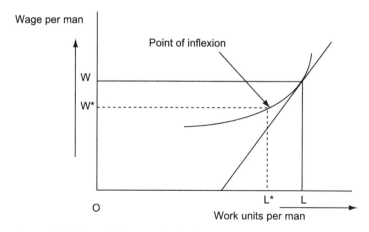

Figure 3.2 Wage–efficiency relationship.

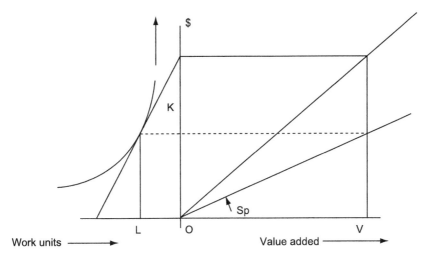

Figure 3.3 General equilibrium.

The location of the firm on the wage–efficiency function determines the wage cost per work-unit faced by the firm. With the supply price of capital (finance) fixed exogenously, the line for the factor–price ratio is as shown in the left-hand quadrant of Figure 3.3 and the firm attains the highest isoquant (given by the production function) at the point of tangency with the factor-price line as portrayed. At this point the firm uses OK units of capital and OL units of labor (efficiency units). Ignoring the target value of the gearing ratio for simplification, the firm must supply OK amount of capital out of profits. The value added corresponding to the most profitable point on the isoquant should be sufficient to support both this volume of investible profits and the wage bill corresponding to the supply of OL amount of work-units at the established wage cost per efficiency unit. The general equilibrium is shown in Figure 3.3. A 45°-line translates the value added produced by the isoquant to the X-axis of Figure 3.3 (the units are adjusted so that a unit of capital has the same value as a unit of output). The line with a slope of S_p shows the value of investible profit corresponding to the value of output. As shown OK amount of investible profit produced by the amount of output OV leaves an amount just sufficient to meet the cost of the wage bill to provide for OL amount of work units.[4]

Dynamics of the firm

While the static equilibrium of the system at a point of time as described in the last sub-section gives an idea of the interrelationships of the system, the dynamic movement of the firm from period to period is governed by expect-ations, which are revised as the latter are only partially fulfilled. The firm adjusts in the direction to which the pressure towards the general equilibrium of the system points.[5] Thus, if the expectations about financing the investment has been too rosy, the firm will be faced with a shortage of labor units to produce the desired output and the investment ratio has to be adjusted downward. Of course new expectations are formed for the ensuing period and these might swamp the adjustment dictated by the realized magnitudes of the current period. Any observed trend value of a variable in our equation (1) or (1a) over a calendar period is thus a statistical average of a succession of decisions based on expectations and their revision.

The cyclical predictions of the model

It is generally accepted in the economic literature that the rate of investment of the firm is very sensitive to *expectations* of market trends. This sensitivity to the *perception* of the future by entrepreneurs makes the investment ratio follow a typically cyclical pattern. Since the share of wages in our theory is ultimately determined by the investment ratio, it will have a cyclical pattern—though it would be anticyclical. The investment ratio increases in periods of optimism and thus the share of wages (and in our model *a*) falls. This has the effect *ceteris paribus* of *reducing* the value of employment elasticity.

Consider now the second labor market variable: the wage–employment trade-off. It has been recognized increasingly in modern labor economics that labor is also a *quasi-fixed* factor. We have discussed above that entrepreneurs have the option of increasing the flow of labor units either by hiring more workers, or by eliciting more work-units from the existing workforce by increasing the wage per worker. In many economies including India, a distinction has to be made between the permanent core of workers and contract labor of various types. The firm operates with at least a core body of tenured workers whose size is slow to respond to changes in the current demand for labor. This is because the cost of hiring-and-firing of "permanent" workers is significant. Like the stock of fixed investments the firm's stock of the "permanent" workers is built up more on their perception of *expected* demand. If current demand deviates from the expected demand, firms adjust the labor input for the period in question by varying the flow of labor units per worker rather than the stock of labor. If expectations are buoyant, firms would build up the stock of labor, and there would be less concern with an increase in wage per worker to elicit a larger inflow of labor units per worker. This will *ceteris paribus* tilt the wage–employment trade-off towards employment increase. Conversely, when there is a downward trend in expected growth, firms would tend to be more inclined to reduce the size of their labor force (through normal attrition of the quasi-fixed part and retrenchment of the non-tenured component) and meet their demand for labor input by increasing the wage per worker. Thus, the trade-off would show a bias to wage growth.

It is then seen that the cyclical behavior of the wage–employment trade-off is *pro-cyclical*—the tilt to employment tends to increase in periods of optimistic expectation and decrease in times of gloomy prospects. Thus as far as the impact on employment elasticity is concerned, the two elements of our decomposition model work in opposite directions with respect to economic cycles. In the upswing the wage share tends to fall, leaving a smaller pie of value added to be taken in the form of either employment or wage increase, but the trade-off leans towards a larger share for employment growth. The net result on employment elasticity depends on the relative strength of these two effects.

Lastly, it is likely that the variable considered exogenous in our decomposition model—the ratio of producer prices to consumer prices (DRER)—will also have a cyclical swing. It can be expected to decline during the downswing and pick up during the upswing. This cyclical movement might be imposed on a longer-term secular swing—in which case, with a downward secular trend, DRER would decline less in an upswing. This is, as we will see, what happened in the 1980s and the 1990s in the case of India. This cyclical movement of the DRER would then have a pro-cyclical impact on employment elasticity, since the DRER term in equation (1a) is negative. However, any cyclical pattern in the movement of this variable might be overshadowed by longer-term trends in the world market (for tradable goods) or in domestic policies (for non-tradables).

3 Decomposition of the factors determining employment elasticity: empirical results

The methodology of decomposition expounded in the last section is now applied to the time series for the organized manufacturing sector as given in the Annual Survey of Industry (ASI) data set. Equation (1) is applied to growth rates separately for the four periods distinguished in Section 2. The results are presented below in Table 3.2. Note that for each period the compound growth rates of the variables in the first five columns are calculated, and the value of the last variable a is calculated as a residual using equation (1). This is because, as explained the equation (1) must hold over a discrete period of time (in our case over the years covered by each of the four cycles). The value of a tends to adjust itself in each period to secure the equilibrium of the firm.

Table 3.2 Proportionate growth rates of selected variables for four periods

Period	$\dot{W}$	$\dot{v}$	$\dot{L}$	$\dot{P}_p$	$\dot{P}_c$	a	Output effect	Price effect	Employment elasticity
I (1974–80)	2.63	3.99	3.95	7.10	4.72	1.02	4.07	2.52	0.99
II (1980–6)	3.51	6.31	−1.01	6.32	8.91	0.90	5.68	−3.20	−0.16
III (1986–96)	1.83	10.65	3.54	9.10	9.56	0.76	8.10	−2.68	0.33
IV(1996–2002)	0.88	1.75	−2.74	3.07	6.92	1.11	1.93	−3.53	−1.42

Note: The values of growth rates are compound rates. a is calculated as a residual using the decomposition equation. The output and price effects are also calculated from equation (1) as defined.

We can see at once the enormous differences in employment elasticities—just about unity in the first period, turning strongly negative in the second period, and recovering to a value of just over 0.3 in the third period. In the last period of post-reform years, the employment elasticity turned negative in a more substantial way than before, even as the output growth faltered.

Period I can be considered to be the period of "benign" growth in terms of the variables treated in our analysis. The economy experienced a moderately high rate of output growth at around 4% per annum. This was, however, supplemented by a favorable trend in the producer prices relative to consumer prices. Since the value of a was just over unity, the share of wages in gross value added grew at the same rate as output, so that in terms of real wage bills the growth rate was over 6% per annum, including the real output growth plus the relative increase in producer prices. It is seen from the value of $\dot{w}$ and $\dot{L}$ that this growing cake was shared between wage growth and employment growth, with the result that employment elasticity was high at around unity.

The subsequent periods register major deviations from this standard. Of the non-labor market variables the impact of the price-effect over all the three succeeding periods leads to a significant difference. The price-effect turned negative after the "benign" first period, and quantitatively it was in all periods a significant "leakage" from the growth in the real output. While this factor was a persistent negative influence in all three periods, the cyclical swings in employment elasticity were the net result of the way the actual magnitudes of the two labor market variables worked out in these periods.

Period II has been called the period of "jobless growth" in India. In spite of a healthy rate of growth of output the employment elasticity turned negative (employment actually fell). It can be seen from Table 3.2 that while the price effect turned significantly negative, real wage growth relative to output growth fell only slightly behind the ratio of the previous period, while a decreased somewhat as the investment rate showed an upward movement. The substantial "leakage" from the wage bill growth meant that the real wage growth relative to output growth could be maintained at nearly its previous level only if there was a large decrease in employment growth—which in fact turned negative. Thus, the gap between $\dot{L}$ and $\dot{W}$ turned from a positive value of 1.32 in Period I to a huge negative value of −4.84 in Period II (see Table 3.2) signifying a massive movement upward on the wage–efficiency function.[6] The period of benign growth preceding it had seen an accumulation of excess labor in manufacturing, driven in part by the policies of government in alliance with a trade union movement biased towards a policy of expanding and protecting employment in the formal sector. When the dominance of this institutional support in favor of those already in employment eased, employers responded with policies which met the demand for labor by eking out more efficient units of labor from a reduced stock.[7]

The succeeding two periods of boom and slump saw the labor market variables working out much as had been predicted in our theoretical discussion in the last section. In the upswing of the post reform years of Period III the uplift in the investment ratio resulted in a sharp reduction of the share of wages (a drastic reduction of a).[8] This would have pushed employment elasticity to further lower levels; but the negative impact of price effect moderated significantly in this period, which was a factor pulling in the opposite direction. At the same time there was a tilt in the wage–employment trade-off to employment growth, as employers, buoyed up by optimistic expectations and an erosion of the excess stock of labor from the last period, sought to build up their labor complement. The net result was a positive if low value of employment elasticity.

As far as the bias towards employment growth is concerned, one of the elements in the story quite clearly is that the excess capacity of the labor force, which might have been a legacy of the previous years, had been largely eliminated during the period of "jobless growth." With the strong output growth registered in this period it was necessary to increase the size of employment over time. Nevertheless, the relatively low employment elasticity suggests that employers might have been wary of the critical role of job security legislation. Not only was labor used more efficiently, employers in this period are widely reported to have used a variety of other methods of organizing production that helped to moderate the increase in "permanent" employment. A major development discussed in the literature was the increasing use of subcontracting. Ramaswami constructed an index of subcontracting by taking "the value of goods sold in the same condition as purchased *plus* the value of work done by concerns on material supplied"—both sets of information given for the registered factories surveyed in the ASI. Although not covering all types of subcontracting, the data showed that "subcontracting intensity" rose from 10% in 1989–90 to 12.3% in 1994–5, and the real value of subcontracting grew at a compound growth rate of 10.9%—a faster rate than total output in manufacturing (ibid., Table 3.4, p. 135).

The downswing of Period IV saw a large recovery of the value a and the wage share as the investment ratio slumped. This would have *ceteris paribus* increased employment elasticity; but again this possibility was swamped by the drastic increase in the negative value of the price effect. Real wage growth did moderate—cut to half its value of the previous boom – but the rate of output growth had fallen even further to a very low level. The large negative value of the price effect and the increase in the $\dot{w}/\dot{v}$ ratio could only be accommodated by a sharp reduction in employment growth. Such a shift in the wage–employment trade-off, this time against employment growth, is in line with our a priori expectations, and we see a large negative employment elasticity for the period.

There has been an upswing in the formal manufacturing sector starting in 2002–3. As mentioned in the endnotes, the latest available data is for the year 2004–5. The number of years is too few to give a reliable quantitative decomposition for this period, but the trends are clear and consistent with the cyclical prediction of our model as discussed in Section 2 above. First, prediction based on the hypothesis of labor as a quasi-fixed factor is that in periods of optimism the wage–employment trade-off would tilt towards employment growth. This is what we find in the current boom with a reversal of the magnitude $\dot{L}$ minus $\dot{w}$ from negative to positive values. Second, in accordance with our hypothesis about the close relationship between profit share and investment rate, the ongoing boom has seen a significant decline in a, and hence the share of wages in value added. Lastly, we expected that the DRER would be more favorable to producer goods in the upswing—at least relative to its trend value. In fact, the indications are that the DRER has swung to a positive value in the current boom, apparently reversing a negative trend since the 1980s.[9]

Relative importance of the wage–employment trade-off and the "price-effect"

The two most important variables affecting employment elasticity would thus seem to be the wage–employment trade-off and the "price-effect" (which translates the leakage from the wage-bill due to movements of the DRER) The former is a labor market variable while the latter is at least partly exogenous to the system. It will be recalled from equation (1) that the magnitude of the price effect is given by $[a\dot{P}_p - \dot{P}_c]$. While a in our hypothesis is influenced by the investment rate, the relative movement of the prices ($\dot{P}_p$ and $\dot{P}_c$) or the DRER is exogenous to the system. Both the wage–employment trade-off and the DRER had a structural break after the period of the "benign growth" of the pre-reform Period I. After this break both seemed to have followed a pro-cyclical pattern—even as the cycle in the DRER followed a downward trend.

As far as the wage–employment trade-off is concerned, the point made above and the consensus in the literature summarized in the endnotes suggests that the break with experience of Period I was largely due to the move away from the previous dirigist regime with the alliance of the state with politically based centralized unions. What was the reason for the reversal of the trend in DRER which shifted from being of positive to negative value after the first period?

The trend in the DRER would have a close relationship to the movement in the prices of wage goods (most notably, food, in the Indian context) relative to the prices of manufactured goods produced in the formal sector (comprising both consumer goods for the middle-class markets and producer goods). The structural break in the DRER in Period II had its roots both in the markets for food and manufactured goods. Ajit Ghose (1994) had pointed out in an early contribution that the early 1980s saw the abandonment of the policy of the pre-reform years which sought to stabilize the price of food at a low level through a policy of low minimum prices at which food was procured by the State and then distributed through "fair price" shops. The increase in the minimum procurement price of food was an aspect of the gradual reform of macro-economic policy started in Period II. However, insofar as administered prices and subsidies remained in the agricultural sector, food is in effect a non-tradable. The relative price of consumer goods would then be heavily influenced by the inflation rate in the domestic economy relative to the inflation rate in India's trading partners. Thus, the change in the value of the DRER would be shaped by macro-economic and exchange rate policies. In the absence of compensating measures the increase in DRER would be reflected in an appreciation of the real effective exchange rate (REER)[10] Another contributing factor of significance might be the worldwide decline in the terms of trade of manufactures against primary commodities in the last two decades of the twentieth century, noted by such writers as Kaplinsky.

The relative importance of the wage–employment trade-off and of the price-effect in different periods can be quantified from our estimation of the decomposition model (Table 3.2). The trend values of the DRER (which is a component of the price-effect and determines its sign) and of the employment elasticity are also included in the table for reference. The wage–employment trade-off can best be measured by the difference between $\dot{L}$ and $\dot{w}$. A negative sign of the value signifies that there is a tilt towards wage growth, while a positive value indicates that employment growth is preferred. Thus other things being equal, a positive value of the first term would favor an increase in employment elasticity, while a negative value would signify that the bias towards wage growth reduces employment elasticity.

The data shows the major importance of the price-effect (associated with the movement of DRER) in the changing values of employment elasticity. In particular the negative values of employment elasticity in Periods II and IV were in no small measure due to the negative price-effect. It should be emphasized, however, that although the negative trend in the DRER was significant in both these periods, the tilt in the wage–employment trade-off towards wage growth was also substantial—in fact a more important *relative* change compared to the previous period.

4 Desegregation: some selected issues

We have so far dealt with the whole of organized (formal) manufacturing as a single entity. It is now important to extend the story to cover some critical issues involving a more disaggregated view of this sector. These are: (i) the

Table 3.3 The relative importance of the wage–employment trade-off and the DRER effect

Period	$\dot{L}$ minus $\dot{W}$	Price-effect $[a\dot{P}_p - \dot{P}_c]$	DRER	Employment elasticity
I 1974–80	1.32	2.52	2.38	0.99
II 1980–6	−9.52	−3.20	−2.59	−0.16
III 1986–96	1.71	−2.68	−0.46	0.33
IV 1996–2002	−3.62	−3.53	−3.85	−1.42

difference between the publicly and privately owned units in manufacturing; and (ii) individual sub-sectors distinguished by key characteristics such as technology and trade-orientation.

Public and private sub-sectors

The Public Sector was a significant part of organized manufacturing in Period I. The high employment elasticity observed in this period was at least partly due to the influence exerted by the All-India unions, with strong affiliation to political parties, in favor of expanding "good jobs" in the formal sector. Since the wage-gap was already very high in favor of the formal sector, the interest of unions was more in the direction of increasing its membership of the privileged workers—rather than the OECD type of bias towards the wage increase of "insiders."

The reform period saw a decline in the public sector as the state controlled pattern of manufacturing growth was gradually whittled down. The following table gives the results of the decomposition analysis separately for the public and private sector establishments in the ASI time series.

The data in Table 3.4 show the slower growth rate of output in the public sector undertaken, as well as the attempt to reduce over-manning. The relatively high growth rate of wages in this sub-sector is probably partly an attempt to reduce the excess capacity built up among the workers. As pointed out earlier the increase in wage per man-hour would probably be less. However, the broad conclusions arrived at above for all manufacturing, without making the public–private distinction, are not altered.

The composition of industry

New technology and greater openness are the two characteristics of the reform period. Accordingly, it is useful to classify the industries at the 2-digit

Table 3.4 Proportionate growth rates for the public and the private sectors, 1986/7–1994/5

Sub-sector	$\dot{w}$	$\dot{v}$	$\dot{L}$	$\dot{P}_p$	$\dot{P}_c$	a	Output effect	Price effect	Employment elasticity
Public	2.38	5.58	−0.11	9.28	9.43	0.79	4.40	−2.12	−0.02
Private	1.60	10.97	3.55	9.28	9.43	0.72	7.90	−2.75	0.32
All manufacturing	1.50	9.68	2.77	9.28	9.43	0.72	7.00	−2.73	0.29

Note: The figures for all manufacturing differ from those given in Table 3.4 because we could not include the high growth year of 1995–6 because of lack of data.

"Public" includes establishments wholly owned by state and/or local governments as well as those owned jointly with the private sector. Employment in joint-sector establishments was around 10% of the total in all public manufacturing in 1987–8.The private sector variables are calculated as residuals and therefore include "unspecified" units.

level of the NIC classification in terms of the dual characteristics of the level of technology, and exposure to the world markets. The latter in turn involves the degree of import penetration and/or the proportion of output exported. We used the input–output table for the Indian economy constructed by the Planning Commission for 1991 to undertake such a classification. The results are given in Table 3.5.

It is seen that in 1991 the high-technology sub-sectors had not yet started to play a significant role in exports. Rather, trade liberalization measures allowed some of these groups to establish themselves with a sizable "import penetration" ratio (sector 1 in the table). The industries classified as using medium-low technology were of two types: NIC groups 31–4 (code 2a) was domestically oriented, although making use of a not insignificant proportion of imports. However, a group had emerged (group 38), consisting a variety of new "other manufacturing" which exported a substantial proportion of its

Table 3.5 Classification of industries by technology level and exposure to trade, 1991

Technology level plus exposed ratio	NIC code	Import penetration	Export ratio	Exposed ratio	Size of sector (%)	Sector code
High exposed	30+35 to 37	29.50	6.05	33.76	31.77	1
Medium domestic	31 to 34	11.08	3.83	14.48	23.86	2a
Medium exposed	38	25.31	28.37	46.50	5.46	2b
Low domestic	20, 22, 27	1.35	2.98	4.29	15.55	3a
Low exposed	23 to 26; 28+29	2.73	15.79	18.09	23.35	3b
	All	14.30	8.54	21.62	100.00	

Source: Planning Commission 60 × 60 Input–output table, 1991.

Definitions
Import penetration = (Value of import)/(value of output − value of export)*100
Export ratio = (Value of export)/(value of output)*100
Exposed ratio = (Value of import + value of export)/(value of output)*100

NIC codes: 30: Basic Chemicals and chemical products
    35–6: Machinery and equipment other than transport equipment
    37: Transport equipments and parts

    31: Rubber, plastic, petroleum and coal products
    32: Non-metallic mineral products
    33: Basic metals and alloys industries
    34: Metal products and parts except machinery

    38: Other manufacturing industries

    23: Cotton textiles
    24: Wool, silk and man-made fiber textiles
    25: Manufacture of Jute and other vegetable fiber
    26: Textile products including wearing apparel.

    28: Paper and paper products
    29: Leather and leather products
    20–1: Food products
    22: Beverages, Tobacco and related products
    27: Wood and wood products

output, and also had a high import penetration. This was then the sub-sector with the highest degree of globalization (our "exposure ratio"). However, its overall importance in terms of the total share in value added in all manufacturing was only around 5% in 1991. Low-technology manufacturing, as is to be expected, had very low import penetration. One sub-group (3b) had a significant export ratio, and indeed accounted for nearly a quarter of the total output of manufacturing. These included textiles and textile products, paper and lather products. Industry groups 20, 22, and 27—food and beverages and wood products—were the truly domestic industries at this date, with a share of 15% of total manufacturing.

It might be of some interest to look at the trends in the key variables studied above for all variables, separately for the industry groups just distinguished. The data are reproduced in Table 3.6.

The first point to note is that there is a clear difference in the rates of growth in industry groups of different levels of technology. The higher technology sub-groups—1, 2a, and 2b—had a significantly higher rate of output growth. The group of "new" industries identified above (2b) as leading the charge in export markets, suffered from a relatively lower trend in producer prices (compared to the trend in consumer prices), so that some of its growth was "lost" in the declining terms of trade. Both the low-technology industry groups—the more "exposed" as well as the less so—had a decidedly lower rate of growth.

Turning to labor market outcomes, domestically oriented low-technology sub-group (3a) seems to have suffered the least from the adverse price (DRER) effect, and labor's share declined the least in this industry group. Thus the wage bill growth was nearly on a par with output growth. The tilt to employment growth as against wage growth was the least pronounced in this group. A reasonable hypothesis is that these older domestically oriented industries continued to experience some of the old power of "insiders." Thus, in spite of the rate of output growth being the second lowest, the growth rate of real wages was highest in this group.

It is, however, remarkable that all three sub-groups with the highest "exposure ratios"—groups 1, 2b, and 3b—had the lowest rate of growth of real wages. In the two exports-oriented groups, 2b and 3b, in fact the growth

Table 3.6 Trends in selected variables by industry groups 1986/7–1996/7

Period III	Industry group	$\dot{W}$	$\dot{V}$	$\dot{L}$	$\dot{P}_p$	$\dot{P}_c$	α
	1	1.58	12.83	4.73	8.49	9.56	0.74
	2a	2.38	11.22	3.01	8.71	9.56	0.75
	2b	0.44	16.57	7.54	5.27	9.56	0.80
	3a	2.51	7.58	3.27	9.79	9.56	0.88
	3b	0.66	6.86	2.75	10.40	9.56	0.75

rate of real wages was barely positive. The wage–employment trade-off had swung heavily in favor of employment growth even as the share of wages declined significantly. We can conclude with some confidence that if the aim of liberalization had been to promote labor-intensive growth and reduce the power of those already in employment, our first cut at the evidence shows that the policy certainly succeeded to some extent in its objectives.

5 Conclusions

The review of the Indian experience in formal manufacturing over the last quarter of the century revealed the enormous fluctuation in employment elasticity from period to period. Starting with the period of "benign" growth in the last half of the 1970s, when employment elasticity was nearly unity, employment growth turned somewhat *negative* in the period of jobless growth in the 1980s. It picked up to a reasonable, but not unduly high, value of 0.33 during the reform period, when output growth was also high, but it slumped badly to a substantial negative figure in the latest post-reform years of 1996–2001 when output growth also stumbled.

We have learnt from the decomposition model that there are three sets of factors affecting employment elasticity, given the rate of growth of real value added: (i) the trend in the share of wages as measured by our a; (ii) the wage–employment trade-off; and (iii) the trend in the domestic real exchange rate or the relative movement over time of the producer price index relative to the consumer price index. The last variable is, for the present analysis, more in the nature of an exogenous factor, influenced by macro-economic and related policies. The first two are labor market variables. At first sight they might both seem be related to the strength or weakness of workers' organizations such as trade unions, but this would be overlooking the different decision-making processes at the firm level that affect the two variables.

The model has a strong suggestion that the employment elasticity resulting from the interaction of these factors will have a cyclical pattern. This is because expectations about future market conditions play a critical role in the model with two factors—capital and labor, which are both quasi-fixed. As predicted, the employment elasticity does show a cyclical pattern—and four phases are distinguished. They correspond reasonably well to different periods of the recent political economy of Indian development culminating in the reform period (1986–96) and the immediate post-reform period of 1996–2002. The relative importance of the three key factors in the fluctuating trend of employment elasticity over the four periods are discussed—particularly in terms of the changes in labor market institutions.

While the illustrative case of India is of interest in itself, some of the findings are of general importance for many economies in the globalizing world.

First, a strong finding was that the downward trend in the DRER has been persistent for the last two decades of the past century. The DRER is of course closely related to the terms of trade of manufactured products and to that of primary commodities (particularly cereals). This turning of the terms of trade against the latter has been noted in the literature.

Second, the close relationship between the investment rate and the share of wages (or with *a*) is established in the Indian case and we have provided evidence of the importance of growing importance of internal finance to the boom in investment in the reform period. Although economies would differ in the importance of this connection, it is probably of general importance, and would indeed be found to be of particular importance in the determination of employment elasticity in most economies.

Third, the wage–employment trade-off is a key determinant. It is influenced partly by employer perception of the expected demand for labor relative to the perceived cost of altering the complement of permanent workers. Institutions on the labor side play an important role in the decisions about this trade-off. Some of the theoretical issues as well as possible empirical differences between regions of the world were discussed in Mazumdar (2003). In the present paper the Indian case illustrates how difficult it might be to reduce the perception of labor as a quasi-fixed factor, once it has been established in the industrial culture.

In the last section of the paper we looked at some selected issues for disaggregated sub-sectors of formal manufacturing. The analysis was applied separately, for example, to groups of industry classified by trade exposure and technology. An important result is that while the elasticity of employment recovered in all categories in the reform period (Period III) compared to the previous one, revealingly the tilt to employment growth (as against wage growth) was more important in the industries with a higher trade exposure.

Notes

* This work is part of a larger research project on globalization, labor markets, and inequality in Asia funded by the International Development Research Center, Ottawa.

1 See, e.g., Eichner (1973). The author notes the affinity of the theoretical tradition to the empirical literature which has found from surveys of business pricing decisions that firms set prices on the basis of the "cost plus" concept. The "plus" margin is in its turn set by the necessity to generate the profit share which finances the investment ratio. The affinity of these ideas to the Kalecki models of the firm have been stressed by Asimakopoulos (1971) among others.

2 The wage–efficiency relationship, as applied to the industrial sector in particular, should not be interpreted in physical or nutritional terms. Rather, the incentive structure, which includes the selection and deployment of labor, is the dominant factor influencing this relationship. The incentives involved in a regime which elicit more efficiency units per worker would usually entail higher wages per man, for supervisory labor as much as for production workers. A classic study of the operation of this set of factors is to be found in Reynolds and Gregory (1965) discussing the impact on manufacturing firms in Puerto Rico following the increases in the minimum wage by the US and Commonwealth governments. The spectacular fall in employment growth relative to output growth in the immediate aftermath of

the minimum wage hike could not be traced to any major changes in production techniques involving more labor-saving machinery. Rather, it came from better personnel policies and production standards leading to a sharp reduction in the use of labor relative to *both* capital and labor. The evidence illustrates the extended range over which efficiency unit per worker could be achieved with a higher wage per man, associated with the requisite manpower policy.

3 See Mazumdar (2003) for a more extended discussion of the labor market theories relevant to this set of decisions.

4 In the medium-to-long run the firm will alter its technique of production in response to changes in the wage cost per efficiency unit if it is perceived to be long-lasting. This possibility is easily handled in terms of the model portrayed in Figures 3.2 and 3.3. The wage–efficiency curves portrayed in these figures relate to the varying use of different efficiencies relating to one "machine" or technique of production. If the wage cost increases beyond a certain point it would no longer be profitable to persist with this technique. The firm might then decide to invest in a superior technique and there will be another wage–efficiency curve relating to this superior machine. This new curve will lie above the old one and slightly to the north-east of it. For the same supply of efficiency units the wage per man is now higher. This is partly because the superior technique requires labor of higher quality, and partly because labor productivity is higher with the new technique, and wage share cannot fall below a certain level without reducing worker incentives. The movement of the wage–efficiency curve to the north-east is because labor with superior technique starts at a higher wage with a larger supply of efficiency units, and unless the response of a larger volume of efficiency units to wage increase is drastically different, the point of inflexion showing the least-cost point on the wage–efficiency function would be to the right of that of the lower curve.

The wage–efficiency curve of Figure 3.2 can then, in the longer run, be interpreted as an *envelope* to the successive curves related to each individual technique of production.

5 See Mazumdar and Sarkar (2008), Appendix to Chapter 7 for an example of a partial dynamic model and its testing with ASI data.

6 Several researchers, including Nagaraj (1992). Papola (1992), Bhalotra (1998), and Uchikawa (2002), have all pointed out the weakness in the analysis which refers only to *number of workers* rather than man-days worked. According to Uchikawa's latest research average annual working days in all manufacturing rose from 273 during the first period, to 300 days in the second period, to 309 days during the third period. (Uchikawa's periods are fairly close to our first three periods distinguished in Table 3.2). Thus, the wage cost per man-hour of work did not increase at nearly the same rate as average earnings or average product wage per man.

Why did the number of man-hours per worker start to increase at the beginning of the second period? Uchikawa's explanation is that "the manufacturing sector had redundant workers in the late 1970s. Although growth rates of GVA (gross value added) declined, man-days increased during the recession period between 1978–9 and 1982–3." (ibid, 38). Strong labor unions, still powerful at the end of the second period prevented retrenchment of redundant workers. Thus, when industry recovered at the beginning of the 1980s, there was enough "surplus" labor available to increase the flow of labor in terms of hours of work required. The textile strike and its aftermath indicated above eased the way to elimination of the surplus labor which was being carried. The employer response to the changed climate of labor deployment in Indian manufacturing was to increase the flow of labor per worker from a reduced rationalized labor force.

7 There has been an alternative view advanced in the earlier literature which

suggested that the shift in the wage–employment trade to wage increase might have been due to the strengthening of job security legislation (World Bank 1989; Fallon and Lucas 1993). Recent research has, however, leaned towards the view that this period saw the beginning of the change in the system which drastically reduced the power of centralized unions. We have already referred to the work of Rodrik and Subramanian in which they sought to document evidence that the period saw an "attitudinal" shift in Indian policy making to a more "pro-business" slant. Uchikawa (2002) has pointed out how the membership of the major unions declined after the large-scale job losses following the closure of textile mills in Bombay in the early 1980s. Tirthankar Roy has written on the shift in bargaining on labor matters from industry-based to plant-based institutions through the 1980s. There was indeed a lowering of the ceiling of the size of establishments which came under the purview of the job security legislation, but this was one part of the carrot-and-stick policy of the government to soften the major blows administered to centralized unions (see Mazumdar and Sarkar 2008, Chapter 7, for a survey of this literature).

8 Careful work by Uchikawa (2002) has shown that there was a sharp acceleration in gross investment in the first half of the 1980s. The gross fixed capital stock in ASI industries increased at the rate of 10.1% per annum at 1980–81 prices. A regression equation estimated for the time-series of capital stock showed that a multiplicative dummy for the post-1990 period was significant at the 5% level, confirming the acceleration of investment after the economic reforms. The rate of growth of the capital stock was about *three times* the rate of growth of employment. There are several reasons for this spurt in investment, some of them having to do with the easing of control over the stock market which encouraged the corporate sector to shift their sources of finance from term lending to paid-up capital. The share of the latter rose suddenly from 7.1% in 1992–3 to 29.6 in 1993–4 (Uchikawa).

9 The relevant growth rates for the variables in our decomposition model are given in the following table for the years 2001–2 to 2004–5 for what they are worth. We should caution that they should be taken only as indicators of the ongoing trend since the period is too short for a reliable calculation of compound rates of growth.

$\dot{w}$	$\dot{V}$	$\dot{L}$	$\dot{P}_p$	$\dot{P}_c$	a	Output effect	Price effect	Employment elasticity
0.85	12.54	3.54	6.56	3.95	0.44	5.47	−0.8	0.28

10 Ahmad Ahsan's econometric work showed that over the period 1980–2002 there was a robust relationship between exchange rate appreciation and the DRER—after controlling for time trends. A summary of this work can be found in Mazumdar and Sarkar (2008), Chapter 8.

References

Asimakopoulos, M. (1971) "The Determinants of Investment in Keynes's Model." *Canadian Journal of Economics* 4(3): 382–8.

Bhalotra, S. R. (1998) "The Puzzle of Jobless Growth in Indian Manufacturing." *Oxford Bulletin of Economics and Statistics* 60(1): 5–32.

Eichner, A. S. (1973) "A Theory of the Determination of the Mark-up." *Economic Journal* 83(332): 1184–200.

Fallon, P. and R. E. B. Lucas (1993) "Job Security Regulations and the Dynamic Demand of Industrial Labour in India and Zimbabwe." *Journal of Development Economic* 40: 241–75.

Ghose, A. K. (1994) "Employment in Organized Manufacturing in India." *Indian Journal of Labor Economics* 37(2), April–June: 141–62.

Government of India (2002) "Report of the Special Group on Targeting Ten Million Employment Opportunities per Year over the 10th Plan Period." Reproduced in *Planning Commission Reports on Labor and Employment*, New Delhi: Academic Foundation.

Kalecki, M. (1941) "A Theory of the Long-run Distribution of the Product of Industry." *Oxford Economic Papers (Old Series)*, 5, June: 31–41.

——. (1971) "Selected Essays on Dynamics of the Capitalist Economy, 1933–1970." London: Cambridge University Press.

Mazumdar, D. (2003) "Trends in Employment and the Employment Elasticity in Manufacturing, 1971–92: An International Comparison." *Cambridge Journal of Economics*, 27(4): 563–82.

—— and S. Sarkar (2008) *Globalization, Labor Markets and Inequality in India*. London: Routledge.

Morawetz, D. (1974) "Employment Implications of Industrialization in Developing Countries." *Economic Journal*, 84(335): 491–542.

Nagaraj, R. (1994) "Employment and Wages in Manufacturing Industries: Trends, Hypotheses and Evidence." *Economic and Political Weekly* 29(4), January 22: 177–86.

Papola, T. S. (1992) "Labor Institutions and Economic Development: The Case of Indian Industrialization." In *Labor Institutions and Economic Development in India* edited by T. S. Papola and G. Rodgers, IILS Research Series no. 97, ILO, Geneva.

Reynolds, L. and P. Gregory (1965) *Wages, Productivity and Industrialization in Puerto Rico*. Homewood, Ill: Richard D. Irwin.

Rodrik, D. and A. Subramanian (2004) "From Hindu Rate of Growth to Productivity Surge: The mystery of the Indian growth transition." NBER Working Paper 1036, March. Cambridge, Mass.: National Bureau of Economic Research. hhttp://www.nber.org/papers/w10376

Roy, T. (2002) "Social Costs of Reforms: A study of job loss with special reference to declining industries in 1990–98." In Uchikawa (2002): 99–126.

Uchikawa, S. (ed.) (2002) *Economic Reforms and Industrial Structure in India*. New Delhi: Manohar.

——. (ed.) (2003) *Labour Market and Institutions in India: 1990s and Beyond*. Tokyo: Institute of Developing Economies.

Uchikawa, U. (2001) "Investment Boom and Underutilisation of Capacity in the 1990s." *Economic and Political Weekly*, August 25.

World Bank (1989) *India: Poverty, Employment and Social Services: A World Bank Country Study*, Washington DC: World Bank.

4 Wage determination and wage inequality inside a Russian firm in late transition

Evidence from personnel data, 1997–2002[*]

Thomas Dohmen, Hartmut Lehmann, and Mark E. Schaffer

1 Introduction

The literature on wage formation and wage inequality in Russian labor markets, limited in scope and often constrained by data quality, has left many controversial issues unresolved. One of the more fundamental issues is the question of which considerations drive managers in the wage determination process. Are Russian wages, for example, formed mainly by institutional factors related to industrial relations and internal labor markets as stressed by Clarke (2002) and Kapeliushnikov (2002) among others, or are managers in their wage decisions mainly led by the interplay of conditions in local labor markets, labor market institutions, and considerations to achieve an optimal level of turnover of the workforce?

The first approach, which for shorthand we may call the industrial relations approach to wage determination in Russia, is aptly summarized by Clarke (2002): "The pattern of change in the structure of wages in Russia is consistent with the supposition that employers follow the line of least resistance and in the first instance adjust their hiring and management practices to a relatively stable level and structure of wages, raising money wages uniformly more or less in line with inflation, although with a lag that is the longer the more hard-pressed is the employer, so that differentials emerge corresponding to the relative prosperity of firms." Clarke's argumentation takes recourse to two strands in the literature on wage formation, the industrial relations institutional literature, which sees the wage structure in a firm as the result of bargaining between production managers, human resource managers and top management, and the early literature on internal labor markets (Dunlop 1957; Doeringer and Piore 1971). Both these strands point to the protection of the workforce in the firm from shocks that occur in the outside labor market by maintaining a stable and "fair" relative wage structure also in times of economic hardship. Can wage differentiation in Russia during transition really be explained well by this approach? Are local labor market conditions really as irrelevant as maintained by Clarke?

The second approach to the analysis of Russian wage formation extends standard models of wage determination in capitalist economies to Russia, and assigns an important role to local labor market conditions in the wage formation process. No matter how much bargaining power of workers and employers is assumed in the models underlying the studies, i.e. independently of whether both agents are assumed to have substantial bargaining power as in the studies of Brainerd (2002), Luke and Schaffer (2000), and Commander, Dhar, and Yemtsov (1996), whether employers decide unilaterally over wage levels and structure (Lehmann, Wadsworth, and Acquisti 1999), or whether the assumption of competitive labor markets is maintained, local labor market conditions are assumed to have a major impact on the decision-making process as well as on outcomes.

Having unique longitudinal personnel data from a Russian manufacturing firm, which includes wages and bonuses of each employee, we provide new evidence on the issue of wage formation and differentiation in Russia. If the "industrial relations school" is right, then firms that have increasing profits should attempt to maintain real wage levels as much as is feasible in times of inflation and reverse real wage losses when inflation subsides. Local labor market conditions should play a very subordinate role, if any. We are fortunate to have personnel data for the years 1997–2002, a period that includes an episode of high inflation in the aftermath of the August 1998 financial crisis. Given our longitudinal personnel data and the profit situation of the firm, we are able to provide direct evidence on the validity of the prediction put forth by Clarke and others from the "industrial relations school" of Russian wage formation.

To see whether and how important labor market conditions affect wages, we need information about the local labor market in which the firm operates. The information we use is taken from regional Rosstat data and from a sample of 33 industrial firms in the same region where the firm is active. We also interviewed the director general of the firm (CEO), after we had analyzed the personnel wage data, to obtain confirmation or clarification on the motives of management regarding its wage policies.

The main results in the final analysis provide little evidence for the prediction put forth by Clarke and others of the "industrial relations school"; our results, rather, show that local labor market conditions are one of the main driving forces determining the management's wage policies in this Russian firm. In the firm at hand, top management, in particular the CEO, unilaterally determine wages in spite of official bargaining between management and trade union representatives. Before the financial crisis in 1998, labor turnover was very high in the firm. This turnover was driven by voluntary quits as employees saw better opportunities outside the firm. However, as of 1996, orders for the firm's products showed a very robust upturn and the firm was in desperate need of qualified production workers, engineers, etc. To attract these qualified employees and to retain them, top management offered real wages far above the regional and sector averages. After the financial crisis of

August 1998, outside opportunities in the local labor market were substantially reduced. This enabled top management to extract rents from the firm's employees through the erosion of real wages via the high inflation that manifested itself during and after the financial crisis. It curbed earnings most for those who earned the highest rents, resulting in a tremendous compression of real wages that was still in place at the end of the reported period. While nominal wages are never cut in this firm, long-lasting real earnings losses were very substantial, and this despite a very strong profit performance.

The remainder of the paper is organized as follows. The next section introduces the firm under study and describes the personnel data set. Section 3 presents the main results of our analysis and establishes some robust evidence about the evolution of wages and total compensation in the firm over the period that encompasses the financial crisis and high inflation. A final section concludes.

2 The firm and its personnel data

Our particular firm is located in a provincial city in Russia and operates in the "machine building and metal working" sector. After having converted production lines from Soviet times "nearly 100%", according to the director general of the firm (CEO),[1] it produces well equipment for gas and oil production and smith-press equipment. More than 90% of its production is destined for the Russian market. It has no local competitors, but nationally it has to compete with more than five firms, among them firms from the European Union. The firm was founded in the middle of the last century and was privatized in 1992. A decade later more than half of the shares were owned by managers and workers, about 20% by former employees and roughly a quarter by other Russian entities. By that time the active shareowners were the members of the board of directors and top management, to whom dividends are paid as well as to those workers who own "privileged shares."[2] While there is collective bargaining on paper at this firm, trade union representatives have virtually no influence on wage policy and wages are set unilaterally by top management. Essentially all important decisions are taken by top managers and in particular by the CEO of this firm.

The firm has an unusual profit performance in the reported period in relation to the sector in which it operates. As Figure 4.1 shows, the profitability of our firm and the profitability of the sector move in opposite directions in the years 1997–2003. Equally important is the fact that our firm, while having declining profits in the three years after 1997, is able to maintain positive profits throughout, i.e. there is clearly no dramatic negative impact on profits brought on by the crisis of August 1998. The firm is also unusual in its wage policies compared with the machine-building and metal-working sector, the oblast where it is located, and the whole economy. Figure 4.2 shows a real monthly wage paid by our firm in 1997 and 1998 that is more than 50% higher

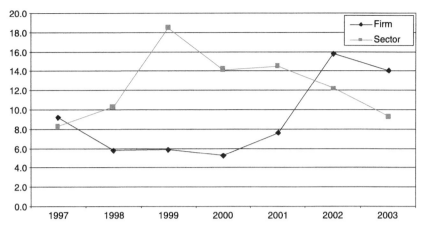

Figure 4.1 Profitability (profit/sales in %).

Source: Rosstat, own calculations.

Notes: The figure shows the percentage of profits relative to sales for the firm and the average percentage of profits to sales for the machine building and metal working sector.

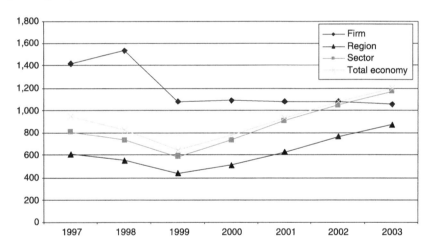

Figure 4.2 Real monthly wage in thousand 1997 rubles.

Source: Rosstat, own calculations.

Notes: The figure shows average real monthly wages in thousands of 1997 rubles for the firm, the region in which the firm is located, the machine building and metal working sector and the entire Russian economy.

than the wage paid in the sector and more than double the wage paid in the region. In the aftermath of the crisis we see a precipitous fall of the real wage in our firm, while wages in the economy at large, the region, and the sector show a more moderate fall. After the crisis the real wage profile in the firm stays flat but shows a continuous rise for the three aggregates. By 2003 the average real wage in the economy and the sector exceed that in our firm. It is noteworthy, however, that the average regional wage remains below the firm's average wage even in 2003.

The firm that we analyze is clearly not representative of the industrial sector in Russia, in that it is more successful than most firms in this sector over the indicated period, and in that collective bargaining is not relevant for wage and employment outcomes. The personnel data of the firm in question are, however, well suited for testing hypotheses emanating from the various schools of thought regarding wage determination by management in Russian firms, since the firm belongs to the minority of prosperous enterprises where workers' institutional influences are very limited and thus do not confound this process of wage determination.

The construction of the personnel data proceeded as follows. We created an electronic file based on records from the personnel archive of the firm, and constructed a year-end panel data set for the years 1997–2002.[3] We have records of all employees who were employed at any time during this period.[4] The data contain information on individuals' demographic characteristics such as gender, age, marital status, and number of children, on their educational attainment, retraining, and other skill enhancement activities before joining the firm and during tenure at the firm. We also know the exact date when each employee started work at the firm as well as his/her complete working history before that date. We can trace each employee's career within the firm. In addition we also know whether someone worked full-time or part-time. For those who separated from the firm we can distinguish between voluntary quit, transfer to another firm, individual dismissal, group dismissal, and retirement.

In Russian firms the workforce is often divided into five employee categories: administration (i.e. management) which we label "managers;" accounting and financial specialists whom we label "accountants;" engineering and technical specialists (including programmers) whom we subsume under the term "engineers;" primary and auxiliary production workers, whom we label "production workers;" and finally, service staff.[5]

For the years 1997–2002 we have monthly wages averaged over the year, and information on the three types of bonus paid to the workforce: (1) a monthly bonus amounting to a fixed percentage of the wage; (2) an extra annual bonus whose level depends on "the results of the year" (i.e. a form of profit sharing); (3) an annual bonus labeled "other bonus." While production workers never receive a monthly bonus, the bonus labeled "other bonus" is paid to production workers only. Wages are reported by the firm as the employee's average monthly wage in rubles for the year (or fraction of the year, if not employed for the full 12 months), with no adjustment for inflation. The monthly bonus is reported as a percentage of the average monthly wage, and the corresponding ruble figure is recovered by applying the percentage to the nominal monthly wage. The other two bonuses are reported in nominal rubles. The inflation rate in Russia during this period was irregular

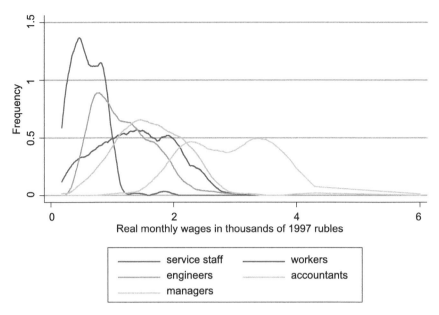

Figure 4.3 Real wage distributions in 1997.

Source: Records from the personnel file, national CPI deflator from Rosstat, own calculations.

Notes: The figure plots the smoothed density functions of the real wage distributions in 1997 for the five employee categories in 1997 rubles, estimated using a Gaussian kernel. The bandwidth is chosen to minimize the mean integrated squared error under the assumption that the data are Gaussian.

and sometimes quite high—the price level more than doubled between the start of the financial crisis in July 1998 and April 1999, and was 0–2% per month before and after—and so some care is required to construct appropriate deflators. Because nominal average monthly wage and the nominal monthly bonus are averages for the year, they are deflated into 1997 constant rubles using an annual average CPI, i.e. the average price level for the year relative to the average price level in 1997. The other two bonuses are paid around the end of the year, and so these are converted into 1997 constant rubles using the CPI price level for December of the corresponding year, i.e. the December price level in that year relative to the average 1997 price level.[6]

3 Main results

Employment

Table 4.1 shows that employment grew steadily from 3,032 employees to 3,221 employees during the period January 1997 to December 2002, with the exception of the post-crisis year 1999. Yet, the composition of the workforce hardly changed throughout the period.

Table 4.1 Composition of workforce (in %), 1997–2002

Year	Service staff	Engineers	Production workers	Accountants	Managers	Total	Absolute number of employees
1997	7.1	24.8	62.1	2.2	3.8	100	3032
1998	7.0	24.4	62.6	2.1	3.8	100	3081
1999	6.9	24.6	62.6	2.1	3.8	100	3077
2000	7.0	24.4	62.8	2.1	3.8	100	3110
2001	6.9	24.0	63.2	2.0	3.8	100	3175
2002	6.9	23.7	63.6	1.9	3.8	100	3221

Source: Personnel records of the firm, own calculations.

Notes: The table shows the composition of the workforce in terms of the five employee categories in percentages. The absolute number of employees is displayed in the rightmost column.

Turnover rates, calculated as the sum of hires and separations during a given year normalized by the stock at the beginning of the year, were particularly large in 1997 and 1998 (see Table 4.2). After the crisis they fell quite dramatically, in 2002 reaching less than half the level of 1997. This secular pattern holds for all employee categories, but turnover was especially turbulent for accountants, production workers, and service staff, and much more modest for engineering staff throughout the period. In addition, while there was a large turnover of managers in the crisis year, there are few managers who enter or leave the firm after 1998.

The fall in turnover rates after the crisis year of 1998 comes about because of a fall in separation *and* hiring rates (see Table 4.2). The bulk of the separations (about 80%) throughout the period are voluntary quits. Therefore the fall in the separation rate in the post-crisis year suggests that the financial crisis restrained many employees from quitting. The firm's employees seem to have been continuously confronted with a more limited array of outside options compared with the situation before the crisis as we now show.[7]

Table 4.3 that summarizes turnover in a sample of industrial firms from the city where our firm resides can tell us something about local labor market conditions in the period 1998–2001.[8] The turnover patterns presented in the regional sample are similar to those for the firm in the years 1998–2001. In particular, separation rates fall by similar percentages for all employee categories, while the fall in inflows is more pronounced for our firm than for the regional sample. If we take the turnover rate as an indicator of local labor market conditions, we can infer that outside opportunities have diminished in a substantial fashion for all employee types compared to the period before the crisis. These diminished opportunities can also be seen by movements of the unemployment rate in the given oblast. While the local unemployment rate was roughly six percentage points lower than the Russian average in 1998, it was two percentage points higher in 2001. The relative magnitudes of the

Table 4.2 Hiring and separation rates (in %), 1997–2002

Year	Service staff			Engineers			Production workers			Accountants			Managers			All employment		
	In	Out	Total	In	Out	Total	In	Out	Total	In	Out	Total	In	Out	Total	In	Out	Total
1997	13.7	14.2	27.8	7.8	7.8	15.5	16.4	15.2	31.5	19.1	23.5	42.6	10.8	9.9	20.7	13.9	13.2	27.1
1998	13.3	13.3	26.5	6.3	5.8	12.1	18.0	16.1	34.1	20.0	23.1	43.1	16.1	13.4	29.5	14.7	13.5	28.2
1999	7.6	5.7	13.3	5.3	4.9	10.3	11.8	11.8	23.7	11.1	14.3	25.4	4.3	4.3	8.7	9.6	9.5	19.1
2000	9.3	7.4	16.7	6.4	5.7	12.1	10.7	7.6	18.3	8.2	0.0	8.2	3.5	0.0	3.5	9.2	6.7	15.9
2001	7.8	6.8	14.6	5.7	5.1	10.8	11.5	7.4	19.0	13.6	19.7	33.3	5.0	1.7	6.7	9.6	6.5	16.2
2002	5.4	3.6	9.0	2.9	3.0	5.9	8.7	7.8	16.5	8.1	9.7	17.7	0.0	0.0	0.0	6.7	6.1	12.8

Source: Personnel records of the firm, own calculations.

Note: The table shows hirings, separations, and total turnover as a percentage of employment for all five employee categories for the years 1997 until 2002.

Table 4.3 Hiring and separation and turnover rates (in %) in sample of industrial firms in the region, 1998–2001

Year	Service staff			Engineers			Production workers			Accountants			Managers			All employment		
	In	Out	Total	In	Out	Total	In	Out	Total	In	Out	Total	In	Out	Total	In	Out	Total
1998	9.2	21.6	30.8	10.8	13.0	23.8	11.3	12.8	24.1	3.1	4.4	7.5	2.1	5.4	7.5	10.9	12.6	23.5
1999	13.2	15.5	28.7	8.6	7.5	16.1	13.1	13.1	26.2	4.1	3.9	8.0	3.6	4.2	7.6	11.5	11.2	22.7
2000	10.1	13.4	23.5	8.3	9.3	17.6	13.1	10.1	23.2	4.7	4.5	9.2	2.6	0.1	2.7	11.2	9.8	21.0
2001	7.2	10.1	17.3	9.1	5.3	14.4	10.9	8.2	19.1	1.8	1.2	3.0	1.7	1.4	3.1	10.2	7.5	17.7

Source: CERT Russian regional data base, own calculations.

Note: The table shows average hirings, separations, and total turnover as a percentage of employment for employee categories in a sample of 33 firms located in the same region as our firm.

unemployment rate as well as the presented regional turnover patterns of industrial firms demonstrate that local labor market conditions were decisively worse after the crisis year of 1998 and did not recover as rapidly as in the Russian Federation in general.[9]

Wage structure

Figure 4.3 plots kernel density estimates of the real wage distributions for different employee categories in 1997. It is immediately obvious that there is substantial heterogeneity in wages within employee categories. Moreover, real wage distributions for different employee categories overlap, so that many high-paid production workers, for example, earned at least as much as lower paid managers. Service staff had the lowest mean wages in 1997, followed, somewhat surprisingly, by engineers, then production workers, and accountants. Managers had the highest wages on average. This ranking of employee group-specific wage distributions remains unchanged throughout the observation period.

Estimates from OLS regressions of log wages in 1997, reported in Table 4.4, show that service staff earn on average 52% less than production workers, while the latter earn around 6% more than engineering staff. Accountants and managers earn approximately 50 and 95% more than production workers (see column (1)). The estimated coefficients in column (1) also illustrate that workers with longer tenure and more education receive higher wages. Women earn significantly less than men, while marital status and the number of children do not have a significant impact on wages. The mentioned factors determine the wage structure throughout the observation period, but the size

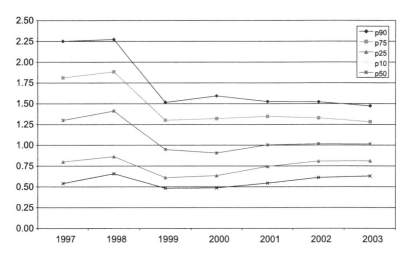

Figure 4.4 Distribution of basic real wage in rubles—all employees.

Source: Records from the personnel file, own calculations.

Table 4.4 Determinants of wages, 1997

	Dependent variable: log (real wage) in 1997					
	All employees (1)	Service staff (2)	Engineers (3)	Production workers (4)	Accountants (5)	Managers (6)
Tenure in years	0.028*** [0.007]	0.020 [0.028]	0.026* [0.014]	0.030*** [0.010]	0.027 [0.041]	0.007 [0.026]
Tenure squared/100 in years	−0.136** [0.067]	−0.269 [0.251]	−0.188 [0.134]	−0.119 [0.089]	−0.471 [0.481]	0.021 [0.237]
Tenure cube /1,000 in years	0.025 [0.016]	0.083 [0.055]	0.04 [0.033]	0.014 [0.021]	0.171 [0.152]	−0.007 [0.058]
Age in years	0.034 [0.038]	0.013 [0.176]	0.012 [0.074]	−0.005 [0.049]	−0.479 [0.290]	−0.588 [0.424]
Age squared/100 in years	−0.033 [0.103]	−0.009 [0.469]	−0.001 [0.198]	0.08 [0.133]	1.579* [0.819]	1.541 [1.059]
Age cube /1000 in years	−0.001 [0.009]	−0.001 [0.041]	−0.002 [0.017]	−0.01 [0.012]	−0.162** [0.075]	−0.131 [0.087]
Basic professional	0.037 [0.029]	0.014 [0.087]		0.036 [0.033]		
Secondary general	0.079*** [0.028]	−0.027 [0.089]		0.076** [0.032]		
Secondary professional	0.097*** [0.030]	0.028 [0.104]	−0.123 [0.277]	0.100*** [0.036]	0.615 [0.390]	
Higher incomplete	0.164** [0.069]	−0.088 [0.469]	−0.065 [0.284]	0.180 [0.114]	1.406** [0.559]	0.035 [0.167]
Higher	0.122*** [0.038]	0.187 [0.273]	−0.073 [0.277]	0.110 [0.069]	0.977** [0.396]	−0.042 [0.053]
1 if female	−0.319*** [0.019]	−0.236*** [0.071]	−0.155*** [0.030]	−0.428*** [0.027]	0.584** [0.284]	−0.044 [0.060]
1 if single	0.021 [0.070]	0.476 [0.467]	−0.038 [0.167]	0.074 [0.093]	0.109 [0.236]	
1 if divorced or widowed	−0.009 [0.035]	0.014 [0.093]	−0.081 [0.074]	−0.005 [0.050]	0.004 [0.132]	−0.056 [0.071]
1 if 1 child	−0.011 [0.053]	0.434 [0.507]	−0.064 [0.086]	0.035 [0.071]	0.078 [0.207]	0.418 [0.253]
1 if more than 1 child	0.042 [0.057]	0.487 [0.498]	−0.055 [0.096]	0.080 [0.076]	0.052 [0.236]	0.444* [0.254]
Service staff	−0.731*** [0.034]					
Engineers	−0.064** [0.030]					
Accountants	0.401*** [0.060]					
Managers	0.662*** [0.051]					
Constant	−0.622 [0.456]	−1.281 [2.150]	−0.015 [0.924]	−0.252 [0.583]	3.422 [3.383]	7.886 [5.539]
Observations	3040	213	790	1838	76	123
R-squared	0.35	0.1	0.06	0.24	0.49	0.16

Note: OLS Estimates. Standard errors in brackets
* significant at 10%; ** significant at 5%; *** significant at 1%

of the effects is attenuated over time.[10] For example, while employees with university degrees earned about 13% higher wages than employees with only basic education (conditional on employee category) in 1997, their wage mark-up falls to only 11% in 2002. It is also striking that wage tenure profiles are much flatter in 2002 than in 1997. The conditional gender wage gap is reduced between 1997 and 2002 from 27 to 15%, and, with the exception of managers, wage differences between employee categories have also diminished by 2002, an issue to which we return later.

Columns (2) to (6) show wage regressions for the different employee categories. In 1997 the conditional gender wage gap was nearly twice as large for production workers as it was for service staff and nearly three times as large in comparison with the gender gap for engineers. Female accountants, on the other hand, experienced a wage premium over their male counterparts when one controls for other factors. Column (5) also makes clear that the larger returns to higher incomplete education compared with the returns to completed higher education for all employees was entirely driven by this relationship for accountants. That accountants who started but did not finish university had higher wages on average than accountants who completed university might strike one as counterintuitive. Confronted with this result, the firm's CEO stated that newly hired university graduates specializing in financial matters received low wages as the supply of these graduates was large, while experienced accountants who had worked long in the firm and some of whom might not have finished higher studies received higher wages. In the case of production workers, we obtain the expected result that workers with secondary and secondary professional education command higher wages than those with basic professional education or less.

Real total compensation was determined by the same factors as wages. This is not surprising since wages made up the lion's share of total income in all years as Table 4.5 shows. In the crisis year of 1998, the wage share rose to more than 90% of total income and then declined to slightly more than three-quarters of total income in 2002. The shares of all bonus components fell in the crisis year but subsequently more than recovered in the remaining years.

Table 4.5 Shares of monthly compensation components

Year	Monthly wage	Monthly bonus	Extra bonus	Other bonus
1997	0.830	0.080	0.051	0.039
1998	0.916	0.059	0.000	0.025
1999	0.870	0.066	0.043	0.021
2000	0.854	0.066	0.042	0.038
2001	0.797	0.081	0.098	0.025
2002	0.776	0.095	0.088	0.041

Source: Personnel records of the firm, own calculations.

Nominal and real rigidity

An inspection of the data reveals that the firm never cuts nominal wages.[11] Real wages, however, fall markedly in the aftermath of the financial crisis in 1998. Figures 4.4 and 4.5 show that real wages and real monthly compensation (measured as the sum of real monthly wages and the monthly share of all real bonus payments for the year) in the upper half of the respective distribution fell most, both in absolute and in relative terms, and recovered least in post-crisis years. As a result, kernel density estimates of the wage distributions in 2002, plotted in Figure 4.6, are clearly to the left of the real wage distributions in 1997, for all employee categories. The real wage distributions in 2002 also appear more compressed. Exactly the same secular patterns can be observed for the real monthly compensation distributions, i.e. between 1997 and 2002 we see a shift to the left of these distributions and their compression.[12]

Who bears the burden of the shock? Individual wage mobility

Even though average real wages fall, not all employees are affected by the crisis in the same way. This becomes evident from Figure 4.7, which plots the kernel density estimate of the distribution function of real wage growth between 1997 and 2002. These heterogeneous real wage growth rates cause substantial relative wage mobility inside the firm as transition rates between quintiles of the wage distribution in 1997 (the origin state) and in 2002 (the destination state), calculated for the balanced panel of those who were continuously employed during the entire period, as Table 4.6 reveals. For example, only 35% of all employees who found themselves in the third

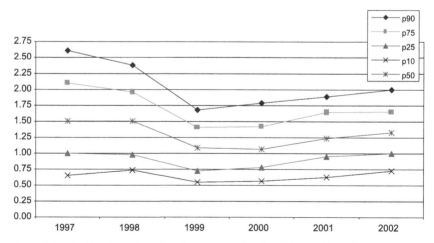

Figure 4.5 Distribution of total real compensation in rubles—all employees.

Source: Records from the personnel file, own calculations.

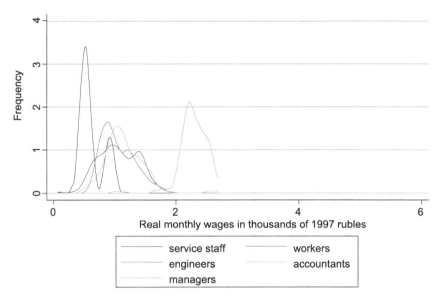

Figure 4.6 Real wage distributions in 2002.

Source: Records from the personnel file, national CPI deflator from Rosstat, own calculations.

Notes: The figure plots the smoothed density functions of the real wage distributions in 2002 for the five employee categories in 1997 rubles, estimated using a Gaussian kernel. The bandwidth is chosen to minimize the mean integrated squared error under the assumption that the data are Gaussian.

quintile of the wage distribution in 1997 remain there in 2002, while 41% move up in the wage distribution and 24% move down. This pattern is observed for all employment groups, but is particularly marked for production workers.[13] The transition patterns are also very similar albeit slightly stronger for total compensation. Thus, the firm substantially realigned real wages and total compensation during the inflationary period following the financial crisis, especially for the core group of the firm, the production workers.

In order to assess whether particular characteristics systematically determine relative wage growth, we regress the growth rate of real wages between 1997 and 2002 on various individual and job characteristics. We restrict the sample to full-time employees who were continuously employed during the entire observation period.

Table 4.7 contains the regression results with three different specifications of the wage growth equation. Specification (1) estimates wage growth as a function of a cubic in tenure and age, dummies for highest educational attainment, and demographic dummies. This specification assumes that wage growth does not depend on an individual's position in the firm-level wage distribution in 1997. The tenure–wage growth profile can be characterized as follows: tenure and wage growth are inversely related up to approximately 20 years, between

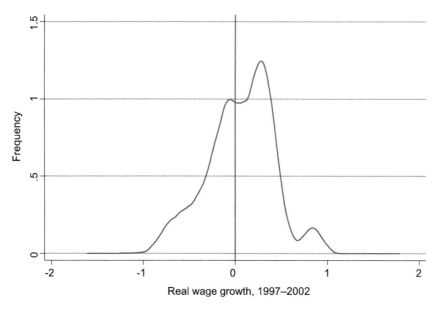

Figure 4.7 Real wage growth, 1997–2002.

Source: Records from the personnel file, CPI deflator from Rosstat, own calculations.

Notes: The figure plots the smoothed density functions of the distribution of real wage growth between 1997 and 2002 for the all employees who stayed with the firm during the entire period. Wages were deflated using the national CPI. The density function is estimated using a Gaussian kernel. The bandwidth is chosen to minimize the mean integrated squared error under the assumption that the data are Gaussian.

Table 4.6 Transition probabilities between quintiles of real wages in 1997 and 2002 (in %); all continuous employees

		Quintile in real wage distribution (2002)					
		1	*2*	*3*	*4*	*5*	*N (1997)*
Quintile in	1	**57.89**	*30.47*	*8.59*	*1.39*	*1.66*	361
real wage	2	28.5	**34.35**	25	*10.28*	*1.87*	428
distribution	3	4.81	19.24	**34.87**	35.27	*5.81*	499
(1997)	4	0.73	5.13	12.96	**49.39**	*31.78*	409
	5	0	0.49	4.62	22.38	**72.51**	411

Source: Personnel records of the firm, own calculations.

21 and 30 years of tenure, wage growth remains flat at roughly minus 22%, and wage growth then turns slightly more negative for longer-tenured employees. On this measure, the firm seemed to favor those employees who have been hired more recently. Holding other factors constant, female employees earn a substantial premium if the results of the model in column 1 are to be believed.

Specification (2) adds dummies for the employee's position in the firm-level

Table 4.7 Real wage growth, 1997–2002

	(1)	(2)	(3)
Tenure in years	−0.038***	−0.029***	−0.020**
	[0.013]	[0.009]	[0.009]
Tenure squared/100 in years	0.160**	0.155***	0.101**
	[0.077]	[0.053]	[0.052]
Tenure cube /1,000 in years	−0.022*	−0.022**	−0.013
	[0.013]	[0.009]	[0.009]
Age in years	0.04	−0.001	−0.016
	[0.052]	[0.036]	[0.034]
Age squared/100 in years	−0.119	−0.005	0.039
	[0.124]	[0.086]	[0.081]
Age cube /1,000 in years	0.011	0.000	−0.003
	[0.010]	[0.007]	[0.006]
Basic professional	0.000	−0.008	0.000
	[0.028]	[0.019]	[0.019]
Secondary general	−0.012	0.024	0.016
	[0.024]	[0.017]	[0.016]
Secondary professional	0.032	0.097***	0.037**
	[0.023]	[0.016]	[0.019]
Higher incomplete	0.056	0.144***	0.066*
	[0.057]	[0.039]	[0.040]
Higher	0.023	0.131***	0.047**
	[0.024]	[0.017]	[0.022]
1 if female	0.087***	−0.035***	−0.050***
	[0.016]	[0.012]	[0.012]
1 if single	−0.061	−0.045	−0.057
	[0.080]	[0.055]	[0.053]
1 if divorced or widowed	−0.015	−0.043**	−0.044**
	[0.027]	[0.019]	[0.018]
1 if 1 child	0.098	0.056	0.045
	[0.062]	[0.043]	[0.041]
1 if more than 1 child	0.063	0.059	0.047
	[0.064]	[0.044]	[0.042]
Position in firm-level wage distribution:			
1st decile		0.563***	
		[0.022]	
2nd decile		0.218***	
		[0.024]	
3rd decile		0.119***	
		[0.023]	
4th decile		0.033	
		[0.023]	
6th decile		−0.098***	
		[0.022]	

(*Continued overleaf*)

Table 4.7 Continued

	(1)	(2)	(3)
7th decile		−0.090*** [0.023]	
8th decile		−0.184*** [0.024]	
9th decile		−0.195*** [0.023]	
10th decile		−0.304*** [0.024]	
Position in employee category specific wage distribution: 1st decile			0.559*** [0.021]
2nd decile			0.251*** [0.020]
3rd decile			0.183*** [0.022]
4th decile			0.134*** [0.020]
6th decile			0.01 [0.022]
7th decile			−0.088*** [0.021]
8th decile			−0.193*** [0.022]
9th decile			−0.154*** [0.020]
10th decile			−0.291*** [0.021]
Service staff			0.286*** [0.018]
Engineers			0.151*** [0.018]
Accountants			−0.078** [0.039]
Managers			−0.089*** [0.028]
Constant	−0.425 [0.699]	−0.056 [0.482]	0.015 [0.459]
Observations	1824	1824	1824
R-squared	0.07	0.56	0.61

Source: Personnel records of the firm, own calculations.

Note: Standard errors in brackets
* significant at 10%; ** significant at 5%; *** significant at 1%

wage distribution in 1997. This model might still be too simplistic, since it assumes that all employees were confronted with the same wage distribution in 1997. As we have seen, however, the locations and the spreads of the wage distributions for the five employee categories were very different in 1997. To take account of this, specification (3) adds controls for the location in the employee category-specific wage distribution and dummies for employee categories. The results of specifications (2) and (3) are similar, and we concentrate our discussion on the results of specification (3).

The impact of tenure, while somewhat attenuated, remains negative throughout the tenure distribution. Secondary professional and higher educational attainment imply higher wage growth, while female employees experience smaller wage growth than their male counterparts. The latter result, reversing the estimated wage growth premium for female employees in specification (1), can be explained by the fact that women find themselves in 1997 in employee and wage segments that exhibit the highest growth throughout the reported period.

The coefficients on the decile dummies strongly confirm our contention that employees positioned in 1997 in the lower deciles of their respective wage distribution experienced relative gains in the reported period. Location in the lower four deciles implies stronger wage growth than for those employees who were positioned in 1997 in the median decile. These relative gains are monotonically decreasing as we go from the bottom to the fourth decile. In contrast, employees positioned in 1997 in the highest four deciles of their wage distribution are confronted with relative wage losses. Relative to production workers, service staff and engineers have wage gains over the period, while accountants and managers have wage losses.

In Table 4.8 we remove the assumption that wage growth is equi-proportionate for each quantile across all employee categories, and estimate wage growth regressions for each employee category separately.[14] The results show clear differences in the returns to the various deciles for the five employee categories. In particular, the relative returns for service staff show a much larger spread across the wage distribution than for other employee categories. In addition, production workers experience positive wage growth higher up in the wage distribution than other employees. The overall result is, however, very clear, no matter what the employee category: employees who find themselves in 1997 in the lower part of their respective wage distribution experience substantially higher wage growth than those who are located in the upper part.

The estimated effect of all of these determinants on the growth of total compensation are very similar, which is not surprising given that the different bonus payments only account for a small share of total compensation.

Extraction of rents and approaching the outside option

The falling outside opportunities after the crisis of 1998 made it possible for top management to use inflation to erode the rents that the firm's employees

Table 4.8 Real wage growth 1997–2002 by employee category

	Service staff (1)	Engineers (2)	Production workers (3)	Accountants (4)	Managers (5)
Tenure in years	−0.143** [0.069]	0.013 [0.011]	−0.027** [0.013]	−0.239 [0.157]	−0.025 [0.024]
Tenure squared/100 in years	0.982* [0.553]	−0.082 [0.066]	0.141* [0.075]	1.683 [1.089]	0.093 [0.142]
Tenure cube /1,000 in years	−0.209 [0.134]	0.015 [0.012]	−0.019 [0.013]	−0.335 [0.231]	−0.008 [0.025]
Age in years	−0.234 [0.148]	−0.02 [0.033]	0.046 [0.055]	−0.532 [1.170]	0.914* [0.468]
Age squared/100 in years	0.55 [0.348]	0.042 [0.076]	−0.103 [0.132]	1.08 [2.834]	−1.978* [1.029]
Age cube /1,000 in years	−0.042 [0.027]	−0.003 [0.006]	0.007 [0.010]	−0.071 [0.225]	0.141* [0.075]
Basic professional	0.058 [0.050]	−0.460*** [0.146]	−0.018 [0.023]		
Secondary general	0.004 [0.052]		−0.001 [0.019]		
Secondary professional	0.057 [0.063]	−0.012 [0.026]	0.028 [0.024]	0.172 [0.447]	−0.066 [0.068]
Higher incomplete	−0.029 [0.235]		0.053 [0.103]	−0.011 [0.813]	
Higher	0.125 [0.163]	−0.005 [0.026]	−0.039 [0.047]	0.337 [0.483]	−0.025 [0.068]
1 if female	−0.036 [0.041]	0.006 [0.011]	−0.111*** [0.021]	−0.29 [0.427]	−0.015 [0.028]
1 if single	−0.247 [0.230]	0.031 [0.075]	0.139 [0.087]		
1 if divorced or widowed	−0.101* [0.056]	−0.016 [0.029]	−0.025 [0.026]	−0.441** [0.192]	0.002 [0.028]
1 if 1 child	−0.066 [0.051]	−0.028 [0.035]	0.232*** [0.073]	0.067 [0.166]	−0.013 [0.020]
1 if more than 1 child		−0.012 [0.039]	0.219*** [0.074]		
Position in employee category specific wage distribution:					
1st decile	0.617*** [0.085]	0.403*** [0.022]	0.674*** [0.032]	0.466 [0.294]	0.419*** [0.041]
2nd decile	0.287*** [0.080]	0.213*** [0.022]	0.270*** [0.029]	0.264 [0.275]	0.278*** [0.047]
3rd decile	−0.037 [0.082]	0.161*** [0.022]	0.202*** [0.034]	−0.003 [0.363]	0.254*** [0.043]

4th decile	0.259*** [0.088]	0.085*** [0.022]	0.137*** [0.030]	0.052 [0.286]	0.103** [0.043]
6th decile	−0.083 [0.083]	−0.087*** [0.023]	0.086** [0.035]	0.107 [0.310]	−0.147*** [0.045]
7th decile	−0.314*** [0.084]	−0.140*** [0.022]	−0.033 [0.031]	−0.175 [0.262]	−0.116*** [0.043]
8th decile	−0.550*** [0.085]	−0.186*** [0.023]	−0.162*** [0.034]	−0.043 [0.344]	−0.123*** [0.039]
9th decile	−0.621*** [0.084]	−0.189*** [0.022]	−0.086*** [0.030]	0.042 [0.274]	−0.158*** [0.050]
10th decile	−0.761*** [0.084]	−0.287*** [0.023]	−0.241*** [0.032]	−0.096 [0.295]	−0.268*** [0.044]
Constant	4.054* [2.070]	0.224 [0.438]	−1.018 [0.733]	8.929 [16.054]	−14.044** [7.005]
Observations	151	611	934	36	92
R-squared	0.83	0.75	0.53	0.69	0.9

Standard errors in brackets
* significant at 10%; ** significant at 5%; *** significant at 1%

enjoyed before the crisis. Table 4.9, shows that the large positive differences between mean wages in the firm and mean wages in the sample of industrial firms located in the same local labor market turned either negative towards the end of the period or were tremendously reduced. The convergence of average wages in the firm towards average wages in the local labor market started after 1999 when employees' rents peaked. The extraction of rents during the period of real wage adjustment was quite relentless as a comparison of the entries for 1999 and the entries for 2002 reveals. If we link these relative wage movements to the information that we provided about local labor market conditions, it seems plausible that top management uses these local labor market conditions as an important element in its calculus regarding wage setting. This conjecture is confirmed by the CEO when asked directly about the determination of wage levels. According to him, three

Table 4.9 Differences between wages in firm and average wages in sample of industrial firms in the region in 1997 rubles, 1998–2002

Year	Service workers	Engineers	Workers	Accountants	Managers
1998	100	133	379	792	1468
1999	346	391	803	805	1898
2000	123	−28	261	223	1056
2001	81	−82	195	279	805
2002	−61	−24	119	150	551

Source: Personnel records of the firm, CERT Russian regional data base, own calculations.

dimensions are relevant for wage determination: the characteristics of a worker, i.e. her/his qualification, tenure, seniority, and work experience in general; labor market conditions, in particular the wage level in the region, and the wage level in the sector; and the price of the order in whose production the employee is engaged.

In sum, given our evidence on the time patterns of regional turnover, the regional unemployment rate, declining relative wage gaps, and the statement by the CEO of the firm, we are confident that local labor market conditions are of paramount importance in the calculus of top management when it comes to wage setting. It is also our conjecture that in this Russian firm the causal effect runs from turnover to wages and not vice versa. This might seem counterintuitive as one would surmise that high wages would cause a fall in turnover. However, the efficiency wage models that explained the causal effect going from wages to turnover (see, e.g., Salop, 1979) are embedded in a mature capitalist economy that finds itself in a steady state. The Russian economy in the 1990s was clearly not in a steady state but in great turmoil with a tremendous amount of labor reallocation taking place. The CEO of our firm paints the following picture of this dramatic period when explaining the development of wages in the firm: "Higher than regional wages contributed to retaining and attracting highly qualified personnel after difficult crisis years in the beginning of the 1990s, when episodes of forced downsizing due to the output decline took place. Later, in 1995–1996, the firm started to receive orders, production growth began, and there was a need for qualified personnel. Since economic improvement happened all over the country, the only way to retain and attract personnel was to pay high wages. After the 1998 crisis, it was economically expedient to stabilize wages at the regional level."[15] In the final analysis, market forces work in the case of our Russian firm and that in a relentless fashion.

Inequality

A comparison of the Figures 4.3 and 4.6 reveals that real wage distributions become more compressed. The difference in the median wage and wages for an employee at the 90th percentile of the distribution is reduced by slightly less than 15 percentage points during the period from 1997 to 2002. The gap between the wage of an employee at the 10th percentile of the wage distribution and the median wage narrowed by 37 percentage points from 1997 to 2002. Hence, the fall in wage inequality comes about by relative wage gains of employees in the lower part of the wage distribution. Gini coefficients reported in column (1) of Table 4.10 corroborate the decline in inequality of wages and total compensation for the entire workforce. The Gini coefficients in columns (2)–(6) show that wage and compensation inequality falls also within all employee categories in the aftermath of the financial crisis. However, this process of wage and compensation compression is not monotonic for all employee categories.

The Gini coefficient can be written as $G = (2/\mu)\,\text{cov}[y,F(y)]$, where y is income, $F(y)$ is the distribution function of y, and μ is mean income (see, e.g., Lambert, 2001). A simple algebraic manipulation then arrives at the decomposition of G into its components by income source:

$$G = \sum_{k} R_k\,G_k\,S_k \tag{1}$$

where R_k is the rank correlation of income source k with the distribution of total income, G_k is the Gini of income source k and S_k is the share of component k in total income.[16] The decomposition of the Gini coefficient by income source is particularly interesting in our context to establish the contribution of the various components to inequality. The kth component of equation (1) divided by G, i.e., $R_k G_k S_k / G$, gives us the share of income source k in total inequality. Dividing this expression by S_k shows the inequality component as a fraction of its income share. Finally, $(R_k G_k S_k / G) - S_k$ approximates the impact of a 1% change of income source k on overall inequality.

The upper panel of Table 4.11 presents the Gini coefficients for the different compensation components. Inequality in wages and in the extra bonus gradually falls with the exception that inequality in the extra bonus was zero in the crisis year 1998 since no extra bonus was paid at all. The other two bonus types show a more erratic behavior. The compression in total compensation is less pronounced than the compression in wages, not least because the Gini coefficients of bonuses were far higher than the Gini coefficients of wages (see top panel of Table 4.11). Despite this large difference

Table 4.10 Evolution of earnings inequality measured by Gini coefficients

Year	(1) Entire workforce	(2) Service staff	(3) Engineers	(4) Workers	(5) Accountants	(6) Managers
Panel (a): Wages						
1997	0.2801	0.2474	0.2294	0.2507	0.1912	0.1367
1998	0.251	0.1484	0.2239	0.2003	0.1417	0.1082
1999	0.2453	0.0853	0.1954	0.1854	0.1267	0.1202
2000	0.2456	0.0649	0.1786	0.1945	0.1705	0.072
2001	0.2189	0.055	0.1679	0.1792	0.1583	0.0438
2002	0.1995	0.1618	0.1437	0.1725	0.1409	0.0482
Panel (b): Total compensation						
1997	0.2928	0.2416	0.2293	0.2456	0.1903	0.1488
1998	0.2547	0.1474	0.2248	0.2015	0.1423	0.1077
1999	0.2444	0.0855	0.1964	0.1823	0.131	0.1202
2000	0.2464	0.0669	0.1792	0.1972	0.1787	0.073
2001	0.2271	0.0684	0.1681	0.1778	0.1696	0.0447
2002	0.2211	0.162	0.1455	0.1845	0.1454	0.0484

Source: Personnel records of the firm, own calculations.

Table 4.11 Gini decomposition by income source

Year	Monthly wage	Monthly bonus	Extra bonus	Other bonus
Gini by income source				
1997	0.2802	0.8069	0.63	0.725
1998	0.251	0.7933	—	0.7027
1999	0.2453	0.7846	0.5467	0.7788
2000	0.2457	0.7759	0.5488	0.7271
2001	0.219	0.7658	0.352	0.7367
2002	0.1996	0.758	0.2724	0.7209
Gini correlation of income source with distribution of total income				
1997	0.9752	0.6052	0.5787	0.2968
1998	0.9893	0.4063	—	0.4621
1999	0.9895	0.2838	0.5298	0.371
2000	0.9775	0.3499	0.3805	0.5315
2001	0.9711	0.5007	0.6761	0.192
2002	0.9586	0.5955	0.8062	0.3527

Source: Personnel records of the firm, own calculations.

between the Gini coefficients of bonus payments and the Gini coefficient of wages, bonuses contributed little to overall inequality for two reasons. First, their shares were small relative to the share of wages (see Table 4.5). Second, the rank correlations of all bonus payments with the distribution of total income were far weaker than the nearly perfect rank correlation of wages (see bottom panel of Table 4.11). Wages contributed slightly less to overall inequality than their share in total income, as Table 4.12 demonstrates, and therefore had a (hypothetical) attenuating impact on overall inequality in all years as the bottom panel of Table 4.13 reveals. Monthly bonus payments, in contrast, "aggravated" overall inequality in all years apart from 1999.

The general entropy index, which is given by

$$GEI(a) = \left[\frac{1}{Na(a-1)}\right] \sum_i \left[\left(\frac{x_i}{\mu}\right)^a - 1\right]$$ (2)

where N is the number of observational units, x_i is the level of earnings of the ith observational unit, and μ is mean earnings, allows us to assess whether the change in inequality is mostly driven by changes at the bottom or by changes at the top of the distribution, by varying the parameter a. The index is more sensitive to changes at the top of the distribution the larger is a.[17] Since the fall in the general entropy index for a parameter value of −1 is more pronounced than for a value of 1, we conclude that the relative gains at the bottom of the wage and the compensation distributions are the more important driving factors of the fall in overall inequality. If we give more weight to

Table 4.12 Contributions of source incomes on inequality

Year	Monthly wage	Monthly bonus	Extra bonus	Other bonus
Share of source income in total inequality				
1997	0.7749	0.1333	0.063	0.0288
1998	0.8929	0.0756	—	0.0315
1999	0.8643	0.06	0.0513	0.0245
2000	0.8324	0.0731	0.0354	0.0591
2001	0.7462	0.1364	0.1021	0.0153
2002	0.6707	0.1947	0.0875	0.047
Inequality components as a fraction of income shares				
1997	0.9333	1.6677	1.2451	0.7349
1998	0.9748	1.2748	—	1.275
1999	0.9932	0.911	1.185	1.1823
2000	0.9745	1.1016	0.8473	1.5682
2001	0.936	1.6878	1.0476	0.6227
2002	0.8649	2.041	0.9928	1.1495
Impact of 1% change in income source on inequality				
1997	−0.0554	0.0534	0.0124	−0.0104
1998	−0.0231	0.0163	—	0.0068
1999	−0.0059	−0.0059	0.008	0.0038
2000	−0.0218	0.0067	−0.0064	0.0214
2001	−0.051	0.0556	0.0046	−0.0093
2002	−0.1048	0.0993	−0.0006	0.0061

Source: Personnel records of the firm, own calculations.

Table 4.13 General Entropy Index (GEI) and its decomposition into within and between parts

Year	(1) Total	(2) GEI(−1) Within	(3) Between	(4) Total	(5) GEI(+1) Within	(6) Between
Panel (a): Wages						
1997	0.1904	0.1515	0.0389	0.1263	0.0914	0.0348
1998	0.1379	0.097	0.0409	0.1001	0.0637	0.0363
1999	0.1151	0.07	0.0451	0.0958	0.0538	0.042
2000	0.1082	0.0626	0.0456	0.0938	0.0539	0.0399
2001	0.095	0.0528	0.0421	0.076	0.0444	0.0315
2002	0.0762	0.0544	0.0217	0.0645	0.0399	0.0245
Panel (b): Total compensation						
1997	0.195	0.1453	0.0497	0.1446	0.086	0.0348
1998	0.1379	0.0976	0.0402	0.1061	0.0636	0.0363
1999	0.1144	0.0688	0.0456	0.0991	0.0525	0.042
2000	0.1086	0.0651	0.0434	0.0987	0.0546	0.0399
2001	0.1017	0.0554	0.0462	0.0853	0.0435	0.0315
2002	0.0941	0.0636	0.0304	0.0826	0.0433	0.0245

Source: Personnel records of the firm, own calculations.

wages in the lower part of the distribution, our measure of overall wage inequality, GEI(–1) indicates that inequality fell by 62% between 1997 and 2002. If, on the other hand, the index is more sensitive to wages in the upper part of the distribution then measured overall wage inequality fell by "only" 44% (see columns (1) and (4) of panel (a) of Table 4.13). Falling inequality is mostly driven by compression within the lower part of the wage distribution in all employee categories except for managers.

The general entropy index can also be additively decomposed into the "within" and "between" parts of inequality. This decomposition reveals that inequality within employee categories dominate overall wage inequality in 1997, while in 2002 within and between group inequality are of roughly equal magnitude. The *GEI(–1)* and *GEI(1)* measures indicate that within-inequality fell, respectively, by 69 and 60% and that between-inequality was reduced by 37 and 1% respectively. Most of the compression in the overall wage distribution between 1997 and 2002 occurred because there was tremendous compression of wages within employee categories. These patterns also hold for inequality of total compensation as the statistics in the bottom panel of Table 4.13 demonstrates. We take these patterns as additional evidence that local labor market conditions strongly impact on the setting of wages in our firm.

4 Conclusions

Having a rich personnel data set of one Russian firm for the years 1997–2002 at our disposal, we can trace out the evolution of wages, total compensation and employment in a period that included an episode of high inflation during and in the aftermath of the financial crisis of 1998. The observed evolution points to "price" rather than "quantity" adjustment within the firm during the crisis as employment remained stable but real wages and real compensation fell substantially. Our evidence thus shows that the firm did not refrain from substantially cutting real wages, taking advantage of a high-inflation environment.

The downward adjustment of earnings led to persistent welfare losses among employees since real wages and real compensation levels had not recovered to pre-crisis levels by 2002, even though the firm's financial situation was then better than before the crisis. The firm, which was a high-wage firm prior to 1998, made use of the high inflation that manifested itself during and in the aftermath of the financial crisis in order to extract rents from employees. These welfare losses were, however, not spread evenly across all employees, since the firm curbed earnings most for those who earned the highest rents, resulting in a tremendous compression of real wages. Wage growth regressions spanning the years 1997–2002 show disproportionate wage growth for those employees located in the lowest four deciles of the wage distribution in 1997, while employees positioned in the highest four deciles were confronted with relative wage losses. Relative to production workers, service staff and engineers saw wage gains over the period, while accountants and managers had small wage losses.

The firm was in a position to extract rents from its employees because of a fall in outside opportunities in the local labor market as evidenced by dramatically falling separation rates after 1999. At the bottom end of the firm's wage distribution there are, however, smaller rents before the crisis and the firm seems to pay wages closer to the opportunity cost for employees at that end of the distribution throughout the reported period.

Our analysis provides strong evidence for the hypothesis that top managers take local labor market conditions into account when deciding on wage levels. In times of very high labor turnover they are willing to pay higher than average real wages to attract and retain skilled workers. On the other hand, being reluctant to cut nominal wages, they relentlessly cut real wages when market conditions make this possible. All in all, our evidence clearly shows that market forces strongly influence the wage policies of our firm and that considerations for a stable internal labor market are of less concern.

Notes

* The authors are very grateful to Vladimir Gimpleson and Rostislaw Kapeliushnikov for useful discussions. Dohmen and Lehmann acknowledge financial support from the Deutsche Forschungsgemeinschaft (DFG) within the research program "Flexibilisierungspotenziale bei heterogenen Arbeitsmärkten" (DFGSP1169). Lehmann and Schaffer are grateful to the European Commission for financial support within the 6th Framework Project "Economic and Social Consequences of Industrial Restructuring in Russia and Ukraine" (ESCIRRU). Schaffer also thanks the William Davidson Institute and the US Department of State (Title VIII) for financial support.
1 Interviews were held with the CEO in the spring of 2002 and in April 2007.
2 Interview with CEO in April 2007.
3 We also have wage data for all months in 2003 except for December. However, since we lack data on yearly bonuses for 2003, we do not use the compensation data for 2003 in this paper.
4 Information for top managers is missing for reasons of confidentiality.
5 Only production workers are subdivided into levels, primary production workers having eight and auxiliary production workers having six levels.
6 We have available monthly data on CPI inflation in Russia overall and in the oblast where the firm is located. Results using wages and bonuses deflated by the national CPI are essentially identical to those using the oblast CPI. We use the former in what follows.
7 One element in an array of outside opportunities was the "suitcase trade" between Russia and, e.g., China or Turkey, consisting in buying and selling certain types of goods informally. Such opportunities were severely reduced after the crisis, resulting in a dramatic fall in the number of "suitcase traders" throughout Russia (Eder, Yakovlev, and Çarkoglu, 2003).
8 We have a balanced panel of 37 firms that represent roughly 15% of industrial employment in this city only for these four years.
9 The sample of firms is not representative in terms of development of total employment in the region, since we have a balanced panel. However, the estimated inflow and outflow rates are indicative of falling outside opportunities after the crisis.

10 The regression results for 2002 are not presented here but are available on request.

11 According to top management the firm never contemplated cutting nominal wages, since such cuts might have resulted in even higher quit rates than those observed before the crisis.

12 The real monthly compensation distributions are not shown here but can be provided by the authors.

13 Transition matrices showing wage and compensation dynamics for different employee categories are available from the authors on request.

14 We have a very small number of observations for accountants. This low number is responsible for the insignificance of virtually all coefficients in column 4 of Table 4.8.

15 Cited from the interview of April 2007.

16 This decomposition is due to Lerman and Yitzaki (1985) who show that.

$$G = (2 / \mu) \sum_{k=1}^{K} \text{cov}(y_k, F) = \sum_{k=1}^{K} [\text{cov}(y_k, F) / \text{cov}(y_k, F_k)] [2 \, \text{cov}(y_k, F_k) / \mu_k] [\mu_k / \mu].$$

17 GEI(a) encompasses several well-known inequality measures: for example, GEI(0) corresponds to the mean log deviation, GEI(1) to the Theil index, and GEI(2) to one-half of the square of the coefficient of variation. We use a modified version of the Stata module "descogini" by Alejandro Lopez-Feldman for our calculations. See Lopez-Feldman (2005).

References

Brainerd, E. (2002) "Five Years After: The Impact of Mass Privatization on Wages in Russia, 1993–1998." *Journal of Comparative Economics* 30(1): 160–90.

Clarke, S. (2002) "Market and Institutional Determinants of Wage Differentiation in Russia." *Industrial Labor Relations Review* 55(4): 628–48.

Commander, S., S. Dhar, and R. Yemtsov (1996) "How Russian Firms Make Their Employment Decisions." In Enterprise *Restructuring and Economic Policy in Russia*, edited by S. Commander, Q. Fan and M. E. Schaffer. Washington, DC: EDI/World Bank, 52–83.

Doeringer, P. B. and M. J. Piore (1971) *Internal Labor Markets and Manpower Analysis*. Lexington, MA: Heath Lexington Books.

Dunlop, J. T. (1957) "The Task of Contemporary Wage Theory." In *New Concepts in Wage Determination*, edited by G. W. Taylor and F. C. Pierson. New York: McGraw Hill, 117–39.

Eder, M., A. Yakovlev, and A. Çarkoglu (2003) "The Suitcase Trade between Turkey and Russia: Microeconomics and institutional structure." Working Paper WP4/2003/07, Moscow: Higher School of Economics.

Kapeliushnikov, R. (2002) *Rossiiski Rynok Truda: Adaptatsia bez Restrukturizatsii*. Moscow.

Lambert, P. J. (2001) *The Distribution and Redistribution of Income*, Manchester and New York: Manchester University Press.

Lehmann, H., J. Wadsworth, and A. Acquisti (1999) "Grime and Punishment: Job insecurity and wage arrears in the Russian Federation." *Journal of Comparative Economics* 27(4): 595–617.

Lerman, R. I. and Shlomo Yitzaki (1985) "Income Inequality Effects by Income

Source: A new approach and applications to the United States." *The Review of Economics and Statistics*, 67(1): 151–6.

Lopez-Feldman, A. (2005) "DESCOGINI: Stata module to perform Gini decomposition by income source". http://ideas.repec.org/c/boc/bocode/s456001.html

Luke, P. and M. E. Schaffer (2000) "Wage Determination in Russia: An econometric investigation." IZA Discussion Paper 143, Bonn.

Salop, S. C. (1979) "A Model of the Natural Rate of Unemployment." *American Economic Review* 69(1): 117–25.

5 Education and youth unemployment in South Africa

David Lam, Murray Leibbrandt, and Cecil Mlatsheni

1 Introduction

The problem of high youth unemployment is a global phenomenon. Accord-ing to an International Labor Office (ILO) study in 2004, youth (15–24) make up nearly half (47%) of the world's unemployed, 88 million out of 186 million, even though youth are only 25% of the world's working age population. Of the world's 550 million working poor who cannot lift themselves above US \$1 per day poverty measure, 150 million are youth. The ILO estimated in 2004 that halving global youth unemployment would increase global GDP by US \$2.2 trillion, 4% of global GDP. These statistics lend weight to the notion that youth unemployment is a problem worthy of attention. In addition, one may argue that addressing unemployment in general would also lower poverty levels and add to GDP (World Bank 2006).

South Africa is an important case study of the problem of youth unemploy-ment. The country has had a pervasive unemployment problem for the last forty years. Standing, Sender, and Weeks (1996) report that unemployment rose sharply in the 1970s and that this rise continued through the 1980s and 1990s. Another longstanding characteristic of South African unemployment is lengthy unemployment duration. In the mid-1990s nearly two-thirds of the unemployed had never worked for pay (Standing, Sender, and Weeks 1996). This feature of the unemployed has persisted. The 2005 Labor Force Survey indicates that 40% of unemployed individuals (by the strict definition) have unemployment durations exceeding three years, while 59% of the unemployed have never had a job at all. These findings accord with the earlier findings of Kingdon and Knight (2000) who found that in 1997, 37% of the *searching* unemployed experienced unemployment durations of more than three years. Things are even bleaker for the non-searching unemployed and non-participants. Dinkelman (2004) examined the transition patterns between dif-ferent labor market states of African cohorts living in KwaZulu-Natal during the period 1993–8 and found that fewer than 10% of those who were in this non-searching group in 1993 were employed in 1998. In sum, chronic unemployment is a longstanding feature of the South African labor market and this has created an unfavorable climate for youth to enter the labor market.

Research focusing explicitly on youth unemployment in South Africa is not new. Studies of youth unemployment prior to the mid-1990s (see Everatt and Sisulu 1992, Truscott 1993 and Van Zyl Slabbert 1994, among others) mainly focused on two issues. First, they detailed the bleak circumstances of youth. This literature provides a moving account of the role that youth played in the fight against apartheid and the negative consequences of this commitment for their personal prospects. Most pertinent for this paper is the discussion of the deficiency in educational accumulation of these youths and its likely negative effect on their employment prospects. Indeed, given the political turbulence and consequent educational disruption of youth in the 1980s there were fears that this youth cohort would become a "lost generation" (Riordan in Everatt and Sisulu 1992). A number of subsequent papers have analyzed various dimensions of youth unemployment in South Africa, including Wittenberg and Pearce (1996), Mhone (2000), and Mlatsheni and Rospabe (2002).

Deficiency in youth education and labor market preparedness is still a relevant concern in contemporary South Africa. The March 2005 Labor Force Survey reveals that 42% of African youth who are between 15 and 24 years of age had stopped their studies and entered the labor market. What is troubling is that more than 60% of these youth have less than a matric (complete secondary) qualification, while 33% have nothing more than a complete matric. As 59% of this group experience unemployment, it is a puzzle why many of these youth quit school before they acquire matric. With such a high unemployment rate, there should be a strong case for further studies even for those that do have a matric certificate. Resource constraints is one obvious candidate to explain this outcome. Indeed, resource constraints are prolific in the developing country context and limit educational attainment on two fronts. First, many individuals wishing to pursue further studies simply cannot afford to do so. Second, even those individuals that obtain funding for further studies may opt for earlier entry into the labor market, even at low pay in mediocre jobs, in order to supplement family income (World Bank 2006). This is especially the case when there are younger siblings in need of support.

Human capital theory assumes that individuals have perfect forsight about future earnings for every level of education. In reality, however, youth are plagued by a great deal of uncertainty. This is especially true of those from less privileged backgrounds. Youth are uncertain about the value of their abilities and schooling as well as the timing of job offers and earnings after studies. In addition, they have no control over future labor demand and they are uncertain about their longevity. Concerns about longevity are likely to be prominent in areas where illness, gang activity, and crime are rife (World Bank 2006). This uncertain reality and the real constraints facing South African youth need to be given attention. However, it is hard to believe that these concerns override the strong signals coming to youth about the value of staying in school.

In this paper we offer a more detailed interrogation of the role of education in youth employment and unemployment. A more detailed review (Lam, Leibbrandt, and Mlatsheni 2008) reveals that there are a large number of youth who leave school only to join the ranks of the unemployed and that some of these youth remain unemployed for a number of years. At the same time, the review indicates that complete secondary education and tertiary education are increasingly important in facilitating a move into employment; hence the puzzle alluded to earlier as to why these youth do not at least complete secondary education.

The paper homes in on this issue using a youth panel survey that holds the possibility of throwing a fresh perspective on youth labor market transitions. We make use of a newly collected longitudinal youth data set, the Cape Area Panel Study (CAPS). In Section 3 we describe these data and analyze transitions from school into the labor market in urban Cape Town. In Section 4 we use probit regressions to investigate the role of education in the transition from unemployment to work. In Section 5 we draw some conclusions. Given that CAPS focuses on Cape Town, Section 2 contextualizes the Cape Town youth labor market in the national context using a descriptive analysis of 2001 Census data. This section provides a broad overview of the contemporary youth unemployment situation in South Africa. Also, it makes the case that an analysis of youth unemployment in Cape Town will generate insights that are useful at the national level and for the youth unemployment discussion in general.

2 Youth unemployment in Cape Town in a national perspective

By way of introducing the sections using the CAPS, we now turn our attention to a comparison of Cape Town and the rest of South Africa using the 2001 census 10% micro-data set. This is the largest data set available to us for a post-2000 analysis. We restrict our comparison to the age ranges 14–22 years old because this coincides with the age ranges of the youth that were included in the first wave of CAPS. According to the 2001 census, Cape Town makes up just over 6% of South Africa's population and 11.3% of the urban population in the 14 to 22 age group.

Table 5.1 compares a population breakdown by race for this age cohort in Cape Town and the rest of South Africa. It shows that Africans make up the overwhelming majority (82%) of the South African population while the shares of coloureds and whites are almost equal at 8% and 7% respectively. The composition of the Cape Town population is very different, however. Almost half of the population of Cape Town is coloured, while 35% is African and 14% is white. Comparison of Cape Town's racial composition with that of the rest of the urban areas indicates that Cape Town's unique history has resulted in something of a reshuffling of the African and coloured race groups. The racial profile of the rest of urban South Africa is similar to the profile of the country as a whole but the shares of Africans and whites are affected by the overrepresentation of Africans in rural areas.

Table 5.1 Population percentages of youth aged 14–22, Cape Town versus the rest of South Africa

Population group	Cape Town	Rest of South Africa		Total South Africa
		Urban	All	
Black African	35	74	85	82
Coloured	49	10	6	8
Indian or Asian	2	5	2	2
White	14	12	7	7
Total	100	100	100	100

Source: 10% microsample of the 2001 census.

Table 5.2 Levels of education of 14–22-year-olds, Cape Town, and the rest of South Africa

Education level	Cape Town (%)	Rest of South Africa (%)	
		All	Urban
No schooling	1.4	4.0	2.1
Some primary	9.4	17.1	11.9
Complete primary	9.5	11.3	9.5
Some secondary	55.0	51.7	53.1
Grade 12 / Std 10	21.5	13.9	20.2
Higher	3.2	2.0	3.2
Total	100	100	100

Source: 10% microsample of the 2001 census.

Table 5.2 shows that the education profile of youth aged 14–22 in Cape Town is very similar to that of the rest of urban South Africa, with the main difference being that there is a lesser share of the Cape Town population with no schooling or some primary schooling and a slightly higher share with incomplete secondary and complete secondary schooling. The effect of including the rural areas of South Africa in the comparison is to increase the shares of the lower education groups. Many of the youth in this age range are still in school. Table 5.3 breaks down the activities of these youth for Cape Town and the rest of South Africa. The table also shows the racial breakdown of the Cape Town figures. As the rest of the country is dominated by Africans, the figures from the rest of the country are driven by Africans. In addition, the share breakdown of whites and coloureds in Cape Town is very similar to that of the whites and coloureds in the rest of South Africa. Therefore, we do not report racial breakdowns for the rest of the country. The table shows that the population group with the highest proportion of youth engaged in studies is the white group (65%), followed by Africans (52%), and coloureds (43%). Also evident is the fact that a very small percentage of white

Table 5.3 Employment status of 15–22-year-old youth in Cape Town and the rest of South Africa, 2001 census

Employment status	Cape Town (%)				Rest of the country (%)	
	African	Coloured	White	Total	All	Urban
Employed	10	23	26	19	8	10
Unemployed	28	22	4	21	17	21
Scholar or student	52	43	65	49	59	57
Home-maker or housewife	1	2	1	1	1	1
Pensioner or retired	0	0	0	0	0	0
Unable to work	1	1	1	1	1	1
Seasonal worker not working	0	1	0	1	1	1
Does not choose to work	3	4	2	3	6	5
Could not find work	5	5	1	4	7	5
Total	100	100	100	100	100	100

Source: 10% microsample of the 2001 census.

Note: This table covers ages 15–22 because employment status is captured for those 15 years and older in the 2001 census.

youth are unemployed (4%) compared to African youth (28%) and coloured youth (22%).

The key points from these tables are the following: while youth unemployment in Cape Town may be lower than in other parts of South Africa, it follows the same patterns. Most importantly, the role of education in a successful move into employment seems to be very similar in the urban Cape Town labor market as it is elsewhere in the country. Moreover, the racial marker is as strong in Cape Town as it is elsewhere. At the same time, the presence of a substantial coloured population occupying an intermediate position between Africans and whites allows for additional subtlety in exploring the interactions between race and education. Thus, there is real interest in what can be learned from the school/labor market transitions and the unemployment/ employment transitions of Cape Town's youth. It is to this that we now turn.

3 Transitions between school and the labor market in the Cape Area Panel Study

While much can be learned from analysis of large cross-sectional data sets such as the census, these data sets provide only a limited picture of the experience of young people when they first enter the labor market. In this section we take advantage of recently collected longitudinal data, the CAPS, for a richer picture of the dynamics of transitions from school to work.

Details about the design of CAPS, a collaborative project of the University of Cape Town and the University of Michigan, are available in Lam, Seekings, and Sparks (2006).[1] Wave 1 of CAPS, which was collected in 2002, included 4,752 young people aged 14–22, living in 3,304 households. CAPS was designed as a stratified two-stage clustered sample with stratification on the predominant population group living in each sample cluster. CAPS oversampled areas classified as predominantly African and white in order to produce larger samples of African and white respondents than would be present in a simple random sample. As discussed above, Cape Town is the only major city in South Africa to have substantial numbers of white, coloured, and African residents, providing unique opportunities for the study of the changing nature of inequality after the abolition of apartheid.[2]

Wave 1 of CAPS contains two major sources of data. First, the survey includes a household questionnaire, in which demographic data on the entire household is collected. Second, the survey includes a detailed young adult questionnaire, which collects data on schooling, employment, and fertility of household members between the ages of 14 and 22. It also includes a basic numeracy and literacy skills test administered to each youth respondent. The results of this test will be used in the analysis below. CAPS youth respondents were interviewed a second time in either 2002 or 2003, a third time in 2005, and a fourth time in 2006. We use data from all waves in our analysis below, taking advantage of the retrospective reports on monthly employment and job search provided in each wave. Overall attrition between Wave 1 and Wave 4 was about 20%, with lower attrition among younger respondents and among the coloured sample, which has strong roots in Cape Town. The African attrition rate was about 25%, with most of the attrition resulting from migration back to the Eastern Cape, a predominantly rural province that serves as the main sending region for Africans living in Cape Town.

A major focus of this section is the comparison of transitions from school to work for African, coloured, and white youths. These three population groups were subject to very different treatment under apartheid. Many of these apartheid-era differences are likely to continue affecting young people in the post-apartheid period. Whites had advantages in a wide range of areas, including significantly higher expenditures on schooling, privileged access to the labor market, unrestricted residential mobility, and better access to most social services. Africans had the least access to services and the most restrictions on work and migration, with a large gap in expenditures on schooling. The coloured population, which is heavily concentrated in Cape Town, occupied an intermediate status under apartheid, with higher expenditures on schooling, fewer restrictions on residential mobility, and better access to jobs.

Patterns of schooling and work

This section provides an overview of some key patterns in school enrollment, grade attainment, and labor force activity that form the backdrop for understanding transitions from school to work. Table 5.4 shows several important indicators of schooling for CAPS respondents aged 16–17 and 21–22 in CAPS Wave 1 in 2002. The results are broken down by gender and population group. Although all of these young people are above the age of compulsory enrollment, 86% of African females and 89% of African males aged 16–17 are enrolled. This is higher than the enrollment rate for coloured youth, although coloured grade attainment exceeds African grade attainment by half a grade for females and a full grade for males. White enrollment at age 16–17 is over 95% for both males and females, with white males having almost two grades more schooling than African males. The fact that Africans have relatively high enrollment rates but are significantly behind in grade attainment is evidence of the high rates of grade repetition in predominantly African schools. As shown by Anderson, Case, and Lam (2001) and Lam, Ardington, and Leibbrandt (2007), grade repetition is a fundamental feature of African schooling. As seen in Column 4, 49% of African males aged 16–17 are two or more years behind their appropriate grade for age (assuming a school starting age of seven), compared to only 7% of white males and 27% of coloured males.

Looking at respondents aged 21–22 in Table 5.4, 31% of African males are enrolled in some kind of educational program. About two-thirds of these are still enrolled in secondary school (not shown), another manifestation of the high rates of grade repetition. As seen in Table 5.4, white males have a schooling advantage of more than two full grades over African males at age 21–22, with 88% of white males having passed the grade 12 matriculation exam, compared to only 34% of African males. Another important feature of Table 5.4 is the fact the females have higher schooling than males in all three population groups and both age groups. As pointed out by Anderson, Case, and Lam (2001), girls move through school faster than boys in South Africa, with lower rates of grade repetition and higher final grade attainment.

Figure 5.1 looks at transitions from school to work using both the retrospective histories from Wave 1 and the longitudinal data on work and school reported in 2003, 2004, and 2005. For each single year of age from 12 to 23 the sample is divided into four possible activities: (1) enrolled but not working; (2) enrolled and working; (3) working but not enrolled; (4) not working and not enrolled. Enrollment includes post-secondary schooling and formal training programs, in addition to primary and secondary school. Work is defined broadly, and includes any work done during the year. This includes work during school vacations, so it is important to keep in mind that the work/school combination does not necessarily imply that work was being combined with school. The sample used in Figure 5.1 is respondents who were age 23–25 in 2005.

Looking at the results for males in Figure 5.1, we see large differences in the transitions from school to work across population groups. While being in school without working is by far the predominant activity for all three groups at age 14, by age 17 some sharp differences have emerged. Significant

Table 5.4 Percentage enrolled and grade attainment, Cape Area Panel Study wave 1, 2002

| Population group | Age 16–17 in Wave 1 | | | | Age 21–22 in Wave 1 | | | |
	N (1)	Currently enrolled (%) (2)	Mean number of grades completed (3)	Two or more grades behind (%) (4)	N (5)	Currently enrolled (%) (6)	Mean number of grades completed (7)	Passed matric (%) (8)
African female	287	86.2	8.51	31.6	249	27.5	10.43	36.0
African male	190	89.0	7.86	49.3	199	30.7	10.12	34.2
Coloured female	283	79.5	9.14	15.4	206	14.2	10.75	53.5
Coloured male	254	72.9	8.71	27.2	138	14.6	10.47	44.7
White female	71	99.2	9.70	0.9	70	63.4	12.81	98.9
White male	74	95.3	9.63	7.5	41	72.1	12.62	87.9
Total	1159	82.9	8.88	22.8	903	28.9	10.92	53.7

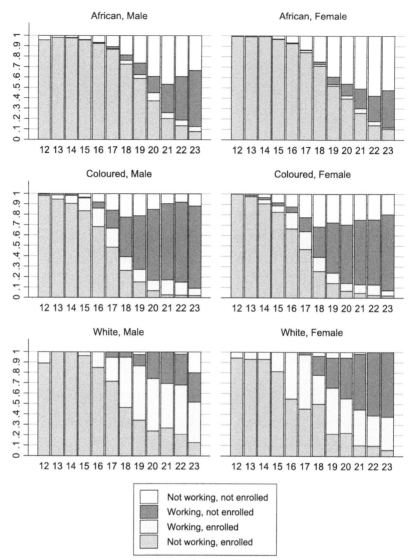

Note: Working and enrolled refer to any time during year.

Figure 5.1 Transitions from school to work CAPS respondents age 23–25, 2005.

proportions of white males are working during years when they are still in school, with 45% of white boys in the work and school category at age 17. In contrast, African males have extremely low rates of work. The percentage of African boys who work during years when they are still in school is negligible, never exceeding 5%. The transition from school to work for coloured males is characterized more by a sharp transition than it is for either white or African males. Relatively small proportions of coloured males work during the years they are in school, with the proportion working exceeding the proportion enrolled at age 18. The proportion of coloured males enrolled in school drops below that of both Africans and whites by age 16.

The patterns for males in Figure 5.1 are broadly similar to the results for females, with males having somewhat higher percentages working at most ages. One of the striking features of Figure 5.1 is that differences across population groups are much larger than differences between males and females within a given population group.

The large racial differences in transitions from school to work are further demonstrated in Table 5.5, which shows three measures of work activity for CAPS respondents aged 16–17 and 21–22 in 2002. Columns 2 and 6 show the percentage of young people who were currently doing any work for pay or family gain at the time of the Wave 1 survey. Columns 3 and 7 show the percentage who did any work during the 12 months prior to the Wave 1 survey, while columns 4 and 8 show the percentage who report having every done any work for pay or family gain. As in Figure 5.1, work is defined broadly. Table 5.5 reinforces the stark racial differences in employment experience shown in Figure 5.1. Only 1% of African females and 7% of African males aged 16–17 report having ever done any work, compared to 28% of coloured females, 38% of coloured males, and over 50% of white males and females. By age 21–22, only 26% of African females and 37% of African males have ever worked, compared to 84–96% for the other groups.

Summarizing the patterns in Figure 5.1, Table 5.4, and Table 5.5, we see that African teenagers in Cape Town tend to have high rates of school enrollment, high rates of grade repetition, and low rates of employment. These patterns are very similar to those that would be found for African youth in all of South Africa (Anderson, Case, and Lam 2002). Limited labor market opportunities, driven in part by extreme spatial segregation that is a legacy of apartheid, presumably plays an important role in explaining both the low employment and the high school enrollment. Coloured youth have significantly higher employment rates than African youth, a possible reflection of both closer geographic proximity to jobs and the legacy of the coloured labor preferences that existed in the Western Cape under apartheid. There appears to be more of a trade-off between school enrollment and work among coloured youth, especially for males. Whites have both the highest rates of employment and the highest levels of school enrollment and schooling attainment, an indication that work and school in the teenage years are not entirely incompatible.

Employment transitions after leaving school

One of the unique features of the CAPS data is that we have collected monthly data on school, work, and job search covering the period from

Table 5.5 Percentage currently working, worked in last 12 months, and ever worked, Cape Area Panel Study wave 1, 2002

| Population group | Age 16–17 in Wave 1 | | | | Age 21–22 in Wave 1 | | | |
	N (1)	Currently working (%) (2)	Worked in last 12 months (%) (3)	Ever worked (%) (4)	N (5)	Currently working (%) (6)	Worked in last 12 months (%) (7)	Ever worked (%) (8)
African female	287	0.4	1.4	1.4	248	13.2	21.8	26.2
African male	190	3.2	5.0	7.1	198	25.5	31.6	37.1
Coloured female	283	11.2	20.8	28.5	205	50.9	70.3	84.2
Coloured male	254	14.2	27.2	38.1	138	62.5	80.0	90.9
White female	71	20.8	50.5	54.5	70	59.5	77.3	93.7
White male	73	27.3	41.4	50.1	41	63.0	89.6	95.6
Total	1158	11.9	22.3	28.9	900	45.8	61.6	71.7

August 2002 through the time of the Wave 4 interview in 2006. These data are collected retrospectively in each wave of the survey. Figure 5.2 shows how these data can be used to follow the transitions of young people into the labor market after leaving school. The sample used in Figure 5.2 is all of respondents who left school (identified as three consecutive months out of school) and were observed in the monthly calendars for at least 36 months after leaving school. The figure shows the proportion of males in each population group that were working in each month since leaving school, as well as the four months prior to leaving school.

As shown in the top panel of Figure 5.2, about 35% of coloured men were working in the first month after leaving school (typically January after the end of their last year in school). About 25% of coloured men were already working during the last four months before leaving school. The percentage of coloured men with jobs rises rapidly during the first 6 months out of school, reaching about 50% after 6 months, with about 60% working after 12 months. African men start at a much lower base, with only about 10% working in the first month after leaving school. This rises slowly to about 25% after 12 months. This suggests that dropping out of school in order to work is a relatively unimportant cause of leaving school for Africans. Africans continue to find jobs at a relatively slow rate in the next two years, with about 40% working in month 24 and about 50% working in month 36 (note that the sample remains constant across months).

There is a significant divergence in the line for "ever worked" from the line for "current work." For coloured men, for example, there is very little increase in the percentage currently working from month 12 to month 24, even though the percentage who had ever worked increases by about 15 percentage points. Similarly, African men have about a 20 percentage point increase in the percentage who have ever worked between month 24 and month 36, about double the increase in the percentage currently working. This suggests that there is considerable turnover in the youth labor market, with the flow of new entrants into employment being offset by the exit of men who were previously working. Since CAPS has data on all labor force transitions, we plan to explore this potentially important labor market volatility in future research.

The second panel of Figure 5.2 shows the proportion of African and coloured youth who were searching for work (and did not have a job) in each month. The proportion searching jumps sharply in the first month after leaving school, rising to about 20% for both African and coloured males. Coloured males secure jobs at a higher rate, so the proportion searching begins to fall after the first few months. African males are much less likely to find jobs, with the proportion searching remaining around 20% over the first six months out of school. The proportion of coloured men searching for work is always lower than the proportion of African men searching for work, a reflection of the greater success that coloured men have in finding jobs.

The bottom panel shows the proportion of active labor force participants, the sum of the proportion currently working, and the proportion searching.

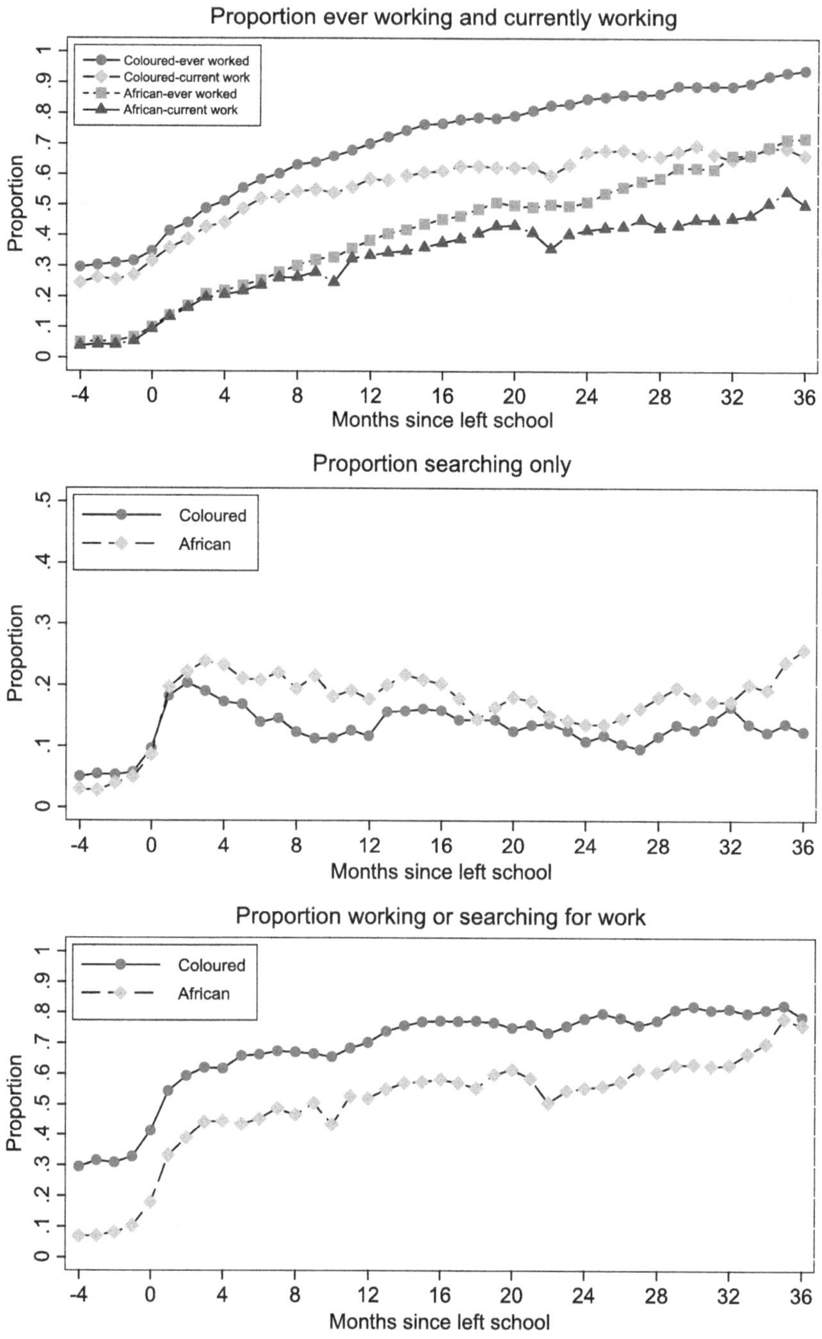

Figure 5.2 Work and job search by months since left school. Males out of school at least 36 months.

The curves are roughly parallel for African and coloured males for the first 24 months, with the coloured curve about 15 percentage points higher in every month. The African curve rises at a slightly more rapid rate than the coloured curve in the third year. This is primarily a reflection of a more rapid increase in search among African men, although it also partly due to a more rapid increase in employment among African men. An interesting feature of this graph is that following a sharp increase in participation in the first month after leaving school, there is a slow but steady increase in labor force participation during the next 36 months. By 36 months after leaving school, about 80% of both African and coloured men are working or searching for work.

Figure 5.3 shows the monthly labor force transitions for women. The proportion of women working is lower than the proportion of men working in every month after leaving school. Coloured women also show a larger discrepancy than coloured men between the proportion currently working and the proportion who have ever worked. This suggests that women have more movement in and out of the labor force. Coloured women have a sharper increase in job search after leaving school than African women, and coloured women are considerably more successful in finding jobs. The bottom panel of Figure 5.3 shows the same kind of parallel patterns for coloured and African women that was observed for men in Figure 5.2, with coloured participation about 15–20 percentage points higher than African participation for the first two years out of school. As with men, there is a convergence in participation rates in the third year out of school. This is partly driven by a decline in participation among coloured women after month 28, a decline that coincides with increasing participation by African women.

4 Modeling transitions to work

CAPS has a rich set of information about young people and their households that can be used to analyze the determinants of early labor market success. In this section we present the results of probit regressions in which we analyze the probability of being employed in each month after leaving school. The analysis is based on the same monthly work histories used to construct Figures 5.2 and 5.3. Table 5.6 presents summary statistics for the dependent and independent variables in the regressions. The sample consists of all CAPS young adult respondents who were out of school from zero to 48 months, with an observation corresponding to one person-month. The total number of individuals contribution person-months is 1,944, a little under half of the original CAPS sample. The total number of person-months observed is 41,983. The dependent variable equals one if the respondent was working in a month and zero if the respondent was not working, whether or not the respondent was searching for work. As suggested by the previous results in this paper, the mean of the "currently working" variable differs dramatically across racial groups, with a mean of 0.29 for Africans, 0.52 for coloureds, and 0.70 for whites. Large differences in schooling are also evident,

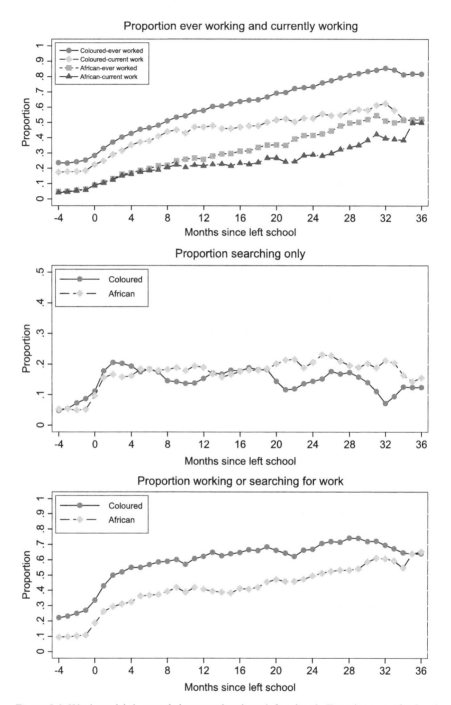

Figure 5.3 Work and job search by months since left school. Females out of school
at least 36 months.

Table 5.6 Descriptive statistics for variables in probit regressions, CAPS respondents out of school 0–48 months, 2002–2006

Variable	African	Coloured	White	Total
Currently working	0.29 (0.45)	0.52 (0.50)	0.70 (0.46)	0.48 (0.50)
Male	0.47 (0.50)	0.47 (0.50)	0.51 (0.50)	0.48 (0.50)
Grade 10 or 11	0.36 (0.48)	0.28 (0.45)	0.23 (0.42)	0.29 (0.45)
Grade 12 or higher	0.36 (0.48)	0.44 (0.50)	0.68 (0.47)	0.45 (0.50)
Literacy and numeracy score	−0.45 (0.86)	0.22 (0.80)	1.14 (0.64)	0.16 (0.92)
Poor health in 2005	0.07 (0.25)	0.04 (0.20)	0.02 (0.15)	0.05 (0.21)
Months since leaving school	14.1 (10.3)	15.5 (11.0)	13.4 (10.0)	14.9 (10.7)
Age in months	21.3 (2.1)	20.1 (2.1)	20.9 (2.2)	20.5 (2.2)
Age in months squared	458.7 (90.1)	408.4 (86.1)	441.5 (94.1)	425.1 (90.6)
Number of individuals	861	910	173	1,944
Number of person-months	17,394	21,506	3,083	41,983

Note: Standard deviation in parentheses; descriptive statistics use sample weights

with 36% of Africans having passed matric compared to 44% of coloureds and 68% of whites.

One interesting feature of CAPS is the literacy and numeracy evaluation (LNE) that was administered to all respondents in Wave 1. This was about a 20-minute self-administered written test with 45 questions covering basic reading and mathematics skills. Respondents could choose to take the test in English or Afrikaans. There was no version in Xhosa, the home language of most African respondents. The English test was taken by 99% of African respondents, 43% of coloured respondents, and 64% of white respondents. Although most Africans took the test in a second language, it is worth noting that English is the official language of instruction in African schools and is used for many tests such as the grade 12 matriculation exam. English language skills are also likely to pay off in job search. We use the LNE scores as a measure of cumulative learning at the time of the 2002 interview. Performance on the test reflects a combination of many factors, including innate ability, home environment, and the quantity and quality of schooling to that point. The LNE scores in Table 5.5, which have been standardized to a mean of zero and standard deviation of one, show enormous racial differences in test scores. The mean score for Africans is 0.7 standard deviations below the mean for coloureds and over 1.5 standard deviations below the mean score for whites. As shown in Lam, Ardington, and Leibbrandt (2007), the LNE scores for Africans and whites barely overlap.

Looking at another key variable in Table 5.6 that will be included in our regressions, the variable "poor health in 2005" indicates that the respondent reported that they were in poor or fair health in 2005 (other choices were good, very good, or excellent). We see that 7% of Africans reported having fair or poor health, compared to 4% of coloureds and 2% of whites. Since the sample was aged 17–25 in 2005, the 7% figure for Africans is relatively high.

This may reflect the impact of HIV/AIDS, although the evidence is only indirect. CAPS does not do HIV testing and does not ask directly about HIV status.

Probit regressions for monthly employment

Table 5.7 presents probit regressions analyzing the probability of being employed in each month after leaving school. For each regression, the first column shows the probit coefficients and the second column shows the marginal effects, evaluated at the sample means. Repeated monthly observations are used for each respondent, so the standard errors are adjusted to account for correlated errors at the individual level. Probit 1 only includes dummies for African and white (coloured is the omitted category), a dummy for male, the number of months since leaving school, and a quadratic in monthly age.

Table 5.7 Probit regressions for working in months after leaving school, Cape area panel study

Variable	Probit 1		Probit 2		Probit 3	
	(1)	(2)	(3)	(4)	(5)	(6)
African	−0.911***	−0.337***	−0.836***	−0.313***	−0.733***	−0.278***
	[0.058]	[0.019]	[0.059]	[0.020]	[0.064]	[0.023]
White	0.365***	0.145***	0.314***	0.125***	0.202*	0.0804*
	[0.11]	[0.043]	[0.12]	[0.045]	[0.12]	[0.047]
Male	0.225***	0.0895***	0.242***	0.0959***	0.216***	0.0857***
	[0.053]	[0.021]	[0.055]	[0.022]	[0.055]	[0.022]
Months since leaving school	0.010***	0.0038***	0.014***	0.006***	0.014***	0.006***
	[0.002]	[0.001]	[0.002]	[0.001]	[0.002]	[0.001]
Age in months	0.823***	0.328***	0.554***	0.221***	0.542***	0.216***
	[0.18]	[0.072]	[0.19]	[0.075]	[0.19]	[0.074]
Age squared	−0.015***	−0.006***	−0.01**	−0.004**	−0.009**	−0.004**
	[0.004]	[0.002]	[0.005]	[0.002]	[0.004]	[0.002]
Grade 10 or 11			0.116	0.0462	0.0331	0.0132
			[0.082]	[0.033]	[0.083]	[0.033]
Grade 12 or higher			0.406***	0.161***	0.263***	0.105***
			[0.085]	[0.033]	[0.090]	[0.035]
Literacy and numeracy score					0.152***	0.0607***
					[0.039]	[0.016]
Poor health in 2005					−0.265**	−0.104**
					[0.12]	[0.047]
Constant	−10.74***		−7.812***		−7.598***	
	[1.89]		[1.95]		[1.93]	
Observations (person-months)	41,983		41,983		41,983	

Notes: Robust standard errors adjusting for repeated observations per individual in brackets. Marginal effects evaluated at means in parentheses.

* significant at 10%; ** significant at 5%; *** significant at 1%
Omitted categories: Coloured, Grade 9 or less.

Looking at the marginal effects in Column 2, Africans have a 34 percentage point lower probability of working than coloureds, evaluated at the sample means, while whites have a 15 percentage point higher probability of working than coloureds. Males have a 9 percentage point higher probability of working than females. The probability of working rises at an average rate of 0.4 percentage points per month.

Probit 2 adds schooling variables. The schooling variables in the regression indicate the highest grade attained at the time the respondent left school, with schooling Grade 9 or below as the omitted category. The point estimate implies a marginal effect of having completed grade 10 or 11 of 5 percentage points, but it is not statistically significant at conventional levels. There is a large effect of completing grade 12 (when there is a standardized matriculation exam), implying a 16 percentage point increase in the probability of working compared to those with less than grade 10. In contrast to the view sometimes expressed in South Africa, completing secondary school does appear to have a substantial effect on successfully finding a job after leaving school.

Probit 3 adds the score on the LNE administered in 2002. We see that the test score is a strong predictor of early labor force outcomes. A one standard deviation increase in the test score is associated with a 6 percentage point higher probability of working. Controlling for the LNE score considerably reduces the estimated impact of schooling. The estimated marginal effect of completing Grade 12 drops from 16 percentage points in Probit 2 to 10 percentage points in Probit 3. The point estimate for the impact of having Grade 10 or 11 (compared to Grade 9 or less) falls from 0.05 in Probit 2 to 0.01 in Probit 3, and remains statistically insignificant. These results suggest that the labor market does reward the skills that are captured in the LNE score. The precise mechanism for this is unclear, however. It could indicate that those who achieve better LNE scores are better motivated and work more effectively at job search. Alternatively, it could mean that employers are somehow able to perceive the greater ability of those with higher test scores, choosing them first out of the pool of new labor force entrants.

Probit 3 also looks at the impact of health on the probability of working. Those who reported being in poor or fair health were 10 percentage points less likely to be working after leaving school compared to those who said they were in good, very good, or excellent health. We cannot be sure of the extent to which this represents the impact of HIV/AIDS, since we do not have direct information on HIV status. The results suggest that poor health does affect the employment of some South African youth, although with only 7% of Africans reporting that their health is fair or poor, health does not appear to play a major role in explaining the low employment rates of African youth.

5 Conclusion

This paper looks at the early labor force experience of young people in South Africa using data from the 2001 census and the CAPS, a new longitudinal study in metropolitan Cape Town. Census data indicate that young people have difficulty making the transition from school to work, with especially high rates of unemployment among the African population. The situation of Africans in Cape Town is very similar to the situation of Africans in the entire country, as shown in our comparison of census data with CAPS data. CAPS data show that only 25% of African men aged 21–22 were working at the time of the CAPS Wave 1 interview in 2002, and only 37% had ever worked for pay. In contrast, 91% of coloured men and 95% of white men had ever done work for pay in 2002. Racial differences appear even before youth finish school, with white youth much more likely than any other group to work during the years they are enrolled in school. Among men aged 16–17, the percentage who had ever done any work in CAPS Wave 1 was only 7% for Africans, 38% for coloureds, and 50% for whites.

Using CAPS to look at month-by-month transitions from school to work, we see that coloured youth are much more likely to be working during the last four months before leaving school than are African youth. Both groups experience a sharp jump in labor force participation immediately after leaving school. Coloured youth are much more likely to find jobs, however, resulting in a quick decline in the percentage searching for work. African men have a slow but steady increase in the percentage working during the first three years after leaving school, but still lag well behind coloureds. By the 36th month after leaving school, about 50% of African men are working, compared to 70% of coloured men. African women also lag well behind coloured women in finding work after leaving school, but begin to close the gap after three years.

Our probit regressions provide strong evidence about the importance of schooling and ability in early labor market outcomes. We estimate significant effects of schooling on the probability of being employed during the first four years after leaving school. Those who leave school with Grade 12 or higher are 16 percentage points more likely to find work than those who leave school with less than Grade 10. When we include the results of the literacy and numeracy test that was administered to CAPS respondents in 2002, we estimate a large impact of the test score on the probability of finding work. Including the LNE score cuts the estimated impact of completing Grade 12 to 10 percentage points, implying that a large part of the apparent impact of schooling is captured by our measure of ability. This may indicate that employers do not use schooling alone as a signal, but are also able to discriminate on the basis of ability. These scores do not provide a direct measure of ability in the sense that the LNE scores themselves are driven by a mix of ability, schooling, and life experience up to the time that the test was taken in 2002 (Lam, Ardington, and Leibbrandt 2007). Thus, although the inclusion of this variable in the regression cuts the direct impact of completed schooling, embodied in this variable is a longer-run legacy of disadvantaged schooling. In particular, the large racial differences in the LNE scores may reflect large differences in school quality, differences that may be contributing to the large racial differences in early labor market success.

Notes

1 Technical documentation and background information is available on the CAPS website, www.caps.uct.ac.za.
2 As in most South African household surveys, CAPS response rates were high in African and coloured areas and low in white areas. Household response rates were 89% in African areas, 83% in coloured areas, and 46% in white areas. Young adult response rates, conditional on participation of the household, were quite high, even in white areas. Given household participation, response rates for young adults were 93% in African areas, 88% in coloured areas, and 86% in white areas (Lam, Seekings, and Sparks 2006).

References

Anderson, K. G., A. Case and D. Lam (2001) "Causes and Consequences of Schooling Outcomes in South Africa: Evidence from survey data". *Social Dynamics* 27(1): 37–59.

Dinkelman, T. (2004) "How Household Context Affects Search Outcomes of the Unemployed in KwaZulu-Natal, South Africa: A panel data analysis." *South African Journal of Economics* 72: 3.

Everatt, D. and E. Sisulu (1992) *Black Youth in Crisis*. Braamfontein: Ravan Press.

International Labour Office (2004) "Key Indicators of the Labour Market." International Labour Office database.

Kingdon, Ge. and J. Knight (2000) "Are Searching and Non-searching Unemployment Distinct States when Unemployment is High? The case of South Africa." University of Oxford: Centre for the Study of African Economies.

Lam, D., C. Ardington, and M. Leibbrandt (2007) "Schooling as a Lottery: Racial differences in schooling advancement in urban South Africa." ERSA Working Paper No. 56. July.

—— , M. Leibbrandt, and C. Mlatsheni (2008) "Education and Youth Unemployment." SALDRU Working Paper, UCT.

—— , J. Seekings and M. Sparks (2006) "The Cape Area Panel Study: Overview and technical documentation for Waves 1–2–3." University of Cape Town, December 2006.

Mhone, G. C. Z. (2000) "Promoting Youth Employment in South Africa." NIEP Occasional Paper Series No. 19, February.

Mlatsheni, C. and S. Rospabe (2002) "Why is Youth Unemployment so High and Unequally Spread in South Africa?" DPRU Working Paper No. 02/65.

Standing, G., J. Sender, and J. Weeks (1996) "Restructuring the Labour Market: The South African challenge." An ILO Country Review. International Labour Office, Geneva.

Truscott, K. (1993) "Youth Education and Work: The need for an integrated policy and action approach." CASE, University of Witwatersrand.

Van Zyl Slabbert, F. (1994) *Youth in the New South Africa*. Pretoria: HSRC Press.

Wittenberg, M. and C. Pearce (1996) "Youth Unemployment: Some perspectives from the South African Living Standards and Development Survey". In L. Chisholm et al., *Out-of-School Youth Report: Policy and Provision for Out-of-School and Out-of-Work Youth*, University of the Witwatersrand: Education Policy Unit.

The World Bank (2006): "Development and the Next Generation." World Development Report 2007.

6 Analysis of attrition patterns in the Turkish Household Labor Force Survey, 2000–2002[*]

İnsan Tunalı

1 Introduction

Attrition is recognized as a major issue by users of panel data sets (an early example being Hausman and Wise 1979). Data collection agencies have methods for adjusting for non-response, but attrition (initial response followed by non-response at a later round of the survey) may cause additional problems which are typically not handled well by standard reweighing schemes (Ridder 1992). There is a large literature on attrition and its consequences in widely used panel data sets. A representative sample may be found in Verbeek and Nijman (1996), and the Spring 1998 special issue of the *Journal of Human Resources*: see, in particular, Fitzgerald et al. (1998), MaCurdy, Mroz, and Gritz (1998), van den Berg and Lindeboom (1998), and Zabel (1998).

Starting with 2000, the Household Labor Force Surveys (HLFSs) administered by the Turkish Statistical Institute (TURKSTAT; formerly the State Institute of Statistics, SIS) have been conducted continuously, using a rotating sample frame designed to yield quarterly estimates (SIS, 2001a). The rotation plan calls for a total of four interviews over a period of six quarters. To be precise, the selected household is interviewed in two subsequent quarters, skipped for the next two, and then interviewed again in two subsequent quarters. Thus, it is possible to form estimates of quarterly and annual transitions between labor market states. This is a major breakthrough that allows tracking of labor market dynamics.[1] However, to date, only two papers have addressed the subject (Taşçı and Tansel 2005; Tansel and Taşçı 2006).

The sampling frame adopted by the New HLFS is address-based. The survey protocol does not require following households (or individual members, so-called splits) who move to another location. Furthermore, if there is a different household at a previously visited address, the newly arrived household is included in the survey. In essence TURKSTAT deals with attrition in the HLFS by using substitute households in place of attritors when available, and reweighing the cross-section sample so that it is representative of the (projected) population. This could be problematic if attrition and/or substitution probabilities depend on labor market states occupied by members of the respondents. In fact Tunalı and Baltacı (2004) have argued that cross-section estimates of standard measures of labor market outcomes (participation rate, unemployment rate, etc.) formed for the period 2000–2 are biased, on the grounds that the statistics are influenced by the number of times a household has been interviewed.

Based on the information in the non-response forms filled by the field staff of TURKSTAT, almost all the attrition takes the form of migration rather than refusal to respond. There is good reason (and ample evidence in the labor economics literature) to believe that individuals, even households, respond to labor market conditions by moving. This certainly was the case in the 1960s and 1970s in Turkey (Tunalı, 1996). It probably was the case in the period following the February 2001 crisis, when Turkey's economic growth rate (as measured by annual changes in real GNP) swung from −9.5% between 2000–1 to +7.9% between 2001–2 (World Bank, 2006, 26).

The objective of this paper is to document the patterns in attrition observed in the HLFS over the period 2000–2. Towards that end I examine the likelihood of attrition within 3, 12, and 15 months of the initial survey by focusing on observed characteristics of the household head. I focus on the household head because standard reweighing schemes (such as those used by TURKSTAT) are designed to match the cross-section distributions of observables such as sex, age and education of the household head with those in the population. Since the links between attrition and labor market out-comes are my main concern, I confine my working sample to (around 47,000) households headed by prime-age (20–54-years-old) individuals, identified as the household head in the first round of the survey. For the subset of (23,790) households which were designated for four interviews, the cumulative prob-ability of attrition is 8% by 3 months, 18.3% by 12 months, and 24.7% by 15 months. These large magnitudes call for an investigation of the determin-ants of attrition, so that their implications for labor market statistics can be understood. In what follows I show convincingly that the labor market state occupied by the household head in the first round influences and is influenced by attrition in subsequent rounds, even when I control for a broader set of household characteristics than those used by TURKSTAT. My results send an important lesson to data collection agencies that insist on simplistic reweighing schemes and policy makers who rely on statistics produced in this manner.

A short formal statement of the problem and its consequences are provided in section 2. Sections 3 and 4 are devoted to data related issues: I discuss the HLFS survey, data problems, and the solutions I adopted. I then define attrition formally and give some summary statistics. The estimation and test-ing methodology is the subject of section 5. Sections 6 and 7 contain the empirical results. The concluding section highlights the key findings and their implications.

2 Attrition and its consequences

To illustrate the source of the problem, consider a two-round panel and let y_{ij} = labor market state of individual i at round j, $j = 1,2$; x_i = fixed characteristics of individual i; $D_i = 1$ if the individual is present at both rounds, 0 otherwise. For brevity I ignore the subscript for the individual and define $f(y_1, y_2 \mid x, D)$ as the joint distribution of labor market states conditional on x and D. In general $f(y_1, y_2 \mid x, D = 1) \neq f(y_1, y_2 \mid x)$, a feature which renders the balanced panel problematic for the purposes of drawing inferences on labor market dynamics. The problem can be attributed to the fact that

$$P(D = 1 \mid y_1, y_2, x) \neq P(D = 1 \mid y_1, x) \neq P(D = 1 \mid x). \tag{1}$$

Equation (1) captures the notion that the attrition process may be influenced by the labor market states occupied by respondents who are observationally identical otherwise (that is, they have the same x). This type of attrition is known as *non-ignorable* attrition (see Rubin 1976; Little and Rubin 1987). In this case even cross-section estimates of labor market outcomes could be affected by attrition, because in general

$$f_2(y_2 \mid x, D = 1) \neq f_2(y_2 \mid x, D = 0) \neq f_2(y_2 \mid x). \tag{2}$$

Tunalı and Baltacı (2004) provide evidence of non-ignorable attrition in the Turkish HLFS. They focus on three labor market states: not in the labor force, employed, and unemployed. They study the steady-state marginal distributions of membership in labor market states $f(y \mid x)$ in the reweighed cross-section as well as steady-state conditional distributions $g(y_2 \mid y_1, x, D = 1)$ which capture the transition probabilities between the three states. They show that all the distributions are influenced by the number of times an individual is observed (controlling for survey round). They also estimate the magnitudes of the biases in the cross-section estimates reported by TURKSTAT by relying on data from individuals who enter the survey sample for the first time, on the assumption that they constitute a "fresh" sample representative of the population.

The current paper places equation (1) in the limelight. I treat attrition as a choice variable at the household level. I express the attrition probability as a function of household characteristics as well as indicators for the survey round. By including a successively longer list of observables (in x), I illustrate the existence of possible venues for extending the standard reweighing schemes. By including information on the labor market state occupied by the household head in the first round (y_1) as a determinant of attrition, I am able to test for the presence of non-ignorable attrition.

3 Data and measurement issues

Household Labor Force Surveys which have nationwide representation have been conducted in Turkey since October 1988. Between 1989 and 1999 the survey was conducted bi-annually, during the months of April and October, with the second full week of the month as the reference week. Reliance on a low sampling frequency and a fixed reference week meant that changes in labor market conditions could not be tracked accurately by the HLFS. The "New" HLFS was designed to respond to this concern and was launched in 2000. It featured a rotating sampling frame (similar to the Current Population Survey conducted in the USA) and a sliding reference week which allows continuous tracking. The design hinges on a total of four visits to the same address, over a period of six quarters. According to the standard pattern, a household is interviewed in two subsequent quarters, allowed to rest for the next two, and returns to the sample for another two. This rotation plan is often abbreviated as "in–in–out–out–in–in" or simply "2–(2)–2." With this rotation plan it is possible to study attrition at three different intervals, namely 3, 12, and 15 months following the initial interview.

In this paper I rely on twelve rounds of the HLFS from the period 2000–2. Each round of the survey includes around 70,000 individuals from 18–20,000 households. The full data set consists of about 890,000 individual records. The rotation plan provides 50% overlap in the sample between subsequent quarters and same quarter one year apart. However not all rounds furnish information at all attrition intervals. First, the steady-state for the standard rotation plan 2–(2)–2 was not reached until 2001: Q2. By design earlier rounds do not provide information at all attrition intervals. Second, I do not have data beyond 2002: Q4. This ushers in censoring. Table 6.A1 in the appendix provides detailed information on the rotation plan and the observation plan to which I turn next.

There is no question that the switch from the original HLFS to the New HLFS posed challenges for TURKSTAT. Since the surveys had been conducted via Computer Assisted Personal Interviews (CAPI) for some time, the proper infrastructure was already in place. Table 6.A1 provides a glimpse of the planning that went into the survey. Each round of the HLFS contains eight sub-samples identified by a distinct *rotation number*. The rotation number determines the number and timing of subsequent visits to the household. In addition, the year and quarter at which each interview *round* took place is known. Household IDs end with either odd or even numbers, and this assignment is consistent with rotation number and round. Furthermore the visit number is recorded at the time of the survey. With this information in hand, it is possible to determine the maximum number of recorded visits as well as the expected number of (total) visits to a given household. Consistency checks on the raw data exposed coding errors in the visit number. These mistakes were easily corrected using information on the rotation number and round which uniquely determine the visit number (see Table 6.A1 in the appendix).

A household was classified as an "attritor" if a scheduled interview did not take place in a subsequent round. A similar scheme was used to detect individual household members who attrited. There were a total of 66,467 households (headed by someone of age 15 or older) and 184,339 individuals (of age 15 or older) who were eligible for the analysis, although not all were subjected to the full rotation plan. About 26% of eligible households and 31.6% of eligible individuals attrited sometime during the observation window.[2] The survey protocol of the HLFS allows for substitution of a departing household by a new one that took residence at the previously visited address between two rounds of the survey. The new household is given a new household ID, but the visit counter is not reset. This practice is consistent with the use of an address-based sampling frame. Since this paper is about attrition patterns in the original sample, the departing households were classified as attritors and substitute households were excluded from the working sample. It is also possible for a household to leave the address for some time, to return later. The returnee households were classified as attritors when they did not show up in the data as scheduled and were excluded from subsequent analysis.

Investigation of substitution yields additional clues about the magnitude of attrition. To begin with, the number of substitute households is less than the number of attriting households (8,492 versus 11,618). One might argue that substitution may correct for the distortions introduced by attrition; however, not all attriting households were replaced. Furthermore a significant share of substitute households (1,001) attrited themselves and some of these were replaced by other substitute households as part of the protocol. Since the total includes multiple substitutions for the same household, double counting is present. Unfortunately, the exact number cannot be determined without a marker for the address.

Second, there might be initial non-response followed by response; that is, some households classified as substitutes may actually be returnees who were absent in the initial round of the survey. Given the fact that a total of 3,688 attritors (amounting to 31.7% of all attriting households) returned to their original addresses during the period under study, there is good reason to believe that a sizeable subset of those classified as substitutes may be returnees themselves. Since the HLFS sample frame is address-based, it is impossible to distinguish returnees from substitutes in the absence of information about migration history. Conveniently this paper is about attrition patterns in the sample subjected to the first round of the interview, so the approach adopted below serves us well.

Further examination of the data revealed that some departures from the survey protocol did take place in the field. In some rare instances, the ID of a departing household appears to have been given to the new household at the old address. In other instances the ID numbers of individual members were messed up as a result of departures from, or new arrivals to, the household. Since the analysis of attrition patterns in the current paper is confined to prime-age household heads, the latter do not concern us here. As for the former, in theory the problem cases can be identified using a computer program that keeps track of changes in the household roster. However, legitimate life cycle events and coding errors that are part and parcel of panel data proved difficult to distinguish.[3] In the end I decided not to do any corrections.

4 Definitions and summary statistics on attrition

Let $A(m)$ denote the indicator of attrition after m months. We set $A(m) = 1$ if the household is not found at the same address m months after the initial visit, and $= 0$ otherwise, $m = 3, 12, 15$. By definition, households interviewed for the first time cannot attrit. For notational convenience we set $A(0) = 0$ for everyone. The risk sets $R(m)$, $m = 3, 12, 15$ respectively consist of all households who did not attrit until month m. If household h attrits in month m_h^*, it is excluded from the risk set at higher intervals; that is, household h belongs to risk set $R(m)$ iff $m_h^* > m$. Individual attrition indicators and risk sets are also computed, following the same logic. Table 6.A2 in the appendix shows the risk sets computed in this manner, using the information in Table 6.A1, as well as summary statistics on the attrition indicators. Note that technically speaking the pre-steady-state rotation plan allows us to study $A(9)$ for a subset of households interviewed in the first quarter of year 2000.

In what follows I study household level attrition patterns for households whose head was 20–54 years old at the time of the first interview. These households form a subset (71.3%) of all households (see Table 6.A2). Households I study are slightly more likely to attrit, but not by much. I focus on the subset because my main objective is to establish the links between labor market status and attrition at a time when the head is likely to be economically active. Labor market attachment of older household heads is low, and attrition behavior of their households may have other explanations. Households whose heads are younger (age < 20) are extremely rare (114 among 66,467), and these are typically single-person households who are attrition-prone. As seen in Table 6.A2, incidence of attrition is higher at the individual level, something we expect. However, due to the challenges posed by the coding errors mentioned above, analysis of individual level attrition is undertaken as a separate project. From this point on, all references to attrition is confined to households with a 20–54-year-old head. For brevity, I drop the qualifier and refer to them as households.

My working sample consists of 47,373 distinct households. Given the rotation plan and the observation window 2000–2, different subsets of households qualify for studying attrition behavior at different intervals. The risk sets are respectively 47,373 for studying $A(3)$, 25,324 for studying $A(12)$, and 19,437 for studying $A(15)$. Recall that (pre-steady-state segment of) the rotation plan allows us to compute $A(9)$ as well. However, the risk set is considerably smaller (3,414) and unlike the other cases, there is no time-series variation in exposure to attrition risk. Under the circumstances I did not feel confident investigating $A(9)$ behavior. Based on the totals (see final column of bottom block in Table 6.A2), about 8.8% of the households attrit before the second round (by month 3). Conditional on survival until the second round and inclusion in the sample frame, an additional 11% attrit before the third round (by month 12); that is, six months after the second interview. Conditional on survival until the third round and inclusion in the sample frame, an additional 7.8% of the households attrit before the fourth and final round (by month 15). These magnitudes underscore the importance of our undertaking. By investigating its determinants, we stand to improve our understanding of the implications of attrition for labor market statistics computed on the HLFS data.

The explanatory variables I rely on in the attrition regressions were constructed from a subset of the 56 survey questions which all 12 rounds have in common, using specifications in the labor economics literature as a guide. The complete list is given in Table 6.1 along with some descriptive statistics on the working samples. All variables are measured at the initial round of the survey.[4] Due to censoring, households (originally) interviewed in 2000 constitute close to one-half of the households in our working sample for $A(3)$. Those interviewed in 2001 and 2002 respectively account for 30 and 21% of the working sample. In the $A(3)$ sample households interviewed in the first to third quarter have above average (27.5% or more), while those interviewed in the fourth quarter have below average (15%) representation. Observations in the $A(12)$ sample are almost evenly split between 2000 and 2001, and the four quarters of the year. In the $A(15)$ sample, households interviewed in 2001 are underrepresented, because those interviewed in the last quarter are not eligible for analysis.

Nearly 80% of households come from an urban location (defined as having a population of 20,000 or over). In the HLFS sampling frame rural households are underrepresented by design, and this is reflected in our working samples.[5] To provide a picture of the households, we focus on the $A(3)$ working sample. The average household consists of 4.2 individuals. However, there is considerable variation. An overwhelming majority of the households consist of a nuclear family, while 12.1% are extended households. More than 90% of the household heads are married, and about 8% are female. The average age of household heads is about 39, and average education is 7.3 years. Since I study prime-age heads, labor market attachment is very high in my working sample. At the initial round of the survey 79% are employed, while 6.9% are unemployed.

5 Econometric methodology

In testing for the presence of non-ignorable attrition, I follow the approach in Fitzgerald et al. (1998) closely. They conduct two tests, which I term FGM

Table 6.1 Summary statistics on the working samples (initial visit). Household heads, age 20–54

Variable *denotes dummy variables	A(3)				A(12)				A(15)			
	Mean	Std dev.	Min.	Max.	Mean	Std dev.	Min.	Max.	Mean	Std dev.	Min.	Max.
*yr 2000 (reference year)	0.49	0.50	0	1	0.48	0.50	0	1	0.56	0.50	0	1
*yr 2001	0.3	0.46	0	1	0.52	0.50	0	1	0.44	0.50	0	1
*yr 2002	0.21	0.41	0	1	—	—	—	—	—	—	—	—
*q1 (reference quarter)	0.29	0.45	0	1	0.25	0.43	0	1	0.29	0.45	0	1
*q2	0.29	0.45	0	1	0.25	0.43	0	1	0.29	0.45	0	1
*q3	0.28	0.45	0	1	0.25	0.43	0	1	0.28	0.45	0	1
*q4	0.15	0.36	0	1	0.26	0.44	0	1	0.14	0.35	0	1
age	39.06	8.31	20	54	39.11	8.27	20	54	39.30	8.20	20	54
sch	7.34	3.78	0	17	7.24	3.74	0	17	7.12	3.68	0	17
*female (reference male)	0.078	0.27	0	1	0.074	0.26	0	1	0.070	0.26	0	1
*urban (reference rural)	0.80	0.40	0	1	0.79	0.41	0	1	0.78	0.41	0	1
*non-participant1 (reference)	0.142	0.35	0	1	0.140	0.35	0	1	0.139	0.35	0	1
*emp1	0.790	0.41	0	1	0.796	0.40	0	1	0.803	0.40	0	1
*unemp1	0.069	0.25	0	1	0.065	0.25	0	1	0.058	0.23	0	1
*single	0.035	0.18	0	1	0.030	0.17	0	1	0.026	0.16	0	1
*married (reference)	0.91	0.28	0	1	0.92	0.27	0	1	0.92	0.26	0	1
*divorced	0.017	0.13	0	1	0.014	0.12	0	1	0.013	0.11	0	1
*widow	0.037	0.19	0	1	0.037	0.19	0	1	0.037	0.19	0	1
Household size	4.18	1.76	1	25	4.22	1.76	1	23	4.27	1.76	1	23
Number of observations	47,373				25,324				19,437			

and BGLW, which are in turn attributable to Fitzgerald, Gottchalk, and Moffit (1998) and Becketti et al. (1988). For the FGM test, binary outcome equations for attrition status need to be estimated. Under the null hypothesis of ignorable attrition, the coefficient(s) on the lagged value(s) of the labor market state occupied by the individual are zero. For the BGLW test, two binary labor market outcome equations (participate or not, unemployed or not) have to be estimated, as a function of individual and household characteristics, as well as dummies for attrition status in future rounds. Under the null hypothesis of ignorable attrition, the coefficient(s) on attrition dummies should be zero.

Let $A_h(m)$ denote the attrition status of household h as of m months after the initial interview. To implement the FGM test, I estimate Probit models of the form

$$Pr\{A_h(m) = 1 \mid y, x, z; h \in R(m)\} = \Phi[\beta'y(0) + \gamma'x + \delta'z] \qquad (3)$$

for $m = 3, 12, 15$. All explanatory variables are measured at the initial survey round. Here, $y(0)$ is a vector that contains indicators of the labor force status of the household head, x denotes the vector of other individual and house-hold characteristics, z denotes indicators that identify the survey round, $R(m)$ denotes the risk set, and $\Phi(.)$ denotes the standard normal c.d.f. We estimate the unknown parameters β, γ, δ using maximum likelihood. If the null hypothesis that $\beta = 0$ is rejected, we have evidence that attrition is non-ignorable.[6]

As I argued in the introduction, the survey protocol of HLFS does not call for following movers. Consequently, there is strong reason to believe that attrition and migration go hand in hand. Although the results are not pub-lished, TURKSTAT officials carefully review the non-response forms filled by the field staff. Their impression is that the bulk of attrition is attributable to migration rather than non-response. I shed further light on this issue by estimating models which mimic the specifications used in reduced form migration equations. If determinants of attrition turn out to be the same as the determinants of migration, our expectations will be fulfilled.

To implement the BGLW test, I focus on two binary labor market out-comes $y_h(0)$ recorded for the household head at the initial survey round: labor force participation (LFP) and unemployment (Unemp) conditional on LFP = 1. I estimate Probit models of the form

$$Pr\{y_h(0) = 1 \mid A(k), k \leq m, x, z; h \in R(m)\}$$
$$= \Phi[\Sigma_{k \leq m} a_k A(k) + \theta'x + \lambda'z] \qquad (4)$$

for $m = 3, 12, 15$. Here $A(k)$'s denote the binary indicators of (future) attri-tion status. All other explanatory variables are measured at the initial survey round. As before, x denotes the vector of other individual and household characteristics, z denotes indicators that identify the survey round, $R(m)$ denotes the risk set, and $\Phi(.)$ denotes the standard normal c.d.f. We estimate the unknown parameters a, θ, λ using maximum likelihood. If the null hypothesis that $a = 0$ is rejected, we have evidence that attrition is non-ignorable.

As Fitzgerald, Gottchalk, and Moffit (1998: 263) underscore, FGM and BGLW tests are related: ". . . the BGLW method is an indirect test of the same restriction as the direct method of estimating the attrition function itself."[7] The BGLW version of the test is attractive because the estimated equation is a standard equation from the labor economics literature, augmented by indicators of future attrition status. As such, it can be used routinely to check for the presence of attrition bias in cross-section estimates. If the ultimate aim is to correct the bias in cross-section (or panel) estimates, the FGM methodology is preferable, because it provides the weights needed for the correction (see Fitzgerald, Gottchalk, and Moffit 1998).

6 Results from the FGM tests (based on Fitzgerald, Gottchalk, and Moffit 1998)

At each attrition interval, the same set of four models was estimated. Each model is nested under the subsequent ones. Model 1 (baseline) includes year and quarter dummies only. These variables capture the common component of the time-series variation in attrition. In Model 2 a set of household charac-teristics are added to the model. This list includes variables that TURKSTAT uses for reweighing, such as age gender of the household head, and location (urban versus rural). In Model 3 indicators for the labor market status of the household head at the initial round are added. Taking non-participants as the reference category, we explore whether households in which heads are employed (unemployed) display different attrition behavior. If the answer is yes, we have evidence of non-ignorable attrition. In Model 4 information on schooling and marital status of the household head and household size (number of people residing in the household) are included. The functional forms of multiple valued variables (age, schooling, and household size) are initially specified as third-degree polynomials. After independent tests on Model 4 results, the functional forms are simplified and the resulting specifi-cation is reported as Model 5.

Complete results from Probit estimates of attrition probability at 3, 12, and 15-month intervals are reported in Tables 6.A3–6.A5 collected in the appendix. The sample sizes are the respective risk sets identified in the third panel of Table 6.A2. At the bottom of each table incremental Likelihood Ratio test statistics that exploit the nesting properties of the subsequent models are reported. In Models 1–4 this statistic is used to test whether added variables are jointly statistically significant. In Model 5 the same statistic is used to test whether excluded variables are jointly statistically significant. Here, we focus on the key findings using two summary tables. The FGM tests of the null hypothesis that attrition is ignorable ($\beta = 0$) against the alternative that it is non-ignorable ($\beta \neq 0$) are based on the final specification (Model 5). The results are reported in Table 6.2. There is very strong evidence that attrition is systematically linked with labor force status at the time of the initial interview. With non-participants as the reference category, at the 3-month mark employed individuals are less, and unemployed individuals are more likely to attrit. At the 12-month mark, unemployed individuals are more likely to attrit. Attrition at the 15-month mark is ignorable, possibly because response to labor-market draws has already taken place. Recall, however, that the samples are not fully nested, and investigations of longer interval behavior are carried out on considerably smaller samples.

The magnitudes involved are not negligible.[8] Based on the results reported in Table 6.A3 for Model 5, attrition probabilities of unemployed household heads are 2.1 percentage points higher than the average ($= 8.8\%$) at the 3-month mark. This amounts to a 24% increase in attrition probability. Based on the results reported in Table 6.A4, this probability is even higher at the 12-month mark: 4.9 percentage points above the average ($= 11\%$), which translates to a 45% increase. Arguably, incidence of unemployment triggers mobility, so that job search can be extended beyond the local labor market. Notably, employed household heads have below-average attrition probabilities at the 3-month mark, by a margin of 1 percentage point (an 11% decrease in relative terms).

Table 6.3 contains a summary of the broader qualitative results based on Model 5 estimated at 3, 12, and 15-month intervals. In this table I report the signs of the statistically significant coefficients taking the 5% level as my standard. Zeros in the table mark the non-significant coefficients. At the bottom of the table I also report results from LR tests of the joint significance of the full model. Although all models are statistically significant at the 0.001 level, goodness of fit of the full model deteriorates as the attrition interval increases. Thus the attrition process becomes less and less selective (the survivors look more and more similar) as attriting households leave the risk set.

Table 6.2 FGM tests of the null hypothesis that attrition is ignorable versus not Signs (*p*-values*) from the probit estimates for model 5 reported in Tables 6.A3–6.A5

Labor force status during the initial visit	A(3)	A(12)	A(15)
Employed	—	0	0
	(0.037)	(0.476)	(0.729)
Unemployed	+	+	0
	(0.001)	(<0.001)	(0.565)
Reference: non-participant			
Joint test *p*-value	<0.001	<0.001	0.60
Observations	47,373	25,324	19,437

* Based on the standard normal and the Chi-squared c.d.f.

Table 6.3 Attrition patterns as of 3, 12, and 15 months, households with 20–54-year-old heads. Qualitative results from the probit estimates for model 5 reported in Tables 6.A3–6.A5

Variable *denotes the characteristics of the household head	A(3)	A(12)	A(15)
Yr 2001	0	+	0
Yr 2002	+	n.a.	n.a.
q2	+	0	+
q3	0	+	0
q4	0	0	0
*age	–	–	–
*age2	0	n.a.	n.a.
*age3	n.a.	n.a.	n.a.
*female	–	0	0
Urban	+	+	+
*empl	–	0	0
*unempl	+	+	0
*sch	–	—	+
*sch2	+	+	n.a.
*sch3	n.a.	n.a.	n.a.
*single	+	+	0
*divorced	+	0	0
*widow	0	0	0
Household size	—	—	—
household size 2	+	+	+
household size 3	—	n.a.	n.a.
Observations	47,373	25,324	19,437
Log-likelihood w/o covariates	–14,089	–8,797	–5,338
Log-likelihood w/ full set of covariates	–13,652	–8,587	–5,235
LR test: Chi-sq (d.f.)	874 (19)	420 (16)	206 (15)

Reported signs ("+" or "–") denote the signs for statistically significant coefficients at the 5% level or lower while "0" denotes non-significance; n.a. = not available (excluded).

As far as the characteristics of the household head are concerned, the sign patterns in Table 6.3 are broadly consistent with the notion that attrition and migration go hand in hand. Being young and being single (rather than married) render attrition more likely. Consistent with a relocation cost-based reasoning, small households are more likely to attrit. The cubic polynomial we relied on in Table 6.A3 revealed that attrition probability was higher for below average size households (< 4.2 members), practically constant in the middle range (5–10 members), and dropped sharply for very large households.

Holding the age of the household head constant, differences in educational attainment distinguish attritors (migrants). Using the numbers in Table 6.A4

Model 5 for the purposes of illustration, the quadratic form we estimated suggests that the likelihood of household attrition is below average for poorly educated heads, and above average for high-school graduates and higher. Attrition probability is lowest when the head has around five years of schooling. In fact five-year primary school graduates actually dominated the labor force in 2000 (SIS 2001b). However high school and university graduates claim an increasing share of recent cohorts of labor market entrants (Tunalı and Başlevent 2006).

Does location matter? If the migration interpretation is invoked, it should. In this paper we rely on a narrow distinction.[9] We find that households residing in urban areas are more likely to attrit. Broadly speaking, this finding is in line with the recent trends in migration, whereby moves between urban areas have come to dominate the internal migration flows.[10] Note, however, that migration studies typically focus on a longer (5-year, 10-year) time horizon than we do. Since new job opportunities are typically located in urban areas, our finding is consistent with job-search arguments.

The signs of the quarter dummies—which mark the timing of the initial survey—are consistent in identifying the round associated with the third quarter as the time during which attrition is highest. With the first quarter as the reference period, when the initial interview takes place in the second quarter, we see that the average 3-month attrition probability is augmented by 3.3 percentage points and the average 15-month probability is augmented by 2.7 percentage points. We also see that when the initial interview takes place in the third quarter, the average 12-month move probability is augmented by 1.7 percentage points. This pattern is attributable to the fact that the employment level is highest in the third quarter.[11] The year dummies also help us establish a connection between employment prospects and attrition. With year 2000 as the reference, we see that the 3-month attrition probability on average was the same in 2001 (the year of the economic crisis), but higher in 2002 (the year following the crisis, when the economy began its rebound but employment continued to decline) by about 1.3 percentage points. Consistent with this finding, we see that the 12-month attrition probability is 1.4 percentage points higher in the case of households interviewed in 2001.

7 Results from the BGLW tests (based on Becketti et al., 1988)

The results from the BGLW test are collected in the appendix, in Tables 6.A6 and 6.A7. The rotation design yields three different samples for each outcome under study. Sample sizes are determined by the expected number of visits to the address (see Table 6.A1). The largest sample on which the participation decision is studied turns out to be the same as the risk set used for the attrition Probits at the 3-month mark (Table 6.A3). The samples associated with the expected number of visits 3 and 4 are larger than the corresponding risks sets (for attrition probits at the 12- and 15-month marks). This is because longer interval attrition probabilities are estimated as *conditional* on survival in the previous round. The restriction does not apply to the participation probability, where attrition dummies mark if and when "future" attrition took place. The respective samples for the unemployment outcome are smaller, because only participants contribute to them.

On each sample, two models were estimated. Model I serves as the baseline and includes attrition indicators along with dummies that identify the initial survey round. As with the attrition models, not all survey rounds contribute to the sample. The extended model augments the baseline model with the usual list of explanatory variables used in reduced form specifications motivated by the standard formulations of the participation decision and the unemployment outcome. As in the FGM version, independent tests were used to simplify the polynomial specifications. Model II contains the simplified version of the extended model, which leads to the same substantive conclusions as the excluded full version. Since the focal point of the paper is attrition, in what follows I concentrate on the top panel of Tables 6.A6 and 6.A7 and refrain from detailed discussion of the determinants of participation and unemployment in the extended model. Suffice it to say that the patterns are as expected, and the models fit very well.

Summary findings are collected in Table 6.4. Recall that the steady-state

Table 6.4 BGLW Tests of the null hypothesis that attrition is ignorable versus not Signs (*p*-values*) from the probit estimates for model II reported in Tables 6.A6–6.A7

	Outcome at initial round	
	Participant	Unemployed
Future attrition status (expected visits = 4)		
Attritor at 3 months	0	+
	(0.22)	(<0.001)
Attritor at 12 months	0	+
	(0.40)	(<0.001)
Attritor at 15 months	0	0
	(0.23)	(0.30)
Joint test *p*-value	0.23	<0.001
Observations	23,790	20,523
Future attrition status (expected visits = 3,4)		
Attritor at 3 months	0	+
	(0.38)	(<0.001)
Attritor at 12 months	0	+
	(0.21)	(<0.001)
Joint test *p*-value	0.27	<0.001
Observations	27,578	23,726
Future attrition status (expected visits = 2,3,4)		
Attritor at 3 months	0	+
	(0.17)	(<0.001)
Observations	47,373	40,668

* Based on the standard normal and Chi-squared c.d.f.

rotation plan involves four visits to each address. The top panel informs us about the consequences of attrition when we examine the subset of the sample which is supposed to deliver to this requirement. Using the *p*-values as our guide, in the participation equation we do not see any evidence of selective (non-ignorable) attrition. From the unemployment equation we learn that attrition 3 months as well as 12 months after the initial survey is selective of participants who were unemployed at the initial round. There is no evidence of additional selectivity in the final round. Viewed together, the patterns from the two equations corroborate the findings from the FGM test: there is a strong association between being unemployed at the time of the initial survey and attrition 3 or 12 months later.

The remaining panels of Table 6.4 use information from a broader set of households. When we include households which should have been visited three times, impacts of attrition behavior at 3 and 12 months can be studied. When we include all households slated for a repeat visit, only the impact of attrition at the 3-month mark can be investigated. The results from the broader samples reinforce the conclusions drawn from the smallest sample.

8 Conclusions

This paper offers a micro-econometric analysis of attrition patterns in the "New" Turkish HLFS which has been conduced since 2000. For this purpose 12 rounds of micro data collected (on a quarterly basis) over the period 2000–2 were used. In general, attrition is a phenomenon which can be attributed to demographic and economic factors, including conditions in the labor market. The purpose of conducting frequent household labor force surveys is to reflect the changing conditions in the labor market. If attrition is related to the pre-attrition labor force status of individuals, this could result in bias in the labor market indicators. Our findings confirm a systematic link between labor force status and subsequent attrition. Compared to the average household headed by a 20–54-year-old, those headed by an unemployed individual at the time of the initial survey are 24% more likely to attrit 3 months later. Conditional on being present during the second interview that takes place at the 3-month mark, households headed by an unemployed individual are 45% more likely to attrit 12 months after the initial survey. These large magnitudes underscore the strong links between attrition behavior and adverse experiences in the labor market. Although the effect is milder, there is evidence that good draws make attrition less likely: households headed by an employed individual are 11% less likely to attrit at the 3-month mark.

Arguably the most important feature of the "New" HLFS which distinguishes it from the older version is its short panel component. The rotation design is similar to those used in better-known surveys, such as the Current Population Survey conducted in the USA. Consequently it provides information on changes in the labor force statuses of individuals at quarterly and annual intervals. If we classify individuals of working age as outside the labor force, employed, or unemployed at a given point in time, knowledge of changes in the (quarterly, yearly) transition rates will provide us with extremely important clues on the links between the conditions in the labor market and the broader economics conditions. Unfortunately the TURK-STAT does not publish predictions based on the panel dimension of the data. This might be attributable to difficulties associated with attrition.

The attrition process removes individuals (households) from the sample on the basis of their (household head's) labor market status and may render the remaining HLFS sample unrepresentative. In fact TURKSTAT substitutes attriting households by new ones if they move to an original address on their list, and reweighs the cross-section for the purposes of the quarterly (and more recently monthly) indicators it publishes. Construction of weights in the face of attrition is a vigorously debated subject by survey statisticians, applied econometricians and labor economists. Unbiased estimation of cross-section and transition indicators requires full understanding of the demographic and economic determinants of attrition, and suitable corrective measures. This investigation is meant to contribute to this endeavor, so that indicators on transition dynamics could be included among the information published on the basis of the HLFS.

Notes

* Earlier versions were presented at the Conference on "Labor Markets in Transition and Developing Economies: Emerging Policy and Analytical Issues," Ann Arbor, May 25–7, 2007, the 14th Annual Conference of the Economic Research Forum, Cairo, December 28–30, 2007, and workshops at Bilkent, Bilgi, and Koç Universities. Research assistance from Emre Ekinci and Berk Yavuzoğlu, and funding from TÜBİTAK via grant no: 106K160 are gratefully acknowledged. I would like to thank Dr Ömer Demir, the president of Turkish Statistical Institute (TURKSTAT), for granting me access to the raw data from the Household Labor Force Survey (HLFS) and TURKSTAT staff Hasibe Dedeş, Didem Sezer and Enver Taştı for their willingness to respond to my endless questions about the HLFS. Finally, I am grateful to Aysıt Tansel, Jackie Wahba, Berk Yavuzoğlu, conference and workshop participants for their comments on earlier versions.

1 TURKSTAT officials do not think so. They argue that many European data collection agencies pay repeat visits to the same address not because they intend to exploit the panel dimension of the data, but because they want to enhance the stability of the sample.

2 These figures were obtained by summing the fraction of attritors after 3, 12, and 15 months given in the first two panels of Table 6.A2. The third panel is associated with the working samples of this paper and is analysed in some detail in section 4.

3 Examination revealed that in 14.7% of eligible households, in some subsequent round the age of the household head differed from the average by more than two years. In 4.1% of the eligible households the sex of the household head changed somewhere along the line. Inspection of a random sample of individual records revealed that most of these were legitimate changes. For a summary discussion of these issues in other contexts, see Deaton (1997: 37–9).

4 In theory, richer specifications that use information on changes in status (for

example, marital status or labor force status) can be estimated. In practice, collinearity is likely to emerge as a serious challenge.

5 Arguably labor markets in urban locations are more complex, and the sampling frame strives to capture this. I was unable to obtain the sampling weights from TURKSTAT. Since I do not aim to arrive at valid estimates for the population as a whole, this is not a handicap.

6 Technically speaking it is possible to include additional lagged values of y (labor force status) when we study attrition over longer intervals (12, 15 months). Fitzgerald, Gottchalk, and Moffit (1998) refer to expanded specifications involving the lagged terms "dynamic attrition" models. These could be useful when constructing weights. Since I focus on whether attrition is ignorable, I rely on the simpler version.

7 Using the terminology which was fashionable in the early 1980s, equation (4) is the "reverse regression" counterpart of equation (3). Reverse regressions were used to conduct an alternative test of discrimination until Goldberger (1984) established the strong distributional requirements needed for that interpretation. Goldberger's criticisms do not apply to the BGLW test, because no attempt is made to link the parameter (vector) a in equation (4) with the parameters in equation (3).

8 The derivatives were calculated by multiplying the reported slopes by the values of the standard normal density at the average attrition probability for that round (yielding 0.16, 0.19, and 0.15 respectively).

9 To push the migration interpretation further, one would need richer geographic demarcations. Unfortunately TURKSTAT did not include province and regional identifiers in the raw data to which I was granted access.

10 Gross flows data from the 2000 General Census which are available on the TURKSTAT web site (www.tuik.gov.tr) support this conclusion.

11 For the period 2000–6, regression of total quarterly employment (millions) on year and quarter dummies yields the following estimated equation:

$$TOTEMP = 20 - .0075 \ YR01 - .075 \ YR02 - .25 \ YR03$$

$$+ .17 \ YR04 + .54 \ YR05$$

$$+ .81 \ YR06 + 2.2 \ Q2 + 2.7 \ Q3 + 1.4 \ Q4.$$

Regression of employment-population ratio on the same set of regressors yields:

$$EMPPOPRATIO = .44 - .0094 \ YR01 - .019 \ YR02$$

$$- .031 \ YR03 - .030 \ YR04$$

$$- .031 \ YR05 - .034 \ YR06 + .042 \ Q2 + .052 \ Q3 + .023 \ Q4.$$

References

Becketti, S., W. Gould, L. Lillard, and F. Welch (1988) "The Panel Study of Income Dynamics after Fourteen Years: An Evaluation." *Journal of Labor Economics* 6(4): 472–92.

Deaton, A. (1997) *The Analysis of Household Surveys: A Microeconomic Approach to Development Policy*. Published for the World Bank, Baltimore and London: Johns Hopkins University Press.

Fitzgerald, J., P. Gottschalk, and R. Moffitt (1998) "An Analysis of Sample Attrition in Panel Data." *Journal of Human Resources* 33(2): 251–99.

Goldberger, A. S. (1984) "Reverse Regression and Salary Discrimination." *The Journal of Human Resources* 19(3): 293–318.

Hausman, J. A. and D. A. Wise (1979) "Attrition Bias in Experimental and Panel Data: The Gary Income Maintenance Experiment." *Econometrica* 47(2): 455–73.

Little, R. and D. Rubin (1987) *Statistical Analysis with Missing Data.* New York: Wiley.

MaCurdy, T., T. Mroz, and R. M. Gritz (1998) "An Evaluation of the NLSY." *Journal of Human Resources* 33(2): 345–436.

Ridder, G. (1992) "An Empirical Evaluation of Some Models for Non-Random Attrition in Panel Data." *Structural Change and Economic Dynamics* 3(2): 337–55.

Rubin, D. (1976) "Inference and Missing Data." *Biometrika* 63: 581–92.

SIS (2001a) *Hanehalkı İşgücü Anketi: Kavramlar ve Yöntemler* [Household Labor Force Survey: Concepts and Methods]. Devlet İstatistik Enstitüsü Matbaası: Ankara.

SIS (2001b) *Hanehalkı İşgücü Anketi Sonuçları: 2000* [Household Labor Force Survey Results: 2000]. Devlet İstatistik Enstitüsü Matbaası: Ankara.

Tansel, A. and H. M. Taşçı (2006) "Explaining Unemployment Duration for Men and Women in a Developing Country: The Case of Turkey." Mimeo.

Taşçı, H. M. and A. Tansel (2005) "Transitions in the Turkish Labor Market: Evidence from Individual Level Data." Economic Research Forum Discussion Paper, Cairo and Bonn; IZA Discussion Paper.

Tunalı, İ. (1996) "Migration and Remigration of Male Household Heads in Turkey, 1963–73." *Economic Development and Cultural Change* 45(1): 31–67.

—— , and R. Baltacı (2004) "Attrition in the New HLFS, 2000–2002." Mimeo.

—— , and C. Başlevent (2006) "Female Labor Supply in Turkey." In *The Turkish Economy: The Real Economy, Corporate Governance and Reform and Stabilization Policy,* edited by S. Altuğ and A. Filiztekin, 92–127. London: Routledge.

van den Berg, G. and M. Lindeboom (1998) "Attrition in Panel Survey Data and the Estimation of Multi-State Labor Market Models." *Journal of Human Resources* 33(2): 458–78.

Verbeek, M. and T. Nijman (1996) "Incomplete Panels and Selection Bias." In *The Econometrics of Panel Data,* edited by L. Matyas and P. Sevestre. Dordrecht: Kluwer.

World Bank (2006) *Turkey Labor Market Study.* Report No. 33254-TR. Poverty Reduction and Economic Management Unit (Europe and Central Asia Region).

Zabel, J. E. (1998) "An Analysis of Attrition in the Panel Study of Income Dynamics and the Survey of Income and Program Participation with an Application to a Model of Labor Market Behavior." *Journal of Human Resources* 33(2): 479–506.

Table 6.A1 Rotation plan of the HLFS 2000–2 and the observation plan of the present study*

Rotation number	2000				2001				2002			
	1	2	3	4	1	2	3	4	1	2	3	4
01	E1x	—	—	—	—	—	—	—	—	—	—	—
02	(E1>)	(E2x)	—	—	—	—	—	—	—	—	—	—
03	O1x	(E1>)	(E2x)	—	—	—	—	—	—	—	—	—
04	(O1>)	(O2x)	(E1>)	(E2x)	—	—	—	—	—	—	—	—
05	[E1>]	(O1>)	(O2x)	[E2>]	[E3x]	—	—	—	—	—	—	—
06	{E1}	{E2>}	(O1>)	(O2x)	{E3>}	{E4x}	—	—	—	—	—	—
07	[O1>]	{E1>}	{E2>}	[O2>]	[O3x]	{E3>}	{E4x}	—	—	—	—	—
08	{O1>}	{O2>}	{E1>}	{E2>}	{O3>}	{O4x}	{E3>}	{E4x}	—	—	—	—
09	—	{O1>}	{O2>}	{E1>}	{E2>}	{O3>}	{O4x}	{E3>}	{E4x}	—	—	—
10	—	—	{O1>}	{O2>}	{E1>}	{E2>}	{O3>}	{O4x}	{E3>}	{E4x}	—	—
11	—	—	—	{O1>}	{O2>}	{E1>}	{E2>}	{O3>}	{O4x}	{E3>}	{E4x}	—
12	—	—	—	—	{O1>}	{O2>}	{E1>}	{E2>}	{O3>}	{O4x}	{E3>}	{E4x}
13	—	—	—	—	—	{O1>}	{O2>}	[E1>]	[E2>]	{O3>}	{O4x}	[E3c]
14	—	—	—	—	—	—	{O1>}	{O2>}	(E1>)	(E2c)	{O3>}	{O4x}
15	—	—	—	—	—	—	—	[O1>]	[O2>]	(E1>)	(E2c)	[O3c]
16	—	—	—	—	—	—	—	—	(O1>)	(O2c)	(E1>)	(E2c)
17	—	—	—	—	—	—	—	—	—	(O1>)	(O2c)	E1c
18	—	—	—	—	—	—	—	—	—	—	(O1>)	(O2c)
19	—	—	—	—	—	—	—	—	—	—	—	O1c
Visit counter	1	1,2	1,2	1,2	1,2,3	1,2,3,4	1,2,3,4	1,2,3,4	1,2,3,4	1,2,3,4	1,2,3,4	1,2,3,4
Expected no. of total visits	1,2,3,4	2,4	2,4	2,3,4	3,4	4	4	3,4	2,3,4	2,4	2,4	1,2,3,4

Source: SIS (2001a) and own calculations (three rows at the bottom).

* Legend: O = odd number; E = even number; > = subsequent visit planned; x = exits from survey; c = censored. Total number of planned visits: no mark = 1 visit; (parentheses) = 2 visits; [bracket] = 3 visits; {brace} = 4 visits.
Visit counter shows possible visit number values in a given round.
Expected number of total visits shows number of times address should be in the sample.

Table 6.A2 Risk sets and proportion of attritors [$p(A) = 1$] by *observation unit*, attrition type [$A(m)$] and survey round

	2000				2001				2002				Total
	Q1	Q2	Q3	Q4	Q1	Q2	Q3	Q4	Q1	Q2	Q3	Q4	
All individuals													
$A(3)$: at risk	26,244	25,669	24,770	12,587	13,397	14,201	14,009	14,376	13,670	13,391	12,025	0	184,339
$p(A=1)$	0.0831	0.1151	0.0910	0.0725	0.0789	0.0917	0.0944	0.0949	0.0797	0.1328	0.0990	0	0.0944
$A(9)$: at risk	13,474	0	0	0	0	0	0	0	0	0	0	0	13,474
$p(A=1)$	0.1092												0.1092
$A(12)$: at risk	12,158	11,482	11,534	11,674	12,340	12,899	12,686	13,012	0	0	0	0	97,785
$p(A=1)$	0.1286	0.1150	0.1244	0.1266	0.1334	0.1332	0.1484	0.1235	0	0	0	0	0.1294
$A(15)$: at risk	10,594	10,161	10,099	10,196	10,694	11,181	10,803	0	0	0	0	0	73,728
$p(A=1)$	0.0853	0.0881	0.0957	0.0882	0.0806	0.1204	0.0838	0	0	0	0	0	0.0919
All households													
$A(3)$: at risk	9,439	9,244	8,914	4,585	4,759	5,201	5,028	5,252	4,887	4,816	4,342	0	66,467
$p(A=1)$	0.0749	0.1049	0.0720	0.0624	0.0727	0.0808	0.0817	0.0864	0.0722	0.1296	0.0799	0	0.0837
$A(9)$: at risk	4,857	0	0	0	0	0	0	0	0	0	0	0	4,857
$p(A=1)$	0.0681												0.0681
$A(12)$: at risk	4,408	4,181	4,204	4,299	4,413	4,781	4,617	4,798	0	0	0	0	35,701
$p(A=1)$	0.0980	0.0897	0.1035	0.1042	0.1072	0.1094	0.1282	0.0965	0	0	0	0	0.1048
$A(15)$: at risk	3,976	3,806	3,769	3,851	3,940	4,258	4,025	0	0	0	0	0	27,625
$p(A=1)$	0.0709	0.0686	0.0738	0.0704	0.0607	0.1080	0.0561	0	0	0	0	0	0.0730
Households headed by 20–54-year-old individuals													
$A(3)$: at risk	6,833	6,505	6,365	3,276	3,385	3,665	3,553	3,788	3,488	3,405	3,110	0	47,373
$p(A=1)$	0.0771	0.1101	0.0743	0.0687	0.0750	0.0849	0.0850	0.0913	0.0771	0.1389	0.0846	0	0.0878
$A(9)$: at risk	3,414	0	0	0	0	0	0	0	0	0	0	0	3,414
$p(A=1)$	0.0723												0.0723
$A(12)$: at risk	3,169	2,928	2,998	3,051	3,131	3,354	3,251	3,442	0	0	0	0	25,324
$p(A=1)$	0.0985	0.0943	0.1081	0.1105	0.1159	0.1139	0.1387	0.1020	0	0	0	0	0.1104
$A(15)$: at risk	2,857	2,652	2,674	2,714	2,768	2,972	2,800	0	0	0	0	0	19,437
$p(A=1)$	0.0763	0.0758	0.0767	0.0711	0.0647	0.1178	0.0629	0	0	0	0	0	0.0783

Table 6.A3 Probit estimates of attrition at 3 months, households with 20–54-year-old heads. Dependent variable: $A(3) = 1$ if attritor, $= 0$ else

Variable *denotes the characteristics of the household head	Model 1	Model 2	Model 3	Model 4	Model 5
Yr 2001	0.002	0.005	0.001	−0.003	−0.003
	(0.019)	(0.020)	(0.020)	(0.020)	(0.020)
Yr 2002	0.090**	0.094**	0.088**	0.080**	0.079**
	(0.021)	(0.021)	(0.021)	(0.021)	(0.021)
q2	0.204**	0.205**	0.208**	0.207**	0.207**
	(0.021)	(0.021)	(0.021)	(0.022)	(0.022)
q3	0.022	0.023	0.027	0.027	0.026
	(0.022)	(0.023)	(0.023)	(0.023)	(0.023)
q4	0.052	0.049	0.051	0.047	0.047
	(0.028)	(0.028)	(0.028)	(0.028)	(0.028)
*age		−0.162**	−0.161**	−0.077	−0.027**
		(0.055)	(0.055)	(0.057)	(0.010)
*age2		0.338*	0.337*	0.157	0.023
		(0.147)	(0.148)	(0.153)	(0.013)
*age3		−0.239	−0.24	−0.116	
		(0.129)	(0.129)	(0.133)	
*female		0.073*	0.066*	−0.086*	−0.088*
		(0.030)	(0.033)	(0.044)	(0.044)
urban		0.302**	0.298**	0.247**	0.246**
		(0.023)	(0.023)	(0.024)	(0.024)
*empl			−0.02	−0.063*	−0.060*
			(0.029)	(0.029)	(0.029)
*unempl			0.133**	0.130**	0.132**
			(0.039)	(0.039)	(0.039)
*sch				0.012	−0.026**
				(0.019)	(0.010)
*sch2				−0.284	0.276**
				(0.241)	(0.052)
*sch3				2.298*	
				(0.956)	
*single				0.185**	0.189**
				(0.046)	(0.045)
*divorced				0.218**	0.218**
				(0.064)	(0.064)
*widow				−0.028	−0.039
				(0.062)	(0.062)
household size				−0.174**	−0.174**
				(0.033)	(0.033)
household size2				2.029**	2.020**
				(0.535)	(0.535)
household size3				−6.759**	−6.734**
				(2.495)	(2.496)
constant	−1.452**	0.834	0.827	−0.039	−0.572**
	(0.018)	(0.655)	(0.656)	(0.691)	(0.182)
Observations	47,373	47,373	47,373	47,373	47,373
Log-likelihood w/o covariates	−14,089	−14,089	−14,089	−14,089	−14,089
Log-likelihood	−14,019	−13,826	−13,814	−13,649	−13,652
LR test: Incremental Chi–sq. (d.f)	139 (5)	386 (5)	24 (2)	330 (9)	6 (2)

Note: Standard errors are in parentheses. Asterisks denote statistical significance at the 5 (*), and 1% (**).
All quadratic terms are scaled by 1/100, all cubic terms by 1/10,000.

Table 6A4 Probit estimates of attrition at 12 months, households with 20–54-year-old heads. Dependent variable: $A(12) = 1$ if attritor, $= 0$ else

Variable *denotes the characteristics of the household head	Model 1	Model 2	Model 3	Model 4	Model 5
Yr 2001	0.077**	0.083**	0.078**	0.074**	0.075**
	(0.021)	(0.021)	(0.021)	(0.021)	(0.021)
q2	−0.016	−0.017	−0.015	−0.014	−0.014
	(0.030)	(0.030)	(0.030)	(0.030)	(0.030)
q3	0.085**	0.084**	0.088**	0.092**	0.092**
	(0.029)	(0.030)	(0.030)	(0.030)	(0.030)
q4	−0.008	−0.01	−0.009	−0.011	−0.011
	(0.030)	(0.030)	(0.030)	(0.030)	(0.030)
*age		−0.175*	−0.187**	−0.11	−0.011**
		(0.072)	(0.072)	(0.075)	(0.001)
*age2		0.400*	0.427*	0.258	
		(0.195)	(0.195)	(0.200)	
*age3		−0.32	−0.337*	−0.217	
		(0.170)	(0.170)	(0.175)	
*female		0.113**	0.149**	0.055	0.057
		(0.039)	(0.043)	(0.059)	(0.059)
urban		0.271**	0.270**	0.237**	0.234**
		(0.029)	(0.029)	(0.029)	(0.029)
*emp1			0.062	0.031	0.026
			(0.038)	(0.038)	(0.037)
*unemp1			0.265**	0.264**	0.260**
			(0.051)	(0.052)	(0.051)
*sch				−0.002	−0.027*
				(0.023)	(0.012)
*sch2				−0.085	0.267**
				(0.300)	(0.067)
*sch3				1.437	
				(1.214)	
*single				0.165**	0.219**
				(0.064)	(0.059)
*divorced				0.038	0.055
				(0.094)	(0.093)
*widow				−0.01	−0.012
				(0.079)	(0.078)
household size				−0.134**	−0.059**
				(0.044)	(0.018)
household size 2				1.650*	0.381**
				(0.696)	(0.146)
household size 3				−5.711	
				(3.217)	
constant	−1.281**	1.087	1.176	0.38	−0.922**
	(0.024)	(0.868)	(0.870)	(0.908)	(0.104)
Observations	25,324	25,324	25,324	25,324	25,324
Log-likelihood w/o covariates	−8,797	−8,797	−8,797	−8,797	−8,797
Log-likelihood	−8,782	−8,660	−8,645	−8,584	−8,587
LR test: Incremental Chi–sq. (d.f)	29 (4)	244 (5)	31 (2)	123 (9)	8 (4)

Note: Standard errors are in parentheses. Asterisks denote statistical significance at the 5 (*), and 1% (**).
All quadratic terms are scaled by 1/100, all cubic terms by 1/10,000.

Table 6.A5 Probit estimates of attrition at 15 months, households with 20–54-year-old heads. Dependent variable: $A(15) = 1$ if attritor, $= 0$ else

Variable *denotes the characteristics of the household head	Model 1	Model 2	Model 3	Model 4	Model 5
Yr 2001	0.034	0.041	0.04	0.036	0.036
	(0.028)	(0.029)	(0.029)	(0.029)	(0.029)
q2	0.176**	0.177**	0.177**	0.174**	0.174**
	(0.034)	(0.034)	(0.034)	(0.035)	(0.035)
q3	−0.008	−0.004	−0.004	−0.001	0
	(0.036)	(0.036)	(0.036)	(0.036)	(0.036)
q4	0.021	0.018	0.019	0.015	0.017
	(0.046)	(0.047)	(0.047)	(0.047)	(0.047)
*age		−0.128	−0.13	−0.078	−0.005**
		(0.092)	(0.092)	(0.095)	(0.002)
*age2		0.287	0.29	0.175	
		(0.245)	(0.246)	(0.252)	
*age3		−0.216	−0.217	−0.136	
		(0.214)	(0.214)	(0.219)	
*female		0.157**	0.167**	0.136	0.141
		(0.049)	(0.055)	(0.076)	(0.075)
urban		0.279**	0.279**	0.238**	0.236**
		(0.036)	(0.036)	(0.037)	(0.037)
*emp1			0.017	−0.01	−0.016
			(0.047)	(0.047)	(0.046)
*unemp1			0.043	0.046	0.039
			(0.069)	(0.069)	(0.068)
*sch				0.027	0.021**
				(0.029)	(0.004)
*sch2				−0.281	
				(0.387)	
*sch3				1.668	
				(1.568)	
*single				0.021	0.044
				(0.087)	(0.082)
*divorced				0.12	0.116
				(0.114)	(0.113)
*widow				−0.066	−0.067
				(0.099)	(0.098)
household size				−0.086	−0.085**
				(0.046)	(0.021)
household size 2				0.633	0.576**
				(0.646)	(0.158)
household size 3				−0.353	
				(2.435)	
constant	−1.488**	0.173	0.181	−0.421	−1.413**
	(0.029)	(1.108)	(1.108)	(1.152)	(0.115)
Observations	19,437	19,437	19,437	19,437	19,437
Log-likelihood w/o covariates	−5,338	−5,338	−5,338	−5,338	−5,338
Log-likelihood	−5,316	−5,266	−5,266	−5,233	−5,235
LR test: Incremental Chi-sq. (d.f)	42 (4)	101 (5)	0 (2)	67 (9)	4 (5)

Note: Standard errors are in parentheses. Asterisks denote statistical significance at the 5 (*), and 1% (**).
All quadratic terms are scaled by 1/100, all cubic terms by 1/10,000.

Table 6.A6 Probit estimates of the 1st visit participation outcome, 20–54 year-old household heads. Dependent variable: LFP = 1 if participant, = 0 if not

Columns grouped under *Expected number of visits* (models I and II for each aggregation: 4; 3,4; 2,3,4).

Variables	4 — I	4 — II	3,4 — I	3,4 — II	2,3,4 — I	2,3,4 — II
* Characteristic of the household head						
Attritor at 3 months	-0.002	-0.056	0.005	-0.037	-0.014	-0.042
A(3) = 1, A(12) = A(15) = 0	(0.038)	(0.046)	(0.034)	(0.042)	(0.025)	(0.030)
Attritor at 12 months	0.069*	0.036	0.074*	0.049		
A(3) = 0, A(12) = 1, A(15) = 0	(0.035)	(0.042)	(0.032)	(0.039)		
Attritor at 15 months	-0.05	-0.056				
A(3) = A(12) = 0, A(15) = 1	(0.039)	(0.047)				
Yr 2001	0.008	-0.017	-0.01	-0.033	-0.011	-0.045*
	(0.022)	(0.027)	(0.019)	(0.023)	(0.017)	(0.020)
Yr 2002					-0.076**	-0.061**
					(0.019)	(0.022)
q2	0.076**	0.166**	0.075**	0.161**	0.088**	0.169**
	(0.027)	(0.033)	(0.027)	(0.032)	(0.019)	(0.023)
q3	0.016	0.072*	0.016	0.070*	0.066**	0.135**
	(0.027)	(0.032)	(0.027)	(0.032)	(0.019)	(0.023)
q4	0.016	0.081	-0.019	0.044	0	0.059*
	(0.035)	(0.042)	(0.026)	(0.031)	(0.023)	(0.028)
*age		0.278**		0.278**		0.284**
		(0.014)		(0.013)		(0.010)
*age2		-0.436**		-0.434**		-0.437**
		(0.017)		(0.016)		(0.012)
*female		-1.793**		-1.765**		-1.711**
		(0.052)		(0.047)		(0.035)

(Continued overleaf)

Table 6.A6 Continued

Variables	Expected number of visits					
	4		3,4		2,3,4	
* Characteristic of the household head	I	II	I	II	I	II
urban		−0.315**		−0.334**		−0.292**
		(0.033)		(0.030)		(0.023)
*sch		−0.086**		−0.079**		−0.069**
		(0.013)		(0.012)		(0.009)
*sch2		0.707**		0.659**		0.638**
		(0.078)		(0.071)		(0.054)
*single		−0.458**		−0.507**		−0.481**
		(0.067)		(0.060)		(0.045)
*divorced		0.211*		0.209*		0.174**
		(0.089)		(0.081)		(0.057)
*widow		−0.287**		−0.250**		−0.268**
		(0.070)		(0.064)		(0.048)
household size		0.029**		0.022**		0.022**
		(0.008)		(0.007)		(0.005)
constant	1.057**	−2.154**	1.062**	−2.168**	1.052**	−2.440**
	(0.022)	(0.271)	(0.021)	(0.249)	(0.015)	(0.187)
Observations	23,790	23,790	27,578	27,578	47,373	47,373
Log-likelihood w/o covariates	−9,518	−9,518	−11,152	−11,152	−19,316	−19,316
Log-likelihood	−9,510	−6,416	−11,142	−7,612	−19,294	−13,300
LR test: Incremental Chi–sq (d.f.)	15 (7)	6,188 (10)	20 (6)	7,059 (10)	44 (6)	11,988 (10)

Note: Standard errors are in parentheses. Asterisks denote statistical significance at the 5 (*), and 1% (**). All quadratic terms are scaled by 1/100.

Table 6.A7 Probit estimates of the first visit unemployment outcome, 20–54-year-old household heads. Dependent variable: unemp = 1 if participant, = 0 if not (conditional on LFP =1)

Variables	Expected number of visits					
	4		3,4		2,3,4	
* Characteristic of the household head	I	II	I	II	I	II
Attritor at 3 months	0.213**	0.219**	0.198**	0.208**	0.168**	0.183**
	(0.045)	(0.046)	(0.041)	(0.042)	(0.030)	(0.031)
$A(3) = 1, A(12) = A(15) = 0$ Attritor at 12 months	0.210**	0.210**	0.209**	0.214**		
	(0.040)	(0.041)	(0.037)	(0.038)		
$A(3) = 0, A(12) = 1, A(15) = 0$ Attritor at 15 months	0.047	0.053				
	(0.051)	(0.052)				
$A(3) = A(12) = 0, A(15) = 1$						
Yr 2001	0.149**	0.166**	0.179**	0.198**	0.187**	0.205**
	(0.028)	(0.029)	(0.024)	(0.025)	(0.021)	(0.022)
Yr 2002					0.298**	0.316**
					(0.023)	(0.024)
q2	-0.127**	-0.125**	-0.127**	-0.123**	-0.167**	-0.169**
	(0.034)	(0.035)	(0.034)	(0.035)	(0.024)	(0.024)
q3	-0.140**	-0.144**	-0.142**	-0.146**	-0.179**	-0.185**
	(0.034)	(0.035)	(0.034)	(0.035)	(0.024)	(0.025)
q4	-0.109*	-0.108*	-0.041	-0.036	-0.065*	-0.064*
	(0.047)	(0.047)	(0.033)	(0.034)	(0.029)	(0.030)
*age		-0.029		-0.021		-0.038**
		(0.016)		(0.015)		(0.011)
*age2		0.036		0.026		0.047**
		(0.020)		(0.019)		(0.014)
*female		0.211*		0.195*		0.211**
		(0.093)		(0.085)		(0.063)

(*Continued overleaf*)

Table 6.A7 Continued

Variables *Characteristic of the household head	Expected number of visits					
	4		3,4		2,3,4	
	I	II	I	II	I	II
urban		0.308** (0.037)		0.305** (0.033)		0.336** (0.025)
*sch		-0.055** (0.004)		-0.058** (0.004)		-0.064** (0.003)
*single		0.368** (0.078)		0.353** (0.073)		0.325** (0.056)
*divorced		0.261* (0.130)		0.282* (0.117)		0.464** (0.080)
*widow		0.144 (0.138)		0.144 (0.125)		0.039 (0.095)
household size		0.015 (0.008)		0.019* (0.008)		0.020** (0.006)
constant	-1.479** (0.029)	-0.909** (0.294)	-1.491** (0.027)	-1.029** (0.272)	-1.445** (0.019)	-0.645** (0.205)
Observations	20,523	20,523	23,726	23,726	40,668	40,668
Log-likelihood w/o covariates	-5,386	-5,386	-6,449	-6,449	-11,368	-11,368
Log-likelihood	-5,337	-5,190	-6,386	-6,201	-11,227	-10,834
LR test: Incremental Chi-sq (d.f.)	97 (7)	293 (9)	126 (6)	370 (9)	281 (6)	786 (9)

Note: Standard errors are in parentheses. Asterisks denote statistical significance at the 5 (*), and 1% (**).
All quadratic terms are scaled by 1/100.

Part II
Formality, informality, and labor market regulation

7 Monopsonistic competition in formal and informal labor markets *

Ted To

". . . if in fact much of the sector is voluntary, in the sense of workers preferring their present job to one in the formal sector, then the informal job must
be at least of equal quality measured along a broader set of relevant job
characteristics."

William F. Maloney, 2004

1 Introduction

The workhorse of urban labor theory in development economics is the for-
mal/informal model of labor market segmentation. The seminal Harris and
Todaro (1970) model has been extended over the years to cope with various
empirical puzzles, not explained in the original framework. However, one
issue stands out that cannot be explained in a competitive framework.[1] Specifically, there is considerable evidence suggesting that many workers choose
to work in the informal sector even though formal sector jobs may be available to them.[2] Indeed, Bosch and Maloney (2005) show that for Mexico,
Argentina, and Brazil, workers move in either direction between the informal
sector and the formal sector.

This presents a problem because wages in the informal sector are often
(although not always) lower than in the formal sector (Marcouiller, de Castilla,
and Woodruff 1997). In a competitive model, if workers have the freedom to
move between the formal and informal sectors, then in equilibrium, formal
and informal wages would equalize (Fields 2005, 2007); that is, the law of one
price implies that the integration of the formal and informal labor markets
will result in equality of formal and informal wages.

More generally, the existence of wage dispersion not explained by differences in worker ability is problematic for any competitive model of the labor
market. Evidence of wage dispersion in the developed world abounds. Slichter (1950) was an early attempt to quantify the degree of inter-industry
wage dispersion and subsequently there have been numerous contributions
(for a handful of examples, see Dickens and Katz 1987, Gibbons and Katz
1992, and Krueger and Summers 1988). Even within industries, there is
evidence that wages vary significantly (Dunlop 1957; Groshen 1991). More

recently, Abowd, Kramarz and Margolis (1999) showed, using French matched employer–employee data, that wage differentials are mostly the result of differences in individual characteristics. However, a significant portion can only be explained as being due to differences in firm characteristics. In developing countries, there is a small but growing literature demonstrating the existence of wage dispersion unexplained by differences in worker ability (Arbache 2001; Cragg and Epelbaum 1996; Moll 1993; Teal 1996).

The alternative to perfect competition are various forms of imperfectly competitive labor markets. Within the realm of imperfectly competitive models of labor markets are efficiency wage models (Albrecht and Vroman 1998), job search models (Burdett and Mortensen 1998), and oligopsony/monopsonistic competition models (Bhaskar, Manning, and To 2002). Because they are dynamic models, efficiency wages and search involve a good deal of technical machinery and as such are more cumbersome for policy analysis.

Since, at the end of the day, development economists are interested in policy analysis, I model imperfectly competitive formal and informal labor markets using a "monopsony-type" model of the labor market.[3] Spacial models like those used in Bhaskar and To (1999) and Bhaskar, Manning, and To (2002) are useful for certain types of analysis. However, because of the difficulty of dealing with entry and exit when employers are heterogeneous (Bhaskar and To 2003), such models are less useful for looking at dichotomous outcomes in labor markets. For this analysis I will use an alternative formulation where employers interact with one another in a symmetric fashion, similar to the well-known Dixit–Stiglitz model of monopolistic competition.[4]

I consider only two sectors of the labor market—the formal labor market and the informal labor market. The formal labor market is subject to regulation and taxation while the informal labor market is not. The informal market as I model it is not the "staging area" notion of an informal labor market but one where workers are free to choose between formal and informal jobs. Under oligopsony, it is assumed that the number of employers in both the formal and informal labor markets is fixed. Under monopsonistic competition, formal and informal employers are free to enter and exit as long as it is profitable to do so.

Without entry or exit, a reduction in the payroll tax results in increased formal wages, an increase in formal sector employment, and a decrease in informal sector employment. Overall, the effect on total employment depends on the relative magnitudes of the formal and informal wages. If formal wages are greater, then a payroll tax decrease results in lower total employment. If informal wages are greater, then a payroll tax decrease results in higher total employment. An increase in the minimum wage does the same.

With free entry and exit, a reduction in the payroll tax results in increased formal wages, more formal sector employers enter, formal sector employment increases, and informal sector employers exit. However, the effect on total employment depends on both the relative wages and the establishment level elasticity of labor supply. As without free entry and exit, if the formal sector wage is greater than the informal sector wage, then total employment falls; but if the informal sector wage is greater than the informal sector wage *and* if the establishment level elasticity of labor supply is sufficiently high (i.e. jobs are highly substitutable), then total employment will rise. Again, a marginal increase in the minimum wage gives rise to qualitatively similar (although quantitatively different) employment effects.

In a recent and related contribution, Galiani and Weinschelbaum (2006) construct a model with some similarities and use it to conduct various policy experiments. In their model, workers choose between working in the competitive formal and informal sectors. Rather than having heterogeneous preferences, workers have heterogeneous abilities. The choice between formality and informality is driven by a fixed cost of participating in the formal market—low-ability workers prefer informal employment to formal employment because the formal participation costs are large relative to the magnitude of their labor endowment (ability).

In the next section, I present a Dixit–Stiglitz model of oligopsonistic competition. In section 3, I analyze the effect of a payroll decrease and a minimum wage increase on formal, informal, and total employment. In section 4, rather than fixed numbers of employers, formal and informal employers can freely enter and exit the market. Finally, in section 5, I offer some conclusions and suggestions for future research.

2 The model

To ensure that labor supply is imperfectly elastic, I assume that different jobs have different non-wage characteristics. These include the job specification, hours of work, distance of the firm from the worker's home, the social environment in the workplace, etc. The importance of non-wage characteristics has been recognized in the theory of compensating differentials, which is a theory of vertical differentiation. Some jobs are good while other jobs are bad, and wage differentials compensate workers for these differences in characteristics. I assume that jobs are *horizontally differentiated* so that workers have heterogeneous preferences over these characteristics. McCue and Reed (1996) provide survey evidence of horizontal heterogeneity in worker preferences. Heterogeneous preferences over non-wage characteristics ensure that each employer has market power in wage setting, even if it competes with many other employers.

Suppose that a representative worker has utility function:

$$U = I^a L^{1-a} \tag{1}$$

where I is money income, L represents the utility that the worker derives from leisure, and a determines the representative worker's preferences between income and leisure. If w_j is the wage rate at job j and l_j is the time spent at job j, then assume total income is

$$I = \sum_{j=1}^{N} w_j l_j$$

and utility from leisure is

$$L = 1 - \left(\sum_{j=1}^{N} l_j^p \right)^{\frac{1}{p}}$$

where $(\Sigma l_j^p)^{1/p}$ represents the aggregate disutility of labor supplied, N is the number of employers, and p determines the elasticity of labor supply. The term $(\Sigma l_j^p)^{1/p}$ can also be thought of as a labor quantity index,[5] similar to the wage index that will later be defined. Assume U is concave; a sufficient condition for concavity is $p > 1$.

Consider this to be the reduced form utility function for the labor market as as a whole where workers have heterogeneous preferences over jobs and work only for a single employer. For example, Anderson, de Palma, and Thisse (1992) have demonstrated for the product market that consumers with heterogeneous preferences and who consume just a single variety of a product can be represented in aggregate with a constant-elasticity-of-substitution representative utility function similar to that given above.

Given a set of wage offers, the worker maximizes utility by choosing how to allocate her work time among the N employers. Her first-order condition is:

$$\frac{\partial U}{\partial l_k} = a w_k \left(\frac{L}{I} \right)^{1-a} - (1-a) \left(\frac{I}{L} \right)^a \left(\sum_{j=1}^{N} l_j^p \right)^{\frac{1}{p}-1} l_k^{p-1} = 0. \tag{2}$$

Multiplying by l_k, summing over all k and some straightforward manipulation shows that

$$L = 1 - a \tag{3}$$

or at a utility maximum, the utility from leisure activities is constant at $1 - a$. The representative worker's problem in this case becomes the simpler one of maximizing income subject to the condition that total disutility equals a (i.e. $(\Sigma l_j^p)^{1/p} = a$).

Using the methods in Dixit and Stiglitz (1977), it is straightforward to show that labor supply is given by:

$$l_k = a \left(\frac{w_k}{\tilde{w}} \right)^{\frac{1}{p-1}} \tag{4}$$

where $\tilde{w}$ is a wage index given by:

$$\tilde{w} = \left(\sum_{j=1}^{N} w_j^{\beta} \right)^{\frac{1}{\beta}} \tag{5}$$

and $\beta = \rho/(\rho - 1)$. When N is relatively large, the effect of a change in w_k on $\tilde{w}$ is approximately zero. As such, the establishment level elasticity of labor supply is approximately

$$\varepsilon = \frac{1}{\rho - 1} \tag{6}$$

Since $\rho > 1$, labor supply is not infinitely elastic at the establishment level, as would be the case under perfect competition.

Assume that there are n_f and n_i employers (where $n_f + n_i = N$) in the formal and informal labor markets where formal sector employers are numbered $k = 1, 2, \ldots, n_f$ and informal sector employers are numbered $k = n_f + 1$, $n_f + 2, \ldots, N$. In the formal labor market, in addition to the wage, employers are subject to a payroll tax of t_f per dollar per hour. Employers have marginal revenue products of ϕ_f and ϕ_i. Note that I make no assumptions about the relative magnitudes of ϕ_f and ϕ_i so that, employers in the formal labor market may or may not be more productive than employers in the informal labor market.

Employer k chooses w_k to maximize its profit:

$$\pi_k = (\phi_k - (1 + t_k)w_k)l_k \tag{7}$$

where $t_k = t_f$ if employer k is a formal market employer and $t_k = 0$ if employer k is an informal market employer. Employer k's first-order condition is:

$$(\phi_k - (1 + t_k)w_k)\frac{\partial l_k}{\partial w_k} - (1 + t_k)l_k = 0$$

implying an equilibrium wage of

$$w_k^* = \frac{\phi_k}{(1 + t_k)\rho} \tag{8}$$

Since $\rho > 1$, workers are paid less than their marginal product net of the payroll tax, t_k. Denote the equilibrium formal and informal wages by w_f^* and w_i^*. Note that depending on the relative magnitudes of $\phi_f/(1 + t_f)$ and ϕ_i, workers in the formal labor market may or may not be paid more than those in the informal labor market. Since all formal market employers pay wage w_f^* and informal market employers pay w_i^*, establishment level employment is given by:

$$l_\tau^* = a \left(\frac{w_\tau^*}{(n_f w_f^{*\beta} + n_i w_i^{*\beta})^{\frac{1}{\beta}}} \right)^{\frac{1}{\rho-1}} \tag{9}$$

where $\tau = f, l$.

Under a minimum wage, as long as $w_m < \phi_f/(1 + t_f)$, the marginal revenue product of labor net of payroll taxes will be greater than the marginal cost of labor and therefore a formal sector employer will hire as many workers as are willing to work for it at w_m so that

$$l_f^m = a \left(\frac{w_m}{(n_f w_m^\beta + n_i w_i^{*\beta})^{\frac{1}{\beta}}} \right)^{\frac{1}{\rho-1}} \tag{10}$$

Informal employment under a minimum wage is given by l_i^* where w_f^* is replaced by w_m.

3 No Entry or Exit

Suppose that the numbers of formal and informal sector employers are fixed at n_f and n_i. Since the government policies on which I focus affect equilibrium wages in a straightforward manner, I begin by looking at how a change in the formal or informal wage rate affects formal, informal, and total employment.

The equilibrium expressions for formal and informal employment are symmetric, so without loss of generality, consider just the comparative statics with respect to the formal wage. Differentiating (9) with respect to w_f^* yields:

$$\frac{\partial l_f^*}{\partial w_f^*} = \frac{l_f^* \varepsilon}{w_f^*} \frac{n_i w_i^{*\beta}}{n_f w_f^{*\beta} + n_i w_i^{*\beta}} > 0 \tag{11}$$

and

$$\frac{\partial l_i^*}{\partial w_f^*} = -\frac{l_i^* \varepsilon}{w_f^*} \frac{n_f w_f^{*\beta}}{n_f w_f^{*\beta} + n_i w_i^{*\beta}} < 0. \tag{12}$$

Since there is no entry or exit, if establishment level formal employment increases, then total formal employment increases. Similarly, since establishment level informal employment falls, total informal employment must fall.

Looking at total employment, $E = n_f l_f^* + n_i l_i^*$,

$$\begin{aligned}
\frac{\partial E}{\partial w_f^*} &= n_f \frac{\partial l_f^*}{\partial w_f^*} + n_i \frac{\partial l_i^*}{\partial w_f^*} \\
&= \frac{(n_f l_f^* + n_i l_i^*)\varepsilon}{w_f^*} \left(\frac{n_f w_f^{*\beta-1}}{n_f w_f^{*\beta-1} + n_i w_i^{*\beta-1}} - \frac{n_f w_f^{*\beta}}{n_f w_f^{*\beta} + n_i w_i^{*\beta}} \right)
\end{aligned} \tag{13}$$

The function $n_f w_f^{*b}/(n_f w_f^{*b} + n_i w_i^{*b})$ is strictly increasing in b if $w_f^* > w_i^*$ and strictly decreasing in b if $w_f^* < w_i^*$. Thus, the overall employment effect will depend on the relative magnitudes of w_f^* and w_i^*. If $w_f^* > w_i^*$, then the overall employment effect must be negative. Conversely, if $w_f^* < w_i^*$, then the overall employment effect must be positive.

Regardless of whether total employment increases or decreases in response to an increase in the formal wage rate, it should be clear that worker surplus increases. With no entry or exit, workers can choose from the same set of jobs and non-wage characteristics. But for formal sector jobs, the wage rate has gone up, so total worker surplus must increase. More precisely, utility maximizing work choices imply that utility from leisure is fixed at $1 - a$, so the effect on worker utility depends on the effect of wage changes on total income. Differentiating $I = n_f w_f^* l_f^* + n_i w_i^* l_i^*$,

$$\frac{\partial I}{\partial w_f^*} = n_f \left(l_f^* + w_f^* \frac{\partial l_f^*}{\partial w_f^*} \right) + n_i w_i^* \frac{\partial l_i^*}{\partial w_f^*}$$

$$= n_f l_f^* > 0.$$

3.1 Payroll taxes

How then does this relate to changes in tax policy? Since equilibrium wages are a decreasing function of the rate of payroll taxation (i.e. $\partial w_f^*/\partial t_f = -\phi_f/p(1 + t_f)^2 < 0$), a decrease in the payroll tax will lead to an increase in the formal sector wage rate, leading to an increase in formal sector employment and a decline in informal sector employment. Total employment will decrease if $w_f^* > w_i^*$ and increase if $w_f^* < w_i^*$. As discussed earlier, regardless of whether total employment increases or decreases, worker income (and utility) must increase.

However, the increased worker utility must be balanced against potentially lost tax revenues (assuming that tax receipts are used for welfare enhancing purposes) and lost profits. To do so, I look at changes in worker income rather than utility. This has the advantage that incomes, tax receipts, and profits are all in monetary terms and are therefore more directly comparable.

Total tax receipts are $T = t_f n_f w_f^* l_f^*$. Differentiating gives,

$$\frac{\partial T}{\partial t_f} = n_f w_f^* l_f^* + t_f n_f \left(l_f^* + w_f^* \frac{\partial l_f^*}{\partial w_f^*} \right) \frac{\partial w_f^*}{\partial t_f} \tag{14}$$

$$= n_f w_f^* l_f^* [1 - (1 + \varepsilon)v]$$

where $v = t_f/(1 + t_f)$ is the elasticity of the formal wage with respect to changes in the rate of payroll taxation. The tax elasticity of the formal wage is 0 when $t_f = 0$ and, assuming that the rate of payroll taxation cannot exceed 100%, reaches its maximum of 1/2 when $t_f = 1$ and is negative when $t_f < 0$ (a wage subsidy). Thus, when the tax rate is low or negative, a payroll tax

146   *T. To*

decrease will result in lower tax revenues; but if the tax rate is high and the establishment labor supply elasticity is high, then a "Laffer" effect is possible and a tax reduction may result in increased tax revenues. It is interesting to note, though, that as long as $\varepsilon \leq 1$ and t_f is bounded by 1, a Laffer effect is not possible.

Finally, since there is no entry or exit, producer surplus is affected by payroll tax changes. A type τ firm's indirect profit function is $\pi_\tau = \dfrac{\phi_\tau}{1+\varepsilon} l_\tau^*$. Hence, the effect of a decrease in the payroll tax on total profits $\Pi = n_f \pi_f^* + n_i \pi_i^*$ is:

$$\frac{\partial \Pi}{\partial t_f} = \left(n_f \frac{\phi_f}{1+\varepsilon} \frac{\partial l_f^*}{\partial w_f^*} + n_i \frac{\phi_i}{1+\varepsilon} \frac{\partial l_i^*}{\partial w_f^*} \right) \frac{\partial w_f^*}{\partial t_f} \tag{15}$$

$$= - n_f w_f^* l_f^* \frac{n_i w_i^{*\beta}}{n_f w_f^{*\beta} + n_i w_i^{*\beta}} v$$

so that total profit rises with a payroll tax decrease.

An overall measure of the change in total surplus can be had by adding the effect of a tax change on total income, tax receipts, and total profits. This gives,

$$\frac{\partial I}{\partial t_f} + \frac{\partial T}{\partial t_f} + \frac{\partial \Pi}{\partial t_f} = - n_f w_f^* l_f^* \left(\varepsilon + \frac{n_i w_i^{*\beta}}{n_f w_f^{*\beta} + n_i w_i^{*\beta}} \right) v \tag{16}$$

If there is no requirement for a balanced budget, this implies that a wage subsidy (negative payroll tax) can increase total surplus. Of course, in order to be truly surplus enhancing, the government must have alternative means for financing these wage subsidies and provide for government services.

3.2 Minimum wage

For a minimum wage increase, as long as $w_m < \phi_f/(1+t_f)$ (i.e. it is still profitable for formal sector employers to operate), the same comparative statics determine the employment and income effects.

With a minimum wage increase, since formal sector employment increases and the wage increases, payroll tax receipts must increase.

$$\frac{\partial T}{\partial w_m} = t_f n_f \left(l_f^m + w_m \frac{\partial l_f^m}{\partial w_m} \right) \tag{17}$$

$$= t_f n_f l_f^m \left(1 + \frac{n_i w_i^{*\beta}}{n_f w_m^\beta + n_i w_i^{*\beta}} \varepsilon \right)$$

The effect on employer profitability, for a just binding minimum wage is:[6]

$$\frac{\partial \Pi}{\partial w_m}\bigg|_{w_m = w_f^*} = n_f \frac{\partial \pi_f^m}{\partial w_m}\bigg|_{w_m = w_f^*} + n_i \frac{\phi_i}{1 + \varepsilon}\frac{\partial l_i^*}{\partial w_m}$$

$$= -n_f l_f^* \left(\frac{n_f w_f^{*\beta}(1 + t_f) + n_i w_i^{*\beta}}{n_f w_f^{*\beta} + n_i w_i^{*\beta}}\right)$$

(18)

The overall effect of a just binding minimum wage on the sum of income, tax receipts and total profits is:

$$\frac{\partial I}{\partial w_m}\bigg|_{w_m = w_f^*} + \frac{\partial T}{\partial w_m}\bigg|_{w_m = w_f^*} + \frac{\partial \Pi}{\partial w_m}\bigg|_{w_m = w_f^*} = t_f n_f l_f^* (1 + \varepsilon) \frac{n_i w_i^{*\beta}}{n_f w_f^{*\beta} + n_i w_i^{*\beta}}$$

In other words, a minimum wage increases total income and payroll tax receipts by more than employer profits are reduced so that a just binding minimum wage is welfare increasing. However, unlike a wage subsidy, a minimum wage actually improves the government's fiscal balance sheet. Thus, a judiciously chosen minimum wage could be employed in conjunction with a welfare-enhancing tax cut that would not adversely affect the government's finances.

4 Free Entry and Exit

Now consider free entry, so that n_f and n_i adjust to eliminate profits. Assume that because of limited capital available for formal enterprises, formal employers have a fixed production cost of $c_f(n_f)$ that is increasing in the number of formal employers, n_f. On the other hand, informal employers' capital requirements are much more flexible and as a result, they have a constant fixed production cost of c_i. Free entry and exit imply equilibrium employment:

$$l_k^* = \frac{c_k \beta}{\phi_k}$$

(19)

where $c_k = c_f(n_f)$ if firm k is a formal market employer and $c_k = c_i$ if firm k is an informal market employer. Note that this implies that under monopsonistic competition, informal market establishment sizes remain constant.

The equilibrium number of employers in free entry, n_f^* and n_i^*, is given by the solution to equations (9) and (19), i.e. n_f^* and n_i^* solve:

$$(n_f w_f^{*\beta} + n_i w_i^{*\beta})\left(\frac{c_f(n_f)\beta}{\phi_f a}\right)^p = w_f^{*\beta}$$

(20)

and

$$(n_f w_f^{*\beta} + n_i w_i^{*\beta}) \left(\frac{c_i \beta}{\phi_i a}\right)^p = w_i^{*\beta} \tag{21}$$

These can be straightforwardly solved for n_i as a function of n_f:

$$n_i^f(n_f) = \left[\left(\frac{\phi_i a}{c_f(n_f)\beta}\right)^p - n_f\right] \left(\frac{w_f^*}{w_i^*}\right)^{\beta}$$

and

$$n_i^i(n_f) = \left(\frac{\phi_i a}{c_i \beta}\right)^p - n_f \left(\frac{w_f^*}{w_i^*}\right)^{\beta}$$

To consider conditions under which a solution exists, differentiate each of these with respect to n_f,

$$\frac{\partial n_i^f}{\partial n_f} = -\left[\left(\frac{\phi_f a}{c_f(n_f)\beta}\right)^p \frac{c_f'(n_f)p}{c_f(n_f)} + 1\right] \left(\frac{w_f^*}{w_i^*}\right)^{\beta}$$

and

$$\frac{\partial n_i^i}{\partial n_f} = -\left(\frac{w_f^*}{w_i^*}\right)^{\beta}.$$

Note first that since $c_f(n_f)$ is increasing in n_f, $\partial n_i^f/\partial n_f < \partial n_i^i/\partial n_f < 0$. Thus, a necessary condition for a solution is that $n_i^f(0) > n_i^i(0)$ for which $[\phi_f/c_f(0)]^p$ $[\phi_f/(1 + t_f)]^\beta > (\phi_i/c_i)^p \phi_i^\beta$ is both necessary and sufficient. Next, note that in order that there is an intersection, two conditions must be satisfied: (i) $c_f'(n_f)/$ $[c_f(n_f)]^{p+1}$ should not fall too quickly, and (ii) the difference between $n_i^f(0)$ and $n_i^i(0)$ is not too large. An illustrative example is:

$$c_f(n_f) = \rho \left(\frac{1}{K - n_f}\right)^{\frac{1}{\rho}}$$

for some constant K and $n_f < K$. In this case, $c_f'(n_f)/[c_f(n_f)]^{p+1}$ is constant at 1. As long as the difference between $n_i^f(0)$ and $n_i^i(0)$ is not too large, then (20) and (21) intersect. Conditions for the existence of an equilibrium where there are both formal and informal enterprises is illustrated in Figure 7.1. The non-bold line represents $n_i^i(n_f)$. The solid, bold curve represents an example of n_i^f where n_i^f and n_i^i intersect so that there is a solution such that $n_f^* > 0$ and $n_i^* > 0$. The dashed bold curves represent examples of n_i^f where n_i^f and n_i^i do not intersect and where the above conditions do not hold.

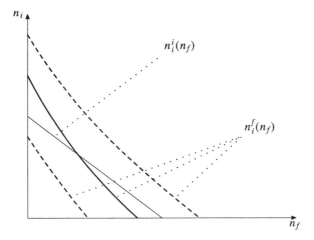

Figure 7.1 Equilibrium number of employers

4.1 Payroll taxes

Having established conditions for the existence of an equilibrium where both n_f^* and n_i^* are positive, I can now consider how n_f^* and n_i^* change in response to a change in the rate of payroll taxation. Totally differentiating (20) and (21) with respect to n_f^*, n_i^*, and w_f^* and rewriting in matrix notation:

$$
\begin{bmatrix}
w_f^{*\beta}\left(\dfrac{c_f(n_f^*)\beta}{\phi_f a}\right)^\rho\left(1+\dfrac{n_f^* w_f^{*\beta}+n_i^* w_i^{*\beta}}{n_f^* w_f^{*\beta}}\rho\xi_f\right) & w_i^{*\beta}\left(\dfrac{c_f(n_f^*)\beta}{\phi_f a}\right)^\rho \\[4mm]
w_f^{*\beta}\left(\dfrac{c_i\beta}{\phi_i a}\right)^\rho & w^{*\beta}\left(\dfrac{c_i\beta}{\phi_i a}\right)^\rho
\end{bmatrix}
\begin{bmatrix}
dn_f^* \\[2mm]
dw_f^* \\[2mm]
dn_i^* \\[2mm]
dw_f^*
\end{bmatrix}
$$

$$
=
\begin{bmatrix}
-\beta w_f^{*\beta-1}\left[n_f^*\left(\dfrac{c_f(n_f^*)\beta}{\phi_f a}\right)^\rho-1\right] \\[4mm]
-\beta w_f^{*\beta-1}\, n_f^*\left(\dfrac{c_i\beta}{\phi_i a}\right)^\rho
\end{bmatrix}
\tag{22}
$$

where ξ_f is the formal-employer, fixed-production-cost elasticity with respect to n_f^*. Let D be the determinant of the first matrix; after some simplification,

$$
D = \frac{w_f^{*\beta}\, w_i^{*\beta}}{n_f^*}\left(\frac{c_i\beta}{\phi_i a}\right)^\rho \rho\xi_f > 0
$$

Using Cramer's rule and simplifying, an increase in the formal-employer wage rate (e.g. from a payroll tax decrease) will have the following effects on the number of employers in the formal and informal labor markets:

$$\frac{dn_f^*}{dw_f^*} = \frac{\beta w_f^{*\,\beta-1}\, w_i^{*\,\beta}\left(\dfrac{c_i\beta}{\phi_i a}\right)^{\!p}}{D} > 0 \tag{23}$$

and

$$\frac{dn_i^*}{dw_f^*} = -\frac{\beta w_f^{*\,2\beta-1}\left(\dfrac{c_i\beta}{\phi_i a}\right)^{\!p}\left[1 + n_f^*\left(\dfrac{c_f(n_f^*)\beta}{\phi_f a}\right)^{\!p}\dfrac{n_f^*\, w_f^{*\,\beta} + n_i^*\, w_i^{*\,\beta}}{n_f^*\, w_f^{*\,\beta}}\,p\xi_f\right]}{D}$$

$$= -\frac{\beta w_f^{*\,2\beta-1}\left(\dfrac{c_i\beta}{\phi_i a}\right)^{\!p}(1 + p\xi_f)}{D} < 0 \tag{24}$$

(The second line of (24) follows from (20).)

Since establishment-level employment in the formal (informal) sector is increasing (constant) and the formal (informal) number of employers increases (decreases) with an increase in the formal sector wage rate, total formal (informal) employment increases (decreases). By extension, since a decrease in the payroll tax leads to an increase in the formal sector wage, a payroll tax decrease results in an increase in formal sector employment and a decrease in informal sector employment.

In other words, a decrease in the payroll tax reduces formal sector employer costs, prompting entry. As a result of this entry, fixed production costs in the formal sector increase and establishments must grow in order to continue breaking even. The shift of workers to the formal sector reduces informal sector labor supply, reducing the profitability of informal sector enterprises resulting in exit from the informal sector.

The formal sector employers become both larger and more numerous while informal sector employers remain the same size but some exit. The overall employment effect therefore depends on the relative magnitudes of these effects. After some manipulation, the overall effect can be computed as:

$$\frac{\partial E}{\partial w_f^*} = \left(n_f^*\frac{\partial l_f^*}{\partial n_f^*} + l_f^*\right)\frac{dn_f^*}{dw_f^*} + l_i^*\frac{dn_i^*}{dw_f^*} \tag{25}$$

$$= \frac{n_f^*\, l_f^*\, \varepsilon}{w_f^*\, \xi_f}\left[(1 + \xi_f) - \frac{w_f^*}{w_i^*}(1 + p\xi_f)\right]$$

Since $p > 1$, it follows that if $w_f^* \geq w_i^*$ then a decrease in the payroll tax will result in a decline in total employment. However, if w_i^* is greater than w_f^* and p is close to 1, then a decrease in the payroll tax will result in an increase in total employment.

It is also straightforward to consider the effect of a payroll tax decrease on total surplus. Since free entry and exit imply zero profits, policy changes have no effect on producer surplus. As before, the utility from leisure will be constant at $L = 1 - a$ so that worker utility depends only on total income, $I = n_f^* w_f^* l_f^* + n_i^* w_i^* l_i^*$. Differentiating this with respect to w_f^* and some manipulation and substitution reveals,

$$\frac{\partial I}{\partial w_f^*} = n_f^* l_f^* + w_f \left[l_f^* + n_f^* \frac{\partial l_f^*}{\partial n_f^*} \right] \frac{dn_f^*}{dw_f^*} + w_i^* l_i^* \frac{dn_i^*}{dw_f^*} \tag{26}$$

$$= 0$$

In other words, cutting payroll taxes, while redistributing jobs and income between different workers, results in no change in total worker income.

As a result, the effect of a payroll tax decrease depends only on its effect on total tax receipts, $T = t_f n_f^* w_f^* l_f^*$. After differentiating and some simplification,

$$\frac{\partial T}{\partial t_f} = n_f^* w_f^* l_f^* + t_f \left[n_f^* l_f^* + w_f^* \left(l_f^* + n_f^* \frac{\partial l_f^*}{\partial n_f^*} \right) \frac{dn_f^*}{dw_f^*} \right] \frac{\partial w_f^*}{\partial t_f} \tag{27}$$

$$= n_f^* w_f^* l_f^* \left[1 - \left(1 + \frac{(1 + \xi_f) \, \varepsilon}{\xi_f} \right) v \right]$$

Thus, when the payroll tax is low (i.e. v is small), the effect of a tax decrease is to reduce tax receipts and therefore total surplus falls; but if the payroll tax is high, the establishment level labor supply elasticity is highly elastic and the fixed-production-cost elasticity is low, then a reduction in the payroll tax can increase tax receipts, increasing total surplus.

4.2 Minimum wages

Now consider the effect of a minimum wage on entry, exit, and employment. With minimum wages, provided that $w_m < \phi_f / (1 + t_f)$, the profit-maximizing calculus changes and as a result, free entry instead implies:

$$[\phi_f - (1 + t_f)w_m] \, l_f = c_f (n_f)$$

or

$$l_f^m = \frac{c_f (n_f^m)}{\phi_f - (1 + t_f)w_m} \tag{28}$$

Like the analysis of payroll taxes, a minimum wage will increase the size of formal sector establishments under free entry and exit.

Together, (28) and (9) imply:

$$(n_f^m w_m^\beta + n_i^* w_i^{*\beta}) \left(\frac{c_f(n_f^m)}{a}\right)^\rho = w_m^\beta [\phi_f - (1 + t_f) w_m]^\rho \tag{29}$$

Totally differentiating (29) and (21) with respect to n_f^m, n_i^m, and w_m and evaluating at $w_m = w_f^*$:

$$\begin{bmatrix} w_f^{*\beta} \left(\dfrac{c_f(n_f^*)}{a}\right)^\rho \left[1 + \dfrac{n_f^* w_f^{*\beta} + n_i^* w_i^{*\beta}}{n_f^* w_f^{*\beta}} \rho\xi_f\right] & w_i^{*\beta} \left(\dfrac{c_f(n_f^*)}{a}\right)^\rho \\ w_f^{*\beta} \left(\dfrac{c_i\beta}{\phi_i a}\right)^\rho & w_i^{*\beta} \left(\dfrac{c_i\beta}{\phi_i a}\right)^\rho \end{bmatrix} \begin{bmatrix} \dfrac{dn_f^m}{dw_m} \\ \dfrac{dn_i^*}{dw_m} \end{bmatrix}$$

$$= \begin{bmatrix} -\beta w_f^{*\beta-1} n_f^* \left(\dfrac{c_f(n_f^*)}{a}\right)^\rho \\ -\beta w_f^{*\beta-1} n_f^* \left(\dfrac{c_i\beta}{\phi_i a}\right)^\rho \end{bmatrix} \tag{30}$$

Let D_m be the determinant of the first matrix:

$$D_m = w_f^{*\beta} \left(\frac{c_f(n_f^*)}{a}\right)^\rho w_i^{*\beta} \left(\frac{c_i\beta}{\phi_i a}\right)^\rho \left(\frac{n_f^* w_f^{*\beta} + n_i^* w_i^{*\beta}}{n_f^* w_f^{*\beta}}\right) \rho\xi_f > 0.$$

Again, we can use Cramer's rule to derive the effect of a change in the minimum wage on the equilibrium number of firms. After simplifying:

$$\left.\frac{dn_f^m}{dw_m}\right|_{w_m = w_f^*} = 0 \tag{31}$$

and

$$\left.\frac{dn_i^*}{dw_m}\right|_{w_m = w_f^*} = -\frac{\beta w_f^{*\beta-1} n_f^*}{w_i^{*\beta}} < 0 \tag{32}$$

Interestingly, an increase in a just binding minimum wage results in no exit of formal employers but induces exit among informal employers.

Although at the establishment level, a minimum wage reduces formal sector profitability and induces exit, in aggregate, a minimum wage results in exit from the informal sector, resulting in an increase in labor supply to the formal sector, thereby increasing profitability. In net, these opposing effects cancel with the result that there is no entry or exit to the formal labor market. However, this result must be kept in perspective. Similar to the envelope theorem arguments used in Card and Krueger (1995) and Rebitzer and Taylor (1995), at the margin, a minimum wage will have a negligible effect on formal employer profitability but a large enough increase in the minimum wage will undoubtedly result in the exit of formal sector employers. Since some informal sector workers move to the formal sector, labor supply in the informal sector falls, reducing profitability of informal sector employers, resulting in firm exit in the informal sector.

Using these results, consider total employment:

$$E = n_f^m l_f^m + n_i^* l_i^*$$

Differentiating this with respect to w_m and simplifying,

$$\left.\frac{\partial E}{\partial w_m}\right|_{w_m = w_f^*} = n_f^* \frac{\partial l_f^m}{\partial w_m} + l_i^* \frac{dn_i^*}{dw_m} \tag{33}$$

$$= \frac{n_f^* l_f^*}{(\rho - 1) w_f^*}\left[1 - \rho \frac{w_f^*}{w_i^*}\right]$$

Similar to the effects of a payroll tax decrease, since $\rho > 1$, if $w_f^* > w_i^*$ then $\partial E / \partial w_m|_{w_m = w_f^*} < 0$ and in aggregate, employment falls. On the other hand, when $w_i^* > w_f^*$, if ρ is sufficiently small, then $\partial E / \partial w_m|_{w_m = w_f^*} > 0$ and a minimum wage can, at the margin, result in an increase in total employment.

As before, since in equilibrium the disutility from work is constant, whether or not worker surplus increases depends on how total worker income changes as a result of a minimum wage. Differentiating income, $I = n_f^m w_m l_f^m + n_i^* w_i^* l_i^*$,

$$\left.\frac{\partial I}{\partial w_m}\right|_{w_m = w_f^*} = n_f^* \left(l_f^* + w_f^* \left.\frac{\partial l_f^m}{\partial w_m}\right|_{w_m = w_f^*}\right) + w_i^* l_i^* \left.\frac{dn_i^*}{dw_m}\right|_{w_m = w_f^*} \tag{34}$$

$$= 0$$

Similar to the effect of a payroll tax cut or hike, a just binding minimum wage redistributes income between different workers but total income remains constant.

Since employment in the formal sector has increased, payroll tax receipts must increase. This can be evaluated precisely by differentiating, $T = t_f n_f^m w_m l_f^m$,

$$\left.\frac{\partial T}{\partial w_m}\right|_{w_m = w_f^*} = t_f n_f^* \left(l_f^* + w_f^* \left.\frac{\partial l_f^m}{\partial w_m}\right|_{w_m = w_f^*}\right) \tag{35}$$

$$= t_f n_f^* l_f^* (1 + \varepsilon)$$

Since tax receipts increase with the imposition of a just binding minimum wage, total surplus must increase as a result. In contrast to a cut in the rate of payroll taxation, a just binding minimum wage unambiguously increases total surplus. A minimum wage redistributes income between different workers, keeping total income the same but higher formal employment leads to higher tax receipts.

5 Conclusions

In this chapter, I considered an alternative model for looking at formal and informal labor markets in developing countries. Empirical evidence suggests that in many developing countries, workers often willingly transition in either direction between the formal and informal sectors. The traditional, competitive "Harris–Todaro" framework cannot be reconciled with voluntary participation in informal labor markets unless the formal and informal labor markets are fully integrated; but full integration of competitive markets requires equalization of the formal and informal wage rates and this is not corroborated by the evidence. I offer oligopsony and monopsonistic competition as an alternative modeling technique that: (1) can capture the notion that some workers voluntarily work in the informal sector, and (2) is tractable enough to conduct interesting policy exercises.

Nevertheless, there are at least two directions that future research should take. First, in order to be fully satisfactory, a model of developing economy labor markets should be able to explain under-/unemployment. One might interpret changes in unemployment as being the negative of the change in employment. However, this interpretation has the clear drawback that unemployment is purely voluntary. Maloney (2004) acknowledges that the informal sector is likely itself to be heterogeneous with a voluntary tier and an involuntary tier. One possible solution may be to construct a hybrid model which incorporates features of both oligopsony/monopsonistic competition and the Harris–Todaro framework.

Second, a feature of the model constructed here is that there are no spillover wage effects; that is, one would expect that following a policy change that affects the formal sector wage, wages in the informal sector would also be affected through competitive linkages between the formal and informal labor markets. For example, if the payroll tax is reduced and formal wages rise, it would not be unreasonable to believe that informal sector employers might raise their wages in an effort to retain workers. Indeed, Gindling and Terrell (2005) find that in Costa Rica, informal sector wages can rise in response to an increase in the minimum wage. One way to capture such wage spillovers is to allow marginal revenue products of labor to vary depending on either the number of establishments or total employment in each sector.

Finally, it may be interesting to consider a combination of oligopsony and monopsonistic competition. In particular, formal sector jobs are sometimes equated with government jobs. As such, the number of "formal establishments" is in some sense fixed but one would certainly expect free entry and exit of informal establishments.

Notes

* I thank John Greenlees, Ravi Kanbur, and conference participants for helpful comments and suggestions.
1 See Fields (2005, 2007) for very good overviews of this literature.
2 Maloney (2004) provides a comprehensive discussion of the evidence.
3 There is little work in development using monopsony-type models of the labor market. Two exceptions are Basu, Chau and Kanbur (2005) where they use a model of monopsony to look at the effects of minimum wage legislation in developing countries where the level of the minimum and enforcement are both endogenous and Basu, Chau and Kanbur (2006) where they examine the effect of employment guarantees under perfect competition and under monopsony/oligopsony.
4 Because of its tractability, variations of the Dixit–Stiglitz model have been in use in the IO, trade, economic geography, and development literatures for decades.
5 It is inaccurate to think of 1 as the total amount of labor/leisure available and $1 - (\Sigma l_j^\rho)^{1/\rho}$ as the quantity of leisure since it is possible for total labor supply to exceed 1. For example, when equilibrium wages are equal across all establishments, if $\rho > \ln N/\ln N + \ln \alpha$ then $\Sigma l_j > 1$. It would be more accurate to think of 1 as being a bound on the disutility from supplying leisure.
6 Keep in mind that the comparative static for the formal sector is found by differentiating (7) since under a (not too large) minimum wage the firm's constrained maximum has it hiring as many workers as are willing to work at the minimum and its indirect profit function is not given by $\phi_f l_f /(1 + \varepsilon)$.

References

Abowd, J., F. Kramarz, and D. Margolis (1999) "High Wage Workers and High Wage Firms." *Econometrica* 67(2): 251–333.

Albrecht, J. W. and S. B. Vroman (1998) "Nash Equilibrium Efficiency Wage Distributions." *International Economic Review* 39(1): 183–203.

Anderson, S., A. de Palma, and J.-F. Thisse (1992) *Discrete Choice Theory of Product Differentiation*. Cambridge, MA: MIT Press.

Arbache, J. S. (2001) "Wage Differentials in Brazil: Theory and Evidence." *Journal of Development Studies* 38(2): 109–130.

Basu, A. K., N. H. Chau, and R. Kanbur (2005) "Turning a Blind Eye: Costly Enforcement, Credible Commitment and Minimum Wage Laws." Working paper.

——— . (2006) "A Theory of Employment Guarantees: Contestability, Credibility and Distributional Concerns." Working paper.

Bhaskar, V., A. Manning, and T. To (2002) "Oligopsony and Monopsonistic Competition in Labor Markets." *Journal of Economic Perspectives* 16(2): 155–74.

Bhaskar, V. and T. To (1999) "Minimum Wages for Ronald McDonald Monopsonies: A theory of monopsonistic competition." *Economic Journal* 109(455): 190–203.

——— . (2003) "Oligopsony and the Distribution of Wages." *European Economic Review* 47(2): 371–99.

Bosch, M. and W. Maloney (2005) "Labor Market Dynamics in Developing Countries: Comparative Analysis using continuous time Markov processes." World Bank Policy Research Working Paper 3583.

Burdett, K. and D. T. Mortensen (1998) "Wage Differentials, Employer Size, and Unemployment." *International Economic Review* 39(2): 257–73.

Card, D. and A. B. Krueger (1995) *Myth and Measurement: The New Economics of the Minimum Wage*. Princeton, NJ: Princeton University Press.

Cragg, M. I. and M. Epelbaum (1996) "Why Has Wage Dispersion Grown in Mexico? Is it the Incidence of Reforms of the Growing Demand for Skills?" *Journal of Development Economics* 51: 99–116.

Dickens, W. and L. Katz (1987) "Inter-industry Wage Differences and Theories of Wage Determination." NBER Working Paper 2271.

Dixit, A. K. and J. E. Stiglitz (1977) "Monopolistic Competition and Optimum Product Diversity," *American Economic Review* 67(3): 297–308.

Dunlop, J. T. (1957) "The Task of Contemporary Wage Theory." In *New Concepts in Wage Determination*," edited by G. W. Taylor and F. C. Pierson New York: McGraw Hill, 117–39.

Fields, G. S. (2005) "A Guide to Multisector Labor Market Models." Mimeo.

——. (2007) "Modeling Labor Market Policy in Developing Countries: A selective review of the literature and needs for the future." Mimeo.

Galiani, S. and F. Weinschelbaum (2006) "Modeling Informality Formally: Households and Firms." Working paper.

Gibbons, R. and L. Katz (1992) "Does Unmeasured Ability Explain Inter-industry Wage Differentials?" *Review of Economic Studies* 59: 515–35.

Gindling, T. H. and K. Terrell (2005) "Legal Minimum Wages and the Wages of Formal and Informal Sector Workers in Costa Rica." *World Development* 33(11): 1905–21.

Groshen, E. (1991) "Sources of Intra-industry Wage Dispersion: How much do employers matter?" *Quarterly Journal of Economics* 106: 869–84.

Harris, J. R. and M. P. Todaro (1970) "Migration, Unemployment and Development: A two-sector analysis." *American Economic Review* 60: 126–42.

Krueger, A. B. and L. H. Summers (1988) "Efficiency Wages and the Inter-industry Wage Structure." *Econometrica* 56: 259–93.

Maloney, W. F. (2004) "Informality Revisited." *World Development* 32(7): 1159–78.

Marcouiller, D., V. R. de Castilla, and C. Woodruff (1997) "Formal Measures of the Informal-Sector Wage Gap in Mexico, El Salvador, and Peru." *Economic Development and Cultural Change* 45(2): 367–92.

McCue, K. and W. R. Reed (1996) "New Empirical Evidence on Worker Willingness to Pay for Job Attributes." *Southern Economic Journal*, 62(3): 647–53.

Moll, P. G. (1993) "Industry Wage Differentials and Efficiency Wages: A dissenting view with South African evidence." *Journal of Development Economics* 41: 213–46.

Rebitzer, J. and L. Taylor (1995) "The Consequences of Minimum Wage Laws: Some new theoretical ideas." *Journal of Public Economics* 56(2): 245–55.

Slichter, S. (1950) "Notes on the Structure of Wages." *Review of Economics and Statistics* 32: 80–91.

Teal, F. (1996) "The Size and Sources of Economic Rents in a Developing Country Manufacturing Labour Market." *Economic Journal* 106: 963–76.

8 Entrepreneurial entry in a developing economy

John Bennett and Saul Estrin

1 Introduction

In this paper we model the process of entrepreneurial entry by new firms, both formal and informal, in a developing economy.[1] Building on characterizations of the entry process and the distinction between formal and informal status, we establish the conditions under which entry and survival of either type takes place when a new opportunity becomes available for exploitation. We analyze whether an innovating firm (the "leader") will initially be formal or informal; how the leader may adapt (into or out of formality) once profitability becomes known; and the choice between formality and informality for a second firm (the "follower"). We also consider how finance constraints may affect the pattern of entry.

There is already a large literature on the choice between formal and informal status in a developing economy. In the two-sector model of Lewis (1954) a reservoir of surplus labor is reduced as the high-productivity sector grows to absorb it. Harris and Todaro (1970) formalize this view of segmented labor markets in a tradition that has been surveyed and extended by numerous authors including Loayza (1994) and Fields (2005). Papers in this tradition tend to view the informal sector as passive, supplying labor to the formal sector at a relatively low fixed wage. A second strand in the literature, originating in the ILO Report on Kenya (1972), suggests that, far from disappearing, the informal sector could instead provide a basis for employment creation and growth.[2] Maloney (1999, 2004) takes this approach further, drawing primarily on Latin American experience to argue that the informal sector is probably better viewed as entrepreneurial. To quote Maloney (2004, 1), "as a first approximation we should think of the informal sector as the unregulated developing country analogue of the voluntary entrepreneurial small firm sector found in developing countries." Our paper follows this lead in the specific context of entrepreneurial entry.

Various contributions have sought to model the interaction between the formal and informal sectors, treating their relative size as endogenous. Rauch (1991) defines a firm as formal at or above a certain size, in which case it must meet a minimum wage constraint. The relative size of firms in the two sectors, and therefore the scale of the informal sector, is found to be sensitive to the gap between the minimum and the market-clearing wage. De Paula and Scheinkman (2006) also study the determinants of informal sector activity, deducing that informal sector firms will be smaller and have a higher cost of capital, results supported by their empirical work on Brazil.

Our approach differs from the literature in its focus on *de novo* entry, allowing us to concentrate on the choice of formal versus informal status when the industry, as well as the firm, is being created by the entry process.[3] We follow Hausmann and Rodrik (2003) and Bennett and Estrin (2006) in arguing that, while innovation in developing countries will typically be through the imitation of existing production methods in developed economies, such technology is not common knowledge. Rather, the transfer of technology to new economic and institutional environments requires adaptations, and there is an associated uncertainty about the future profitability of the new ventures in a developing economy (see also Hausmann, Hwang, and Rodrik 2006). Hence, we model entrepreneurs that set up firms in a "new" industry, the profitability of which is initially unknown.

We analyze the choice of legal status (formal or informal) both at the point of entry, and subsequently, once the potential profitability of the industry is revealed. Firms can enter formally or informally, and change their status in either direction once the profitability of the industry becomes known and entrepreneurs have reevaluated their prospects in the light of this information. By analyzing the choice of status from the time at which the industry is first set up in the developing economy, and providing a simple dynamic formulation, we are able to bring the roles of uncertainty and experimentation into the analysis. Such issues may be critical in the life cycle of an industry, but are excluded when a static approach is taken. Also, we are able to allow strategic behavior in the choice of formality/informality status, given that the acquisition of either status involves a sunk cost, which is higher in the case of formality.

Our approach is to characterize the essential features of formal and informal sector firms in a parsimonious manner. In our model both the formal and informal sector pay a fixed wage per worker, but the formal sector labor cost includes an additional element which can represent either the cost of supplying social benefits or the minimum wage that must be paid to formal sector workers. We also assume formal firms are larger and, in much of the analysis, more productive. For ease of analysis we model a fixed-coefficient technology, in which formal sector firms are not assumed to be more capital intensive. Their productivity advantage is instead captured in terms of higher output per worker (and capital).

There are two periods and two entrepreneurs in the model, which is solved by backward induction. In the second period the leader is already an incumbent, and may be formal or informal (or may exit). Depending on the realization of profitability and the values of other parameters, entry by the follower may occur, either formally or informally, and we formulate the Nash equilibrium that obtains. In the first period the leader decides whether to enter, and, if so, whether the firm should be formal or informal. He or she takes into account the equilibrium that will obtain in period 2 for all possible realizations of profitability of the industry.

Some of our results would have been expected intuitively, such as that a higher minimum wage in the formal sector is conducive to the growth of the informal rather than the formal sector. Others might not have been predicted. For example, in terms of comparative statics, a higher realized productivity may have a non-monotonic effect on the number of informal firms, and for intermediate realizations may lead to multiple equilibria and churning of both the number of firms and their status. Moreover, credit constraints can affect the balance of entry in a way that may be found surprising: credit constraints may stimulate informal entry even when they do not prevent formal entry.

In Section 2 we outline the model and our main assumptions. Because even our stylized and simple framework generates many cases, we do not assume productivity differences between formal and informal sector firms and an upward sloping capital supply curve simultaneously. Rather, in Section 3 we consider the evolution of the industry with a perfectly elastic capital supply, but with the formal sector assumed to be more productive than the informal. Then in Section 4 we do the converse, analyzing the case of an upward-sloping capital supply curve on the assumption that productivity in the two sectors is the same. Section 5 concludes.

2 The set-up

We consider an innovation in a developing economy in the form of imitation of a technique that already exists in developed economies. The transfer of technology to the new economic and institutional environment requires adaptation, and there is an associated uncertainty about the future profitability of the venture (see Hausmann and Rodrik 2003). When an entrepreneur sets up a firm in a particular 'new' industry, the profitability is initially unknown. We focus on a simple example, with two entrepreneurs, two time periods, fixed input proportions, and a constant price of output. In effect, we are making the small open economy assumption. Although price is fixed, the suitability of the industry to local conditions makes profitability unknown before entry occurs.

In the industry that we analyze, there are no incumbent firms at time $t = 0$, but the leader, entrepreneur A, may innovate, setting up a firm (also called A) to enter the industry and produce at $t = 1$. The firm may be either informal or formal at $t = 1$. Its activity at $t = 1$ reveals the profitability of the industry, which is then common knowledge. At $t = 2$ entrepreneur A may then exit the industry, or keep the firm at its original formality/informality status, or switch status. We assume that the follower, entrepreneur B, observes that A has entered at $t = 1$ and then, when A's profitability is revealed, may enter at

$t = 2$, either formally or informally. Thus, there may be one or two firms in the industry at $t = 2$, with both firms being formal, or both informal, or one formal and the other informal. There are no further time periods in the model.

We follow Rauch (1991) in using firm size, measured in terms of employment, as a defining characteristic of formality, an informal firm employing one unit of labor, while a formal firm employs two. Factor proportions are fixed: an informal firm requires k units of capital, and a formal firm $2k$. If firm A enters informally at $t = 1$ it purchases k units of capital. If it switches to formality at $t = 2$ it must purchase k. If it enters formally at $t = 1$ and then switches to informality it disposes of its unused capital freely.

Rauch (1991) and Loayza (1994) regard the requirement to pay minimum wages as an essential characteristic of the formal sector. We model this by assuming that whereas the market wage w is paid in the informal sector, the formal sector pays an increment s, where $w + s \equiv \bar{w}$ can be interpreted as the minimum wage. Alternatively, s may be regarded as the cost of supplying social benefits to formal sector workers. We write $\bar{w}$ in place of $w + s$ where this is more consistent with the exposition.

To reflect shortage of capital, we assume that the unit price r_t of capital at time t may be increasing in K_t, the aggregate amount of capital bought at t:

$$r_t = 1 + [K_t - 1]\, \rho, \text{ where } \rho \geq 0. \tag{1}$$

Since capital is assumed to be bought in units of k, this implies that if k units are bought the price is unity, if $2k$ are bought the price per unit is $1 + \rho$, and if $3k$ are bought it is $1 + 2\rho$. If $\rho = 0$ then $r_t = 1$.

In addition to the social cost s, we characterize informality in terms of size. Being larger is a potential benefit to a firm: if the industry is profitable, the extra size associated with formality will enable it to earn further profits (whereas if the industry is not profitable, the firm is not obliged to be formal). We allow for one further difference: as noted by de Paula and Scheinkman (2006) and Straub (2005), a formal firm may enjoy a productivity benefit β. Thus we assume that although it uses twice as many inputs as an informal firm does, its output is 2β that of the informal firm, where $\beta \geq 1$. Formality may also enable the firm to sell output to the government, presumably at a price that is at least as high as that for private sales. The parameter β may be interpreted as reflecting this differential.

We assume that the profitability of the industry depends on the value taken by a stochastic term θ, which may represent demand or cost factors. θ captures the idea that, although the industry may exist in other countries, its suitability to local conditions and institutions can only be discovered by experimentation. At $t = 1$, θ is stochastic, being uniform over $[0, 2\Theta]$; but, given that entrepreneur A sets up his or her firm at $t = 1$, either informally or formally, the value of θ is common knowledge at $t = 2$. This represents the idea that the suitability of the industry to local conditions and institutions is discovered by experimentation. Apart from θ at $t = 1$, everything in the model is common knowledge.

At $t = 1$ firm A's respective profits if is informal and if it is formal are

$$\pi_{1i}^A = \theta - w - k;$$
$$\pi_{1f}^A = 2[\beta\theta - w - s - (1 + p)k].$$

At $t = 2$, if A is informal it does not have to purchase any capital, regardless of the status it chose at $t = 1$, and so its profit is

$$\pi_{2i}^A = \theta - w. \tag{2}$$

If, however, A is formal at $t = 2$ its profit depends on its status at $t = 1$, because a switch from informality to formality involves the purchase of an extra unit of capital. Its profit also depends, through the price of capital, on the behavior of firm B at $t = 2$. Thus, A's profit at $t = 2$ is

$$\pi_{2f}^A = 2(\beta\theta - w - s) - r_2 k \text{ if A informal at } t = 1; \tag{3}$$
$$= 2(\beta\theta - w - s) \text{ if A formal at } t = 1. \tag{4}$$

At $t = 2$ firm B's profit is

$$\pi_{2i}^B = \theta - w - r_2 k \text{ if B informal}; \tag{5}$$
$$\pi_{2f}^B = 2[\beta\theta - w - s - r_2 k] \text{ if B informal.} \tag{6}$$

We assume that at $t = 1$ firm A makes decisions so as to maximize the expected present value of its profit stream, applying a discount factor $\sigma \in (0, 1]$. At $t = 2$ both A and B independently maximize profits. We solve the model by backward induction. We begin by considering $t = 2$, first on the assumption that A entered formally at $t = 1$, and then assuming that A entered informally at $t = 1$. In each of these two cases we consider the behavior of A and B for all possible realizations of θ. For each such realization A must choose between exit, informality, and formality, while B must choose between staying out, informality, and formality; and we determine the Nash equilibrium in each case. Then we consider $t = 1$. Here, taking into account all the potential outcomes at $t = 2$, A must decide whether to enter, and, if so, whether to take informal or formal status.

Even this simple framework would generate a large number of different cases, and so we simplify our analysis as follows. First, we include the productivity benefit of formality, i.e. we assume that $\beta > 1$; but we assume that the price of capital is fixed, i.e. that $p = 0$, so that $r_t = 1$. Then we change each of these assumptions: we assume that there is no productivity benefit ($\beta = 1$) but that the supply curve of capital is upward-sloping ($p > 0$). In this case the profit of each firm depends on the behavior of the other and so there is strategic interaction. In describing the firms' choices at $t = 2$ we use X to indicate exit, I informal status, F formal status, and SO staying out of the industry.

3 Formality gives a productivity advantage

In this section we assume that $\beta > 1$ but $\rho = 0$. Since in this case neither firm's behavior affects the profit of the other, we focus on one firm—the leader, firm A—in isolation. We begin by examining A's behavior at $t = 2$, first on the assumption that it entered formally at $t = 1$, and then on the assumption that it entered informally at $t = 1$. A comparison follows. In the next section, where, because the supply curve of capital is assumed upward sloping, there is strategic interaction, we bring the follower, firm B, explicitly into the analysis.

3.1 Firm A at t = 2 after formal entry at t = 1

If A entered formally at $t = 1$, it will not acquire additional capital at $t = 2$. Neither firm's behavior at $t = 2$ affects the profit of the other, so that for each possible realization of θ we have a dominant-strategy equilibrium. If it stays in production, A's profits at $t = 2$ are given by (2) or (4); that is, they are $\theta - w$ if it chooses I, but $2(\beta\theta - w - s)$ if it chooses F.

The unit cost of output with formality, relative to that under informality, is raised by the existence of the social cost s, but lowered by the productivity benefit β. Given that A acquired k units of capital at $t = 1$, its unit cost of output at $t = 2$ is w if it chooses I, but $(w + s)/\beta$ if it chooses F. If $w \geq (w + s)/\beta$, A does not choose I for any realization of θ at $t = 2$, whereas if $w < (w + s)/\beta$ A may choose either I or F, depending on the realization of θ. Even if the unit cost is greater for formality, the higher output that formality allows may make it more profitable than informality.

Hence, comparing A's profit levels across its options at $t = 2$, and rewriting the unit cost inequality, it is found that if

$$s \leq (\beta - 1)w, \tag{7}$$

I is never chosen—A chooses either X or F. Then A's dominant strategy is X if $\theta < (w + s)/\beta$, but F if $\theta \geq (w + s)/\beta$. If, however, (7) does not hold, i.e. if $(\beta - 1)w < s$, A may, depending on the realization θ, choose any of the three options, X, I, or F. A's dominant strategy is then X if $\theta < w$; I if $w \leq \theta < (w + 2s)/(2\beta - 1)$; but F if $(w + 2s)/(2\beta - 1) \leq \theta \leq 2\Theta$.

Given that (7) may or may not hold, there are two possibilities.

(a) $s \leq (\beta - 1)w < (\beta - 1)(w + k)$. In this case neither firm will choose to be informal at $t = 2$. If $0 \leq \theta < (w + s)/\beta$, then A chooses X; if $(w + s)/\beta \leq \theta < (w + s + k)/\beta$, it chooses F. Given A's profits at $t = 2$ for each range of realization of θ, we obtain its expected profit $E\pi_2^A(f)$ at $t = 2$, given that it enters formally at $t = 1$ (with the expectation being taken at the beginning of $t = 1$):

$$2\Theta E\pi_2^A(f) = \int_{(w+s)/\beta}^{2\Theta} 2(\beta\theta - w - s)d\theta = \frac{1}{\beta}(w+s)^2 + 4\Theta\,[\beta\Theta - (w+s)] \quad (8)$$

The limits on the integral here define the range of θ values for which F is chosen by A at $t = 2$, and $2(\beta\theta - w - s)$ is the profit earned for each realization of θ in this range. For (8) to be valid, we assume

$$2\Theta > (w+s)/\beta. \qquad (9)$$

By assuming that Θ is this large, we ensure that in the equilibrium at $t = 2$ the outcome {F,F} is a possibility. If we restricted Θ to taking a lower value, then {F,F}, and perhaps other outcomes, would be ruled out by assumption. A similar assumption to (9) is made below for each of our other cases.

(b) $(\beta - 1)w < s \le (\beta - 1)(w + k)$. Under these conditions A may choose informality at $t = 2$. The following choices then obtain. If $0 \le \theta < w$, A chooses X; if $w \le \theta < (w + 2s)/(2\beta - 1)$, it chooses I; if $(w + 2s)/(2\beta - 1) \le \theta$ it chooses F. Thus, in case (b) we obtain

$$2\Theta E\pi_2^A(f) = \int_w^{(w+2s)/(2\beta-1)} (\theta - w)d\theta + \int_{(w+2s)/(2\beta-1)}^{2\Theta} 2(\beta\theta - w - s)d\theta$$

$$= \frac{1}{2}\frac{(w+s)^2}{(2\beta - 1)} + \frac{1}{2}w^2 + 4\Theta\,[\beta\Theta - (w+s)]. \qquad (10)$$

The first integral relates to the range of θ for which I is chosen, and the second for which F is chosen. For (10) to be valid, we assume

$$2\Theta > (w + 2s)/(2\beta - 1)$$

Within each case, (a) and (b), $E\pi_{2f}^A$ is increasing in Θ and β, and decreasing in w and s; and it is independent of k.

3.2 Firm A at $t = 2$ after informal entry at $t = 1$

Assuming now that the leader, firm A, entered informally at $t = 1$, its profit at $t = 2$ is the same as if it enters formally at $t = 1$, except in one respect: if it chooses F at $t = 2$ it must then spend k to expand its capital stock (its profit then is $2(\beta\theta - w - s) - k$, as given by (3) with $r_2 = 1$).

Comparing A's profits across its three options, it is found that if

$$s + \frac{k}{2} \le (\beta - 1)w, \tag{11}$$

it does not choose I at $t = 2$ for any realization of θ. The term $k/2$ appears in (11) but not in (7) because of the additional expenditure k that is required to obtain the output associated with F. If (11) holds, A's dominant strategy is X if $\theta < (w + s + \frac{k}{2})/\beta$, but F if $\theta \ge (w + s + \frac{k}{2})/\beta$.

If, however, (11) does not hold, i.e. if $s + \frac{k}{2} > (\beta - 1)w$, A's dominant strategy is X if $0 < w$; I if $w \le \theta < (w + 2s + k)/(2\beta - 1)$; but F if $(w + 2s + k)/(2\beta - 1) \le 0$.

There are again two possibilities.

(c) $s + \frac{k}{2} \le (\beta - 1)w < (\beta - 1)(w + k)$. If $0 \le \theta < (w + s + \frac{k}{2})/\beta$, A chooses X. Otherwise it chooses F. Thus, A's expected profit $E\pi_{2i}^A$ at $t = 2$ when it enters informally at $t = 1$, is given by

$$2\Theta E\pi_{2i}^A = \int_{(w + s + \frac{k}{2})/\beta}^{(w + s + k)/\beta} (\theta - w)\,d\theta + \int_{(w + s + k)/\beta}^{2\Theta} [2(\beta\theta - w - s) - k]\,d\theta$$

$$= 2\Theta\,[2\beta\Theta - 2(w + s) - k] + \frac{k}{2\beta^2}\left[s + \frac{3}{4}k - (\beta - 1)w\right] \tag{12}$$

$$+ \frac{1}{\beta}(w + s + k)(w + s)$$

For (12) to be valid, we assume

$$2\Theta > (w + s + k)/\beta.$$

(d) $(\beta - 1)w < s + \frac{k}{2} \le (\beta - 1)(w + k)$. In this case $(w + 2s + k)/(2\beta - 1) < (w + s + k)/\beta$. Thus, if $0 \le \theta < w$, A chooses X; if $w \le \theta < (w + 2s + k)/(2\beta - 1)$ it chooses I; if $(w + 2s + k)/(2\beta - 1) \le \theta$ it chooses F. This yields

$$2\Theta\,E\pi_2^A\,(i) = \int_w^{(w + 2s + k)/(2\beta - 1)} (\theta - w)\,d\theta + \int_{(w + 2s + k)/(2\beta - 1)}^{2\Theta} [2(\beta\theta - w - s) - k]d\theta$$

$$= 2\Theta[2\beta\Theta - 2(w + s) - k] + \frac{1}{2}w^2 + \frac{1}{2(2\beta - 1)}(w + 2s + k)^2 \tag{13}$$

For (13) to be valid, we assume

$$2\Theta > (w + 2s + k)/(2\beta - 1)$$

As in cases (a) and (b), within each case (c) and (d), $E\pi_{2i}^A$ is increasing in Θ and β, and decreasing in w and s; it is independent of k.

3.3 A's choice of status at t = 1

We assume that A's objective at the start of $t = 1$ is to maximize the present value of its expected profit stream. If A enters formally at $t = 1$ this present value is

$$EV^A (f) = 2(\beta\Theta - w - s - k) + \sigma E\pi_2^A (f),$$

where $\sigma \in (0, 1]$ is a discount factor. If A enters informally at $t = 1$ the present value is

$$EV^A (i) = \Theta - w - k + \sigma E\pi_2^A (i),$$

Thus, denoting by Δ_1 the net gain in expected $t = 1$ profit from choosing formality rather than informality at $t = 1$; and denoting by Δ_2 the net gain in expected $t = 2$ profit from choosing formality rather than informality at $t = 1$,

$$\Delta_1 = (2\beta - 1)\Theta - w - 2s - k > 0;$$
$$\Delta_2 = E\pi_2^A (f) - E\pi_2^A (i), \tag{14}$$

Given that A enters, it prefers formality (informality) if

$$EV^A (f) - EV^A (i) = \Delta_1 + \sigma\Delta_2 > (<) 0, \tag{15}$$

From (14),

$$\Delta_1 \gtrless 0 \text{ as } \Theta \gtrless (w + k + 2s)/(2\beta - 1) \tag{16}$$

However, under the present assumptions $\Delta_2 > 0$ in all cases because formal entry at $t = 1$ involves the purchase of more capital than informal entry at $t = 1$ does. This additional capital may then be used profitably at $t = 2$, and it is assumed that there are no costs of disposal if it is not used. The following combinations of cases (a)–(d) are mutually consistent.

I. *Low Social Costs:* $s < s + \frac{k}{2} \leq (\beta - 1)w$. This combination of parameter values, which can also be interpreted as a relatively low minimum wage ($\bar{w} + k/2 < \beta w$) obtains when cases (a) and (c) hold together. A will not choose to be informal at $t = 2$, regardless of its formality/informality status at $t = 1$. From (8) and (12),

$$\Delta_2 = k - \frac{k}{4\beta^2 \Theta} \left[(1 + 2\beta) s + (1 + \beta)w + \frac{3}{4}k \right].$$

II. *Intermediate Social Costs:* $s \leq (\beta - 1)w < s + \frac{k}{2}$. This combination, which can be interpreted as representing an intermediate value of the minimum wage ($\bar{w} \le \beta w < \bar{w} + k/2$), obtains when (a) and (d) hold together. If A enters formally at $t = 1$ it will not choose informality at $t = 2$; but if it enters informally at $t = 1$ it may choose either status at $t = 2$. From (8) and (13),

$$\Delta_2 = k - \frac{1}{4\beta\,(2\beta - 1)\Theta}\,\{2[(\beta - 1)w - s]^2 + \beta k(k + 4s + 2w)\},$$

III. *High Social Costs:* $(\beta - 1)w < s < s + k/2$. These inequalities, which represent a high minimum wage ($\beta w < \bar{w}$) obtain when (b) and (d) hold together. From (10) and (13),

$$\Delta_2 = k - \frac{1}{4(2\beta - 1)\Theta}\,(s + k)\,(2w + 3s + k),$$

Since $\Delta_2 > 0$, we have from (16) that a sufficient condition for formal entry at $t = 1$ to be preferred is that

$$\Theta \ge (w + k + 2s)/(2\beta - 1),$$

Using (15), we find that $d[EV^A(f) - EV^A(i)]/d\Theta > 0$; i.e. a higher Θ favors formality at $t = 1$. Also, $EV^A(f) - EV^A(i)$ is increasing in β and σ, and decreasing in w, s, and k. There is a critical value of Θ, which we denote by $\bar{\Theta}$, at which $EV^A(f) - EV^A(i) = 0$. We write $\bar{\Theta} = \bar{\Theta}^I$ for low, $\bar{\Theta} = \bar{\Theta}^{II}$ for medium, and $\bar{\Theta} = \bar{\Theta}^{III}$ for high social costs. Thus we obtain[4]

$$\bar{\Theta}^I < \bar{\Theta}^{II} < \bar{\Theta}^{III}, \tag{17}$$

The minimum value of Θ for which A will choose formality at $t = 1$ is greatest in the high social cost case and smallest in the low social cost case. Holding w constant, an increase in the minimum wage rate $\bar{w}$ reduces the relative attractiveness of formality for A at $t = 1$ and increase $\bar{\Theta}$.

The first lemma summarizes the main conclusions so far.

Lemma 1 *Suppose that $\beta > 1$ and $\rho = 0$. If $s \le (\beta - 1)w$, A will not choose informality at $t = 2$, while if $(\beta - 1)w < s$ informality may be preferred for A at $t = 1$ or $t = 2$. A sufficient condition for A to prefer formal entry at $t = 1$ is that $\Theta \ge (w + k + 2s)/(2\beta - 1)$.*

We have seen that if $s \le (\beta - 1)w$, the social cost (or excess of the minimum wage over the market wage) s being small, informal entry allows A, as leader, to explore the profitability of the industry without sinking a large investment. Given that there is no strategic interaction at $t = 2$, there is no competitive disadvantage to making this choice. The potential disadvantage, however, is that if the realization of θ is relatively high then A will have forgone potential profits at $t = 1$.

Note that for various ranges of parameter values A takes up the option of informality, but would not be willing to operate formally. The point here is not just that having the option of informality raises the expected present value of the profit stream, but also that the existence of the informal option can be the critical factor that raises the present value of the profit stream above zero, inducing entry and enabling formal status possibly to be attained. This can happen in two ways. First, the entrepreneur may take up the option of informal status at $t = 1$ as a potential "stepping-stone" to formality at $t = 2$, should conditions turn out to be favorable. Alternatively, the entrepreneur may choose formality at $t = 1$ only because, should conditions then be revealed to be only mildly favorable, the option of informality may be taken up at $t = 2$, as a "consolation prize."

Proposition 1 *Informality may be a stepping stone or a consolation prize.*

We now focus on some comparative statics. Using (17), we can interpret the shift from I to II to III as an increase in s. Putting this together with our results that $d\bar{\Theta}^I/ds$, $d\bar{\Theta}^{II}/ds$ and $d\bar{\Theta}^{III}/ds$ are each positive, we obtain a comparative statics result that spans all combinations of parameter values (see the next lemma). This can also be interpreted as an increase in the minimum wage $\bar{w} = s + w$. Conversely, if we increase w with $\bar{w}$ held constant, we move from III to II to I; and within each of the three parameter ranges it is found that a higher level of the informal wage rate w is associated with a lower value of $\bar{\Theta}$. We therefore obtain the following lemma.

Lemma 2 *Suppose that $\beta > 1$ and $\rho = 0$. Then, with held w constant, an increase in the minimum wage rate $\bar{w}$ reduces the attractiveness of formality relative to informality for A at $t = 1$ and increases the value of Θ that is necessary for A to choose formality at $t = 1$. With $\bar{w}$ held constant, an increase in the informal wage rate w has the opposite effects*

It is also worth stressing, however, that the wedge s between w and $\bar{w}$ can actually enhance the role of informality. Suppose, in particular, that s is reduced to zero (e.g., the minimum wage law is repealed). This increases the profits from formal operation at both $t = 1$ and $t = 2$. However, it also increases the present value of the expected profit stream for firm A if it enters *informally* at $t = 1$—because A may switch to formality at $t = 2$, and the profits from formality have been raised. Put differently, the existence of s reduces the benefits that experimentation will produce if θ turns out favorably. While its removal favors formality relative to informality at $t = 1$, it also favors informal entry relative to no entry at $t = 1$. For some parameter values (ones for which formality at $t = 1$ is not chosen), a minimum wage law that binds only on the formal sector may be the decisive factor that prevents entrepreneur A from entering informally, thereby preventing the industry from starting. Removal of the minimum wage law can thus enhance the role of informality as a stepping stone.

4 Increasing supply price of capital

We now assume that $\rho > 0$, whereas $\beta = 1$. This has a significant effect on the analysis in that there is a now mutual dependence between A's and B's profits at $t = 2$, and so there can be strategic interaction. The general nature of the above analysis survives, but two main additional considerations enter the picture. One is that firms do not always have dominant strategies, and for a given realization of θ there may not be a unique pure-strategy Nash equilibrium. The other is that the introduction of an exogenous constraint can, because of strategic behavior by A, have interesting effects on the pattern of entry and status. Again we begin by considering $t = 2$, first given that the leader, firm A, entered formally and then given that it entered informally at $t = 1$. A comparison follows.

4.1 Behavior at $t = 2$ when firm A formal at $t = 1$.

Given that $\rho > 0$, if A enters formally at $t = 1$ it is found that at $t = 2$ there is no range of parameter values for which informality is dominated for a firm for all possible realizations of θ. Also, although any purchase of capital by B affects the price of capital, since A does not buy any capital (having already acquired $2k$ at $t = 2$), neither firm's behavior can affect the profits of the other. For each possible realization of θ, we therefore have a dominant strategy equilibrium.

If A entered formally at $t = 1$ it will not acquire additional capital at $t = 2$. If it stays in production, its profits at $t = 2$ are given by (2) or (4); that is, they are $\theta - w$ if it chooses I, but $2(\theta - w - s)$ if it chooses F. Assuming it enters, firm B's profits at $t = 2$ are given by (5) with $r_2 = 1$ or (6) with $r_2 = 1 + \rho$; that is, they are $\theta - w - k$ if it chooses I, but $2[\theta - w - s - (1 + \rho)k]$ if it chooses F.

A's dominant strategy is X if $0 \leq \theta < w$; I if $w \leq \theta < w + 2s$; and F if $w + 2s < \theta$. B's dominant strategy is SO if $0 \leq \theta < w + k$; I if $w + k \leq \theta < w + (1 + 2\rho)k + 2s$; and F if $w + (1 + 2\rho)k + 2s < \theta$. Together, these strategies imply that there are two cases.

(i) $k \geq 2s$. Then, if $0 \leq \theta < w$, we have {X,SO}. If $w \leq \theta < w + 2s$, we have {I,SO}. If $w + 2s \leq \theta < w + k$, we have {F,SO}. If $w + k \leq \theta < w + (1 + 2\rho)k + 2s$, we have {F,I}. If $w + (1 + 2\rho)k + 2s \leq \theta$, we have {F,F}.

(ii) $k < 2s$. Then, if $0 \leq \theta < w$, we have {X,SO}. If $w \leq \theta < w + k$, we have {I,SO}. If $w + k \leq \theta < w + 2s$, we have {I,I}. If $w + 2s \leq \theta < w + (1 + 2\rho)k + 2s$, we have {F,I}. If $w + (1 + 2\rho)k + 2s \leq \theta$, we have {F,F}.

For both these cases, with firm A entering formally at $t = 1$, its expected profit $E\pi_2^A$ (f) at $t = 2$ is given by

$$2 \, \Theta \, E\pi_2^A \, (f) = \int_w^{w + 2s} (\theta - w) \, \mathrm{d}\theta + \int_{w + 2s}^{2\Theta} 2(\theta - w - s) \, \mathrm{d}\theta$$

$$= 2s^2 + w^2 + 2sw + 4\Theta \, [\Theta - (w + s)] \tag{18}$$

This is valid provided that

$$2\Theta > w + 2s.$$

Formal entry at $t = 1$ yields A an expected profit stream with present value

$$EV^A(f) = 2[\Theta - w - s - (1 + p)k] + \sigma \, E\pi_2^A(f).$$

4.2 Behavior at t = 2 when firm A informal at t = 1

If A enters informally at $t = 1$, then, because each firm may choose to buy capital at $t = 2$, and the supply price of capital is increasing, the profits of each firm depend on the behavior of the other firm. These profits, which are obtained from (2)–(6), using (1), are presented in Table 8.1, where firm A is represented in the rows and B in the columns. There is no range of parameter values for which informality is dominated for all possible realizations of θ, and so, in the absence of dominant strategies, we examine the Nash equilibria for all realizations of θ.

The best responses for each firm are easily obtained (see Bennett and Estrin, 2007). Putting these responses together, it is found that there are two cases, depending on whether $pk \gtrless 2s$. We write $\{\ldots\}$ to denote the status of the two firms at $t = 2$, with the first entry in the brackets referring to A's choice and the second B's.

(iii) $pk \geq 2s$. If $0 \leq \theta < w$, we have $\{X,SO\}$. If $w \leq \theta < w + k$, we have $\{I,SO\}$. If $w + k \leq \theta < w + 2s + k$, we have $\{I,I\}$. If $w + 2s + k \leq \theta < w + (1 + p)k$, there are two pure-strategy equilibria, $\{I,I\}$ and $\{F,SO\}$. If $w + (1 + p)k \leq \theta < w + 2s + (1 + p)k$, we have $\{I,I\}$. If $w + 2s + (1 + p)k \leq \theta < w + 2s + (1 + 3p)k$, we have $\{F,I\}$. If $w + 2s + (1 + 3p)k \leq 0$, we have $\{F,F\}$.

(iv) $pk < 2s$. If $0 \leq \theta < w$, we have $\{X,SO\}$. If $w \leq \theta < w + k$, we have $\{I,SO\}$. If $w + k \leq \theta < w + 2s + (1 + p)k$, we have $\{I,I\}$. If $w + 2s + (1 + p)k \leq \theta < w + 2s + (1 + 3p)k$, we have $\{F,I\}$. If $w + 2s + (1 + 3p)k \leq 0$, we have $\{F,F\}$.

Table 8.1 Profits at $t = 2$ when A informal at $t = 1$ ($\beta = 1$; $\rho > 0$)

		SO	B I	F
	X	0 0	0 $\theta - w - k$	0 $2[\theta - w - s - (1 + p)k]$
A	I	$\theta - w$ 0	$\theta - w$ $\theta - w - k$	$\theta - w$ $2[\theta - w - s - (1 + p)k]$
	F	$2(\theta - w - s) - k$ 0	$2(\theta - w - s) - (1 + p)k$ $\theta - w - (1 + p)k$	$2(\theta - w - s) - (1 + 2p)k$ $2[\theta - w - s - (1 + 2p)k]$

In case (iv), the number of informal firms rises at first with θ, but then falls as formality becomes highly profitable, and in both (iii) and (iv) there is an intermediate value of θ that gives the pure-strategy equilibrium {I,I}. However, in case (iii), for θ in the next higher range, it is found that there are two pure-strategy equilibria, {I,I} and {F,SO}. For the range of θ above that we again find a single pure-strategy equilibrium, {I,I}.

The two pure-strategy equilibria occur when $pk \geq 2s$ and $w + 2s + k \leq 0 < w + (1 + p)k$. If B stays out, the lack of pressure on the price of capital makes formality for A, which requires the purchase of additional capital k, an attractive proposition; and, since A is buying capital, B does not find it profitable to buy capital at the same time, given that the price will be driven up. This gives the pure-strategy equilibrium {F,SO}. However, if B enters informally, buying capital k to do so, A will not find it profitable to add to its capital stock and become formal because the price of capital will be higher when both firms make a purchase. Given that A is not purchasing capital, B finds it profitable to enter, though only informally because θ is only in an intermediate range. This gives the pure-strategy equilibrium {I,I}.

We assume that when there are two pure-strategy equilibria a mixed-strategy equilibrium obtains. Hence, the outcome may be any of: {F,SO}, {I,I}, {I,SO} and {F,I}. Consequently, looking at the whole range of θ values, as demand takes higher values the number of informal firms may rise from 0 to 1 to 2, but then may fall to 1 or even 0 before, for the two highest ranges of θ, we have 1 and 0 informal firms. Also, since {F,I} and {I,SO} are possible outcomes but are not pure-strategy equilibria, 'churning' (turbulence) may be a characteristic of an intermediate realization of θ.

Proposition 2 *Suppose that $\beta = 1$ and $p > 0$, and that the leader, firm A, enters informally at $t = 1$. Then an intermediate range of realizations θ of profitability exists for which there are two pure-strategy equilibria at $t = 2$. With a mixed-strategy equilibrium in this range there may be churning, with no settled behavior with regard to formality and informality.*

For both these cases, (iii) and (iv), with firm A entering informally at $t = 1$, its expected profit $E\pi_{2i}^A$ at $t = 2$ is given by[5]

$$2\Theta E\pi_2^A(i) = \int_w^{w + 2s + (1 + p)k} (\theta - w)\, d\theta + \int_{w + 2s + (1 + p)k}^{w + 2s + (1 + 3p)k} [2(\theta - w - s)$$

$$- (1 + p)k]\, d\theta + \int_{w + 2s + (1 + 3p)k}^{2\Theta} [2(\theta - w - s) - (1 + 2p)k]\, d\theta \qquad (19)$$

$$= \frac{1}{2}[2s + (1 + p)k]^2 + 2pk\,]2s + (1 + 3p)k] +$$

$$2\Theta \{2\Theta - [2(w + s) + (1 + 2p)k]\} + (w - pk)[w + 2s + (1 + 3p)k]$$

The first integral covers the range of θ in which A remains informal. The second and third integrals cover range of θ in which A switches to formality, buying an additional k units of capital. The second integral relates to B choosing informal, buying k units of capital, so that the unit price of capital is $1 + p$; the third integral relates to B choosing formality, buying $2k$ units of capital, so that the unit price of capital is $1 + 2p$. For (19) to be valid we assume that

$$2\Theta > w + 2s + (1 + 3p)\, k, \tag{20}$$

Informal entry at $t = 1$ earns A a profit stream with expected present value,

$$EV^A(i) = \Theta - w - k + \sigma\, E\pi_{2i}^A. \tag{21}$$

4.3 A's choice between formality and informality

Assuming that A enters, it prefers formality (informality) if

$$EV^A(f) - EV^A(i) = \Theta - w - 2s - (1 + 2p)\, k + \sigma\, \Delta > (<)\, 0, \tag{22}$$

where $\Delta = E\pi_2^A(f) - E\pi_2^A(i)$. From (18) and (19),

$$\Delta = (1 + 2p)\, k - \frac{1}{2\Theta}\left\{ (2\, s + w)\,(1 + 2p)\, k + \left[\frac{1}{2}(1 + p)^2 + p(1 + 3p)\right] k^2 \right\}.$$

Given (21), $\Delta > 0$; that is, by entering formally at $t = 1$ firm A earns a higher expected profit at $t = 2$ than if it entered informally at $t = 1$. From (22), a sufficient condition for firm A to prefer formality at $t = 1$ is therefore that

$$\Theta > w + 2s + (1 + 2p)\, k.$$

As in Section 3 $d[EV^A(f) - EV^A(i)]/d\Theta > 0$; that is, a higher Θ favors formality at $t = 1$. Also, $EV^A(f) - EV^A(i)$ is increasing in σ, and decreasing in w, s, k, and p. There is a critical value of Θ, which we denote by $\bar{\Theta}$, at which $EV^A(f) - EV^A(i) = 0$. Firm A prefers formality (informality) at $t = 1$ if $\Theta > (<)\bar{\Theta}$.

The comparative statics are similar to those of Section 3, but with an additional parameter p. If A enters formally at $t = 1$ it pays unit capital cost $1 + p$ and so its expected profit falls when p is raised; but since it then does not expand further, its profitability at $t = 2$ is unaffected. If A enters informally at $t = 1$ its unit capital cost is unity, independent of p. Then, using (20), a higher p at $t = 2$ is found to reduce A's (and B's) profitability. Also, if A enters informally at $t = 1$ a higher value of p can make case (iii) rather than (iv) obtain; i.e. it results in the possibility of churning.

4.4 Finance constraints

In general, we may expect finance constraints to lead to less investment, but our concern here will be with whether there may be any more interesting effects, particularly on the behavior of the leader, firm A. We assume that capital investment requires up-front expenditure, which must be financed, but that labor costs do not require such expenditure, being met ex post by sales revenue.

In our model A purchases up to k units of capital at $t = 2$, while B purchases up to $2k$ units of capital at $t = 2$. Suppose, however, that the amount of finance available at $t = 2$ is enough for a total of only $2k$ units of capital to be bought then. We focus on the case in which it is known with certainty, at $t = 1$, that if the constraint binds at $t = 2$, it will bind equally, in the sense that at $t = 2$ each firm will be able to buy at most k units of capital. Since A will never wish to buy $2k$ units of capital at $t = 2$, this is equivalent to a constraint solely on B that only k units of capital may be bought.

If A enters formally at $t = 1$ the constraint cannot bind at $t = 2$ and so our earlier analysis still holds. If, however. A enters informally at $t = 1$ the constraint binds at $t = 2$ if both firms want to be formal then: A's choice between exit, continued informality, or a switch to formality will be unaffected, but B will be restricted to staying out or informality. Instead of (19), we have

$$2\Theta E\pi_2^A(i) = \int_w^{w + 2s + (1 + p)k} (\theta - w)d\theta + \int_{w + 2s + (1 + p)k}^{2\Theta} [2(\theta - w - s)$$

$$- (1 + p)k]\,d\theta = \frac{1}{2}[w + 2s + (1 + p)k]^2 + \frac{1}{2}w^2 + \qquad (23)$$

$$2\Theta\,\{2\Theta - [2(w + s) + (1 + 2p)k]\,\}.$$

If A enters formally at $t = 1$ its expected profit at $t = 2$ is unaffected by the existence of the constraint; but the constraint has an impact if A enters informally at $t = 1$. Let Ω denote the difference between A's expected profit at $t = 2$ when the constraint exists and when it does not. From (19) and (23),

$$2\Theta\Omega = \int_{w + 2s + (1 + 3p)k}^{2\Theta} pk\,d\theta = pk\,\{2\Theta - [w + 2s + (1 + 3p)k]\,\}.$$

Given (20), $\Omega > 0$: the existence of the constraint raises the present value of A's expected profit stream. The constraint prevents B from being formal at $t = 2$, limiting the potential competition facing A. This benefit to A only occurs if it enters informally at $t = 1$. This gives our third proposition.

Proposition 3 *The existence of a common constraint on finance at $t = 2$ can* encourage entry by the leader, firm A, at *t = 1*, but it does so by raising the return to informal, rather than formal entry at *t = 1*.

For example, the value $\bar{\Theta}$ of Θ above which formality is preferred is made greater by the existence of the finance constraint. It may thus occur that in the absence of the finance constraint A would enter formally, but with the constraint – which only binds strictly on B – A chooses to enter informally. Indeed, it may be that in the absence of the finance constraint A would not enter at all, but with the constraint A would enter informally. The constraint restricts the competition that would potentially occur at *t = 2* if, at *t = 1*, A entered informally. The expected present value of the profit stream for A resulting from informal entry at *t = 1* is therefore raised, whereas that for formal entry and that for staying out are unaffected. The finance constraint can therefore result in informality being a stepping stone.

We could also suppose that there is a finance constraint at *t = 1*. There are two forms of this assumption that are consistent with the above analysis. First, it may be that there are *2k* units of finance available at *t = 1* but that, since A is the only firm at this time, it can have all of this finance if it wants it. Second, it may be that only *k* units of finance are available per (potential) firm at *t = 1*. This does not affect the critical part of the story above, for we still have that informality is chosen at *t = 1*. Although with this interpretation we lose the result that the constraint encourages informality (it now *forces* informality) we still have following result:

Corollary 1 *A k unit finance constraint on each firm in each period can encourage entrepreneurial entry.*

5 Conclusions

We have examined decisions with respect to formality or informality for entrepreneurs in a new industry for a developing economy. By focusing on the decisions *ab initio* we have been able to deal with issues such as experimentation and strategic behavior that may be critical for both entry and the choice of status. Using a simple framework for tractability, our analysis has enabled us to establish conditions under which different configurations of firm status will occur for the leader and the follower, and we have derived the comparative statics for parameters such as the minimum wage rate and a characterization of *ex ante* prospects about the profitability of the industry. We have shown that there is not a simple monotonic relationship between the number of informal firms and the realized profitability of the industry.

One of the aims of our analysis was to explore whether the existence of the informal option could boost entry and the long-term development of an industry, including its formal sector. Our findings indicate some clear benefits for developing countries from the existence of the option of informal status, in contrast to the views of, e.g., Loayza (1994), for whom the informal sector is regarded as a phenomenon likely to constrain economic growth. We have shown that informality allows a leader to explore, without significant sunk costs, the potential profitability of the industry; that is, informality may be a stepping stone, enabling an entrepreneur to experiment cheaply in an uncertain environment. We have shown that there are circumstances under which, without this option, the industry would not become established.

Informality may alternatively be a consolation prize, that is, it may be the equilibrium status if, once uncertainty has been resolved, the profitability of the industry is relatively low. This is perhaps closer to the traditional view of the sector. However, even in our simple two-firm model there may be multiple equilibria, with churning of entry and status. This can occur when the realized profitability of the industry is at an intermediate level. In this particular case the existence of the informal option creates instability.

We have also shown that in the entrepreneurial context the existence of finance constraints can actually encourage entry—even if the constraints fall equally on each firm in each period. A constraint can act in a similar way to a patent, limiting subsequent competition by a follower, and thus raising the expected present value of the profit stream for a leader.

Notes

1 See Bennett and Estrin (2007) for an earlier version which deals with the derivations in more detail.
2 This view is confirmed for Kenya more recently by Bigsten, Kimyu, and Lundvall (2004).
3 Weak institutions, and, in particular, high levels of taxation and regulation burdening formal firms, combined with an inability to enforce property rights, including those of the state, have been regarded in the literature as the main cause of the emergence of the informal sector (see, e.g. Loayza 1994). In this paper we take as given that institutions are weak and that informality, as well as formality, is an option for potential entrants.
4 See Bennett and Estrin (2007) for the details.
5 To calculate this expected profit we must solve for the mixed-strategy equilibrium that is discussed in the text. Since firm A's profit from remaining informal is independent of B's behavior, this is the expected profit that must obtain for A in this equilibrium.

References

Bennett, J. and S. Estrin (2006) "Regulatory Barriers and Entry in Developing Economies." CEDI Working Paper 06–02, Brunel University.
—— , (2007) "Informality as a Stepping-stone: Entrepreneurial entry in a developing economy." IZA Discussion Paper 2950.
Bigsten, A. K. Lundvall, and P. Kimuyu (2004) "What to Do with the Informal Sector?" *Development Policy Review* 22: 701–15.
Fields, G. S. (2005) "A Guide to Multisector Labor Market Models." World Bank, Social Protection Working Paper No 0505.
Harris, J. and M. Todaro (1970) "Migration, Unemployment, and Development: A two sector analysis." *American Economic Review* 40: 126–42.

Hausmann, R. J. Hwang, and D. Rodrick (2006) "What You Export Matters." Harvard University, mimeo.

Hausmann, R. and D. Rodrick (2003) "Economic Development as Self-discovery." *Journal of Development Economics* 72: 603–33.

International Labour Office (1972) *Employment, Incomes, and Equality: a Strategy for Increasing Productive Employment in Kenya*. Geneva: ILO.

Lewis, W. A. (1954) "Economic Development with Unlimited Supplies of Labour." *Manchester School*, 22: 139–91.

Loayza, N. V. (1994) Labor Regulations and the Informal Economy." Policy Research Working Paper 1335, Washington DC: World Bank.

Maloney, (1999) "Does Informality Imply Segmentation in Urban Labor Markets? Evidence from sectoral transitions in Mexico." *The World Bank Economic Review* 13: 275–302.

Maloney, (2004) "Informality Revisited." *World Development* 32: 1159–78.

Paula, A. de, and J. Scheinkman, (2006) "The Informal Sector." UCLA Department of Economics working paper.

Rauch, J. E. (1991) "Modelling the Informal Sector Informally." *Journal of Development Economics* 35: 33–47.

Straub, S. (2005) "Informal Sector: The credit market channel." *Journal of Development Economics* 78: 299–321.

9 Multiple-job-holding in Tanzania[*]

*Theis Theisen**

1 Introduction

Individuals in developing countries often rely on various sources of monetary income. Leibbrand, Woolard, and Woolard (2000) provide empirical evidence that this is the case in South Africa. Glick (1999) documents that, in the case of Guinea, monetary earnings often are supplemented through extensive engagement in home production. Theisen (2005a) finds that Tanzanian formal sector workers often participate in informal production, and Reardon (1997) documents that households in sub-Saharan Africa derive income from various sources. This suggests that studies of labour markets in developing countries should start from the presumption that multiple-job-holding is the norm rather than the exception. Except for Glick (1999), Joliffe (2004), and Theisen (2005a), this is, however, not the state of the art in the economics literature. Hence, my main aim is to investigate the extent of multiple-job-holding in the African context, and to examine which factors that drive individuals into multiple-job-holding.

My attention to multiple-job-holding in developing countries was triggered by the observation that the real wages of the Tanzanian formal sector workers declined in much of the period from the early 1970s to the commencement of the restructuring period in the late 1980s. How are individuals who are experiencing large declines in real wages able to cope in their daily lives? Has their material standard of living deteriorated correspondingly, or have lower real wages induced workers to increase their working hours, either in their main job or in additional jobs? In particular, has formal sector workers' participation in informal production increased?[1]

Glick (1999) and Joliffe (2004) address some of these questions, but due to data limitations they both had to use reduced form models. By contrast, since the appearance of the seminal article of Shishko and Rostker (1976) studies of multiple-job-holding in industrial countries have usually been based on structural form models. This methodological difference is largely due to the problems of observing what people in developing countries earn in the informal sector. Deaton (1997: 29) emphasizes the difficulties in income measurement in developing countries. The present paper suggests a new way around this problem. The suggested method permits the estimation of a structural form multiple-job-holding model. To my knowledge, structural models of multiple-job-holding have not previously been estimated on data from developing countries. This distinguishes the present paper from the companion paper of Theisen (2005a).

The structural form approach places the present paper in the tradition of Shishko and Rostker (1976), but drawing on Gronau (1977) it also incorporates home production. On the other hand, while Shisko and Rostker (1976) and most of the multiple-job-holding literature from developed countries estimate labour supply equations, the present paper is limited to participation in multiple-job-holding. This limitation is mainly due to the available data, and is related to the measurement problems pointed out above.

I focus exclusively on whether workers holding a job in the formal sector also hold additional jobs in the informal sector. Previous papers of Gindling (1991), Pradhan and van Soest (1995), and Funkhauser (1996) have examined determinants of participation in the informal and formal sectors in Brazil, Bolivia, and Central America. All these contributions rest, however, on the assumption that an individual will work either exclusively in the formal sector, or exclusively in the informal sector, and they abstract from home production. Consequently, the present paper complements this vein of the literature.

In section 2 we establish a theoretical model, which is used as a vehicle for deriving conditions for participation in informal production, as well as labour supply functions for time allocated to such production, conditional on the individual holding a job in the formal sector. In section 3 the econometric model is developed, and we present and discuss the approach used to tackle the problem of measuring earnings from informal production. Section 4 contains a descriptive analysis of participation in informal production. Two main forms of participation are distinguished: home production for own consumption and income-generating informal activities. In section 5 we estimate an earnings function that subsequently is used for predicting the "wage rate" in informal production. In section 6 the main estimation results are presented, and some results are discussed in more detail in section 7. Section 8 summarizes and provides some suggestions for further research.

2 Theoretical model

Consider an individual with the utility function $U(X, L)$, where X is a Hicksian aggregate good, and L is leisure. Utility is maximized subject to two constraints. First, there is a goods constraint. When the unit price of the aggregate good is normalized to 1, the goods constraint takes the form $X = V + W\bar{N} + ZF(H)$, where V is non-labour income, W is the formal sector wage rate, $\bar{N}$ is hours worked in the formal sector, Z is a productivity index, and $F(H)$ is a function for which we assume that $F(0) = 0$ and that $F(H)$ is increasing and concave in H ($F_H > 0$ and $F_{HH} \le 0$; subscripts denoting partial derivates). The goods constraint lays out that goods consumption can be "financed" from three sources: (a) non-labour income (V), (b) formal sector wage earnings ($W\bar{N}$), and (c) home production ($ZF(H)$). Our home production function corresponds closely to that of Gronau (1977), and the model implies that home-produced goods and goods bought in the market are perfect substitutes in consumption. Factors of production other than household time, such as capital, land, skills, etc., may affect the productivity index, but are not specified.

Utility maximization is subject to a time constraint, $L + H + \bar{N} = T$, where T is time available, with L, H, $\bar{N}$ and T all non-negative. Formal sector working-time is assumed to be determined from the demand side of the labour market; hence it is exogenous to the individual, as indicated by the bar above N. In addition, we assume that an individual who wants a formal sector job typically must agree to work full time. This is in accordance with the observation that part-time jobs are practically non-existent in the Tanzanian formal sector.[2]

When combined, the goods constraint and the time constraint yield the budget constraint $ABCDE$ in Figure 9.1. With the indifference curves drawn in the figure, utility is maximized at Q. We focus, however, on participation in home production (and other forms of informal production). Consider therefore the situation at D in Figure 9.1, where the individual is working $\bar{N}$ hours in the formal sector. The crucial question is whether he or she will participate in home production. The answer follows directly from Figure 9.1, which shows that the individual will participate in home production only if the indifference curve at D slopes less than the home production function. Denoting marginal utilities of the aggregate good and leisure by U_X and U_L, the participation condition takes the form:

$$\frac{U_L(V + W\bar{N}, T - \bar{N})}{U_X(V + W\bar{N}, T - \bar{N})} \begin{cases} \geq ZF_H(0) & \Rightarrow \quad \text{no participation } (H = 0) \\ < ZF_H(0) & \Rightarrow \quad \text{participation } (H > 0) \end{cases}. \tag{1}$$

Condition (1) implies that the individual will participate in home production if the utility forgone by one hour less leisure falls short of the utility gained through the output from an extra hour in home production. This is the case if, at D in Figure 9.1, the value of the marginal productivity in home production ($ZF_H(0)$) exceeds the individual's shadow wage, $W^* = U_L/U_X$. Furthermore, for a participant in home production, utility can be gained through increasing hours in home production up to Q in Figure 9.1. At Q the value of the marginal productivity equals the shadow wage. Hence, for a participant in home production we have the first-order condition:

$$\frac{U_L(V + W\bar{N} + ZF(H), T - \bar{N} - H)}{U_X(V + W\bar{N} + ZF(H), T - \bar{N} - H)} = ZF_H(H). \tag{2}$$

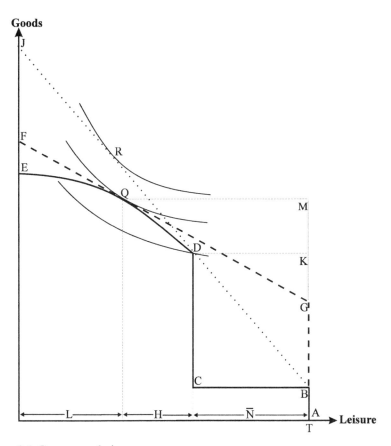

Figure 9.1 Consumer choice.

This yields the conditional supply function for hours worked in home production:

$$H = f(\hat{W}, \hat{V}) - \bar{N}, \tag{3}$$

where $\hat{W} = ZF_H(H)$ is the value of the marginal productivity in home production, which is equivalent to the concept of a "virtual wage rate" used in the following. In Figure 9.1, the virtual wage corresponds to the slope of the linearized budget constraint GQF supporting the optimum at Q. $\hat{V}$ in equation (3) is "virtual non-earned income," which equals the distance AG in Figure 9.1. Virtual income equals total income minus the income that the individual would have earned if working $(\bar{N} + H)$ hours at the virtual wage rate. Mathematically, $\hat{V} = V + (\bar{W} - \hat{W})H + (W - \hat{W})\bar{N}$, where $\bar{W} = ZF(H)/H$ is the average "wage rate" in home production.[3] Killingsworth (1983: 88–91) discusses the use of virtual concepts, which have the great advantage that the conditional supply function can be written on the simple structural form given by equation (3), where $f(\hat{W}, \hat{V})$ is the (total) labour supply function, conditional on holding a full-time formal sector job. Since $\hat{W}$ and $\hat{V}$ generally are functions of H, equation (3) gives the supply of labour to home production only on implicit form. This complication is handled in section 3 by imposing additional restrictions on the home production function.

Figure 9.1 illustrates only one of the cases that may occur: a worker who is "under-employed" in the formal sector. Since the virtual wage at the optimum (Q) falls short of the formal sector wage, the worker would have preferred to work more than $\bar{N}$ hours in the formal sector, and to reduce hours in home production. Due to the restriction on $\bar{N}$ this is not possible. Hence, the individual is under-employed in the formal sector.

A case with "over-employment" in the formal sector occurs if $F(H)$ is strongly concave. The individual may then want to work only a few hours in home production, and combine this with a formal sector job—in order to obtain a desired volume of goods. The utility of such an individual could be increased by reducing the number of hours worked in the formal sector, and expanding hours in home production, but the restriction on $\bar{N}$ precludes such a reallocation. Hence, the individual is in effect overemployed in the formal sector. In Section 4 we examine empirically over-employment and underemployment in the formal sector job.

The model can be extended to a multiperson household. Since the available data preclude exploiting the finer structure of a multiperson model, we do not pursue such a strategy. Consequently, we include incomes earned by household members other than the one in focus in the exogenous non-earned income variable, and hours devoted to home production by household members other than the one we focus on are taken as exogenously given. Other multiple-job-holding papers, such as Shiskho and Rostker (1976) and Conway and Kimmel (1998), tacitly follow a similar strategy.

Theisen (2005a, Appendix A) shows how the model can be extended to multiple goods. In such a model, home production of some goods may exceed consumption, so that there will be a surplus to sell on the market. The individual is then in effect part-time self-employed. Home production and self-employment are, however, distinguished only by whether $X_H^i < X^i$ or $X_H^i > X^i$, where i indexes goods. The individual may also engage in part-time employment in a second (informal) job. Under assumptions stated in Theisen (2005a), there is, however, no need to distinguish between home production, part-time self-employment, and part-time employment as an informal sector worker. Consequently, the real value of wage income earned in an informal sector job may be aggregated with output from home production and self-employment to an aggregate good. Hence, in the following we use the general term informal production rather than home production, and proceed as if the individual participates in informal production of a single aggregate good. This facilitates substantially the econometric analysis.

3 Econometric model

We parametrize the r.h.s. of the participation condition by assuming that informal production is proportional to hours allocated to such production ($X_H = ZH$), implying that the virtual and average wage rates in the informal sector coincide. This may seem restrictive, but it is in line with the vast majority of labour supply and multiple-job-holding studies.[4]

In parametrizing the l.h.s of the participation condition we start from:

$$U(X, H + \bar{N}; R, \varepsilon) = \left(\frac{\omega_{\hat{V}}(H + \bar{N}) - \omega_{\hat{W}}}{(\omega_{\hat{V}})^2} \right)$$

$$\exp \left\{ \frac{\omega_{\hat{V}}(\omega_0 + \omega_{\hat{V}} X + \omega'_R R + \varepsilon) - \omega_{\hat{W}}}{\omega_{\hat{V}}(H + \bar{N}) - \omega_{\hat{W}}} \right\}, \qquad (4)$$

where the ω_i's ($i = 0, \hat{W}, \hat{V}$) are parameters, and ω'_R is a row vector of parameters. The stochastic term, ε, can be interpreted as a taste shifter known to the individual worker, but unknown to the researcher. R is a column vector of taste shifters known not only to the individual worker, but also to the researcher. For further discussion, see Pencavel (1986).

Our parametrizations lead to the participation condition:

$$\omega_0 + \omega_{\hat{V}} \hat{V}^k + \omega_{\hat{W}} \hat{W}^k + \omega'_R R^k - \bar{N}^k + \varepsilon^k$$

$$\begin{cases} \leq 0 & \Rightarrow \quad \text{Non- participation} \\ > 0 & \Rightarrow \quad \text{Participation} \end{cases} \qquad (k = 1, \ldots, K), \qquad (5)$$

where k indexes individuals. For a non-participant in informal production, the l.h.s. of condition (5) is negative, and can be interpreted as the latent supply (H^k_*) of hours to informal production. For a participant in informal production, the l.h.s. of condition (5) is positive, and gives the actual (= latent) hours supplied to informal production. Hence, we obtain the conditional latent informal labour supply function:

$$H^k_* = \omega_0 + \omega_{\hat{V}} \hat{V}^k + \omega_{\hat{W}} \hat{W}^k + \omega'_R R^k - \bar{N}^k + \varepsilon^k \qquad (k = 1, \ldots, K), \qquad (6)$$

where the dependent variable appears only on the l.h.s., while it appeared on both sides of equation (3).

Next, define the indicator, $\tilde{H}^k_*$, equal to 1 if an individual participates in informal production, equal to 0 in case of non-participation. This yields the participation model:

$$\tilde{H}^k_* = \begin{cases} 0 \text{ if } H^k_* \leq 0 \\ 1 \text{ if } H^k_* > 0 \end{cases} \qquad (k = 1, \ldots, K), \qquad (7)$$

with H_*^k given by equation (6). Assuming a logistically distributed error-term (ε^k), relationship (7) together with (6) constitutes a logit model.

With data on the virtual wage rate and human capital variables, one could use the sub-sample of those working in the informal sector for estimating a virtual wage equation, which in turn could be used to predict the virtual wages for all individuals. Such a procedure was pursued by Shishko and Rostker (1976), and has become standard in multiple-job-holding studies based on data from developed economies. In multiple-job-holding studies conducted on data from developing countries, researchers have typically not had access to virtual wage data. Hence, Glick (1999), Jolliffe (2004), and Theisen (2005a) all relied on reduced-form approaches. This methodological difference reflects the greater difficulties in measuring the virtual wage rate in developing countries than in developed countries. These measurement problems are related to the fact that individuals in developing countries often hold several informal jobs simultaneously, switch back and forth between informal activities over time, and are heavily engaged in home production, for which the volume is hard to measure and the value is difficult to impute. Such complications led Deaton (1997: 29–30) to a sceptical view on income measurement in developing countries. Similar complications arise in the measurement of informal sector working hours. Since the virtual wage usually is calculated as the ratio between the incomes earned and hours worked in the informal sector, these measurement problems imply that virtual wage data often are unavailable. These measurement problems are also the main reason why we carry out a participation study rather than estimating an informal labor supply function.

A reduced-form approach provides a possible solution to the problem of a non-observable virtual wage. Theisen (2005a) demonstrates that it gives consistent estimates, but only under restrictions that are unlikely to be completely fulfilled. Hence, we pursue here an approach based on the structural form of the participation function, taking as the starting point that wages can be modelled by sector-specific Mincer-type earnings functions:

$$Ln\hat{W}_j^k = \eta_j + \sigma_j'S^k + e_j^k \qquad (j = -2, -1, 0, 1, 2; k = 1, \ldots, K), \qquad (8)$$

where j indexes sector of employment ($j = -2$ for home production, $j = -1$ for the (monetary) informal sector, $j = 0$ for the private formal sector, $j = 1$ for the parastatal sector, and $j = 2$ for the public sector). $Ln\hat{W}_j^k$ is the natural logarithm of the hourly wage that can be earned by individual k in sector j, the η_j's are constant terms, the σ_j''s are row vectors of parameters, S^k is a column vector of explanatory variables, and the e_j^k's are stochastic error terms.

When data on the virtual wage are unavailable, it is impossible to estimate the informal sector earnings function directly. The informal sector is, however, a sub-sector of the private sphere of the economy, encompassing three sub-sectors: (a) the private formal sector, (b) the (monetary) informal sector, and (c) the (non-monetary) home production sector. If workers flow freely between the formal and informal parts of the private sector, it can be argued that competition between workers about jobs, and between employers about workers will tend towards an equilibrium where an individual with a given set of characteristics earns an (untaxed) "wage rate" in the informal (private) sector that is (approximately) equal to the after-tax wage he or she could earn in the formal private sector. If this wage-equalization process works smoothly, earnings functions in the formal and the informal parts of the private sector will tend to be similar. Hence, we assume: $(\eta_{-2}, \sigma'_{-2}) = (\eta_{-1}, \sigma'_{-1}) = (\eta_0, \sigma'_0)$. Gindling (1991) found empirical evidence that the last equality may hold as an approximation, but the results of Funkhauser (1996) for Central America imply 15–20% lower returns to schooling in the informal than in the formal sector. The assumption of wage-equalization can also be seen as an extension of the result that a common virtual wage rate applies in all sub-sectors of informal production, cf. Theisen (2005a). In terms of Figure 9.1 our assumption implies that workers in the private part of the formal sector face a budget constraint ABCDJ. For workers in the government or parastatal sectors, however, the budget constraint may look very different. We return to the implications of this in section 5.

One complication remains: since the parameters (η_0, σ'_0) of equation (8) must be estimated from the sub-sample of workers holding a job in the formal private sector, OLS is likely to lead to sample selection bias. Lee (1983) demonstrated that this problem can be solved through a two-step procedure, which was applied inter alia by Trost and Lee (1984) and Lassibille and Tan (2004). In the first step, the allocation of workers to sectors of formal employment is modeled. With three sectors of formal employment, the following multinomial logit model is used:

$$P_j = \frac{\exp(a'_j Y)}{1 + \sum_{j=1,2} \exp(a'_j Y)} \qquad (j = 1, 2), \qquad (9)$$

where P_j denotes the probability that a worker is allocated to sector j ($j = 1, 2$) rather than to sector 0, Y is a vector of covariates, and the coefficient vector for the private sector, a_0, is normalized to zero; cf. Green (2000).

The estimation results for the multinomial logit model are used to generate the following selection term for the private sector earnings function:

$$\hat{\lambda} = \varphi[J(\hat{a}'_j Y_j)]/F(\hat{a}'_j Y_j), \qquad (10)$$

where φ is the standard normal density function, F is the logistic marginal distribution, and J equals $\Phi^{-1}F$, where Φ is the cumulative distribution function of the standard normal distribution.

In the second stage we include the selection term defined in equation (10) in the earnings function. Hence, omitting sector indexes, we obtain the earnings function:

$$Ln\hat{W}^k = \eta + \sigma' S^k + \tau \lambda^k + \tilde{e}^k \qquad (k = 1, \ldots, K), \qquad (11)$$

where τ is an unknown parameter to be estimated, and $\tilde{e}^k$ is an error-term. The relationship between the error terms of equations (8) and (11) are given by $E(e_0^k|\text{Sectoral choice}) = \tau \lambda^k + \tilde{e}^k$. Application of ordinary least squares to equation (11) will give consistent estimates of all parameters in the earnings function, and allows us to test for the presence of sample selection.

Our econometric approach can be summarized as follows: first, we employ a multinomial logit model for the allocation of workers to their formal sector of employment. Second, we estimate an earnings function from the sub-sample of workers in the private formal sector, as well with as without a selection term, and test for sample selection. Third, we use the estimated private sector earnings function to predict the virtual wage for all individuals. The predicted virtual wages are used for calculating virtual non-earned income. Fourth, we estimate the logit model given by relationships (7) and (6).

From the presumption that leisure is a non-inferior good, it follows that the virtual income parameter ($\omega_{\hat{V}}$) will take a negative sign. The parameter $\omega_{\hat{W}}$, which captures the uncompensated wage effect, cannot be signed from the above assumptions. Finally, the coefficient affiliated with formal sector working time is expected to be -1.

4 Data collection, descriptive analysis, and assessment of modeling assumptions

Data were collected in three steps. First, five towns (Dar es Salaam, Dodoma, Iringa, Morogoro, Mzumbe) were chosen as places to conduct interviews. Second, 45 formal sector organizations were selected. Finally, workers to be interviewed were selected within each organization. At the last stage, managers were asked to assist in selecting workers randomly within their organization. In order to avoid strategic selection by the manager, workers were selected "on-the-spot," after enumerators had arrived at the workplace. This resulted in a sample of 261. Because of non-response to questions concerning participation in informal production, the analyses in the following are, however, based on a sample of 247.

The sample contains only workers holding a formal sector job. Such a sample delimitation is natural, since our focus is on whether workers are multiple-job-holders. Restricting the sample as just described is in line with Shisko and Rostker (1976) and Conway and Kimmel (1998), and it enables us to address multiple-job-holding with a sample of modest size.

Formal sector workers were asked about their participation in home production for own consumption, and in income-generating informal production. Data on home production cover six important goods (maize, rice, fruit, vegetables, eggs, milk). Data on participation in income generating informal production cover agricultural commodities for sale, catering, working as craftsmen, etc. Some ways of earning monetary incomes are in effect informal part-time self-employment (agriculture), which is distinguished from home production mainly by the scale of the activity and by the fact that output is sold in the market. Other informal ways of earning monetary incomes (private teaching) come very close to holding a second job as a part-time wage earner. A complete list of informal income-generating activities is provided in Theisen (2005a).

The sample of size 247 contains 157 participants (64%) in informal production and 90 non-participants (36%). Of the 157 participants 145 took part in home production, and 59 in income generating informal production. Of the 59 participants in income-generating informal production 47 participated also in home production. These observations demonstrate the importance of multiple sources of income and consumption goods in the livelihood strategies of Tanzanian households.

Participation rates were 66% for men but 58% for women. Among women with children below school age the participation rate was 49%, while it was 73% for women without small children. Among public sector workers 72% participated in informal production, compared to 58% in the parastatal sector and 63% in the private sector. Finally, while only 43% of formal sector workers in Dar es Salaam participated in informal production, the corresponding number for the other (smaller) towns was 72%. Consequently, livelihood strategies differ substantially with the size of the urban area.

Among home production participants, 88 persons (61%) produced only one good, 32 (22%) produced two, 19 (13%) three, 10 (7%) four, but nobody produced more than four of the six goods examined. These observations of multiple goods production are in accordance with the arguments that Tanzanians in their livelihood strategies often rely on a multitude of income sources. In the theoretical model, by contrast, proportional informal production functions implied that each individual in optimum either would participate in only one form of informal production, or not participate at all. If stochastic elements are added to the model, however, participation in multiple forms of informal production may occur.

Answers to open-ended questions revealed that formal sector workers of almost all kinds participated in home production. In income-generating informal production, however, there seems to be a distinct pattern of specialization: skilled blue-collar male workers holding formal sector jobs as mechanics, carpenters, etc. usually carried out the same type of work in the informal sector. Workers in formal sector administrative positions were often engaged in informal trade, or in large-scale agricultural production, such as running a farm. Unskilled female workers earned extra by doing laundry, selling ice cream, selling pancakes, and other activities similar to household work. In summary, these observations indicate that formal sector workers who earned monetary incomes informally usually participated in activities where they have a comparative advantage.

In order to examine the relative importance of underemployment and overemployment in the main job, respondents were asked if they would like to work overtime in their formal sector job. Of the 197 who responded to this question (with a clear yes or no), 176 (90%) answered the question in the affirmative, indicating that the vast majority participated in informal production because of underemployment in their formal sector jobs. Hence, we disregard the possibility—emphasized by Conway and Kimmel (1998)—that individuals may participate in informal production because they find less displeasure by working in the informal than in the formal sector.

Table 9.1 provides definitions and descriptive statistics for variables in the participation functions. There is limited variation in formal sector working hours. The impact coefficient of this variable may therefore be hard to identify with our data. We return to this in section 6.

Table 9.1 Definitions and descriptive statistics of variables in the participation functions

Variable	Definition	Mean	Std dev.
Informal work	Binary variable equal to 1 if respondent participates in some form of informal production, otherwise 0	0.6356	0.4822
Virtual income	Total household expenditures minus monetary incomes earned by the respondent through informal work minus the income the respondent would have earned by working the hours actually worked in the formal sector at the virtual wage rate. Measured on a monthly basis in 1,000 Tanzanian shillings, 1991	10.1308	17.8486
Virtual wage rate	The wage rate that the respondent is predicted to earn if working in the private sector. Tanzanian shillings, 1991	9.2104	5.2056
Age	Age of respondent, measured in years	35.1336	8.0770
Size	Number of persons in the respondent's household	3.7652	2.4581
Female	1 if respondent is female, 0 if male	0.2713	0.4455
Mother	1 if respondent is female and has children below 7 years of age, 0 if not	0.1660	0.3728
School-aged	Number of children in respondent's household between 7 and 15 years of age	1.0850	1.3453
Dar es Salaam	1 if respondent lives in Dar es Salaam, 0 if not	0.3077	0.4625
Hours	Hours worked per day in the formal sector	8.0121	0.4640
Public	1 if respondent holds a full-time job in the public sector, 0 if not	0.3482	0.4774
Parastatal	1 if respondent holds a full-time job in the parastatal sector, 0 if not	0.4170	0.4941

5 Predicting the virtual wage rate

The first step in predicting the virtual wage rate amounts to estimating the parameters of the earnings function (11), using the sub-sample of private sector workers. Table 9.2 provides definitions and descriptive statistics of variables entering the earnings function, including the selection variable calculated from estimated parameters of the multinomial logit model, for which estimation results are shown in Appendix Table 9.A1.

The estimated function in Table 9.3 fits the data very well. The selection-term coefficient is insignificant at standard levels of statistical significance, indicating that there is no sample selection bias. Hence, we use the earnings function without the selection for predicting the virtual wage. Table 9.3 shows that all independent variables, except experience squared, have a statistically significant impact on earnings, and carry the signs usually found in earnings function studies. Hence, the estimated earnings function seems to provide a reasonably good basis for predicting the virtual wage.

Based on the assumption $(\eta_{-2}, \sigma'_{-2}) = (\eta_{-1}, \sigma'_{-1}) = (\eta_0, \sigma'_0)$ our proxy for the

Table 9.2 Definitions and descriptive statistics of variables in the earnings function. Sub-sample of formal private sector workers, $n = 58$

Variable	Definition	Mean	Std dev.
$Ln\hat{W}^k_p$	The natural logarithm of salary	1.8542	0.5570
Schooling	Years of formal schooling	8.3621	3.1992
Experience	Age minus years of formal schooling minus 7	18.4483	8.8460
Expsq	Experience squared divided by 100	4.1724	4.0736
Female	1 if respondent is female, otherwise zero	0.2241	0.4207
Dar es Salaam	1 if respondent lives in Dar es Salaam, otherwise zero	0.3276	0.4734
Lambda	λ calculated by means of equation (10)	0.3557	0.2209

Table 9.3 Estimation results for the earnings function*

Variable	Without selectivity correction		With selectivity correction	
	Coefficient	Standard error	Coefficient	Standard error
Constant	0.1441		−0.0570	
Schooling	0.1311***	(0.0161)	0.1364***	(0.0321)
Experience	0.0434*	(0.0222)	0.0439*	(0.0226)
Expsq	−0.0512	(0.0475)	−0.0511	(0.0480)
Female	−0.2441*	(0.1274)	−0.2337*	(0.1391)
Dar es Salaam	0.2517**	(0.1054)	0.2467**	(0.1094)
Lambda	—	—	0.0874	(0.4489)
	$R^2 = 0.6373$	$F(5,52) = 18.28$	$R^2 = 0.6376$	$F(6,51) = 14.95$

* Standard errors in parentheses. Significance at 10% level indicated by *, at 5% level by **, and at 1% level by ***.

virtual wage can be determined from the parameter estimates in Table 9.3 (without selectivity correction). For job-holders in the formal private sector, the predicted virtual wage deviates only randomly from their actual formal sector wage. The picture is very different for the 189 individuals holding a job in one of the two other formal sectors. For 80% of the public sector workers, and in particular for the more educated, the predicted virtual wage exceeded their formal sector wage. For parastatal sector workers the picture is more mixed: those at very low and very high formal sector wages earned higher wages in their formal sector job than their predicted virtual wage. These results, in particular for the public sector, are in line with the "compressed wage structure" observed by Knight and Sabot (1990) in the Government and parastatal sectors of Tanzania.

6 Empirical results

The three variants of the participation function (A, B, and C) reported in Table 9.4 all exhibit an acceptable fit (log-likelihood, Chi-square or McFadden's pseudo-R^2), and acceptable predictive properties (share of cases correctly predicted).[5]

In each of the estimated equations, the coefficients affiliated with five explanatory variables are significantly different from zero. The impact coefficients of Virtual income carry the predicted negative sign, and they are different from zero at standard levels of statistical significance. Living in the country's largest city reduces the probability of participating in informal sector activities, as implied by the strongly negative and statistically significant coefficient of the variable Dar es Salaam. The estimated coefficients of variables Female and Mother are statistically significant. The negative Mother-coefficient is in accordance with the findings of Glick (1999). The positive Female-coefficient must be interpreted in view of the fact that the share of women holding a formal sector job is rather small. The positive, and statistically significant, coefficient of the Age-variable implies that participation in informal production is an increasing function of Age. This is discussed in more detail below.

The positive, coefficient of the Hours-variable in column A of Table 9.4 needs to be noted, even if it is statistically insignificant. The theoretical model predicts this coefficient to be −1. In evaluating the estimation result it is, however, important to take into account that our data exhibit very little variation in formal sector working time. Hence, the Hours-variable comes close to being a second constant. The impact coefficient of such a variable is hard to identify. Consider, therefore, the results in column B from re-estimating the participation equation with the Hours-variable excluded. A pairwise comparison of coefficients in A versus B reveals that the impact coefficients of other variables change very little when the Hours-variable is left out, and the fit drops only negligibly. Taken together, these observations have led us to focus on the participation equation where the Hours' variable is

Table 9.4 Estimation results for structural-form logit model*

	A	B	C
Constant	−2.2494	−1.4221	−1.4199
	(2.9831)	(0.8117)	(0.8110)
Virtual income	−0.0290***	−0.0292***	−0.0290***
	(0.0062)	(0.0108)	(0.0106)
Virtual wage rate	−0.0026	−0.0032	–
	(0.0372)	(0.0372)	
Hours	0.0995	–	–
	(0.3453)		
Size	0.0675	0.0692	0.0692
	(0.0652)	(0.0650)	(0.0649)
Female	1.1540**	1.1614**	1.1711**
	(0.5591)	(0.5571)	(0.5455)
Mother	−1.4726**	−1.4919**	−1.4948**
	(0.6168)	(0.6122)	(0.6110)
School-aged	0.1162	0.1114	0.1120
	(0.1298)	(0.1289)	(0.1287)
Age	0.0629**	0.0629**	0.0621***
	(0.0252)	(0.0252)	(0.0234)
Dar es Salaam	−1.1987***	−1.2211***	−1.2256***
	(0.3470)	(0.3384)	(0.3343)
Public	0.3617	0.3500	0.3450
	(0.4215)	(0.4199)	(0.4159)
Parastatal	0.1055	0.0795	0.0685
	(0.4145)	(0.4049)	(0.3842)
Log-likelihood	−137.0322	−137.0739	−137.0776
Log-likelihood (Slopes = 0)	−162.0055	−162.0055	−162.0055
Chi-squared	49.94661	49.86304	49.85567
Pseudo R^2	0.1541	0.1539	0.1539
Correct predictions	0.7166	0.7206	0.7166
Sample size	247	247	247

* Standard errors in parentheses. Significance at 10% level indicated by *, at 5% level by **, and at 1% level by ***.

excluded. Notice, however, that the arguments for excluding the formal sector working-time variable from the participation equation are due only to properties of the data, reflecting properties of the Tanzanian formal sector labour market. From a theoretical point of view, there is no doubt that the Hours' variable belongs in the participation equation. In order to identify the impact of formal sector working hours on participation in informal production, however, a data set with much more variation in the Hours-variable is needed.

7 Discussion of the main results

The statistically significant income-coefficient carries the expected negative sign, implying that leisure is a normal good. Using the results in column B of

Table 9.4 to calculate the probability of participation in informal production for a man working in the private sector outside Dar es Salaam, with all children above 7 years, and with average age, family size, virtual income, and virtual wage, yields a participation probability of 0.673.

For a better grasp of the relationship between participation in informal production and income, the participation rate is in Figure 9.2 plotted as a function of virtual income, using the results in column B of Table 9.4. The same man referred to above (indicated by MEN in the figure) has a predicted participation probability of almost 0.8 if his virtual income is very low, but 0.35 if his income is at the high end of the income distribution. The income variations in Figure 9.2 are, however, large. An increase in virtual income from the average (approximately 10 in Figure 9.2) to twice the average results in only a few percentage points' drop in the participation probability. Hence, income has a clear impact on participation, but it takes a large increase in income to reduce drastically participation in informal production.

We have followed the normal practice of including socio-economic variables in the participation function. The correlation matrix *does not* indicate serious problems related to the taste shifters. Nevertheless, as a robustness check, the participation equation has been re-estimated with taste shifters left out, one or two at a time. Table 9.5 shows that this in most cases has little impact on the estimated Virtual-income coefficient. There is one exception, however:

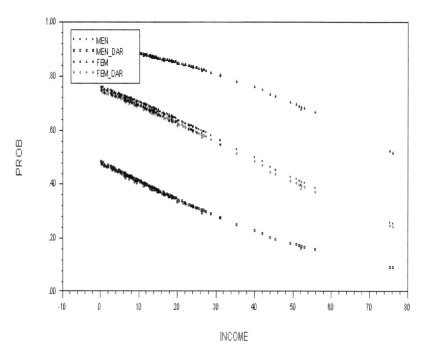

Figure 9.2 Probability of participation in the informal sector as a function of virtual income.

Table 9.5 Estimated income and wage coefficients when different (groups of) taste shifters are left out of the participation equation. Standard errors in parenthesis

	Virtual income	*Virtual wage rate*
Basic equation	−0.0292 (0.0108)	−0.0032 (0.0372)
Size	−0.0287 (0.0108)	−0.0035 (0.0372)
Female	−0.0283 (0.0106)	−0.0214 (0.0359)
Mother	−0.0310 (0.0108)	−0.0097 (0.0367)
School-aged	−0.0292 (0.0108)	−0.0050 (0.0371)
Age	−0.0269 (0.0107)	−0.0031 (0.0338)
Dar es Salaam	−0.0346 (0.0107)	−0.0246 (0.0360)
Sector dummies	−0.0285 (0.0105)	−0.0030 (0.0352)

leaving out Dar es Salaam gives an estimate of the Virtual income coefficient outside the 95% confidence interval of the estimate in the basic equation. The magnitude of the deviation between the estimated coefficient in the basic equation and the re-estimated equations is, however, in all cases less than 20% (except for the statistically insignificant coefficients of the virtual wage). Hence, the estimated impact parameters of economic variables are quite robust towards the specification of taste shifters.

From Table 9.3 we see that the virtual wage depends heavily on schooling. As mentioned in section 3 some researchers have found that the virtual wage rate in developing countries may fall short of the wage in the formal private sector by 10–20%. We therefore carried out a sensitivity analysis to assess whether our results would be substantially changed if the virtual wage is made less strongly dependent on schooling. Specifically, we assumed in the sensitivity analysis that the schooling parameter in the virtual wage function is 25% smaller than in Table 9.3, while all other parameters are unchanged. In a specification equal to that in column B of Table 9.4 this led to a negligible change (−0.0292 to −0.0294) in the Virtual income coefficient. Hence, we conclude that the inference drawn from our estimation results with respect to the impact of virtual income seems to be robust towards measurement errors in the virtual wage.

In order further to assess the robustness of our estimates, let us compare the results for Specification B in Table 9.4 with results obtained by Theisen (2005a) in estimating a reduced-form participation equation with a similar specification, and from the same data. The income parameter, $\omega_{\hat{v}}$, in the structural form model is identified also in the reduced form model, cf. Theisen (2005a). In the reduced form estimation, a probit model was used, and the income coefficient was estimated to −0.0168, with a standard deviation of 0.0062. However, as explained by Maddala (1983: 23) the probit coefficient has, due to differences in the variance of the logistic and normal distributions, to be multiplied by $\pi/\sqrt{3}$ in order to be made comparable to the logit coefficient. Multiplying −0.0168 by $\pi/\sqrt{3}$ gives a coefficient of −0.030, which is practically identical to our estimate of −0.029 in Specification B. This provides additional evidence that our estimate of the income coefficient is robust.

The statistically significant coefficient of the Age-variable carries a positive sign, implying that individuals are more likely to participate in informal production, the higher their age. This is in accordance with the results of Pradhan and van Soest (1995), and with interpreting age as a measure of human capital acquired through experience. We do not subscribe to this interpretation, which corresponds poorly with the weak correlation between education and participation in informal production in our sample. A more likely explanation may be that Tanzanians have strong incentives to engage in informal production as they approach retirement, because pensions are far from sufficient to cover the costs of living after retirement. This interpretation is supported by the observation that 43% of the individuals in the sample envisaged income from informal production as an important source of living after retirement, while only 31% envisaged pension incomes among the important sources of income after retirement. This in turn implies that there may be a relationship between the low level of retirement benefits and the size of the informal sector. Indeed, the fact that the increase in retirement benefits for many years had fallen short of inflation may partly explain the growth of the informal sector in Tanzania.

8 Conclusions

We have estimated structural-form functions explaining multiple-job-holding in the form of participation in informal production, in addition to holding a job in the formal sector. These participation functions complement the work of Gindling (1991), Pradhan and van Soest (1995), and Funkhauser (1996). While these papers focus on individuals' choice of primary sector of work, the focus in the present paper has been on multiple-job-holding in the form of informal sector participation, conditional on holding a job in the formal sector. The present paper also complements the reduced form multiple-job-holding studies of Glick (1999), Joliffe (2004), and Theisen (2005a). To my knowledge, structural form participation functions of multiple-job-holding in developing countries have not previously been estimated. Strong assumptions were needed to come around measurement problems. The way we solved these measurement problems is of interest in itself, and the results seem to be robust.

The empirical results show that leisure is a normal good. Consequently, we expect that formal-sector-workers who experience declining real wages in their main job may compensate partly by increasing their participation in informal production. This is in accordance with the view of Fields (1975) that the informal sector plays the role of a buffer sector. To some extent this may reduce the need for government interventions in order to alleviate poverty problems in periods of economic recession.

The estimation results show that living in Dar es Salaam and being the mother of a small child affect participation negatively, while female gender and high age have an opposite effect. Comparing these results with Shishko and Rostker (1976) and Conway and Kimmel (1998) provide interesting insights: first, income, gender, and presence of small children have a negative effect on labour supplied to a second job both in Tanzania and in the USA. On the other hand, while age affects Tanzanian formal-sector workers' participation in informal production positively, Shishko and Rostker (1976) and Conway and Kimmel (1998) found a strong negative effect of age on the probability of US workers holding a second job. These differences can most likely be attributed to differences in pension systems. Specifically, Tanzanians' participation in informal production may function as a "substitute" for a pension system. The same may be the case in many other developing countries. In developed countries such as the USA, by contrast, the negative impact of age on participation suggests that workers when they approach retirement first withdraw from their second job, then from their main job. These differences in the transition from a full-time formal sector job to retirement should be paid more attention to in future research.

Notes

* This paper derives from a collaborative project with the late Ram Jogi. I am indebted to Ram Jogi and Elia W. Mwakagali for their efforts in data collection. Otto Andersen, S. Quamrul Ahsan, Jonathan Baker, Kristin Dale, Magnus Hatlebakk, Jochen Jungeilges, and Ingrid Leiprecht are thanked for comments to earlier versions of the paper.

1 The concept of the informal sector is fairly well established. In brief, it is usually taken to include small-scale enterprises, largely operating without a business permit, without paying taxes, and without adhering to a number of other regulations; cf. Feige (1990). The informal sector is also economically important. Schneider and Enste (2002) estimate that 54% of the African labour-force hold a job in the informal sector.

2 See Deardorff and Stafford (1976) and Oswald and Walker (1993) for theoretical analysis of restrictions on working hours, and Biddle (1988) and Moffitt (1982) for empirical evidence.

3 From Figure 9.1, $\hat{V} = AG = AB + BK + KM - MG = V + W\overline{N} + ZF(H) - \hat{W}(\overline{N} + H) = V + (ZF(H) - \hat{W}H) + (W - \hat{W})\overline{N} = V + (ZF(H)/H - \hat{W})H + (W - \hat{W})\overline{N} = V + (\overline{W} - \hat{W})H + (W - \hat{W})\overline{N}$

4 The labour supply study of Moffitt (1984) is one of the few assuming an endogenous hourly wage. I am not aware of multiple-job-holding studies based on similar assumptions.

5 Theisen (2005b) obtained similar results for a specification where the ratio between virtual income and the virtual wage rate entered instead of the two variables separately.

References

Biddle, J. (1988) "Intertemporal Substitution and Constraints on Labour Supply." *The Review of Economics and Statistics* 70: 347–51.

Conway, K. S. and J. Kimmel (1998) "Male Labour Supply Estimates and the Decision to Moonlight." *Labour Economics* 5: 135–66.

Deardorff, A. V. and F. P. Stafford (1976) "Compensating and Cooperating Factors." *Econometrica* 44, 671–84.

Deaton, A. (1997) *The Analysis of Household Surveys. A Microeconometric Approach to Development Policy*, Baltimore, Maryland, USA: Johns Hopkins University Press.

Feige, E. L. (1990) "Defining and Estimating Underground and Informal Economies: The new institutional economics approach." *World Development* 18: 989–1002.

Fields, G. S. (1975) "Rural Urban Migration, Urban Unemployment and Underemployment, and Job-search Activity in LDCs." *Journal of Development Economics* 2: 165–87.

Funkhauser, E. (1996) "The Urban Informal Sector in Central America: Household Survey Evidence." *World Development* 24: 1737–51.

Gindling, T. H. (1991) "Labour Market Segmentation and the Determination of Wages in the Public, Private-formal, and Informal Sectors in San Jose, Costa Rica." *Economic Development and Cultural Change* 39, 585–606.

Glick, P. (1999) "Simultaneous Determination of Home Work and Market Work of Women in Urban West Africa." *Oxford Bulletin of Economics and Statistics* 61: 57–84.

Green, W. H. (2000) *Econometric Analysis*, fourth edition. Upper Saddle River, NJ: Prentice Hall.

Gronau, R. (1977) "Leisure, Home Production, and Work—the Theory of the Allocation of Time Revisited." *Journal of Political Economy* 85: 1099–1123.

Jolliffe, D. (2004) "The Impact of Education in Rural Ghana: Examining Household Labor Allocation and Returns On and Off the Farm." *Journal of Development Economics* 73: 287–314.

Killingsworth, M. R. (1983) *Labour Supply*. Cambridge: Cambridge University Press.

Knight, J. B. and R. H. Sabot (1990) *Education, Productivity, and Inequality: The East African Natural Experiment*. Oxford: Oxford University Press.

Lassibille, G. and J-P. Tan (2004) "The Returns to Education in Rwanda." *Journal of African Economies* 14: 92–116.

Lee, L-F. (1983) "Generalized Econometric Models with Selectivity." *Econometrica* 51: 507–12.

Leibbrandt, M., C. Woolard, and I. Woolard (2000) "The Contribution of Income Components to Income Inequality in the Rural Former Homelands of South Africa: A decomposable Gini analysis." *Journal of African Economics* 9, 79–99.

Maddala, G. S. (1983) *Limited-dependent and Qualitative Variables in Econometrics*. Cambridge, New York: Cambridge University Press.

Moffitt, R. (1982) "The Tobit Model, Hours of Work and Institutional Constraints." *Review of Economics and Statistics* 64, 510–15.

——. (1984) "The Estimation of a Joint Wage-Hours Labor Supply Model." *Journal of Labour Economics* 2: 550–66.

Oswald, A. and I. Walker (1993) "Labour Supply, Contract Theory and Unions." IFS working paper W93/21, London.

Pencavel, J. (1986) "Labour Supply of Men: A Survey." In *Handbook of Labor Economics*, edited by, O. Ashenfelter and D. Layard. Amsterdam: North-Holland, 1: 3–102.

Pradhan, M. and A. van Soest (1995) "Formal and Informal Sector Employment in Urban Areas of Bolivia." *Labour Economics* 2: 275–97.

Reardon, T. (1997) "Using Evidence of Household Income Diversification to Inform Study of the Rural Nonfarm Labor Market in Africa." *World Development* 25: 735–47.

Schneider, F. and D. H. Enste (2002) *The Shadow Economy: An International Survey.* Cambridge: Cambridge University Press.

Shishko, R. and B. Rostker (1976) "The Economics of Multiple Job Holding." *American Economic Review* 66: 298–308.

Theisen, T. (2005a) "Tanzanian Formal Sector Worker's Participation in Informal Production." *Applied Economics* 37: 2469–85.

—— . (2005b) "Multiple-job-holding in Africa: The case of Tanzania." Working paper 2005: 3, Agder University College: Department of Economics and Business Administration, School of Management.

Trost, R. P. and L-F. Lee (1984) "Technical Training and Earnings: a Polychotomous Choice Model with Selectivity." *The Review of Economics and Statistics* 66: 151–6.

Appendix

The covariates in the multinomial logit model for the allocation of workers to sectors of formal employment are show in Table 9.A1, along with descriptive statistics.

The dependent variable in the multinomial logit model is an integer equal to 0 if the respondent is employed in the private sector, 1 if employed in the parastatal sector, and 2 if employed in the public sector. Estimation results are shown in Table 9.A2. A likelihood ratio test refutes the null hypothesis

Table 9.A1 Sample means by sector for correlates in the multinomial logit model for sector allocation of workers. Sample standard deviations of continuous variables in parentheses

| Covariates | Sub-sectors | | | |
	Private sector N = 58	Parastatal sector N = 103	Public sector N = 86	All sectors N = 247
Secondary*	0.1724	0.2427	0.3372	0.2591
University**	0.1034	0.3786	0.2326	0.2632
Age	33.8103	35.5631	35.5116	35.1336
	(8.6277)	(7.7582)	(8.0684)	(8.0770)
Female	0.2241	0.2621	0.3140	0.2713
Small children	0.6552	0.6796	0.6512	0.6640
Married***	0.7241	0.6990	0.7442	0.7206
Dar Es Salaam	0.3276	0.4563	0.1163	0.3077

* Secondary is a dummy variable equal to 1 if the respondent's highest level of education is lower or upper secondary school, 0 if not.

** University is a dummy variable equal to 1 if the respondent's highest level of education is a university degree, 0 if not.

*** Married is a dummy variable equal to 1 if the respondent is married, 0 if not.

Table 9.A2 Estimation results for multinomial logit model*

	Parastatal sector		Public sector	
	Coefficient	*Std dev.*	*Coefficient*	*Std dev.*
Constant	−1.3104		−0.9639	
Secondary	0.9152**	0.4390	1.1216**	0.4425
University	2.0313***	0.5030	1.2649**	0.5532
Age	0.0258	0.0237	0.0299	0.0256
Female	0.5386	0.4303	0.7922*	0.4289
Small children	0.1831	0.4359	−0.2234	0.4049
Married	−0.2640	0.5040	0.0542	0.4696
Dar Es Salaam	0.6840*	0.3598	−1.3290***	0.4766
Log-likelihood		−234.6481		
Log-likelihood (Slopes = 0)		−264.8623		
Chi.-Sq.		60.4284		
Pseudo R²		0.1586		
Percentage of correct predictions		53.0364		

* Standard errors in parentheses. Significance at 10% level indicated by *, at 5% level by **, and at 1% level by ***.

that the covariates have no impact on the allocation of workers to formal sectors of employment. Notice in particular that the education coefficients are positive and statistically significant at conventional levels of significance, indicating a strong tendency for educated individuals to be allocated to the parastatal or the public sector.

10 Regulation of entry, informality, and policy complementarities

Mariano Bosch

1 Introduction

Easy access to legal firm registration has been identified as one of the major determinants of the existence of informality. In his influential book, "The Other Path," de Soto (1989) argues that informality is the rational response of agents to the inefficiencies and high entry costs in the formal sector. A major worldwide data collection effort is being made at the World Bank Doing Business project to measure and monitor the evolution of a number of indicators on the barriers to legally operate a business. These new data have shown tremendous differences in the ease of starting businesses across the globe. The bureaucratic costs of establishing a firm in a OECD country average around 5% of gross national income (GNI); in sub-Saharian Africa it is around 150%. It is well known that the excessive red tape in developing economies leads to an oversized unofficial or informal economy. Djankov et al. (2002) argue that a 1% increase in start-up costs increase the level of informality by 6.5%. Furthermore, policy is being shifted towards a lower regulation of entry environment. According to the Doing Business website, between April 2006 and June 2007, 98 countries undertook reforms towards a less regulated environment. Some of those reforms are already being evaluated. In Mexico a municipality-level reform reducing drastically the time and expenses needed to open a firm (SARE) has proven to be successful in fostering the registration of new formal firms (see Kaplan, Piedra, and Seira 2006, and Bruhn 2006).

There is much literature detailing how regulation can drive firms into the unofficial economy, where they can avoid some or all of these regulations. See, for example, Johnson, Kaufmann, and Zoido-Lobaton (1997) and Friedman et al. (1999). On the theoretical front, there are numerous papers dealing with the impact of policy regulations in labor markets with informal jobs.[1]

Similarly, a new generation of models has analyzed labor markets in developing countries under search frictions.[2] However, these new sets of models have paid little attention to the impact of start-up costs in developing economies and the effect that search frictions may have in propagating policy effects.[3]

This paper presents a search and matching model that analyzes the possible effects of regulation of entry in an economy with informal jobs. The model builds on an occupational choice framework. Agents are heterogeneous in their managerial ability. Depending on their competence as managers, agents decide what occupation they pursue. They have three choices. They can become formal managers, informal managers, or workers in search of a job. Those entrepreneurs who decide to open formal firms have to pay an initial start-up cost. This brings about two advantages over informal entrepreneurs. First, they benefit from higher productivity workers, and, second, they can manage bigger firms. Finally, workers direct their search towards one of the two sectors, the returns to search in each sector thus equalizing.

In this framework, the effects of start-up costs operate through two channels. First, from the firms' point of view, an increase in the burden of regulation forces some entrepreneurs to establish informal firms. Formal firms are then replaced by informal firms. As a result, the number of potential jobs in the economy decreases, because informal firms are relatively smaller. Because of search frictions, this triggers a second effect. More agents choose to be informal entrepreneurs instead of firm workers because the returns to search are too low due to the scarcity of jobs. Overall, both effects increase the size of the informal sector; however, while substitution of formal firms by informal firms results in a net destruction of jobs, the expansion of the informal sector creates new jobs. The interaction of those forces will determine the overall effect on the unemployment rate. This gives rise to the scope of policy complementarities (see Orszag and Snower 1997, 1999) where the impact of one particular policy may have different effects, depending on whether or not other policies are put into place. I argue that to increase start-up costs raises unemployment if, in the face of steeper regulations, the expansion of the informal sector is small. This occurs when unemployment benefits are relatively high or the monitoring of the labor market is low.

This paper borrows from Fonseca, Lopez-Garcia, and Pissarides (2001) and Pissarides (2003), who analyze the impact of start-up costs in developed economies where compliance is full. They argue that higher start-up costs lead to less entrepreneurship, less job creation, and more unemployment. This paper shows that allowing for informal firms that do not comply with regulations, the implications of higher start-up costs are radically different from those in developed countries. Higher start-up costs will indeed reduce the number of formal entrepreneurs, but informal entrepreneurs will take their place. Net, a larger proportion of agents will become entrepreneurs. This is consistent with the oversized microfirm sector often common in developing economies. Moreover, the overall impact of start-up costs on unemployment is ambiguous, since formal jobs are being destroyed but informal entrepreneurship is fostered. It is this ambiguity that gives rise to policy complementarities in this context.

The remainder of the paper is as follows. Section 2 presents the model,

Section 3 studies the comparative statics of the model, Section 4 illustrates the range of policy complementaries. Section 5 concludes.

2 Concepts and notation

This model focuses on the entrepreneurial decision of the agents to justify the existence of the informal sector. I assume an economy consisting of a continuum of infinitely lived individuals in the unit interval. Agents in this economy choose their occupation among three different possible options. Agents may become formal entrepreneurs, informal entrepreneurs, or workers in search of a job offered by the entrepreneurs (both formal and informal). An entrepreneur (formal or informal) can manage several jobs at the same time, but workers can only occupy one job at any moment in time.

Agents in the economy are identical except in their managerial ability, which is the only source of heterogeneity in this model. There is a distribution of managerial ability with c.d.f. $F(a)$, which is continuous in the interval $[0,a_0]$. a_0 being the best manager in the economy. Hence, agents can be identified by their managerial ability a. The choice between the two kinds of entrepreneurship and becoming a worker is made by the agent attending to the present discounted value (PDV) of each of the options. If agent a opens a formal firm he would post a jobs with productivity p_f and has to bear some start-up costs k, which account for the loss of wealth he has to undertake in order legally to set up a formal firm. If agent a chooses to be an informal entrepreneur, he avoids the start-up costs but only posts δa jobs ($\delta < 1$) and enjoys lower productivity workers $p_i < p_f$. Finally, the individual can become a worker and obtain U.

There are a number of ways one can justify the productivity gap between formal and informal workers. De Soto (1989) argues that the threat of confiscation makes informal investors reduce their investments in capital. On the other hand, formal entrepreneurs face taxes and have social security contributions to fulfill when they hire workers, which generates incentives to pursue more capital-intensive technologies than their informal counterparts. The parameter $\delta < 1$, however, embodies the idea that for the same managerial ability informal entrepreneurs would open a lower quantity of vacancies. There are mainly two arguments that justify the introduction of this parameter. First, there is a visibility argument. Informal firms would try to conceal their existence to government officials as much as possible in order to avoid penalties. Second, informal labor markets cannot enforce contracts. Therefore, the cost for an informal entrepreneur of managing jobs is bound to be greater than in the formal sector.[4] Overall δ captures, somehow, the level of tolerance that a society has to the informal sector. I will refer to δ as a "monitoring" parameter. The higher the δ, the lower the monitoring activities by the government and the easier it is to become informal.

At any given time formal entrepreneurs post $n_f + v_f$ jobs, of which n_f are occupied and v_f are vacant. Similarly for informal firms there would be n_i

occupied jobs and v_i vacant jobs. Occupied jobs in formal and informal firms produce a constant output of p_f and p_i ($p_i < p_f$) respectively. When a negative shock arrives, jobs are destroyed immediately and the agent becomes unemployed, whereas entrepreneurs post new vacancies to replace those jobs. Wages in both sectors are established by a Nash bargaining solution, which implies sharing the surplus of the match according to the bargaining power of each of the parties. I assume that workers have information about the state of both the formal and the informal labor markets so that they can direct their search towards one or the other. This assumption gives rise to two different market tightness parameters, $\theta_f = (v_f/u_f)$ and $\theta_i = (v_i/u_i)$, which fully characterize the arrival rate of workers to jobs given by $q(\theta_k)$, $k = f,i$ and the arrival of jobs to workers given by $\theta_k q(\theta_k)$, $k = f,i$. where $q(\theta_k)$ satisfies the following conditions,

$$\lim_{\theta_k \to 0} \theta_k q(\theta_k) = \lim_{\theta_k \to \infty} q(\theta_k) = 0, k = f,i \tag{1}$$

$$\lim_{\theta_k \to 0} q(\theta_k) = \lim_{\theta_k \to \infty} \theta_k q(\theta_k) = \infty, k = f,i$$

The entrepreneurial decision

Agents in this economy decide between three different outcomes: become a formal manager, become an informal manager, or enter the labor force in search of a job. In order to make that decision, agents in the economy look at their expected payoff in the three different states.

Let V_f and V_i be the PDV of opening a vacancy in the formal sector and the informal sectors respectively. Similarly, U corresponds to the PDV of unemployment. The PDV of unemployment or vacancies does not depend on managerial ability a. The expected payoffs for agents with managerial ability a of the three options are $aV_f - k$, $\delta a V_i$, and U for formal entrepreneurship, informal entrepreneurship and joining the pool of workers, respectively.

Given those payoffs, I can define two managerial ability thresholds. First, there is one managerial ability that makes the agent indifferent to whether a formal firm or an informal firm is opened. Second, there is one managerial ability that makes the agent indifferent to whether s/he becomes a worker or opens a firm (formal or informal). I start with the former.

I define managerial skill I that leaves the agent indifferent to whether opening a formal firm enjoying high productivity workers with the start-up costs (k) or opening an informal firm and hiring less productive workers:

$$IV_f - k = I\delta V_i \tag{2}$$

$$I = \frac{k}{V_f - \delta V_i}$$

Expression (2) simply states that the income flow from the *I* formal jobs have to cover the entry costs (*k*) and the manager's loss of expected returns from opening δI in the informal sector.

Similarly, I can define the threshold managerial skill *R* that leaves the agent indifferent as to opening a firm (formal or informal) or becoming a worker,

$$\delta RV_i \quad = U, \text{ in the case of an informal firm} \tag{3}$$

$$RV_f - k = U, \text{ in the case of a formal firm}$$

This decision framework gives rise to three different scenarios, which I plot in Figures 10.1, 10.2, and 10.3. This set of figures plots the managerial ability of the agent (*a*) in the horizontal axis and the PDV of the three different options the agents have, give an overall level of market tightness in each sector. Obviously, the agent chooses the occupation that returns a higher PDV for his level of managerial ability. In this locus, the PDV of being unemployed is a horizontal line as it is independent of the managerial ability of the worker. The PDV for being a formal or informal entrepreneur is a linear and increasing function of *a*. The better the manager (higher *a*), the more jobs the entrepreneur will open. However, in order to become formal, entrepreneurial agents have to pay *k*. As formal jobs are more productive than informal jobs, the formal entrepreneur path is steeper and one crosses the informal entrepreneur PDV line only once, which will determine the marginal agent given by equation (2). Similarly, both lines will only once cross the

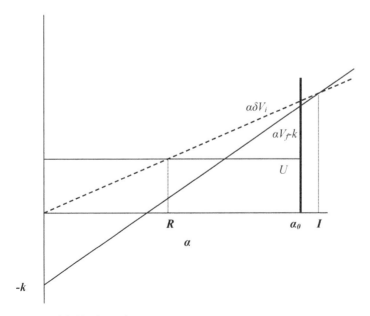

Figure 10.1 No formal sector.

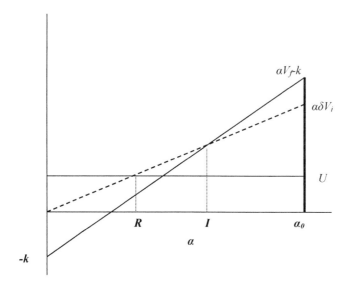

Figure 10.2 Formal and informal sectors.

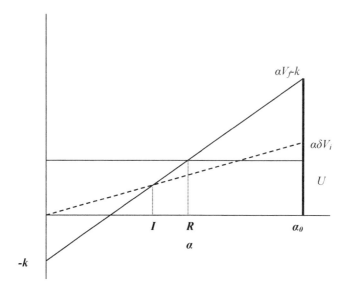

Figure 10.3 No informal sector.

unemployment line. The choice of the agent between the three possible out-comes is given by the upper frontier formed by the U, $aV_f - k$ and δaV_i lines.

Figure 10.1 depicts a scenario where $I > a_o$. This means that the threshold between formal and informal entrepreneurship is to the right of the most skilled manager. In other words, not even the best manager in the economy would like to be formal. Therefore, all the firms in this economy will establish themselves as informal firms. Then, the threshold managerial ability between becoming a worker or an entrepreneur (R) is given by the equality between the unemployment and the informal entrepreneurship lines. There would be $1-F(R)$ informal managers and $F(R)$ informal workers.

Figure 10.2 plots the scenario in which $I < a_o$ and $IV_f - k = \delta IV_i > U$. Thus, some firms will be opened formally as for agents $1-F(I)$ that is the best available option. Similarly, as $\delta IV_i > U$, there is a managerial ability range in which agents choose to be informal entrepreneurs up to the point where they would rather be workers (crossing the point between the informal entre-preneurship and the unemployment lines). This determines the threshold managerial ability that makes the agent indifferent as to being an entre-preneur, in this case informal, and being a worker. This economy would consist of $1-F(I)$ formal entrepreneurs, $F(I)-F(R)$ informal entrepreneurs, and $F(R)$ workers.

Finally, Figure 10.3 plots the scenario in which $I < a_o$ but $R > I$. In this economy no agent wants to be an informal entrepreneur because the PDV of opening an informal firm is dominated by the PDV of becoming a worker up to managerial ability I and by the PDV of being a formal entrepreneur there-after. Some agents want to be formal entrepreneurs, as long as $aV_f - k > U$ for some $a < a_o$. Hence, this economy would consist of $1-F(R)$ formal entre-preneurs and $F(R)$ workers, in this case, formal workers.

Of course, the most interesting scenario is one in which formal and informal firms operate simultaneously in the economy. Therefore, I will focus on case 2 in the following sections.

Payoffs: directed search

In this model workers are homogeneous in everything but their managerial skill which affects neither their ability to find a job, nor their productivity. I consider that workers have information about the state of both the formal and the informal labor markets so that they can direct their search towards one or the other. The flow values for searching in each sector are,

$$rU_f = b + \theta_f q(\theta_f)(W_f - U_f) \tag{4}$$
$$rU_i = b + \theta_i q(\theta_i)(W_i - U_i)$$

where b is the income when unemployed or the value of leisure and $\theta_k q(\theta_k)$ $k = f,I$ is the arrival rate of jobs to the unemployed in the respective sectors.[5]

Similarly, W_f and W_i show the PDV for the worker when employed in formal and informal jobs respectively. Workers earn a wage (w_f and w_i), but with rate λ they are returned to the unemployment pool.

$$rW_f = w_f + \lambda(W_f - U_f) \tag{5}$$
$$rW_i = w_i + \lambda(W_i - U_i)$$

For firms, the PDV of positing formal or informal vacancies V_f, V_i satisfies,

$$rV_f = q(\theta_f)(J_f - V_f) \tag{6}$$
$$rV_i = q(\theta_i)(J_i - V_i)$$

where $q(\theta_f)$ and $q(\theta_i)$ are the arrival rate of workers to vacancies for formal and informal firms respectively and J_f and J_i are the PDV of occupied jobs in each of the sectors, expressed as,

$$rJ_f = p_f - w_f + \lambda(V_f - J_f) \tag{7}$$
$$rJ_i = p_i - w_i + \lambda(V_i - J_i)$$

where p_f and p_i are the productivities of workers in formal and informal jobs.

Following the literature, the standard Nash sharing rule determining wages applies to both sectors.[6] I assume that the bargaining power of workers is the same in both sectors and is equal to β.

$$W_f - U_f = \frac{\beta}{(1-\beta)}(J_f - V_f) \tag{8}$$

$$W_i - U_i = \frac{\beta}{(1-\beta)}(J_i - V_i)$$

Using expressions (4) to (7) and attending to the sharing rule, equation (8), it is straightforward to obtain expression for the surpluses of jobs in the formal and informal sectors.

$$S_f = \frac{p_f - b}{(1-\beta)q(\theta_f) + r + \lambda + \beta\theta_f q(\theta_f)} \tag{9}$$

$$S_f = \frac{p_i - b}{(1-\beta)q(\theta_i) + r + \lambda + \beta\theta_i q(\theta_i)}$$

Equation (9) allows us to express the value of vacancies and unemployment as a function of the market tightness of each sector. Using (4) and (5), the flow value of unemployment can be expressed as

$$rU_f = b + \frac{\beta\theta_f q(\theta_f)(p_f - b)}{(1-\beta)q(\theta_f) + r + \lambda + \beta\theta_f q(\theta_f)} \tag{10}$$

$$rU_i = b + \frac{\beta\theta_i q(\theta_i)(p_i - b)}{(1-\beta)q(\theta_i) + r + \lambda + \beta\theta_i q(\theta_i)}$$

Similarly, for vacancies, using (6) and (7),

$$rV_f = \frac{(1 - \beta)q(\theta_f)(p_f - b)}{(1 - \beta)q(\theta_f) + r + \lambda + \beta\theta_f q(\theta_f)} \tag{11}$$

$$rV_i = \frac{(1 - \beta)q(\theta_i)(p_i - b)}{(1 - \beta)q(\theta_i) + r + \lambda + \beta\theta_i q(\theta_i)}$$

Expressions (10) and (11) have very intuitive interpretations. The value of unemployment when searching both in the formal and informal sectors increases the market tightness of the respective market; that is, the higher the number of vacancies per worker, the greater the chances for the worker to find a job and the greater the option value of searching. The same effect in reverse goes for firms: the higher the market tightness, the tougher it is to find workers to fill vacancies and, therefore, the lower the value of the vacancies. I can now express the threshold managerial abilities as functions of θ_f and θ_i.

In the case of directed search, there are two different values of unemployment, depending on which sector the agent is searching in. Therefore, the managerial ability that makes the agent indifferent between being a worker or an informal manager will be defined by

$$R = \frac{\max[U_f, U_i]}{\delta V_i} \tag{12}$$

If searching in the formal sector is optimal ($U_f > U_i$), R is increasing in both θ_f, as the value of search increases and θ_i, as the value of opening an informal firm decreases. Similarly, if the option of searching in the informal sector is preferred ($U_f < U_i$), R is increasing in θ_i as, on the one hand, the value of unemployment increases, and in parallel the value of informal vacancies decreases.[7]

For I, defined in equation (2), an increase in θ_f decreases the value of formal vacancies, which implies an increase of the marginal manager I, who is indifferent between opening an informal firm or a formal one. Additionally, I is negatively related to θ_i for similar reasons.

Equilibrium

All the variables of the system are expressed as functions of θ_i and θ_f. The first equilibrium equation captures the equality between the two search options. In equilibrium the expected return of the search in the formal market has to be equal to the expected return of search in the informal sector.

$$rU_f = rU_i = rU \tag{13}$$

that is,

$$\frac{\beta \theta_f q(\theta_f)(p_f - b)}{(1 - \beta)q(\theta_f) + r + \lambda + \beta \theta_f q(\theta_f)} = \frac{\beta \theta_i q(\theta_i)(p_i - b)}{(1 - \beta)q(\theta_i) + r + \lambda + \beta \theta_i q(\theta_i)}$$

Equation (13) is referred to as the equality of returns curve, ER. It portrays a positive relationship between θ_i and θ_f. In other words, as the probability of obtaining a job in one of the sectors increases, so does the other, leaving the expected return from search in each of the sectors equal. Another immediate result of equation (13) is that $\theta_i > \theta_f$. The intuition of this result is simple, as the productivity of the match is greater in the formal $(p_f > p_i)$ sector and the expected returns from search have to be equal across sectors; necessarily the probability of finding a job in the informal sector has to be greater; that is, the queues for formal jobs are longer.

The second equilibrium equation of the model is a market clearing condition. It states that the workers have to be either working or searching for jobs in one of the sectors,

$$F(R) = n_f + n_i + u_f + u_i \tag{14}$$

where n_f, n_i, u_f, and u_i are the number of workers employed and the number of searchers for formal and informal jobs respectively. Values for n_f, n_i, u_f, and u_i, and u_i can be derived from the steady state conditions of the employment equations. The equation determining the evolution of employment in each formal (informal) firm is

$$\dot{n}_f(a) = [a - n_f(a)]q(\theta_f) - \lambda n_f(a) \tag{15}$$

$$\dot{n}_i(a) = [\delta a - n_i(a)]q(\theta_i) - \lambda n_i(a)$$

Adding up across firms,

$$\dot{n}_f = [\int_I^{a_0} a \, dF(a) - n_f]q(\theta_f) - \lambda n_f \tag{16}$$

$$\dot{n}_i = [\int_R^{I} a \, dF(a) - n_i]q(\theta_i) - \lambda n_i$$

In the steady state $\dot{n}_f = \dot{n}_i = 0$, so the equilibrium values for n_f and n_i are,

$$n_f = \frac{q(\theta_f)}{q(\theta_f) + \lambda} \int_I^{a_0} a \, dF(a) \tag{17}$$

$$n_i = \frac{q(\theta_i)}{q(\theta_i) + \lambda} \int_R^{I} a \, dF(a)$$

Similarly, unemployment in the formal and informal sectors can be defined as,

$$u_f = \frac{[\int_I^{a_0} a \, dF(a) - n_f]}{\theta_f} \tag{18}$$

$$u_i = \frac{[\int_R^I a \, dF(a) - n_i]}{\theta_i}$$

where the numerator in both expressions are just the number of vacancies in each sector. Using equations (14), (17), and (18) I obtain the second equilibrium condition of the model.

$$F(R) = \frac{\theta_f q(\theta_f) + \lambda}{\theta_f q(\theta_f) + \theta_f \lambda} \int_I^{a_0} a \, dF(a) + \frac{\theta_i q(\theta_i) + \lambda}{\theta_i q(\theta_i) + \theta_i \lambda} \int_R^I a \, dF(a) \tag{19}$$

Equation (19) shows the combinations of θ_i and θ_f consistent with the allocation of the labor force across sectors and it is referred to subsequently as the steady state (SS) condition. Intuitively, equation (19) establishes a negative relationship between θ_i and θ_f. If market tightness increases in the formal sector, for instance, this would imply higher incentives for agents to become workers (higher R) and at the same time would increase I as entrepreneurs would find the formal sector relatively less attractive than the informal sector. This would increase the term on the left-hand side and lower the first term on the right-hand side. Therefore, in order to balance the equation, θ_i should decrease to generate some extra jobs in the informal sector, establishing a negative relationship between θ_i and θ_f.[8]

The equilibrium of the model is depicted graphically in Figure 10.4. The central locus shows the relationship between θ_f against θ_i, from the equality of returns (ER) condition, equation (13) and the SS condition, equation (19). I also plot two auxiliary graphs which depict the values of cut-off points I and R in the managerial distribution from the formal entrepreneurship curve (FE), equation (2) and the informal entrepreneurship (IE) curve, equation (3). Note that the equilibrium will always be located below the 45-degree line as is implied by $\theta_i > \theta_f$ in equation (13).

In equilibrium the size of the informal sector can now be computed in two different ways. First, the size of the informal sector can be measured as the ratio of total informal posted jobs divided by total posted jobs given by,

208   *M. Bosch*

$$\pi_1 = \frac{n_f + v_f}{n_f + v_f + n_i + v_i} = \frac{\displaystyle\int_I^{a_0} a\, dF(a)}{\displaystyle\int_I^{a_0} a\, dF(a) + \int_R^I a\, dF(a)} \tag{20}$$

Similarly, the informal sector can also be measured as the ratio of informal occupied jobs over total occupied jobs[9]

$$\pi_w = \frac{n_f}{n_f + n_i} = \frac{\dfrac{q(\theta_f)}{q(\theta_f) + \lambda}\displaystyle\int_I^{a_0} a\, dF(a)}{\dfrac{q(\theta_f)}{q(\theta_f) + \lambda}\displaystyle\int_I^{a_0} a\, dF(a) + \dfrac{q(\theta_i)}{q(\theta_i) + \lambda}\displaystyle\int_R^I a\, dF(a)} \tag{21}$$

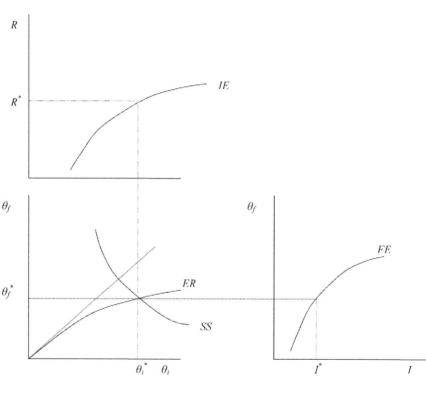

Figure 10.4 Equilibrium.

The fact that market tightness is different in each market makes these two measures differ. In equilibrium, $\theta_i > \theta_f$, which necessarily implies that $\pi_1 > \pi_2$, that is the percentage of informal posted jobs is greater than the percentage of informal occupied jobs.

Unemployment rate in the economy is given by

$$u = F(R) - n_f - n_i \qquad (22)$$

3 Comparative statics

I explore now how higher start-up costs affect the equilibrium. Figure 10.5 presents the results of an increase in start-up costs (k). An increase in k shifts the SS curve down: for the same market tightness in the informal sector,

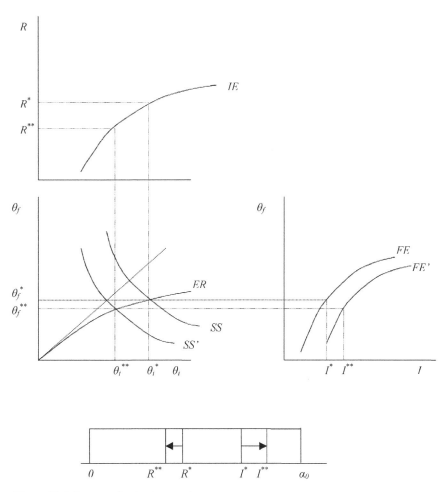

Figure 10.5 Increase in start-up costs.

market tightness in the formal sector decreases. The ER curve is unaltered. Therefore the new equilibrium is at a lower θ_f and θ_i. Similarly the FE curve in the $[I,\theta_f]$ locus is also shifted to the right. Overall, I obtain lower θ_f and θ_i, lower R, and higher I. These results imply an increase in the size of the informal sector, both in the proportion of total jobs posted π_1, and the proportion of formal workers to informal workers π_2.[10]

The intuition is as follows, as start-up costs increase, a number of managers become informal (shift in I): this provokes a reduction in vacancies in the formal sector and an increase in vacancies in the informal sector which reduces θ_f and increases θ_i. In the face of shortage of formal jobs, there is a reduction in the expected return of search in the formal market, and an increase of the expected return of search in the informal sector. This generates a transfer of unemployed workers looking for a job in the formal sector to the informal labor market to achieve the equalization of returns to search again. Both the increase in k and the new patterns of search of the unemployed increase I, shrinking the number of formal entrepreneurs that are replaced by informal entrepreneurs. Finally, at the other end of the distribution, the reduction of market tightness in both labor markets induces workers to give up search and start up their own informal firm, which additionally enlarges the informal sector (decrease in R).

The effect of higher start-up costs on unemployment is ambiguous. There are three forces at play here. First, formal entrepreneurs have been replaced by informal entrepreneurs (the difference between I^* and I^{**}) which produces a reduction in total formal jobs in the economy. This increases unemployment. Second, R has decreased, so that there are more informal entrepreneurs in the economy posting jobs reducing unemployment. Finally, there are fewer workers in this economy, hence reducing unemployment. Therefore, the overall effect will be determined by the interaction between these three effects. Intuitively, the pressure on unemployment comes from the fact that some jobs in the formal sector are being destroyed (lower n_f) and not replaced by new informal jobs. However, changes in the occupational choice of agents releases some of those pressures.

The overall effect of start-up costs on unemployment is ambiguous and will depend upon the value of specific parameters. I will explore the effect of the different parameters in the next section.

4 Quantitative examples: policy complementarities

In this section I explore the quantitative consequences of the model. I focus on the effect of start-up costs on two main variables: the size of the informal sector and the unemployment rate. I have argued that higher start-up costs will lead to an increased informal sector; however, the effect on the unemployment rate is ambiguous. The overall effect on the unemployment level would depend on the forces destroying employment, (substitution of formal firms by informal firms) and the forces creating employment (the appearance of new informal firms). The other policy parameters, namely unemployment benefits (b) and monitoring of the informal sector (δ), will determine the overall impact of start-up costs on unemployment.

To illustrate the mechanism I compute some numerical examples. For the sake of simplicity I assume a uniform distribution of managerial ability between 0 and 1. The formal sector is 50% more productive than the informal sector ($p_f = 1.5$ and $p_i = 1$), informal entrepreneurs can only open 50% of the vacancies they would have had, had they chosen to be formal ($\delta = 0.5$). The exogenous job destruction rate λ is set to 0.1 for both sectors. Bargaining power is established to be equally distributed, $\beta = 0.5$, in both sectors and income when unemployed is $b = 0.1$. Finally, the matching technology can be summarized by a Cobb Douglas function such as

$$q(\theta) = 20^{1/2} \tag{23}$$

I start by comparing our baseline model with the Fonseca, Lopez-Garcia, and Pissarides (2001) model, where informality is not considered to be an option. This is presented in Table 10.1. The Fonseca, Lopez-Garcia, and Pissarides (2001) model returns an economy where 49% of the agents choose to be workers and the other 51% decide to be entrepreneurs. This gives an unemployment rate of 10.64%. In our baseline model 44% of the population joins the labor force in search for a job, 13% are informal entrepreneurs and the other 43% are formal entrepreneurs, giving an unemployment rate of 7.48%. Therefore, for this set of parameters, when the informal entrepreneurship option is available, a number of agents that were previously formal entrepreneurs find it more profitable to avoid start-up costs and do their business underground. To be more precise, the segment of agents from 0.57 to 0.49 in the unit interval representing managerial ability choose this option. Furthermore, some agents in the Fonseca, Lopez-Garcia, and Pissarides (2001) model were workers who decide to be informal entrepreneurs when this option is available. These are the agents between 0.49 and 0.44 managerial ability. Employment in the formal sector has declined from 0.38 to 0.34; this has been partly compensated by the appearance of an informal economy, which now also generates jobs. Although overall employment is lower in our baseline model, the fact that R is lower, and therefore, that there are fewer agents looking for jobs, forces the unemployment rate lower. Finally, the size of the informal sector measured as the ratio of informal/total jobs posted, equation (20), is 15% whereas the ratio of informal/total jobs

Table 10.1 Comparison between FLP and base-line model

	θ_f	θ_i	n_f	n_i	u	R	I	π_1	π_2
All Formal	0.0317		0.38		10.64	0.49			
Base line model	0.0581	0.0941	0.34	0.03	7.48	0.44	0.57	15%	8%

occupied, equation (21), is slightly lower 8% .This is due to the fact that market tightness in the formal sector is lower, and the formal have higher queues than the informal jobs.

Table 10.2 shows the effects of an increase in start-up costs on the main variables of the model. The effects follow closely the dynamics described in the previous section. As k increases, I goes from 0.56 to 0.78 and R falls from 0.44 to 0.38; that is, overall entrepreneurship increases, informality increases, wage employment $(n_f + n_i)$ falls from 0.37 to 0.30 and, in this case, unemployment falls. Although there is no ambiguity in the effects of start-up costs on informality, the effects on unemployment will depend on which other policies are in place in a given country. The key element in the response of unemployment is how the informal sector will expand, or in other words, how many workers will give up search and engage in informal entrepreneurship. Differences in the monitoring of the informal sector, δ, and the extent of unemployment benefits, b, will determine this response and whether the job creation forces outweigh the job destruction forces when start-up costs increase. I quantitatively explore this issue.

Figures 10.6 and 10.7 show the impact of start-up costs on the size of the informal sector and the unemployment rate for different values of the monitoring parameter, δ. Focusing on the impact of size of the informal sector, it is clear that start-up costs increase the size of the informal sector for any value of δ. However, interestingly, the impact of start-up costs on informality varies significantly with δ. For low values of δ, that is, strong monitoring, the expansion of the informal sector in the face of increased start-up costs is weaker than for high values. This implies that the expansion of the informal sector does not compensate for the loss of jobs in the formal sector and therefore unemployment rises. Conversely, as δ approaches one and the informal sector is widely accepted in the country, the increased start-up costs significantly expand the informal sector and lower the unemployment rate. Therefore, a higher δ strengthens the job-creating forces in the presence of start-up costs and weakens the job destruction forces.

Figures 10.8 and 10.9 present similar exercises for unemployment benefits, b. First, note that both figures include a dashed line which represents the behavior of a model where only the unemployed searching in the formal sector have access to unemployment benefits.[11]

Table 10.2 Increase in start-up costs

k	θ_f	θ_i	n_f	n_i	u	R	I	π_2
10	0.0581	0.0941	0.34	0.03	7.48%	0.44	0.56	8%
11	0.0544	0.0880	0.30	0.05	7.36%	0.43	0.62	14%
12	0.0504	0.0813	0.27	0.07	7.24%	0.41	0.67	21%
13	0.0461	0.0742	0.23	0.09	7.12%	0.40	0.73	28%
14	0.0415	0.0666	0.19	0.11	6.99%	0.38	0.78	37%

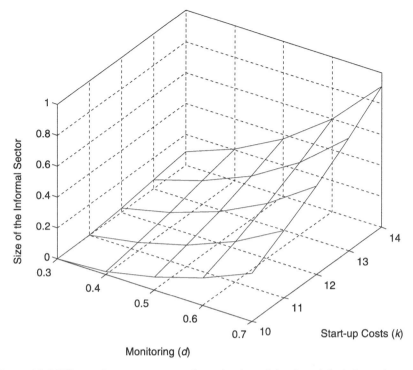

Figure 10.6 Effects of start-up costs and monitoring of the size of the informal sector.

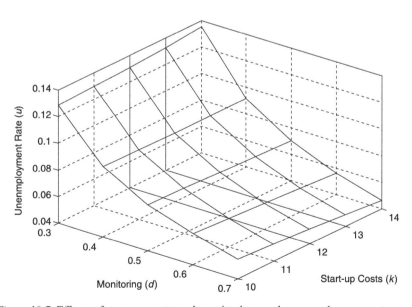

Figure 10.7 Effects of start-up costs and monitoring on the unemployment rate.

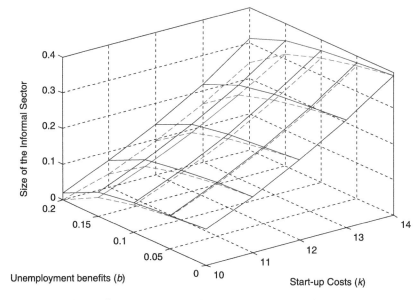

Figure 10.8 Effects of start-up cost and unemployment benefits on the size of the informal sector.

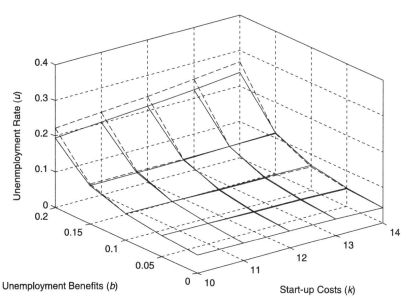

Figure 10.9 Effects of start-up costs and unemployment benefits on the unemployment rate.

Similarly to the effects of δ, the effects of start-up costs on unemployment vary with b. High values of unemployment benefits are associated with an increasing relationship between informality and unemployment, whereas that relationship is negative for low values of b. In essence, the reasoning behind this asymmetric behavior is similar to the previous case. The weak expansion of the informal sector when benefits are high provokes the unemployment level to increase and vice versa.

This illustrates how combinations of policies may be key when addressing the optimal policy mix to achieve particular outcomes. For instance, developing countries may be in a situation with high start-up costs and low monitoring and low unemployment benefits, all contributing to an oversized informal sector and relatively low unemployment rate. Trying to reduce the informal sector by increasing monitoring alone will rapidly increase unemployment, making this policy politically unavailable. Increasing monitoring at the same time as changing the incentives to become formal by decreasing start-up costs will have a greater impact on informality and will soften the impact on unemployment.

5 Conclusions

This paper presents a labor market search model that allows for the existence of the informal sector in the economy where agents may open formal or informal firms. The model is constructed in the spirit of the literature considering the existence of the informal sector not as a residual sector of a dualistic labor market but as a viable option for agents who weigh the advantages and disadvantages of the different options offered in the labor market.

I have argued that increases in labor market regulations, and in particular, start-up costs, expand the informal economy. There are two channels through which that expansion of the informal sector occurs. The direct effect is a substitution of formal firms by informal firms. This triggers an indirect effect through the search process. In the face of a diminishing number of jobs in the formal sector, workers shift their search towards the informal sector, which in turn makes the informal entrepreneurship option more attractive, providing the incentives for workers to become informal entrepreneurs, further expanding the informal sector.

However, changes in the size of the informal sector have ambiguous effects on the unemployment rate as destruction of jobs in the formal sector may be only partially or totally compensated by creation of jobs in the informal sector. I argue that parameters such as income when unemployed and tolerance to informality will determine whether increases in the size of the informal sector are going to be positive or negative for the level of unemployment.

Notes

1 See Fields for a review of traditional static models (1990, 2004).
2 For models with informal jos and search frictions, see Fugazza and Jaques (2002) and Kolm and Larsen (2002) and (2004), Boeri and Garibaldi (2006), Kugler (1999), and Albrecht, Navarro, and Vroman (2006).
3 An exception is Antunes and Cavalcanti (2007). Using a general equilibrium model, they argue that regulation costs and not the level of enforcement account for differences in the size of the informal sector between te USA and Mediterranean Europe. However, for a developing country such as Peru, contract enforcement and regulation costs are equally important in accounting for the size of the informal sector.
4 Pissarides (2003) considers that the number of entrepreneur vacancies open depends on the value of the vacancy. This would also explain why informal entrepreneurs open fewer vacancies than formal ones.
5 It might be argued that informal workers do not enjoy unemployment benefits. However, this equation refers to the search process of the agent and hence the authorities would not be able to distinguish between the search for formal jobs and the search for informal jobs. I relax this assumption in the simulation and obtain qualitatively very similar results.
6 The Nash sharing rule implies that the surplus of job formation $(S_k = W_k - U_k + J_k - V_k, k = i, f)$ is divided between the worker and the firm according to the bargaining power of each of the parts, β.
7 In practice, in equilibrium $rU_f = rU_i$.
8 See Bosch (2004) for proofs.
9 This expression refers to the proportion of total jobs that are informal. Another way of measuring informality could be the proportion of agents (including entrepreneurs) that are informal, such as $[n_i + F(I) - F(R)]/(n_f + n_i + 1 - F(R))$.
10 From equation (20) it is immediately seen that the size of the informal sector has increased. Looking at equation (21) it can be shown that the number of informal jobs has increased but there is an ambiguity as to the number of formal jobs, as the number of total jobs posted is lower but market tightness is also lower. However, it can be shown that the absolute number of formal jobs has also decreased. See Bosch (2004) for proofs.
11 This minor modification of the model addresses earlier concerns on the interpretation of the b parameter.

References

Albrecht, J. W., L. Navarro, and S. B. Vroman (2006) "The Effects of Labor Market Policies in an Economy with an Informal Sector." IZA Discussion Paper 2141.
Antunes, A.R. and T.V. Cavalcanti (2007) "Start Up Costs, Limited Enforcement, and the Hidden Economy." *European Economic Review* 51: 203–24.
Boeri, T. and P. Garibaldi (2006) "Shadow Sorting." CEPR discussion paper DP5487.
Bosch, M. (2004) "Start up costs, Informality and Policy complementarities." Mimeo: LSE.
Bruhn, M. (2006) "License to Sell: The Effect of Business Registration Reform on Entrepreneurial Activity in Mexico." Job Market Paper MIT.
De Soto, H. (1989) *The Other Path*. New York: Harper & Row.
Djankov, S., R. La Porta, F. Lopez-de-Silanes, and A. Shleifer (2002) "The Regulation of Entry." *Quarterly Journal of Economics* 117(1): February, 1–37. 57.

Fields, G. S. (2006) "A Guide to Multisector Labor Market Models." Washington, DC : World Bank Labor Market Conference, November 18–19.

——. (1990) "Labor Market Modelling and the Urban Informal Sector: Theory and evidence." In Paris: OECD, The Informal Sector Revisited.

Fonseca, R., P. Lopez-Garcia, and C. Pissarides (2001) "Entrepreneurship, Start-Up Costs and Employment." *European Economic Review* 45: 692–705.

Friedman, E., S. Johnson, D. Kaufmann, and P. Zoido-Labton (1999) "Dodging the Grabbing Hand: The determinants of unofficial activity in 69 countries." Discussion paper, Washington DC: World Bank.

Fugazza, M. and J. F. Jaques (2002) "Labor Market Institutions, Taxation and the Underground Economy." *Journal of Public Economics* 88(1–2): January, 395–418.

Johnson, S., D. Kaufmann, and A. Shleifer (1997) "The Unofficial Economy in Transition." Brookings Papers on Economic Activity, Fall, Washington DC.

Kaplan, D. S., E. Piedra, and E. Seira (2007) "Entry Regulation and Business Start-Ups: Evidence from Mexico" (June). World Bank Policy Research Working Paper 4322.

Kolm, A. S. and B. Larsen (2002) "Moral Cost, the Informal Sector and Unemployment." Working Paper 1-2001. Compenhagen Business School: Department of Economics.

——. (2004) "Does Tax Evasion Affect Unemployment and Educational Choice?." Working Paper 4-2004 Department of Economics. Copenhagen Business School.

Kugler, A. (1999) "The impact of Firing Cost on Turnover and Unemployment: Evidence from the Colombian labor Market Reforms." *International Tax ad Public Finance* 6: 389–410.

Orszag, M., and D. J. Snower (1997) "From Unemployment Benefits to Unemployment Support Accounts," Discussion Paper, Department of Economics, Birkbeck College, University of London.

——. (1999) "Anatomy of Policy Complementarities." IZA Discussion Papers 41, Institute for the Study of Labor (IZA).

Pissarides, C. (2003) "Company Start-Up Costs and Employment, in Knowledge, Information, and Expectations." In *Modern Macroeconomics: In Honor of Edmund S. Phelps*, edited by P. Aghion, R. Frydman, J. Stiglitz, and M. Woodford. Princeton: Princeton University Press.

11 Can social programs reduce productivity and growth?

A hypothesis for Mexico

Santiago Levy[*]

1 Introduction

Mexico's low growth has become a critical area of concern. In the last decade the average growth rate of per capita GDP was 2.1%; and for the last five years 0.4%. Productivity growth has also been slow.[1] This lackluster performance has generated a search for explanations. Attention has focused on monopolistic practices in the telecommunications sector; low lending to firms by commercial banks; uncertain supply conditions associated with public energy monopolies; labor market rigidities derived from onerous firing regulations; and low levels of education of the workforce.

Without diminishing the merit of these explanations or weighing their relative importance, in this paper I highlight another source of low growth and stagnant productivity overlooked so far: social programs that induce workers and firms into low productivity jobs and socially inefficient investments respectively. The paper points out that social programs segment workers and firms into a formal and an informal sector, and that this segmentation not only has negative social implications—as similar workers receive different social benefits—but also reduces growth and productivity. This matters greatly for Mexico for a simple but powerful reason: the majority of firms and workers are informal. If social programs cause informality, and if the distortions associated with informality reduce productivity and growth, then social programs can harm productivity and growth, more so if they are expanding rapidly as is the case in Mexico.

Section 2 describes the relevant characteristics of Mexico's social programs and labor market. Section 3 exploits the standard two-sector model to analyze the impact of social programs on labor productivity and the allocation of investment. Section 4 concludes.

2 Social security and social protection

Mexico provides social benefits to workers based on labor status. On one hand, social security is a right of salaried workers only, and an obligation of firms only with respect to the salaried workers they hire.[2] Coverage involves a wide set of benefits: (i) health insurance, (ii) day-care services; (iii) life insurance; (iv) disability pensions; (v) work-risk pensions; (vi) sports and cultural facilities; (vii) retirement pensions; (viii) housing loans; and (ix) severance pay. Benefits are paid out of workers' and firms' contributions, and are bundled in the sense that workers and firms must pay for all of them, regardless of whether workers desire all or only a subset.

On the other hand, the self-employed and non-salaried workers benefit from various health, housing, day care and, more recently, pension programs—grouped here under the label of social protection—which differ from social security in two relevant senses: benefits are unbundled and paid out of general revenues.[3]

Associating coverage of social security with "formality" and lack thereof with "informality," the labor force divides into a formal and an informal sector, with formal/informal workers receiving social security/social protection benefits.[4] In principle, this division should coincide with salaried and non-salaried workers; but this is not so, since as a result of evasion of social security laws there are salaried workers with social protection benefits that add to informal employment. Table 11.1 describes the magnitudes of each in 2006. Note that 36% of salaried workers evade social security laws.

A critical feature of Mexico's labor market is large-scale mobility of workers between sectors. Here, I summarize the results of an exercise where the length of stay in the formal sector—measured by affiliation with IMSS—of 9 million individual workers is followed from July 1997 to July 2006.[5] Interestingly, only 16.2% of low-wage workers were enrolled with IMSS for 10 complete years over the decade, as opposed to 51.6% of high wage workers. At the other end, of all low-wage workers enrolled in IMSS in 1997, almost 19.5% were in the formal sector for only one year over the decade; this contrasts with 5.9% of high-wage workers. All in all, the average low wage worker who in 1997 was enrolled in IMSS had social security coverage for only 4.9 out of the 10 years during which he could have been covered, or 49% of his working time; the corresponding average for high-wage workers is 7.7 years, or 77% of his working time.

More generally, workers in Mexico have spells of formality with social

Table 11.1 Mexico's labor force, 2006 (thousands of workers)

	Number	*Share*
I. Formal	14,079	33.9
II. Informal	25,777	62.2
(a) non-salaried	17,685	—
(b) salaried (evasion)	8,092	—
III. Open Unemployment	1,600	3.8
IV. Total	41,456	100.0

Source: Levy (2008).

Note: the table excludes public sector workers.

security coverage, and spells of informality with social protection coverage; these transits are more frequent, the lower the worker's wage. These results are confirmed using the national employment surveys, which are also panel data sets that follow workers' formal–informal transits (although for only a year). According to these data, in 2005, 16% of low-wage workers who began the year in the formal sector ended it in the informal; and 10% who started the year in the informal sector ended it in the formal. Calderon-Madrid (2006) computes transition matrices for Mexican workers between formality and informality for years of high and low GDP growth (1997, 2001, and 2005) and finds similar results, suggesting also that the phenomenon is not a result of the business cycle.[6] On the other hand, transits from formality and informality into open unemployment are very small, and spells of open unemployment are very short; see IDB (2004). There is no unemployment insurance in Mexico.

In sum, there appear to be no substantive barriers for workers to enter the formal sector.[7] The formal–informal dichotomy is a characterization of the legal status of workers at a point of time, not a permanent separation of individual workers into two mutually exclusive subsets. The problem for Mexican workers is not accessing a formal job; the problem is that permanence in formality is very erratic.

3 Social programs and productivity

3.1 Static general equilibrium

This section describes a framework to identify the efficiency effects of social security and social protection programs. The labor force L is divided into salaried and non-salaried employment, with social security and social protection coverage, or into formal and informal employment, L_f and L_i, respectively. Assume that all are unskilled low-wage workers.

In the absence of evasion (see below), informal employment includes two types of worker: the self-employed and those with a non-salaried labor relation with a firm. The self-employed might own productive assets (say, a half hectare of land, a mixer to make fruit juices for sale in city streets) and may exploit those assets on their own; critically, the amount of time they devote to work with these assets depends on the wages they could earn working as salaried or non-salaried employees for somebody else (which measures the opportunity cost of their own time). Alternatively, the self-employed might own no productive assets at all but still work on their own (washing cars in the street, say).

Informal workers, however, can also borrow working capital and sell products in the streets (contraband, newspapers, candy), or work for a firm selling its products door-to-door or in the streets (cosmetics, food, lottery tickets). Because their effort cannot be monitored (as hours worked are variable and the workplace is mobile), when employed by a firm these workers receive a "commission" and not a wage. As a result, they are non-salaried; but in a labor market characterized by mobility across sectors, the level of these commissions depends on the wages and benefits in salaried employment as the latter measure the opportunity cost of their time. The key point is that the decisions of workers with or without productive assets to devote part or all of their time to various forms of non-salaried work depends on the earnings they can obtain in these occupations and the benefits derived from social protection programs vis-à-vis the wages and benefits of social security.

Firms divide between formal and informal, respectively hiring salaried and non-salaried workers. I initially take the number of firms in each sector as given and assume that there is no evasion of social security laws. As a result, all firms hiring salaried workers are formal, while all the self-employed or workers in a non-salaried contractual relation with a firm together constitute the informal sector. Firms' output is given by:

$$Q_f = Q_f(K_f, L_f) \tag{1a}$$

$$Q_i = Q_i(K_i, L_i) \tag{1b}$$

where K_f, K_i is the (fixed) capital stock in each sector.

Let T_f be the costs of social security benefits and w_f be the formal wage, formal firms' cost of hiring a worker are $w_f + T_f$.[8] Formal firms hire workers up until the point where the value of their marginal product, MPL_f, equals $w_f + T_f$. For various reasons, however, formal sector workers might not attach a value to social security benefits equivalent to their costs. Let $\beta_f \in [0,1]$ be workers' valuation coefficient of social security benefits so that their utility from a formal job is $w_f + \beta_f T_f$.[9] Clearly, if workers value social security fully, so that $\beta_f = 1$, formal firms' labor costs equal formal workers' utility; conversely, if workers undervalue these benefits, so that $\beta_f < 1$, there is a wedge between what the formal firm pays and what the worker receives. This wedge is equal to $(1 - \beta_f)T_f$ and is equivalent to a tax on salaried employment (not on labor).

In the informal sector, non-wage costs of labor are absent. Firms (including firms owned by the self-employed) hire workers so that the MPL_i equals w_i, where this wage is interpreted as equivalent to the commissions paid for non-salaried labor; or to the remunerations obtained by the self-employed net of the quasi-rents on their own productive assets (if they own any); or to the remunerations earned by the self-employed parking or washing cars or in any other occupation requiring only labor inputs. At the same time, informal workers receive benefits from social protection programs whose costs per worker are T_i, valued at $\beta_i T_i$ with $\beta_i \in [0,1]$. Critically, neither self-employed workers nor workers in non-salaried relations with firms pay for T_i; so while it may be the case that $\beta_f T_f > \beta_i T_i$, so workers value more social security than social protection benefits, it is also the case that the former are costly and the latter free. Of course, it may also be that $\beta_f T_f < \beta_i T_i$.

Equilibrium is represented by:[10]

$$p^w \, \partial \, Q_f / \partial \, L_f - (w_f + T_f) = 0 \tag{2a}$$

$$p^w \, \partial \, Q_i / \partial \, L_i - w_i = 0 \tag{2b}$$

$$w_i + \beta_i T_i = w_f + \beta_f T_f \tag{2c}$$

$$L_i + L_f = L \tag{2d}$$

where (2a,b) are the profit-maximizing conditions for formal and informal firms, (2c) is the utility maximizing condition for workers, and (2d) the equilibrium condition in the labor market.

Figure 11.1 depicts the distribution of employment with the demand for formal labor D_f drawn from the left hand side and the demand for informal labor D_i from the right-hand side. D_f and D_i result from the aggregation of individual firm demand curves for labor in each sector and in the case of D_i includes the demand for self-employment.

What is the impact of social programs? Consider first the case where social security is fully valued and there are no social protection programs. This is obtained by solving (2) with $\beta_f = 1$ and $T_i = 0$. In this case the equilibrium is at point A, with L_f^* workers employed in the formal sector and L_i^* (not drawn, but equal to $(L - L_f^*)$) in the informal.

Informal workers receive a wage of w_i^*, and formal workers receive w_f^*. However, when the value of the social security benefits received by formal workers is considered, worker's utility is the same across sectors. Note that the MPL in the formal sector, $w_f^* + T_f$, is equal to the MPL in the informal, w_i^*, so that the allocation of labor is efficient. A well-functioning social security system, interpreted here as $\beta_f = 1$, maximizes output at world prices and the productivity of labor (and workers' wages). Note also that when

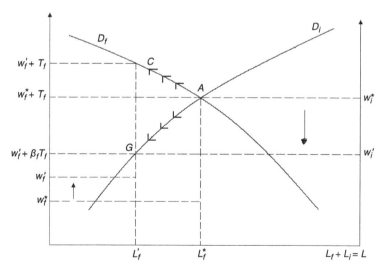

Figure 11.1 Social security with a formal and an informal sector.

$\beta_f = 1$ informal employment is the same with or without social security, as is the level of output of informal firms.

Evidently, informality in the sense of lack of social security coverage is inevitable in a legal framework that excludes non-salaried labor from the obligations of social security, because in any economy there are many valid reasons for non-salaried employment relations: because firms and workers find it profitable to engage in such relations for risk-sharing or effort-eliciting reasons; and because workers might also find it profitable to work on their own. Informality in this context is as efficient as formality, except that informal workers consume a different bundle of goods than formal workers: formal workers freely dispose of their wage w_f^* and are forced to consume benefits worth T_f to them, while informal workers freely dispose of their wage w_i^* and may or may not use part of their wages to purchase health insurance, save for a retirement pension, and so on.

Consider now the solution to (2) when $\beta_f < 1$, but assume still that there are no social protection programs (so $T_i = 0$). Note in Figure 1 that at $(w_f^* + \beta_f T_f) < w_i^*$ formal workers are less well-off than informal ones. This induces workers to move out of the formal sector with formal employment falling from L_f^* to L_f' (and informal employment increasing); but with fewer formal workers w_f inevitably increases, from w_f^* to w_f'. A key point here, however, is that formal firms still have to incorporate into their labor costs the full amount of social security contributions, T_f, regardless of whether workers value them fully or not; inevitably, their labor costs increase. This induces formal firms to move from point A to point C, where MPL_f is equal to $(w_f' + T_f)$. On the other hand, if more workers are now in the informal sector, they can only be employed if their wages fall from w_i^* to w_i'; this allows informal sector firms to increase their employment from point A to G, where the $MPL_i = w_i'$, and induces more workers to be self-employed. Note that at w_f' and w_i' workers are indifferent between formal and informal employment because $(w_f' + \beta_f T_f) = w_i'$.

In this equilibrium the productivity of formal workers is $w_f' + T_f$, while that of informal workers is w_i'. Since w_f and w_i moved in opposite directions, formal workers are now more productive than informal workers; but this is not the result of them being more educated; nor is it the result of a barrier to entry into formal employment. The differences in productivity between similar workers are caused by an undervalued social security system.

The shift from w_f^*, w_i^* to w_f', w_i' impacts quasi-rents on capital. In the formal sector the future flow of quasi-rents on K_f and the price of capital goods falls. The opposite happens in the informal one; productive assets in the informal sector become more valuable: the half-hectare of low-quality land exploited by a rural worker; the mixer or stove used by urban workers to make food for sale in city streets. At $\beta_f = 1$, these assets would probably not be used; at $\beta_f < 1$ they are valuable.

Figure 11.2 depicts what happens when social protection programs are introduced, so that (2) is now solved with $T_i > 0$.[11] At points G and C formal

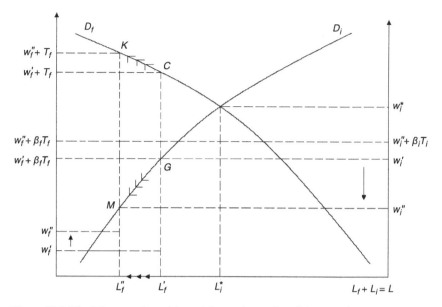

Figure 11.2 The labor market with social security and social protection.

workers would be receiving $(w_f' + \beta_f T_f)$, while informal workers $(w_i' + \beta_i T_i)$ $> (w_f' + \beta_f T_f)$; but this makes formal workers relatively worse off, inducing them to move to the informal sector. As the supply of labor to the formal sector falls, wages there increase from w_f' to w_f''. As a result, formal firms' labor costs are higher and they reduce formal employment, which falls from L_f' to L_f''. However, the additional workers in the informal sector can only be employed there if wages fall from w_i' to w_i''.

What is the effect of social protection programs on labor productivity? In the formal sector the productivity of workers is $w_f'' + T_f$ as firms are at point K. In the informal it is just w_i'' as firms are at point M. The result is that the productivity difference widens (contrast distance KM versus distance CG). Differently put: social protection programs generate productivity losses additional to the ones created by an undervalued social security system. The intuition is simple: $\beta_f < 1$ acts as a tax on salaried employment in the formal sector; $T_i > 0$ worsens things as it acts as a subsidy to informal employment.

I highlight a result from Figure 11.2 that may be initially surprising but that is not really so: with social protection programs informal and formal workers are both better off. Despite the fact that wages in the informal sector fall, they now receive benefits that they were not getting before; and because there are fewer formal sector workers, their wages increase. So it is the case that $w_i'' + \beta_i T_i = (w_i'' + \beta_i T_i) > (w_f' + \beta_f T_f) = w_f'$. It is noteworthy that workers are better off despite that fact that they are less productive and the economy is less efficient. This happens because there are benefits for which (apparently) nobody is paying.[12]

Since the *MPL* in each sector is $(w_f + T_f)$ and w_i respectively, using (2c) I obtain:

$$MPL_f - MPL_i = [(1 - \beta_f)T_f + \beta_i T_i] > 0 \qquad (3)$$

This expression identifies the two components of the productivity loss: the first is the output loss in the formal sector caused by incompletely valued social security, and it is greater, the lower the value of β_f. The second is the output loss in the formal sector caused by social protection, and it is greater the higher is the value of β_i. Note that β_f and β_i have opposite effects: improving the valuation of social security augments productivity as formal employment increases; but improving social protection lowers productivity by inducing overemployment in the informal sector. The total productivity loss is the value of GDP forgone because there are too many workers employed in low-productivity jobs in the informal sector, and too few workers employed in high-productivity jobs in the formal sector. This is:

$$\text{Annual GDP Loss} = p^w \{ [Q_f^*(., L_f^*) + Q_i^*(., L_i^*)]$$
$$- [Q_f''(., L_f'') + Q_i''(., L_i'')] \} \qquad (4)$$
$$= p^w \int_{L_f}^{L_f^*} [\partial Q_f / \partial L_f - \partial Q_i / \partial L_i] dL$$

which, using (3) is approximated by:

$$\text{Annual GDP Loss} \approx [(1 - \beta_f)T_f + \beta_i T_i] \Delta L \qquad (5)$$

where $\Delta L(T_f, T_i, \beta_f, \beta_i)$ is the difference between L_f^* and L_f'' in Figure 11.2 and consists of two components: the shift from L_f^* to L_f' as a result of $\beta_f < 1$, and the shift from L_f' to L_f'' as a result of $T_i > 0$.

3.2 Evasion and informal salaried employment

When $\beta_f < 1$ firms and workers have incentives to evade social security laws, generating salaried employment without social security coverage, labeled here L_{if}. Whether or not this occurs depends on the gains from evading, which are positive when $\beta_f < 1$ even if there are no social protection programs ($T_i = 0$), on one hand; and the penalties associated with evading the law, on the other hand. Let $F > T_f$ be the fine imposed on a firm hiring salaried workers but not registering them with IMSS; and $\lambda \in [0,1]$ be the probability of being fined. It is natural to assume that λ increases with the level of evasion, measured here by the number of workers hired by firms but not registered with IMSS.

For their part, workers accept salaried employment without social security benefits only if the firm compensates them with a higher wage than w_i; call this w_{if}, the wage paid to salaried workers by firms evading social security. At the same time, evading workers receive social protection benefits as I assume that these programs cover all workers without social security, regardless of whether this is because they are non-salaried or because they are salaried but illegal workers (as is the case in Mexico). Since the worker values social security benefits in $\beta_f T_f$ it follows that $(w_{if} + \beta_i T_i) = (w_f + \beta_f T_f)$ for workers to accept salaried employment without social security. The (expected) cost of labor to firms hiring informal salaried workers, on the other hand, is $w_{if} + \lambda F$. Equilibrium in the labor market with evasion of social security is given by:

$$p^w \partial Q_f (L_f + L_{if}) / \partial L_f - (w_f + T_f) = 0 \tag{6a}$$

$$p^w \partial Q_f (L_f + L_{if}) / \partial L_{if} - [w_{if} + \lambda F + (\partial \lambda (L_{if}) / \partial L_{if}) . F . L_{if}] = 0 \tag{6b}$$

$$p^w \partial Q_i / \partial L_i - w_i = 0 \tag{6c}$$

$$w_i + \beta_i T_i = w_{if} + \beta_i T_i \tag{6d}$$

$$w_{if} + \beta_i T_i = (w_f + \beta_f T_f) \tag{6e}$$

$$\lambda = \lambda(L_{if}) ; \lambda' > 0 ; \quad \lambda(0) = 0 \tag{6f}$$

$$L_i + L_{if} + L_f = L \tag{6g}$$

Informal employment $(L_i + L_{if})$ now results from a legal design that excludes non-salaried workers from social security; from a social security system that does not work well; from social protection programs; and from the response of firms and workers to these circumstances through evasion of social security. The latter is not a minor issue in Mexico since, as can be seen from Table 11.1, in the absence of evasion in 2006 social security coverage would have been at least 55% higher than it was!

Depending on the mix of legal and illegal employment, firms hiring salaried workers, can be classified as fully formal ($L_f > 0$, $L_{if} = 0$), fully informal ($L_f = 0$, $L_{if} > 0$), and mixed ($L_f > 0$, $L_{if} > 0$). Aside from all other parameter values, this depends critically on the probability that the firm is detected, λ. Equation (7) suggests a plausible form for λ:

$$\lambda(L_{if}) = \begin{cases} 0 \text{ if } (L_f + L_{if}) < \underline{L} \\ L_{if}^a \text{ if } (L_f + L_{if}) \in [\underline{L}, \overline{L}] ; \quad a > 1 \\ 1 \text{ if } (L_f + L_{if}) > \overline{L} \end{cases} \tag{7}$$

where $\underline{L}$ is perhaps 9 or 10 workers, and $\overline{L}$ 50. The combination of (6) and (7) generates a distribution of firms by size of employment: fully informal firms with up to 10 salaried workers (here labeled micro and small firms); mixed firms hiring between 9 or 10 and 50 workers combining registered and unregistered workers (here labeled medium-size firms); and fully formal firms with 50 workers or more registering all their workers (large firms).

Table 11.2 shows the number and distribution of registered firms with IMSS by number of salaried workers, which I take here to be the set of formal firms, and the number and distribution of firms by number of salaried workers employed according to the Economic Census, published by INEGI which I take here to be the set of all firms.

The contrast is sharp and revealing. At one extreme there are approximately 35,000 large firms (50 workers or more) that account for about 46% of total salaried employment (about 7.4 million workers), and 63% of all formal employment. At the other extreme there are about 2.7 million micro and small firms (five workers or less) that account for 32% of salaried employment (5.1 million workers); but only around 530,000 of those firms are registered with IMSS, accounting for 10% of formal employment (1.1 million workers). I conclude that evasion of social security (or illegal salaried employment receiving social protection benefits) is concentrated mostly in small firms, although a non-negligible amount occurs in medium-size firms.

3.3 New investments and growth

Depending on production functions and parameter values, (6) and (7) admit a large number of solutions. In some cases informal salaried employment will coexist with formal salaried employment in the same industry; in some others the whole industry might consist only of informal firms; and yet in some others only formal firms might be present. In parallel, the wage rates given by (6) also determine the level of non-salaried and self-employment.

To gain further insights, I shift to a partial equilibrium analysis and ignore non-salaried and self-employment in the informal sector. I analyze a simple case with only two firms hiring salaried labor, one fully formal and one fully informal, both producing the same good.[13] Assume that wage rates are given, and that both firms have access to the same technology in the sense of knowing the same information about production blueprints. Note from (6a) and (6b) that $(w_f + T_f) > (w_{if} + \lambda F)$. Since average labor costs are lower for the informal firm, the formal firm will have a higher capital/labor ratio.

It is critical to highlight, on the other hand, that the response of labor costs to changes in employment differs between firms. To see this, contrast from (6a) and (6b) the marginal costs of hiring one more worker (or MCL, marginal cost of labor):

$$MCL_f = w_f + T_f \quad \text{so that } \partial MCL_f / \partial L_f = 0 \tag{8a}$$

$$MCL_i = w_{if} + \lambda F + \partial \lambda(L_{if}) / \partial L_{if} . F . L_{if} \text{ so that } \partial MCL_i / \partial L_{if} > 0 \tag{8b}$$

This result is important: formal firms can expand employment at constant labor costs, while informal firms that initially have a cost advantage because they evade social security contributions face increasing (expected) labor costs. This is because hiring more workers increases the probability of being fined,

Table 11.2 INEGI versus IMSS registries of workers and firms, 2003

Size		INEGI (1)		IMSS (2)		Difference (1)–(2)	
Number of workers)		Number of firms	Workers	Number of firms	Workers	Number of firms	Workers
From	to						
0	2	2,118,138	3,011,902	350,459	488,727	1,767,679	2,523,175
3	5	581,262	2,078,023	183,432	686,515	397,830	1,391,508
6	10	153,891	1,135,021	95,886	725,253	58,005	409,768
11	15	47,601	604,387	38,855	494,430	8,746	109,957
16	20	24,361	433,741	21,342	379,795	3,019	53,946
21	30	25,171	627,011	22,399	556,830	2,772	70,181
31	50	20,927	812,729	19,125	743,225	1,802	69,504
51	100	16,100	1,135,608	15,337	1,077,909	763	57,699
101	250	10,898	1,683,740	10,526	1,629,298	372	54,442
251	500	4,029	1,379,532	3,804	1,314,357	225	65,175
501	more	2,636	3,199,628	2,626	3,082,169	10	117,459
Total		3,005,014	16,101,322	763,791	11,178,508	2,241,223	4,922,814

Source: Levy (2008).

and the fine is imposed on all workers hired, not only on the last worker hired who caused the firm to be caught. There is, so-to-speak, an endogenous limit to the expansion of informal firms; their cost advantage is rapidly eroded with size.[14] Informal firms will, on average, be smaller than formal firms.

Differences in labor costs will influence investment decisions. I want to make three points: (1) social programs increase the relative profitability of investments in informal vs. formal firms; (2) investments in the informal sector are biased in the direction of creating new firms rather than expanding existing ones; and (3) informality increases the economy's incremental capital–output ratio, ICOR, and reduces the rate of growth.

I tackle the first point noting that investment alternatives in the informal sector are to augment the capital stock in established firms but remaining informal (option A); to create a new informal firm (option B); or to invest while turning formal and registering with IMSS the additional workers hired and paying a cost of registration of C (option C). On the other hand, investment alternatives in the formal sector are expanding the firm (option D); or creating a new firm (option E). Let one unit of investment "I" purchase one unit of capital K, assume there are no indivisibilities, and let ΔL^k ($k = A,B,C,D,E$) be the additional labor required in the firm to expand output with the additional investment.[15] The additional profits made by investing "I" in each case are:

$$\Pi^A = \{p^w[(K_i + I), (L_{if} + \Delta L^A)] - [w_{if} + \lambda(L_{if} + \Delta L^A)F](L_{if} + \Delta L^A)\}$$
$$\quad - \{p^w(K_i, L_{if}) - [w_{if} + \lambda(L_{if})F]L_{if}\} \tag{9a}$$

$$\Pi^B = p^w(I, \Delta L^B) - [w_{if} + \lambda(\Delta L^B)F]\Delta L^B \tag{9b}$$

$$\Pi^C = \{p^w[(K_i + I), (L_{if} + \Delta L^C)] - [w_{if} + \lambda(L_{if})F]L_{if} - (w_f + T_f)\Delta L^C - C\}$$
$$\quad - \{p^w(K_i, L_{if}) - [w_{if} + \lambda(L_{if})F]L_{if}\} \tag{9c}$$

$$\Pi^D = \{p^w[(K_f + I), (L_f + \Delta L^D)] - (w_f + T_f)(L_f + \Delta L^D)\}$$
$$\quad - \{p^w(K_f, L_f) - (w_f + T_f)L_f\} \tag{9d}$$

$$\Pi^E = p^w(I, \Delta L^E) - (w_f + T_f)\Delta L^E - C \tag{9e}$$

Note from (9a) that if the informal firm grows its marginal and average costs of labor increase as there are more workers in the same firm. In turn, (9b) measures profits investing "I" on a new informal firm with lower average labor costs. The change in profits if the informal firm expands and becomes formal is given by (9c).[16] In the case of expansion of the formal firm, (9d), note that there are no additional costs of formality, while these need to be paid if a new firm is set up (9e); in these last two cases all workers are formal.

How do social programs impact (9)? I answer this writing $\Pi^k = \Pi^k (T_f, T_i, \beta_f, \beta_i)$ and calculating the impact on the profitability of each investment option of changes in the parameters defining social programs. The results are in Table 11.3.

Table 11.3 Social programs and the profitability of investment options

Social program/investment option	T_f	β_f	T_i	β_i
A	−	−	+	+
B	−	−	+	+
C	−	+	−	−
D	−	+	−	−
E	−	+	−	−

Note: These are general equilibrium effects of $\partial\Pi^k / \partial SP^i$, where SP^i refers to the corresponding parameter of social programs.

Concentrating on the valuation of social security and resources for social protection programs (columns for β_f and T_i) the table shows that deteriorating social security services makes investments in the informal sector more profitable than in the formal one; the same happens if more resources are allocated to social protection programs. In both cases the reason is the same: the wage for informal salaried labor, w_{if}, falls relative to the wage for formal labor, w_f.

Of course, in each option the change in profits from the additional investment of "I" needs to be compared with the cost of capital (or credit) to firms. To focus sharply on the effects of social programs, assume that there are no imperfections in the credit market so that all firms can access capital at the rate r^*. I next compare the rates of return on each investment option, $r^k = \Pi^k/I$, k = A,B,C,D,E with r^*. A bias in social programs in favor of informality, in the sense of $\beta_f < 1$ and/or $T_i > 0$, increases the profitability of investments in the informal sector relative to the formal one, and a larger share of the economy's investment resources will flow to the informal sector. In this context, note that expression (5) measuring the GDP loss associated with social programs was calculated for a given distribution of the capital stock between the formal and the informal sector. However, investment changes this distribution overtime, and it can do so in the direction of augmenting or reducing (5). My first point is that fostering social protection augments it.

The analysis suggests as well that some industries are more prone to informality than others. In general, informality is more likely in salaried activities with decreasing, constant, or mildly increasing returns, as well as in activities where indivisibilities in investment are unimportant. It is difficult to think that cars or steel could be profitably produced by illegal firms, but it is easy to think that clothing, shoes, jewelry, furniture, food, and a myriad of products and services can be profitably produced by illegal firms. This is important as it emphasizes that informality also biases the sectoral composition of output within salaried activities. This can be captured by writing (9) not only for firms choosing between investing and being formal or informal in the production of a given good, but for each industry or relevant product aggregation. The first effect that I discuss here would then be reflected not only in a bias towards informality in a given sector, but in the bias of aggregate investment towards activities/industries where the conditions facilitating informality are present.[17]

I turn to the second point relative to the distribution of investments in the informal sector between expanding or creating new firms. Inspection of (9a,b,c) suggests that if there are constant or decreasing returns to scale, $\Pi^B > \Pi^A$ and $\Pi^B > \Pi^{C}$.[18] The reason is clear: $\Pi^B > \Pi^A$ because the expanded labor force working in one informal firm is more costly than the labor force working separately in two informal firms (i.e. $\lambda(\Delta L) < \lambda(L_{if} + \Delta L)$). The same reason explains why $\Pi^B > \Pi^C$: investing in a new informal firm has lower labor costs than investing in the existing informal firm while turning formal (more so if the registration costs of formality are high).[19] On the other hand, if there are increasing returns to scale, the investment could be channeled to the same firm, if the cost advantages of larger size dominate the disadvantage of more costly labor. Finally, for sufficiently strong returns to scale (or advantages of size) the firm could register some workers with IMSS (if $\Pi^C > \Pi^B > \Pi^A$); this is facilitated if C is low. There are clearly many possibilities, but from the point of view of productivity the important cases occur when economies of scale or advantages of size are unexploited as investment is channeled into new informal firms because social programs make this the most profitable alternative.

To make my third point, assume that the total investment resources available to the economy are exogenously given, I^*. Next, rank the rates of return on all investment projects available in two scenarios: in case 1 when $\beta_f = 1$ and $T_i = 0$, and in case 2 when $\beta_f < 1$ and $T_i > 0$. Letting these rates of return be r^1_j and r^2_j, respectively, for $j = 1,2, \ldots$ N, investment resources can be distributed according to:[20]

$$I^* = \sum_{j=1}^{r^1_j \geq r^*} I^j\,(r^1_{\,j}) \quad \text{or} \quad I^* = \sum_{j=1}^{r^2_j \geq r^*} I^j\,(r^2_{\,j}) \tag{10}$$

so that the *same* aggregate investment results in a different distribution of the capital stocks across firms and activities. In case 1 only projects where labor is efficiently allocated are chosen, resulting in the maximum additional GDP from investing I^* or, differently put, in the lowest incremental capital-output ratio, ICOR. This implies that when $\beta_f < 1$ and $T_i > 0$, the mix of privately chosen investment projects results in a higher ICOR, and a lower rate of growth of GDP.

To sum up: given the cost of credit, technology, and other parameters, the direction in which new investments flow depends on social programs. These programs can distort investment decisions as much as imperfections in the capital markets and induce investment into the formal sector in larger and more capital intensive firms; or into the informal sector in smaller and more labor intensive firms. What the analysis shows is that if resources for social programs are tilted in favor of social protection, more investments will be channeled to the informal sector; that some of these investments will take place in the form of very small firms; and that this will lower the economy's growth rate.

4 Concluding remarks

This paper argues that social programs are a source of informality and, in turn, that informality lowers the productivity of workers and distorts the investment decisions of firms. However, I am evidently not advocating the removal of social programs. My point is different. It is that the formal/informal segmentation of firms and workers associated with social security/social protection programs division is bad economic policy (aside from bad social policy). Mexico is caught in a self-made dilemma between increasing workers' welfare through various forms of social intervention, on one hand; and appropriate incentives to workers and firms to seek high-productivity jobs and socially efficient investments, on the other. Unless Mexico escapes from this dilemma, both workers' welfare and productivity will suffer.

In parallel, I argue that reforming social programs is required effectively to reach the government's social objectives. Today similar workers are subject to different treatments; social security and social protection are not the same (or the same worker to different interventions as he transits between labor statuses). It is not the same to force workers to save for retirement in one case, and give them the option to do so in the other; it is not the same to force workers to save for a housing loan in one case, and give them the option to obtain one in the other; it is not the same to force workers to purchase life, health, and disability insurance in one case, and give them the option to do so in the other; and it is not the same to bundle all these obligations into a single one in one case, and unbundle them as any combination of options in the other.

A reform of social programs that contributes to growth, productivity and equity has two prerequisites. First, these programs must not discriminate in the nature of benefits on the basis of workers' labor status. Second, they must be paid for with the same sources of revenue. Changing policy to achieve this requires an understanding of the political forces that sustain the current equilibrium—in particular, the link between social programs and political legitimacy—and a gradual transition strategy; but a good place to begin is to recognize that Mexico has been moving in the opposite direction.

Notes

* I thank Ravi Kanbur for very valuable comments and suggestions. The usual disclaimers apply.
1 Bassi et al. (2006) found that the average product per worker in Mexico grew at an average rate of 1.4% between 1995 and 2004, substantially below OECD countries.
2 The Federal Labor Law distinguishes between salaried and non-salaried workers, where the former are defined as those performing subordinated work for a boss

(firm) in exchange for a wage. Workers engaged with firms under risk-sharing or effort-eliciting contracts receiving a commission or profit-sharing are not salaried. Firms hiring non-salaried workers are not obligated to affiliate their workers to social security.

3 In 2007, the Government spent approximately 1.7% of GDP in social protection programs; see Levy (2008).

4 I follow Guha-Khasnobis, Kanbur, and Ostrom (2006) defining formality with respect to a "governance structure". In this case, informal workers and firms are those that avoid the governance structures of salaried labor (for example, the obligation to purchase health insurance, save for retirement, and so on).

5 The exercise begins on July 1, 1997 when the current Social Security Law came into effect, when there were 9 million workers affiliated with the Instituto Mexicano del Seguro Social (IMSS), of which 3 million earned more than 3 mw ("high") and 6 million 3 mw or less ("low"). The exercise measures number of years in formality, defined here as being registered with IMSS, given that the worker was formal in 1997. Workers with 56 years of age or more in 1997 are excluded from the data base, so departures from formality are not due to retirement; when the worker is not in the formal sector he is in the informal, openly unemployed, has dropped out of the labor force, or migrated abroad; see Levy (2008).

6 See Gong, Soest, and Villagomez (2004), Navarro and Schrimpf (2004), and Bosch and Maloney (2006). Duryea et al. (2006) study nine middle-income countries and find that labor mobility is highest in Mexico.

7 Evidence also suggests that minimum wages are not binding; see Maloney and Nuñez (2004) and Bell (1997).

8 T_f is usually expressed as a fraction of the wage but is easier to express it in absolute terms. T_f includes all other costs associated with hiring a formal worker: labor taxes and the contingent costs of severance pay regulations.

9 Levy (2008) discusses these reasons in the case of Mexico, and provides evidence that suggests that β_f is approximately 0.25, while T_f is approximately 35% of w_f.

10 I do not index goods by sector or firm. Output is a Hicks-composite of many goods whose relative prices are exogenous (say, because all goods are traded, p^w). Attention is centered here in the market for factors.

11 The government introduces these programs to provide social benefits for workers excluded from social security; but the attempt to correct for the design flaws and operational problems of social security with these programs generates three problems. (1) They further reduce social security coverage as they depress salaried employment. (2) They are not bundled, so while health insurance coverage is extended, for instance, the number of workers forced to save for retirement pensions falls (as is the number of workers covered by disability or work-risk insurance). (3) They induce workers into lower productivity jobs. This last point is the one emphasized in this paper, but from the point of view of social policy it is important to note that social protection programs extend protection to workers along some dimensions but reduce it along others.

12 Of course, social protection programs must be paid for, but this is done from general taxes or other sources like oil rents; the point is that their costs are not internalized by workers and firms in the informal sector.

13 Think of products such as jeans, shoes, toys, or shirts produced in a maquiladora plant and the backyard of a house respectively.

14 This depends on the steepness of $\lambda(L_{if})$. Note too that the advantage of informality is rapidly lost because size not only increases expected labor costs but also the probability of being fined by the tax authorities for evading income taxes. This could be modeled as informal firms facing de facto an output price that is inversely proportional to output even if they produce traded goods. The pressure for smallness would now come from both the output price and the cost of labor.

15 Put Differently, $I/\Delta L^k$ is the capital/labor ratio of the new investment, which may or may not be equal to the capital/labor ratio existing in the firm (so firms can grow by capital deepening or widening).

16 C could just be a one-time registration cost; but there could be other costs also. For instance, an illegal firm in the backyard of a house can pay for its electricity at the usually lower rate for household consumption, but as a registered firm it would have to pay at the usually higher commercial rate. (In the extreme, as a formal firm it could perhaps not steal electricity, but it could do so as an informal one.)

17 In general, one would expect a bias in favor of services and commerce vis-à-vis manufacturing. Note also that if the degree of tradeability across sectors differs, then social programs will also distort the allocation of investments between traded and non-traded sectors; see Levy (2008).

18 The expression is inexact since, as noted, the capital/labor ratio associated with the expansion of the existing firm need not equal the one in the existing firm. The idea is more general and encompasses any advantage associated with larger firm size even if there are constant returns to scale: economies of scope, more resilience to negative output shocks, more labor training, lower cost of credit, more technology adoption, and so on.

19 This also suggests that attempts to reduce informality by lowering C while leaving the rest of the incentive structure favoring informality intact will not have strong results (more so if T_i is raised in parallel).

20 Note that N is a very large number as it refers to all potential investments projects of existing or new firms.

References

Bassi, M., C. Fox, G. Márquez, and J. Mazza (2006) "Creando Buenos Empleos: Políticas Públicas y Mercado de Trabajo". Mimeo, Banco Interamericano de Desarrollo.

Bell, L. A. (1997) "The Impact of Minimum Wages in Mexico and Colombia". *Journal of Labor Economics* 15: 103–35.

Bosch, M. and W. Maloney (2006) "Gross Worker Flows in the Presence of Informal Labor Markets: The Mexican Experience". Washington, DC: World Bank.

Calderon-Madrid, A. (2006) "Mobility of Workers between Formal and Informal Job Status: An Empirical Assessment of Earnings Variations and Exit Hazards in Mexico's Urban Labor Market". El Colegio de México.

Duryea, S., G. Marquez, C. Pages, and S. Scarpetta (2006) "For Better or for Worse: Job and Earnings Mobility in Nine Middle and Low Income Countries". Inter-American Development Bank.

Gong, X., A. Soest, and E. Villagomez (2004) "Mobility in the Urban Labor Market: A Panel Data Analysis for Mexico". *Economic Development and Cultural Change* 53(1): 1–36.

Guha-Khasnobis, B., R. Kanbur, and E. Ostrom (2006) "Beyond Formality and Informality". In Linking the Formal and Informal Economy: Concepts and Policies, edited by B. Guha-Khasnobis, R. Kanbur, and E. Ostrom. Oxford University Press.

Inter-American Development Bank (2004) *Good Jobs Wanted: Labor Markets in Latin America*, Washington, DC.

Levy, S. (2008) "Good Intentions, Bad Outcomes: Social Policy, Informality and Economic Growth in Mexico", Brookings Institution Press.

Maloney, W. and J. Nuñez Mendez (2004) "Measuring the Impact of Minimum

Wages: Evidence from Latin America." In *Law and Employment: Lessons from Latin America and the Caribbean*, edited by J. Heckman and C. Pages. University of Chicago Press.

Navarro, S. and P. Schrimpf (2004) "The Importance of Being Formal: Testing for Segmentation in the Mexican Labor Market." Department of Economics, University of Chicago.

12 Minimum wages in Kenya[*]

Mabel Andalón and Carmen Pagés

1 Introduction

Policies to set "living wages" are a popular but contentious instrument. As Blanchard (2002) suggests, the main reason for instituting minimum wages is to empower workers whose wages are constrained by the excessive market power of employers. Two other arguments in favor of minimum wage setting relate to efficiency/wages and the fact that minimum wages increase workers' purchasing power, which in turn can stimulate labor demand (Levin-Waldman, 1997). The efficiency-wage argument states that higher wages can increase workers' productivity, which in turn allows employers to pay higher wages. One reason for an increase in productivity might be that higher wages allow workers to improve their nutrition and their human development. Another version of this argument is that minimum wages force managers to provide on-the-job training, which makes workers more productive. Yet, it may also be argued that in the absence of well-developed incentives to provide training, firms may just become more selective, hiring workers with higher productivity rather than incurring the cost of training them. For its part, the purchasing power argument requires that low-wage businesses benefit from the higher consumption of low-income workers, which may not necessarily be the case. In the absence of that link, the effects are likely to be small, as increased sales are not likely to compensate for higher wage costs.

Minimum wages might also help to lift the working poor out of poverty by raising their wages. The empirical literature in Latin America (Morley, 1995) and other developing countries (Lustig and Mcleod, 1997) provides evidence that poverty falls as the minimum wage rises. Drawing on the "new economics of the minimum wage", more recent evidence reviewed in Deveraeux (2005) also suggests a decreasing in poverty that is achievable with negligible side-effects. However, a theoretical model developed by Fields and Kanbur (2007) suggests that poverty can actually decrease, increase, or remain unchanged, depending on the degree of poverty aversion, the elasticity of labor demand, the ratio of the minimum wage to the poverty line, and the extent of income sharing.

Yet, despite its potential benefits, minimum wages might also bring undesirable side effects. The standard competitive model predicts that forcing the price of labor above the market price leads to job losses in firms where regulations are enforced, and an increase in employment in the uncovered sector. In a model with fixed but imperfect levels of enforcement, which better characterize the labor market in Kenya (see Omolo and Omitti, 2004), positive, negative, or mute responses of employment to minimum wages can prevail within well-defined ranges of minimum wages and enforcement intensities (Basu, Chau, and Kanbur, 2007).

The empirical evidence on the effects of minimum wages on employment is quite mixed; see Neumark and Washer 2007 for a review of the literature on this issue. In developed countries a number of studies have failed to find significant negative impacts (see, for example, Card and Krueger, 1994 and Dickens, Machine, and Manning, 1999). Yet others find sizeable negative effects (see, for example, Brown, Gilroy, and Khon, 1982 and Neumark, Schweitzer, and Wascher, 2000). Most of the evidence for developing countries points to negative employment effects, in particular when wages are set at relatively high levels in relation to the median wage. Bell (1997) and Maloney and Nuñez (2004) find the negative employment effects of an increase in minimum wages in Colombia. Cowan, Micco, and Pagés (2004) and Montenegro and Pagés (2004) find negative employment effects in Chile. Gindling and Terrel (2005) find that an increase of multiple minimum wages reduces employment in Costa Rica. Rama (2001) also finds similar negative effects in Indonesia. Bhorat (2000) finds that mandatory wage increases in South Africa would result in significant job losses in low-pay occupations, such as low-paid domestic work and farm work. Jones (1997) finds a decline in manufacturing employment and an increase in employment in the informal sector in Ghana. In contrast, Lemos (2004) finds little evidence of adverse employment effects in Brazil, and Bell (1997) finds no effects in Mexico where the minimum wage is set at a lower level relative to the median wage.

Kenya has held an active minimum wage-setting policy since independence. There are as many as 17 minimum wage orders, setting a large number of minimum wage floors that vary by occupation, sector of activity, and location. Minimum wages are updated annually and apply to all salaried employees who are at least 18 years old and work in the formal sector. The self-employed are not covered by statutory minimum wages. A different wage grid applies to agricultural employees and to workers in other activities.

Evidence of the effect of minimum wages in Kenya is hampered by the scarcity of data. In a descriptive paper, Omolo and Omitti (2004) find that the minimum wage policy in Kenya has failed to contribute to sustained poverty reduction. Moreover, using aggregate time series data, they find a negative correlation between minimum wages and modern private sector employment. This paper contributes to the literature of the effects of minimum wages on the Kenyan labor market by: (i) examining the performance of the legislation of minimum wages in Kenya, both in terms of its coverage and enforcement, and (ii) estimating the effects on wages and employment using micro data. Our findings based on the 1998/9 labor force data indicate that minimum wages were better enforced and had stronger effects in the non-agricultural industry. More specifically, our results suggest that (i) non-compliance affected one in four salaried workers in agriculture and one in six in non-agricultural activities in urban areas, (ii) minimum wages were associated with higher wages for low-educated workers and women in urban areas who work in non-agricultural activities, while no such effects were found for workers in agriculture, and (iii) higher minimum wages were associated with a lower share of workers in formal activities, and a higher share of workers in self-employment in a given occupation and location.

The rest of the paper is organized as follows: Section 2 describes the institutions for minimum wage setting in Kenya. Section 3 presents the data used in this study. Section 4 examines the enforcement and wage effects of minimum wages. Sections 5 and 6 report some estimates of its effects on the wage level and distribution and the structure of employment, respectively. The last section concludes.

2 Institutions for minimum wage-setting

Minimum wages in Kenya are specified as part of a national wage policy set in place before independence and guided by the Regulation of Wages and Conditions of Employment Act (CAP 229). The objective of such policy has been to reduce poverty as well as to protect and promote the living standards of workers (Omolo and Omitti, 2004). Two wage boards: the Agricultural Wages Advisory Board (AWAB) and the General Wages Advisory Board (GWAB) give recommendations on the wages that might be published on May 1 of each year and on the employment conditions of workers. The GWAB has the authority to appoint wage councils to set statutory working conditions and minimum wages in different occupations. There are 17 such wage councils, but most of them have only updated statutory wages on an ad hoc basis and so they are often outdated. The AWAB sets statutory minimum wage orders for agricultural workers while the GWAB sets wage floors for workers in other industries who are not covered by specific wage boards. The boards have a tripartite structure (dominated by the Ministry of Labor, the central organization of trade unions and the Federation of Kenyan Employers) and are chaired by an independent member (usually a labor market or industry expert). Given the advisory status of the boards, the Ministry of Labor can modify their proposals without consultation. Since 2002, the government has not specified the statutory minimum wages for workers below 18 years of age in order to discourage the employment of children.

Within agriculture and non-agricultural activities in urban areas (hereafter general order), statutory minimum wages vary by age and occupation. In addition, for the general order, minimum wages also vary by location, distinguishing three separate urban areas with different minimum wage levels.

These geographical areas are: Nairobi and Mombassa, other municipalities, and other towns. The classification of occupations retains the colonial job classification in Kenya—with a few additions and no subtractions over time—implying that some wage categories may be irrelevant for the current job market. Tables 12.1 and 12.2 list the schedule of minimum wages specified by the agricultural and general order, respectively, for the years 1997–2004. These minimum wages only apply to workers aged 18 years or older. Within occupation and locations, minimum wages increase with the skill level and with city size. Despite the many values of the minimum wages, relative minimum wages have been kept constant by virtue of multiplying all minimum wages by the same growth factor.[1] Therefore, different minimum wages across occupations have not contributed to modify relative wages across occupations or locations.

In real terms, minimum wages fell sharply from the period 1991 to 1994 and then increased afterwards at a rate of 2% a year. However, in 2004 real minimum wages had not recovered the 1991 level (Figure 12.1). In the last years (since 1998) real minimum wages have grown in line with real GDP per capita, but much below the growth rate of real wages in the private sector (Figure 12.1). The evolution of the real minimum wage is almost identical if rather than a price index for the lower income group, available only for Nairobi, an overall CPI index, obtained from the World Development Indicators (WDI) is used.

The stabilization of inflation in 1995 brought real gains in minimum and average wages. However, the relaxation of wage guidelines in mid-1994 was followed by an upward adjustment of real wages in both the public and the private sectors (Kulundu Manda, 2002), which was not accompanied by similar adjustments in the minimum wage. In fact, compared to the average wage, minimum wages for general laborers declined from 0.35 of the average wage in the private sector in 1994, to 0.17 in 2004 (Figure 12.2). Given this evolution it is quite unlikely that minimum wages are behind the sharp increase in average wages experienced since 1994.

3 Data

In this study, we rely on aggregate data from the Central Bureau of Statistics (*Economic Survey*, various years) and micro-data from the 1998/9 Integrated Labour Force Survey (ILFS), a nationally representative survey conducted during the months of December 1998 and January 1999 to 11,040 households. At the individual level there are records for 52,016 individuals. The main purpose of this survey was to gather information on the labor force, the informal sector, and child labor in Kenya.[2]

In the analysis that follows, the term "salaried" or "paid employees" refers to all workers working for someone else, in exchange for a wage or a salary. Salary is defined as income from paid employment before adding other benefits and allowances, and before deducting taxes and other compulsory

Table 12.1 Gazetted monthly basic minimum wages for agricultural industry, 1997–2004, Kenyan shillings

Occupation	1997	1998	1999	2000	2001	2002	2003	2004
Unskilled employees 18 years and above	1,095	1,259	1,347	1,428	1,535	1,642	1,888	2,096
Stockman, herdsman, and watchman 18 year and above	1,263	1,453	1,555	1,648	1,772	1,896	2,180	2,420
Skilled and semi-skilled employees								
House servant or cook	1,249	1,436	1,537	1,629	1,751	1,874	2,155	2,392
Farm foreman	1,973	2,269	2,428	2,574	2,767	2,961	3,405	3,780
Farm clerk	1,973	2,269	2,428	2,574	2,767	2,961	3,405	3,780
Section foreman	1,278	1,470	1,573	1,667	1,792	1,917	2,205	2,448
Farm artisan	1,309	1,505	1,610	1,707	1,835	1,963	2,257	2,505
Tractor driver	1,387	1,595	1,707	1,809	1,945	2,081	2,393	2,656
Combine harvester driver	1,528	1,757	1,880	1,993	2,142	2,292	2,636	2,926
Lorry driver or car driver	1,604	1,845	1,974	2,092	2,249	2,406	2,767	3,701
Average	1,362	1,567	1,676	1,777	1,910	2,199	2,529	2,870

Source: Economic Survey, Central Bureau of Statistics, from Ministry of Labor and Human Resource Development

Table 12.2 Gazetted monthly basic minimum wages for non-agricultural industry in urban areas excluding housing allowance (general order), 1998–2000 and 2002–2004, Kenyan shillings

Occupation	Nairobi area, Mombasa, and Kisumu			Other municipalities plus Mavoko and Ruiru town councils			All other towns		
	1998	1999	2000*	1998	1999	2000*	1998	1999	2000*
General laborer	2,697	2,886	3,059	2,488	2,662	2,822	1,439	1,540	1,632
Miner, stone cutter, turnboy, waiter, cook	2,912	3,116	3,303	2,593	2,764	2,930	1,663	1,779	1,886
Night watchman	3,008	3,279	3,412	2,790	2,985	3,164	1,717	1,837	1,947
Machine attendant	3,056	3,270	3,446	2,844	3,043	3,226	2,306	2,467	2,615
Machinist	3,488	3,732	3,956	3,264	3,492	3,702	2,669	2,856	3,027
Plywood machine operator	3,639	3,894	4,128	3,359	3,594	3,810	2,778	2,972	3,150
Pattern designer	4,154	4,445	4,712	3,797	4,063	4,307	3,238	3,465	3,673
Tailor, driver (medium vehicle)	4,578	4,898	5,192	4,208	4,503	4,773	3,751	4,014	4,255
Dyer, crawler, tractor driver, salesman	5,054	5,408	5,732	4,715	5,045	5,348	4,256	4,554	4,827
Saw doctor, caretaker (building)	5,593	5,985	6,344	5,222	5,588	5,923	4,865	5,206	5,518
Cashier, driver (heavy commercial)	6,086	6,512	6,903	5,726	6,127	6,495	5,369	5,745	6,090
Artisan (ungraded)	3,639	3,894	4,128	3,359	3,594	3,810	2,778	2,972	3,150
Artisan Grade III	4,578	4,898	5,192	4,208	4,503	4,773	3,758	4,021	4,262
Artisan Grade II	5,054	5,408	5,732	4,715	5,045	5,348	4,256	4,554	4,827
Artisan Grade I	6,086	6,512	6,903	5,726	6,127	6,495	5,369	5,745	6,090
Average	4,241	4,538	4,809	3,934	4,209	4,462	3,347	3,582	3,797

(Continued overleaf)

Table 12.2 Continued

Occupation	Nairobi area, Mombasa and Kisumu			Other municipalities plus Mavoko and Ruiru town councils			All other towns		
	2002	2003	2004	2002	2003	2004	2002	2003	2004
General laborer	3,518	3,905	4,335	3,246	3,603	3,999	1,877	2,083	2,312
Miner, stone cutter, turnboy, waiter, cook	3,800	4,218	4,682	3,371	3,742	4,154	2,169	2,408	2,673
Night watchman	3,925	4,357	4,836	3,639	4,039	4,483	2,240	2,486	2,759
Machine attendant	3,987	4,426	4,913	3,711	4,119	4,572	3,008	3,339	3,706
Machinist	4,551	5,052	5,608	4,259	4,727	5,247	3,482	3,865	4,290
Plywood machine operator	4,749	5,271	5,851	4,383	4,865	5,400	3,623	4,022	4,464
Pattern designer	5,420	6,016	6,678	4,954	5,499	6,104	4,224	4,689	5,205
Tailor, driver (medium vehicle)	5,972	6,629	7,358	5,490	6,094	6,764	4,894	5,432	6,030
Dyer, crawler, tractor driver, Salesman	6,593	7,318	8,123	6,151	6,828	7,579	5,552	6,163	6,841
Saw doctor, caretaker (building)	7,297	8,100	8,991	6,813	7,562	8,394	6,347	7,045	7,820
Cashier, driver (heavy commercial)	7,940	8,813	9,782	7,471	8,293	9,205	7,005	7,776	8,631
Artisan (ungraded)	4,749	5,271	5,851	4,383	4,865	5,400	3,623	4,022	4,464
Artisan Grade III	5,972	6,629	7,358	5,490	6,094	6,764	4,903	5,442	6,041
Artisan Grade II	6,593	7,318	8,123	6,151	6,828	7,579	5,552	6,163	6,841
Artisan Grade I	7,940	8,813	9,782	7,471	8,293	9,205	7,005	7,776	8,631
Average	5,534	6,142	6,818	5,132	5,697	6,323	4,367	4,848	5,381

Source: Economic Survey, 2001 and 2005. Central Bureau of Statistics from Ministry of Labor and Human Resource Development.

* Provisional

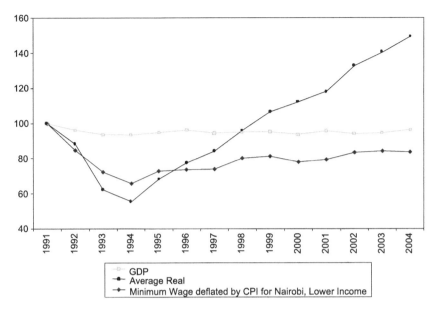

Figure 12.1 Evolution of minimum wage, GDP per capita, and average wage in real terms.

Source: Own calculations based on Economic Survey (Central Bureau of Statistics), various years.

Notes: Minimum wages correspond to the values for general laborers in Nairobi and Mombassa deflated with a price index for the lower income group in Nairobi. Average wages are for the private sector deflated with CPI from World Development Indicators, World Bank.

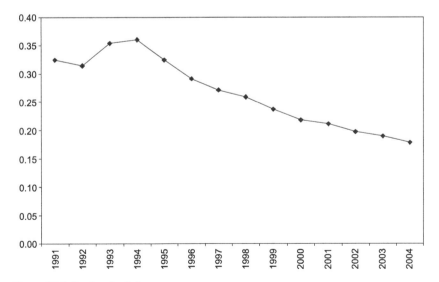

Figure 12.2 Ratio of minimum to average wage.

Source: Own calculations based on Economic Survey (Central Bureau of Statistics), various years.

Notes: Minimum wages correspond to the values for general laborers in Nairobi and Mombassa deflated with a price index for the lower income group in Nairobi. Average wages are for private sector workers deflated with CPI from World Development Indicators, World Bank.

deduction. The self-employed is comprised of people that run their own business (i.e. working employers who hire employees, and own-account workers who hire no employees). Unskilled workers are those who work in elementary occupations according to ISCO-88. Low-educated workers are people who have completed secondary schooling or less.

The formal sector includes public and private establishments operating organized businesses as well as farm-related economic activities that are mainly located in rural areas. The informal sector, also referred to as "*Jua Kali*," covers all small-scale activities that are normally semi-organized and unregulated, and use low and simple technology.

Panels I and II of Table 12.3 report summary statistics for the entire population and for those who work. For the latter, we restrict the sample to people between 18 and 64 years old.[3] Data indicates a high share of children (42%) and of low-educated people (8%), and a majority of the people living in rural areas (74%). Out of those who live in urban areas 35.7% are concentrated in the largest cities: Nairobi and Mombassa.

Regarding those in work, one in four workers are self-employed, 33.6% are paid employees, and a large majority of employed workers are in unpaid work (43%). Out of those in salaried jobs, one-quarter are in the informal sector, 55% lived in urban areas, 14% were engaged in agricultural activities, and 30% are public sector employees.

Panel III of Table 12.3 presents wage indicators for salaried workers aged 18–64 who earned positive wages in the month of reference and worked full time. Restricting the sample this way yields 3,331 observations. Median earnings are lower in the informal compared to those in the formal sector, however, wage inequality is higher in the informal sector.

4 Incidence and compliance of minimum wages

Minimum wages in Kenya are said to suffer from inadequate enforcement. Omolo and Omitti (2004) indicate that "[even] the government itself does not adhere to the minimum wage regulations" (16). Using microdata from the 1998/9 ILFS—the last cross section of household data available— it is possible to estimate the degree of coverage and enforcement of the minimum wage in that year. These calculations are performed separately for general order (non-agricultural activities in urban areas) and agricultural minimum wages.

We determine the specific minimum wage that applies to each worker based on the reported sector of activity, geographical location, and occupation according to the ISCO-88 classification for occupations (Elias and Birch, 1994). It is quite difficult to match the list of occupations specified in the minimum wage schedule with those in the ISCO-88 classification. For example, the minimum wage schedule lists at least four different minimum wages for clerical jobs. Thus, it distinguishes between junior clerks, typists, cashiers, and general clerks. Given these difficulties, we use the following

Table 12.3 Descriptive statistics

Variables	Kenya
I. Percentage of population	
aged 0 to 14 years old	42.26
aged 15 to 24 years old	20.00
aged 25 to 64 years old	33.82
aged over 65 years old	3.92
women	50.08
enrolled in schooling	27.58
no education	26.56
primary education	51.33
secondary education	17.09
undergraduate and postgraduate	0.92
retired	0.43
in urban areas	25.91
Nairobi and Mombasa	35.77
Other Municipalities	51.84
All other towns	6.15
sample	52 016
II. Percentage of workers (18 to 64 years)	
self employed	24.63
paid employees:	33.60
informal sector	26.81
full time	79.99
in urban areas	55.73
Nairobi and Mombasa	40.82
Other Municipalities	49.47
All other towns	5.82
agriculture[#]	14.23
manufacturing	14.06
construction	4.59
hotels and restaurants	5.05
transports and communications	8.2
financial services	6.14
public sector	29.92
sample	17 145

	Total	Formal	Informal
III. Labor market indicators*			
in 10th percentile real earnings distribution	7.36	7.87	6.73
in 25th percentile real earnings distribution	8.01	8.23	7.22
in 50th percentile real earnings distribution	8.52	8.69	7.79
in 75th percentile real earnings distribution	8.97	9.03	8.29
in 90th percentile real earnings distribution	9.35	9.44	8.78
in average real earnings distribution	8.79	8.93	8.18
sample[§]	3 331	2 409	804

Source: Own calculations based on 98/9 ILFS data.

\# The fractions of the activities do not add up to 1 because there are some activities not reported here.

* The sample used is full time paid employees aged 18–64 years with positive earnings

§ The difference between formal and informal and total is due to missing values in status of employment.

methodology to match workers to minimum wage categories: for all workers for whom there is no clear match to the minimum wages categories we assign them to the general laborer minimum wage. This is the wage that according to the minimum wage regulation applies to all workers except when other orders specify a higher minimum wage. For workers for whom a match between the ISCO occupation and the minimum wages schedule is made and the minimum wages schedule specifies a higher minimum wage than that for general laborers, we replace the general minimum wage with the higher minimum wage specified under the law. Finally, when the minimum wages distinguishes different levels of minimum wages for workers within the same occupation group, we assign the lower minimum wage within the category. For example, in the case of clerks, this implies that all non-clearly assigned workers in clerical jobs are given the "junior clerk" minimum wage level.[4]

There are several additional sample restrictions. According to the Regulation of Wages and Conditions of Employment Act, the GWAB is responsible for setting minimum wages for workers in non-agricultural activities living in rural areas. However, the information on the minimum wages that apply to these workers is not available and so we had to eliminate these people from the analysis.[5] Of the 3,331 workers who earned positive wages in the month of reference and worked full time, 1,661 were engaged in non-agricultural activities in rural zones. The self-employed are also not included in these calculations as earnings data for these workers is not available in the survey.[6] Unpaid family workers are excluded for the same reason. Additional restrictions due to missing data on status of employment yield a sample of 1,772 observations. Non-compliance rates (reported below) would be much higher if this large group was included in the calculations.

We find substantial non-compliance rates. About 24% of the salaried workers in agriculture and 17% of salaried workers in non-agricultural activities in urban areas earned monthly wages below the statutory minimum (see Table 12.4, *Fraction below*). Non-compliance was particularly high among workers in the higher-skill occupations in urban zones such as dyers, crawlers, tractor drivers, salesmen, saw doctor, or caretakers where it reached 67%. Among the different types of workers, non-compliance was similar for men and women in agriculture, but much higher for women (25%), relative to men (7%), in the general order (Table 12.5). Non-compliance was also higher for less-educated workers, particularly in agriculture and for young workers (18–25 years old) both in agricultural and in general order (Tables 12.6 and 12.7). Within the general order regime, non-compliance was higher in municipalities other than Nairobi and Mombassa (Table 12.8).

The ILFS data allows the percentage of workers whose earnings are at the minimum wage level to be identified. This percentage is usually identified by the term "Fraction." Only a small fraction of salaried workers received monthly wages equal to the statutory minimum. If Fraction is measured as all workers whose earnings are within a range of plus/minus 2% of

Table 12.4 Minimum wage indicators: fraction below, fraction at MW, fraction affected, and Kaitz index

Occupation	Obs.	Occupation share	Fraction below	Fraction at +/- 2%	Fraction at +/- 5%	Fraction affected	Minimum to median ratio (median group)	Minimum to median ratio (median salaried)
I. Agricultural industry	510	100	0.245	0.003	0.068	0.081	0.768	0.392
unskilled	281	54.61	0.276	0.003	0.049	0.049	0.630	0.315
stockman, herdsman and watchman	159	29.57	0.265	0.000	0.114	0.147	0.727	0.363
house servant or cook	32	7.73	0.141	0.000	0.059	0.086	0.410	0.359
farm foreman, farm clerk	18	4.73	0.035	0.000	0.000	0.064	0.336	0.567
farm artisan	5	0.76	0.182	0.182	0.182	0.000	0.753	0.376
tractor driver	8	1.22	0.207	0.000	0.000	0.000	0.659	0.399
lorry or car driver	7	1.37	0.000	0.000	0.091	0.091	0.283	0.461
II. General order	1212	100	0.176	0.021	0.029	0.051	0.529	0.767
general laborer	593	48.73	0.136	0.015	0.020	0.041	0.415	0.622
miner, stone cutter, turnboy, waiter,cook	9	0.66	0.298	0.000	0.000	0.000	0.549	0.686
machine attendant, shoe cutter	167	13.12	0.201	0.066	0.080	0.083	0.560	0.728
machinist, junior clerk	138	10.63	0.068	0.006	0.013	0.025	0.567	0.831
plywood machine operator, copy-typist, shop assistant	172	16.02	0.074	0.000	0.012	0.086	0.570	0.869
pattern designer	2	0.2	1.000	0.000	0.000	0.000	1.296	0.972
dyer, crawler, tractor driver, salesman	62	6.79	0.675	0.037	0.046	0.019	1.612	1.227
saw doctor, caretaker (building)	20	1.16	0.678	0.072	0.072	0.072	1.342	1.342
cashier/driver(heavy commercial)	40	2.01	0.340	0.048	0.077	0.049	0,721	1.441
artisan (upgraded)	9	0.68	0.052	0.000	0.000	0.000	0.640	0.880

Source: Authors' calculations based on ILFS data.

Notes: Fraction below is the percentage of workers paid below their corresponding statutory minimum. Fraction at +/- x% is the fraction of salaried workers that received monthly wages within a rage of plus/minus 2 and 5% of the statutory minimum wage. Fraction affected is the proportion of people earning a real wage between the 1998 and the 1999 minimum wage. The minimum to median ratio is also known as the Kaitz index.

Table 12.5 Minimum wages variables by gender

Occupation	Gender	Obs.	Occupation share	Fraction below	Fraction at +/-2%	Fraction at +/-5%	Fraction affected	Minimum to median ratio (median group)	Minimum to median ratio (median salaried)
A. Agricultural industry*									
unskilled		510	100	0.245	0.003	0.068	0.081	0.768	0.392
	male	209	39.03	0.270	0.002	0.042	0.037	0.630	0.315
	female	72	15.58	0.292	0.007	0.068	0.077	0.552	0.315
all other occupations	male	184	35.06	0.207	0.004	0.096	0.101	0.620	0.388
	female	45	10.33	0.213	0.000	0.071	0.186	0.779	0.389
B. General order&									
general laborer		1212	100	0.176	0.021	0.029	0.051	0.529	0.767
	male	377	30.66	0.069	0.015	0.022	0.037	0.357	0.615
	female	216	18.07	0.249	0.014	0.017	0.048	0.551	0.634
all other occupations	male	477	39.67	0.215	0.027	0.040	0.059	0.628	0.907
	female	142	11.60	0.215	0.024	0.031	0.062	0.688	0.893

Source: Authors' calculations based on ILFS data.

Notes: See Table 12.4 for definitions of the variables reported in this table.
* all other occupations in Agricultural industry refers to workers other than unskilled workers in Table 12.1.
& all other occupations in general order refers to workers other than general labourers in Table 12.2.

Table 12.6 Minimum wage indicators by education level

Occupation	Education	Obs.	Occupation share	Fraction below	Fraction at +/- 2%	Fraction at +/- 5%	Fraction affected	Minimum to median ratio (median group)	Minimum to median ratio (median salaried)
A. Agricultural industry*									
unskilled		510	100	0.245	0.003	0.068	0.081	0.768	0.392
	Low	258	49.95	0.292	0.004	0.054	0.053	0.630	0.315
	High	23	4.67	0.100	0.000	0.000	0.000	0.420	0.315
all other occupations	Low	166	30.28	0.297	0.000	0.131	0.170	0.819	0.369
	High	63	15.11	0.033	0.009	0.009	0.020	0.253	0.427
B. General order\&									
general laborer		1212	100	0.176	0.021	0.029	0.051	0.529	0.767
	Low	207	16.49	0.307	0.019	0.027	0.075	0.737	0.641
	High	386	32.24	0.048	0.013	0.017	0.024	0.320	0.613
all other occupations	Low	180	13.23	0.316	0.045	0.053	0.053	0.684	0.855
	High	439	38.04	0.180	0.020	0.032	0.062	0.614	0.921

Source: Authors' calculations based on ILFS data.

Notes: See Table 12.4 for definitions of the variables reported in this table.
* all other occupations in Agricultural industry refers to workers other than unskilled workers in Table 12.1.
\& all other occupations in general order refers to workers other than general labourers in Table 12.2.

Table 12.7 Minimum wage indicators by age

Occupation	Age	Obs.	Occupation share	Fraction below	Fraction at +/- 2%	Fraction at +/- 5%	Fraction affected	Minimum to median ratio (median group)	Minimum to median ratio (median salaried)
A. Agricultural industry*									
unskilled		510	100	0.245	0.003	0.068	0.081	0.768	0.392
	18–25	85	15.43	0.408	0.000	0.064	0.013	0.839	0.315
	26–45	145	28.73	0.203	0.003	0.053	0.065	0.594	0.315
	46–64	51	10.45	0.281	0.010	0.017	0.058	0.617	0.315
all other occupations	18–25	58	8.91	0.463	0.000	0.106	0.140	1.008	0.378
	26–45	135	28.84	0.155	0.005	0.094	0.130	0.614	0.384
	46–64	36	7.64	0.109	0.000	0.056	0.056	0.369	0.415
B. General order&									
general laborer		1212	100	0.176	0.021	0.029	0.051	0.529	0.767
	18–25	117	0.10	0.317	0.020	0.029	0.066	0.661	0.628
	26–45	401	0.07	0.088	0.016	0.018	0.037	0.382	0.621
	46–64	75	0.32	0.088	0.003	0.017	0.024	0.375	0.618
all other occupations	18–25	104	0.09	0.558	0.065	0.077	0.102	1.280	0.960
	26–45	436	0.36	0.125	0.018	0.031	0.057	0.594	0.892
	46–64	79	0.06	0.217	0.015	0.018	0.004	0.591	0.887

Source: Authors' calculations based on ILFS data

Notes: See Table 12.4 for definitions of the variables reported in this table.
* all other occupations in Agricultural industry refers to workers other than unskilled workers in Table 12.1.
& all other occupations in general order refers to workers other than general labourers in Table 12.2.

Table 12.8 Minimum wage indicators by location

Occupation	Obs.	Fraction below	Fraction at +/− 2%	Fraction at +/− 5%	Fraction affected	Minimum to median ratio (median group)	Minimum to median ratio (median salaried)
Area 1: Mombasa and Nairobi general labourer	177	0.073	0.000	0.005	0.053	0.450	0.674
Area 2: Other municipalities general labourer	368	0.214	0.031	0.038	0.038	0.440	0.622
Area 3: All other towns general labourer	48	0.008	0.000	0.000	0.000	0.189	0.360

Source: Authors' calculations based on ILFS data

Notes: See Table 12.4 for definitions of the variables reported in this table.

the statutory minimum wage, it is found that only 0.3% of the workers in agricultural activities, and 2.1% of workers in urban areas had earnings within that range (see Table 12.4, *Fraction at + /–2 %*) Even when this interval is increased to plus/minus 5% of the minimum wage, the share of workers whose earnings fall in that range is not very large: 6.8% for agricultural and 2.9 for urban workers. The fraction at the minimum wage is higher for men, less educated, and young workers.

The number of workers whose wage and employment status are potentially influenced by the minimum wage increases somewhat if we adopt as a measure of the importance of the minimum wage the *fraction affected*, that is the proportion of workers whose wages are just above the 1998 minimum wage, but below the wage set the following year in May 1, 1999.[7] These workers could potentially have lost their jobs after the following update if the wage in 1998/9 reflected their productivity. According to this measure, 8.1% of the workers in agriculture and 5.1 in general order were at risk of being affected by the minimum wage increase. This percentage is higher for women, less educated, and younger workers.

The ratio of the minimum to the average wage is a widely used measure to assess the toughness of the minimum wage. This measure is often called the *Kaitz ratio*. Another often-reported measure is the ratio of the minimum wage relative to the median wage in the economy. Measures referred to the median wage are more appropriated in countries with high earnings inequality or in instances where the minimum wage could be affecting the average wage. Based on this latter indicator, minimum wages in Kenya are 0.39 and 0.76 of the median wage for agricultural and general order respectively (see last column in Tables 12.4–12.8) By way of comparison Maloney and Nuñez Mendez (2004) find this indicator to be 0.68 in Colombia, a country in which minimum wages are considered to be high and binding. This ratio is lower for the unskilled occupations in both the agricultural and general order. However, a number of minimum wages for semiskilled or skilled occupations are set at levels that are very high relative to the median wages (above two-thirds of the median).

Based on the 1998/9 levels—there were 18 minimum wages that were higher than 70% of the median wage for all employees (Table 12.9). Levin-Waldman, 1997 suggests setting minimum wages at the median of the unskilled labor wages. In Kenya, most minimum wages in urban areas are way above that range; and while minimum wages in rural areas appear low, many are above this threshold when compared to the wages of unskilled laborers for agricultural areas (Table 12.9).

5 Incidence of the minimum wage on wage level and distribution

The analysis in the previous section yields a mixed picture. While wages are set at quite high levels relative to the median wage, non-compliance is high and the fraction of workers that receive wages at the minimum is relatively

Table 12.9 Minimum wages relative to the median for all salaried workers 1998/9

Occupation	Mombassa, Nairobi and Kisumu	Other municipalities	All other towns
general laborer	0.674	0.622	0.360
general miner, stone cutter	0.728	0.646	
machine attendant/shoe cutter	0.764	0.711	0.577
junior clerk/tractor driver	0.872	0.816	0.667
machine operator/copy-typist/ shop assistant	0.910	0.840	0.695
artisan (upgraded)	0.910	0.840	
salesman/tractor driver	1.264	1.179	1.064
caretaker	1.398	1.306	1.216
cashier/driver(heavy)	1.522	1.432	1.342

Agricultural Industry

Occupation	Median all salaried	Median unskilled in Agriculture
unskilled	0.315	0.630
house servant	0.359	0.718
stockman, herdsman and watchman	0.363	0.727
farm artisan	0.376	0.753
tractor driver	0.399	0.798
lorry or car driver	0.461	0.923
farm foreman or farm clerk	0.567	1.135

Source: Authors' computations based on 98/9 ILFS data.

small. The latter suggest that minimum wages may not be affecting the level or the distribution of wages in a noticeable way.

The Labor Force data (1998/9) indicates that across occupations there is a strong positive relation between the level and the percentage of non-compliance of the minimum wage, as shown in Figure 12.3. The former suggests that attempts to raise the minimum wage to significant levels in relation to the median wage lead to increasing non-compliance, thus reducing the scope for effects of the minimum wage on wages.

A common way to judge whether minimum wages have an influence in the overall wage distribution is to assess the shape of the distribution and see whether a large number of workers are bunched around the minimum wage level. If minimum wages do not exert any influence, the distribution of the logarithm of wages would display a typical Normal curve. If instead, the minimum wage is exerting a significant influence, many workers would receive wages at the minimum level and the wage distribution would show a spike at the minimum wage. In addition, there would be few workers with earnings immediately below the statutory minimum, as their wages would have been

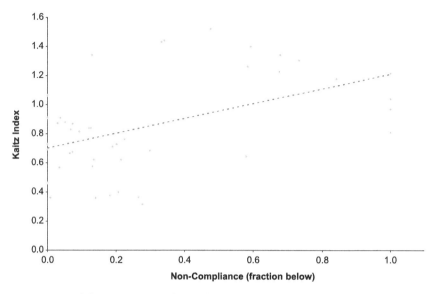

Figure 12.3 Minimum wage level (relative to median wage for salaried population) and percentage of non-compliance by occupation–location pairs.

Source: Authors' elaboration from Labor Force data for period 1998/9.

Notes: Each data point corresponds to the ratio of the minimum to the median wage and the non-compliance rates for one occupation–location pair (for example, unskilled workers in agricultural sector). For each occupation–location pair, the minimum to median wage ratio is computed dividing by the median wage of overall salaried employment.

pushed up by the effect of establishing a wage floor. To accommodate the fact that Kenya has a large number of minimum wages, we present two curves in the same graph. The first presents the distribution of minimum wages; the second is a histogram of the wage distribution. Spikes in the distribution of minimum wages indicate minimum wage levels that, at least in principle, are applicable to many workers. These are the levels of the minimum wage that are likely to exert a higher influence in the distribution of wages, and the ones on which we focus our attention.

Figures 12.4 and 12.5 present the distribution of wages and minimum wages in the agricultural sector for formal and informal salaried workers respectively. We focus first on the distribution of minimum wages. The solid line in the figure indicates how many workers are subjected to each level of minimum wages. The spikes in this curve indicate that in agriculture, two minimum wage levels apply, at least in principle, to a large number of workers. These are the statutory wages for unskilled workers and for stockman, herdsman, and watchman. In comparison, minimum wages for other occupations are applicable only to a small number of salaried agricultural workers. We then assess whether the distribution of wages displays spikes at any of the two minimum wage levels mentioned above, either in the formal

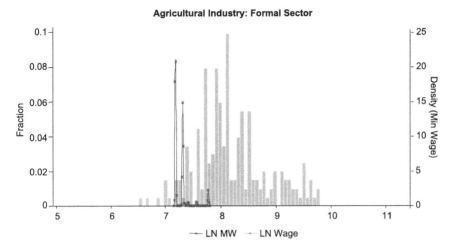

Figure 12.4 Minimum wages in agricultural industry. Formal sector 1998/9: distribution of wages and minimum wages.

Source: Authors' calculations based on 1998/9 ILFS data.

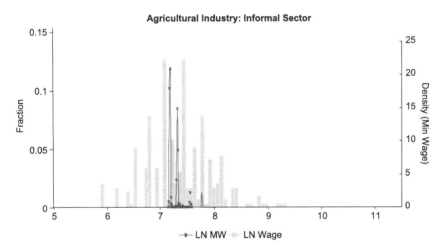

Figure 12.5 Minimum wages in agricultural industry. Informal sector 1998/9: distribution of wages and minimum wages.

Source: Authors' calculations based on 1998/9 ILFS data.

or informal wage distribution. This would indicate that statutory minimum wages alter the wage distribution. An examination of Figures 12.4 and 12.5 shows that there are no noticeable spikes in the wage distribution at the two mentioned minimum wage levels in the formal or in the informal sector, even though compliance levels are higher in the formal sector. Thus, there is no indication of substantive effects of minimum wages on agricultural wages.

In contrast, there appears to be a spike at the minimum wage for general laborers in municipalities other than Nairobi and Mombassa in the distribution of general order formal wages in urban areas (Figure 12.6) which is not evident in the figure for informal employment (Figure 12.7). Figure 12.6 also reveals higher compliance with the minimum wage in the formal relative to the informal sector. The distribution of wages for formal workers lies mostly at the right of the minimum wage for general laborers. Instead, non-compliance is high and minimum wages appear not to affect the distribution of wages in the informal sector (Figure 12.7).

The former findings suggest that minimum wages might be pushing up the level of urban wages for formal workers in urban areas—particularly in municipalities other than Nairobi and Mombassa. However, they should be taken only as indicative as a visual inspection of the wage distribution does not provide conclusive evidence about the relationship of minimum wages and earnings controlling for individual characteristics and other factors that influence the wage level. We do so by estimating the following specification separately for agricultural and general order:

$$\ln W_{ioj} = a + \beta \ln MW_{oj} + X_i \Gamma + \tau_o + \tau_j + \tau_s + \varepsilon_{ioj} \tag{1}$$

where W_{ioj} is the monthly real wage of worker i in occupation o and location j; MW_{oj} is the monthly real minimum wage for occupation o and location j; X_i is a vector of personal characteristics (level of education, gender, and age);

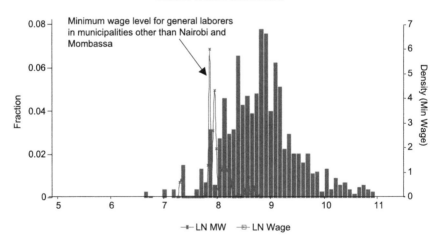

Figure 12.6 Minimum wages in general order (urban areas). Formal sector 1998/9: distribution of wages and minimum wages.

Source: Authors' calculations based on 1998/9 ILFS data.

General Order: Informal Sector

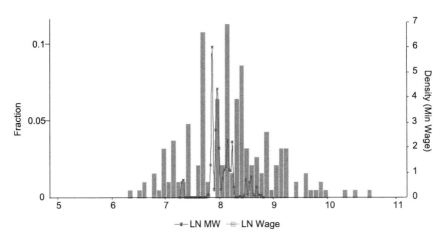

Figure 12.7 Minimum wages in general order. Informal sector 1998/9: distribution of wages and minimum wages.

Source: Authors' calculations based on 1998/9 ILFS data.

τ_o, τ_j, and τ_s are sets of indicator variables for occupation, location and sector of employment (formal or informal) respectively and ε_{ioj} is the error term. In some specifications we also include interactions of the minimum wages with personal characteristics and the sector of employment. Notice that by controlling by occupation and location we can compare differences in minimum wages within occupations across locations in which minimum wages are set at higher levels relative to locations where they are set at a lower rate.

The first and the fourth columns in Table 12.10 report the simple correlation between the level of wages and minimum wages, for agricultural and general order minimum wages. Such correlation is found to be positive and statistically significant for agricultural activities; however, it may well be driven by reverse causality: higher wages determine higher minimum wages. Columns (2) and (4) in Table 12.10 examine the correlation between wages and minimum wages controlling for a number of individual and job characteristics that explain the level of wages across occupations. Once these effects are taken into account, the minimum wage is no longer significant in explaining the level of wages for the average worker.

However, minimum wages may be relevant for explaining the wage level of workers of certain types, particularly those whose wages are more likely to be close to the minimum wage. To account for such a possibility, we add interactions between the minimum wage level and individual characteristics of workers (age, gender, education level, and whether formal or informal). We report the results in columns (3) and (6) of Table 12.10. Given

Table 12.10 Effect of minimum wages on wages. Dependent variable: Natural logarithm of real wages

Variables	Agricultural			General order		
	1	2	3	4	5	6
ln MW	1.960* [0.256]	0.396 [0.213]		0.054 [0.084]	0.165 [0.156]	1.016** [0.388]
education		0.609*** [0.118]	5.369 [6.129]		0.600*** [0.110]	5.962*** [2.098]
gender (1 = female)		-0.120*** [0.028]	-0.135*** [0.025]		-0.183*** [0.048]	-0.421*** [0.115]
18–25		-0.293*** [0.037]	5.132** [1.431]		-0.359*** [0.051]	-2.219 [1.603]
46–64		0.001 [0.079]	-2.281 [2.332]		0.240*** [0.066]	2.9 [1.701]
stockman, herdsman and watchman			0.068 [0.040]			
house servant			0.472*** [0.055]			
farm foreman, farm clerk			0.529 [0.559]			
farm artisan			-0.063 [0.099]			
tractor driver			0.152 [0.092]			
lorry or car driver			0.543* [0.253]			
miner, stone cutter, turnboy, waiter, cook					-0.295 [0.186]	-0.328** [0.156]
machine attendant, shoe cutter					-0.07 [0.055]	-0.104 [0.063]
machinist, junior clerk					-0.222*** [0.067]	-0.285*** [0.065]
playwood machine operator, copy-typist,					-0.024 [0.062]	-0.142* [0.070]
shop assistant					0.018 [0.135]	-0.126 [0.201]
pattern designer						

	(1)	(2)	(3)	(4)	(5)	(6)
dyer, crawler, tractor driver, salesman					-0.452*** [0.124]	-0.651*** [0.194]
sawdoctor, caretaker (building)					-0.590*** [0.160]	-0.869*** [0.157]
cashier, driver (heavy commercial)					-0.02 [0.157]	-0.117 [0.155]
artisan (upgraded)					-0.032 [0.053]	-0.177* [0.104]
other Municipalities					-0.276*** [0.030]	-0.264*** [0.033]
all other towns					-0.202** [0.080]	-0.115 [0.092]
formal		0.597*** [0.029]	1.364 [4.551]		0.347*** [0.073]	1.367 [2.198]
lnMW*education			-0.657 [0.834]			-0.681** [0.260]
lnMW*gender			0.002 [0.021]			0.043*** [0.014]
lnMW*18–25			-0.747*** [0.199]			0.234 [0.203]
lnMW*46–64			0.314 [0.325]			-0.333 [0.213]
lnMW*formal			-0.107 [0.631]			-0.127 [0.275]
Constant	-6.644*** [1.862]	4.504** [1.527]	7.326*** [0.030]	8.185*** [0.679]	6.970*** [1.290]	0.247 [3.121]
Observations	507	493	493	1208	1162	1162
R-squared	0.1	0.44	0.46	0.00	0.35	0.37

Source: Authors' estimates based on ILFS data.

Standard errors in brackets

* significant at 10%; ** significant at 5%; *** significant at 1%

Omitted categories: incomplete secondary education or less. male. 26–45 years, and Nairobi and Mombasa (General Order).

Omitted occupations: Unskilled in Agricultural Industry and General Laborer in General Order that minimum wages vary only by occupation, in agriculture, the level effect of the minimum wage is absorbed by the inclusion of occupation effects. The coefficients on the interactions between the minimum wage and the personal characteristics indicate whether minimum wages affect some workers more than others. The only coefficient that is statistically significant is the inter-action with age. The negative sign suggests that in agriculture, minimum wages exert a stronger upward push on wages for the adult population than for younger workers.

The level effect of the minimum wage can be recovered for workers in urban areas because minimum wages vary by location within occupation. Its coefficient suggests that minimum wages exert an upward push on the wages of less educated workers The results also suggest that minimum wages exert a higher push on the wages of women, thereby contributing to reduce the gender earnings gap.

6 Minimum wages and employment

Evidence on the effect of minimum wages on employment in Kenya is scarce. To our knowledge, only one study explored this issue and concluded that minimum wages reduce employment (Omolo and Omitti 2004). Their find-ings are based on an estimated negative correlation between changes in the minimum wage and changes in employment using aggregate data. However, a negative correlation does not establish causality. It could well be, for example, that the causality goes in the opposite direction; that is, periods of low employment growth, and in general poor output growth, lead to lower increases in the minimum wage.

Given the problems associated with using aggregate time series data, the economic literature relies on repeated cross-sectional or longitudinal data at the individual level to estimate the effect of minimum wages on employment. Unfortunately, there is not much labor market micro data available in Kenya. To our knowledge, in the last 10 years there was only one labor force survey that covered urban areas. Nonetheless, the presence of a large number of minimum wage levels across occupations and locations provides important cross-sectional variation that we can exploit with the 1998/9 ILFS data to relate employment to the multiple minimum wages.

Figure 12.8 relates the ratio of the minimum, for each occupation–location pair, to the median wage for all salaried workers with the share of formal salaried employment, the share of informal salaried, and the share of self-employment in total employment for each location–occupation pair. We restrict the analysis to urban areas, since the wage analysis suggests that these are the areas where minimum wages are more likely to be binding and also because in urban areas we can exploit the occupation–location variation. Total employment includes salaried, self-employment, unpaid work and apprentices. The number of data points in these figures is constrained by: (i) the number of occupation–location pairs for which a minimum wage is

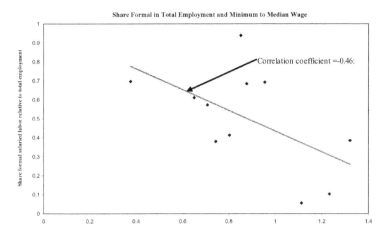

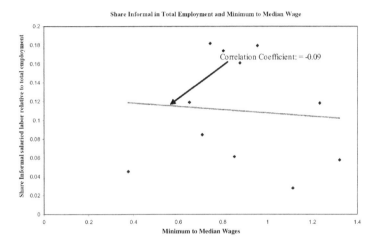

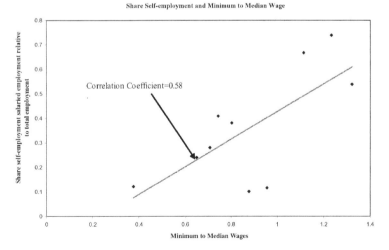

Figure 12.8 Minimum wage and structure of employment.

Source: Authors' computations based on 1998/9 ILFS data.

Notes: Occupation–location cells with more than 35 observations. The analysis is for non-agricultural sectors only.

defined, and (ii) the number of occupation–location pairs for which a sufficiently large number of observations are available in the survey.[8] These data suggest a negative relationship between the level of the minimum wage—in relation to the median—and the share of formal salaried employment in total employment within occupation–location cells. It also suggests a strong positive association between the share of self-employment and the minimum to median wage ratio. Notice, for example, that the correlation coefficient between the share of formal salaried employment and the minimum to median wage ratio is −0.46 while the correlation between the share of self-employment and the minimum wage in the cross-section of occupations–locations is equal to 0.58. In contrast, the correlation with informal salaried employment is very small and negative (−0.09), indicating that minimum wages could actually reduce employment for salaried informal workers. We formalize these results by estimating the following regression:

$$S_{oj} = a + \beta_1 K_{oj} + \varepsilon_{oj} \tag{2}$$

Results are presented in Tables 12.11 and 12.12. The dependent variable S_{oj} is the share of formal salaried (columns 1 and 4), informal salaried (columns 2 and 5), and self-employed workers (columns 3 and 6) in total employment. K_{oj} is the minimum to median wage ratio and ε_{oj} is the error term. The results in Table 12.11 are based on occupation–location-specific minimum to median wages while the results on Table 12.12 are based on the ratio of the occupation-location specific minimum wage to the median wage for all salaried workers. The results in Table 12.11 indicate that, assuming a minimum cell size of 10 observations, a 10-percentage point increase in the minimum to median wage reduces the share of formal salaried employment by 4.1 points, while increasing the share of self-employment by 4.7 points. These results are statistically significant at the 5% level for self-employment and at the 10% level for salaried employment. In contrast, minimum wages are found to have a marginal effect on informal salaried employment. The level of significance increases and the size of the coefficients becomes larger—but of similar magnitude—if the threshold for the cell size is increased to 35 observations (columns 4–6).

Results become weaker if, rather than measuring the level of the minimum wage with occupation–location-specific minimum to median wage ratios, they are instead measured with the ratio of each minimum wage to the median wage of all salaried workers.[9] Using this methodologically better measure leads to much smaller estimates of the association between minimum wages and formal and self-employment. These estimates also suggest a decline in informal salaried employment as a result of higher minimum wages. Yet, given the number of observations, none of these coefficients are statistically significant at conventional levels.

However, increasing the threshold for cell size to at least 35 observations increases the size and significance of effects for formal employment and

Table 12.11 Structure of employment and minimum to median wage ratio for each occupation–location pair

	Share salaried formal in total employment	Share informal in total employment	Share self-employed in total emp.	Share salaried formal in total employment	Share informal in total employment	Share self-employed in total emp.
	Cell size > 10	Cell size > 10	Cell size > 10	Cell size > 35	Cell size > 35	Cell size > 35
Kaitz (minimum/median)	−0.412*	0.014	0.468**	−0.471	0.007	0.516**
	(0.08)	(0.84)	(0.03)	(0.05)	(0.92)	(0.02)
Constant	0.741***	0.121**	0.036	0.738***	0.111**	0.054
	(0.00)	(0.02)	(0.78)	(0.00)	(0.04)	(0.67)
Observations	15	15	15	10	10	10
R-squared	0.218	0.003	0.316	0.391	0.001	0.493

Source: Elaborated by the authors from ILFS data.

Absolute value of t-statistics in parentheses
* significant at 10%; ** significant at 5%; *** significant at 1%

Table 12.12 Structure of employment and ratio of minimum to median wage (Median wage for all salaried employees)

	Share salaried formal in total employment	Share informal in total employment	Share self-employed in total emp.	Share salaried formal in total employment	Share informal in total employment	Share self-employed in total emp.
	Cell size > 10	Cell size > 10	Cell size > 10	Cell size > 35	Cell size > 35	Cell size > 35
Kaitz (minimum/median)	−0.116	−0.102	0.272	−0.559**	−0.02	0.593**
	(0.62)	(0.12)	(0.20)	(0.04)	(0.79)	(0.02)
Constant	0.592**	0.215***	0.088	0.929***	0.132	−0.139
	(0.01)	(0.00)	(0.63)	(0.00)	(0.08)	(0.47)
Observations	15	15	15	10	10	10
R-squared	0.02	0.18	0.122	0.423	0.009	0.5

Source: Elaborated by the authors from ILFS data.

Absolute value of t-statistics in parentheses
** significant at 5%; *** significant at 1%

self-employment. The direction and size of the estimates is now in line with those presented on Table 12.11. A 10% increase in the minimum to median ratio would lead to approximately a 5.6 percentage points decline in the share of formal employment and a 5.9 percentage points increase in the share of self-employment. In sum, the evidence suggests that minimum wages in Kenya increase the share of self-employment and reduce the fraction of workers in formal salaried jobs.

7 Conclusions

This paper has briefly reviewed the main arguments in favor of and against minimum wages. While efficiency–wage arguments may be an important part of the story, the main reason for instituting minimum wages is not to fight poverty or inequality: there are other instruments to achieve that goal. Instead, the main justification is to empower workers whose wages are constrained by the excessive market power of employers. To the extent that there is enforcement, the most important argument for not fixing minimum floors is that this instrument can price many workers out of formal employment. Most of the evidence for developing countries points to negative employment effects.

The analysis developed in this paper, based on cross-sectional data for 1998/9, indicates that minimum to median wage ratios were quite high, particularly for workers in more skilled occupations. At the same time, non-compliance affected one in four salaried workers in agriculture and one in six in urban areas. Non-compliance was higher for women, youth, and workers with a low level of education attained.

A number of reasons may be behind the relatively low enforcement level of minimum wages in Kenya. On the one hand, the existence of many different categories of minimum wage makes it very difficult for workers and firms to know them. On the other, minimum wages are set at levels that are high in relation to the median wage—especially for semiskilled and more skilled occupations. Finally, the classification of occupations used for the minimum wage is outdated, implying that many occupations may no longer be adequate for the requirements of today's labor market.

The evidence indicates that minimum wages pushed up wages set by the general order, but not by the agricultural order. The indication would then be that relatively low minimum wages, combined with non-compliance, limited the effect of the minimum wage in the agricultural sector. In contrast, minimum wages in the general order appear to have raised wages for low-educated workers and women, leading to seemingly strong adverse effects on formal sector employment. Our estimates indicate that a 10 percentage point increase in the minimum to median wage ratio would be associated with a decline in the share of formal employment of between 1.1 and 5.5 percentage points—and an increase of between 2.7 and 5.9 points in the share of self-employment.

This paper has provided some initial steps towards an evidence-based diagnostic of the effectiveness of minimum wage policies in Kenya. Up-to-date techniques to investigate the effect of minimum wages on poverty, inequality, and employment require longitudinal micro data, or in its defect, a series of consecutive household level surveys. Such data is not available in Kenya. Improving the frequency of data collection to at least one labor force survey every two years would go a long way towards developing better labor market policies.

Notes

* Background work for this paper was performed while Carmen Pagés was at the World Bank. The authors are deeply indebted to Sara Lemos, Sumana Dhar, Gary Fields, and the Government of Kenya for valuable comments and discussions. The authors are also grateful to participants at the Second IZA/World Bank Conference on Employment and Development (Bonn, 2007) and at the Cornell/Michigan Conference on Labor Markets in Developing and Transition Economies: Emerging Policy and Analytical Issues (Ann Arbor, 2007)
1 In other words, with very few exceptions, the ratio of any minimum wage to the average minimum wage has been constant over the last years.
2 For further details about the survey design and main results please see: Republic of Kenya (2002).
3 We excluded workers below 18 years because the official publications on minimum wages of the CBS solely report minimum wages for unskilled, stockman, herdsman, and watchman in agricultural activities in this age group. Moreover, to discourage child employment, there has been no statutory minimum wage for workers 18 or younger since 2002.
4 This implies that our results somewhat underestimate the minimum wage and non-compliance level in a few occupations.
5 All the results are presented separately for workers in the agriculture industry (in rural and urban areas) and employees in non-agricultural activities (in urban areas only). The former group is affected by the minimum wages set by the AWAB (agricultural order) and the latter by the minimum wages set by the GWAB (general order).
6 The self-employed are, however, included in the analysis to measure the employment effects of minimum wages on the informal sector.
7 When reporting fraction affected, wages are expressed in constant prices of October 1997.
8 In Figure 12.8, we do not consider occupation–location cells for which the number of observations available in the survey is below 35.
9 The latter measure is better from a methodological point of view because it minimizes reverse causality. This arises from the fact that a higher share of informal or self-employment in total employment may reduce the median wage, and therefore increase the minimum to median wage in a given occupation–location.

References

Basu, A. K., N. H. Chau, and R. Kanbur (2007) "Turning a Blind Eye: Costly Enforcement, Credible Commitment and Minimum Wage Laws." IZA Discussion Paper 2998.
Bell, L. A. (1997) "The Impact of Minimum Wages in Mexico and Colombia." Part 2:

Labor Market Flexibility in Developing Countries. *Journal of Labor Economics* 15(3): S102–S135, July.

Bhorat, H. (2000) "Are Wage Adjustments an Effective Mechanisms for Poverty Alleviation? Some simulations for domestic and farm workers." Paper presented at the *Trade and Industrial Policy Secretariat (TIPS) 2000 Annual Forum.* Development Policy Research Unit, University of Cape Town, Cape Town.

Blanchard, O. (2002) "Designing Labor Market Institutions." Paper presented at the conference *Beyond Transition: Development Perspectives and Dilemmas,* April 12–13, Warsaw (available at web.mit.edu/blanchar/www/).

Brown, C., C. Gilroy, and A. Kohen (1982) "The Effect of the Minimum Wage on Employment and Unemployment." *Journal of Economic Literature* 20(2): 487–528, June.

Card, D. and A. B. Krueger (1994) "Minimum Wages and Employment: A Case Study of the Fast-Food Industry in New Jersey and Pennsylvania." *The American Economic Review* 84(4): 772–93, September.

Cowan, K., A. Micco, and C. Pagés (2004) "Labor Market Adjustment in Chile." *Economía, Journal of the Latin American and the Caribbean Economic Association* 5(1): 219–66, Fall.

Deveraux, S. (2005) "Can Minimum Wages Contribute to Poverty Reduction in Poor Countries?" *Journal of International Development* 17: 899–912.

Dickens, R., S. Machin, and A. Manning (1999) "The Effects of Minimum Wages on Employment: Theory and Evidence from Britain." *Journal of Labor Economics,* 17(1): 1–22, January.

Elias, P. and M. Birch (1994) "ISCO 88 (COM) A Guide for Users". Mimeograph. Institute for Employment Reseach. University of Warwick. (available at http://www2.warwick.ac.uk/fac/soc/ier/research/isco88/englishisco.doc)

Fields, G. and R. Kanbur (2007) "Minimum Wages and Poverty with Income-sharing." *Journal of Economic Inequality* 5(2): 135–47, Forthcoming, August.

Gindling, T. H. and K. Terrell (2005) "The Effects of Multiple Minimum Wages throughout the Labor Market." Mimeo.

Jones, P. (1997) "The Impact of Minimum Wage Legislation in Developing Countries where Coverage is Incomplete." Working Paper WPS/98–2. Centre for the Study of African Economies. Institute of Economics and Statistics. University of Oxford.

Kulundu Manda, D. (2002) "Globalisation and the Labour Market in Kenya." The Kenya Institute for Public Policy Research and Analysis (KIPPRA) Discussion Paper 6. Nairobi.

Lemos, S. (2004) "Minimum Wage Policy and Employment Effects: Evidence from Brazil." *Economía, Journal of the Latin American and the Caribbean Economic Association* 5(1): 219–66, Fall.

Levin-Waldman, O. M. (1997) "Linking the Minimum Wage to Productivity." Working paper 219. Annandale-on-Hudson, NY: The Jerome Levy Economics Institute.

Lustig, N. C. and D. McLeod (1997) "Minimum Wages and Poverty in Developing Countries: Some Empirical Evidence." In *Labour Markets in Latin America,* edited by S. Edwards and N. C. Lustig. Washington: The Brookings Institution Press, pp. 62–103.

Maloney, W. F. and J. N. Mendez (2004) "Measuring the Impact of Minimum Wages: Evidence from Latin America." In *Law and Employment: Lessons from Latin American and the Caribbean,* edited by J. J. Heckman and C. Pagés. Chicago: The University of Chicago Press.

Montenegro, C. E. and C. Pagés (2004) "Who Benefits from Labor Market Regulations? Chile, 1960–1998," in *Law and Employment: Lessons from Latin American and the Caribbean* edited by J. J. Heckman and C. Pagés. Chicago: The University of Chicago Press.

Morley, S. A. (1995) "Structural Adjustment and the Determinants of Poverty in Latin America." In *Coping with Austerity: Poverty and Inequality in Latin America*, edited by N. Lustig. Washington, DC: Brookings Institution.

Neumark, D. and W. Wascher (2007) "Minimum Wages and Employment." IZA Discussion Paper 2570.

——, M. Schweitzer, and W. Wascher (2000) "The Effects of Minimum Wages Throughout the Wage Distribution." NBER Working Paper 7519. Cambridge: Massachusetts.

Omolo, J. O. and J. M. Omitti (2004) "Is Minimum Wage Policy Effective in Kenya?" Institute of Policy Analysis and Research Discussion Paper 054/2004. Nairobi.

Rama, M. (2001) "The Consequences of Doubling the Minimum Wage: The Case of Indonesia." *Industrial and Labor Relations Review* 54(4): 864–81, July.

Republic of Kenya (2002) "The 1998/99 Integrated Labour Force Survey Report." Nairobi: Ministry of Planning and National Development.

World Bank (2004) Statistics retrieved January 2004, from World Development Indicators Online (WDI).

13 Labor market flexibility

Insurance versus efficiency and the Indian experience

Errol D'Souza

Introduction

The issue of flexibility in the labor market has attracted much attention in policy debates in India. The lack of flexibility in the labor market is often cited as the reason for poor performance of the labor market in terms of employment generation and productivity growth. A popular view is that increased integration of the economy and technological change require structural change in the organization of production in firms and the lack of flexibility in the labor market does not permit accommodation of this change; yet the link between the claimed hindrances to the allocative function of the labor market and the slow growth of the formal industrial sector has only been attempted to be demonstrated in a few select articles that are in approach either empirical or theoretical. This paper reviews this literature and draws lessons about the impact of regulations in formal labor markets on employment and output growth.

The literature has focused exclusively on numerical flexibility—adjustment of the numbers employed in response to fluctuating product market demand—and even though functional flexibility—the ability of a firm to reallocate employees among a wide range of tasks and to initiate changes in work practices and reorganization of job boundaries—is an important issue (section 9A of the Industrial Disputes Act of 1947) the focus has been more on the effect of labor regulation on output and employment. This is mainly because the path of development envisaged a reliance on the manufacturing sector to draw surplus labor out of agriculture into more productive employment. The success of labor institutions is thus measured by the effect they have had on generating jobs rather than whether they have enabled the use of more flexible forms of work organization that are supportive of lean production systems.

Legislation's effect on employment

The important piece of legislation that has attracted all the attention is the Industrial Disputes Act (IDA) of 1947 which applies to establishments employing 50 or more workers in the organized sector. The IDA was amended under pressure from the trade unions in 1976 and 1982. The 1976 amendment of the IDA requires that if a firm employs 300 or more workers, then the workers cannot be laid off or retrenched without the permission of the government. The 1982 amendment of the IDA made this provision of government permission applicable to all firms employing 100 or more workers. This provision is known as Chapter V-B of the IDA which stipulated prior permission from government for layoff, retrenchment, or closure. There is an exception for retrenchment resulting from power shortages or natural disaster but the penalty for retrenchment or closure without permission includes a fine and a prison sentence for the employer.[1]

Realizing that the amendments lend themselves to a natural experiment, Fallon and Lucas (1991, 1993) argue that if new job security regulations impose higher costs on changing the level of employment, then the change in employment levels should prove even slower following enactment of the new laws. Second, apart from the cost of adjusting the labor force, the new regulations can increase the effective cost of employing a given level of employees and result in diminished employment by the firm. Fallon and Lucas use industry data from the Annual Survey of Industries for the period 1959–81 and find no change in the speed of employment adjustment but a drop in labor demand after 1976 that is significant at 5% in 11 of 35 industries. Their estimates reveal a negative effect on labor demand of job security regulation in 25 out of 35 sectors using a 25% level of significance. They conclude that employment would have been 17.5% higher in India in the organized sector if there had been no job security provision. This conclusion is not warranted as, first, the negative estimate on labor demand is significant at only a very high level of significance in a majority of the sectors and, second, they average the coefficients across all sectors (including the sectors with insignificant coefficients) to obtain an estimate of a 17.5% drop in labor demand. Clearly, they are drawing the conclusion about the negative impact on employment of labor regulation that their estimates do not portray.

In a more exhaustive study, Dutta Roy (2004) reinvestigates the impact of job security legislation on employment. Dutta Roy derives estimates for 16 industry groups that accounted for over 77% and 84% respectively of total employment and value added of the registered manufacturing sector over the period 1960–94. Dutta Roy first demonstrates the existence of significant rigidities in employment adjustment in the Indian labor market. For 10 industries the response of employment to a disequilibrium in the industry's own market in the preceding period is insignificant. These industries include chemicals and chemical products, structural clay products, miscellaneous food products, sugar, paper and paper products, no-electrical machinery, electrical machinery, railroad equipment, and motor vehicles. Barring cement and nonferrous basic metals where about 90% of the disequilibrium arising in any period is corrected in the subsequent period, the average for the four other industries—iron and steel, rubber and rubber products, textile products, and tobacco—is less than 40%. The results reveal that across all industries it takes on average about 5 to 6 years for most of the adjustment to be completed. This evidence of rigidities in adjustments is also found by Bhalotra (1998), who shows that it takes time to adjust employment; in her study it was estimated that it takes almost 6 years in Indian factories for 90% of the adjustment in employment to its optimal level to be completed. This rigidity in employment also calls into question the Fallon and Lucas conclusion about the fall in employment that coincides with the time of the amendment to the IDA in 1976.

Dutta Roy then investigates whether the rigidities in employment are due to the inherent characteristics of the industries or whether job security regulations have exacerbated the rigidities. She investigates whether the pre- and post-1976 and pre- and post-1982 periods when the IDA amendments came into effect results in an enhancement of flexibility and a change in the adjustment coefficients after the implementation of the new job security regulations. Prior to the amendments in job security regulations, 10 industries were characterized by rigidities in adjustment. Seven of these did not reveal any change due to changes in job security regulations: textile products, miscellaneous food products, tobacco, non-electrical machinery, railroad equipment, motor vehicles, and paper and paper products. The net impact of the job security regulations amendments of 1976 and 1982 is ambiguous in the case of two industries—petroleum refinery products and sugar—and it is favorable in the structural clay products industry. By contrast six industries showed flexibility in employment in the pre-job security regulation amendment period. The amendments did not have any impact on employment practices in three industries: iron and steel, chemical and chemical products, and rubber and rubber products. In two industries—non ferrous basic metals and electrical machinery—amendments to job regulations favorably impacted on employment flexibility, whereas in the sole case of the cement industry, flexibility was impaired as a result of labor market regulations. The results indicate that a major proportion of industries reveals rigidities attributable to industry-specific characteristics and the imposition of job security regulations is not the primary cause of observed rigidities in employment adjustment in the registered manufacturing sector.

Intermediation of other factors

The question that arises, however, is whether job security regulations were responsible for a high rate of growth of wages which in turn adversely impacted on employment. This possibility needs to be considered, given that there was a mismatch between output growth in the 1980s and employment growth. Indeed the World Bank (1989) and Ahluwalia (1991) explain the employment decline as a result of a high rate of growth of wages. The World Bank (1989) study calculated a 5.7% decline in employment on account of wage growth in the 1980s. However, this estimate overlooks the fact that employers can match staffing to workload fluctuations through two routes:

1   by adjusting the numbers employed;
2   by adjusting the number and timing of hours worked.

The former is akin to a flexibility on the extensive margin—the flexibility of numbers derived from the ability to adjust the headcount. Here, additional workers can be returned to the external labor market when work levels fall and their services are no longer required. Flexibility on the intensive margin, by contrast, can be achieved without changes in employment levels through changes in the timing of working hours (work-time flexibility) or through changes in the range of tasks employees perform (functional flexibility). Looking at the period 1979–87 Bhalotra (1998) found that actual hours grew at a trend rate of 1.64% p.a. and this was significantly different from zero in 14 of the 18 industries in the sample. The increase in time worked from 1979 to 1987 was equivalent to a shift from a 5- to a 6-day week. Thus, a sixth of official working time was being lost in 1979 and this was recuperated over the course of the 1980s. The significant increase in days worked per worker implies that rapid rises in earnings (wage rates per day multiplied by days worked) translates into a lower growth in wage rate. Apart from hours of work Bhalotra argues that the Bank omits other variables that affect employment such as productivity and cyclical demand effects. These omissions are serious, especially as the period was marked out by a growth in productivity (Ahluwalia, 1991). The specification implies that employment (N) may be written as a function of output (Y), real wages (w), productivity (A), hours worked, (H), and cyclical demand effects (D), or,

$$N = f(Y, w, A, H, D)$$

Estimating this equation it was found by Bhalotra (1998) that the trend wage growth of 4.2% p.a. during the 1979–87 period implied a decline in employment of 1.18% p.a. which is substantially smaller than the 5.7% p.a. decline featured in the World Bank report. The growth in work intensity (H) has a strong negative effect on employment and total factor productivity (A) also exercises a powerful drag on employment.

Bhalotra also finds that capital accumulation exerts a strong positive effect on employment—the effect of capital accumulation on employment growth is that it more than offsets the adverse impact on employment due to growth in work intensity and efficiency associated with technical progress. If we ignore cyclical fluctuations and concentrate on trends, then, if no capital accumulation had taken place, the employment decline of the period can be attributed 26% to be due to the increase in wage rates, 15% to work intensification, and 59% to technical progress that is labor-augmenting and makes labor more efficient resulting in a lesser requirement of labor per unit of capital. Capital accumulation effects on employment are so strong that they dampen most of these negative effects on employment—employment that would have declined by about 7.13% p.a. without capital accumulation ended up declining by just about 0.3% p.a. over the period.

Implementation effects at decentralized levels

That job security regulations are passed at the central level but state govern-ments have the right to amend them under the Indian constitution implies that state government amendments to labor regulations could have an important impact on explaining their manufacturing performance. Besley and Burgess (2004) follow up this lead and read the text of each state amendment to the Industrial Disputes Act of 1947 and classify each as pro-worker, pro-employer, or neutral. Each pro-employer amendment (e.g. pro-hibiting strikes to maintain industrial peace) is coded as a minus one, each neutral amendment as a zero, and each pro-worker amendment (e.g. time frame for workers to receive payments on being laid off being reduced) is coded as a one. After obtaining the direction of amendments in a given year in this fashion, they then cumulate the scores over time to arrive at a quantita-tive picture of how the regulatory environment evolved over time. They use this as their measure of labor regulation. They then develop an econometric analysis of whether labor regulation can account for the cross-state pattern of manufacturing performance between 1958 and 1992. They find that states with more pro-worker legislation have lower levels of employment in registered manufacturing.

The four pro-worker states that Besley–Burgess identify on the basis of the index they develop are Gujarat, Maharashtra, Orissa, and West Bengal. Maharashtra and Gujarat are two of India's most industrialized states and are perceived as good locations for setting up manufacturing plants. It needs to be explained as to why these two states are considered as priority states for industrial establishments if they are pro-labor. Conversely Kerala which cannot claim a comparable industrial relations climate is identified as pro-employer and hardly attracts manufacturing activity. Second, a survey on investment climate faced by manufacturing firms (Dollar, Iarossi, and Mengistae, 2002) indicated that while in all states firms indicated that there was over-manning and that they would like to reduce employment, the extent of over manning reported was lowest in Maharashtra and Gujarat. Third, there is a need to make a distinction between legislation and enforcement in the context of a developing society. The Dollar, Iarossi, and Mengistae (2002) study found that small and medium enterprises received twice as many fac-tory inspections a year in states such as Kerala (classified as pro-employer by Besley and Burgess) as did states such as Maharashtra and Gujarat (clas-sified as pro-employee). Fourth, states such as Andhra Pradesh, Rajasthan, and Tamil Nadu that had been classified as pro-employer have had de-clining secondary sector employment elasticities in the recent reform period (1994–2000) compared to the 1984–94 period whereas pro-employee states such as Maharashtra, Gujarat and Orissa have witnessed an acceleration in secondary employment during this period (their employment elasticities have increased)—see Table 12 of Bhattacharya and Sakthivel (2003). The classification of states as being pro-labor or pro-employer as done by Besley and Burgess thus is at variance with the way these states should have performed or been considered as manufacturing destinations by firms.

The econometric analysis of Besley and Burgess also throws up questionable results. They do panel regressions for 16 states over the period 1958–1992. The dependent variable is the log of registered manufacturing output per capita or the log of total employees and this is regressed on their measure of labor regulation, other exogenous variables such as development expenditure per capita, installed electricity capacity per capita, etc., a state-fixed effect (to capture state-specific factors) and a year fixed effect (to capture common shocks such as central government amendments to the Industrial Disputes Act). Although they cluster their standard errors by state to deal with serial correlation concerns, their high values of R^2 of over 0.92 indicate that the problem might persist. In a panel regression it is well known that systematic unobserved temporal effects can be quite important and to take care of this, the regression is estimated with a time trend on the right-hand side. The estimates with and without this time trend are reported in Table 13.1 below:

Table 13.1 Estimated effect of various factors on log registered manufacturing output per capita

Technique	OLS	OLS with state time trends
Independent variables		
Labor regulation (t-1)	−0.014*	0.0002
	(2.67)	(0.01)
Log development expenditure per capita	0.184	0.241**
	(1.55)	(2.28)
Log installed electricity capacity per capita	0.082	0.023
	(1.51)	(0.69)
Log state population	0.310	−1.419
	(0.26)	(0.61)
Congress majority	−0.0009	0.020**
	(0.09)	(2.08)
Hard left majority	−0.050*	−0.007
	(2.97)	(0.77)
Janata majority	0.008	−0.020
	(0.34)	(0.60)
Regional majority	0.006	0.026
	(0.70)	(1.11)
Adjusted R^2	0.94	0.95
Observations	491	491

Source: Besley and Burgess (2004).

Figures in brackets are *t*-statistics. * denotes significant at 1% and ** significant at 5%.

It transpires that once the time trend is introduced, labor regulation is no longer a significant variable in the explanation of manufacturing output and employment. Instead, development expenditure (state spending on social and economic services—health, education, infrastructure, and administration) is now the driving variable that explains output growth among states. In Indian states public expenditure is known to crowd in private capital formation (Athukorala and Sen 2002) and as we saw earlier it is capital accumulation that has the biggest impact on employment growth in India (Bhalotra 1998). Besley and Burgess, however, conclude: "The fact that our results are not robust to state-specific time trends does raise the question of whether the effects that we are picking up are those due to labour regulations *per se* or the consequences of a poor climate of labour relations—union power and labour/management hostility—which affect the trend rate of growth within a state. This goes to interpretation of the finding" (Besley and Burgess 2004: 125). Yet they conclude that the "analysis suggests that labour market institutions in India have had an important impact on manufacturing development."

The estimation techniques used by Besley and Burgess is also questionable. They estimate by the technique of ordinary least squares which is likely to lead to unsatisfactory estimates. In practice actual employment deviates from its desired level due to adjustment costs associated with training, hiring and firing. Besley and Burgess recognize this: "Labour regulation will typically create adjustment costs in hiring and firing labour . . ." (101). In that case employment and output will depend on its lagged values. We have already seen that it takes almost 6 years for adjustments in employment to be completed (Bhalotra 1998). As a result employment and its lagged values will be functions of the state-fixed effects, making OLS estimates biased and inconsistent. In addition, unobserved state characteristics may well be correlated with one or more of the other regressors. One of the ways to proceed, then, is first to differentiate the regression equation to order to be rid of the correlation between the state-fixed effect and lagged values of employment (or output) and other right-hand side variables and then to use an instrument for the lagged, differenced employment (or output) term as it would be correlated with the transformed error term in the regression. The generalized method of moments estimator proposed by Arellano and Bond (1991) uses such a procedure to provide consistent and efficient estimates and such a procedure was warranted instead of the OLS used by Besley and Burgess.

Composition of contracts in formal sector

It is well known that factories in India employ both regular and casual workers as the adjustment costs for the former would be larger than for the latter. Thus, in addition to varying work intensity, firms take care of cyclical fluctuations by varying the composition of the workforce as between permanent and non-permanent employment. Despite job security regulations, firms are able to vary employment by varying the composition of the contracts (permanent versus non-permanent) offered to the workforce. This means that employment flexibility is quite pronounced even if it could be claimed that the regulatory environment is quite stringent. Deshpande et al. (2004) conducted a study of employment practices in a sample of 1,307 factories belonging to nine industries and 10 states in 1998. They found that between 1991 and 1998 small establishments employing 10–19 and 20–49 workers increased their employment fastest at approximately 6% p.a. However, restrictions of firing (that apply to larger firms) could not have been a factor impacting on employment decisions because firms employing between 200 and 499 workers increased employment at only a slightly lower rate of 5.28%. Again, some employers—13% of the respondents—did not change their employment over the period 1991–8 whereas 27% reported fewer employees and 60% increased employment. That the same regulatory set-up allowed some to decrease and others to increase employment implies again that regulation is not important to hiring-and-firing decisions. Deshpande et al. also found that the share of permanent workers declined over the years of liberalization and that the larger the firm, the higher the share of non-permanent temporary and casual workers (Table 4.1 in Deshpande et al. 2004). One would have expected the industrial relations climate and type of political incumbent to have an effect on the propensity to employ non-permanent workers. Deshpande et al. find that Kerala and Bengal can be clubbed with Maharashtra in having lower growth in non-permanent employment, which implies that it is not just the existence of unions but the effectiveness of administration that is the binding factor. Despite the high unionization, Kerala, for instance, has witnessed a growth in employment in the secondary sector in the latter half of the 1990s that is higher than the all-India average (Bhattacharya and Sakthivel 2003).

Besley and Burgess, by concentrating on labor regulation, implicitly assume that enforcement is without cost and complete. Legal rules comprising regulation do not specify the least-cost method of ensuring that legal standards are adhered to. Typically, enforcement rarely takes a penal form and legal actions are invoked selectively. Mostly, the enforcement system is one of compliance with direct negotiations and bargaining between enforcement official and violator that results in discretionary flexible enforcement that takes into account the offender's difficulties in complying with the law. As regulatory politics scholars emphasize (Hutter 1989) there is a distinction between a deterrence model of enforcement where firms that violate administrative laws are sought to be punished, and a bargaining model where enforcement is more discretionary and seeks to persuade regulated firms to improve their performance. That establishments were able to vary their employment and that the share of permanent workers declined over the 1990s indicates that there is a variability in enforcement that is important in determining employment. Moreover, as Harriss-White (2003: 18) puts it: "In practically every 'organized' firm, including state-run corporations, unorganized labour is selectively incorporated into the labour process." The proportion of unorganized labor in the corporate sector has been estimated to be between 40 and 85% (Bhowmik 1998). In a survey of registered firms in the garment industry in Ahmedabad it was found that 50% of workers did not have written contracts and about 10% did not receive any benefits (Jhabvala and Kanbur 2004). It is because enforcement is discretionary that this is possible.

In order to employ unorganized labor in a registered firm, some cost to circumvent enforcement has to be incurred (see Dasgupta and Marjit (2004) for a formal model on these lines). If there was no circumvention cost the firm could employ at the competitive wage in the informal sector, w_I. Without loss of generality let the marginal circumvention cost per unit of labor be linear in the employment of such labor, i.e. cL_I. Then, the marginal cost of employing labor on informal contracts is $w_I + cL_I$. Higher levels of enforcement will result in a larger value of c. If all labor were to be employed on these contracts, then the interaction of the marginal cost of informal contract labor curve w_IA and the marginal revenue productivity or demand curve BC would determine the extent of informal employment at point E (Figure 13.1). However, workers on formal contracts are able to bargain a higher wage w_F than the informal wage, say, owing to unionization or by resorting to influences on establishments through the apparatus of the state which intervenes in the labor market to strengthen the position of workers owing to its past historic association with organized labor in the Independence movement and its goals of establishing a socialist and equitable society. We would expect formal wages to be increasing in prices as workers seek to protect real wages and in circumvention costs as higher circumvention costs imply that workers on formal contracts can leverage the better climate of enforcement to bargain for higher wages. The firm accordingly employs OM workers on informal contracts and MN on formal contracts.

Figure 13.1 indicates that if enforcement increases the curve, w_IA will rotate counterclockwise—the dashed line beginning at w_I. Total employment would decline but informal employment could even increase if the formal wage increased sufficiently in response to the increased enforcement so as to cause a substitution of formal contract workers with informal contract workers by the firm. The point of interest here is that differences in enforcement result in differences in employment.

We could also interpret the parameter c as a more stringent regulation that is pro-labor in the spirit of Besley and Burgess and conclude that less employment is associated with pro-labor regulation. However, that is an argument that does not pose the counterfactuals appropriately enough. If there is a rise in capital accumulation, the demand for labor curve shifts to the right and employment increases. The empirical data points to employment growth being associated with capital formation (Bhalotra 1998) and as demonstrated by Ramaswamy (2002) it was the liberalization of capacity licensing and entry regulation that led to high rates of capital formation and employment especially in import- competing industries such as consumer durables.

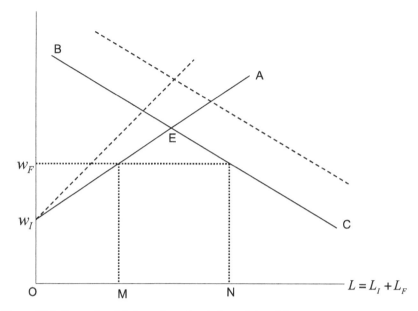

Figure 13.1 Formal and informal contracts in registered firms.

Employment may not have grown in India pre-liberalization because capacity constraints imposed by a system of industrial licensing did not allow the demand for labor curve *BC* to shift out to the position of the dashed line on its right. In India lending by banks and financial development institutions was also often by virtue of the fact that the establishment had been issued a license by the government. In such a situation employment growth was more a function of imposed capacity constraints than of labor regulation.

The conventional view is that job security regulations and unions are the main cause of rigidity and unemployment. The restriction on firing is in this view akin to generating rents equal to the welfare difference between an employed and an unemployed worker. These restrictions increase workers' bargaining power by making it more difficult for employers to resist wage demands by refusing to employ the workers any longer. Firing costs are a device to protect the rents of incumbent employees. However, the historical line of causation is the reverse—job security regulations that are blamed for rigidities in the labor market were often instituted as a response to the threat of unemployment and income insecurity. The arrival of organized labor on the Mumbai scene, for instance, goes back to 1917 when there was a wave of large-scale strikes in textiles and other industries in response to the erosion of income owing to wartime inflation. The interwar period saw many strikes where workers joined campaigns but drifted away once the strikes were over. The colonial state, however, intervened on the part of labor and passed the Trade Disputes Conciliation Act of 1934 and appointed labor officers to mediate in disputes. As that was a period of economic depression with unfavorable conditions for bargaining, state involvement in labor relations was welcomed by workers as more beneficial to them than the returns possible through unions. Trade unions in turn embraced the state (Sherlock 2001) and this was not driven by rent-seeking as much as a search for social insurance.

As stated by Datta-Chaudhuri (2000), "The modalities of labour use in the organized sector in India are dictated primarily by the state, not by the market or by the results of collective bargaining . . . The state plays a dominant role through labour laws, labour judiciary and administrative officers to administer social justice keeping in view the power position and susceptibilities of workers . . . to eventually lead to a just industrial society." Given that human capital is the most important asset for most individuals in India, the demand for insurance against labor income risk translated into a demand for job security that was accommodated by the state in a situation where insurance markets for such needs do not exist. "The paramount concern of Indian workers, and thus of their trade unions, relates to the question of job security" (Datta-Chaudhuri 2000) and this risk aversion towards unemployment and income insecurity lies behind institutions such as chapter V-B of the IDA. The foundation of the idea is social insurance and not rent-seeking. Today, job security may create efficiency losses but it should not be lost sight of that it also creates insurance benefits that are probably substantial (and unmeasurable) and may even offset the efficiency losses. Of course, it may be objected that if labor market risk is so all encompassing, then, why can we not leave it to firms and employees to take care of it themselves through insurance contracts and wage bargains? We turn to this next.

State intervention and markets

Basu (2002) argues that legislation against retrenchment or dismissal of labor as in the IDA of 1947 can backfire because of failure to distinguish between what is good *ex ante* and what is good *ex post*. A law that makes retrenchment difficult is of course good for workers who are already employed. However, firms will be more wary of employing workers, making labor a less valuable input and decreasing the demand for labor. As a result, wages will fall and workers who benefit from more secure jobs lose out by having lower wages. Thus, workers may be worse off as a result of legislation meant to make them better off. A formal statement of this argument is in Basu, Fields, and Debgupta (2001). Basu recommends on this basis that contracts between firms and employees should not be exogenously fixed by law (such as the restrictions on firing) but that there should be free contract between workers and firms, which depending on preferences (including risk aversion), would see some contracts with low wages and long tenure for employees and some contracts with high wages and firing rights with employers. This argument that free contracts lead to efficiency is an outcome of the traditional, perfectly competitive story in which workers and firms implicitly bargain for the efficient level of employment security. This is a very unsatisfactory way of carrying out the analysis because in a competitive model, when wages adjust, the unemployment rate remains unchanged or zero.

A satisfactory model for the analysis of employment protection must be able to demonstrate not only that wages are endogenous but also that equilibrium unemployment is possible because labor markets such as credit markets do not clear. Such an explanation is provided by efficiency wage models. In one variant of these models, workers are paid in excess of their marginal contribution and reservation wages in order to reduce shirking and increase labor productivity at the risk of involuntary unemployment (Shapiro and Stiglitz 1984). In another version which is the deferred payment incentive version, the wage is initially less than the worker's marginal product and then increases as tenure in employment increases in order to induce effort over time. In both variants the threat of termination and loss of the efficiency wage deter employee shirking. However, efficiency wage models also do not consider the possibility that when efficiency wages exceed workers' marginal contributions, firms have an incentive to terminate workers before the wages are paid. The response to this moral hazard is to introduce employment protection. Hence, labor protection laws may be necessary to deter employer opportunism.

The problem of employment protection in an efficiency wage set-up is best addressed in a simple two-period framework. At time t_0 the firm and the worker agree to a contract to be executed in period t_1. The contract states that the firm will pay the worker ($w > 0$) if the worker expends effort ($e > 0$) but the worker will be terminated from service without compensation ($w = 0$) if the worker is caught shirking ($e = 0$). The worker's disutility of effort is e. The effort provided by the worker is not easily observable by the employer or verifiable by a third party such as a court. The output generated due to the effort expended by the worker, however, is observable and verifiable.

At time t_1 the worker has the options of either working or shirking. If effort is expended, the firm's gross benefit is y and if the worker shirks, then expected output is py where $(1 - p)$ is the probability of detecting a shirking worker. The firm also has two options before it[2]—to fulfill the contract or to behave opportunistically and terminate the worker. If the firm is opportunistic and the contract is terminated by it, then it captures the full rents generated from the employee's efforts. If the firm honors the contract, it pays the worker for effort or fires a shirking worker detected with probability $(1 - p)$. Hence, the worker can be dismissed for two reasons—employer opportunism and verifiable shirking. The expected payoffs of the firm are in the lower left-hand corner of each cell in Table 13.2 and that of the worker in the upper right-hand corner of each cell.

Table 13.2 depicts the opportunism faced by both firms and workers. The worker has an incentive to shirk if the wage is too low and monitoring is imperfect and the firm has an incentive to exploit the worker. When both firm and worker anticipate the other will behave opportunistically, the worker will

Table 13.2 Efficiency wages when firms and workers are opportunistic

			Worker	
			Work	Shirk
Firm	Honor contract		$w - e$	pw
		$y - w$		$p(y - w)$
	Terminate		$-e$	0
		y		py

shirk and the firm will fire the worker and neither benefits from engaging in a contract. Employer reputation effects may result in the efficient contractual outcome where workers supply effort and firms honor the contract and compensate workers; but to expect all firms to have reputational capital is unwarranted and so employment protection legislation can play the role of restraining opportunistic behavior by firms and workers. Of course, it must be kept in mind that labor protection laws can reduce the effectiveness of efficiency wages and reduce worker productivity if it is a blunt instrument. An employment protection legislation, while alleviating the worker's fear that he may be opportunistically terminated, must at the same time allow the firm to terminate the worker if he is caught shirking. If there is third-party verifiable evidence of shirking, then legislation should be such as to induce the expectation in the worker that termination of his services will occur.

There is of course the second variant of efficiency wages where workers are given deferred payments in order to elicit a performance bond in the form of effort over time (Lazear 1981). Here, even if the worker is fired with verifiable evidence, he loses compensation due to him in the future. Also, the fact that compensation is deferred gives an incentive to employers to terminate services before the full term is served. To safeguard against this type of opportunism, contractual safeguards in the form of a penalty on the firm in case of premature firing is called for. This function is typically performed by severance packages which specify a fraction of the worker's contractually established wage benefits to be paid to the worker if the firm chooses to terminate his services. In the product market when firms may behave opportunistically with respect to quality, warranties are used to signal quality attributes. Similarly, in labor markets when firms *and* workers may behave opportunistically, *third-party* enforcement of employment protection legislation is called for. This legislation should not be written in stone but should accommodate firing in case shirking by workers is established and severance payments in case firms wish to terminate workers regardless of shirking.

Employment protection involves a whole range of measures apart from severance payments. These are designed so as to limit the employer's ability to dismiss workers without delay or cost. The idea is to protect both workers and employers from opportunistic behavior—tying their hands so as to make both better off by deterring them from short-termism. Some forms of employment protection need not entail immediate financial gains to either party. Administrative procedures such as writing to an employee concerned giving reasons for dismissal, specifying lengths of time that the employer has to wait for a response, and notices of termination where the length of notice varies by tenure and includes a cooling-off period during which the notice may be issued but not become effective, etc., are employment protection measures that do not entail a direct transfer from the employer to the worker. These are often wise to include in employment protection legislation so as to delay dismissals and induce employers to negotiate over termination and not behave opportunistically. One could argue that this increases job tenures and gives power to established workers with adverse effects on job creation. However, given opportunism, the only way that workers and firms will invest in a job is if there are speed breakers to opportunism. The unintended consequence that this may reduce turnover is an outcome that is an indirect cost of the gains to protection. Employment protection is usually thought of as creating redistribution towards labor, especially established workers, and is held responsible for creating rent seeking and efficiency losses. However, such policies also create immense insurance benefits by deterring opportunism.

The challenge is to ensure that the efficiency losses are contained while the insurance gains are furthered. Employment protection should not be so rigid that it prevents change and preserves the status quo. It should not be so blunt that it is unable to distinguish between termination for shirking and opportunistic termination. Serious employment protection is counter-productive when it is protectionist to vested interests and does not promote economic progress. Datta-Chaudhuri (2001) appropriately quotes Justice Mehta, a former Chief Justice of a High Court, when he states that the view taken by many judgments "that to favour labour is the only goal of the statute (the IDA) is counter productive in as such as it ultimately harms the cause of labour itself."

Conclusion

Indian governments have intervened in organized labor markets to strengthen the position of workers vis-à-vis employers. Job security regulations have been central to government interventions in the labor market. Their impact on employment and output growth in the registered manufacturing sector is important because a measure of success in development is the extent to which the manufacturing sector is able to draw surplus labor out of agriculture. Amendments to the legislation in the form of the Industrial Disputes Act have provided opportunities to study the impact of job security legislation on employment and output. The empirical evidence suggests that job security legislation in India has on balance not had the negative effects its critics argue. Rigidities in employment adjustment—it takes about 5 to 6 years for employment adjustment to be completed—are more due to the inherent characteristics of the industries than to job security regulation.

Employers in India in the 1980s, termed the period of jobless growth, matched staffing to workload fluctuations by adjusting the timing of hours worked (work-time flexibility). The increase in time worked from 1979 to 1987 was equivalent to a shift from a 5- to a 6-day week. At the same time, productivity increases due to infrastructure investment and trade liberalization increased the efficiency of labor while reducing its requirement per unit of capital. Capital accumulation, however, has been the driving force that has offset the negative effects of the growth in work intensity and productivity. Also, apart from work intensity, firms have managed to be flexible by changing the composition of contracts via changes in the share of permanent to non-permanent temporary and casual workers.

Implementation of labor legislation is a state subject and states can amend central legislation. However, identifying state amendments as being pro-labor or pro-employer is a task that can result in paradoxes. Maharashtra and Gujarat in one exercise are labeled as pro-worker states when another study reports the extent of overmanning in these states as being the lowest. These states are also perceived as good locations for setting up manufacturing units. Also, it is not just the legislations, but the enforcement that is crucial to the extent to which firms are deterred by labor legislation. More stringent labor legislation and better enforcement can both deter employment generation. However, at the same time as labor legislation was being tightened, regulations on entry and capacity made the licensing system and capacity the main constraints on expansion of firms in the registered manufacturing sector. Delicensing along with capital accumulation affected employment growth more than labor legislation.

Job security regulations are often seen as a source of rigidity resulting in rents for organized labor. However, these regulations often emerged as a response to the threat of unemployment and income insecurity and are more a social insurance than rent-seeking. Over time, and arguably the IDA amendment in 1982 is an example, rent-seeking became more entrenched. To mitigate this effect demands have arisen to reduce employment protection that have dampened incentives for investment on the job. However, markets if left to themselves will not be able to devise contracts that provide an efficient level of employment security. In a temporal world if workers trade off working with shirking, employers can similarly trade off honoring a contract with termination of employees. Opportunistic behavior is often difficult to observe or to verify. In product markets, opportunism can be nipped through signals such as the offer of warranties. In labor markets, both firms and workers are susceptible to opportunism and to verify breach of contract is difficult. A meaningful way to encourage workers to invest in a job and employers to honor contracts is to legislate for employment protection. The difficult task, in reality, is of course to ensure that employment protection does not become protectionist and an enemy of economic progress.

Notes

1 Of course, there are enforcement failures. As many labour leaders have voiced in the past, (a) who has ever been penalized? and (b) is the fine (usually a small sum of something like Rs. 5,000/-) really a deterrent?
2 For simplicity assume that at time t_1 the worker's effort decision is made simultaneously with the decision of the firm as to whether to honour the contract.

References

Ahluwalia, I J. (1991) "Productivity and Growth in Indian Manufacturing." New Delhi: Oxford University Press.

Arellano, M. and S. Bond (1991) "Some Tests of Specification for Panel Data: Monte Carlo evidence and an application to employment equations." *Review of Economic Studies* 58: 277–97.

Athukorala P. and K. Sen (2002) "Saving, Investment, and Growth in India." New Delhi: Oxford University Press.

Basu, K. (2002) "Ideology, Economics and Labour Market Policy." In *Facets of the Indian Economy—The NCAER Golden Jubilee Lectures*, edited by R. Mohan. New Delhi: Oxford University Press, pp. 248–64.

——, G. S. Fields, and S. Debgupta (2001) "Retrenchment, Labor Laws and Government Policy: An analysis with special reference to India." Paper written for the World Bank, Washington DC: Shrinking Smartly Research.

Besley, T. and R. Burgess (2004) "Can Labor Regulation Hinder Economic Performance? Evidence from India." *Quarterly Journal of Economics*, 91–134, February.

Bhalotra, S. (1998) "The Puzzle of Jobless Growth in Indian Manufacturing." *Oxford Bulletin of Economics and Statistics* 60(1): 5–32.

Bhattacharya, B. B. and S. Sakthivel (2003) "Economic Reforms and Jobless Growth in India in the 1990s." *The Indian Journal of Labour Economics* 46(4): 845–65.

Bhowmik, S. K. (1998) "The Labour Movement in India: Present problems and future perspectives." *The Indian Journal of Social Work* 59(1): 147–66.

Dasgupta, I. and S. Marjit (2004) "Evasive Reform: Informalisation in a Liberalised Economy with Wage-setting Unions." EGDI and UNU-WIDER Conference on *Unlocking Human Potential: Linking the Informal and Formal Sectors*, 17–18 September, 2004, Helsinki.

Datta-Chaudhuri, M. (2000) "Labour Markets as Social Institutions in India." In *Institutions, Incentives and Economic Reforms in India*, edited by S. Kähkönen and A. Lanyi. New Delhi: Sage Publications, pp. 449–68.

Deshpande, L. K., A. N. Sharma, A. K. Karan, and S. Sarkar (2004) *Liberalisation and Labour—Labour Flexibility in Indian Manufacturing*. New Delhi: Institute for Human Development.

Dollar, D., G. Iarossi, and T. Mengistae (2002) "Investment Climate and Economic Performance: Some Firm Level Evidence from India." Development Research Group, The World Bank, Working Paper 143.

Dutta Roy, S. (2003) "Employment Dynamics in Indian Industry: Adjustment lags and the impact of job security regulations." *Journal of Development Economics* 73: 233–56.

Fallon, P. R. and R. E. B. Lucas (1991) "The Impact of Changes in Job Security Regulations in India and Zimbabwe." *The World Bank Economic Review* 5(3): 395–413.

—— and —— (1993) "Job Security Regulations and the Dynamic Demand for Industrial Labour in India and Zimbabwe." *Journal of Development Economics* 40: 241–75.

Harriss-White, B. (2003) *India Working—Essays on Society and Economy*. Cambridge University Press, UK.

Hutter, B. (1989) "Variations in Regulatory Enforcement Styles." *Law and Policy* 11: 153–74.

Jhabvala, R. and R. Kanbur (2004) "Globalisation and Economic Reform as Seen from the Ground: SEWA's Experience in India." In *India's Emerging Economy—Performance and Prospects in the 1990s and Beyond*, edited by K. Basu. New Delhi: Oxford University Press, pp. 293–312.

Lazear, E. (1981) "Agency, Earnings Profiles, Productivity, and Hours Restrictions." *American Economic Review*, 71: 606–20, September.

Ramaswamy, K. V. (2003) "Liberalization, Outsourcing and Industrial Labour Markets in India: Some Preliminary Results." In *Labour Market and Institution in India—1990s and Beyond*, edited by S. Uchikawa. New Delhi: Manohar Publications, pp. 155–75.

Shapiro, C. and J. E. Stiglitz (1984) "Equilibrium Unemployment as a Worker Discipline Device." *American Economic Review* 74(3): 433–44.

Sherlock, S. (2001) "Labour and the Remaking of Bombay." In *Organising Labour in Globalising Asia*, edited by J. Hutchison and A. Brown. London: Routledge, pp. 147–67.

World Bank (1989) "India: Poverty, Employment and Social Services: A World Bank Study." Washington DC: World Bank.

14 Labor productivity growth, informal wage, and capital mobility[*]

A general equilibrium analysis

Sugata Marjit and Saibal Kar

1 Introduction

This paper looks at the impact of growth in the productivity of workers in both the formal and informal sectors, on the informal wage and employment. It is now more or less established that the recent surge in the Indian growth rate is much more related to a productivity boost than to a rise in investment (see, for example, Guha-Khasnobis and Bari 2003; Marjit 2005, etc.). If such income growth precipitates on the lower deciles of the income groups, then it is expected that the social consequences of the overall increase in the growth rate must be reflected on the quality of life of the poor people. It is clearly a difficult task to measure such impact at the micro level and in terms of the various indicators of human development, and therefore, we argue that the informal wage is a good indicator to capture the income element, given that most of the workforce in India is absorbed in this segment. Hence, for example, one may like to know how a productivity growth in the skilled sector affects the wages of unskilled workers involved in the informal sector, or how a productivity growth of unskilled workers working in the organized/formal sector affects their informal counterpart. Before we provide further details on the plan of work, let us briefly visit the existing literature dealing with informal labor markets in developing countries.

Several empirical papers by Marjit and Maiti (2006), Sinha and Adam (2006), Olofin and Folawewo (2006) contained in a recent volume edited by Guha-Khasnobis and Kanbur (2006) discuss various aspects of the informal labor market and its role in the development process. Goldberg and Pavcnik (2003) and Marjit, Ghosh, and Biswas (2006) point out the asymmetric impact of reform policies on the size of the informal sector. Marjit (2003), Marjit, Kar, and Beladi (2007) argue that liberal trade policies that contract the size of the import-competing sector and create an excess supply of workers in the informal segment can still lead to a rise in the informal wage if capital is also allowed to relocate to the informal sector. Empirical evidence supporting these claims is provided in Marjit and Kar (2005) and Marjit and Maiti (2006). The theoretical structure dealing with formal–informal interaction in some of the abovementioned works captures the dual labor market by including a high fixed wage formal sector with a lower flexible wage informal segment, in line with the earlier treatments of Carruth and Oswald (1981), Agenor and Montiel (1997), Marjit (2003), etc.

While the main focus of the earlier papers was to investigate the trade policy induced relative price effects on real informal wage, the current paper highlights the productivity issue explicitly. It finds that the degree of capital mobility between the formal and the informal sector is quite critical in determining whether the benefit of a productivity growth in the formal sector percolates to the informal workers and/or whether productivity growth of the informal workers is eventually translated into an increase in their wages. In the process, we extend Jones (1971) and demonstrate that the condition under which the mobile factor gains from its own productivity growth is altered as soon as we bring in some degree of mobility in a model where capital is sector-specific.

The spillover effects of productivity growth on informal wages may perhaps be best understood by dwelling upon the aspects of free mobility of labor and capital, and on the vertical linkage between the formal and the informal sectors, of which we focus on the issue of factor mobility only. The linkage effect is discussed in the appendix. These, however, need to be supplemented by demand side effects when growth in income spills over to the non-traded informal activities. Yet, we look at the supply side effects only, partly because the demand effect is quite standard and also due to the fact that the demand effect may not be very significant.

In a recent paper, Foster and Rosenzweig (2004) argue that greater agricultural productivity induced higher wage in the rural economy increases the cost of production in rural industries. At the same time, greater demand for rural non-traded goods encourages rural industrialization. In the case of India, the mix of such effects has worked against rural industrialization. Thus, they show that the role of demand in rural industrialization is less significant compared to the supply side effects. While the overall demand effect in the entire economy cannot be undermined, in the current context we are interested in identifying the supply side outcomes. In fact, using these elements as building blocks, our study offers a general equilibrium model of production for a small open economy and looks at the labor productivity growth in formal and informal sectors. We derive a set of results, by considering the short run when capital is sector specific, and the longer run when capital moves gradually across sectors.

Higher productivity growth in the skilled sector in the short run has an unfavorable impact on the informal wage, whereas in the longer run, it may not have any impact. Productivity growth in the unskilled sector is likely to have opposite effects on informal wages in the short and in the long run. Productivity growth in the informal sector will be retained in higher wages in the short run provided Jones's (1971) condition holds. As we introduce some degree of capital mobility, the condition changes and the possibility of a rising informal wage is eventually guaranteed by a higher elasticity of capital mobility. With full mobility of capital the informal wage must rise.

The paper is structured as follows. The second section offers the basic framework and results. The third section attempts a simple econometric exercise to corroborate some of the theoretical claims and discusses certain policy issues. The last one concludes.

2 The model

We have a three sector economy, X uses skilled labor and capital; Y uses unskilled labor and capital. X and Y are produced by the formal/organized segment of the labor market. While the skilled wage is market determined, unionized bargaining determines the level of fixed wage for the unskilled in the formal sector. One point should be noted here. One can easily endogenize the fixed wage by invoking a utility maximizing union without any perceptible change in the direction of the results. Thus, exogeneity of fixed unskilled wages is not a crucial assumption and can be relaxed. Z is produced with informal workers and capital. The informal wage is market determined and is less than the fixed wage in the formal sector. In the short term, capital does not flow between the formal and the informal segments; but there is perfect mobility of capital within the formal sectors producing X and Y. Markets are competitive and technology is neo-classical. We assume exogenously given commodity prices, consistent with the small open economy assumption.

The following equations describe the model.

The competitive price conditions are given by:

$$w_S a_{SX} + r a_{KX} = P_X \tag{1}$$

$$\overline{w} a_{LY} + r a_{KY} = P_Y \tag{2}$$

$$w a_{LZ} + R a_{KZ} = P_Z \tag{3}$$

and, the full employment conditions imply:

$$a_{KX} X + a_{KY} Y = \tilde{K} \tag{4}$$

$$a_{LY} Y + a_{LZ} Z = L \tag{5}$$

$$a_{SX} X = S \tag{6}$$

$$a_{KZ} Z = K_Z \tag{7}$$

Note that equations (1) and (2) determine w_S and r. Then, from (4) and (6) we determine X and Y. Further, (3), (5), and (7) determine w, R, and Z. (a_{KX}, a_{SX}, a_{KY}, a_{LY}) are determined by the wage-rental ratios, w_S / r and $\overline{w} / r$. It is easy to check that for (5) and (7) to hold, simultaneously an increase in w must increase R also. A rise in w, given that $a_{LY} Y$, reduces demand for labor in the informal sector. Hence, R must rise to absorb the excess. On the other hand,

(3) suggests that (w, R) should be negatively related. These relationships together analytically determine w and R and hence Z from (7) (see Figure 14.1).

This structure refers to the short-run with no mobility of capital between the formal and the informal segments, i.e. $r \neq R$. We now look at the consequence of a secular decline in a_{SX}, a_{LY}, and a_{LZ} on w, the informal wage. Note that

$$a_{SX} = f\left(\frac{w_S}{r}, t\right) \tag{8}$$

where t denotes some sort of productivity parameter and $\hat{a}_{SX} = -a < 0$ denotes the elasticity of a_{SX} with respect to t, given w_S / r.

Let us trace the general equilibrium consequence of a drop in a_{SX}. A decline in a_{SX} must increase w_S as r is pegged from (2). Note that this should raise X and reduce Y. From (5) it is straightforward to argue that there will be an excess supply of labor in the informal segment following a production contraction in Y. Thus, w will go down and R will increase. The size of informal output and employment will expand but informal workers will be poorer.

A secular decline in a_{LY} on the other hand, raises r and squeezes down, w_S, reducing X and increasing Y. Interestingly, though, this may or may not increase the demand for informal labor as a_{LY} drops and Y increases. If the elasticity of factor substitution is strong enough, employment in Y will increase, drawing workers from the informal segment. This should raise w and reduce R in turn.

The last exercise on which we dwell is the direct effect of a secular decline in

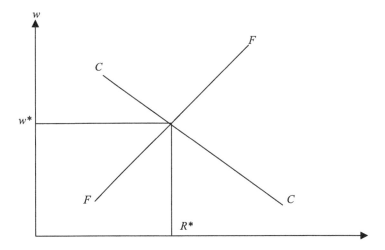

Figure 14.1 Determination of wage and rental rate

Note: CC refers to the Competitive Condition, FF refers to the Full-Employment Condition.

a_{LZ} on w. Given Y, whether such a change increases w depends on the elasticity of substitution. With weak substitution elasticity, wages can go down.

Note that while productivity growth in the skilled sector cannot increase w, more productive unskilled workers in the formal sector may raise w.

The long run

Suppose capital can move freely between the formal and the informal sectors with $r = R$. Also, equations (4) and (7) are now conjoined as (9).

$$a_{KX}X + a_{KY}Y + a_{KZ}Z = \bar{K} \qquad (9)$$

Note that w is insulated from changes in supply of informal workers as capital moves in and out to remove any gap between r and R.

A drop in a_{SX} now increases w_S without any impact on r or w. The short-run negative effect on w is now mitigated by the full mobility of capital, as X draws in the retrenched capital out of Y. On the other hand, a drop in a_{LY} will increase r, reducing both w_S and w. The informal sector and the skilled sector both have to accommodate a higher r in the process.

Finally, we show that a drop in a_{LZ} must increase w. This is also an unambiguous result. As $\bar{w}$ is frozen, any tendency of increase in the return to capital in the formal sector is countered by the movement of capital into the sector. Thus, the benefit rests with the informal workers. In fact, the rate of increase in w will be greater than the rate of growth in productivity.

3   A heuristic exercise

In this section, we try to assess the above theoretical conjectures in terms of some empirical evidence drawn from the data on informal wage, formal sector productivity, and capital accumulation in Indian industries. As noted in the theoretical section, labor productivity growth in the skilled sector should not benefit the informal workers. In fact, it can worsen if capital is sector-specific. On the other hand, labor productivity growth in the unskilled segment may increase unskilled informal wages. In terms of a preliminary empirical exercise we use data on informal wages, labor productivity in the organized sector, and fixed assets for the unorganized manufacturing for various NSS (National Sample Survey of India) rounds between 1989/90 and 2000/1 across various provinces in India. We first construct an index to classify the provinces according to the skill content in their organized production system, i.e. the states are classified as relatively skilled and relatively unskilled in terms of the participation of skilled workers in the organized manufacturing within each state. The number of skilled workers in any state is obtained by taking the difference between the total employees across all industry types less the number of wage earners in that state. The degree of "skill concentration" in each state may therefore, be simply stated as the share of skill in total employment.[1] Furthermore, the states have been ranked as High Concentration (Rank 1) or Low Concentration (Rank 2) as per the respective skill concentrations greater than or less than the all-India average given in the last but one column in Table 14.A1. Interestingly, most of the states do not display any appreciable increase in the skill concentration, and some have actually registered lower skill concentration despite continuing above the national average during the period (1989/90 to 2000/1). Using this information, we construct a Skill-Dummy for each state (value 1, if the skill concentration ratio is above the national average, or value 0, if the skill concentration ratio is below it). Subsequently, we run a set of pooled regressions with real informal wage (manufacturing) as the dependent variable. The data is available from the three rounds of NSSO, i.e. 1989–90, 1994–5, and 2000–1 (see Appendix 3). The gross value added (GVA) per worker in the organized manufacturing is available from the Annual Survey of Industries for various states, the real fixed assets in the informal sector (available from NSSO) as a proxy for capital stock and the skill dummy as three explanatory variables. The GVA per worker in this structure represents the average productivity of labor in each state. The actual values of GVA per worker, the level of real informal fixed assets, and the real informal wage are shown in Table 14.A2 in Appendix 3.

The regression result offers interesting, though exploratory, evidence on the relationship between annual growth of real informal wages and the growth in GVA per worker in the formal sector. For the relatively "unskilled" states (i.e. for the skill dummy taking the value of 0), the relationship is positive and significant. However, the coefficient of real fixed assets is not significant. On the other hand, a growth in the productivity of unskilled workers in the organized sector does have a positive influence on the growth of real informal wages, a distinct possibility in our theoretical structure.

The main point of our analysis is the focus on capital mobility between the formal and informal sectors as an important policy variable. Let us briefly discuss a few possible policy options which might make the "informal sector" more receptive to productivity augmenting effects in the "formal sector". It follows from our analysis that if informal labor has to derive the maximum benefits of its own productivity growth, then more capital needs to flow into this sector. Otherwise, the stringent capital constraint will push the wage down as the labor requirement per unit of output falls due to a productivity improvement. Since it is well known that the unorganized or the informal sector suffers from the standard moral hazard problem whereby flow of formal investments are rare, the creation of an institution which could relax such constraint by allowing more symmetric information between the agents would help the cause of a large number of poor workers involved in this sector. Apart from the well-known peer-monitored group-based lending schemes which come closest to what we have in mind, one could also think of restructuring the emphasis of the credit agencies that in many developing countries act under high degrees of risk aversion and therefore are interested only in very safe activities. This is undoubtedly an area that policy makers may explore beyond the purview of labor market interventions, in order to address the poverty and welfare issues of a large number of workers in the unorganized sector.

The source of productivity growth is also quite important. If the growth in productivity takes place in the formal sector, the greater will be the positive impact on the informal wage provided that capital is relatively sticky in the informal sector. The problem is that footloose capital will require a higher return in the informal sector, pushing down the wages. It is clear from our analysis that a critical degree of capital inflow into the sector will generate higher informal wages. We have also argued that the vertical linkage between the formal and informal sectors is more effective in channeling the productivity growth in the former on to the informal workers through a trickle-down mechanism. Thus, along with capital inflow, the informal workers also enjoy the direct benefits of growth in the formal sector. As we are not proposing a universal theory, a case-by-case approach will perhaps be more relevant towards getting the full implications of our findings.

4 Concluding remarks

This paper starts from a stylized fact that the recent growth in the Indian economy is influenced more by a productivity take-off as compared to other factors. Such productivity growth is largely concentrated in the service sector, which has grown phenomenally over recent years. However, given the fact that the size of the unorganized sector is quite substantial, a number of interesting questions require serious attention. As labor productivity in the formal/organized sector increases, does it help the informal workers? How does the informal wage, a benchmark yardstick for the poor, respond to such changes in the short-run and in the long-run when we account for both labor and capital movement across sectors? We prove that higher productivity of skilled workers should not affect informal wages. More productive unskilled workers in the formal segment may help the informal workers in the short-run but definitely not in the long-run. Thus, capital mobility plays a crucial role in our analysis, when aspects of product market reform, productivity change, and trade-related reform also affect the informal wage. We have argued elsewhere that trade reform should help the informal workers, provided that capital moves more or less freely between the segments. However, as we show here, the productivity impact does have opposite implications. For example, any reform that reduces the cost of capital in the formal sector must help the informal segment when capital is mobile. However, under the same circumstances, a productivity growth in the formal sector will hurt the informal workers. One future task might be to isolate these impacts empirically.

Appendix 1

Effect of a decline in a_{LY} and a_{LZ} with imperfect mobility of capital

$$K_X + K_Y = \tilde{K} \tag{A1}$$

$$\tilde{K} + K_Z = \overline{K} \tag{A2}$$

$$\hat{\tilde{K}} - \hat{K}_Z = \epsilon\,(\hat{r} - \hat{R}) \tag{A3}$$

Differentiating full-employment conditions

$$\lambda_{LY}\hat{Y} + \lambda_{LZ}\hat{Z} + \lambda_{LY}\hat{a}_{LY} + \lambda_{LZ}\hat{a}_{LZ} - \lambda_{LY}a - \lambda_{LZ}\beta = 0 \tag{A4}$$

$$\lambda_{KX}\hat{X} + \lambda_{KY}\hat{Y} = \hat{\tilde{K}} \tag{A5}$$

$$\hat{a}_{KZ}\hat{Z} = \hat{K}_Z \tag{A6}$$

$$\hat{X} = 0 \tag{A7}$$

From (A2), (A4), (A5), (A6), and (A7)

$$\frac{\lambda_{LY}}{\lambda_{KY}}\hat{\tilde{K}} + \lambda_{LZ}\hat{K}_Z - \lambda_{LY}\sigma_y(-\hat{r}) - \lambda_{LZ}\sigma_Z(\hat{w} - \hat{R}) = \lambda_{LY}a + \lambda_{LZ}\beta$$

$$-\frac{\lambda_{LY}}{\lambda_{KY}}s_Z\hat{K}_Z + \lambda_{LZ}\hat{K}_Z + \lambda_{LY}\sigma_Y\hat{r} - \lambda_{LX}\sigma_Z(\hat{w} - \hat{R}) = \lambda_{LY}a + \lambda_{LZ}\beta \tag{A8}$$

Differentiating competitive price conditions,

$$\hat{K}_Z\left(\lambda_{LZ} - \frac{\lambda_{LY}}{\lambda_{KY}}\frac{\lambda_{KZ}}{\lambda_K}\right) + \lambda_{LY}\,\sigma_Y\,\hat{r} - \lambda_{LZ}\sigma_Z\frac{(\hat{w} - \theta_{LZ}\beta)}{\theta_{KZ}} = \lambda_{LY}\,a + \lambda_{LZ}\beta$$

$$f_Z\hat{K}_Z + \lambda_{LY}\sigma_Y\left(\frac{\theta_{LY}a}{\theta_{KY}}\right) + \lambda_{LZ}\sigma_Z\beta\frac{\theta_{LZ}}{\theta_{KZ}} - \frac{\lambda_{LZ}}{\theta_{KZ}}\sigma_Z\hat{w} = \lambda_{LY}a + \lambda_{LZ}\beta$$

From (A3)

$$-\frac{f_Z\epsilon}{1 + \dfrac{\lambda_{KZ}}{\lambda_K}}\left(\frac{\theta_{LY}a}{\theta_{KY}} - \frac{\theta_{LZ}\beta - \theta_{LZ}\,\hat{w}}{\theta_{KZ}}\right) + \lambda_{LY}\sigma_Y\left(\frac{\theta_{LY}a}{\theta_{KY}}\right)$$

$$+ \lambda_{LZ}\,\sigma_Z\beta\frac{\theta_{LZ}}{\theta_{KZ}} - \frac{\lambda_{LZ}}{\lambda_{KZ}}\sigma_Z\,\hat{w} = \lambda_{LY}a + \lambda_{LZ}\beta$$

$$-\hat{w}\left[\frac{\lambda_{LZ}}{\theta_{KZ}}\sigma_Z + \frac{f_Z \in \theta_{LZ}}{\theta_{KZ}\left(1+\frac{\lambda_{KZ}}{\lambda_K}\right)}\right] = a\left[\lambda_{LY} + \frac{f_Z \in \theta_{LY}}{\theta_{KY}\left(1+\frac{\lambda_{KZ}}{\lambda_K}\right)} - \lambda_{LY}\sigma_Y\frac{\theta_{LY}}{\theta_{KY}}\right]$$

$$+\beta\left[\lambda_{LZ} - \lambda_{LZ}\sigma_Z\frac{\theta_{LZ}}{\theta_{KZ}} - \frac{\theta_{LZ}f_Z \in}{\theta_{KZ}\left(1+\frac{\lambda_{KZ}}{\lambda_K}\right)}\right]$$

$$\hat{w} = \frac{a\left[\lambda_{LY} + \dfrac{f_Z \in \theta_{LY}}{\theta_{KY}\left(1+\frac{\lambda_{KZ}}{\lambda_K}\right)} - \lambda_{LY}\sigma_Y\dfrac{\theta_{LY}}{\theta_{KY}}\right]}{(-)\left(\dfrac{\lambda_{LZ}}{\theta_{KZ}}\sigma_Z + \dfrac{f_Z\theta_{LZ} \in}{\theta_{KZ}\left(1+\frac{\lambda_{KZ}}{\lambda_K}\right)}\right)}$$

$$+\beta\frac{\left[\lambda_{LZ} - \lambda_{LZ}\sigma_Z\dfrac{\theta_{LZ}}{\theta_{KZ}} - \dfrac{\theta_{LZ}f_Z \in}{\theta_{KZ}\left(1+\frac{\lambda_{KZ}}{\lambda_K}\right)}\right]}{(-)\left(\dfrac{\lambda_{LZ}}{\theta_{KZ}}\sigma_Z + \dfrac{f_Z\theta_{LZ} \in}{\theta_{KZ}\left(1+\frac{\lambda_{KZ}}{\lambda_K}\right)}\right)} \qquad (A9)$$

Suppose that, $\in = 0$, $a > 0$, $\beta = 0$ (short-run, only labor productivity in Y goes up).

Then, $\hat{w} > 0$ iff $1 < \sigma_Y(\theta_{LY}/\theta_{KY}$

Similarly, for $\in = 0$, $a = 0$, $\beta > 0$, $\hat{w} > 0$ iff $1 < \sigma_Z(\theta_{LZ}/\theta_{KZ}$.

Thus, strong elasticities of substitution will increase w.

Let us divide the numerator and denominator in RHS of (A9) by $\in \ne 0$

Then, let $\in \to \infty$ (the perfect mobility case)

$a > 0$, $\beta = 0 \Rightarrow \hat{w} < 0$

$a = 0$, $\beta > 0 \Rightarrow \hat{w} > 0$

This proves the argument in the text.

Appendix 2

Vertical linkage and productivity impact

We follow Marjit (2003).

$$\overline{w}a_{LY} + ra_{KY} + P_m a_{my} = P_y \tag{A10}$$

$$wa_{Lm} + ra_{Km} = P_m \tag{A11}$$

$$wa_{LZ} + ra_{KZ} = P_Z \tag{A12}$$

M is capital-intensive.

In this model, r is positively related to P_m as M is capital intensive and LHS in (A10) is an increasing function of P_m. Therefore, a drop in a_{LY} must raise P_m and r reducing w—the same effect that we derive in the model without vertical linkage. If M is labor intensive, r is declining in P_m. In that case, one does not know whether the LHS in (10A) is declining in P_m. If it is still increasing in P_m, then a drop in a_{LY} will raise P_m and w via the Stolper–Samuelson result. Therefore, we do have a different outcome. However, if LHS in (A10) is declining in P_m, a drop in a_{LY} will reduce P_m and w.

Appendix 3

Table 14.A1 State-wise skill concentration rank in India

States	Skill concentration (rank)		
	1989–90	*1994–5*	*2000–1*
Himachal Pradesh	32.64 (1)	34.98 (1)	24.33 (1)
Madhya Pradesh	30.37 (1)	30.49 (1)	24.59 (1)
Delhi	29.21 (1)	29.84 (1)	31.80 (1)
Maharashtra	27.05 (1)	28.47 (1)	30.31 (1)
Karnataka	26.03 (1)	24.84 (1)	24.24 (1)
Haryana	24.13 (1)	27.42 (1)	27.70 (1)
Orissa	23.81 (1)	23.73 (2)	22.96 (2)
Rajasthan	23.60 (1)	26.06 (1)	24.38 (1)
West Bengal	21.84 (2)	22.17 (2)	20.01 (2)
Bihar	21.82 (2)	23.01 (2)	22.37 (2)
Punjab	21.70 (2)	25.14 (1)	22.70 (2)
Gujarat	21.33 (2)	26.03 (1)	26.37 (1)
Uttar Pradesh	20.64 (2)	23.09 (2)	26.16 (1)
Tamil Nadu	20.19 (2)	20.01 (2)	18.56 (2)
Kerala	17.44 (2)	16.37 (2)	16.08 (2)
Assam	16.90 (2)	18.31 (2)	17.83 (2)
Andhra Pradesh	14.42 (2)	15.21 (2)	15.78 (2)
All-India average	**23.13**	**24.42**	**23.31**

Source: ASI, various years

Pooled regression results

Pooled Regression Equation (Random Effects Model):

$$Ln(I_w) = a + (\beta_1 + \gamma_1 D_s) Ln(Y_F) + \beta_2 Ln(I_{FA})$$

such that,

$$Ln(I_w) = 0.07 + (0.61^* + 0.D_s) Ln(Y_F) + 0.11 Ln(I_{FA})$$

R-squared: 0.33,   Adj.   *R*-Squared: 0.29,   Prob $>F = 0.00$, $\rho = 0$,
Hausman $= 0.00$, * = significant at 5% level

where

I_w = informal wage
a = constant
Y_F = formal average productivity of labor
I_{FA} = informal fixed assets
D_s = skill dummy (which takes value = 1 for skilled formal labor, value = 0 for unskilled formal labor)

Table 14.A2 State-wise real GVA/worker, real fixed assets and real wage (informal)

States	Real GVA per worker (formal)			Real fixed assets ('000) (informal)			Real wage (informal)		
	1989–90	1994–5	2000–1	1989–90	1994–5	2000–1	1989–90	1994–5	2000–1
Andhra Pradesh	55,859	93,600	99,091	112,699	119,314	298,122	2,535	7,441	7,037
Assam	121,584	102,492	118,578	15,260	24,942	31,404	2,665	5,324	7,181
Bihar	154,334	174,546	221,411	171,383	138,364	195,048	3,308	5,293	7,974
Gujarat	117,194	229,594	283,751	163,235	219,203	300,510	3,607	10,739	12,663
Haryana	109,689	150,910	223,213	50,051	52,169	157,014	6,852	9,175	11,028
Himachal Pradesh	115,405	188,139	354,982	56,235	16,102	33,121	4,460	6,748	12,009
Karnataka	120,800	173,724	194,272	77,874	101,751	215,801	2,671	6,342	8,392
Kerala	106,577	78,337	108,657	60,789	44,697	159,397	4,446	7,530	9,718
Madhya Pradesh	147,232	217,470	265,189	76,709	92,499	189,710	2,958	7,966	8,249
Maharashtra	185,831	268,129	315,094	209,950	303,671	608,403	4,038	10,974	12,695
Orissa	170,424	158,313	212,283	44,574	53,120	72,085	2,438	5,781	6,592
Punjab	116,263	117,541	130,473	90,991	32,617	230,536	2,071	8,026	11,274
Rajasthan	103,813	196,273	251,614	129,626	63,960	237,915	2,958	8,008	12,177
Tamil Nadu	106,940	135,241	149,697	140,946	94,346	487,575	4,214	6,812	9,945
Uttar Pradesh	116,773	192,203	214,509	312,029	220,188	565,231	3,490	6,036	8,405
West Bengal	67,296	98,239	106,662	164,692	125,816	327,097	3,250	6,828	8,358
Delhi	105,609	222,398	191,485	81,516	126,654	433,640	8,741	11,139	14,783

Notes

* An earlier version of this paper was presented at the "Cornell–Michigan Conference on Labor Market in Transition and Developing Economies" at the University of Michigan, Ann Arbor. The authors are indebted to the conference participants, in particular to Ravi Kanbur and Jan Svejnar and to Ronald Jones for helpful comments. We are also indebted to Pranab Kumar Das and Dibyendu Maiti for suggestions with the empirical section. Research assistance by Mahasweta Kundu and Archita Banik is also acknowledged. The usual disclaimer applies.
1 See Table A1 in Appendix 3 for a ranking of the states according to skill concentration as defined here.

References

Agenor, R. and P. Montiel (1997) "Development Macroeconomics," second edition, NJ: Princeton University Press.

Carruth, A. and A. Oswald (1981) "The Determination of Union and Non-Union Wage-rates." *European Economic Review* 16(2): 285–302.

Foster, A. and M. R. Rosenzweig (2004) "Agricultural Productivity Growth, Rural Economic Diversity, and Economic Reforms: India, 1970–2000." *Economic Development and Cultural Change* 52: 509–42.

Goldberg, P. K. and N. Pavcnik (2003) "The Response of the Informal Sector to Trade Liberalization." NBER working paper 9443, Cambridge: MA.

Guha-Khasnobis, B. and R. Kanbur (eds.) (2006) "Informal Labor Markets and Development." NY: Palgrave-MacMillan.

——, and F. Bari (2003) "Sources of Growth in South Asian Countries." In *The South Asian Experience with Growth*, edited by Isher Judge Ahluwalia and J. Williamson. Oxford University Press.

Jones, R. W. (1971) "The Specific- Factor Model in Trade, Theory and History." In *Trade, Balance of Payments and Growth*, edited by J. N. Bhagwati et al. Amsterdam: North Holland.

Marjit, S. (2003) "Economic Reform and Informal Wage—A general equilibrium analysis." *Journal of Development Economics* 72(1): 371–8.

——. (2005) "Financial Sector Reform for Stimulating Investment and Economic Growth—The Indian Experience." Policy paper prepared for the Ministry of Finance, Government of India and the ADB, New Delhi.

—— and S. Kar (2005) "Pro-market Reform and Informal Wage-theory and the Contemporary Indian Perspective." *India Macroeconomics Annual.*

—— and D. S. Maiti (2006) "Globalization, Economic Reform and Informal Labor." In *Informal Labor Markets and Development*, edited by B. Guha-Khasnobis and R. Kanbur. NY: Palgrave-MacMillan.

——, S. Kar, and H. Beladi (2007) "Trade Reform and Informal Wage." *Review of Development Economics* 11(2): 313–20.

——, S. Ghosh, and A. K. Biswas (2006) "Informality, Corruption and Trade Reform." *European Journal of Political Economy* (forthcoming).

Olofin, S. O. and A. O. Folawewo (2006) "Skill Requirements, Earnings and Labor Demand in Nigeria's Urban Informal Sector." In *Informal Labor Markets and Development*, edited by B. Guha-Khasnobis and R. Kanbur. NY: Palgrave-Macmillan.

Sinha, A. and C. Adam (2006) "Trade Reforms and Informalization: Getting Behind Jobless Growth in India." In *Informal Labor Markets and Development*, edited by B. Guha-Khasnobis and R. Kanbur. NY: Palgrave-MacMillan.

Part III

Trade and labor

15 Trade and labor standards

New empirical evidence

Yiagadeesen Samy and Vivek H. Dehejia

1 Introduction

Should labor standards be imposed in international trade? This issue, despite not being a new one, has been at the forefront of trade negotiations in recent years because of concerns arising out of the increasing globalization of the world economy, and is not likely to go away anytime soon. The debate over the inclusion of labor standards in international trade is a reflection of how to improve the lot of the poor in developing countries. Labor interests in high-standard or developed countries view the adoption of core labor standards[1] (CLSs) as a necessary condition for improving labor standards but they are not clear on how the likely increase in production costs due to improved standards will be shared. For example, in a closed economy, firms will have a tendency to shift the increase in costs on to the consumers through higher prices. However, in a world characterized by free trade and where prices are determined on international markets, the firm (or its workers) will have to bear the cost of the labor standards. Developing or low-standard countries thus view the imposition of labor standards as disguised protectionism as it will rob them of their competitive advantage, which is largely based on labor costs. Labor groups in high-standard countries also argue that low-standard countries benefit from an unfair source of comparative advantage (the so-called conventional wisdom), and they fear that there will be a race to the bottom of standards as trade flows represented by imports from low-standard countries intensify.

Not surprisingly, both the USA and France tried (without success) to put labor standards on the agenda during GATT talks, as well as during WTO conferences in Singapore and Seattle in 1996 and 1999 respectively. The European Union also brought this issue at the WTO conference in Doha in 2001 and it was rejected by the developing countries. In fact, in Doha, the WTO indicated that it would hold talks about labor standards and was asked to take note of work under way at the ILO on the social dimensions of globalization. Both WTO and ILO member states have committed themselves to the observance of CLSs (as reflected in the WTO Singapore Ministerial Declaration of 1996 and the ILO Declaration on Fundamental Principles and Rights at Work of 1998). They have also agreed that labor standards should not be used for protectionist intents and that ignorance of, and deliberate violations of CLS to achieve comparative advantage, should be avoided. Regarding the "race to the bottom" of standards across countries, one can argue against this possibility at a theoretical level by pointing out that even though labor standards may be distortionary, they can also enhance efficiency. Hence, there exist incentives for countries to increase rather than reduce the level of their standards. Because of this, and for political economy reasons,[2] one should not expect countries to be dragged into a "race to the bottom" of standards. Several papers (for example, Portes 1990, Fields 1995, and Aggarwal 1995) have discussed the issue of what should constitute a labor standard. In this paper, labor standards will be loosely defined as a set of enforceable rules and regulations governing workers' rights, and our focus will be on the empirical impact of these standards on trade.

The rest of the paper proceeds as follows. In Section 2, we briefly examine the relationship between labor standards, comparative advantage, and trade. In Section 3, we review the empirical literature on trade and labor standards, and use the latest available data to examine whether the conventional wisdom that low labor standards influence trade performance holds. We also verify whether openness to trade has positively impacted labor standards, focusing on child labor in particular. Section 4 concludes the paper.

2   Trade, comparative advantage, and labor standards

Early studies, for instance by Johnson (1969) and Brecher (1974a and 1974b), considered minimum wages and their welfare implications but did not consider other internationally accepted labor standards such as the number of hours worked, the freedom from forced labor, or unionization. Alam (1992), on the other hand, was one of the first to provide a more general framework for the economic analysis of the impact of labor standards, at constant goods prices, on a country's comparative advantage. Alam concludes that the impact of labor standards (minimum wages and occupational safety and health) on comparative advantage is non-neutral in most cases, even though some of his results are counterintuitive in the sense that the impact of labor standards is sometimes neutral or non-neutral in the wrong direction.

Brown, Deardoff, and Stern (1996) focus on the welfare and other effects of standards and whether it is in a country's interest to implement common international standards. Most of their analysis is graphical and relies on the Heckscher–Ohlin trade model. The different models in Brown, Deardoff, and Stern (1996) show that the effects of labor standards are dependent on the technology of production of goods and standards, and also on whether the standards are endogenous (in which case the existence of a market failure will not lead to a socially optimal level of the standard). If the market fails to yield the socially optimal level of the standard, intervention on the part of the government may not necessarily correct the failure. All these results, according to them, suggest that the international harmonization of labor cannot be supported since market failures are not similar across countries and cannot, therefore, be overcome by similar measures. Including labor standards into multilateral trade negotiations, the so-called social clause, should therefore be dealt with extreme caution.

Dehejia and Samy (2004), building on the work of Brown, Deardoff, and Stern (1996), formally investigate the links between labor standards and comparative advantage through their effects on the terms of trade. In their model, two countries (I and II) produce two traded goods ("x" and "y") and each good uses two factors of production, labor (L) and capital (K). With fixed factor endowments in each country, perfect competition in commodity and factor markets, identical technology and preferences, and perfect mobility of factors within each country, differences in relative overall endowments drive comparative advantage in such a model. For instance, suppose country I is capital abundant relative to country II. Suppose also that good "x" is capital intensive while good "y" is labor intensive. Let the price of good "x" be denoted by p_x and the price of good "y" by p_y. In autarky, country I will then produce good "x" at a relatively lower price. Autarky price ratios will be such that $(p_y/p_x)^{II} < (p_y/p_x)^{I}$ and international equilibrium will then imply that $(p_y/p_x)^{I} = (p_y/p_x)^{II}$. By the Heckscher–Ohlin theorem, good "x" will be exported by the capital-abundant country (country I) and good "y" will be exported by the labor-abundant country (country II). In equilibrium, the terms of trade p ($= p_y/p_x$) must be such as to clear the market for both goods. In other words, world production must be equal to world consumption or the value of exports of a country must be equal to the value of its imports. By Walras's law, clearance of the market for good "x" implies clearance of the other and one is thus able to write down the following equation for the terms of trade:

$$p = \frac{Q_x^I - C_x^I}{Q_y^{II} - C_y^{II}} \tag{1}$$

where C denotes the consumption of goods "x" and "y", Q refers to production levels, and the superscripts refer to countries I and II. Given Cobb–Douglas production functions and preferences for goods "x" and "y", one can express the terms of trade in terms of overall endowments, and technological and preference parameters.[3] Suppose that a labor standard is imposed in country I only and uses a fraction of output "x" which is produced; that is, it is withdrawing resources away from one of the tradable sectors. Hence, if λ is the fraction of output "x" which is used to finance the labor standard, only $(1 - \lambda)$ of output "x" is available for trade. The fact that the labor standard is using some of the output of "x" implicitly implies that it is using some amount of capital and some amount of labor.[4] The terms of trade are now equal to

$$p = \frac{(1-\lambda)\,Q_x^I - C_x^I}{Q_y^{II} - C_y^{II}} \tag{2}$$

It transpires that the labor standard will lead to an improvement or deterioration in the terms of trade depending on whether it is imposed in the import or export sector. Dehejia and Samy (2004) also consider the possibility that the same quantities of tradable goods "*x*" and "*y*" are produced and that a fraction of output "*x*", for example, is used to finance the standard. The impact on the terms of trade in this case depends on the capital-labor intensity of the tradables. These results have interesting implications. First, countries that are large enough to influence their terms of trade may impose labor standards for terms of trade gains. Second, countries can also impose labor standards on their trading partners in order to lead to deterioration in the latter's terms of trade and an improvement in theirs. Third, the absence of coordination implies that the world optimum will not be reached as countries will have an incentive to under- or overprovide standards for terms of trade gains.

Now that we have briefly discussed relationships between labor standards, comparative advantage, and trade, in the next section we empirically examine whether labor standards have an impact on export performance, and also whether globalization (in terms of trade openness) has affected labor standards.

3   Trade and labor standards: empirical findings

In this section, we consider two issues from an empirical perspective: (1) the conventional wisdom that countries with lower standards obtain (unfair) advantages in trade (leading to a race to the bottom of standards across countries as they lower their standards to remain competitive), and (2) the relationship between trade openness and labor standards (with a particular focus on child labor, which tends to permeate debates on trade and labor standards).

3.1 Existing studies

Several studies have attempted to examine the empirical relationship between trade and labor standards. Aggarwal (1995) investigates whether labor standards were being suppressed by developing countries so that they can reduce production costs and encourage exports. She thus examines the export patterns of 10 developing countries to the USA and finds no positive relationship between lower standards and better export growth rates. Rather, she notices a tendency for labor standards in developing countries to be higher in export-oriented sectors compared to less export-oriented and non-traded sectors. A qualitative OECD (1996) study on trade, employment, and labor standards finds no evidence that countries with low labor standards (proxied by freedom of association and collective bargaining rights) can achieve better export performance, both in the aggregate and for labor-intensive goods. The study, which is mainly based on plots, also finds that countries that have liberalized trade do not necessarily face a worsening of their labor standards.

Mah (1997) examines the relationship between CLS and the export performance of (non-OECD) developing countries by regressing export shares of GDP on the ratification of core ILO conventions for a group of 45 developing countries. Overall, his results show that higher labor standards have a negative impact on export performance. Mah's analysis contains two major weaknesses. First, the ratification of core conventions, which is essentially a binary index, is the only indicator used to capture the labor standards variables. This is misleading for two reasons: first, ratification of conventions does not necessarily mean that standards are being enforced, and second, it is quite possible that countries that ratify conventions will do so because they have already attained the standards that are being asked of them in the first place (hence, the act of ratification becomes a purely symbolic gesture). The second problem with Mah's analysis has to do with the lack of control variables for other determinants of comparative advantage, which may lead to biased estimates. Hence, while labor standards may be an important factor, it is possible that other country characteristics that are missing in his analysis can be important determinants of the volume of trade.

Van Beers (1998) uses a measure of labor standards stringency from the OECD employment outlook (which takes into account employment protection rights, working time, minimum wages, fixed term contracts, and employees' representational rights—but not CLS) for 18 OECD countries to estimate a bilateral gravity equation. His analysis leads to a number of interesting findings: first, when aggregate exports is considered as a dependent variable, the measure of strictness of labor standards is not a significant factor in explaining bilateral trade flows; second, when trade flows are divided into labor-intensive and capital-intensive groups, the stringency of labor standards does not affect the exports of labor intensive goods; third, when trade flows are divided in terms of skill-intensity, stricter labor standards tend to reduce the exports of both labor and capital-intensive goods produced with skilled labor. The results are counterintuitive since they seem to indicate that labor standards have a stronger impact on skilled labor. On the other hand, the debate on trade and labor standards is usually about the opposite case, namely that countries whose comparative advantage lies in the export of unskilled labor-intensive goods will lose from forced harmonization (or what Bhagwati has called straitjacketing) of standards that apply in high-skill abundant countries. Unfortunately, Van Beers does not provide an explanation for this, and given that his analysis is restricted to the OECD countries, it is hard to tell whether the results would hold for a larger sample of developing countries.

Rodrik (1996) and Dehejia and Samy (2004) do a much better job at controlling for other determinants of comparative advantage by including control variables for the labor and human capital endowments, and using cross-sectional data for developed and developing countries. The other improvement is the use of a wider range of indicators for labor standards other than simply ILO conventions ratified. The results of both of these papers confirm that factor endowments (in accordance with the Heckscher–Ohlin theorem) are important determinants of comparative advantage while the conventional wisdom does not seem to hold. Rodriguez and Samy (2003) and Dehejia and Samy (2004) are to our knowledge the only studies that have so far considered time series data to investigate the issue of trade and labor standards. However, due to data limitations, the time series analysis is carried out for Canada and the United States in the context of the NAFTA. Rodriguez and Samy (2003) apply time-series analysis with structural breaks to US data for the period 1950–98 to estimate a model with endogenous breaks, and using various indicators for labor standards. Their results show that the conventional wisdom may or may not hold for the USA. Dehejia and Samy (2004) provide time-series results for Canada by estimating a vector auto-regressive model, using a number of indicators for labor standards and also controlling for the usual determinants of comparative advantage. They obtain very weak evidence for the conventional wisdom.

Busse (2002) obtains mixed evidence regarding the effect of labor standards on comparative advantage; more precisely, the effect on comparative advantage depends on the type of standard and in the case of union rights or forced labor, for example, he finds evidence in favor of the conventional wisdom for labor intensive exports. The ratification of core ILO conventions is not significant in his analysis. Flanagan (2003) considers the issue of trade and labor standards using panel data. Even though this is a brave attempt at exploiting the advantages inherent in panel data, the problem is that the author focuses solely on core and non-core ILO conventions ratified as indicators of labor standards, which may or may not reflect the level of enforcement. In fact, Flanagan finds that ratification of ILO conventions is not a good predictor of actual labor standards. In a recent paper, Kucera and Sarna (2006), used a gravity trade model as in Van Beers (1998) and find evidence in favor of the conventional wisdom for labor intensive exports but not total manufacturing exports. Their conclusion is that "possible negative effects through labor costs of stronger FACB rights and democracy are offset by other positive effects of stronger FACB rights and democracy" (879).

3.2 New empirical evidence

Labor standards and export performance

Following Dehejia and Samy (2004) we estimate the following equation in order to analyze the effects of labor standards on export performance:

$$lexp_i = a_0 + a_1 \, popland_i + a_2 \, human_i + a_3 \, labstd_i + \varepsilon_i \tag{3}$$

where *lexp* refers to the log of exports of manufactured goods as a percentage of gross domestic product; *popland* is the population to land ratio; *human* is the literacy rate in the population 15 years and older; *labstd* is any one of the indicators for the labor standard; subscript *i* refers to countries and ε is the disturbance term. The dependent variable is so chosen since concerns about labor standards in developing countries are commonly expressed with regards to manufacturing sectors and factories in developing countries. We also consider an alternative definition of the dependent variable, namely manufacturing exports as a percentage of merchandise exports (*lexp1*), which is a measure of comparative advantage in the manufacturing sector. The proxies for measures of comparative advantage, *popland* (proxy for labor endowment relative to land endowment) and *human* (proxy for human capital), are expected to be positively related to the dependent variable, and we want to check whether a_3 is significantly different from zero; given that a standard may affect productivity and is also costly, the effect on export performance remains unclear. It is important to note that there is no appropriate measure for physical capital stock as an additional control. Not only is it difficult to find such a measure but including per capita GDP as a proxy (as others have done) did not add much to the regression, since the human capital variable is already picking up some of this effect; the significance of the labor standards, which is our main focus, did not change when per capita GDP was included.

We consider cross-sectional macro data for developing countries (excluding all OECD countries), and the variables are all averaged over the period 1990–2001, unless otherwise indicated. Other studies (for example, Mah 1997; Van Beers 1998; Dehejia and Samy 2004) consider a specific year because of data limitations. If we were to again consider a specific year, we could well end up with more observations than we have; however, the findings could be specific to that particular year and hence we present results that use data averaged over time when available. We are also constrained by the availability of data for more recent years but the time period considered covers the recent developments that have taken place regarding this issue (as discussed in the introduction). The different proxies for the labor standard variable are as follows. We construct an indicator for the number of core ILO conventions ratified, *cconv*, (using ratification information from ILOLEX, a database of international labor standards from the ILO). The main problem with this indicator is that it may not reflect the degree of enforcement of the standard.

We consider two proxies for hours worked; namely, the normal weekly hours of work (statutory working week) based on the labor regulations that are in effect in each country (*hour1*) and actual hours worked in the manufacturing sector (*hour2*). We have more data on the former than the latter. The indicator of civil liberties (*civilb*) from Freedom House (2007) is also considered. The computation of this index (on a scale of 1 to 7, with small values indicating more rights) is based on questions such as presence of trade unions, the effectiveness of collective bargaining, and freedom from exploit-ation by employers or union leaders. We recognize that some of the questions used to calculate the civil liberties index have nothing to do with labor stand-ards, such as questions regarding religious freedom and the rule of law. A proxy for child labor (denoted by *child*) is also considered and measured as working children aged 10–14 as a percentage of age group. Again, this proxy is not perfect since it ignores children under the age of 10 who work, not an unlikely possibility in developing countries.

We also have data for the violation of freedom of association and collective bargaining (FACB) rights. The measure of FACB rights violation is based on 37 evaluative criteria that address *de jure* and *de facto* problems with FACB and are constructed by coding violations of these rights (see Kucera 2004, and Kucera and Sarna, 2006). The evaluation criteria are based on rights defined by the ILO Conventions on freedom of association and collective bargaining and other related ILO documents, and was used to evaluate violation of FACB rights from various reports such as the *Annual Survey of Violations of Trade Union Rights*, the US State Department's *Country Reports on Human Rights Practices*, and ILO Reports. This variable is denoted by *union1* and *union 2* (unweighted and weighted versions respect-ively)[5] on a scale of 0 (best) to 10 (worst). Given the high correlation between the unweighted and weighted index, we did not expect results to vary signifi-cantly using either measure, and this was confirmed in the empirical analysis. One possible shortcoming of this measure is that it could be non-random. For example, Latin American countries' trade unions tend to file more com-plaints with the ILO (Neumayer and Soysa, 2006). In order to deal with this potential problem, regional dummies were included in the regressions but did not alter the results significantly.

All of these indicators have been used in previous studies but are not without their problems, as discussed above. Summary statistics and correl-ation matrices for the variables used to estimate equation (3) are provided in Appendix A. Table 15.1 below shows the results, after applying White's test for heteroscedasticity, when equation (3) is estimated for developing countries over the period 1990–2001. Column (1) shows the results for the benchmark model without the labor standards. The remaining columns show the results when each indicator is added to the benchmark model one at a time in order to assess their individual effects. The natural determinants of comparative advantage (represented by *popland* and *human*) are significant and of the right sign in most of the regressions. As for the proxies for labor standard, only *child* is significant with a negative sign, indicating that an increase in child labor is associated with a reduction in export performance, thus contra-dicting the conventional wisdom.

The results reported above did not change when different combinations of labor standards were tried in the regressions. When the dependent variable was replaced by *lexp1*, the results remained the same, except for *civilb* which again contradicted the conventional wisdom. The results did not change

Table 15.1 Estimated coefficients for equation (3)—developing countries (1990–2001)

	(1)	(2)	(3)	(4)	(5)	(6)	(7)	(8)
Constant	2.26**	2.46**	2.48	1.36**	1.89**	3.32**	2.34**	2.36**
	(10.78)	(8.32)	(0.81)	(2.32)	(5.81)	(7.25)	(8.94)	(8.85)
popland	0.01**	0.03**	0.03**	0.01	0.02**	0.01	0.02**	0.02**
	(1.85)	(4.61)	(5.03)	(1.41)	(8.41)	(1.23)	(6.83)	(6.88)
human	0.01**	0.01**	0.01**	0.02**	0.01**	0.01**	0.01**	0.01**
	(4.02)	(3.51)	(4.56)	(4.88)	(4.32)	(3.37)	(3.83)	(3.87)
cconv	—	-0.04	—	—	—	—	—	—
		(-1.05)						
log (hour1)	—	—	-0.08	—	—	—	—	—
			(-0.11)					
log (hour2)	—	—	—	0.02	—	—	—	—
				(0.15)				
civilb	—	—	—	—	0.06	—	—	—
					(-1.24)			
child	—	—	—	—	—	-0.02**	—	—
						(-2.66)		
union1	—	—	—	—	—	—	-0.01	—
							(-0.51)	
union2	—	—	—	—	—	—	—	-0.01
								(-0.54)
R^2	0.33	0.35	0.36	0.37	0.35	0.27	0.28	0.27
N	127	121	119	51	125	124	118	119
F-Stat	7.79	5.89	7.09	5.93	8.04	8.45	7.63	7.69

Note: Except where indicated otherwise, the figures in parentheses are the *t*-values. Standard errors are White-robust. *(**) indicates 10(5)% level of significance.

when only low-income developing countries (with a GDP per capita of less than $6 000) were considered. Also, as discussed above, regional dummies, when included, did not change the results significantly. Overall, therefore, the evidence is rather weak that countries with low labor standards obtain a comparative advantage in trade, confirming the evidence reported in previous studies discussed above. In fact, trade is determined primarily by the natural determinants of comparative advantage, and in those cases where standards matter, they go against the commonsense conclusion that low standards provide (unfair) advantages in trade.

Labor standards and trade openness: an examination of child labor

The second issue that we address is whether globalization (measured by openness to trade) has had a positive or negative impact on labor standards. Countries that are more open to trade face more competitive pressures and critics of globalization are worried that this will translate in a race to the bottom as countries lower their standards to remain competitive. On the other hand, proponents of globalization argue that countries that are more integrated in the world economy are more likely to have higher standards because of higher income resulting from deeper integration, assuming these standards are like normal goods. At a theoretical level, many have pointed out that the level of labor standards is ultimately a domestic choice and is a reflection of a country's level of economic development, factor endowments, and values (see, for example, Bhagwati (1995)) and that trade should not be a major factor in that equation. However, to the extent that the level of income (and income distribution) is influenced by openness to trade, then labor standards may be affected as a result. For example, in Casella's (1996) model, labor standards respond to the level of income and trade may lead to a leveling up of labor standards. On the other hand, we have seen in the theoretical section of the current paper that standards can be used as an economic instrument to influence the terms of trade and that this may force countries in prisoner dilemma-type situations where they all lower standards to remain competitive.

For illustrative purposes only, Appendix B shows the correlation between trade openness (denoted by *trade*) and two of the labor standards (*child* and *civilb*). Outliers for the trade openness variable for countries such as Singapore were removed from the dataset so as not to bias the results and this reduced the sample by a few observations. Both graphs show a positive relationship between openness to trade and better standards for the sample of developing countries over the 1990–2001 period.

Table 15.2 below shows the results for bivariate regressions of trade openness on labor standards (*child*, *civilb*, and *union1*). The trade variable is significant in all cases, but in the case of *union1* supports the views of globalization skeptics.[6] For the rest of this section we will focus on the issue of child labor in order to check whether the correlation between trade openness and child labor remains when other determinants of child labor are controlled for. The abundant theoretical literature and empirical evidence regarding the benefits of open trade regimes on growth and poverty reduction means that one should expect open economies to be characterized by lower levels of child

Table 15.2 Labor standards and trade openness—developing countries (1990–2001)

	DV: child	DV: civilb	DV: union1
Constant	27.22**	5.47**	2.28**
	(7.69)	(17.31)	(3.53)
trade	−0.19**	−0.02**	0.04**
	(−4.47)	(−4.77)	(4.47)
R^2	0.13	0.14	0.12
N	131	143	120
F-Stat	19.32	23.75	16.15

Note: Except where indicated otherwise, the figures in parentheses are the *t*-values. Standard errors are White-robust. *(**) indicates 10(5)% level of significance.

labor. Since the seminal work by Becker (1964), numerous studies have also examined the determinants of child labor at the household level.[7] Our focus here is on the trade–labor linkage and not the determinants of child labor per se. However, in order to check whether trade openness is indeed an important determinant of child labor, one needs to control for other determinants of the latter. Much of the literature on child labor shows that poverty and the extent to which children are able to attend school are the main causal factors; poor families are more likely to send their children to work. Hence, any equation that tries to identify the determinants of child labor should control for a measure of level of development, such as GDP per capita in constant PPP\$ (represented here as *gdp*). We therefore estimate the following equation using ordinary least squares:

$$child_i = a_0 + a_1\, gdp_i + a_2\, trade_i + a_3\, du1_{i+} a_4\, du2_{i+}\, \varepsilon_i \qquad (4)$$

where *du1* and *du2* are regional dummy variables included for African and Asian countries to take into consideration historical and cultural factors, since child labor is more prevalent in these regions, and, once again, ε is the disturbance term. In a recent paper, Edmunds and Pavcnik (2006) have analyzed this issue extensively for 1995 data, and similarly to Dehejia and Gatti, they include a quadratic term for income to account for the fact that a marginal increase in income will have different effects on child labor, depending on the country's level of income. We consider this possibility in the empirical analysis, as well as other controls, but to be consistent with what we did earlier, our dataset covers the period 1990–2001 to guard against picking an unrepresentative year. Summary statistics for the main variables used to estimate equation (4) are provided in Appendix C.

One possible problem with equation (4) is the fact that endogeneity could bias the OLS estimates. It is possible for the level of child labor, to influence the volume of trade by changing the quantity of labor available as well as the allocation of labor across sectors in a given economy. In such a case, instrumental variables (IV) estimation needs to be considered. It is important to point out that our choice of IV estimation as opposed to reduced forms (where the relationship between instruments themselves and child labor would allow one to assess more precisely the source of variation in trade used for identification) is a matter of following convention, and is not based on the results. The levels of development (*gdp*) could also be endogenous, since child labor can have a negative impact on productivity and economic growth by reducing human capital accumulation. To deal with these possible problems, we instrument the level of development with its lagged value (averaged over the 1980s), which is a common procedure. The trade variable is instrumented using "population" averaged over the period 1990–2001, and "distance" to a main economic center represented in this case by the EU (as used in gravity models of trade) and using lagged values of the trade variable. Again, this is a procedure that has been used elsewhere.

Table 15.3 below shows the results for equation (4) based on cross-sectional data averaged over 1990–2001, and after applying White's test for heteroskedasticity. In column (1), the logarithm of GDP and the trade variable are significant determinants of child labor with the expected signs. When the income variable is entered as a squared term in column (2), it is also significant as in Edmunds and Pavcnik (2006) and Dehejia and Gatti (2005). In column (3), we add additional controls from the literature, namely access to credit and education, proxied by the ratio of private credit issued by deposit banks to GDP (denoted by *credit*) and secondary enrolment rates (denoted by *sec*) respectively. Dehejia and Gatti (2005) find that (lack of) access to credit is an important determinant of child labor: theoretically, when children work, family income increases, but future family incomes decrease since the human capital accumulation of children is implicitly reduced when they do not attend school. If households have access to credit (that is, borrowing against future income), they can choose optimally between current and future income. The *credit* variable is widely used as a proxy for the level of development of financial markets and is the same one that is used by Dehejia and Gatti (2005); it is essentially a measure of private credit, and bypasses the role of the government. It transpires that this variable is not significant in our analysis, possibly because the time period considered is too short. Regarding

Table 15.3 Child labor and openness to trade (developing countries 1990–2001)—OLS and IV estimates

Explanatory variables	(1) OLS	(2) OLS	(3) OLS	(4) OLS	(5) OLS	(6) IV-(1)
Constant	88.37** (8.06)	274.74** (4.23)	246.47** (3.84)	243.61** (3.67)	71.51** (6.66)	112.25** (6.80)
$log(GDP)$	−9.02** (−7.04)	−55.41** (−3.61)	−49.88** (−3.25)	−44.52** (−2.71)	−5.68** (−4.11)	−11.84** (−6.00)
trade	−0.07** (−2.66)	−0.07** (−2.62)	−0.04 (−1.65)	−0.07** (−2.84)	−0.06** (−1.95)	−0.01 (−0.27)
$log(GDP)^2$	—	2.86** (3.15)	2.77** (3.04)	2.20** (2.27)	—	—
credit	—	—	0.22 (0.05)	4.70 (0.92)	4.72 (0.82)	—
sec	—	—	−0.26** (−6.38)	—	−0.26** (−6.42)	—
du1	9.26** (3.70)	7.33** (2.95)	4.17* (1.70)	5.18** (2.05)	5.75** (2.27)	1.47** (0.27)
du2	−2.68 (−1.47)	−3.52** (−2.20)	−1.31 (−0.84)	−2.81* (−1.82)	−0.14 (−0.08)	−8.04** (−2.81)
R²	0.69	0.72	0.81	0.79	0.79	0.64
N	121	121	89	102	96	101
F-Stat	65.49	59.66	48.99	49.35	67.64	—

Note: Except where indicated otherwise, the figures in parentheses are the *t*-values. Standard errors are White-robust. *(**) indicates 10(5)% level of significance.

education, the lack of access to schools or a lack of quality in education can lead parents to send their children to work. Hence, the control for education is expected to be negatively related to child labor. As seen in Table 3 below, *sec* is significant and with the right sign. When primary school enrolment rates are considered instead of *sec*, the results did not change significantly.[8] The dummy variable for Africa is also highly significant while the one for Asia is not always and this may be due to the fact that although Asia has the largest number of child workers, in relative terms, Africa has the highest rate of child labor. When only low-income countries are considered (by restricting our sample to countries below a certain threshold for GDP per capita), the results are not significantly different from what is reported in the table.

When IV estimation is considered in column (6) based on the specification in column (1), the trade variable is no longer significant, but it still does not support the argument that trade has led to an increase in child labor. We also conducted IV estimation for specifications using *sec* and *credit*, using lagged values for the education variable and origin of a country's legal system (used in Dehejia and Gatti 2005) as instruments for these variables. Once again, the trade variable lost its significance. Finally, in order to check the quality of instruments used in column (6), we regressed the residuals from equation (8) on the instrumental variables, and since none of the instruments are significant, we concluded that they are good instruments. There is thus no empirical evidence that openness to trade increases child labor. If anything, the results obtained above show that countries that open their economies to trade are more likely to reduce child labor.

4 Conclusion

This paper has briefly reviewed the theoretical literature on trade, labor standards, and comparative advantage, and provided new empirical evidence regarding the latter. The empirical evidence based on cross-sectional data for developing countries over the period 1990–2001 does not support the view that labor standards have affected comparative advantage and export performance. We have also examined the issue of trade openness and labor standards (focusing on child labor), again using the latest available cross-sectional data for developing countries. The evidence seems to favor the view that openness to trade has led to an improvement, not a worsening of standards. The question that will continue to dominate this debate in the coming years is whether (and how) the idea of a social clause, which would incorporate CLS into future trade agreements, can be implemented. In a recent paper, Reddy and Barry (2006) argue that linkage can be made to work as long as it is "unimposed, transparent and rule-based, applied in a manner reflecting a country's level of development, demands adequate international burden-sharing, and incorporates measures that ensure that appropriate account is taken of different viewpoints within each country" (2). Beyond the fact that the practicality of such an approach needs to be investigated further, their proposal has serious implications, not only for national sovereignty, but also for the gains from trade of developing countries in the event that linkage is hijacked by protectionist intents. The empirical evidence to date does not indicate that linkage should be a priority for action (and Reddy and Barry (2006), in fairness, also agree with this). We, however, believe that labor standards are ultimately a matter of domestic policy choice and that there remains a need for great caution when making policy pronouncements on the linkages between trade and labor standards.

Appendix A: Equation (3)

Correlation Matrix

	lexp	*popland*	*human*	*cconv*	*lhour1*	*lhour2*	*civilb*	*child*	*union1*
lexp	1.00								
popland	0.48	1.00							
human	0.49	−0.03	1.00						
cconv	−0.22	−0.17	−0.02	1.00					
lhour1	−0.48	−0.05	−0.49	0.17	1.00				
lhour2	−0.12	0.02	−0.20	0.06	0.42	1.00			
civilb	−0.29	0.11	−0.55	−0.31	0.30	0.27	1.00		
child	−0.42	−0.08	−0.71	−0.07	0.45	0.06	0.53	1.00	
union1	0.45	0.22	0.35	0.07	−0.48	−0.13	−0.52	−0.46	1.00

Note: UNION2 is almost perfectly correlated with UNION1 and is therefore not shown in the above table.

Summary Statistics

Variable	*N*	*Mean*	*Median*	*Maximum*	*Minimum*	*STD*
lexp	161	2.99	3.05	4.97	0.61	0.82
popland	162	3.16	0.58	203.13	0.00	17.25
human	128	74.59	81.57	99.80	13.85	22.13
cconv	143	4.62	5.00	7.17	0.00	1.84
lhour1	139	3.78	3.78	3.87	3.61	0.08
lhour2	58	3.75	3.76	5.53	2.05	0.36
civilb	152	4.06	4.00	7.00	1.00	1.53
child	142	12.81	5.44	53.35	0.00	15.02
union1	132	4.79	5.71	9.52	0.00	3.05
union2	133	5.01	5.49	9.55	0.00	2.97

Appendix B: Labor standards and openness

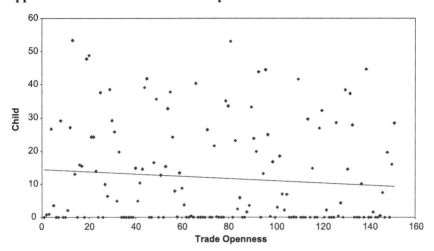

Figure A15.1 Child labor and trade openness: developing countries (1990–2001).

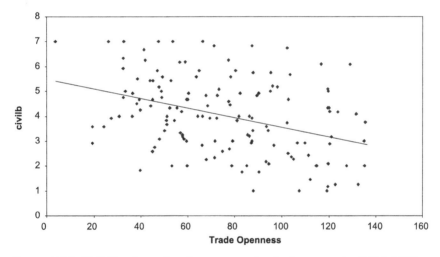

Figure A15.2 Civil liberties and trade openness: developing countries (1990–2001).

Appendix C: Equation (4)

Correlation Matrix

	child	log(gdp)	credit	pri	sec	trade
child	1.00					
log(gdp)	−0.76	1.00				
credit	−0.43	0.59	1.00			
pri	−0.71	0.59	0.34	1.00		
sec	−0.84	0.73	0.46	0.66	1.00	
trade	−0.36	0.32	0.30	0.18	0.39	1.00

Summary Statistics

	N	Mean	Median	Maximum	Minimum	STD
child	130	13.74	7.23	53.35	0.00	15.34
log(gdp)	121	8.00	7.96	10.01	6.13	0.91
credit	111	0.22	0.18	0.86	0.00	0.18
pri	118	0.22	0.18	106.17	24.89	19.33
sec	101	79.43	86.13	91.32	4.79	25.02
trade	130	46.60	47.37	136.37	3.59	29.56

Notes

1 There is international support for CLSs (represented by eight ILO conventions defining four fundamental rights at work) and this shows that they are applicable regardless of a country's level of economic development. CLSs do not set a particular level of working conditions, wages, or health and safety standards to be applied internationally, and are not meant to change the comparative advantage of any country.

2 Indeed, in well-functioning democracies, labor standards legislation just like any other legislation, should represent what the majority of the public desires. It could also be determined by narrowly based lobbies, but by and large the majority of the public favors fairly tight standards so that there exists some political pressure for them.

3 See Dehejia and Samy (2004) for a more detailed exposition.

4 For example, occupational health and safety regulations may require both labor and capital investments.

5 We thank David Kucera from the ILO (who constructed this variable) for sending us this data for the mid-1990s.

6 These are obviously interesting findings that need to be investigated further, namely, taking into account other factors. We do this in the case of child labor only here.

7 For an excellent review of theory and policy regarding child labor, see Brown, Deardorff, and Stern (2003).

8 When average years of schooling were considered instead of *sec* and *pri* (since the latter are highly correlated with child labor, and could in fact be proxying for it), the result did not change substantially.

References

Aggarwal, Mita (1995) "International Trade, Labor Standards, and Labor Market Conditions: An Evaluation of the Linkages," Office of Economics Working Paper, United States International Trade Commission, Washington DC.

Alam, A. (1992) "Labor Standards and Comparative Advantage". Unpublished Doctoral Dissertation, Columbia University.

Becker, G. S. (1964) *Human capital.* New York: Columbia University Press

Bhagwati, J. (1995) "Trade Liberalization and Fair Trade Demands: Addressing the Environmental and Labor Standards Issues." *World Economy* 18(6): 745–59.

Brecher, R. A. (1974a), "Optimal Commercial Policy for a Minimum-Wage Economy," *Journal of International Economics*, 4, 139–49.

—— (1974b), "Minimum Wage Rates and the Pure Theory of International Trade," *Quarterly Journal of Economics*, 88, 98–116.

Brown, D. K., A. V. Deardoff, and R. M. Stern (2003) "Child Labor: Theory, Evidence and Policy," in *International Labor Standards*, edited by K. Basu, H. Horn, L. Roman, and J. Shapiro. Oxford: Blackwell Publishing Ltd.

——, ——, and ——. (1996) "International Labor Standards and Trade: A Theoretical Analysis," In *Fair Trade and Harmonization: Prerequisites for Free Trade? Volume 1, Economic Analysis*, edited by J. N. Bhagwati and R. E. Hudec. Cambridge and London: MIT Press.

Busse, M. (2002) "Do Labor Standards Affect Comparative Advantage in Developing Countries?", *World Development* 30: 1921–32.

Casella, A. (1996) "Free Trade and Evolving Standards." In *Fair Trade and Harmonization: Prerequisites for Free Trade? Volume 1, Economic Analysis*, edited by J. N. Bhagwati and R. E. Hudec. Cambridge and London: MIT Press.

Dehejia, V. and Y. Samy (2004) "Trade and Labor Standards: Theory and New Empirical Evidence." *Journal of International Trade and Economic Development* 13(2): 177–96 (June).

Dehejia, R. and R. Gatti, (2005) "Child Labor: The Role of Financial Development and Income Variability Across Countries." *Economic Development and Cultural Change* 53(4), 913–32.

Edmonds, E. and N. Pavcnik (2006) "International Trade and Child Labor: Cross-country Evidence." *Journal of International Economics* 68: 115–40.

Fields, Gary S., 1995, *Trade and Labour Standards: A Review of the Issues* (Paris, France: Organization for Economic Cooperation and Development).

Flanagan, R. (2003) "Labor Standards and International Competitive Advantage." In *International Labor Standards: Globalization, Trade and Public Policy*, edited by R. Flanagan. Stanford, CA: Stanford University Press.

Freedom House (2007) Freedom in the World: The Annual Survey of Political Rights and Civil Liberties, www.freedomhourse.org.

ILO (1995) *Conditions of Work Digest: Working Time Around The World.* Geneva: International Labour Office.

—— (2004) *A Fair Globalization: Creating Opportunities for All.* Report of the World Commission on the Social Dimension of Globalization, Geneva.

—— (2007) LABORSTA Internet at http://laborsta.ilo.org/

Johnson, H. G. (1969), "Minimum Wage Laws: A General Equilibrium Analysis," *Canadian Journal of Economics*, 2, 599–604.

Kucera, D. (2004) "Measuring Trade Union Rights: A country-level indicator constructed from coding violations recorded in textual sources." ILO Policy Integration Department, Working Paper 50.

—— and R. Sarna (2006) "Trade Union Rights, Democracy, and Exports: A gravity model approach." *Review of International Economics* 14(5): 859–82.

Mah, J. S. (1997) "Core Labor Standards and Export Performance in Developing Countries". *The World Economy*, 20(6): 773–85.

Neumayer, E. and I. Soysa (2006) "Globalization and the Right to Free Association and Collective Bargaining: An empirical analysis." *World Development* 34(1): 31–49

OECD (1996) *Trade, Employment and Labor Standards*. Paris, France: Organization for Economic Cooperation and Development.

Portes, A. (1990) "When More Can Be Less: Labor Standards, Development and the Informal Economy." In *Labor Standards and Development in the Global Economy*. Washington DC.

Reddy, S. G. and C. Barry (2006) "International Trade and Labor Standards: A Proposal for Linkage." Available at SSRN: http://ssrn.com/abstract=799924

Rodriguez, G. and Y. Samy (2003) "Analyzing the Effects of Labor Standards on US Export Performance. A Time Series Approach with Structural Change." *Applied Economics* 35: 1043–51, June.

Rodrik, D. (1996) "Labor Standards in International Trade: Do they matter and what do we do about them?". In *Emerging Agenda for Global Trade: High stakes for developing countries*, edited by R. Z. Lawrence, D. Rodrik, and J. Whalley. Overseas Development Council Essay 20, Washington DC: Johns Hopkins University Press.

Van Beers, C. (1998) "Labour Standards and Trade Flows of OECD Countries," *The World Economy* 21: 1, 57–73.

16 Do foreign-owned firms pay more?

Evidence from the Indonesian manufacturing sector

Ann E. Harrison and Jason Scorse[*]

People who work in so-called "sweatshops" in poor countries go back day after day and are the envy of the even poorer people in the farming communities they left. Preventing them from having those jobs keeps them poor.

David Henderson. The Hoover Institute (2001)

In many cases, sweatshop workers employed by large multinational corporations are trapped in a system of modern day indentured servitude comparable to slavery and denied basic human freedoms like the right to join a union, attend religious services, quit or marry. Menial wages and reports of physical abuse in addition are typical of a new economic world order in which the poor are getting poorer and the rich growing richer.

From the *Citizen Works* website

1 Introduction

The above quotes are emblematic of the continuing debate over whether globalization benefits workers in developing countries. Economic theory does not provide clear and simple answers to this question since there are many competing forces at work. As developing countries liberalize their economies foreign firms may bring new technologies to the host country, thereby raising productivity (Bailey and Gersbach 1995), and they may have incentives to retain workers due to high search and job training costs, reputation effects, and political considerations, all of which would lead to higher wages However, foreign firms may also be concentrated in export sectors which face increased global competition, thereby depressing wages in a "race to the bottom" scenario (Chau and Kanbur 2002, Feenstra 1998). Given the inconclusive nature of the question, it is best addressed empirically at a micro level within developing countries.

Wages in developing countries have been the topic of an extensive literature and numerous empirical studies have examined the links between foreign ownership and wages. Aitken, Harrison, and Lipsey (1996) compared wages and foreign ownership in Mexico, Venezuela, and the USA in the late 1970s through 1990 and consistently found evidence that foreign firms paid more than their domestic counterparts, in the range of 20–30%, even after controlling for size, geographic location, skill mix, and capital intensity. They also found little evidence of wage spillovers from foreign to domestic owned firms in Venezuela and Mexico, despite the belief that an infusion of technological knowledge into developing countries leads to increased productivity within industries.

Using data from 1970 to 1996 Ramstetter (1999) found evidence that average worker productivity was significantly higher in foreign-owned firms in Hong Kong, Indonesia, Taiwan, Malaysia, and Singapore but that in most cases this did not translate into significantly higher wages for employees; a surprising result given the theoretical link between compensation and worker productivity. Using data from Cameroon, Ghana, Kenya, Zambia, and Zimbabwe from 1990 to 1993 Velde and Morrissey (2001) found significant wage premiums in foreign-owned firms, which increased with worker skill level. Lipsey and Sjoholm (2001) used a 1996 cross-section of data on Indonesian manufacturing firms to show that foreign firms paid significantly higher wages, in the range of 20 to 30%, and that the increased presence of foreign firms in a given province led domestic firms to pay higher wages as well, thus leading to an enhanced wage effect. However, they did not control for worker education levels.

Udomsaph (2002) used a similar approach as the one in this paper to posit that many of the wage differentials between foreign-owned and domestic firms uncovered in previous empirical work have been due mainly to the inability to control for worker characteristics. Using data from the Thai manufacturing sector in 1999–2000 he showed that worker heterogeneity is controlled, for unskilled workers received no wage premium, while the premium for high-skilled workers still remained.

One problem with the above studies, however, is that they do not have an extensive time series available, combined with detailed information on worker characteristics, skill levels, and educational achievement. Consequently, it is difficult for previous studies to be able to say conclusively whether higher wages paid by foreign firms are actually the result of foreign wage premia or unobserved quality differentials of workers hired by foreign firms. Using firm level data collected by the Indonesian government, this paper compares the wage rates paid by foreign-owned and domestic firms during the years 1990–1999. In addition, we control for detailed worker characteristics in the years 1995–1997 in order to analyze to what extent worker heterogeneity may be driving any persistent differences. Foreign-owned firms may employ workers with different skill levels that are not picked up by the common aggregate measurements such as "unskilled" and "skilled" common to most studies.

We find that although there is evidence of wage premiums for unskilled workers in foreign-owned firms, this is largely diminished, in the range of 5 to 10%, once education levels and gender enter the equation. However, high wage premiums between 20 and 30% for more skilled workers persist even after controlling for these factors. The results suggest that foreign firms do indeed pay a significant wage premium, even after taking into account differences in worker characteristics such as skill levels and education. Section 2 summarizes the data, Section 3 presents a simple economic model, Section 4 presents the econometric results, and we conclude with Section 5.

2 Data summary

Indonesia has firms that fall within all ISIC categories for manufacturing. Food and beverages, wood products, textiles and garments, chemicals and petroleum products, minerals, and metal sectors have the greatest number of firms. Foreign-owned businesses are dispersed throughout most of Indonesia's manufacturing sectors but are particularly concentrated in textile and garments, metal products, and the chemical and petroleum industries.

The data for this analysis comes from the annual manufacturing survey of Indonesia collected and compiled by the Indonesian government's statistical agency BPS (Badan Pusat Statistik). The completion of this survey is mandatory under Indonesian law and therefore the data captures the entire population of Indonesian manufacturing firms; which ranged from approximately 13,000 in 1990 to over 20,000 in 1999. The survey includes over 400 questions in any given year, the large majority of which remain constant although in certain periods additional questions are included and others removed. Over the 10-year period there is an average of 4.5 observations per firm, reflecting the fact that some firms go out of business while others enter.

There are two obvious sources of measurement error in the data. The first is human error in either filling out the questionnaire or reading the data from it. A fairly significant percentage of the observations include nonsensical entries such as a negative number of workers, a negative age of the firm, or a zero level of output. These observations were dropped. This could potentially bias the results if they were systematic, but an inspection of the data revealed no underlying patterns in the erroneous values.

Another potential source of measurement error is the inclusion of purposefully untruthful information. Given that Indonesia has minimum wage laws there would appear to be an incentive for firms to exaggerate wages in order to feign compliance. However, whether due to ignorance of these laws or a lack of enforcement, a very large percentage of firms reported wages significantly below the minimum for a number of years. Although surprising and sure to engender skepticism on the part of most economists, Currie and Harrison (1997) found self-reported non-compliance rates of up to 50% in Morocco, presumably due to a lack of enforcement or fear of penalties as well.

Figure 16.1 shows the percentage of foreign-owned firms (firms with any positive level of foreign ownership) and domestic firms which report average wages for unskilled workers which fall below the minimum wage between 1990 and 1999. Although a significant percentage of both types of firm exhibit a high degree of non-compliance the domestic firms consistently fail to comply with greater frequency. It is important to keep in mind that this

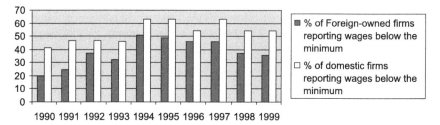

Figure 16.1 Non-compliance with the minimum wage laws 1990–1999.

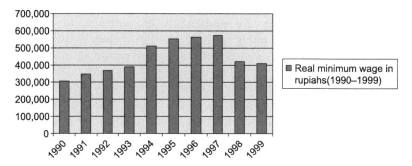

Figure 16.2 Real minimum wage in rupiahs (1990–1999).

does not control for the number of employees, the degree of foreign owner-ship, or the level of divergence from the minimum wage. The absolute number of domestic firms greatly outweighed the number of foreign-owned firms throughout this time period, at approximately 50:1 in 1990 and 16:1 in 1999; the share of foreign-owned firms rising from less than 2% to almost 6%.

Figure 16.2 shows the average real minimum wage throughout the 1990s, which increased steadily until the extreme inflation that accompanied the East Asian crisis at the end of the decade. In most countries with minimum wage laws (e.g. the USA) the nominal levels remain constant for a number of years but in Indonesia the experience is quite different; changes often take place every year or two. This may account for some of the high levels of non-compliance since firms must continually take this new information into account.

Figures 16.3 and 16.4 show that on average the annual real wages for both unskilled and skilled workers were much higher in foreign-owned firms throughout this time period. Not controlling for worker characteristics, wages ranged from double for unskilled workers in 1993 to more than five times for skilled workers in 1999. This does not include overtime pay, health benefits, gifts, or pension plans.

Tables 16.1 and 16.2 present aggregate summary statistics for key variables in the years 1990 and 1999. Notice the increases in the average number of unskilled workers from 124 to 154 (up 24%), the average level of foreign

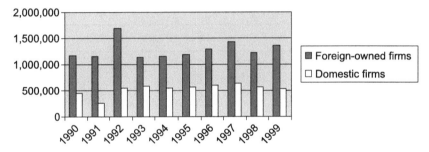

Figure 16.3 Average real wages paid to unskilled workers in rupiahs (1990–1999).

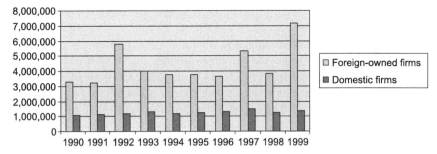

Figure 16.4 Average real wages paid to skilled workers in rupiahs (1990–1999).

Table 16.1 Summary statistics 1990

Variable	# Obs	Mean	Std dev.	Min	Max
Firm ID	11,051				
Unskilled workers	11,051	125	480	2	36,874
Skilled workers	11,051	24	125	0	6,965
% foreign ownership	11,051	1.3	9.9	0	100
% goods exported	11,051	7.9	24.4	0	100
Age of firm (years)	11,022	12	11	0	90
Average wage (prod 000)	11,051	677	362	120	1,920
Average wage (non-prod 000)	11,051	1471	1,024	120	5,509
Capital value (000)	11,051	1578	62,600	0	6,440,000

ownership from 1.3 to 4.4% (up 240%), and the average percentage of goods exported from 7.9 to 11.2% (up 42%). Dividing the firms into domestic and foreign-owned the average number of unskilled workers in foreign-owned firms increased from 416 to 498 (up 20%), the average number of skilled workers actually fell (possibly signaling a shift to low-skilled production) from 95 to 69 (a drop of more than 27%), the average percentage of foreign ownership increased from 67 to 78% (up 16%), the average level of exports increased slightly from 30 to 34% (up 13%), while the percentage of firms with

Table 16.2 Summary statistics 1999

Variable	# Obs	Mean	Std dev.	Min	Max
Firm ID	19,583				
Unskilled workers	19,853	154	577	0	33,797
Skilled workers	19,853	27	113	0	4,009
% foreign ownership	15,784	4.4	18.8	0	100
% goods exported	15,773	11.2	29.4	0	100
Age of firm	15,784	16	18	0	99
Average wage (prod 000)	15,783	2,720	1,406	548	8,069
Average wage (non-prod 000)	12,526	5,481	4,685	555	30,100
Capital value (000)	15,784	1,170	46,800	0	5,340,000

any export activities at all remained in the range of 40 to 50% throughout the decade. At the same time the average number of unskilled workers in domestic firms increased from 118 to 133 (up 13%), the average number of skilled workers stayed almost exactly the same at 24, the average level of exports rose from 7.5% to 9.8% (up 30%), and the percentage of firms with any exports stayed in the range of 11% to 13%.

From these numbers we can see that although the underlying trend during the 1990s was a move to larger firms with a greater average level of exports, on average the foreign-owned firms continued to be both much bigger and much more focused on export production than domestic firms. These increases occurred both within existing firms and new entries, as well as across industries, such that no one source was driving the change. This is true also for the increases in wages.

3 The empirical framework

We begin with the assumption that both domestic and foreign firms in Indonesia face the same labor market. In line with standard economic theory, firms should pay a wage equal to the marginal revenue product of labor; which is the marginal productivity of labor times the price of output. Therefore, assuming two inputs, labor and capital, firms will pay higher wages the more capital they employ (since the marginal productivity of labor is increasing in capital) or the higher their price of output; all else held equal. Although classical theory would typically predict that workers' marginal product decreases with an increase in the total number of workers, numerous empirical studies of firm size have documented that larger firms often pay considerably more (Oi and Idson 1999). This may be due to the fact that bigger firms enjoy economies of scale and therefore are generally more productive. Productivity is also a function of capital vintage, with older firms typically employing older and less productive machinery and therefore, *ceteris paribus*, wages have been shown to decrease with firm age. Finally, firms face a heterogeneous workforce and will pay more for workers with higher skills, and hence productivity, which we assume is highly correlated with levels of education.

This framework would not predict any systematic differences between wages paid by different types of firm once size, age, capital, and worker characteristics are controlled for. However, Card and Krueger (1995) outline how differences in information on worker ability, search and training costs, alternative wages paid by competitors, as well as a desire to prevent shirking may cause firms to pay a variety of wages rates to workers with similar skill levels. For example, a firm that has higher training costs and wants to decrease turnover or a firm that has higher managerial costs and wants to provide incentives for high effort levels, may pay a higher wage. These types of firm behavior have been documented extensively in the labor economics literature and are increasingly being used to explain many common labor market "anomalies." Unfortunately, we do not have much data which can help to illuminate to what degree these added considerations are factoring into firm wage decisions in Indonesia. However, we do know that on average foreign firms in Indonesia spent twice as much on training costs per worker, which suggests that in an econometric analysis foreign ownership might be correlated with a wage premium since it serves as a proxy for a higher investment in workers. In addition, foreign firms may also have very real incentives to pay more due both to political considerations (e.g. in order to win favor with local governments) and for reputation effects (e.g. to counter claims of worker exploitation) which will also be captured in a foreign owner-ship variable. We have no way at present of disentangling all of these potential effects, most of which are not necessarily specific to foreign-owned firms.

For the econometric estimation we will control for capital stock (the total estimated value of all machinery, land, buildings, and vehicles), size (the total number of paid workers), age, as well as the price of output. Since firms did not state the prices they received directly we use the Indonesian Census Bureau's manufacturing index which provides average annual prices for out-put based on five-digit ISIC codes. In order to control for the alternative wage faced by workers, for each province we constructed an average wage variable by firm which is the average wage paid by all other firms in the area. Since minimum wage laws, which differ within provinces, will presumably also effect a firm's decisions to some degree they too are included, even if they are not always binding. Apart from the percentage of foreign ownership, which takes on a value of 0 to 100 and is the primary variable of interest, the percentage of goods exported is the final firm characteristic included in the estimating equation since firms which produce for export often face add-itional levels of competition. Therefore, we estimate separately for both unskilled and skilled workers the following reduced form equation, where ε_{it} is an i.i.d. disturbance term and the signs above the betas indicate the predicted signs of the coefficients:

$$\ln w_{it} = \beta_0 + \overset{+}{\beta_1} \ln \text{altwage}_{it} + \overset{+}{\beta_2} \ln \text{minwage}_{it} + \overset{?}{\beta_3} \text{foreign}_{it}$$
$$+ \overset{?}{\beta_4} \text{exports}_{it} + \overset{+}{\beta_5} \text{kapital}_{it} + \overset{+}{\beta_6} \text{size} + \overset{+}{\beta_7} \text{price} + \overset{-}{\beta_8} \text{age}$$
$$+ \overset{+}{\text{worker}_{it}} + \text{region} + \text{time} + \text{industry} + \varepsilon_{it}$$

Higher worker characteristics, as measured by levels of education (included in a subset of the data from 1995–7), should lead to higher wages although we expect men to receive higher compensation than women which is likely to make female coefficients negative. The dependent variable, the average annual wage, was constructed by dividing total firm wages by the total number of employees per year. All monetary variables are in real terms; rupiahs divided by the CPI. In line with common economic practice, region, time, and industry-level dummy variables are included since there may be particular types of law, constraint, or added cost captured by these variables which need to be controlled for since they could potentially bias the results.

Since all of the variables are annualized, yet capture decisions and changes that occur throughout the year, we use lag variables for foreign ownership, exports, capital, and size, both for convenience and to eliminate any potential endogeneity problems. It is reasonable to assume that even if in the present year these variables changed, the effects on wages would not be felt for at least some time and therefore do not bias our estimates.

4 Results

Table 16.3 shows the results for the entire sample (1990–9), which exclude worker characteristics, for average unskilled wages using both ordinary least squares (OLS) and fixed effects. The Hausman test for non-systematic correlation between the error terms and the independent variables was strongly rejected, so we do not include the random effects results. Robust covariance estimates were computed using White's standard errors and we allowed for clustering at the province level. We checked to see if using logs for both the percentage of foreign ownership and exports significantly affected the results and they did not, so we use the non-log forms throughout.

In the OLS specification all of the coefficients on the independent variables have the expected sign and are all significant at the 1% level besides age and exports. The magnitude of the foreign ownership coefficient suggests that a firm which is 100% foreign-owned would on average pay a wage premium to unskilled workers of 18%. However, in the fixed effects specification, which is likely to be the more accurate model since there are probably unobserved firm characteristics such as management styles or country of main foreign investor which do not change over time and yet influence the estimates, the effect of foreign ownership, while still significant at the 5% level, is severely muted. A firm with 100% foreign ownership would only provide a wage for unskilled workers on average about 5% more than a similar domestic

Table 16.3 Dependent variable: log average wage of unskilled workers (1990–9)

	OLS	Fixed effects
Firm age	−0.00057	
	(0.00046)	
Price of output (log)	0.070	0.023
	(0.0178)**	(0.0099)*
Average wage (log)	0.053	0.021
	(0.0233)*	(0.0083)**
Minimum wage (log)	0.39	0.17
	(0.0773)**	(0.0140)**
% foreign ownership (−1)	0.0018	0.0005
	(0.00024)**	(0.00018)**
Capital stock (log −1)	0.0043	−0.000024
	(0.00089)**	(0.00026)
Firm size (log −1)	0.064	−0.0001
	(0.0074)**	(0.00006)
% goods exported (−1)	−0.00005	−0.00022
	(0.00016)	(0.0033)
Time dummies	Yes	Yes
Industry dummies	Yes	Yes
Province dummies	Yes	No
Number of observations	71,130	71,130
R^2	.2872	.1113

* Indicates significance at the 5% level and ** at the 1% level

firm. Note that the industry dummies are still included in the fixed effects regressions because many of the firms change ISIC code over the course of the 10-year period; almost always reflecting a shift to a similar type of production within the same general manufacturing category.

Table 16.4 shows the results using the same estimators and data but with the average wage for skilled workers as the dependent variable. In the OLS specification all of the coefficients have the expected signs and all are significant at the 1% level except price of output and average wage. The coefficient on foreign ownership is even more pronounced, suggesting a wage premium of 31% for complete foreign ownership. The fixed effects estimates are supported by the Hausman test and all of the significant coefficients have the correct signs. Again, however, the wage premium corresponding to complete foreign ownership is much diminished, down to about 7%.

Table 16.5 presents the OLS estimates of the reduced sample for the years 1995–7 in which detailed worker education variables are included. Education levels for both men and women are provided in a highly disaggregated form, ranging from no school to college for unskilled workers and less than high school to Ph.D. for skilled workers.

All of the coefficients on the main variables have the expected signs and most are significant at the 5% or 1% levels. The only education variables

Table 16.4 Dependent variable: log average wages of skilled workers (1990–9)

	OLS	Fixed effects
Firm age	−0.0019	
	(0.00068)**	
Price of output (log)	0.034	0.030
	(0.022)	(0.015)*
Average wage (log)	0.017	0.022
	(0.022)	(0.012)
Minimum wage (log)	0.404	0.078
	(0.066)**	(0.022)**
% foreign ownership (−1)	0.003	0.0007
	(0.00040)**	(0.00029)*
Capital stock (log −1)	0.006	−0.0006
	(0.0007)**	(0.0004)
Firm size (log −1)	0.150	−0.005
	(0.0097)**	(0.0053)
% goods exported (−1)	0.0010	−0.00004
	(0.00009)**	(0.00009)
Time dummies	Yes	Yes
Industry dummies	Yes	Yes
Province dummies	Yes	No
Number of observations	59,021	59,021
R^2	.2703	.0519

* Indicates significance at the 5% level and ** at the 1% level

which are significant are for female workers and they have the expected negative sign. The effect of foreign ownership is much less than in the unrestricted of sample from 1990–9 but stays at around 9% in both the estimates with and without worker characteristics.

Table 16.6 presents estimates from a random effects regression using the same data, since for this subset the Hausman test fails to reject the lack of correlation between the error term and the independent variables, suggesting that the fixed effect is not appropriate. Again, the signs on the coefficients have the correct sign and the magnitude of the effect of complete foreign ownership increases only slightly to about 10%. The only education variables which are significant are for males and they have the expected positive sign.

Table 16.7 provides the same OLS estimates for skilled workers. Again, all of the coefficients have the expected signs except for the average wage variable, which is also significant at the 5% level. This may be due to the fact that the minimum wage variable is picking up more of the effect since for skilled workers it is typically binding. The average wage premiums for complete foreign ownership are again high, at around 24% in both regressions, down somewhat from the 31% in the entire 10-year sample. Surprisingly, none of the worker characteristic variables are significant. In the random effects

Table 16.5 Dependent variable: log average wages of unskilled workers (1995–7)

	OLS	*OLS w/worker characteristics*
Firm age	−0.004	−0.0004
	(0.0005)	(0.0005)
Price of output (log)	0.053	0.054
	(0.0212)*	(0.0303)*
Average wage (log)	0.030	0.007
	(0.058)	(0.059)
Minimum wage (log)	0.922	0.968
	(0.249)**	(0.238)**
% foreign ownership (−1)	0.0009	0.0009
	(0.0003)**	(0.0003)**
Capital stock (log −1)	0.0018	0.0012
	(0.0007)*	(0.0007)*
Firm size (log −1)	0.043	0.044
	(0.006)**	(0.006)**
% goods exported (−1)	0.0002	0.0002
	(0.0002)	(0.0002)
No school (M)		−0.016
		(0.050)
Some primary (M)		0.032
		(0.050)
Junior high (M)		0.042
		(0.050)
Senior high (M)		0.073
		(0.045)
Some college (M)		(dropped)
College (M)		0.220
		(0.138)
No school (F)		−0.0753
		(0.032)*
Some primary (F)		−0.066
		(0.025)*
Junior high (F)		−0.054
		(0.027)*
Senior high (F)		−0.071
		(0.028)*
Some college (F)		−0.019
		(0.040)
College (F)		(dropped)
Time dummies	Yes	Yes
Industry dummies	Yes	Yes
Province dummies	Yes	Yes
Number of observations	23,451	17,582
R^2	.2703	.3079

* Indicates significance at the 5% level and ** at the 1% level

Table 16.6 Dependent variable: log average wages of unskilled workers (1995–7)

	Random effects
Price of output (log)	0.065
	(0.019)**
Average wage (log)	0.144
	(0.017)**
Minimum wage (log)	0.58
	(0.028)**
% foreign ownership (−1)	0.001
	(0.0002)**
Capital stock (log −1)	0.00009
	(0.0004)
Firm size (log −1)	0.040
	(0.003)**
% goods exported (−1)	0.0003
	(0.00009)**
No school (M)	3.07
	(0.26)**
Some primary (M)	3.09
	(0.26)**
Junior high (M)	3.10
	(0.257)**
Senior high (M)	3.13
	(0.257)**
Some college (M)	2.99
	(0.263)**
College (M)	3.27
	(0.265)**
No school (F)	−0.052
	(0.036)
Some primary (F)	−0.046
	(0.036)
Junior high (F)	−0.053
	(0.036)
Senior high (F)	−0.064
	(0.036)
Some college (F)	0.009
	(0.050)
College (F)	(dropped)
Time dummies	Yes
Industry dummies	Yes
Province dummies	No
Number of observations	17,583
R^2	.2922

** Indicates significance at the 1% level.

Table 16.7 Dependent variable: log average wages of skilled workers (1995–7)

	OLS	OLS w/ worker characteristics
Firm age	−0.002	−0.002
	(0.001)	(0.001)
Price of output (log)	0.010	0.045
	(0.043)	(0.044)
Average wage (log)	−0.178	−0.227
	(0.071)*	(0.072)**
Minimum wage (log)	1.32	1.37
	(0.315)**	(0.417)**
% foreign ownership (−1)	0.0024	0.0024
	(0.0004)**	(0.0004)**
Capital stock (log −1)	0.0059	0.0068
	(0.0006)**	(0.0006)**
Firm size (log −1)	0.151	0.142
	(0.0095)**	(0.0091)**
% goods exported (−1)	0.0009	0.0008
	(0.0002)**	(0.0002)**
High school or less (M)		.420
		(0.3222)
Some college (M)		0.43
		(0.3243)
College (M)		0.49
		(0.344)
Masters (M)		(dropped)
PhD (M)		0.86
		(0.546)
High school or less (F)		−.20
		(0.221)
Some college (F)		−0.14
		(0.224)
College (F)		−0.19
		(0.226)
Masters (F)		(dropped)
Ph.D.(F)		0.56
		(1.012)
Time dummies	Yes	Yes
Industry dummies	Yes	Yes
Province dummies	Yes	Yes
Number of observations	21,579	13,483
R^2	.2624	.2435

* Indicates significance at the 5% level and ** at the 1% level

estimates in Table 16.8 all of the principle coefficients have the expected sign and most are significant at the 1% level. The effect of complete foreign ownership decreases only slightly to a little over 22%.

The foreign wage premium is robust to the inclusion of worker

Table 16.8 Dependent variable: log average wages of skilled workers (1995–7)

	Random effects
Price of output (log)	0.037
	(0.0328)
Average wage (log)	0.158
	(0.0204)
Minimum wage (log)	0.814
	(0.0464)**
% foreign ownership (−1)	0.0023
	(0.0003)**
Capital stock (log −1)	0.0047
	(0.0008)**
Firm size (log −1)	0.134
	(0.005)**
% goods exported (−1)	0.0007
	(0.00018)**
High school or less (M)	−.66
	(0.054)
Some college (M)	−0.65
	(0.549)
College (M)	−0.61
	(0.549)
Masters (M)	−1.05
	(0.58)
Ph.D. (M)	(dropped)
High school or less (F)	.53
	(0.745)
Some college (F)	0.578
	(0.749)
College (F)	0.52
	(0.74)
Masters (F)	0.716
	(0.782)
Ph.D. (F)	1.31
	(1.19)
Time dummies	Yes
Industry dummies	Yes
Province dummies	No
Number of observations	13,484
R^2	.2316

** Indicates significance at the 1% level.

characteristics, particularly for skilled workers. However, we also tested further for robustness by including only those firms which experienced a change in foreign ownership during the 1995–7 period. There are approximately 580 observations for which the mean change in foreign ownership was a little over 4%. About 60% of the firms in this sample increased foreign ownership an average of 38% while the remaining 40% of the observations decreased foreign ownership by an average of near 50%, resulting in a small net gain over all 580 firms. Tables 16.9 and 16.10 provide an OLS and random effects estimate for unskilled and skilled workers using this reduced sample.

In the OLS specification for unskilled workers all the coefficients exhibit the proper signs, yet only price of output, minimum wage, and foreign ownership are significant (at the 5% level). The effect of complete foreign ownership remains near 10% and persists in the random effects specification (the Hausman test again strongly rejects the use of fixed effects) even though it is not significant. The only education variable which is significant is the male college, which exhibits the predicted positive sign.

In the OLS specification for skilled workers the signs are all in the right direction and the effect of foreign ownership is quite high, 34%, and significant at the 1% level. It is also significant in the random effects specification (at the 5% level) with almost as high a magnitude at close to 30%. The coefficients on levels of education are odd, with female levels higher than males, although not significant, and the male Ph.D. variable highly negative. This is most probably due to the fact that less than 1% of the (already small number of) observations contain any entries for masters or Ph.D. workers of either gender.

Next, we decreased the sample to only those firms which operated in the textile, apparel, or footwear sectors, since these have been targeted by anti-sweatshop groups for their low wages and are typically concentrated in the export sector. The percentage of foreign firms in these almost 31,000 observations was a little greater than across the whole sample, at approximately 6.5%. The foreign owned firms exported on average a little over 50% of their output compared to 12% for domestic firms and they were much bigger, employing an average of 1,058 unskilled workers to the 224 in domestic firms, more than four times as much, and 87 skilled workers to 28 in domestic firms, more than three times as much. Again, the average unskilled wage on average was almost double for foreign firms and the average skilled wage almost five times as much without controlling for worker characteristics.

In the simple OLS regressions for the 10-year period without worker characteristics the premium for unskilled workers was actually a little higher than in other specifications, at almost 13%, and the same was true for skilled workers for which the premium was close to 39%; both significant at the 1% level. All of the other primary variables had the predicted signs, and the coefficient on exports is positive and significant at the 5% level in both regressions as well. In Tables 16.11 and 16.12 we report the random effects estimates for the reduced sample for 1995 to 1997 with worker characteristics since once again we failed to reject the Hausman test that the errors are non-systematic. The premium for full foreign ownership decreased to about 9% for unskilled workers and remained significant at the 5% level, while the premium for skilled worker dropped to 28% and was significant at

Table 16.9 Dependent variable: log average wage of unskilled workers (only firms with changes in foreign ownership 1995–7)

	OLS	Random effects
Price of output (log)	.45	.41
	(.211)*	(.263)
Average wage (log)	.28	.31
	(.167)	(.236)
Minimum wage (log)	.65	.60
	(.253)*	(.375)
% foreign ownership (−1)	.001	.001
	(.00048)*	(.00092)
Capital stock (log −1)	.003	.003
	(.006)	(.005)
Firm size (log −1)	.041	.043
	(.0357)	(.0317)
% goods exported (−1)	−.0019	−.0017
	(.0006)**	(.0008)
No school (M)	−.57	−2.46
	(.345)	(1.005)*
Some primary (M)	−.25	−2.27
	(.195)	(.960)*
Junior high (M)	−.27	−2.29
	(.209)	(.955)*
Senior high (M)	−.15	−2.17
	(.234)	(.958)*
Some college (M)	(dropped)	−2.05
		(1.18)
College (M)	2.18	(dropped)
	(1.01)*	
No school (F)	−.48	−.03
	(.417)	(.482)
Some primary (F)	−.25	.11
	(.40)	(.399)
Junior high (F)	−.37	.11
	(.467)	(.397)
Senior high (F)	−.44	.04
	(.458)	(.390)
Some college (F)	−.46	(dropped)
	(.731)	
College (F)	(dropped)	.48
		(.533)
Time dummies	Yes	Yes
Industry dummies	Yes	Yes
Province dummies	Yes	No
Number of observations	580	580
R^2	.2692	.2683

* Indicates significance at the 5% level and ** at the 1% level

Table 16.10 Dependent variable: log average wages of skilled workers (only firms with changes in foreign ownership 1995–7)

	OLS	Random effects
Price of output (log)	.20	.58
	(.185)	(.281)
Average wage (log)	.27	.18
	(.136)*	(.194)
Minimum wage (log)	.54	.70
	(.223)*	(.421)
% foreign ownership (−1)	.0034	.0029
	(.00103)**	(.00118)*
Capital stock (log −1)	.026	.027
	(.0075)**	(.0061)**
Firm size (log −1)	.028	.030
	(.0541)	(.006)
% goods exported (−1)	−.0015	−.0014
	(.00087)	(.0012)
High school or less (M)	−6.22	6.74
	(2.296)*	(28.993)
Some college (M)	−6.27	6.765
	(2.538)*	(28.999)
College (M)	−5.95	6.85
	(2.342)*	(28.997)
Masters (M)	(dropped)	15.80
		(29.341)
Ph.D. (M)	−18.34	−5.13
	(5.211)**	(28.774)
High school or less (F)	−5.81	−4.83
	(43.582)	(28.384)
Some college (F)	−5.91	−4.90
	(43.557)	(28.386)
College (F)	−5.75	−4.81
	(43.471)	(28.383)
Masters (F)	−8.33	−7.64
	(43.441)	(28.509)
Ph.D.(F)	(dropped)	(dropped)
Time dummies	Yes	Yes
Industry dummies	Yes	Yes
Province dummies	Yes	No
Number of observations	564	564
R^2	.2106	.2029

* Indicates significance at the 5% level and ** at the 1% level

the 1% level. The positive coefficient on exports remained significant at the 1% level in both.

In order to see if selection bias may be affecting our results we used Heckman's maximum likelihood estimator. For both production and non-production workers the coefficients on foreign ownership were

Table 16.11 Dependent variable: log average wage of unskilled worker (1995–7) (reduced sample: only textile, apparel, and footwear industries)

	Random effects
Price of output (log)	−.11
	(0.102)
Average wage (log)	0.21
	(0.057)**
Minimum wage (log)	1.03
	(0.087)**
% foreign ownership (−1)	0.0009
	(0.0004)*
Capital stock (log −1)	0.0007
	(0.001)
Firm size (log −1)	0.048
	(0.007)**
% goods exported (−1)	0.0009
	(0.0002)**
No school (M)	−3.24
	(0.926)**
Some primary (M)	−3.19
	(0.925)**
Junior high (M)	−3.18
	(.924)**
Senior high (M)	−3.20
	(.925)**
Some college (M)	−3.42
	(.943)**
College (M)	−3.25
	(0.939)**
No school (F)	−.053
	(0.506)
Some primary (F)	−.051
	(0.505)
Junior high (F)	0.−051
	(0.505)
Senior high (F)	−.046
	(.508)
Some college (F)	.116
	.553
College (F)	(Dropped)
Time dummies	Yes
Industry dummies	No
Province dummies	No
Number of observations	4736
R^2	.30

* Indicates significance at the 5% level and ** at the 1% level

Table 16.12 Dependent variable: log average wage of skilled workers (1995–7) (reduced sample: only textile, apparel, and footwear industries)

	Random effects
Price of output (log)	−.55
	(0.195)**
Average wage (log)	0.30
	(0.066)**
Minimum wage (log)	1.00
	(0.139)**
% foreign ownership (−1)	0.0028
	(0.0007)**
Capital stock (log −1)	0.005
	(0.0024)*
Firm size (log −1)	0.16
	(0.012)**
% goods exported (−1)	0.0013
	(0.0004)**
High school or less (M)	−1.73
	(1.76)
Some college (M)	−1.78
	(1.75)
College (M)	−1.71
	(1.76)
Masters (M)	−3.11
	(2.06)
Ph.D. (M)	−.842
	(2.26)
High school or less (F)	−.607
	(0.922)
Some college (F)	−.63
	(0.929)
College (F)	−.71
	(0.93)
Masters (F)	(dropped)
Ph.D.(F)	13.63
	(14.30)
Time dummies	Yes
Industry dummies	Yes
Province dummies	No
Number of observations	13,484
R^2	.2316

* Indicates significance at the 5% level and ** at the 1% level

significantly higher once firm exiting was taken into account. Over the full sample excluding worker characteristics the wage premiums were 31% and 56% for production and non-production workers respectively, and 22% and 45% in the restricted sample which included worker characteristics; with all coefficients being significant beyond the 1% level. All of the other primary coefficients continued to exhibit the proper signs.

Even with lagged values for exports the model may still suffer from endogeneity and therefore we used an instrumental variables estimator to see how this would affect the results. As an instrument for exports we used the percentage of output within the ISIC sector that is exported at the province level, excluding own firm's exports. The premiums for production workers were significantly higher than the OLS results for both the whole sample and restricted sample with worker characteristics, at 26% and 17% respectively, the former significant at the 1% level and the latter at the 5% level. For non-production workers the premiums were again higher, at 49% and 41% respectively, and both were significant well beyond the 1% level. Again, all of the other primary coefficients had the expected signs.

5 General discussion and conclusion

Wage premiums paid by foreign establishments in Indonesia during the 1990s were found to be robust to the inclusion of worker characteristics, across specifications, within selected industries and in limited samples for which the foreign ownership variable changed significantly. Premiums for unskilled workers were mostly in the range of 5 to 10% and between 20 and 35% for skilled workers. These findings are in line with other similar estimates using data from Central and South America, other parts of Asia, and Africa.

This paper provides strong evidence that foreign-owned companies do pay higher wages on average. The next question is why? As mentioned earlier, the dataset includes limited information on total training costs and foreign firms on average spent much more. This finding would support the view that foreign firms pay higher wages in order to retain workers, given their increased investment in training. However, we have no way of determining whether foreign firms have less turnover than domestic firms since we have no data on hires and fires, only on annual aggregate numbers of workers.

Although hard to quantify, political and social pressure on foreign firms should not be discounted. The antisweatshop movement of the 1990s, with its particular focus on companies such as Nike, which is based in Indonesia, led to a number of large lawsuits, immense negative publicity, and eventually commitments by many firms to increase wages for the poorest workers. A follow-up study will try to determine to what extent this contributed to upward wage pressure.

Empirical studies such as these will surely not put an end to the heated debate surrounding globalization, and well they shouldn't, but they can help to focus inquiry and potentially direct policy. As this study and other studies demonstrate, it is wrong to claim that foreign firms pay the lowest wages in developing countries. In Indonesia, based on simple summary statistics, on average they paid very high wages compared to their domestic counterparts throughout the 1990s.

This being said, aside from the potential reputational and political considerations, perhaps the question of whether foreign firms pay more just because they are foreign is not the best one to ask. If higher productivity is largely responsible for higher wages, which is what most economic theory predicts, maybe it would be more fruitful to investigate the mechanisms, both at the firm level and the institutional level, that promote increased productivity. We may want to know whether productivity is largely a function of access to capital and technology, related to an infant-industry argument or perhaps linked to state-ownership. Given that many firms in developing countries are actually partnerships between various entities—private, both domestic and foreign, as well as public—isolating simply the foreign component may not tell us much. Furthermore, foreign ownership in and of itself is not particularly informative because there are hundreds of potential foreign owners each with varying levels of capital, technology, and management skills. It is probably not accurate to treat foreign ownership originating from Malaysia in the same way as foreign ownership originating from the USA. The exact nature by which productivity gains are correlated with foreign ownership is also unclear. It may simply be a linear function of the percentage of foreign ownership but perhaps there may be discontinuities that come with majority ownership or non-linearities.

All of these questions and issues emphasize how difficult it is to study wage determination, since it is based on very dynamic and complex processes, especially in developing countries such as Indonesia that have recently undergone tremendous change; social, political, and economic. Narrowing the focus of research on more specific determinants of productivity growth within industries, or on the precise channels through which outside pressure may force firms to pay higher wages, might offer the best policy-relevant information. Given that in our model the variables, which economic theory predicts are directly linked to productivity, captured such a large portion of the wage premiums between foreign and domestic firms and were significant in almost all specifications, this leads us to believe that we have an excellent foundation on which to build.

Note

* The authors would like to thank Garrick Blalock for generously sharing his data and expertise on Indonesia.

References

Aitken, B., A. Harrison, and R. Lipsey (1996) "Wages and Foreign Ownership: A comparative study of Mexico, Venezuela, and the United States." *Journal of International Economics* 40(3): 345–71, May.

Baily, M. and H. Gersbach (1995) "Efficiency in Manufacturing and the Need for Global Competition." *Brookings Papers on Economic Activity: Microeconomics* 1995: 307–47.

Card, D. and A. B. Krueger (1995) *Myth and Measurement: The New Economics of the Minimum Wage.* New York: Princeton University Press.

Chau, N. and R. Kanbur (2001) "The Adoption of International Labor Standards Conventions: Who, When, and Why?" in Brookings Trade Forum, edited by S. Collins, and D. Rodrik. Washington DC: The Brookings Institution.

Currie, J. and A. Harrison (1997) "Sharing the Costs: The Impact of Trade Reform on Capital and Labor in Morocco." *Journal of Labor Economics* 15(3): 44–71, July.

Feenstra, R. (1998) "Integration of Trade and Disintegration of Production in the Global Economy." *The Journal of Economic Perspectives* 12(4): 31–50, Autumn.

"Globalization: Sweatshop Labor." *Get Informed at Citizen Works*, Citizen Works. 31 December 2008 <http://www.citizenworks.org/issues/globalization/glob-sweatshops.php>.

Henderson, David. "Free Trade and Sweatshops: Is Global Trade Doing More Harm Than Good?" *San Francisco Chronicle*, 24 June 2001: C8.

Idson, T. and W. Oi (1999) "Firm Size and Wages." In *Handbook of Labor Economics*, edited by D. Card, and A. Orley, Vol. 3. New York: Elsevier.

Lipsey, R. and F. Sjoholm (2001) "Foreign Direct Investment and Wages in Indonesian Manufacturing." National Bureau of Economic Research (Cambridge, MA) Working Paper W8299, May.

Ramstetter, E. D. (1999) "Comparisons of Foreign Multinationals and Local Firms in Asian Manufacturing Over Time." *Asian Economic Journal* 12(2): 163–203, June.

Udomsaph, C. C. (2002) "Premiums to Employment in Establishments with Foreign Direct Investment: Evidence from the Thai manufacturing sector." Working paper, UC-Berkeley Economics Department, October.

Velde, D. W. te and O. Morrissey (2001) "Foreign Ownership and Wages: Evidence from Five African Countries." CREDIT Research Paper 01/19, Centre for Research in Economic Development and International Trade (University of Nottingham), November.

17 Gender inequality in the labor market during economic transition

Changes in India's manufacturing sector[*]

Nidhiya Menon and Yana van der Meulen Rodgers

Introduction

In 1990 and early 1991, a series of international and domestic shocks—including an oil price hike, a reduction in remittances from Indians working in the Middle East, a weakening in investor confidence following the assassination of Rajiv Gandhi, and expanding fiscal and trade deficits—precipitated a financial crisis in India. In return for receiving stand-by assistance from the International Monetary Fund in August 1991, the Indian government agreed to a standard policy prescription of stabilization and structural adjustment policies. Prominent among the policy reforms were substantial reductions in tariff levels on a wide range of imported products. Several new waves of reforms occurred in 1994 and 1997, with a slowdown in the pace of trade liberalization after 1997 as pressures from international agencies and creditors subsided.

During this period of liberalization, the gender wage differential remained unchanged, with women in manufacturing earning 49% of what men earned. This paper analyzes why women's relative wages in manufacturing stagnated during the reform period. Understanding why trade liberalization in India did not contribute to an increase in women's relative wages adds depth to the growing literature on wage structures and women's labor market performance in developing and transition economies. Relatively few studies have gone beyond descriptive analyses of changes in women's relative wages in periods of trade liberalization and increasing trade openness. The few studies that do employ econometric techniques to identify the impact of international trade on gender wage gaps have found conflicting results. In particular, Berik, Rodgers, and Zveglich (2004) find evidence that increasing trade openness is associated with higher residual wage gaps between men and women in two East Asian economies, a sign the authors interpret as increased wage discrimination.[1] Yet Black and Brainerd (2004) reach the opposite conclusion for the USA, with shrinking residual wage gaps associated with greater openness to imports. Hazarika and Otero (2004) also find that increased trade (in this case Mexico) is associated with lower gender earnings differentials. Finally,

Oostendorp (2004) uses data for more than 80 lower- and higher-income economies to show that except for highly-skilled workers in lower-income economies, increased trade is associated with reduced wage gaps.

This paper provides a detailed assessment of India's gender wage differential using four cross-sections of data collected by the National Sample Survey Organization (NSSO). The data include the years 1983, 1987–8, 1999–2000, and 2004, providing us with data coverage before, during, and after the macroeconomic liberalization. We use these data to conduct two decomposition procedures. The first decomposes the wage gap in individual years into a portion explained by measured, gender-specific skill differences, and a residual portion. The second procedure measures the contribution of changes over time in measured and unmeasured gender-specific factors, and in market returns to measured and unmeasured skills.

Results offer detailed evidence that unmeasured gender-specific factors have become more important determinants of gender wage differentials across education groups. Female workers gained relative to their male counterparts in education and experience, and the dispersion in the residual male wage distribution narrowed, which caused average male wages to fall relative to female wages. However, these relative gains for women were offset by a greater importance of unmeasured gender-specific factors, resulting in a stagnation of the aggregate gender earnings differential. These unmeasured factors could encompass growing gender differences in the unobserved skills of new labor market entrants, widening gender disparities in labor force commitment due to intermittency, and increasing wage discrimination by gender. We test this last assertion with industry-level regressions and find support for the hypothesis that increased competition from India's trade liberalization is associated with a widening in the residual gender wage gap in concentrated manufacturing industries.

Our study contributes new results that show the gender-specific repercussions of trade reforms, thus yielding useful evidence for policy makers in other countries that are moving toward less restrictive trade policies. This work will help to justify policy measures that build women's human capital and strengthen the social safety net. In addition, improved enforcement of equal pay and equal opportunity legislation will help to reduce unfair labor market practices that may contribute to observed gender differences.

Data description

To explore the labor market impacts of trade policy reforms, we use four cross-sections of data collected by the NSSO. The data include the years 1983 (38th round), 1987–8 (43rd round), 1999–2000 (55th round), and 2004 (60th round), providing us with coverage that precedes and spans years following trade and fiscal reforms. For each round, we utilize the Employment and Unemployment module—Household Schedule 10. To construct our labor force sample, we retain all individuals of prime working age (ages 15–60) who are employed in the manufacturing sector and who have positive weekly cash wages.[2] Industry-level variables are constructed using India's National Industrial Classification (NIC) system, which is based on international standards. The two earlier rounds of NSSO data use the 1970 NIC codes, while the two later rounds of data use the 1998 NIC codes. There are major differences at all levels of disaggregation beyond the one-digit level between the 1970 and 1998 NIC codes; these are incorporated in our empirical analysis.

Our analysis includes tests involving trade indicators. Data on export and import values across manufacturing industries, from 1980 to 2004, are constructed using the World Bank's Trade, Production, and Protection Database (Nicita and Olarreaga 2006). We construct three measures of trade openness: exports/output, imports/output, and (exports + imports)/output. Although the data source also has information on tariff rates, we used trade shares because the tariff data are plagued with missing values. Data on output across manufacturing industries are obtained from India's Annual Survey of Industries (ASI).[3] Because the domestic output data are in rupees and the trade series are in dollars, we use average annual rupee/US$ exchange rates to convert output into dollars. Finally, ASI data are used to construct an index of domestic concentration across manufacturing industries. This index is based on the number of enterprises relative to output, by industry. All data sources are summarized in Appendix Table 17.A1.

For the industry-level tests of competition and residual wage gaps, the various data series need to be aggregated to the same sets of industries using the same industry codes. We adopted the categorization in the World Bank Trade, Production and Protection series, which uses the ISIC (revision 2) classification at the three-digit level and contains 28 industry categories per year. The NSSO labor data and the ASI production data are converted to this classification scheme using a concordance schedule we created based on information in Sivadasan and Slemrod (2006) and Central Statistical Organization (1970, 1998). The concordance schedule is reported in Appendix Table 17.A2.

Stylized facts: trade liberalization and structural changes in the labor market

Like many developing countries in the post-World War II era, India based its economic development and trade policies on an import substitution industrialization strategy. The country had some of the highest tariff rates and most restrictive non-tariff barriers in the region (Krishna and Mitra 1998, Topalova 2005). However, in 1990 and early 1991, a series of external, political, and macroeconomic shocks—including an oil price hike spurred by the Gulf War, a reduction in remittances from Indians employed in the Middle East, a shake-up in investor confidence following the assassination of Rajiv Gandhi, and growing fiscal and trade deficits—precipitated a financial crisis (Edmonds, Pavcnik, and Topalova 2005). The Indian government requested stand-by assistance from the International Monetary Fund in August 1991, and in return, agreed to what had become a fairly standard policy prescription of stabilization and structural adjustment policies. The government aimed to reduce tariff levels on a wide range of imported products, lower the variation across sectors in tariff rates, simplify the tariff structure, and remove many of the exemptions (Krishna and Mitra 1998, Topalova 2005). Several new waves of reforms occurred in 1994 and 1997, with a slowdown in the pace of trade liberalization after 1997.

Previous studies on India have found negative social impacts resulting from the introduction of trade policy reforms. In particular, evidence from a difference-in-difference approach in Topalova (2005) indicates that in districts that were more exposed to trade liberalization, both the incidence and depth of poverty decreased by less than the reductions observed in other districts that had fewer industries exposed to trade liberalization. India's trade liberalization also appears to have had negative impacts on child well-being. Findings in Edmonds, Pavcnik, and Topalova (2005) suggest that adjustment costs associated with trade liberalization were responsible for smaller declines in child labor and smaller improvements in school attendance in districts exposed to tariff cuts, compared to districts less exposed to the tariff reductions.[4] Trade liberalization also had differential effects on male and female employment. According to Bhaumik (2003), the growth in the workforce share classified as casual accelerated after 1993 as a result of the liberalization policies, with larger increases for female workers compared to their male counterparts in both rural and urban areas. However, not all studies have found negative social impacts for India. In particular, Mishra and Kumar (2005) argue that higher wage premiums in sectors that disproportionately employ unskilled workers led to an increase in their relative income and a decline in overall wage inequality.

Manufacturing industries across the board experienced some degree of tariff reductions during and after the initial sweeping 1991 reform package, and India's imports and exports grew dramatically as a result. Figure 17.1, which reports trends in exports and imports as a share of production, shows that both the aggregate export share and import share jumped sharply after 1991 and continued to rise steadily until the late 1990s. With a slowing in the pace of trade liberalization, the growth in trade ratios eased during the early 2000s, especially for exports. Superimposed onto this diagram are women's relative wages, with results suggesting that in the midst of India's comprehensive trade liberalization, women's relative wages stagnated at about 49% from 1987 through 2004.

During this reform period, male and female employment distributions changed dramatically. Table 17.1, which reports population-weighted employment shares for all individuals of working age, shows a very large shift out of agriculture for female workers. In 1983, almost 90% of female workers were employed in agriculture, and by 2004 this proportion had dropped to 53%. Women shifted into manufacturing as well as the various service industries. Although male workers also moved out of agriculture, the changes were less

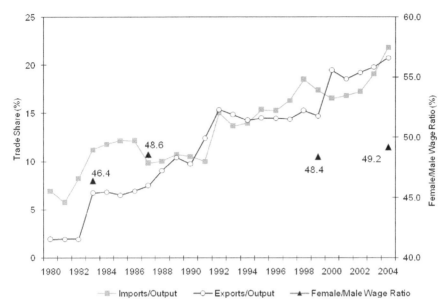

Figure 17.1 Trade ratios and female/male wage ratios, 1980–2004

Source: Authors' calculations based on data sources in Appendix Table 1.

dramatic (from 61 to 51% during the period), with the gain absorbed entirely in services but not in manufacturing. Within manufacturing, India's employment distribution resembles that of many developing countries, with relatively high female representation in low-skilled intensive industries such as garments, food products, beverages, and tobacco, and relatively high male representation in higher-skilled and capital intensive industries such as industrial chemicals, glass, iron and steel, fabricated metals, and machinery.

Trends in the female–male wage ratio and explanations

The analysis of trade liberalization and trends in the gender wage differential continues with a more detailed examination of the evolution of the female–male wage ratio in India's manufacturing sector. Table 17.2 reports results for unadjusted wage ratios by education groups. The top row reports the same (stagnant) aggregate wage ratio series that is illustrated in Figure 17.1. With disaggregation into education groups, the wage ratios rise on average from 1983 to 1987–8 for three of the four groups (those with middle school being the exception). From 1987–8 to 1999–2000 (the post-liberalization era), ratios rise for all groups except those with the highest levels of education (high school and above). However, wage ratios in the 1999–2000 to 2004 time frame increase only for those with high school and above; ratios for women in the remaining groups experience a decline. The most dramatic fall in the 1999/2000–2004 years is experienced by women with primary school

Table 17.1 Employment structure in India by gender, 1983–2004 (in %)

	1983	1987–8	1999–2000	2004
Male				
Agriculture	60.9	60.1	54.7	50.8
Mining	0.8	0.9	0.7	0.1
Manufacturing	11.7	11.3	11.0	11.8
Utilities and construction	4.1	5.4	6.9	8.5
Wholesale and retail trade	7.6	8.0	12.4	11.5
Transport, storage, and communication	3.9	3.8	4.8	5.8
Business and social services	11.1	10.5	9.6	10.6
Sample Size	395,829	433,461	185,416	121,890
Female				
Agriculture	86.8	85.6	76.7	53.2
Mining	0.3	0.3	0.3	0.9
Manufacturing	5.4	5.4	9.0	11.1
Utilities and construction	1.2	2.4	1.9	7.3
Wholesale and retail trade	1.9	1.8	4.3	11.0
Transport, storage, and communication	0.2	0.1	0.3	5.4
Business and social services	4.3	4.3	7.5	11.1
Sample Size	245,344	270,502	80,998	106,199

Source: Authors' calculations based on NSSO data.

Note: The results are population-weighted employment shares for all workers aged 15 to 60 who report a defined industry category.

Table 17.2 Female–male wage ratios in India's manufacturing sector, 1983–2004 (in %)

	1983	1987–8	1999–2000	2004
Unadjusted wage ratios				
All education levels	46.4	48.6	48.4	49.2
Illiterate and some primary	50.9	52.4	53.2	51.9
Primary school	44.0	54.1	54.4	44.8
Middle school	53.9	44.0	54.8	52.2
High school and above	59.2	73.2	57.3	64.4

Source: Authors' calculations based on NSSO data.

Note: Wage ratios are the ratio of the geometric means of female and male weekly cash wages.

education. Hence, the relatively constant female–male wage ratio from 1983 to 2004 hides wide fluctuations which become evident when the analysis is segregated by differing levels of human capital.

The determinants of trends in India's gender wage differential can be divided into four categories: changes in men's and women's observed characteristics, changes in the market returns to observed characteristics, changes in men's and women's unobserved characteristics, and changes in the market returns to unobserved characteristics. We examine each of these possible sources with a battery of descriptive statistics in the remainder of this section, and decomposition analyses in the subsequent section. The first category, observed characteristics, encompasses gender differences in education, experience, employment characteristics, and personal characteristics. In terms of education, sample means in Appendix Table 17.A3 show that in 1983, 72% of female workers and 37% of male workers in manufacturing were illiterate or had less than a primary school education. By 2004, these proportions had fallen to 49% for females and 27% for males. Women also made substantial gains relative to men in attaining secondary school and graduate school educations. Also, women's average level of experience rose slightly during the period while that of men dropped. Hence the sample means point to an improvement in the educational attainment and experience of women relative to men, which contributes to an increase in women's relative wages.

The second explanation for trends in India's overall gender wage differential is changes in the market returns to observed characteristics. To provide evidence of such changes, we use ordinary least squares estimates of a standard human capital equation for male wages. For a given year t, we regress the natural logarithm of real weekly cash wages (w) for male workers on a set of worker characteristics X as follows:

$$w_t = X_t \beta_t + \varepsilon_t. \qquad (1)$$

Within X, we use a set of dummy variables for education level attained; an indicator variable for whether the individual has any technical education; years of potential experience and its square; number of pre-school children in the household; and binary variables for regional location, rural status, marital status, low-caste status, self-employed status, religion, and household headship. The notation ε is a random error term assumed to be normally distributed with variance σ^2. Appendix Table 17.A4 reports coefficient estimates from the male wage regressions for all four survey years. In this table, the excluded education level is no schooling (illiterate), and the excluded regional dummy is the western region of India. The regressions are weighted using sample weights provided in the NSSO data for the relevant years. The weights correct for the fact that the proportion of individuals and households in each sample differs from the proportion in the true population. Use of these weights thus adjusts the coefficients to make them nationally representative. As evident in the table, general education, technical education, and experience have positive effects on wages. Wages are lower for self-employed individuals, for individuals belonging to castes that are perceived as inferior, and for individuals employed in rural areas of India. Furthermore, on average, wages tend to be higher in the western regions as compared to other locations in India.

Coefficient estimates in this appendix table also provide strong evidence of a widening over time in market payoffs to observed skills. The coefficient on the dummy variables for individuals with secondary school and graduate school both rose over time, from 0.46 and 0.82 in 1983 to 0.72 and 1.25 in 2004. Returns to individuals with all other levels of schooling also rose over time compared to individuals who are illiterate. This result is consistent with findings in Kijima (2006) of a widening in the dispersion of returns to observed skills during the period. Because men on average have higher education levels than women in most years, this increase in the premium for higher levels of schooling after 1983 contributes to higher average male wages relative to average female wages. Also acting against women's interests, the wage penalty for self-employment grew more severe during the period, with a coefficient that changed from −0.14 to −0.28. Because women were more likely to be self-employed, this worsening in the wage penalty serves to dampen women's relative overall wages. However, some changes in market returns were in women's favor, especially the increase in the premium for years of experience (from 0.04 to 0.06). With women on average having slightly more experience compared to men during the period, this premium increase boosts women's relative wages.

Gender differences in unobserved characteristics could also influence trends in the female–male wage ratio. This category could encompass unobserved skills of male and female workers, changes in the labor force commitment of female workers due to longer intermittency from the workforce, and wage discrimination by gender. Unobserved factors affect women's relative wages, after accounting for gender differences attributed to observed characteristics. To provide a better sense of the magnitude of this category of wage gap determinants, we calculated the mean female position in the male residual wage distribution, where residual wages measure the portion of wages that cannot be explained by observed productivity attributes. Results, which are found in Table 17.3, can be interpreted as the average woman's ranking in the male wage distribution after controlling for gender differences in observed qualifications. For example, the first entry under the column titled "1983" indicates that the mean female position is 27% of the way up the male residual wage distribution; that is, controlling for gender differences in observed char-

Table 17.3 Mean female position in the male residual wage distribution, 1983–2004 (in %)

	1983	1987–8	1999–2000	2004
Female position in male distribution				
All education levels	27.0	31.1	28.7	24.9
Illiterate and some primary	24.3	24.7	22.8	20.8
Primary school	23.2	32.6	31.8	16.8
Middle school	35.1	31.2	27.5	24.5
High school and above	42.1	48.2	36.4	34.0

Source: Authors' calculations based on NSSO data.

acteristics, a woman with average wages for a female worker earns an amount that is just at the 27th percentile of the male wage distribution.

As evident from Table 17.3, the average female position in the male residual wage distribution improved from 1983 through 1987–8, and then declined to reach a level in 2004 that was lower than the level in 1983. The increase in the mean female position through 1987–8 was true for all educational categories, except for women with middle school. The erosion from 1987–8 to 2004 was experienced by all educational groups, and was particularly marked for women with primary school and for women with high school and above. The analysis was also performed for women at different points in the male distribution (10th percentile, 90th percentile). For most educational groups, the position of women in the male residual wage distribution deteriorated over time.

In addition to gender differences in unobserved characteristics, differences in labor market returns to unobserved qualifications may also affect female–male wage ratios. To depict changes in returns to unobservable skills, Table 17.4 reports trends in the dispersion of residual male wages. A narrowing in the dispersion indicates decreasing returns to unobserved skills. Such declines should help to close the gender wage gap because more women have wages that rank toward the lower end of the male distribution. Therefore, when the male residual dispersion narrows, the average woman receives a relatively higher wage for a given position in the male distribution. The first row of estimates in Table 17.4 shows the difference in log wages between men in the 90th and 10th percentiles of the male residual wage distribution. It is clear that from 1983 to 2004, this difference decreased. Results indicate that the 90th–10th differential declined by 0.45 log points between 1983 and 2004. The decline in the 75–25 spread of 0.53 log points between 1983 and 2004 suggests that the broad trend of decreasing inequality cannot be attributed to changes that were occurring only in the tails of the distribution. Hence, from 1983 to 2004, the narrowing residual wage dispersion occurred throughout

Table 17.4 Residual wage dispersion for men, 1983–2004 (in log points)

	1983	*1987–8*	*1999–2000*	*2004*
Residual wage differential:				
90–10 spread	2.279	2.398	2.295	1.826
90–50 spread	0.851	0.842	0.817	0.714
50–10 spread	1.428	1.556	1.478	1.112
75–25 spread	1.352	1.457	1.084	0.826
75–50 spread	0.515	0.499	0.444	0.382
50–25 spread	0.838	0.958	0.640	0.444

Source: Authors' calculations based on NSSO data.

Note: Male residual wages are the portion of wages which cannot be explained by observed characteristics. Each result represents the difference in log wages between men in the indicated percentiles of the residual distribution.

the male distribution and should have, in principle, raised women's overall relative wages.

Formal decomposition analyses of India's gender wage gap

The previous section lay the groundwork in presenting descriptive evidence showing changes in India's wage structure that often worked in opposing directions to influence the net male–female wage differential. This section uses two decomposition procedures to examine the various explanations more formally. The first technique uses individual cross-sections to examine the degree to which the overall wage gap can be explained by observed productivity characteristics between men and women (Oaxaca 1973; Blinder 1973). This procedure decomposes the wage gap in a particular year into a portion explained by average group differences in productivity characteristics and a residual portion that is commonly attributed to discrimination. For a given year t, the gender wage gap may be decomposed by expressing the natural logarithm of real wages *(w)* for male workers *(i = m)* and female workers *(i = f)* as follows:

$$w_{it} = X_{it}\beta_{it} + \sigma_{it}\theta_{it}. \tag{2}$$

The notation X denotes a set of worker characteristics that affect wages (which we measure with the same variables noted above), and $\sigma_{it}\theta_{it}$ is a standardized error term. The standardized residual θ_{it} is distributed normally with a mean of zero and a variance of one for all years. The female wage equation can then be described using only the male coefficients and standard deviations as follows:

$$w_{ft} = X_{ft}\beta_{mt} + \sigma_{mt}\theta_{ft}. \tag{3}$$

In equation (3), we are using the market returns for male workers to predict the average wage that women would receive, given their observed characteristics, if they were paid the male rates. The gender gap can then be written as

$$w_{mt} - w_{ft} = (X_{mt} - X_{ft})\beta_{mt} + \sigma_{mt}(\theta_{mt} - \theta_{ft}). \tag{4}$$

The left-hand side of equation (4) is the total log-wage differential. On the right-hand side, the first term is the explained gap (the portion of the gap attributed to gender differences in measured productivity characteristics) and the second term is the residual gap (the portion attributed to unobserved returns and the error terms). When this equation is evaluated at the means, the residual gap represents the dispersion in the male residual wage distribution (σ_{mt}) and the average woman's position in the male residual wage distribution (θ_{ft}). In performing the decomposition, the convention in the literature is to use the male coefficients, since it is presumed that male wages better reflect the market payoffs for productivity characteristics than do female wages. The male wage regression coefficients are then applied to female worker characteristics to construct measures of the residual wage gap.

Results from the Oaxaca–Blinder decomposition are reported in Table 17.5. The table shows that in 1983, the total male–female wage gap (in log points) for all education groups stood at 0.767. This gap can be converted to a ratio of geometric means by exponentiating its negative, yielding a female to male wage ratio of only 46.4%. Even though the total wage gap narrowed slightly over time to 0.710 log points in 2004, this end point is equivalent to a relative female wage of 49.2%, which is extremely low by international standards. Table 17.5 also shows that most of the total gender wage gap in India across all education groups remains unexplained by variations in education, experience, and other human capital characteristics. In 1983, 68.2% of the wage gap remained unexplained, and after a slight dip in the mid-1980s, the portion of the wage gap that cannot be explained grew to 78.0% by 2004. After 1987–8, the explained gap steadily fell as women gained relatively more education and experience. However, acting against this improvement was a steady widening in the residual gap between men and women.

The Oaxaca–Blinder decomposition results in Table 17.5 indicate that the increase in the residual wage gap between men and women from 1983 to 2004 occurred across all educational categories in the sample. The largest increases were experienced by those with primary and middle school education. Women with high school and above also experienced an increase in the proportion of the wage gap that is unexplained from 1983 to 2004; however, this increase was more modest in magnitude (and slightly lower than the increase across all education groups) as compared to those experienced by groups with lower levels of education.

Even though the residual gap is commonly attributed to wage discrimination by gender, it may incorporate other economic factors that have little to do with discrimination. The Juhn–Murphy–Pierce (1991) technique provides a more detailed description of the residual wage gap, and the determinants of the total wage differential between men and women. This procedure continues from Equation (4) by expressing the rate of change between year t and year u, and by using the notation Δ for the male–female difference in the variable that follows. The difference in the gender wage gap between two years is then

$$\Delta w_t - \Delta w_u = (\Delta X_t \beta_{mt} - \Delta X_u \beta_{mu}) + (\sigma_{mt} \Delta \theta_t - \sigma_{mu} \Delta \theta_u). \tag{5}$$

The final step is to choose year u as the base year by adding and subtracting the terms $\Delta X_t \beta_{mu}$ and $\sigma_{mu} \Delta \theta_t$. This algebraic manipulation yields the Juhn–Murphy–Pierce decomposition equation, which is as follows:

$$\Delta w_t - \Delta w_u = (\Delta X_t - \Delta X_u)\beta_{mu} + \Delta X_t (\beta_{mt} - \beta_{mu})$$
$$+ \sigma_{mu} (\Delta \theta_t - \Delta \theta_u) + (\sigma_{mt} - \sigma_{mu}) \Delta \theta_t. \tag{6}$$

Table 17.5 Oaxaca–Blinder decomposition of male–female wage gap (in log points)

	1983	1987–8	1999–2000	2004
All education groups				
Total M–F wage gap	0.767	0.721	0.725	0.710
Explained gap	0.244	0.249	0.235	0.156
Unexplained (residual) gap	0.523	0.472	0.490	0.554
% gap unexplained	68.2	65.5	67.6	78.0
Illiterate and some primary				
Total M–F wage gap	0.676	0.646	0.631	0.656
Explained gap	0.132	0.057	0.056	0.077
Unexplained (residual) gap	0.544	0.589	0.575	0.579
% gap unexplained	80.5	91.2	91.1	88.3
Primary school				
Total M–F wage gap	0.822	0.615	0.610	0.804
Explained gap	0.266	0.192	0.167	0.104
Unexplained (residual) gap	0.556	0.423	0.443	0.700
% gap unexplained	67.6	68.8	72.6	87.1
Middle school				
Total M–F wage gap	0.618	0.822	0.602	0.650
Explained gap	0.277	0.328	0.178	0.109
Unexplained (residual) gap	0.341	0.494	0.424	0.541
% gap unexplained	55.2	60.1	70.4	83.2
High school and above				
Total M–F wage gap	0.524	0.312	0.557	0.440
Explained gap	0.201	0.215	0.201	0.133
Unexplained (residual) gap	0.323	0.097	0.356	0.307
% gap unexplained	61.6	31.1	63.9	69.8

Note: The total wage gap is male wages—female wages; the explained wage gap is gender differences in observed characteristics weighted by male coefficients; and the residual wage gap is the portion that cannot be explained by differences in characteristics. All results are in log points, except the unexplained gap as a share of the total wage gap is in percentage points.

On the right-hand side, the first term represents the change in the gender wage gap due to observed worker characteristics, while the second term shows the change due to market returns to these observed characteristics. The third term captures changes in the gender wage gap due to unobserved characteristics. This term is interpreted as changes in the position of women in the male residual wage distribution. The last term represents changes in the gender wage gap due to returns to unobserved characteristics, as reflected in a narrowing or widening in the dispersion of men's residual wages. For each education group, we perform this decomposition for every year of available NSSO data. To avoid possible bias from choosing a particular year to represent the base year u, we use the average across the four years of data to measure year u. This procedure results in four observations for each term of the equation, which are then regressed on a linear spline with a break point in

1987. We chose 1987 as a plausible break point, given that many of the results in the stylized facts section point to 1987 as a pivotal year for structural changes in the labor market.

Coefficients on the time trend variables from these spline regressions represent annual rates of change in the decomposition terms. These results are reported in Table 17.6. The table shows results for the entire 1983–2004 period as well as the 1983–7 and 1987–2004 sub-periods. A negative sign indicates that the male–female gap has become smaller, and a positive

Table 17.6 Annual rates of change in the male–female wage gap (in %)

	1983–7 Sub-Period	1987–2004 Sub-Period	1983–2004 Total
All education levels			
Total change in gap	−0.249	−0.452	−0.298
Change due to observed characteristics	0.148	−2.499	−0.487
Change due to observed returns	−0.080	1.063	0.194
Change due to unobserved characteristics	−0.416	2.845	0.366
Change due to unobserved returns	0.099	−1.860	−0.371
Illiterate and some primary			
Total change in gap	−0.539	0.391	−0.316
Change due to observed characteristics	−0.254	−0.556	−0.327
Change due to observed returns	−0.101	1.222	0.216
Change due to unobserved characteristics	0.027	2.072	0.518
Change due to unobserved returns	−0.211	−2.346	−0.723
Primary school			
Total change in gap	−2.007	4.020	−0.560
Change due to observed characteristics	−0.582	−0.727	−0.616
Change due to observed returns	0.092	−0.713	−0.101
Change due to unobserved characteristics	−1.694	8.593	0.775
Change due to unobserved returns	0.177	−3.134	−0.618
Middle school			
Total change in gap	−0.189	0.430	−0.041
Change due to observed characteristics	−0.641	−0.896	−0.702
Change due to observed returns	−0.298	0.224	−0.173
Change due to unobserved characteristics	0.839	2.695	1.284
Change due to unobserved returns	−0.089	−1.593	−0.450
High school and above			
Total change in gap	1.845	−1.684	0.998
Change due to observed characteristics	0.482	−2.175	−0.156
Change due to observed returns	0.129	−0.135	0.065
Change due to unobserved characteristics	1.069	1.581	1.192
Change due to unobserved returns	0.166	−0.955	−0.103

Note: For each education group, we perform the Juhn, Murphy, and Pierce decomposition for each year of available NSSO data. This procedure results in four observations for each term of the equation, which are then regressed on a linear spline with a break point in 1987. Coefficients on the time trend variables are reported above. A negative sign indicates that the male–female gap has become smaller, and a positive number means the male–female gap has grown larger.

number means the male–female gap has grown larger. In each column and for each education group, the total change in the wage gap must sum to the changes due to the four components (observed characteristics, observed returns, unobserved characteristics, and unobserved returns).

The top row of Table 17.6 indicates that the overall gender wage gap narrowed slightly during the period of analysis, with forces in opposing directions preventing large changes in either direction. Central among these forces for the aggregate wage gap is a strong widening in the wage gap due to unobserved characteristics after 1987 (that is, some combination of increasing gender differences in unobserved abilities, increasing female intermittency, and growing wage discrimination by gender. On average, changes in unobserved gender-specific characteristics caused the wage gap to widen by 2.8% per year between 1987 and 2004. Also contributing to wider wage gaps is the growing dispersion in the returns to education and returns to other observed skills, which caused the total wage gap between men and women to widen by 1.1% per year between 1987 and 2004. Helping women overall is the relative improvement in their educational attainment and in other observed skills. This relative improvement contributed to a narrowing in the total wage gap of about 0.5% per year after 1987. The narrowing in residual male returns had an even larger contribution (about 1.9% annually) in helping to reduce the overall disparity between men's and women's wages.

The remaining results in Table 17.6 for the disaggregated education groups consistently indicate that changes in unobserved gender-specific characteristics are a sizable share of the divergence in (total) male–female wage gaps across all four education groups. This component grows by as much as 8.6% per year for individuals with primary school attainment, far outweighing any other component for that education group. The other common conclusion across all education groups is a narrowing in the wage gap due to women's relative gains in observed characteristics after 1987, and for the entire period as a whole. However, for high-school and college-educated women, this gain in observed skills is not enough to offset the losses in unobserved characteristics, and the total wage gap for the most highly-educated women increases for the period as a whole.

Forces behind the growing gap in unobserved characteristics

An important and interesting question is why the gender gap in unobserved characteristics widens for all education groups after 1987. One explanation is growing gender differences in the unmeasured abilities of new entrants into the labor market. One could argue that an influx of lower-skilled women into the manufacturing labor force during the period may have reduced the average wages of all working women. Under such a scenario, the decomposition analysis would attribute the growing gender wage gap to a widening gap between men and women in unobserved characteristics. Since the NSSO surveys do not follow the same workers over time, we cannot control for changes in unobserved ability as new workers enter the manufacturing sector. Hence, the hypothesis regarding the low ability of new labor market entrants is difficult to test in our data. However, evidence reported in Table 17.1 shows that the large shift for women workers out of agriculture was redirected more toward services than manufacturing. Coupled with large gains across India in women's literacy rates during the period, these broad changes suggest that an influx of lower-skilled women into manufacturing is unlikely to be the main reason behind the growing gap in unobserved characteristics.

A second explanation is growing differences between male and female workers in unmeasured skills as they age. This argument is particularly relevant if women spend time out of the labor force following childbirth. If labor force commitment by men and women diverged during the period of analysis due to women's increasing intermittency, our measure of potential experience would not be able to capture this change. As a consequence, the expanding gap in unobserved characteristics calculated by the decomposition may reflect women's increasing intermittency. However, demographic evidence from the World Bank (2005) suggests that this is unlikely to be the case. The total fertility rate (births per woman) in India decreased from 3.8 in 1990 to 2.9 in 2003. Moreover, the female labor force participation rate for ages 15–64 increased from 42.4% in 1990 to 45.2% in 2003. Finally, the proportion of the labor force that is female increased slightly from 31.2% in 1990 to 32.6% in 2003 (World Bank 2005).

The final explanation for the growing residual wage gap is an increase in wage discrimination against female workers. This result would counter the implications of the neoclassical theory on discrimination. The neoclassical theory of labor market discrimination implies that increased competition from international trade will reduce the wage gap. In a market economy where discrimination is costly, employers are less able to indulge their tastes for discrimination as competitive forces drive down profit margins (Becker 1971). To test this idea, we perform industry-level regressions to test the theoretical model of the gender wage gap and foreign trade competition. The empirics examine the relationship between the male–female wage gap and variations across industry and time in the exposure to competition from international trade, while controlling for changes in worker characteristics and domestic concentration. Our identification strategy centers on comparing India's more concentrated manufacturing industries, where firms enjoyed rents and could indulge in their taste for discrimination, with India's less concentrated manufacturing industries, where firms experienced greater domestic competition and were less able to discriminate.[5]

The residual wage series for male and female workers is constructed following the Oaxaca–Blinder decomposition procedure. We aggregate the residual wages by industry and year, and then estimate the determinants of residual wage gaps between men and women at the industry level as follows:

$$w_{imt} - w_{ift} = \beta_0 + C_{it}\,\beta_1 + T_{it}\,\beta_2 + Y\,\beta_3 + C_{it}\,T_{it}\,\beta_4 + C_{it}\,Y\,\beta_5$$
$$+ T_{it}\,Y\,\beta_6 + C_{it}\,T_{it}\,Y\,\beta_7 + \varepsilon_{it}. \tag{7}$$

The notation w_{imt} denotes total male residual wages in industry i and year t, w_{ift} denotes total female residual wages in industry i and year t; C_{it} measures domestic concentration by industry and year; T_{it} represents competition from international trade by industry and year; and Y represents the year. The final term contains the interaction between domestic concentration and international competition and year $(C_{it}T_{it}Y)$. We focus on this term's coefficient as it represents the impact of international trade competition in concentrated industries over time. All regressions are weighted with industry-level employment shares, and year and concentration are included as continuous variables. We use 28 industry classifications, as shown in Appendix Table 17.A2.

Equation (7) is estimated using a panel data set of industry-level observations over time. These results are reported in Table 17.7 for six different models. The first three models use ordinary least squares, while models 4–6 use fixed effects to control for time-invariant characteristics that are specific to each of the industries. The models differ according to the measurement of trade shares: models 1 and 4 use export shares, models 2 and 5 use import shares, and models 3 and 6 use total trade (exports plus imports) shares.

Results on the interaction term for concentration, trade, and year in Table 17.7 indicate that across model specifications, increasing trade openness in more concentrated industries is associated with higher wage gaps between men and women. The coefficient on this interaction term is positive and statistically significant in all six models. The observed changes in the gender pay differentials are likely to have arisen due to pressures from international trade since, as noted above, more concentrated industries are exposed to less domestic competition.

Discussion and conclusion

If women are bearing a disproportionately large share of the costs of trade liberalization, then a number of policy measures that build women's human capital and strengthen the social safety net may help ease the burden. A policy priority is to achieve gender equality at all education levels so that women have access to the same range of occupational choices as men. Improved educational opportunities also include greater access for working-age women to vocational education; this may be especially useful for women who are displaced as a consequence of increased competition from abroad. Closely related, access to firm-specific training and new programs for accreditation for workers' skills can help to close the gender gap. By building and upgrading skills, vocational education programs and improved opportunities for on-the-job training can help improve women's ability to obtain a

Table 17.7 Test of male–female residual wage gaps and trade competition (in log points; standard errors in parentheses)

	Model 1	Model 2	Model 3	Model 4	Model 5	Model 6
Concentration	0.395	−0.690*	1.489*	0.357	−1.098**	0.896*
	(0.719)	(0.406)	(0.852)	(0.460)	(0.443)	(0.472)
Trade	0.573*	0.462***	0.883***	0.689**	0.425***	0.789***
	(0.321)	(0.110)	(0.240)	(0.289)	(0.152)	(0.267)
Year	0.424	−0.351**	0.263	0.071	−0.314***	0.037
	(0.378)	(0.166)	(0.373)	(0.196)	(0.104)	(0.216)
Concen x Trade	−0.574	−0.756***	−1.213***	−0.732**	−0.562***	−0.997***
	(0.386)	(0.151)	(0.336)	(0.327)	(0.171)	(0.309)
Concen x Year	−0.490	0.307	−0.488	−0.149	0.316***	−0.180
	(0.417)	(0.197)	(0.428)	(0.227)	(0.113)	(0.235)
Trade x Year	−0.305	−0.074	−0.237	−0.224	−0.076	−0.187
	(0.186)	(0.065)	(0.158)	(0.149)	(0.046)	(0.127)
Concen x Trade x Year	0.337*	0.151**	0.343*	0.270*	0.122**	0.263*
	(0.202)	(0.074)	(0.174)	(0.164)	(0.055)	(0.138)
Constant	−0.031	1.304***	−0.446			
	(0.641)	(0.316)	(0.587)			
Number observations	112	112	112	112	112	112
R^2	0.161	0.301	0.157	0.892	0.892	0.894

Note: The dependent variable in all models is the male–female residual wage gap. Models 1–3 estimate OLS regressions. Models 4–6 estimate Fixed Effects regressions, which include 28 industry dummies. In Models 1 and 4, trade is exports/output; in Models 2 and 5, trade is imports/output; and in Models 3 and 6, trade is (exports + imports)/output. All regressions are weighted with industry-level employment shares; year and concentration are both continuous variables. The notation *** denotes statistically significant at the 0.01 level; ** at the 0.05 level, and * at the 0.10 level.

wider range of jobs, which, in turn, can help boost women's relative pay. Additionally, stronger enforcement of India's equal pay and equal opportunity legislation, which dates back to the late 1950s, may reduce discriminatory pay practices that appear to contribute to rising residual wage gaps in the manufacturing sector.

To the extent that productivity enhancing policies are not enough to safeguard women who are adversely affected by trade, improved social safety nets can help to reduce the burden that many low-wage women face. For example, greater public provision of day-care services for very young children and after-school services for school-age children can help to decrease the time and budgetary constraints that India's factory workers experience. Furthermore, women employed in export-producing factories often remit high shares of their income to families in the rural sector, at potentially great personal cost. Poor social safety nets in the rural sector contribute to this reliance on remittances from these women. Policy reforms that create a viable infrastructure in the rural sector, including social security, may help to reduce the dependence on remittances, and so ease the pressure on such workers. By analyzing the effects of India's liberalization on women's compensation, and by highlighting the fact that female employees in manufacturing industries appear to fare less well compared to their male counterparts, this study makes an important contribution to the literature by demonstrating that not everyone benefited equally as a consequence of the reforms.

Notes

*   We are indebted to Narayanan Subramanian, Elizabeth Brainerd, Rachel McCulloch, Joe Zveglich, and participants in the University of Pennsylvania Family Macro workshop for their helpful suggestions. Funding from Brandeis University's Theodore and Jane Norman research grant is gratefully acknowledged. The usual caveat applies.

1   Agesa and Hamilton (2004) apply a similar methodology to data from the United States in the context of the racial wage gap for men, and they also find little evidence that increasing competition from international trade reduces the racial wage gap.

2   To prevent distortions from outliers in the mean regressions, individuals with implausibly high weekly cash wages are dropped from the sample. As the cut-off points, we use the rupee equivalent of US\$ 4,000 in real 1999 dollars. This cutoff amounts to 41,360 rupees for rural and urban samples in 1983; 66,101.45 rupees for the rural sample and 73,732.16 rupees for the urban sample in 1987–8; 614,757.20 rupees for the rural sample and 707,790.42 rupees for the urban sample in 1999; and 705,184.69 rupees for the rural sample and 876, 846.86 for the urban sample in 2004.

3   The ASI cover the years 1980/1 through to 2003/4, where 19801 represents April 1980 through March 1981, and so forth. Because the 2004/5 ASI have not yet been released, we applied the one-year historical average growth rate from 2002/3 to 2003/4 to the base values for 2003/4 in each industry in order to estimate industry-level output and number of establishments for 2004/5. In the regression estimates, we conducted robustness checks that included applying the two-year and three-

year historical average growth rates, and the magnitudes, signs, and significance levels on the key interaction term of interest did not vary substantially.
4 The idea that children bear some of the adjustment costs of trade reforms is consistent with findings in Menon (2007) which finds that states in India that are unionized have higher incidences of labor unrest, disruptions in household earnings, and child labor.
5 This approach was originally developed in Borjas and Ramey (1995) in the context of overall US wage inequality.

References

Agesa, J. and D. Hamilton (2004) "Competition and Wage Discrimination: The Effects of Interindustry Concentration and Import Penetration." *Social Science Quarterly* 85(1): 121–35.

Becker, G. (1971) *The Economics of Discrimination*, second edition. Chicago: University of Chicago Press.

Berik, G., Y. Rodgers, and J. Zveglich (2004) "International Trade and Gender Wage Discrimination: Evidence from East Asia." *Review of Development Economics* 8(2): 237–54.

Bhaumik, S. K. (2003) "Casualisation of the Workforce in India, 1983–2002," *Indian Journal of Labour Economics* 46(4): 907–26.

Black, S. and E. Brainerd (2004) "Importing Equality? The Impact of Globalization on Gender Discrimination." *Industrial and Labor Relations Review* 57(4): 540–59.

Blinder, A. S. (1973) "Wage Discrimination: Reduced Form and Structural Estimates." *Journal of Human Resources* 8(4): 436–55.

Borjas, G. and V. Ramey (1995) "Foreign Competition, Market Power, and Wage Inequality." *Quarterly Journal of Economics* 110(4): 1075–110.

Central Statistical Organization (1970) *National Industrial Classification 1970*. New Delhi, India: Department of Statistics, Ministry of Planning.

——. (1998) *National Industrial Classification (All Economic Activities) 1998*. New Delhi, India: Department of Statistics, Ministry of Planning and Programme Implementation.

Edmonds, E., N. Pavcnik, and P. Topalova (2005) "Trade Liberalization, Child Labor, and Schooling: Evidence from India." Mimeo. Dartmouth University.

Hazarika, G. and R. Otero (2004) "Foreign Trade and the Gender Earnings Differential in Urban Mexico." *Journal of Economic Integration* 19(2): 353–73.

Juhn, C., K. Murphy, and B. Pierce (1991) "Accounting for the Slowdown in Black–White Wage Convergence," in *Workers and Their Wages: Changing Patterns in the United States*, edited by M. Kosters (Washington, DC: American Enterprise Institute Press), pp. 107–43.

Kijima, Y. (2006) "Why did Wage Inequality Increase? Evidence from Urban India." *Journal of Development Economics* 81(1): 97–117.

Krishna, P. and D. Mitra (1998) "Trade Liberalization, Market Discipline and Productivity Growth: New Evidence from India." *Journal of Development Economics* 56(2): 447–62.

Menon, N. (2007) "The Relationship between Labor Unionization and the Number of Working Children in India." Mimeo. Brandeis University.

Mishra, P. and U. Kumar (2005) "Trade Liberalization and Wage Inequality: Evidence from India." International Monetary Fund Working Paper 05/20. Washington, DC: International Monetary Fund.

Nicita, A. and M. Olarreaga (2006) "Trade, Production and Protection 1976–2004." World Bank Database (http://www.worldbank.org/trade).

Oaxaca, R. (1973) "Male–Female Differentials in Urban Labor Markets." *International Economic Review* 14(3): 693–709.

Oostendorp, R. (2004) "Globalization and the Gender Wage Gap." World Bank Policy Research Working Paper 3256.

Sivadasan, J. and J. Slemrod (2006) "Tax Law Changes, Income Shifting and Measured Wage Inequality: Evidence from India." National Bureau of Economic Research Working Paper 12240. Cambridge, MA: National Bureau of Economic Research.

Topalova, P. (2005) "Trade Liberalization, Poverty and Inequality: Evidence from Indian Districts." National Bureau of Economic Research Working Paper 11614. Cambridge, MA: National Bureau of Economic Research.

World Bank (2005) *World Development Indicators, 2005*. Washington DC: World Bank.

Appendix

Table 17.A1 Descriptive and regression analyses: variables and data sources

Variable	Description	Data source
Gender wage gap	Male wages—female wages, by industry (unadjusted wages and residual wages)	National Sample Survey Organization (NSSO) 1983, 1987–8, 1999–2000, 2004
Wage deflator	Wholesale price index for manufactured products	Ministry of Commerce and Industry, Government of India, 1980–1–2004–5
Export value	Dollar value of India's exports, by industry	Trade, Production and Protection Database (Nicita and Olarreaga 2006), 1980–2004
Import value	Dollar value of India's imports, by industry	Trade, Production and Protection Database (Nicita and Olarreaga 2006), 1980–2004
Tariffs	Average tariff rates, by industry	Trade, Production and Protection Database (Nicita and Olarreaga 2006), 1980–2004
Domestic output	Total output, in rupees, by industry	Annual Survey of Industries (ASI), 1980/1–2003/4
Exchange rate	Average annual rupee/US$ exchange rate	Reserve Bank of India, 1980/1–2004/5
Domestic concentration	(1—Number establishments/output), by industry	Annual Survey of Industries (ASI), 1980/1–2003/4

Table 17.A2 Concordance between ISIC revision 2, NIC 1970, and NIC 1998 codes

Labels	ISIC (rev 2)	NIC 1970	NIC 1998
Food products	311–12	200–19	1511–49
Beverages	313	220–4	1551–4
Tobacco	314	225–9	1600
Textiles	321	230–63, 266–9	1711–30
Wearing apparel (except footwear)	322	264, 265	1810
Leather products	323	290, 292–3, 295–9	1820–1912
Footwear (except rubber or plastic)	324	291	1920
Wood products (except furniture)	331	270–5, 279	2010–29
Furniture (except metal)	332	276–7	3610
Paper and products	341	280–3	2101–9
Printing and publishing	342	284–9	2211–30
Industrial chemicals	351	294, 310–11, 316	2411–13, 2430
Other chemicals	352	312–15, 317–19	2421–9
Petroleum refinery	353	304	2320
Miscellaneous petroleum and coal products	354	305–7	2310, 2330
Rubber products	355	300–2	2511–19
Plastic products	356	303	2520
Pottery, china, earthenware	361	322, 323	2691
Glass and products	362	321	2610
Other non-metallic mineral products	369	320, 324–9	2692–9
Iron and steel	371	330–2	2710
Non-ferrous metals	372	333–9, 344	2720–32, 2891–2
Fabricated metal products	381	340–3, 345–9	2811–12, 2893–9
Machinery (except electrical)	382	350–9	2813, 2911–30, 3000
Machinery (electric)	383	360–9	3110–230
Transport equipment	384	370–9	3410–599
Professional and scientific equipment	385	380–2	3311–30
Other manufactured products	390	383–9	3691–9

Source: Created by authors, with reference to data in Sivadasan and Slemrod (2006) and Central Statistical Organization (1970, 1998).

Table 17.A3 Means and standard deviations for wage earners in manufacturing, 1983–2004

	Male 1983	Female 1983	Male 2004	Female 2004
Variable				
Log real weekly cash wages in rupees	3.978 (0.937)	3.211 (0.793)	4.650 (0.872)	3.940 (0.972)
Dummy for illiterate individual	0.215 (0.411)	0.603 (0.489)	0.180 (0.384)	0.432 (0.496)
Dummy for individual with below primary years of schooling	0.151 (0.358)	0.115 (0.319)	0.085 (0.279)	0.060 (0.237)
Dummy for individual with primary school	0.207 (0.405)	0.152 (0.359)	0.171 (0.376)	0.154 (0.361)
Dummy for individual with middle school	0.185 (0.388)	0.061 (0.240)	0.256 (0.436)	0.124 (0.330)
Dummy for individual with secondary school	0.182 (0.386)	0.057 (0.232)	0.192 (0.394)	0.108 (0.310)
Dummy for individual with graduate school	0.059 (0.236)	0.012 (0.109)	0.117 (0.321)	0.123 (0.328)
Years of potential experience for individual	20.546 (12.016)	21.371 (12.512)	19.200 (11.679)	21.792 (12.881)
Years of potential experience for individual squared/100	5.665 (6.011)	6.132 (6.508)	5.050 (5.563)	6.406 (6.317)
Dummy for individual with no technical education	0.935 (0.246)	0.979 (0.142)	0.912 (0.283)	0.937 (0.243)
Dummy for individual who is currently married	0.724 (0.447)	0.595 (0.491)	0.701 (0.458)	0.699 (0.459)
Dummy for scheduled-tribe/scheduled-caste individual	0.177 (0.381)	0.206 (0.405)	0.219 (0.413)	0.286 (0.452)
Dummy for self-employed individual	0.112 (0.315)	0.206 (0.405)	0.098 (0.298)	0.159 (0.366)
Dummy for individual of Hindu religion	0.825 (0.380)	0.768 (0.422)	0.844 (0.363)	0.859 (0.348)
Dummy for households with male heads	0.962 (0.192)	0.785 (0.411)	0.940 (0.238)	0.812 (0.391)
Dummy for rural areas	0.296 (0.457)	0.531 (0.499)	0.432 (0.495)	0.584 (0.493)
Number of pre-school children in household	0.636 (0.863)	0.626 (0.877)	0.502 (0.792)	0.396 (0.721)
Dummy for northern states of India	0.215 (0.411)	0.090 (0.287)	0.264 (0.441)	0.105 (0.306)
Dummy for southern states of India	0.287 (0.452)	0.591 (0.492)	0.266 (0.442)	0.437 (0.496)
Dummy for eastern states of India	0.167 (0.373)	0.093 (0.290)	0.110 (0.313)	0.100 (0.300)
Dummy for western states of India	0.331 (0.471)	0.225 (0.418)	0.360 (0.480)	0.358 (0.480)
Number of observations	14,435	2,517	5,155	1,004

Standard deviations in parentheses. Sample in each year consists of working age population (15–60 years of age) with positive cash wages employed in the manufacturing industry.

Table 17.A4 Coefficient estimates from male wage regressions (in log points; standard errors in parentheses)

	1983	1987–8	1999–2000	2004
Dummy for individual with below primary years of schooling	0.070*** (0.025)	0.054* (0.031)	0.103*** (0.033)	0.141*** (0.044)
Dummy for individual with primary school	0.147*** (0.024)	0.109*** (0.029)	0.068** (0.032)	0.279*** (0.037)
Dummy for individual with middle school	0.196*** (0.025)	0.248*** (0.031)	0.228*** (0.030)	0.355*** (0.036)
Dummy for individual with secondary school	0.460*** (0.028)	0.501*** (0.031)	0.473*** (0.030)	0.715*** (0.040)
Dummy for individual with graduate school	0.818*** (0.039)	0.949*** (0.038)	1.024*** (0.037)	1.246*** (0.050)
Years of potential experience for individual	0.041*** (0.003)	0.047*** (0.003)	0.041*** (0.003)	0.059*** (0.004)
Years of potential experience for individual squared/100	−0.056*** (0.005)	−0.061*** (0.006)	−0.059*** (0.005)	−0.092*** (0.008)
Dummy for individual with no technical education	−0.186*** (0.032)	−0.274*** (0.032)	−0.327*** (0.034)	−0.315*** (0.042)
Dummy for individual who is currently married	0.120*** (0.022)	0.140*** (0.027)	0.093*** (0.023)	−0.068** (0.034)
Dummy for scheduled-tribe/ scheduled-caste individual	−0.091*** (0.020)	−0.035 (0.025)	−0.032* (0.018)	−0.073*** (0.027)
Dummy for self-employed individual	−0.135*** (0.025)	−0.180*** (0.029)	−0.045** (0.021)	−0.278*** (0.037)
Dummy for individual of Hindu religion	0.004 (0.020)	0.009 (0.023)	−0.051** (0.024)	0.013 (0.030)
Dummy for households with male heads	0.044 (0.039)	0.117*** (0.043)	0.147** (0.067)	0.101** (0.045)
Dummy for rural areas	−0.105*** (0.017)	0.185*** (0.028)	−0.007 (0.018)	0.004 (0.023)
Number of pre-school children in household	0.003 (0.009)	−0.003 (0.011)	0.003 (0.012)	0.009 (0.014)
Dummy for northern states of India	−0.065*** (0.021)	0.043* (0.024)	0.159*** (0.022)	0.135*** (0.028)
Dummy for southern states of India	−0.238*** (0.019)	−0.192*** (0.022)	−0.029 (0.021)	−0.072*** (0.027)
Dummy for eastern states of India	−0.203*** (0.022)	−0.047* (0.026)	0.152*** (0.031)	−0.055 (0.037)
Constant	3.461*** (0.062)	3.295*** (0.067)	3.754*** (0.085)	3.806*** (0.081)
Number observations	14,426	12,028	11,150	5,155
Adjusted R^2	0.115	0.148	0.157	0.259

Note: All estimates are from weighted ordinary least squares regressions. The notation *** indicates statistically significant at the 0.01 level; ** at the 0.05 level, and * at the 0.10 level.

Part IV

Human capital, productivity, and gender

18 Multidimensional human capital, wages, and endogenous employment status in Ghana

Niels-Hugo Blunch[*]

1 Introduction

One of the most important ways to improve one's livelihood comes through the acquisition of education and its subsequent return in the labor market. As a consequence, the issue of education—and especially of how to improve it and bring more access to more people—has been at the center of the policy debate in most countries for quite some time. The effect of education on labor market outcomes, especially earnings, has also received considerable interest in the academic literature, which has confirmed the positive association between education and economic success.[1]

Yet, there are still issues related to education and labor market outcomes that would seem to require more attention, both related to the transition into the labor market and among different employment categories and to enumeration. Which types of education are successful in generating employment or self-employment? How are different types and levels of education enumerated? How much of the enumeration is accounted for by basic literacy and numeracy ability and how much by other human capital? These questions are particularly relevant for developing countries. The evidence here is more scarce due to data limitations but at the same time, addressing these questions is even more pertinent due to having fewer resources available for education.

Hence, while much of the human capital literature for developed countries has focused on formal education and within this further focused on higher levels of education, other types and other levels of education may be more relevant. In Ghana, for example, while few people attend tertiary education, technical-vocational education is popular. Also, due to the low levels of formal educational attainment in Ghana, adult literacy programs have been offered for a number of years. The labor market in developing countries also differs from developed countries by having more individuals working either as self-employees or as unpaid family workers. Whereas previous studies have often focused on regular wage employees, a more appropriate approach may be to include all categories of work simultaneously.

Estimating wage and employment status equations simultaneously, this paper examines the three questions posed earlier for the case of Ghana, taking the issues discussed previously into account. First, the set of human capital variables included in the wage and employment equations contain formal education, technical-vocational education, adult literacy programs, and basic literacy and numeracy, thus broadening the more common approach of focusing on formal education only. This will allow for contrasting and comparing the relative impact of different types and levels of education, as well as literacy and numeracy, on wages and employment status. Second, the categories in the employment status equation include regular wage employees, the self-employed, unpaid family workers, and individuals not working. In addition to enabling me to examine the returns to human capital among regular wage employees and the self-employed, this also allows me to examine how different human capital components affect the transition among different labor market categories, say, between unemployment and self-employment or between being an unpaid family worker and being self-employed. In doing so, the empirical analyses account for the endogeneity of employment status using a two-stage procedure, where the employment status is estimated in the first stage, and conditional on employment status, the wage structure is then estimated in the second stage.

2 Conceptual framework

This section presents a theoretical analysis of wages and employment status and how they are affected by skills and schooling. Conditional on employment status (the j subscript), wages are assumed to be a function of skills (S); other observed individual background characteristics including age, gender, and geographical location (B); and unobserved individual characteristics including ability (δ), giving rise to the following wage function:

$$W_j = W_j (S, B, \delta) \tag{1}$$

In (1), an increase in skills leads to an increase in wages also, holding the other factors constant.

I extend this discussion by considering, first, the different routes though which skills may be acquired, and, second, different types of skill. Following Blunch (2006), there are several routes for achieving skills, namely formal schooling obtained during childhood, and adult literacy program participation later in life. Similarly, there are different skills that may affect wages through separate channels. Most importantly, an individual's wages may increase from participation in childhood schooling. This could be due to a direct productivity effect from cognitive skills such as literacy and numeracy in line with a standard human capital explanation or from non-cognitive skills such as socialization or discipline skills (Heckman, Stixrud, and Urzua 2006). Alternatively, earnings capacity may increase either from credentialism or signaling (Spence 1973) obtained from schooling, especially at higher levels.

Wages may also increase from learning about income-generating activities, which is an integral component of adult literacy programs in Ghana (Blunch and Pörtner 2005). In addition to merely learning about different income-generating activities, participants also frequently directly engage in income-generating activities. Under the guidance of the teacher, participants may, for example, engage in pottery, weaving, or groundnut oil extraction. Both the learning and the more practical of these program components may affect wages (failing that, they still may affect the labor supply of participants, especially in terms of moving from being economically inactive to becoming self-employed).

From (1), the wage structure is conditional on employment status, so that employment status clearly affects wages—for example, regular employees might earn higher wages than the self-employed, all other things being equal.[2] While this may be accounted for by merely including employment status as a variable in the vector of other observed background characteristics (*B*), employment status might more appropriately be treated as endogenous. For example, regular employees may be systematically different from individuals who are either self-employed or working as unpaid family workers. Similarly, individuals who are inactive may be systematically different from either of these groups. Additionally, however, the returns to skills and schooling may differ systematically, depending on employment. For example, one might expect that the returns to certain skills may be greater for regular wage employees than for self-employed workers.

These considerations lead me to consider employment status as being governed by a separate process; this depends on five factors: skills (*S*), other observed individual background characteristics described previously (*B*), unobserved individual characteristics, including employment status preferences (*δ*), expected wages if working as a regular wage employee (*W₁*) and as a self-employed worker (*W₂*), and other job characteristics (*η*), giving rise to the following employment status[3] function:

$$E = E (S, P, B, \delta, W_1, W_2, \eta) \tag{2}$$

The pathways through which skills and the other factors affect employment status in (2) include the following. Education may have a non-productivity effect, for example through signaling, connections or networks. For example, an educated individual would seem to be more likely to be working than not working and also more likely to be a regular wage employee than to be either self-employed or working as an unpaid family workers. Parental occupation is likely to affect search cost, so that individuals whose parents were white-collar workers would also seem to be more likely to work and, conditional on working, also more likely to be regular wage employees than to be either self-employed or unpaid family workers. The individual may also have strong preferences for one employment status over another, for example preferring the relative autonomy of self-employment or the job-security of being a regular wage employee. The employment choice is, thus, a trade-off between opportunity and return: the individual simply chooses the employment status, which yields the highest indirect utility in terms of monetary and non-monetary returns, conditional on having access to the employment category in question.[4]

From this discussion, there are several implications for the empirical analyses. First, due to the possibility of employment status being endogenous, this framework highlights the importance of modeling the determinants of wages and employment status simultaneously. Second, the model points to the variables that should be included in the empirical analyses as explanatory variables. These include skills, parental employment status, and other observed individual background characteristics such as age, gender, and geographical location. Third, the model indicates that skills have both direct and indirect effects on wages, the latter coming through the impact on employment status.

Based on the previous discussion I will examine whether basic literacy and numeracy (basic cognitive skills) affect wages, in particular whether they have effects beyond those of schooling itself. Additionally, I will examine what the effect is on the schooling estimates from introducing literacy and numeracy. This effectively amounts to examining, on one hand, the relative importance of basic cognitive skills vis-à-vis schooling for individual earnings capacity, and, on the other, the efficiency of schooling in cognitive skills production.

I will also examine the impact of basic literacy and numeracy and schooling on employment status. As with the wage analyses, the focus is on whether skills have effects beyond those of schooling itself. This effectively amounts to examining the possibility of indirect wage effects—that is, effects coming through the effect on employment status.

For both sets of analyses two additional issues will be examined. First, one may ask whether economic conditions affect the returns to education and literacy and numeracy and/or their effect on employment status. Here, it is possible that both the returns to education and literacy and numeracy and their effect on employment status vary with characteristics such as geographical location; that is, rather than merely including geographical location in equations (1) and (2), these equations could be made conditional on geographical location. For example, I expect the returns to schooling and literacy and numeracy to be higher in areas where the returns to skilled labor are higher and in areas where incomes and/or the cost of living are higher.[5] The insight here is that urban areas are generally better off in terms of economic conditions than rural areas.[6] Second, attitudinal and social factors may affect schooling and skills returns and employment status, especially gender. Certainly, in many developing countries social norms and traditions prescribe "traditional" gender roles, which could, in turn, affect education and labor market outcomes and lead to substantial gender wage and employment status gaps. For example, it might be expected that males both earn more and are more likely to be regular wage employees than females, controlling for other factors.

3 Previous research

Starting with the literature on education and wages, this generally finds large private returns to education.[7] For example, reviewing 133 studies for 98 different countries, Psacharopoulos and Patrinos (2004) calculate the average private returns to a year of education to be 10%. Developing regions generally experience much higher returns to education than OECD countries. The regional average Mincerian return for sub-Saharan Africa, for example, is 11.7%, compared to 7.5% for OECD countries.

These general findings for the (formal) schooling–wage (earnings) relationship also have been established for Ghana. For example, Glewwe (1996, 1999) found that an additional year of schooling increased wages by about 8.5% for government and private sector workers as a whole. Similarly, positive effects of schooling are found on manufacturing sector wages (Teal 2000), non-farm self-employment income (Vijverberg 1995) and on farm and non-farm (i.e. wage income and self-employment) profit (Joliffe 2004).

Studies that have considered cognitive skills in the human capital-wage (earnings) relationship have generally found evidence of a separate effect from these skills, controlling for schooling. Adding controls for cognitive skills to a wage or earnings regression typically leads to a decrease in the estimated effect of formal schooling. In a seminal study of Kenya and Tanzania, Boissiere, Knight, and Sabot (1985) simultaneously considered formal educational attainment and cognitive skills. Introduction of the cognitive skills measures decreased the estimated association between formal educational attainment and log earnings by nearly two-thirds. Similar results are found in Moll's (1998) study of South Africa.[8]

The literature examining the impact of cognitive skills on earnings (wages) in Ghana is much in line with that from other countries. Including English reading and mathematics test scores in a study of public and private sector wages, Glewwe (1996)[9] found a positive and statistically significant effect from numeracy on government sector wages of about 2.5 to 3.5% depending on the specification—but not on private sector wages—even when formal educational attainment is included. English reading skills, on the other hand, were found to affect wages in the private sector positively, by about 3–3.5% but were not found to affect wages in the government sector. Years of schooling and teacher training were positive and statistically significant in the government sector, which was taken to indicate the existence of diploma effects.

The impact of cognitive skills on non-farm self-employment income in Ghana was examined by Vijverberg (1999), using the same data set as Glewwe (1996, 1999). Linear specifications with either schooling or cognitive skills did not yield significant effects of human capital on non-farm self-employment income while interacted models (with years of schooling and cognitive skills) led to "sporadic evidence of positive links between elements of human capital (schooling or skills) and enterprise income" (241).

Summing up, numerous studies find evidence of a positive association between formal schooling and wages. This is true for the general literature and also to some extent for the smaller literature, which examines wage determinants in Ghana. Only a subset of studies, for Ghana and elsewhere, incorporates literacy and numeracy in addition to formal educational attainment. The individual studies generally consider regular wage employment or self-employment separately, or alternatively aggregate employment categories, for example aggregating formal and non-formal (non-farm) employment into non-farm employment, rather than simultaneously examining regular wage employment and self-employment. Lastly, very few studies directly examine the effect of types of schooling other than formal schooling on wages (earnings). Participation in adult literacy programs or technical and vocational education may provide participants with literacy and numeracy and/or other skills, which may positively affect wages via their influence on productivity and therefore also would seem to belong in the human capital–wage relationship.

4 Estimation strategy and issues

From the conceptual framework in section 2, I have suggested that skills can affect wages either directly or indirectly through their impact on employment status. Empirically, the direct effects can be estimated by a Mincer equation (Mincer 1974), augmented with skills, whereas the indirect effects can be estimated by a multinomial logit model of employment status, including skills as explanatory variables. Again, the endogeneity of wages and employment status warrants an estimation strategy that takes this into account.

These considerations lead me to pursue a two-stage estimation procedure. In the first stage, the employment status is estimated by a multinomial logit model. Let the indirect utility of individual i associated with employment status j be given as:

$$v_{ij} = a_{0j} + a_{1j} S_i + a_{2j} B_i + a_{3j} P_i + \varepsilon_{ij} \tag{3}$$

where S_i includes variables for formal educational attainment, adult literacy program participation, and literacy and numeracy, P_i includes variables for parental employment status, and B_i include other (control) variables, including age, gender, and geographical location. ε_{ij} is an error-term capturing unobservables, and j = regular wage employee, self-employed, unpaid family worker, or not working. Individual i chooses employment status j if the indirect utility of status j exceeds that of all the other possible employment categories. Assuming that the errors across choices are independently and identically distributed such that $F(\varepsilon_{ii}) = \exp(e^{-\varepsilon_{ij}})$, this yields the multinomial logit model.

In the second stage, the conditional wage equation is estimated, including the Durbin–McFadden (1984) correction for selectivity (based on the multi-nomial logit model from the first stage):

$$W_{ij} = \beta_{0j} + \beta_{1j} S_i + \beta_{2j} B_i + \beta_{3j} \hat{\lambda}_{ij} + \psi_{ij}, \tag{4}$$

where W_{ij} denotes (log) wages for individual i in employment status j, $\hat{\lambda}_{ij}$ is a vector of selection-terms (inverse Mills ratios) estimated from the first-stage employment equation, ξ_{ij} is an error-term capturing unobservables, and the other variables are defined similarly to equation (3). While the parameter estimates are consistent, the standard errors must be corrected to take the two-stage nature of the estimation procedure into account. This is done by bootstrapping the standard errors. Also, the survey design (see the next section) is explicitly accounted for by incorporating sampling weights and clustering in the estimations throughout. In order to identify the model one or more exclusion restrictions must be imposed; that is, one or more variables should be included in the employment status equation (4) but excluded from the wage equation (3). The parental occupation measures play that role, although this requires the somewhat unrealistic assumption that parental occupation has no independent effect on productivity. Marital status and marital status interacted with gender are included as additional exclusion restrictions. As motivated earlier, wage and employment status equations are estimated for the full sample, for females and males separately, for rural and urban areas separately, and for individuals with no formal education.

5 Data

The empirical analyses of this paper examine household survey data from the fourth round of the Ghana Living Standards Survey. The survey gathered information on income, labor supply, literacy and numeracy, formal educational attainment, and participation in adult literacy courses as well as other information such as age, gender, and geographical location.

One primary dependent variable in this paper is the natural logarithm of the hourly wage rate for the person's main occupation (if any); it is calculated as the average hourly earnings, including all monetary and (monetized) non-monetary payments. The other primary dependent variable in this paper is employment status: working for pay for another enterprise (employee), working for pay for one's own enterprise (self-employed), working but not for pay (unpaid family worker), and not working (economically inactive).

Moving to the explanatory variables, I construct a binary "functional literacy" measure. This measure is if the individual can either write in a Ghanaian language *or* English *and* do written calculations, and zero otherwise (in sensitivity analyses I examine other specifications of cognitive skills). Educational attainment is measured as the highest level completed, ranging from "none" through "university" and also includes technical/vocational training. I consider a set of four binary variables, corresponding to the completion of primary school, middle and junior secondary school, secondary school and above, and technical/vocational training.[10] I also construct a binary measure, indicating whether an individual has ever attended an adult literacy course program.[11] Other explanatory variables include controls for rural–urban location and female gender, as well as age and age squared, marital status, and parental employment status, including white-collar and agriculture.[12]

Turning next to sample restrictions, individuals should have had a chance to complete primary schooling, while at the same time being eligible for participation in adult literacy programs (the lower age limit). Also, individuals should not be "too old," since measurement issues then start to become more important (the upper-age limit). This leads me to restrict the initial sample to adults between 15 and 54 years of age (both included), yielding an initial 10,139 observations for the selection equation for the full sample. Some of these observations are missing on one or more variables, however. This leads to a drop in the estimation sample to 10,003 individuals. Further, 13 individuals report having completed "other" education; since it is not clear exactly what this means and since there are so few of these—leading to extremely thinly populated cells for some of the sub-group analyses—these are also dropped. The final, effective estimation sample for the selection equation therefore contains 9,990 individuals—corresponding to a drop of less than 1.5% relative to the initial sample. Descriptive statistics of the main variables (log hourly wages, employment status, literacy and numeracy, schooling) for the analyses samples are reported in Tables 18.A1 and 18.A2 in the Appendix.

6 Results

In this section, reduced-form estimates of the employment status and wage models are presented and discussed. The models are estimated for the full sample, and for five different sub-samples: females, males, rural areas, urban areas, and for individuals with no formal education completed. Since the focus of the paper is on the effect of literacy and numeracy and schooling, the results for the other explanatory variables—including variables for gender, age, age squared, rural–urban location, and, for the employment status regressions, only (i.e. the exclusion restrictions): marital status, marital status interacted with gender, and variables for parental employment status—are not reviewed here (they are available upon request).

Employment status

Since the multinomial logit model is non-linear, estimated parameters depend on the values of all the other variables in the model. To ease the interpretation of the estimated effects, therefore, the results are presented in Table 18.1 in terms of marginal effects, evaluated at the mean of the other explanatory

Table 18.1 Marginal effects for education and literacy and numeracy from employment status equation

	Full sample	Female	Male	Rural	Urban	No formal education
Regular wage employment						
Primary	0.042*	0.013	0.095*	0.040	0.030	
Middle/JSS	0.109***	0.070***	0.183***	0.088***	0.137***	
Secondary and above	0.467***	0.442***	0.548***	0.461***	0.462***	
Technical/vocational	0.316***	0.241***	0.404***	0.361***	0.332***	
Literacy course	−0.034**	0.010	−0.130***	−0.040***	0.048	−0.009
Literate and numerate	−0.015	0.010	−0.087	−0.013	−0.017	−0.005
Self-employed						
Primary	0.004	0.060*	−0.083	0.034	−0.022	
Middle/JSS	−0.053	0.024	−0.180***	0.010	−0.111**	
Secondary and above	−0.422***	−0.356***	−0.537***	−0.382***	−0.418***	
Technical/vocational	−0.206***	−0.067	−0.352***	−0.263***	−0.197***	
Literacy course	0.106***	0.092**	0.164***	0.111***	0.023	0.097**
Literate and numerate	0.026	0.001	0.105**	0.031	0.008	−0.018
Unpaid fam. worker						
Primary	−0.052***	−0.088***	−0.018**	−0.077***	−0.023***	
Middle/JSS	−0.068***	−0.123***	−0.012	−0.108***	−0.018	
Secondary and above	−0.041***	−0.096***	−0.004	−0.068**	−0.015*	
Technical/vocational	−0.092***	−0.165***	−0.036***	−0.125***	−0.042***	
Literacy course	−0.020	−0.032	−0.017*	−0.046**	0.016	−0.055
Literate and numerate	−0.029*	−0.029	−0.030	−0.031	−0.020	−0.070*
Not working						
Primary	0.005	0.016	0.006	0.002	0.014	
Middle/JSS	0.013	0.029	0.008	0.010	−0.009	
Secondary and above	−0.004	0.010	−0.006	−0.011	−0.030	
Technical/vocational	−0.019	−0.008	−0.017	0.027	−0.094**	
Literacy course	−0.052***	−0.070***	−0.017	−0.025***	−0.086**	−0.033***
Literate and numerate	0.018	0.018	0.013	0.013*	0.029	0.093**
Pseudo-R^2	0.27	0.21	0.32	0.26	0.23	0.23
N	9,881	5,560	4,321	6,382	3,499	3,937

Source: Ghana Living Standards Survey (Round 4, 1998/9).

Notes: Estimations employ robust Huber–White (Huber 1967; White 1980) standard errors and incorporate sampling weights and adjust for within-community correlation/clustering (Froot 1989; Williams 2000). *: statistically significant at 10%; **: statistically significant at 5%; ***: statistically significant at 1%.

variables. Starting from the top of the table, the first set of results is for regular employees, followed by the self-employed, unpaid family workers, and inactive individuals. For each of these categories, the table gives the results for the full sample in the first column and the sub-groups—the female, male, rural and urban samples, and the sample for individuals with no completed formal education—in columns two through six. From Table 18.1 a few overall results stand out in particular.

First, not surprisingly, formal education—especially at the higher levels—predominantly leads to regular wage employment, while adult literacy program participation leads to self-employment. Noticeably, this last result is both substantively large, ranging from about 2% for individuals from urban areas to about 16% for males, and mostly also statistically significant. Note that while it may appear that adult literacy course participation is "bad" for regular wage employment, the preferred estimation sample for judging the effect on adult literacy course participation is the sample of individuals with no formal education. For this estimation sample, the estimated association between adult literacy program participation and formal wage employment is nil, both in substantive and statistical terms.

Second, adult literacy course participation decreases economic inactivity, especially for females and in urban areas. Therefore, while—as we will see later—participation in adult literacy programs does not have a direct effect on wages, conditional on employment status, it does have a substantial indirect effect on wages through its impact on employment status—namely by enabling individuals to move from economic inactivity into self-employment.

Third, employment status is strongly affected by parental employment status (results not shown in the table). Individuals whose parents were white-collar workers are more likely to be regular employees and less likely to be self-employed, unpaid family workers, or not working.

Wages

Turning to the results for the wage equation, the marginal effects of the schooling and literacy and numeracy variables—using Kennedy's (1981) bias correction[13]—are shown in Table 18.2. The table is organized similar to the employment status regression results in Table 18.1, except that now there are only results from the employment categories, which obtain wages—namely regular employees and the self-employed; also, the models are estimated in two flavors: one where everything but literacy and numeracy is included, and one that adds literacy and numeracy.[14] Again, the reason for this is that I want to examine the extent to which literacy and numeracy skills affects the schooling premium and the extent to which literacy and numeracy add additional explanatory power to the wage equations.

From Table 18.2 the first specification, which is estimated for the full sample and includes formal schooling and adult literacy participation, reveals a large positive and statistically significant association between formal education

Table 18.2 Marginal effects for education and literacy and numeracy from wage equation

	Full sample		Females		Males		Rural		Urban		No formal education	
	Only education	+ lit/num	Only education	+ lit/num	Only education	+ lit/num	Only education	+ lit/num	Only education	+ lit/num	Only education	+ lit/num
Regular wage employee												
Primary	0.074	-0.019	0.311	0.256	-0.189	-0.218	-0.175	-0.292	0.374	0.345		
Middle/JSS	0.513***	0.028	1.178***	0.124	0.092	-0.035	0.247	-0.302	0.681**	0.431		
Secondary and above	3.071***	1.649***	5.663***	2.072***	1.968***	1.596***	2.634***	0.895**	3.023***	2.428***		
Technical/vocational	1.124***	0.425	0.959	-0.178	-0.943	-0.021	1.368**	0.025	-0.990	-0.716	-0.518	-0.545
Literacy course	-0.324	-0.312	0.047	0.140	-0.634	-0.633	-0.206	-0.186	-0.346	-0.342		0.264
Literate and numerate		0.519***		0.950***		0.129		0.860		0.165	1.071	1.130
Selection term, self-employment	0.759***	0.741***	1.154**	1.025*	0.654**	0.657***	0.827**	0.774***	0.665*	0.650**	-0.379*	-0.373*
Selection term, unpaid family worker	-0.078	-0.075	0.120	0.134	-0.330*	-0.322*	-0.188*	-0.189*	-0.018	-0.020	0.131	0.138
Selection term, not working/inactive	-0.105	-0.103	-0.051	0.038	0.013	0.013	-0.022	-0.007	-0.124	-0.121		
R^2	0.26	0.27	0.40	0.41	0.23	0.23	0.33	0.35	0.21	0.21	0.21	0.23
N	5,263	1162	2,983	297	2,280	865	3,590	488	1,673	674		149
Self-employed												
Primary	0.185**	0.140*	0.085	0.082	0.137	0.142	0.225**	0.188**	-0.055	-0.103		
Middle/JSS	0.313***	0.190**	0.053	0.033	0.139	0.273	0.397***	0.268**	0.121	0.009		
Secondary and above	0.867***	0.675***	0.759**	0.708*	0.661***	0.850***	0.398**	0.248	1.275***	1.014***		
Technical/vocational	0.614***	0.421	0.051	0.072	-0.936	-0.977	1.091***	0.889***	-0.983	-0.955	0.079	0.071
Literacy course	-0.154*	-0.160*	-0.089	-0.105	-0.322	-0.324	-0.012	-0.019	-0.172	-0.169		0.134
Literate and numerate		0.121		0.026		-0.134		0.115		0.121	0.050	0.055
Selection term, self-employment	0.109*	0.107*	0.246**	0.239*	-0.049	-0.047	0.189**	0.187**	-0.070	-0.079	-0.091	-0.085
Selection term, unpaid family worker	-0.041	-0.041	0.088	0.083	-0.324*	-0.323*	0.035	0.034	-0.156*	-0.156*	0.046	0.040
Selection term, not working/inactive	-0.168***	-0.171**	-0.034	-0.049	0.002	0.002	-0.137***	-0.137**	-0.010	-0.015		
R^2	0.12	0.12	0.10	0.10	0.14	0.14	0.07	0.07	0.06	0.07	0.07	0.07
N	5,263		2,983		2,280		3,590		1,673			2,171

Source: Ghana Living Standards Survey (Round 4, 1998/9).

Notes: Models are estimated using the multinomial selection model developed in Durbin-McFadden (1984). Marginal effects are calculated using Kennedy's (1981) bias correction for binary variables in semi-logarithmic equations. Estimations employ robust Huber–White (Huber 1967; White 1980) standard errors; incorporate sampling weights and adjust for within-community correlation/clustering (Froot 1989; Williams 2000). *: statistically significant at 10%; **: statistically significant at 5%; ***: statistically significant at 1%.

and wages. This is true across all estimation samples. The finding of a large return to formal education accords with the findings in the previous literature reviewed in Section 3 of this paper. Again, while it may appear that adult literacy course participation is "bad" for wages, the preferred estimation sample for judging the effect on adult literacy course participation is the sample of individuals with no formal education. For this sample, the estimated association between adult literacy program participation and wages, while negative, is not statistically significant for regular wage employment. For self-employment, it is positive (but not statistically significant).

Adding literacy and numeracy in the second specification causes a substantial drop in the premium to formal education for wage employees, often also losing statistical significance, while the skills premium at the same time is large and positive. The returns to middle and junior secondary school, for example, drop from about 51% to about 3% in the full sample. This is consistent with earlier findings for Kenya and Tanzania (Boissiere, Knight, and Sabot 1985) and South Africa (Moll 1998). The literacy and numeracy premium ranges from about 13 to 95% for regular wage employment and from 2.6 to about 13% for self-employment; it is mostly statistically significant for the regular wage employees, while it is somewhat imprecisely measured for the self-employed and therefore not statistically significant. R^2 remains constant, indicating very little independent explanatory power in literacy and numeracy, once schooling has been controlled for.

What do these results mean? The finding of an individual skills effect, separate from that of education, confirms that it is not only schooling per se that is important for wages: the cognitive skills obtained from schooling are important, too, possibly through their impact on productivity and therefore on wages. It also confirms that the Ghanaian education system is successful in creating skills; this has been examined more extensively elsewhere, however (Blunch 2006). This is all consistent with a standard human capital explanation.

While literacy and numeracy are important determinants of wages, the results also indicate that education is important, even after controlling for cognitive skills—in accord with the findings in Boissiere, Knight, and Sabot (1985), Moll (1998), and Glewwe (1996). In other words, skills other than basic cognitive skills achieved through schooling are also important. Such skills may include more advanced cognitive skills and non-cognitive skills such as socialization or discipline skills (Heckman, Stixrud, and Urzua 2006); conceptually, these skills would seem to be produced mainly at higher levels of formal education, and through technical-vocational education or adult literacy course participation. Formal education may also generate diploma or signaling effects (Spence 1973), which would also affect wages; conceptually, the signaling effect would only seem to be relevant for higher levels of formal education and then only for regular wage employees. Hence, for secondary education, it is not possible empirically to distinguish between production of more advanced cognitive skills or non-cognitive skills and the "production" of signaling.

Empirically, the results are consistent with the advanced cognitive skills, non-cognitive skills, or signaling explanation for secondary education and the advanced cognitive skills explanation for technical-vocational education. The former is particularly strong for females and individuals from urban areas, while the latter is particularly strong in urban areas. Again, this is also consistent with the returns to these more advanced skills partly coming about through the existence of better economic opportunities in urban areas.

Turning to the differences between regular employees and the self-employed, the drop in the education premium when including cognitive skills is not nearly as dramatic for the self-employed; the statistical significance of estimates is also retained to a greater degree than was the case for regular wage employees. The education premium in self-employment is much lower to begin with, however—for secondary and above for the full sample, for example, less than a third of that of regular wage employees. These results indicate that the returns to human capital generally are lower for the self-employed—which is consistent with this segment of the labor market possibly employing relatively less skilled labor, as is also revealed by the descriptive statistics in Table 18.A2.

In sum, the human capital effects have been deconstructed into two individual groups of effects: basic cognitive skills, and advanced cognitive, non-cognitive skills, or signaling effects, all of which are important in the human capital–wage relationship.

Lastly, the selection terms are frequently statistically significant, supporting the importance of employing the Durbin-McFadden (1984) procedure used here. To further assess the validity of this procedure, tests for the joint significance of the over-identifying variables[15] in the employment status equation were undertaken. The results (not shown) indicate that the set of identifying instruments as a whole are strong predictors of employment status, being statistically significant at 0.01% or better in all cases. Since conceptually the instruments should not affect wages, conditional on employment status, the selectivity correction procedure employed here appears both justified and valid.

Besides these main patterns in the wage regression results, there are also some additional interesting results pertaining to some of the sub-group analyses. For example, the cognitive skills and education premia are substantially higher in urban regular wage employment than in rural regular wage employment. The reason for this is probably that the labor market conditions and economic opportunities more generally are greater in urban than in rural areas, especially as they pertain to skilled workers, and here especially to regular wage employees. Expanding educational opportunities, therefore, have the greatest effect if carried out in an environment with economic opportunities. Alternatively, educational expansion might benefit from associated policies aimed to enable such economic opportunities. Also, in rural areas the results for formal education are strongest and most consistent for technical and vocational education and training. This is consistent with practical skills being more valued in rural areas, which again is in line with signaling and non-cognitive skills mattering mainly for regular wage employment.

Sensitivity analyses

I also performed sensitivity analyses to assess the robustness of the previous results. Specifically, I experimented with several different alternative functional literacy (cognitive skills) measures. In addition to the preferred measure (Ghanaian *or* English writing *and* written calculations), I re-estimated the model for the full sample using Ghanaian *or* English reading *and* written calculations, Ghanaian *and* English reading *and* written calculations, and Ghanaian *and* English writing *and* written calculations. The wage premium to the three alternative functional literacy measures was found to be substantial, although of differing magnitude depending on the measure in question; it was also not always statistically significant. These discrepancies notwithstanding, the results from the sensitivity analyses do not appear to detract from the overall conclusions of the main analyses of there existing large returns to literacy and numeracy, controlling for schooling.

7 Conclusion

This paper examines the determinants of wages in Ghana, focusing on the effect from a set of human capital variables that captures formal and non-formal education and cognitive and non-cognitive skills, treating employment status as endogenous. Previous research has mostly treated human capital as a "black box," typically incorporating measures for formal education but not for non-formal education or literacy and numeracy when examining the association of human capital and wages.

Among the main findings, the introduction of basic literacy and numeracy in the human capital–wage relationship decreases the estimated effects of formal schooling, especially at the lower levels, often rendering the effect statistically insignificant. In turn, this indicates that "cognitive skills matter," not only schooling in and by itself is what matters. At the same time, these results also confirm that the Ghanaian education system is successful in creating basic cognitive skills. This is all consistent with a standard human capital explanation.

Additionally, the continued importance of technical-vocational education and secondary and higher indicate that skills other than basic cognitive skills achieved through schooling are important also. Such skills may include more advanced cognitive skills and non-cognitive skills such as socialization or discipline (Heckman, Stixrud, and Urzua 2006). Formal education may also generate diploma or signaling effects (Spence 1973), which would also affect wages, however. The results are consistent with both explanations for secondary education.

In addition to the direct effects from skills and schooling on wages, however, several indirect effects—coming through the impact on employment status—are established. First, not surprisingly, formal education predominantly leads to more regular wage employment. Second, the opposite is true for self-employment, where workers are less likely to have completed formal education but more likely to have attended an adult literacy program. Third, adult literacy course participation decreases economic inactivity, especially for females, individuals with no formal education, and in urban areas. Therefore, while participation in adult literacy programs does not have a direct effect on wages, conditional on employment status, it does have a substantial indirect effect on wages through its impact on employment status.

What are the policy implications of these results? First, policy makers should care more about educational outputs than education and educational enrollment per se. If educational programs—in the broadest sense, including both formal and non-formal education—do not produce useful skills, such as literacy and numeracy, for example, they should either be adjusted and improved or abandoned in favor of programs that do.

Cost-effectiveness is crucially important in this connection, especially for the developing countries. If adult literacy programs indeed have positive indirect effects on wages, through the effect on employment status—as the evidence here suggests they do, especially for females and in urban areas—they may well be cost-effective relative to formal education; at least they may be a useful complement to formal education, especially for individuals with low stocks of formal human capital. Since participants meet a couple of hours a few times a week, typically of a duration of about two years, and participation is mostly free, except for a small reward to the facilitator (typically in the form of a bike or a sewing machine), the main costs are forgone earnings. At such modest costs even moderate returns in terms of wages (through the decrease in economic inactivity) would seem to make these programs and their further strengthening worthwhile. Indeed, there are other potential effects from these programs which will positively affect peoples' livelihoods in addition to wages, such as increased child health arising from the health component of these programs (Blunch 2006).

A few comments are in order, however, regarding the frequently quite high returns to skills and schooling estimated here. As Glewwe (1991: 318) also notes, since such estimates are conditional on past choices in asset accumulation, estimated returns tend to overestimate the returns to education for the general population. Policy makers, therefore, should not expect quite as massive results if human capital levels were to increase for the economy at large. Even if these estimates are upper-bound estimates of the "true" effects, however, continued investment in human capital in Ghana should remain a priority for Ghanaian policy makers and international development organizations in the future.

Also, while suggestive, the results and analyses here represent only a first attempt at opening the black box in the human capital–wage relationship, however—more research is needed. Above all, the analysis of more and better data is required: do the results here pertain to other (West) African countries—and other developing countries more generally? Also, the measures of literacy and numeracy examined here were arguably crude. Rather than self-reported (binary) measures of literacy and numeracy ability, one would prefer more objective (continuous) test score-based measures.

Similarly, there are obvious timing issues related to the adult literacy course participation measure: it is known if a person participated but not when, in which program, or whether the program was completed. With that information, much richer analyses could be performed. Future research, using more precise measures of participation, could validate the findings here while also more precisely estimating impacts and possible asymmetries in effects from different providers of adult literacy programs.

As researchers, we mostly have simply to accept the data we are given—only rarely do we have the resources available to collect exactly the data we need for a particular analysis. One can only urge national statistical agencies, the World Bank, UNICEF, ILO and others carrying out large-scale household surveys in developing countries to continuously refine their survey instruments, keeping in mind the issues raised here.

Notes

* I thank Bryan Boulier, Donald Parsons, David Ribar, and participants at the XXI Annual Conference of the European Society for Population Economics and the Second IZA/World Bank Conference on Employment and Development for helpful comments and suggestions on earlier versions of this paper. Remaining errors and omissions are my own. The data were kindly provided by the Ghana Statistical Service. The findings and interpretations, however, are those of the author and should not be attributed to the Ghana Statistical Service.

1 See, for example, Card (1999), Psacharopoulos (1973, 1981, 1985, 1994), Psacharopoulos and Patrinos (2004), and Willis (1986).

2 Or vice versa: self-employment may not necessarily be inferior to regular wage employment (Maloney 2004).

3 Due to rationing and barriers to entry into regular wage employment, there might not be much of a choice between this and self-employment. There is still a choice between economic inactivity and self-employment, however. Again, at the other end of the spectrum, there is also still the possibility that self-employment is a sector of choice rather than a marginal sector (Maloney 2004); in turn, this would induce selection for the full range of employment status possibilities.

4 Regular wage employment may require personal connections and networks or self-employment may require credit for start-up costs, for example.

5 While migration for education and/or work purposes may be a potential issue here, incorporating migration would greatly complicate the analyses.

6 Also, some regions are better off than others; most notably the Greater Accra region is better off than the other nine regions in terms of economic conditions. However, since for the analyses here I am mainly interested in the gross returns to education and literacy and numeracy, I want to avoid including variables beyond an absolute minimum.

7 Extensive reviews of this literature are provided in Card (1999), Psacharopoulos (1973, 1981, 1985, 1994), Psacharopoulos and Patrinos (2004), and Willis (1986).
8 One should be careful in interpreting these results as "only—or even mainly—cognitive skills matter," since these skills are produced from schooling. Rather, they both indicate that schooling is successful in producing these skills and that there are additional components of schooling that affect wages in addition to cognitive skills.
9 The results in Glewwe (1999) are similar as far as cognitive skills are concerned (schooling was not included in the specifications where cognitive skills were included).
10 Thirteen individuals in the full sample report having completed "other education." These are dropped since it is not clear what "other education" is.
11 There are, of course, some issues here, related to timing and intensity of participation, and so on. See Blunch (2006) for more discussion of this.
12 A more detailed discussion of both dependent and explanatory variables and their definitions is provided in Blunch (2006).
13 The marginal effects for dummy variables in semi-logarithmic models are not merely given as the estimated coefficients (although some studies treat them as such); therefore, the estimated coefficients are not interpretable "as is." While direct exponentiation (via the formula: marginal effect = exp(coefficient) − 1) is a common way of converting the estimated coefficients of dummy variables from semi-logarithmic models into marginal effects, Kennedy (1981) suggests that this is a biased estimator for the "true" marginal effect. He offers a bias correction—involving the variance of the estimate—which is also used here.
14 Estimating the employment status equation in both flavors revealed that the results generally were quite robust as to whether or not literacy and numeracy was included.
15 Marital status, marital status interacted with gender, and dummy variables for parental employment status.

References

Blunch, N.-H. (2006) *Skills, Schooling and Household Well-Being in Ghana.* Unpublished Ph.D. dissertation. Washington, DC: George Washington University.
—— and C. Pörtner (2005) "Literacy, Skills and Welfare: Effects of Participation in an Adult literacy Program." Working paper UWEC-2005–23, Department of Economics, University of Washington, Seattle.
Boissiere, M., J. Knight, and R. Sabot (1985) "Earnings, Schooling, Ability and Cognitive Skills." *American Economic Review* 73(5): 926–46.
Card, D. (1999) "The Causal Effect of Education on Earnings." In *Handbook of Labor Economics*, edited by O. Ashenfelter and D. Card, Vol. 3. Elsevier Science B. V.
Durbin, J. A. and D. McFadden (1984) "An Econometric Analysis of Residential Electric Appliance Holdings and Consumption," *Econometrica*, 52(2): 345–62.
Froot, K. A. (1989) "Consistent Covariance Matrix Estimation with Cross-sectional Dependence and Heteroskedasticity in Financial Data." *Journal of Financial and Quantitative Analysis* 24: 333–55.
Glewwe, P. (1991) "Investigating the Determinants of Household Welfare in Côte d'Ivoire." *Journal of Development Economics* 35: 307–37.
——. (1996) "The Relevance of Standard Estimates of Rates of Return to Schooling for Education Policy: A Critical Assessment." *Journal of Development Economics* 51: 267–90.

——— . (1999) "The Impact of Cognitive Skills on Wages." In *The Economics of School Quality Investments in Developing Countries: An Empirical Study of Ghana*, edited by P. Glewwe. London: Macmillan.

Heckman, J. J., J. Stixrud, and S. Urzua (2006) "The Effects of Cognitive and Noncognitive Abilities on Labor Market Outcomes and Social Behavior." *Journal of Labor Economics* 24(3): 411–82.

Huber, P. J. (1967) "The Behavior of Maximum Likelihood Estimates under Non-standard Conditions." In Proceedings of the Fifth Berkeley Symposium on *Mathematical Statistics and Probability* Vol. 1, Berkeley, CA: University of California Press.

Joliffe, D. (2004) "The Impact of Education in Rural Ghana: Examining Household Labor Allocation and Returns On and Off the Farm." *Journal of Development Economics* 73: 287–314.

Kennedy, P. E. (1981) "Estimation with Correctly Interpreted Dummy Variables in Semilogarithmic Equations." *American Economic Review* 71(4): 801.

Maloney, W. (2004) "Informality Revisited." *World Development* 32(7): 1159–78.

Mincer, J. (1974) *Schooling, Experience and Earnings*, New York: National Bureau of Economic Research.

Moll, P. G. (1998) "Primary Schooling, Cognitive Skills and Wages in South Africa." *Economica* 65: 263–84.

Psacharopoulos, G. (1973) *Returns to Education: An International Comparison*. Joessey-Bass, Elsevier.

——— . (1981) "Returns to Education: An Updated International Comparison." *Comparative Education* 17: 321–41.

——— . (1985) "Returns to Education: A Further International Update and Implications." *Journal of Human Resources* 20(4): 583–611.

——— . (1994) Returns to Investment in Education: A global update. *World Development* 22(9): 1325–43.

——— and H. A. Patrinos (2004) Returns to Investment in Education: A further update. *Education Economics*, 12(2): 111–34.

Spence, M. A. (1973) "Job Market Signaling." *Quarterly Journal of Economics* 87(3): 55–74.

Teal, F. (2000) "Real Wages and the Demand for Skilled and Unskilled Male Labour in Ghana's Manufacturing Sector: 1991–1995." *Journal of Development Economics* 61: 447–61.

Vijverberg, W. P.M. (1995) "Returns to Schooling in Non-Farm Self-Employment: An Econometric Case Study of Ghana." *World Development* 23(7): 1215–27.

——— . (1999) "The Impact of Schooling and Cognitive Skills on Income from Non-Farm Self-Employment." In *The Economics of School Quality Investments in Developing Countries: An Empirical Study of Ghana*, edited by P. Glewwe. London: Macmillan.

White, H. (1980) "A Heteroskedasticity-Consistent Covariance Matrix Estimator and a Direct Test for Heteroskedasticity." *Econometrica* 48(4): 817–30.

Williams, R. L. (2000) "A Note on Robust Variance Estimation for Cluster-correlated Data." *Biometrics* 56: 645–6.

Willis, R. J. (1986) "Wage Determinants: A Survey and Reinterpretation of Human Capital Earnings Functions." In *Handbook of Labor Economics*, edited by O. Ashenfelter and R. Layard. North-Holland: Elsevier.

Appendix: descriptive statistics

Table 18.A1 Descriptive statistics for employment status from estimation samples (employment status equations)

	Full sample		Females		Males		Rural		Urban		No formal education	
	Mean	Std dev.	Mean	Std dev.	Mean	Std dev.	Mean	Std dev.	Mean	Std dev.	Mean	Std dev.
Regular employee	0.131	0.337	0.062	0.241	0.219	0.413	0.088	0.284	0.209	0.407	0.043	0.204
Self-employed	0.560	0.496	0.565	0.496	0.554	0.497	0.595	0.491	0.495	0.500	0.594	0.491
Unpaid family worker	0.167	0.373	0.222	0.415	0.098	0.297	0.225	0.418	0.060	0.238	0.269	0.443
Not working (reference)	0.142	0.349	0.152	0.359	0.129	0.336	0.091	0.288	0.236	0.424	0.094	0.292
N	9,881		5,560		4,321		6,382		3,499		3,937	

Source: Ghana Living Standards Survey (Round 4, 1998/9).

Notes: Calculations incorporate sampling weights and adjust for within-community correlation/clustering (Froot 1989; Williams 2000).

Table 18.A2 Descriptive statistics for wages, education, and literacy and numeracy (wage equations)

	Full sample		Females		Males		Rural		Urban		No formal education	
	Mean	Std dev.	Mean	Std dev.	Mean	Std dev.	Mean	Std dev.	Mean	Std dev.	Mean	Std dev.
Regular employee												
Hourly wages (cedis)	1375.1	8197.5	876.8	1285.6	1550.5	9496.0	1008.0	1234.0	1656.4	10835.0	542.4	567.7
No formal education	0.133	0.339	0.154	0.362	0.125	0.331	0.167	0.373	0.106	0.308	1.000	0.000
Primary	0.070	0.254	0.067	0.250	0.070	0.256	0.091	0.288	0.053	0.224	0.000	0.000
Middle/JSS	0.372	0.484	0.368	0.483	0.373	0.484	0.384	0.487	0.363	0.481	0.000	0.000
Secondary and above	0.348	0.477	0.333	0.472	0.353	0.478	0.319	0.467	0.370	0.483	0.000	0.000
Technical/vocational	0.078	0.268	0.078	0.268	0.078	0.269	0.039	0.194	0.108	0.311	0.000	0.000
Literacy course	0.028	0.166	0.060	0.238	0.017	0.130	0.024	0.152	0.032	0.177	0.104	0.306
Literate and numerate	0.791	0.406	0.753	0.432	0.805	0.397	0.736	0.441	0.834	0.373	0.042	0.201
N	1,162		297		865		488		674		149	

(Continued overleaf)

Table 18.A2 Continued

	Full sample		Females		Males		Rural		Urban		No formal education	
	Mean	Std dev.	Mean	Std dev.	Mean	Std dev.	Mean	Std dev.	Mean	Std dev.	Mean	Std dev.
Self-employed												
Hourly wages (cedis)	764.0	4714.4	693.4	2719.3	855.4	6435.3	498.1	1085.5	1331.4	8166.3	463.3	842.2
No formal education	0.414	0.493	0.485	0.500	0.323	0.468	0.469	0.499	0.298	0.458	1.000	0.000
Primary	0.152	0.359	0.168	0.374	0.130	0.337	0.155	0.362	0.143	0.351	0.000	0.000
Middle/JSS	0.360	0.480	0.297	0.457	0.441	0.497	0.331	0.471	0.421	0.494	0.000	0.000
Secondary and above	0.049	0.215	0.029	0.167	0.074	0.262	0.036	0.187	0.075	0.263	0.000	0.000
Technical/vocational	0.026	0.159	0.022	0.145	0.032	0.176	0.009	0.093	0.063	0.244	0.000	0.000
Literacy course	0.094	0.292	0.098	0.298	0.088	0.283	0.119	0.324	0.039	0.194	0.160	0.367
Literate and numerate	0.459	0.498	0.345	0.476	0.606	0.489	0.404	0.491	0.577	0.494	0.026	0.159
N	5,263		2,983		2,280		3,590		1,673		2,171	
Unpaid family worker												
No formal education	0.645	0.479	0.707	0.455	0.466	0.499	0.669	0.471	0.479	0.501	1.000	0.000
Primary	0.114	0.318	0.111	0.315	0.121	0.327	0.116	0.320	0.100	0.301	0.000	0.000
Middle/JSS	0.192	0.394	0.158	0.365	0.288	0.454	0.174	0.380	0.313	0.465	0.000	0.000
Secondary and above	0.047	0.211	0.021	0.143	0.120	0.326	0.038	0.191	0.104	0.306	0.000	0.000
Technical/vocational	0.003	0.050	0.002	0.046	0.004	0.062	0.002	0.048	0.004	0.064	0.000	0.000
Literacy course	0.070	0.255	0.085	0.279	0.026	0.160	0.072	0.259	0.051	0.221	0.090	0.286
Literate and numerate	0.231	0.422	0.173	0.379	0.397	0.490	0.208	0.406	0.391	0.489	0.009	0.096
N	1,728		1,283		445		1,504		224		1,093	
Not working												
No formal education	0.266	0.442	0.322	0.467	0.183	0.387	0.327	0.470	0.223	0.416	1.000	0.000
Primary	0.144	0.351	0.157	0.364	0.125	0.331	0.142	0.350	0.145	0.353	0.000	0.000
Middle/JSS	0.452	0.498	0.434	0.496	0.480	0.500	0.464	0.499	0.444	0.497	0.000	0.000
Secondary and above	0.115	0.319	0.073	0.260	0.179	0.383	0.055	0.228	0.158	0.365	0.000	0.000
Technical/vocational	0.022	0.148	0.015	0.121	0.033	0.180	0.012	0.109	0.030	0.169	0.000	0.000
Literacy course	0.016	0.127	0.018	0.133	0.014	0.118	0.018	0.133	0.015	0.123	0.038	0.191
Literate and numerate	0.590	0.492	0.499	0.500	0.726	0.446	0.508	0.500	0.649	0.478	0.065	0.246
N	1,430		824		606		567		863		351	

Source: Ghana Living Standards Survey (Round 4, 1998/9).

Notes: Calculations incorporate sampling weights and adjust for within-community correlation/clustering (Froot 1989; Williams 2000).

19 Wage convergence and inequality after unification: (East) Germany in transition

Johannes Gernandt and Friedhelm Pfeiffer[*]

1 Introduction

German reunification might become a paradigm of convergence and integration of neighbouring regions with unequal starting conditions. One of the most ambitious political goals has been the equalization of living conditions and wages in both parts of Germany. There are various channels through which wages and living conditions may converge. With unification, barriers to labor market competition and migration were removed. Competition for jobs and wages increased and changed the allocation of labor and skills through migration, unemployment and wage adjustments in both German regions. However, wage adjustment takes time, because wage determination deviates from the determination of prices in auction markets (Bewley 1999, Pfeiffer, 2003, among others). While some wages, especially in larger industrial firms, are the result of central wage bargaining, the adaption of other wages, of qualifications and skills follows different pathways, influenced by expectations, migration and unemployment dynamics (Akerlof et al. 1991, Krueger and Pischke 1995, Lechner and Pfeiffer 1993, among others).

This paper investigates the evolution of the wage distribution after reunification in both parts of Germany as well as the wages and the wage distribution of East German migrants and commuters to West Germany. Whether wages and the wage distribution have already converged is a topic of considerable debate among researchers and is discussed in our paper. Our approach is to compare the wage distribution of East German workers, commuters from East to West Germany and migrants from East to West Germany with their statistical twins from the West German workforce. Migration to West Germany, especially among the younger highly skilled workers continues, indicating ongoing transition processes (compare also Burda et al. 1998, Franz and Steiner 2000, Hunt 2006, Uhlig 2006). Our empirical part builds on samples for these groups of workers extracted from the German Socioeconomic Panel (SOEP) 1992–2005. Using regression and non-parametric matching methods, we identify a group of West German workers comparable to the East German workers. Based on this comparison in observables, wages and the convergence (or divergence) of wage distributions in the transition period from 1992 to 2005 are investigated.

Our contribution is related to the issue of rising wage inequality (compare Autor, Katz, and Kearny 2006, among others). For a long time, rising wage inequality in Great Britain and the USA has been contrasted with a stable wage distribution in Europe and especially in Germany (e.g. Prasad 2004). The issue has been highlighted by Krugman (1994), who argues that rising inequality as well as low unemployment rates in the USA and rising unemployment and a stable wage distribution in Europe are two sides of the same coin. In this view, high European unemployment rates are the consequence of rigid labor market regulations that inhibit a downward adjustment of wages. However, findings by Fitzenberger et al. (2001), Kohn (2006), Möller (2005), among others, suggest that wages in Germany have always been flexible to some degree and that wage inequality is rising in East and West Germany already since 1993/4 (Gernandt and Pfeiffer 2007).

Based on samples taken from the SOEP, our findings indicate that between 1992 and 2005 the average gross hourly wage of prime-age dependent workers living and working in East Germany increased by 52%, whereas it increased only by 9% for workers in West Germany. While the group of stayers receives on average between 70 and 75%, migrants receive 95 to 100% and commuters 85% of the wages of their West German statistical twins. Interestingly, wage inequality among East German workers today is higher when compared to their West German colleagues. For prime-age dependent workers, living and working in East Germany, the ratio of wages for high-wage workers, as measured by the ninetieth percentile of the wage distribution, and low-wage workers, as measured by the tenth percentile of the wage distribution, increased from 2.00 to 2.93 between 1992 and 2005, and from 2.40 to 2.85 in West Germany. In terms of price flexibility, labor markets seem to be a long way off from functioning as auction markets and even among two regions as close as East and West Germany wage disparity persists. Significant forces are shaping Germany's wage distribution through commuting and migration and equalization takes time.

The paper is organized as follows: Section 2 gives an overview on migration, unemployment, wages, and productivity after unification in East Germany. Section 3 introduces the data and the samples drawn from SOEP. Section 4 is concerned with the regression and matching methods employed. In section 5 we discuss the empirical results. Section 6 concludes.

2 Migration and aggregate dynamics after unification

In East Germany privatization and restructuring of state enterprises and wage bargaining took place since the formation of a monetary union on July 1, 1990. Because eastern unions were strongly connected with the old system of the former German Democratic Republic, western unions installed a bargaining system similar to the one in West Germany. Since firms were in a process of privatization their bargaining power was rather weak. After reunification, western unions feared wage competition in West Germany through labor migration while western employers were afraid of competition from newly founded firms in East Germany. The result was a rapid rise of wages after reunification and a high rate of unemployment (Akerlof et al. 1991, Sinn and Sinn 1992).

Figure 19.1 shows the development of GDP, the unemployment rate for East Germany and the gross migration flows to West Germany between 1991 and 2005. Nominal GDP in East Germany (without Berlin) was €107 billion in 1991. At that time 7% of the German GDP was generated in the East (2007: €278 billion, 11.5% of GDP). GDP in East Germany first increased rapidly and then stabilized in the mid-1990s. Until 1995 the wage level in East Germany increased to 70% of the western level and remained at that level in the following years. Similarly, labor productivity rose to 70% of the western level, while GDP per capita increased to only 65%. Unemployment rates increased from 10.2% in 1991 to 20.6% in 2005 (and since then decreased to 15.1% in 2007).

Migration to the West (without Berlin) was highest in 1991 with 229,200 persons (compared to 63,800 who migrated from West to East Germany in the same year), decreased to 124,900 persons in 1997, increased again to 192,000 in 2001 and finally decreased to 137,200 in 2005. Between 1989 and 2001, 7.5% of the population in East Germany migrated to West Germany

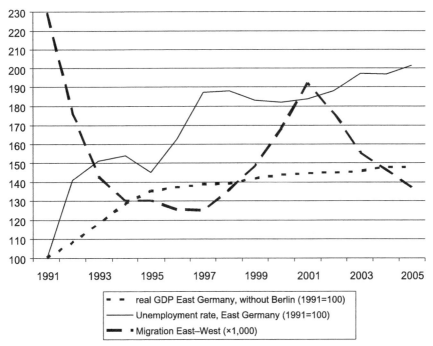

Figure 19.1 GDP and unemployment in East Germany and migration to the West, 1991–2005.

Source: Statistisches Bundesamt, 2006, Statistische Ämter der Länder, 2005; own calculation.

(Brücker and Trübswetter 2007). In 1989, migration reached levels (around 3% of the East German population, Pischke, Staat, and Vögele 1994), nearly as high as before the closing of the border in Berlin in 1963. Favourite destinations in West Germany are neighbouring regions such as Hesse for workers from Thuringia or economically stronger regions such as Bavaria, Baden-Wuerttemberg, or North Rhine-Westphalia (Heiland 2004). Between 1990 and 1995, wage mobility was higher in the eastern than in the western part of Germany (Gernandt and Pfeiffer 2007, Hauser and Fabig 1999, Hunt 2001).

Migrants are often better educated compared to commuters, and commuting sometimes is a first step to migration. Economic incentives for migration from East to West Germany result from job better opportunities and higher wages in West Germany, despite the fact that migrants are likely to lose some of their more specific human capital (Burda et al. 1998, Brücker and Trübswetter 2007, among others). In general, Young and highly skilled workers in East Germany have gained from reunification (Bird, Schwartze, and Wagner 1994, Franz and Steiner 2000), while for workers born between 1935 and 1945 the labor market situation has often changed for the worse (Hauser and Wagner 1996).

3 Data and descriptive analysis

For the purpose of the analysis, we make use of a sample from the German SOEP[1] for the period from 1992 to 2005.[2] We restrict the sample to dependent workers (not self-employed), aged between 25 and 55, who are wage-workers (in a cross-section) and hold German citizenship. All observations with missing information on household residence in 1989, workplace residence between 1992 and 2005, wages, and controls have been excluded.[3] The variable real gross hourly wage is obtained by the division of last month's salary by last month's work hours, including reported overtime.[4] Wages are trimmed by the 2% highest and lowest observations on hourly wages.

For our investigation of wage convergence and inequality, we further extract four samples for each year (see Table 19.1). Sample 1 (referred to as West Germans) contains workers who live in West Germany, who already lived there before unification (1989) and who do not commute to work in East Germany in a cross-section. This is the largest sample. Sample 2 (referred to as East Germans) contains cross-section observations of workers living in East Germany, who lived there before unification and who are working in East Germany. Sample 3 (referred to as Migrants) encompasses former East Germans who migrated to West Germany and who also work in West Germany. The last sample (referred to as commuters) contains East Germans who lived in East Germany before the unification and still live there in the observation period but commute to work to West Germany. Samples 3 and 4 contain the lowest number of observations.

Wages are highest for workers living and working in West Germany (West Germans and Migrants from East Germany), followed by workers who

Table 19.1 Mean real gross hourly wages (€) in the four samples

	West Germans (Sample 1)		East Germans (Sample 2)		Migrants (Sample 3)		Commuters (Sample 4)	
	Number	Euro, 95% confidence interval	Number	Euro (ratio to West Germans), 95% confidence interval	Number	Euro (ratio to West Germans), 95% confidence interval	Number	Euro (ratio to West Germans), 95% confidence interval
1992	1,585	12.96 12.75–13.18	1,582	6.88 (53%) 6.77–6.98	34	11.29 (87%) 9.95–12.63	82	9.31 (72%) 8.74–9.89
1993	1,628	13.24 13.02–13.45	1,415	8.04 (61%) 7.90–8.19	53	10.67 (81%) 9.96–11.78	87	9.25 (70%) 8.63–9.86
1994	1,677	13.24 13.03–13.45	1,341	8.72 (66%) 8.57–8.87	63	11.74 (89%) 10.76–12.72	85	10.15 (77%) 9.52–10.78
1995	1,695	13.52 13.30–13.74	1,309	9.01 (67%) 8.84–9.18	79	11.62 (86%) 10.76–12.47	84	10.90 (81%) 10.15–11.65
1996	1,721	13.55 13.33–13.77	1,245	9.41 (69%) 9.22–9.59	87	11.54 (85%) 10.71–12.37	79	11.25 (83%) 10.55–11.94
1997	1,747	13.35 13.14–13.56	1,173	9.51 (71%) 9.31–9.70	91	11.51 (86%) 10.62–12.40	90	10.61 (79%) 9.89–11.33
1998	1,821	13.58 13.37–13.79	1,092	9.76 (72%) 9.54–9.97	89	12.22 (90%) 11.28–13.16	91	10.87 (80%) 10.07–11.67
1999	1,177	14.01 13.75–14.28	550	9.57 (68%) 9.26–9.87	58	12.45 (89%) 11.20–13.69	69	10.91 (78%) 10.16–11.65
2000	2,150	14.21 14.01–14.41	709	9.85 (69%) 9.58–10.11	86	12.95 (91%) 11.91–13.98	82	10.47 (74%) 9.73–11.22
2001	2,031	14.22 14.01–14.44	676	10.06 (71%) 9.77–10.36	90	12.65 (89%) 11.66–13.65	104	10.65 (75%) 9.84–11.46
2002	3,745	14.07 13.90–14.24	1,375	10.27 (73%) 10.06–10.49	184	12.29 (87%) 11.61–12.96	123	11.90 (85%) 11.15–12.66
2003	3,681	14.45 14.27–14.62	1,275	10.67 (74%) 10.43–10.90	202	12.53 (87%) 11.82–13.24	145	12.25 (85%) 11.50–12.99
2004	3,585	14.28 14.10–14.46	1,252	10.68 (75%) 10.44–10.93	210	12.39 (87%) 11.73–13.06	144	11.78 (82%) 11.07–12.49
2005	3,325	14.14 13.96–14.32	1,167	10.46 (74%) 10.20–10.72	209	12.21 (86%) 11.54–12.88	145	12.04 (85%) 11.32–12.75

Source: Samples taken from the SOEP 1992–2005, see text; own calculations.

commute to West Germany (see Table 19.1 and Figure 19.2). Workers living and working in East Germany earn between 53% (in 1992) and 75% (later on) of West Germans. Former East Germans, who migrated to the West, as well as commuters, earn higher wages. The differences between real wages for West German workers and the three other groups of workers are statistically significant as indicated by the 95% confidence intervals shown in Table 19.1.

In 2005, workers who work and live in West Germany, and also lived there before reunification, earned on average €14.14 per hour, workers who live and work in East Germany, and also lived there before reunification, earned €10.46 (74% of West German wages). Workers who migrated from East to West Germany earned on average €12.21 (86% of West German wages) and workers who commute to work from East to West Germany earned €12.04 (85% of West German wages). The hourly wage of commuters is higher when compared to stayers but lower when compared to migrants. Figure 19.2 shows the evolution of the wage gap relative to West Germans. Migrants earn about 86% of western wages, commuters approached this wage in the last years and East Germans in all years earned the lowest wages. Interestingly, the gap between East Germans, migrants and commuters narrowed. In the econometric part, in section 5, we will compare East Germans, migrants, and commuters to their statistical West German twins.

Figure 19.3 shows the wage distribution for the four samples of workers (West Germans, East Germans, Migrants, and Commuters) for selected years (1992, 1994, and 2005) to illustrate the evolution of wages and their distribution over time. The figures indicate the usual shape of wage distributions and a stronger compression of East German wages. The evolution over time

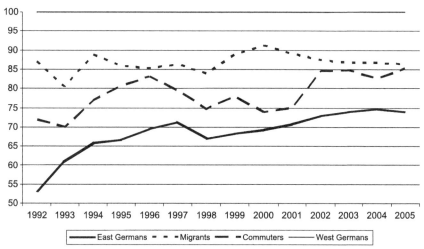

Figure 19.2 Wage convergence between 1992 and 2005: East Germans, migrants, and commuters compared to West Germans.

Source: Samples from SOEP 1992–2005, see text; own calculations.

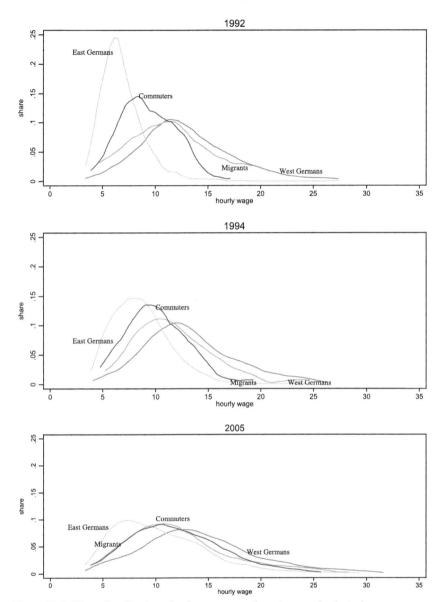

Figure 19.3 Wage distributions for four groups of workers and selected years.

Source: Samples taken from the SOEP 1992–2005, see text; own calculations.

suggests some degree of wage convergence, although a closer look (especially on the right side of the distributions) reveals that considerable differences remain. Wages for East Germans were less dispersed in 1992 compared to 2005. After more than 10 years of convergence the inequality of wages increased again in East Germany and is today even higher than in the West

German wage distribution. The wages of the migrants show a much higher degree of similarity to the wages of the West Germans already in 1992.

The vector of observables for the wage regression and matching procedures contains formal educational qualification, firm size, potential experience, tenure, indicators of economic sectors, an indicator variable which equals one if the worker is born in 1975 or later and zero otherwise, and a variable which indicates whether the worker still works in the job of his first educational qualification. The year 1975 has been chosen because people born after 1975 have started working only after the fall of the Berlin wall. Table 19.2 contains descriptive statistics for some selected variables for the years 1992 and 2005.

On average, workers migrating to the West are youngest (in 2005 31.10% are born after 1974), commuters are younger compared to East Germans who work in East Germany but significantly older than workers who migrate to West Germany. The share of working females is higher in the East (48% in 1992, 53% in 2005) compared to West Germany (43% in 1992, 48% in 2005). In 1992, only 35% of migrants and 18% of commuters were females, so females are under-represented in these groups. In 2005, females were over-represented in the migration sample, while the share of commuting females doubled since 1992 but remains below 50%.

Table 19.2 Descriptive statistics of socio-economic characteristics, 1992 and 2005

	West Germans	*East Germans*	*Migrants*	*Commuters*
1992				
Age (in years)	38.89	39.79	35.65	37.43
Born after 1974 (%)	0	0	0	0
Females (%)	42.71	48.36	35.29	18.29
Low skilled (%)	13.82	1.96	5.88	2.44
Skilled (%)	73.44	65.55	58.82	75.61
High skilled (%)	12.74	32.49	35.29	21.95
Tenure (in years)	10.44	9.32	1.99	1.72
Still in job of first education (%)	61.58	60.62	50.00	45.12
2005				
Age (in years)	41.21	41.99	37.22	39.74
Born after 1974 (%)	9.68	11.57	31.10	16.55
Females (%)	47.76	53.38	54.55	35.86
Low skilled (%)	9.62	4.28	5.26	4.14
Skilled (%)	70.56	64.01	74.16	68.28
High skilled (%)	19.82	31.71	20.57	27.59
Tenure (in years)	11.55	10.80	6.02	8.05
Still in job of first education (%)	62.32	61.27	56.94	57.93

Source: Samples from SOEP 2000–5, see text; own calculations.

Note: Low-skilled: education categories 1 and 2—workers without vocational training; Skilled: education categories 3 and 4—workers with vocational training; High skilled: education categories 5 and 6—workers with a degree from (technical) university.

Formal education has been divided into six categories.[5] According to this definition, East German workers are better educated than West German workers. In 2005, 29.8% (19.8%) of the workforce in our sample who lived in East (West) Germany before unification were high skilled, meaning that they had a degree from technical university or university. On the contrary, only 4.4% (9.6%) were low educated, meaning that they had no vocational training or school degree.

Potential experience is defined as age minus years of education minus 6. It is the time a worker is potentially active in the labor market to gain human capital. We define 17 categories: less than or equal to 3 years of potential experience, 4–6 years, 7–9 years, and so on untill more than 48 years. Tenure is often regarded as a proxy for specific human capital and is divided into 13 categories: less than or equal to 3 years, 4–6 years, 7–9 years, and so on. The highest category is more than 36 years of tenure. Potential experience is comparable between East (21.33 years in 1992, 23.05 years in 2005) and West Germans (21.24 years in 1992, 22.86 years in 2005) while tenure is higher for West Germans (10.44 years in 1992; 11.55 years in 2005) compared to East Germans (9.32 years in 1992, 10.80 years in 2005). Migrants and commuters have the lowest tenure, a result of job changes going hand in hand with migrating or commuting. In 2005, tenure increased, so there seems to be job stability and especially commuters seem to commute to the same employer for a longer time. Migrants to the West change their job more often compared to West and East Germans.

When compared to East Germany, more West German workers are still working in the job of their first educational qualification. In 1992, 50% of migrants and 45% of all commuters were still working in the job of their first occupation training. These shares increased until 2005 as a result of the increasing share of workers who were educated after reunification. Workers who were born before 1975 have potentially been employed in East Germany before unification. They may thus have a higher attachment to the East German labor market and region.

Firm size is measured by 4 four categories.[6] There is a tendency towards smaller enterprises in both German regions. However, in East Germany more workers are employed in firms with fewer than 200 employees (59.3% in 2005), while in West Germany more workers are employed in firms with more than 2,000 employees (48% in 2005). In addition, we control for 11 economic sectors. More East German workers are engaged in agriculture/ mining and construction while more West German workers are engaged in industry sectors and in finance/ business services.

Are these variables enough to identify similar workers in East and West Germany? From our point of view the variables are sensible indicators of human capital. Although their content may differ to some degree, taken together and given the amount and richness of our vector of observables, we think that our matching approach contributes to the understanding of wage convergence. On the one hand, there are possible differences in the meaning of the employment history before reunification and the educational degrees in East Germany. On the other hand, East and West Germans once were unified and despite the separation after World War Two they share the same language, similar working attitudes, and history.

4 An econometric framework

To analyze the evolution of wage convergence and wage inequality in the four groups of workers, we employ a non-parametric matching procedure. The basic idea is to generate samples of West German workers, living and working in West Germany since before reunification, who are similar with respect to the observable characteristics of East German workers. First, we employ a matching procedure to generate a sample of West German workers that is similar to the group of East German workers, living and working in East Germany for each year starting in 1992 and ending in 2005. In these new samples of East and West German statistical twin workers we study wage convergence and the evolution of inequality. Second, we employ a matching procedure to generate a sample of West German workers that is similar to the group of East German workers, who migrated to West Germany. Third, we employ a matching procedure to generate a sample of West German workers that is similar to the group of East German workers, who live in East Germany and commute to work to West Germany. The second and third part of the analysis is restricted to the cross-sections from 2000 to 2005. In earlier cross-sections there are too few observations.

The matching procedure for part one, concerning sample 1 (West Germans) and sample 2 (East Germans) shall be briefly described (for an introduction to the evaluation literature, see Blundell, Dearden, and Sianesi 2005 or Lechner and Pfeiffer 2001). Living in East Germany (currently and before unification) and working in East Germany is our "treatment" group of workers ($D = 1$)). The matched group of workers ($D = 0$) is chosen from the sample of workers who live in West Germany, lived there before unification, and currently work in West Germany.

For the purpose of our investigation we interpret the difference in wages from East German workers and West German statistical twin workers as evidence on wage convergence with respect to the observed characteristics (and not as an average treatment effect). If there no longer remains any difference between the groups compared, then this is interpreted as evidence on wage convergence. Our analysis is not restricted to means or variances, since we compare the evolution of the entire wage distribution over time.

The following matching procedure is used:[7]

1   An observation is drawn from the pool of workers living in East Germany since before reunification.
2   For these workers the nearest neighbour is determined (identified by the

propensity score) from the pool of workers living in West Germany since before reunification.

3 The worker from the West German sample, drawn in step two, is deleted (matching without replacement).

4 Steps 1–3 are repeated for all East German workers.

5 Finally, matches of bad quality are excluded.[8]

This procedure functions well in identifying West German workers who are similar in observable characteristics to the three groups of workers from East Germany. After matching, the two groups of workers are statistically identical with respect to the means of all observed characteristics (the detailed results are available from the authors upon request).

5 Empirical findings on convergence and inequality

Table 19.3 contains the results for four selected cross-sections, 1992, 1994, 2000, and 2005 of West German workers (sample 1 in the first line), East German workers (sample 2, second line), and their West German statistical twin workers (third line). Our measure of wage inequality is the ninetieth to tenth percentile of real gross hourly wage, as well as its two sub-groups, the ninetieth to fiftieth, and fiftieth to tenth percentile of the wage distribution.

Mean wages of East German workers are significantly lower in each cross-section when compared to West German workers in general and their West German statistical twin workers in particular. The differences remain significant, which can be seen by comparing the 95% confidence intervals in Table 19.3 (in brackets). In 2005, East German workers earn about 74% of the wage of their West German statistical twins, starting from 51% in the year 1992. Interestingly there is no measurable difference between the mean wages of West German workers and West German statistical twin workers. Therefore, our findings indicate that the observed wage differentials between East and West German workers are not attributable to differences in the structure of the socio-economic characteristics. For the large group of East German workers, who continue working in East Germany, wage convergence has not taken place after the first 15 years of transition. The labor market returns to similar observed characteristics still differ to a significant degree between East and West Germany.

Our results for commuters and migrants have to be interpreted with caution, since they are based on fewer observations, Table 19.4. Having said this, a clear picture emerges from the matching approach. First, migrants from East to West Germany earn the same wages as their West German statistical twins. A similar set of characteristics results in similar wages. The hypothesis that wages between migrants and West German statistical twins significantly differ, can be rejected in all years as seen by comparing the 95% confidence intervals in Table 19.4 which do overlap. Lower average wages in the group of migrants are therefore caused by differences in individual characteristics,

Table 19.3 Wage convergence and wage inequality: East German workers, West German workers, and West German statistical twins

	Mean wage in €	90/10 percentile	90/50 percentile	50/10 percentile	N
1992					
West Germans	12.96	2.40	1.52	1.57	1,585
	(12.75–13.18)	(2.25–2.54)	(1.48–1.56)	(1.49–1.66)	
East Germans[a]	6.75	2.01	1.46	1.38	904
	(6.61–6.89)	(1.90–2.12)	(1.39–1.52)	(1.33–1.43)	
	(51%)				
West Germans	13.11	2.32	1.52	1.53	904
statistical twins	(12.82–13.40)	(2.17–2.47)	(1.46–1.58)	(1.45–1.61)	
1994					
West Germans	13.24	2.34	1.51	1.55	1,677
	(13.03–13.45)	(2.24–2.44)	(1.46–1.56)	(1.51–1.60)	
East Germans[a]	8.56	2.26	1.45	1.56	805
	(8.37–8.76)	(2.13–2.39)	(1.39–1.51)	(1.50–1.62)	
	(64%)				
West Germans	13.35	2.49	1.58	1.58	805
statistical twins	(13.04–13.66)	(2.36–2.63)	(1.50–1.65)	(1.53–1.64)	
2000					
West Germans	14.21	2.43	1.54	1.58	2,150
	(14.01–14.41)	(2.34–2.52)	(1.50–1.58)	(1.53–1.63)	
East Germans[a]	9.91	2.63	1.62	1.63	606
	(9.61–10.20)	(2.45–2.82)	(1.54–1.70)	(1.52–1.73)	
	(72%)				
West Germans	13.80	2.60	1.60	1.63	606
statistical twins	(13.42–14.19)	(2.38–2.82)	(1.52–1.67)	(1.52–1.75)	
2005					
West Germans	14.14	2.85	1.60	1.79	3,325
	(13.96–14.32)	(2.75–2.96)	(1.56–1.63)	(1.73–1.84)	
East Germans[a]	10.52	2.90	1.70	1.70	1,022
	(10.25–10.80)	(2.71–3.08)	(1.60–1.79)	(1.64–1.77)	
	(74%)				
West Germans	14.16	2.80	1.61	1.74	1,022
statistical twins	(13.83–14.50)	(2.58–3.02)	(1.55–1.67)	(1.62–1.85)	

Source: Samples from SOEP 1992–2005, see text; own calculations; 95% confidence interval and percentage to West German statistical twins in brackets; confidence intervals for percentile ratios are calculated by bootstrapping (1,000 replications); [a] Only East German workers with a matched West German statistical twin.

such as lower tenure or working in smaller companies. Second, commuters earn about 85% of their West German statistical twin workers and the difference in wages is significant (with the exception of the years 2002 and 2005, which can be seen by comparison of the 95% confidence intervals given in Table 19.4 in brackets).

We summarize our findings so far in Figure 19.4. Full wage convergence between East and West German workers has taken place in the group of

Table 19.4 Wage convergence in the groups of migrants and commuters

	Migrants		West Germans statistical twins	Commuters		West Germans statistical twins
	Number	Euro, 95% confidence interval (ratio to West Germans)	Euro, 95% confidence interval	Number	Euro, 95% confidence interval (ratio to West Germans)	Euro, 95% confidence interval
2000	85	12.97 (11.92–14.01) (103%)	12.64 (11.69–13.60)	80	10.46 (9.71–11.22) (83%)	12.63 (11.52–13.74)
2001	89	12.71 (11.71–13.71) (94%)	13.55 (12.50–14.60)	97	10.70 (9.86–11.54) (86%)	12.45 (11.61–13.29)
2002	178	12.36 (11.67–13.05) (95%)	13.02 (12.20–13.85)	120	11.93 (11.17–12.69) (88%)	13.54 (12.56–14.51)
2003	189	12.42 (11.71–13.14) (93%)	13.39 (12.67–14.11)	131	12.20 (11.43–12.97) (84%)	14.55 (13.59–15.51)
2004	205	12.46 (11.79–13.13) (100%)	12.41 (11.71–13.11)	142	11,80 (11.09–12.52) (87%)	13.56 (12.66–14.45)
2005	199	12.28 (11.58–12.97) (97%)	12.68 (11.96–13.40)	141	12.03 (11.30–12.76) (89%)	13.45 (12.52–14.37)

Source: Samples from SOEP 1992–2005, see text; own calculations.

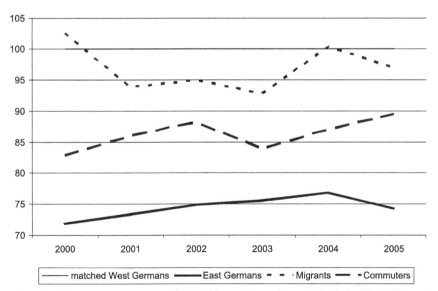

Figure 19.4 Wage convergence of East German workers with their West German statistical twins between 2000 and 2005.

Source: Samples from SOEP 2000–2005, see text; own calculations.

migrants from East to West Germany. Nearly full wage convergence occurred in the group of commuters from East Germany to West Germany. For the largest group of workers, those workers who still work in East Germany, we have to reject the hypothesis of wage convergence.

Our additional analysis deals with the evolution of wage inequality. Among West German workers the ratio of the ninetieth to tenth percentile first decreased from 1984 to 1992, indicating moderate wage compression (Gernandt and Pfeiffer 2007). Since around 1993/4, the year of a severe recession after the unification boom, wage inequality has increased in both parts of Germany. In our samples, (see Table 19.3) over the period from 1992 to 2005 wage inequality, measured by the ninetieth to tenth wage percentile ratio, has increased by 19% (from 2.40 to 2.85) in West Germany and by 44% in East Germany (from 2.01 to 2.90). In West Germany inequality increased stronger below, in East Germany above the median.

Compared to West German workers, wage inequality was lower in the sample of East German workers in 1992. Today, our measures of wage inequality no longer show any significant differences between East and West German workers and between East German workers and their West German statistical twins. In both parts of Germany, the degree of wage inequality seems to have converged. We summarize some of these findings in Figure 19.5. The figure shows the wage distribution for East and West German workers and for the West German statistical twin workers of the East German workers. Figure 19.5 nicely illustrates that there is no difference in the wage distribution between West German workers and the West German statistical twins of East German workers. In addition, it shows that the shape of the wage distribution of East German workers converges to the shape of West German workers.

To further investigate price, composition, and residual factors behind the evolution of wage inequality we employ the Juhn, Murphy, and Pierce (1993) decomposition method. Table 19.5 contains the results for these three factors from 1994 to 2005, with the base year 1994. In East Germany, wage inequality measured by the ninetieth–tenth wage percentile ratio increased by 0.248 log points. A larger part of the increase, 0.159 log points, took place above the median. In West Germany, wage inequality increased by 0.197 log points. A larger part of the increase, 0.141 log points, took place below the median. In West Germany, rising wage inequality is mainly driven by residual (0.101 log points) and price effects (0.028 log points), in East Germany price effects (0.159 log points) are the most important reason for rising wage inequality followed by residual effects (0.087 log points). The evolution of wage inequality in the group of West German statistical twin workers shows more similarities to the development of West German workers as compared to East German workers.

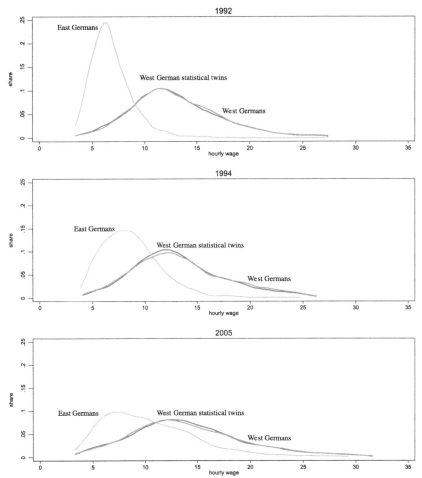

Figure 19.5 The evolution of wage distributions for East and West German workers.

Source: Samples from SOEP 1992–2005, see text; own calculations.

6 Concluding remarks

German reunification might become a paradigm of convergence and integration of neighbouring regions with unequal starting conditions. One of the most ambitious political goals has been the equalization of living conditions and wages in both parts of Germany. What has happened to wages and wage convergence after 15 years of transition? Do labor markets in two neighboring regions such as East and West Germany function in such a way that wage convergence takes place?

In this study, we empirically compare the evolution of wages and wage inequality after reunification in both parts of Germany. In particular, we

Table 19.5 Composition, price and residual effects, 1994–2005

Differential	Total	Quantities	Prices	Unobserved
West Germans				
90–10	0.197	0.028	0.068	0.101
90–50	0.056	−0.007	0.021	0.041
50–10	0.141	0.035	0.047	0.060
East Germans				
90–10	0.248	0.002	0.159	0.087
90–50	0.159	0.024	0.095	0.040
50–10	0.089	−0.022	0.064	0.047
West German statistical twins				
90–10	0.116	−0.028	0.054	0.091
90–50	0.024	−0.035	0.027	0.031
50–10	0.093	0.007	0.026	0.060

Source: SOEP 1994–2005, see text; own calculations.

compare three groups of workers who lived in East Germany in 1989, defined as stayers, migrants, and commuters to West Germany, and groups of West German statistical twin workers, all taken from the SOEP 1992–2005. Regression analysis, non-parametric matching methods, and graphical presentations are employed to study wage convergence and inequality. Our findings indicate that for the largest group of workers, those who still work in East Germany, the hypothesis of wage convergence has to be rejected. After 15 years of transition wages for East and West German workers with similar characteristics did not converge. However, full wage convergence between East and West German workers has taken place in the group of migrants from East to West Germany, and, nearly full wage convergence occurred in the group of commuters from East Germany to West Germany.

Furthermore, wage inequality converged. For prime age dependent employees living and working in East Germany the ratio of wages for high-wage workers, as measured by the ninetieth percentile of the wage distribution, and low-wage workers, as measured by the tenth percentile of the wage distribution, increased from 2.00 to 2.93 and is now similar to wage inequality in the group of West German statistical twin workers. We conclude that labor markets in East and West Germany still exhibit large differences in wages, but that the degree of inequality in the two regions converged.

Notes

* Friedhelm Pfeiffer acknowledges financial support from the German Science Foundation under grants PF 331/2 ("Microeconometric Methods to Assess Heterogeneous Returns to Education") and PF 331/3 ("Wages, Rent-Sharing and Collective Wage Bargaining"). For comments we would like to thank · Alisher Aldashev, Markus Clauss and Pia Pinger. For fine research assistance we thank

Philipp Eisenhauer, Jan Huntgeburth and Carina Leesch. The usual disclaimer applies.
1   See Haisken-DeNew and Frick (2005).
2   SOEP-Samples 4 and 7 have been omitted. Sample 4 focuses on immigrants to West Germany between 1984 and 1993 (mainly foreigners). There are no immigrants to East Germany. Sample 7, which is available only for 2002, 2003, and 2004, is an expansion of the SOEP and contains mostly high-wage earners. Several tests to check the sensitivity of the selected sample have been performed. Inclusion of sample 4 does not alter our findings. Sample 6 is included to exploit the total number of observations available in the SOEP.
3   Since 1999 there are more observations with missing information about household residence in 1989.
4   All wages are deflated with the Consumer Price Index for Germany, base year 2000, Statistisches Bundesamt (2006).
5   These are: without a school qualification and without vocational training; with a school qualification but without vocational training; with a medium school qualification and with vocational training; with highest school qualification and with vocational training; with a technical university degree; with a university degree.
6   These are: small firms with less or equal than 19 employees; medium-sized firms with 20–199 employees; large firms with 200–2,000 employees; very large firms with more than 2,000 employees.
7   Estimation was performed with STATA (psmatch2; see Leuven and Sianesi 2003).
8   Observations are deleted if the difference of the propensity scores exceeds 0.05.

References

Akerlof, G. A., A. K. Rose, J. L. Yellen, H. Hessenius, R. Dornbusch, and M. Guitan (1991) "East Germany in from the Cold: The Economic Aftermath of Currency Union." *Brookings Papers on Economic Activity* 1: 1–105.
Autor, D. H., L. F. Katz, and M. S. Kearny (2006) "The Polarization of the US Labor Market." *The American Economic Review* 96, 189–94.
Bewley, T. (1999) *Why Wages Don't Fall During a Recession*, Cambridge, MA: Harvard University Press.
Bird, E. J., J. Schwarze, and G. G. Wagner (1994) "Wage Effects on the Move Toward Free Markets in East Germany." *Industrial and Labor Relations Review* 47(3): 390–400.
Blundell, R., L. Dearden, and B. Sianesi (2005) "Evaluating the Impact of Education on Earnings in the UK: Models, methods and results from the NCDS." *Journal of the Royal Statistical Society: Series A* 168(3): 473–512.
Brücker, H. and P. Trübswetter (2007) "Do the Best Go West? An analysis of the self-selection of employed east-west migrants in Germany. *Empirica* 34(4): 371–95.
Burda, M. C., W. Hardle, M. Muller, and A. Werwatz (1998) "Semiparametric Analysis of German East-West Migration Intentions: Facts and Theory." *Journal of Applied Econometrics* 13(5): 525–41.
Fitzenberger, B., R. Hujer, T. E. MaCurdy, and R. Schnabel (2001) "Testing for Uniform Wage Trends in West-Germany: A cohort analysis using quantile regressions for censored data." *Empirical Economics* 26: 41–86.
Franz, W. and V. Steiner (2000) "Wages in the East German Transition Process: Facts and Explanations." *German Economic Review* 1(3): 241–69.
Gernandt, J. and F. Pfeiffer (2007) "Rising Wage Inequality in Germany." *Jahrbücher für Nationalökonomie und Statistik* 227(4).

Haisken-DeNew, J. and J. R. Frick (2005) *DTC Desktop Companion to the German Socio-Economic Panel (SOEP)*. DIW Berlin.

Hauser, R. and H. Fabig (1999) "Labor Earning and Household Income Mobility in Reunified Germany: A comparison of the eastern and western states." *Review of Income and Wealth* 45(3): 303–24.

Hauser, R. and G. G. Wagner (1996) "Die Einkommensverteilung in Ostdeutschland—Darstellung und Determinanten für die Jahre 1990 bis 1994." In R. Hauser, *Sozialpolitik im vereinten Deutschland III*. Berlin: Dunker und Humblot, pp. 79–127.

Heiland, F. (2004) "Trends in East-West German Migration from 1989 to 2002." *Demograhic Research* 11(7), 173–94.

Hunt, J. (2001) "Post-Unification Wage Growth in East Germany." *Review of Economics and Statistics* 83: 190–5.

Hunt, J. (2006) "Staunching Emigration from East Germany: Age and the determinants of migration." *Journal of the European Economic Association* 4(5): 1014–37.

Juhn, C., K. M. Murphy, and B. Pierce (1993) "Wage Inequality and the Rise in Returns to Skill." *The Journal of Political Economy* 101(3): 410–42.

Kohn, K. (2006) "Rising Wage Dispersion, After All! The German wage structure at the turn of the century." ZEW Discussion Paper 06–031.

Krueger, A. B. and J.-S. Pischke (1995) "A Comparative Analysis of East and West German Labor Markets: Before and after unification." In: R. Freeman and L. Katz, *Differences and Changes in Wage Structures*. University of Chicago Press, Chicago, pp. 405–45.

Krugman, P. (1994) "Past and Prospective Causes of High Unemployment." *Economic Review*, Federal Reserve Bank of Kansas City, pp. 23–43.

Lechner, M. and F. Pfeiffer (2001) *Econometric Evaluation of Labour Market Policies*. Heidelberg: Physica.

——, ——, and L. Giesecke-O'Shea (1993) "Expected Job Loss in East Germany Shortly Before German Unification." *Empirical Economics* 18: 289–306.

Leuven, E. and B. Sianesi (2003) *PSMATCH2: Stata Module to Perform Full Mahalanobis and Propensity Score Matching, Common Support Graphing, and Covariate Imbalance Testing*, http://ideas.repec.org/c/boc/bocode/s432001.html.

Möller, J. (2005) "Die Entwicklung der Lohnspreizung in West- und Ostdeutschland." *Beiträge zur Arbeitsmarkt und Berufsforschung* 294, IAB Nürnberg, 47–63.

Pfeiffer, F. (2003) *Lohnrigiditäten im gemischten Lohnbildungssystem*. Baden-Baden: Nomos.

Pischke, J.-S., M. Staat, and S. Vögele (1994) "Warum pendeln Ostdeutsche in den Westen?" In H. König and W. Steiner, *Arbeitslosigkeit, Löhne und Weiterbildung*, Baden-Baden: Nomos, pp. 311–43.

Prasad, E. S. (2004) "The Unbearable Stability of the German Wage Structure: Evidence and interpretation." *IMF Staff Papers* 51(2), 354–85.

Sinn, G. and H.-W. Sinn (1992) *Jumpstart. The Economic Unification of Germany*. Cambridge, MA: MIT Press.

Statistisches Bundesamt (2006) *Statistisches Jahrbuch 2006 für die Bundesrepublik Deutschland*, Wiesbaden (Statistisches Bundesamt).

Statistische Ämter der Länder (2005) *Volkswirtschaftliche Gesamtrechnung der Länder*, Reihe 1, Band 1, Wiesbaden.

Uhlig, H. (2006) "Regional Labor Markets, Network Externalities and Migration: The case of German reunification." *The American Economic Review* 96(2): 383–7.

20 Child work and schooling costs in rural Northern India

Gautam Hazarika and Arjun Singh Bedi

1 Introduction

That child labor and schooling are competing activities so that work by children reduces their school attendance, and, thereby, their future welfare, is a prime reason for the objectionability of child labor. Substitutability between child work and schooling suggests the former may be combated by educational interventions such as improvement in the quality of and access to education. Indeed, the International Labor Organization (ILO) holds that "the single most effective way to stem the flow of school-age children into abusive forms of employment is to extend and improve schooling so that it will attract and retain them" (ILO 1998a).

However, empirical studies do not always find a strong negative relation between access to schooling and child work. For example, Grootaert (1999) reports that access to schooling is negatively related to child labor force participation in rural Cote d'Ivoire, but that schooling costs are not statistically significant correlates of child labor in urban Cote d'Ivoire. Recent research into India's South Asian neighbors, Bangladesh and Pakistan, suggests that the failure of some studies to find a strong positive (negative) relation between child work and schooling costs (access to schooling) may be due to two reasons. First, a strong negative relation between school enrollment and schooling costs may not translate to a strong positive relation between child work and schooling costs if children's leisure mitigates the trade-off between their work and schooling (Ravallion and Wodon 2000). Second, all types of child work may not be responsive to changes in schooling costs. Indeed, some types of work may be entirely unresponsive, and if such work makes up a large portion of child work, child labor as a whole and schooling costs may not be strongly associated[1] (Hazarika and Bedi 2003). Both Ravallion's and Wodon's (2000) and Hazarika's and Bedi's (2003) findings suggest that a policy of improving access to schooling shall have limited success in quelling child work.[2] Might this be true of neighboring India as well, where educational interventions have lately been seen as crucial to the suppression of child work?

This study uses data from rural Uttar Pradesh and Bihar, two Northern

Indian states, to estimate the effects of schooling costs upon, separately, child work and school enrollment, in order to assess the extent of contemporaneous trade-off between work and school attendance, and, thereby, the efficacy of a policy of improving access to schooling in reducing child work. The study subsequently acknowledges that children may combine work with schooling, or, for that matter, neither work nor attend school. In other words, it recognizes that a child may occupy one of the four states of "school and no work", "no school and work", "school and work", and "no school and no work". Thus, in order to assess the extent of contemporaneous trade-off between children's work and school attendance, it also estimates the effect of schooling costs upon the probability that a child shall work rather than enroll in school relative to the probability that she shall enroll in school rather than work. Finally, since there may be heterogeneity in the effects of educational policy interventions upon the different types of child work, this study estimates the effects of schooling costs upon, separately, intra-household and extra-household work, and, separately, domestic and economic (both intra-household and extra-household) work.

It is found that not only is there a significant positive relation between child work and schooling costs, and a significant negative relation between school enrollment and schooling costs, but also that the increase in the probability of school enrollment from a decrease in schooling costs is comparable in magnitude to the corresponding decrease in the probability of child work, implying children's work and school attendance are highly substitutable activities. This is implied as well by the uncovering of a positive relation between schooling costs and the probability that a child shall work rather than enroll in school relative to the probability that she shall enroll in school rather than work. Thus, a policy of improving access to schooling may both raise school attendance and reduce child work in rural Uttar Pradesh and Bihar.

The following section discusses the scope of, and policies with regard to, child labor in India. Section 3 discusses empirical issues in the assessment of contemporaneous trade-off between children's work and schooling, as well as the study's empirical strategy. Section 4 describes the utilized data. Section 5 reports the empirical findings. Section 6 presents concluding remarks.

2 Child labor in India: scope, legal framework, and policies

Work, according to the instructional manuals provided to Census and National Sample Survey enumerators by the Government of India, is defined as "participation in any economically productive activity" (Census of India 1981, Vol. 22). This definition includes unpaid intra-household work in a farm or a non-farm enterprise but excludes chores such as cooking, cleaning, caring for cattle, collecting firewood, and child care. By this narrow definition, the Census of India estimates that there were 11.28 million 5–14 year old working Indian children in 1991. A slightly lower figure of 10.4 million working children is obtained from the 55th round of the National Sample

Survey conducted in 1999–2000. Therefore, based on a total of 210 million 5–14-year-old children in 1991, the activity rate of children lies in the range of 5 to 5.2%. In contrast, the ILO estimates that 13.5% of boys and 10.3% of girls were economically active in the period 1981–91 (ILO 1995). More worrisome estimates result from a broadening of the definition of work to include domestic chores, or from the presumption that children not in school must be at work. For instance, UNICEF "cites figures ranging from seventy-five to ninety million child laborers under the age of fourteen" (Human Rights Watch 1996). A government report (Government of India, National Commission on Labor 2001) puts the number of working children at more than 100 million, which translates to an activity rate of about 48%. Thus, estimates of the number of working Indian children range from 10 to 100 million.

India is a signatory to several international conventions designed to secure the rights of children. In addition, Article 24 of the Indian Constitution states that "No child below the age of fourteen years shall be employed to work in any factory or mine or employed in any hazardous employment." Article 39(e) of the Constitution directs the State to ensure that "the tender age of children" is "not abused and that citizens are not forced by economic necessity to enter avocations unsuited to their age or strength". The Child Labor Act of 1986 prohibits the employment of children below age 14 in specified hazardous occupations and processes. A tighter ban on child labor in India came into effect on October 10, 2006, by which even the hiring of children below age 14 as household domestic help or as waiters in restaurants is proscribed. Thus, laws in India offer child workers a measure of protection. However, their enforcement is wanting. For example, based on its investigation of child labor in India between 1996 and 2003, Human Rights Watch found that most government officials responsible for enforcing child labor laws have failed to do so, that illegal employers are almost never persecuted, and that money allocated by the government for the rehabilitation of child workers has remained unspent (Human Rights Watch, 2006). In any case, labor laws may not be depended upon to stamp out child work since unpaid labor in a household farm or non-farm enterprise, the predominant form of child work, is usually beyond the scope of legislation. Recognizing this, policy makers in India and elsewhere are increasingly looking to educational interventions to combat child labor.[3]

The two major child labor and educational programs of the Government of India are the National Child Labor Projects (under the aegis of the National Child Labor Policy of 1987) and the Sarva Shiksha Abhiyan (SSA) program. The National Child Labor Projects (NCLP) are focused on districts where child labor is widespread and attempt to provide educational opportunities to working children. Their strategy includes the establishment of schools supplying non-formal education, the creation of additional income and employment generation opportunities for parents, and the founding of programs to raise public awareness.

The Sarva Shiksha Abhiyan (SSA) program, launched in 2001, aims to ensure that all children will begin completing elementary education (grades 1–5) by 2007 and upper primary education (grades 6–8) by 2010.[4] In addition to its other activities, the program finances the construction and repair of schools, the payment of teachers' salaries, the provision of free textbooks to girls, and the establishment of crèches for the younger siblings of children of school going age. Various reports (Wu, Kaul and Sankar 2005) suggest that the program has been successful in improving the quality of educational inputs and increasing school enrollment. The SSA program has non-partisan political support, and substantial monetary and human resources have been devoted to it. Its 2006–7 budget is 41% higher than in the previous year and it is expected that 500,000 additional classrooms will be constructed and 150,000 new teachers will be appointed (Government of India Union Budget 2006–7). Although it is not focused upon child labor, an expected favorable side-effect of its activities is decline in child work.

3 Empirical concerns and strategy

It shall be argued below that a child's time constraint and her household's budget constraint may limit the empirical methodology suitable to assessing the extent of contemporaneous trade-off between children's work and school attendance.

Assume, as do Ravallion and Wodon (2000), that the parents of, for simplicity, a single child, derive utility in a period from household consumption (C), their child's schooling (S), and her leisure (H). Hence, their utility function may be represented as

$$U = U(C, S, H; Z)$$

where Z represents exogenous household and community characteristics that parameterize the utility function. The child's total available time (T) may be allocated between schooling, leisure, and wage labor (L). This yields the time constraint

$$S + H + L = T.$$

The household's budget constraint may be written as

$$C + t.S = w.L + Y(Z),$$

where t represents the cost of schooling, w denotes the child's wage rate, and Y, taken to be a function of the exogenous household and community characteristics Z, represents household income from sources other than child labor. The time and budget constraints may be combined as

$$w.T + Y(Z) - (w + t).S - w.H - C = 0 \qquad (1)$$

Hence, the parents may be viewed as maximizing $U(C, S, H; Z)$ with respect to C, S, and H, subject to the constraint (1). The Lagrangian function of this optimization problem is

$$Ł = U(C, S, H; Z) + \lambda. [w.T + Y(Z) - C - (w + t).S - w.H], \qquad (2)$$

λ denoting the Lagrange multiplier. Of the four first-order conditions for a maximum, consider, for example,

$$\partial Ł / \partial S = U_2 - \lambda.(w + t) = 0. \qquad (3)$$

(3) yields optimal child school attendance as a function of household consumption, child leisure, the exogenous Z, the child's wage rate, the cost of schooling, and λ, that is

$$S = f(C, H, Z, w, t, \lambda). \qquad (4)$$

Given the household's budget constraint and the child's time constraint, (4) may be rewritten as

$$S = f\{w.L + Y(Z), T - S - L, Z, w, t, \lambda\}$$

so that it is possible that collecting terms shall yield

$$S = S(L, Z, w, t, \lambda). \qquad (5)$$

(5) relates the child's optimal hours at school to her time at work. A negative relation between S and L by this equation, interpretable as evidence of trade-off between children's work and school attendance, will indicate that parents who find it optimal to work their children harder will also find it optimal to have them spend less time at school. Assume (5), augmented to include unobserved and random influences, e, upon S, takes the linear form

$$S = a + b_1.L + b_2.Z + b_3.w + b_4.t + b_5.\lambda + e. \qquad (6)$$

It is clear that all the exogenous variables in the model, namely, Z, w, and t, are explanatory variables in (6). Even if, by some formulation of the model, a subset of these exogenous variables were excluded from (6), λ, the value of the Lagrange multiplier at the optimum, is a function of *all* the exogenous variables in the model. Hence, if, as a necessary prelude to estimation, unobserved λ were substituted by its functional form, S in (6) would be a function of all the exogenous variables in the model. Since L, the child's optimal time at work, is, by dint of being a function of the choice variables S and H, endogenous, the direct effect of L upon S via formulations such as (6) must be estimated by instrumental variables (IV) methods. In other words, this "direct approach" to gauging trade-off between children's work and their schooling must rest upon credible instruments for child work. Suitable instruments must be exogenous, correlated with child work, and absent from (6). However, if *all* exogenous influences are, in fact, explanatory variables in (6), suitable instruments may not be found.

In sum, since it is likely parents simultaneously select children's optimal school attendance and work in a time period, an equation relating school attendance to work, the basis of the aforementioned "direct approach", must be viewed as a first-order condition of optimization to be estimated by IV methods. It is probable, particularly since optimization is constrained by household budgets and children's available time, that this first-order condition shall include all the exogenous variables with any bearing on the optimization. It may be impossible, therefore, to uncover an exogenous variable that is correlated with child work but not a direct influence upon school attendance, that is, to instrument endogenous child work.

While a number of studies estimate equations such as (6), many mistakenly consider child work to be exogenous. While other, more recent, studies treat child labor as endogenous and employ IV methods to identify the true causal effect of child work upon schooling, it is uncertain, in light of the above arguments, that the utilized instruments are valid. For example, Ray and Lancaster (2005) estimate the effect of children's work hours upon their dichotomous school enrollment status in seven countries including Cambodia, the Philippines, and Sri Lanka. Dichotomous school enrollment status is merely an indicator of hours at school. Therefore, a regression equation relating school enrollment status to hours of work would resemble (6), and, hence, finding exogenous variables to instrument endogenous work hours shall, as discussed, prove difficult. Ray's and Lancaster's (2005) instruments include measures of household income and wealth. However, household income and wealth would be factors in the type of parental constrained optimization discussed above and so would appear among the explanatory variables in (6). It is notable that the authors accede that the reader "needs to keep in mind that the evidence from the IV estimates is conditional on the validity of the instruments used here".

Hence, this study adopts the approach, although indirect, of examining the effect of a policy intervention upon children's time in school in a period and, separately, its effect upon their time at work in the same period. This is the very strategy adopted by, for example, Ravallion and Wodon (2000). The finding that the intervention results in both a decrease (increase) in school attendance and a comparable increase (decrease) in work would indicate there is contemporaneous trade-off between them. As discussed in Section 4, the utilized data do not offer a continuous measure of work. Thus, this study estimates the effect of changes in schooling costs upon the probability that a child is enrolled in school in a time period and, separately, upon the probability that she works in that period. If a fall in schooling costs were found to increase the probability of school enrollment while comparably decreasing the probability of child work, it will be inferred that children's work and school attendance are highly substitutable activities so that a policy of improving access to schooling would be effective in steering children away from work toward school. Consequently, the equations

$$work^* = a_1 + \beta_1. \textit{ schooling costs} + \gamma_1. \textit{ other exogenous correlates} + u_1, \quad (7)$$

and

$$school^* = a_2 + \beta_2. \textit{ schooling costs} + \gamma_2. \textit{ other exogenous correlates} + u_2, \quad (8)$$

are estimated, where *work** measures a child's dichotomous participation in work, *school** measures her dichotomous enrollment in school, and the *u* are regression errors. (7) and (8) may be considered solutions to the child's parents' aforementioned constrained optimization problem. Assuming u_1 and u_2 are each normally distributed, the equations may be estimated by probit ML. While the coefficients in vector β_1 are expected to be positive, it is anticipated those in β_2 shall be negative.

There is, in addition, a subsidiary strategy. Since a child may combine work with school, or neither work nor attend school,[5] that is, occupy one of the four states of "school and no work", "no school and work", "school and work", and "no school and no work", children's school enrollment and work are also analyzed by the means of a multinomial logit model. Therefore, it is assumed that

prob. (*not in school and working*)/prob. (*in school and not working*) =

exponent $(a_3 + \beta_3. \textit{ schooling costs} + \gamma_3. \textit{ other exogenous correlates}), \quad (9)$

that

prob. (*in school and working*)/prob. (*in school and not working*) =

exponent $(a_4 + \beta_4. \textit{ schooling costs} + \gamma_4. \textit{ other exogenous correlates}), \quad (10)$

and that

prob. (*not in school and not working*)/prob. (*in school and not working*) =

exponent $(a_5 + \beta_5. \textit{ schooling costs} + \gamma_5. \textit{ other exogenous correlates}). \quad (11)$

The finding that β_3 is positive, that is, an increase in schooling costs raises the probability that a child shall work rather than enroll in school relative to the probability that she shall enroll in school rather than work, will also indicate that there is contemporaneous trade-off between children's work and school attendance.

4 The data

The study's empirical analyses are conducted upon data from the 1997–8 Survey of Living Conditions in rural Southern and Eastern Uttar Pradesh and Northern and Central Bihar, of the Living Standards Measurement Survey (LSMS) series of the World Bank. The Survey covered 2,250 house-holds drawn from 120 villages in 25 districts of Uttar Pradesh and Bihar. With nearly 176 million inhabitants, Uttar Pradesh is India's most populous state. Bihar, with a population of nearly 83 million, is India's third most populous state[6]. By almost any indicator of poverty and socio-economic development, these two states are ranked among the lowest in the Indian Union (Government of India, Planning Commission 2001).

The Survey elicited information about 10–14-year-old children's work activities. Hours within the preceding year in intra-household work pro-ducing a marketable output, and in extra-household work, may be computed. However, only dichotomous participation in household domestic work is known. This study considers child work to include household domestic work since its exclusion would likely seriously bias gender perspectives of India's child labor problem. The inclusion of domestic work is also justi-fied upon grounds of the ILO's warning that "an emphasis on traditional practices over the potential hazards of work for children can result in ignor-ing the extent of the child labor problem" and that "what happens within the family context" may well fall within the purview of labor laws in the future (ILO 1998b), and Nieuwenhuys's (1994) conclusion, based on detailed anthropological study in Kerala, India, that work within the household is not any less demanding or less important for families than market work, and there can be no presumption that poor parents are able to protect their children from excessive drudgery and exploitation. However, the utilized data do not supply a continuous gauge of household domestic work, and so it is necessary to measure child work as a whole in binary fashion. Thus, it will be possible to estimate the effect of schooling costs only upon the probability that a child worked in the preceding year. Since a change in the probability of child work must then, by the study's empirical strategy, be compared to the corresponding change in the probability of school attend-ance, school attendance too is measured dichotomously as current school enrollment.

The data are rich in household and community descriptors. They permit measurement of the costs of schooling in four ways, namely, by the distance in kilometers to the nearest public primary (grades 1–5) school, the distance to the nearest middle (grades 6–8) public or private school, the distance to the nearest secondary (grades 9–10) public or private school, and by the village-average monetary cost of primary schooling. The first three measures pertain to the time, or opportunity, cost of school attendance, while the fourth gauges the direct cost of schooling. Note that the nearest middle and secondary schools need not be in the public sector, though they likely are, given that, of the 104 villages in the Survey in which schools were located, 71.2% had but public schools.

By NSS (1999–2000) data, the economic activity rates of children in Bihar and Uttar Pradesh are, respectively, 5% and 6.4%. In contrast, as shown in Table 20.1, these LSMS data indicate that 12% of children in the two states, albeit in their rural areas, were engaged in economic work in the year preceding the survey, with no substantial difference between the participation rates of boys (12.8%) and girls (11.7%). About 18% of the children participated in household domestic work. Clearly, far more girls (36.6%) than boys (3.8%) performed domestic chores. Thus, ignoring domestic chores shall certainly bias gender perspectives of child work in this region. As regards work as a whole, 27.76% of the children undertook it in the preceding twelve months, with 44.16% of the girls but only 15.14% of the boys doing so. The figures in Table 20.1 show that this substantial gender difference is due to the much higher participation rate of girls in household domestic work. Thus, girls appear doubly burdened in that they engage in economic work at about the same rate as boys besides participating far more substantially in household domestic work. By Table 20.2, about 70% of the children were enrolled in school at the time of the survey. However, with 80.6% of the boys but only 55.8% of the girls enrolled, there is a large gender difference.

Table 20.3 presents sample descriptive statistics. These occasionally differ from corresponding 2001 Census statistics since the data, collected from South and Eastern Uttar Pradesh and North and Central Bihar, are not representative of these states in their entirety. For example, the proportion of Muslims in Bihar and Uttar Pradesh is 15–16% and average family size is

Table 20.1 Work participation rates (per cent) of 10–14-year-old children in rural Uttar Pradesh and Bihar, 1997–8

	Male	*Female*	*Total*
Domestic work—within the household	3.86	36.55	18.08
Economic work—within the household	7.43	7.98	7.67
All intra-household work	11.29	41.00	24.21
Economic work—outside the household	4.29	4.82	4.52
All work	15.14	44.16	27.76
Number	700	539	1239

Table 20.2 School enrollment rates (per cent) of 10–14-year-old children in rural Uttar Pradesh and Bihar, 1997–8

	Male	*Female*	*Total*
Enrolled in school	80.57	55.8	69.8
Number	700	539	1239

Table 20.3 Full sample descriptive statistics

Variable	Mean	Std dev.
Dependent variables		
Working = 1	0.278	0.448
Engaged in intra-household work	0.242	0.429
Engaged in extra-household work	0.045	0.208
Engaged in household domestic work	0.181	0.385
Engaged in economic work	0.116	0.321
Enrolled in school =1	0.698	0.459
Enrolled in school and not engaged in work	0.659	0.474
Not enrolled in school and engaged in work	0.238	0.426
Enrolled in school and engaged in work	0.040	0.195
Not enrolled in school and not engaged in work	0.064	0.244
Child attributes		
Male = 1	0.565	0.496
Age	11.72	1.417
Costs of schooling		
Distance to nearest primary school (kilometers)	0.592	0.918
Distance to nearest middle school (kilometers)	2.771	2.497
Distance to nearest secondary school (kilometers)	5.156	4.300
Village-average annual direct cost of primary schooling (thousands of rupees)	0.328	0.179
Household attributes		
Household head is illiterate = 1	0.454	0.498
Landholding (acres)	2.810	5.931
Transfer payments received by household (hundreds of rupees)	12.54	75.60
Family size	8.251	4.235
Number of children, 0–4 age group	0.860	1.036
Number of children, 5–9 age group	1.362	1.234
Female headed household = 1	0.035	0.183
Number of enterprises run by household	0.542	0.780
Household has a handicraft enterprise	0.014	0.116
Household has a retail enterprise	0.165	0.371
Muslim = 1	0.100	0.300
Hindu, upper caste = 1	0.157	0.364
Hindu, middle caste = 1	0.023	0.149
Community and regional controls		
Village average daily male wage in agriculture (rupees)	24.90	8.177
Access to paved road = 1	0.502	0.500
Access to irrigation = 1	0.262	0.440
Residing in Bihar = 1	0.438	0.496
N	1239	

between 6.16 and 6.25 according to 2001 Census data, whereas Muslims make up a smaller proportion of the sample and the sample mean family is larger. However, these sample statistics match the States' Census figures along other dimensions such as household literacy. It would be safer, however, to view the study's findings as applying only to the mentioned regions of these two states.

5 Results

Table 20.4 presents probit estimates of (7). Given the descriptive statistics in Table 20.1, it is not surprising that boys are 32 percentage points less likely to work than girls. Older children appear more likely to work. The marginal effect of age upon the probability of work ranges from 2 percentage points for boys to 9.5 percentage points for girls. A boy in a household with an illiterate head is 11 percentage points more likely to work whereas an equivalent girl is about 20 percentage points likelier to do so. Children in large families appear less likely to be called upon to work. Somewhat surprisingly, given that, traditionally, mainly girls care for their younger siblings, work by both boys and girls is more likely in households with greater numbers of younger children. Girls in female-headed households are 23 percentage points more likely to work perhaps because they must shoulder more domestic chores as the adult females engage in necessary economic work. A girl's propensity to work significantly decreases in her household's unearned income. There appear to be inter-caste differences in children's propensities to work, although no significant inter-faith differences. For example, upper caste Hindu boys and girls are, respectively, 6 percentage points and 35 percentage points less likely to work. Variables plausibly associated with household demand for child labor, such as landholdings and the type of non-farm enterprises operated by families, are statistically insignificant correlates of child work.

It may be seen that a child's propensity to work is largely significantly related to measures of the costs of schooling. Since most villages have a primary school, it is not surprising that distance to the nearest public primary school has no statistically discernible effect upon child work. On the other hand, distances to the nearest middle and secondary schools and the monetary cost of primary schooling are statistically significant influences upon a child's propensity to work, although there are notable gender differences. The monetary cost of primary schooling is a more pronounced determinant of work by boys than of work by girls. The estimates suggest that reducing the average annual monetary cost of primary schooling by one standard deviation (Rs. 179) would cause the probability of work by the average boy to decrease by 3.7 ($0.179 \times 0.207 \times 100$) percentage points while having no statistically discernible effect upon a girl's propensity to work. In contrast, proximity to schools has a stronger influence upon work by girls. A kilometer reduction in the distance to the nearest middle school would result in a

Table 20.4 Determinants of work probit marginal effects

Variable	(1) Full sample	(2) Boys	(3) Girls
Male	−0.323*** (0.026)	.	.
Age	0.050*** (0.009)	0.020** (0.008)	0.095*** (0.018)
Distance to nearest primary school	−0.016 (0.015)	−0.005 (0.013)	−0.034 (0.030)
Distance to nearest middle school	0.019*** (0.006)	0.010* (0.005)	0.028*** (0.011)
Distance to nearest secondary school	0.012*** (0.003)	0.004 (0.003)	0.026*** (0.007)
Direct cost of primary schooling	0.207*** (0.081)	0.207*** (0.072)	0.106 (0.157)
Household head is Illiterate	0.148*** (0.028)	0.109*** (0.027)	0.204*** (0.050)
Landholding	−0.004 (0.003)	−0.001 (0.003)	−0.007 (0.007)
Transfer	−0.0009* (0.0005)	−0.00003 (0.0003)	−0.002** (0.001)
Family size	−0.031*** (0.006)	−0.031*** (0.007)	−0.033*** (0.011)
Number of children 0–4 age group	0.035** (0.017)	0.036** (0.017)	0.047 (0.030)
Number of children 5–9 age group	0.035** (0.015)	0.023 (0.016)	0.050* (0.027)
Female headed household	0.145* (0.085)	0.047 (0.079)	0.235* (0.126)
Number of enterprises	0.020 (0.021)	0.006 (0.020)	0.053 (0.038)
Handicraft enterprise	0.047 (0.116)	0.101 (0.156)	−0.059 (0.180)
Retail enterprise	−0.042 (0.038)	0.0002 (0.039)	−0.077 (0.074)
Muslim	−0.0003 (0.042)	0.013 (0.045)	−0.009 (0.076)
Hindu—upper caste	−0.181*** (0.026)	−0.063* (0.030)	−0.347*** (0.053)
Hindu—middle caste	0.074 (0.101)	0.025 (0.089)	0.134 (0.194)
Average male wage in agriculture	−0.002 (0.002)	−0.001 (0.002)	−0.004 (0.003)
N	1239	700	539
Log likelihood	−549.40	−254.06	−289.89
Pseudo R²	0.249	0.146	0.241

Notes: The numbers in parentheses are standard errors. Other regressors include indicators of the presence of a paved road, the presence of irrigation, and a state-specific indicator for Bihar. *, **, *** indicate significance at the 10%, 5%, and 1% levels respectively.

1 percentage point decrease in the probability of work by the average boy, whereas the probability that the average girl shall work would fall by as much as 2.8 percentage points. Further, a kilometer reduction in the distance to the nearest secondary school would cause the likelihood of work by the average girl to decrease by 2.6 percentage points while having no significant effect upon a boy's propensity to work.

Table 20.5 presents estimates of (8). It is found that, but for distance to the nearest primary school, the school cost variables are statistically significant correlates of school enrollment, although there are notable gender differences. The monetary cost of primary schooling has a statistically significant retardant effect only upon boys' enrollment. By the estimates, a one-standard deviation reduction in the monetary cost of primary schooling would increase the probability of the average boy's enrollment in school by about 3.3 percentage points. On the other hand, proximity to schools is the stronger influence upon the enrollment of girls. For example, a kilometer reduction in the distance to the nearest middle school would cause the probability of the average girl's enrollment in school to increase by 2.7 percentage points while having no significant effect upon a boy's propensity to enroll.

In sum, a kilometer decrease in distances to the nearest middle and secondary schools would increase the probability of the average girl's school enrollment by, respectively, 2.5 and 2.7 percentage points, and, correspondingly, decrease the probability that she shall work by 2.6 and 2.8 percentage points, respectively, while a one standard deviation decrease in the monetary cost of primary schooling would increase the probability of the average boy's school enrollment by 3.3 percentage points while reducing the probability of his participation in work by 3.7 percentage points. These findings imply that there is a high degree of substitution between children's work and school attendance.

This is implied as well by the multinomial logit estimates and associated marginal effects excerpted in Table 20.6. The marginal effects inform that a kilometer decrease in the distance to the nearest middle school would increase the probability that that the average child shall enroll in school rather than work by 1.9 percentage points while reducing the probability that she shall work rather than enroll in school by 1.2 percentage points. Similarly, a kilometer decrease in the distance to the closest secondary school would raise the probability that she shall enroll in school rather than work by 1.2 percentage points while reducing the probability that she shall work rather than enroll in school by 1.1 percentage points. Further, a one standard deviation decrease in the monetary cost of primary schooling would increase the probability that the average child shall enroll in school rather than work by 1.9 percentage points while reducing the probability that she shall work rather than enroll in school by 3.4 percentage points. Hence, these multinomial logit estimates also indicate that there is considerable trade-off between child work and school attendance in rural Northern India. It is notable, by the estimates in columns 2 and 3, that a lowering of the monetary cost of primary

Table 20.5 Determinants of school enrollment probit marginal effects

Variable	(1) Full sample	(2) Boys	(3) Girls
Male	0.280*** (0.027)	.	.
Age	−0.047*** (0.009)	−0.013 (0.008)	−0.095*** (0.017)
Distance to nearest primary school	−0.010 (0.015)	−0.003 (0.012)	−0.022 (0.028)
Distance to nearest middle school	−0.015*** (0.006)	−0.005 (0.005)	−0.027*** (0.011)
Distance to nearest secondary school	−0.015*** (0.004)	−0.008*** (0.003)	−0.025*** (0.007)
Direct cost of primary schooling	−0.182*** (0.081)	−0.182*** (0.073)	−0.175 (0.148)
Household head is Illiterate	−0.217*** (0.028)	−0.132*** (0.027)	−0.283*** (0.049)
Landholding	0.007* (0.004)	0.005 (0.004)	0.010 (0.007)
Transfer	0.0015* (0.0008)	0.002*** (0.0007)	0.0018 (0.0012)
Family size	0.033*** (0.006)	0.022*** (0.007)	0.043*** (0.011)
Number of children 0–4 age group	−0.039*** (0.017)	−0.012 (0.015)	−0.071*** (0.029)
Number of children 5–9 age group	−0.057*** (0.016)	−0.031** (0.015)	−0.084*** (0.028)
Female headed household	−0.100 (0.082)	−0.155* (0.104)	−0.021 (0.117)
Number of enterprises	−0.022 (0.023)	−0.006 (0.022)	−0.046 (0.038)
Handicraft enterprise	−0.070 (0.139)	−0.047 (0.150)	−0.063 (0.196)
Retail enterprise	0.067 (0.039)	0.036 (0.034)	0.091 (0.075)
Muslim	−0.021 (0.044)	−0.074 (0.052)	0.059 (0.073)
Hindu—upper caste	0.185*** (0.030)	0.132*** (0.023)	0.244*** (0.063)
Hindu—middle caste	−0.017 (0.101)	0.022 (0.072)	−0.138 (0.198)
Average male wage in agriculture	0.003 (0.002)	0.002 (0.002)	0.003 (0.004)
N	1239	700	539
Log likelihood	−564.51	−270.97	−281.62
Pseudo R²	0.256	0.213	0.239

Notes: The numbers in parentheses are standard errors. Other regressors include indicators of the presence of a paved road, the presence of irrigation, and a state-specific indicator for Bihar. *, **, *** indicate significance at the 10%, 5%, and 1% levels respectively.

Table 20.6 Select multinomial logit estimates and marginal effects

Variable	(1) Full sample	(2) Boys	(3) Girls
Probability of school and no work			
Distance to nearest primary school	**−0.008**	**0.0003**	**0.017**
Distance to nearest middle school	**−0.019**	**−0.0003**	**−0.036**
Distance to nearest secondary school	**−0.012**	**−0.002**	**−0.027**
Direct cost of primary schooling	**−0.1073**	**−0.063**	**−0.086**
Probability of no school and work			
Distance to nearest primary school	−0.028	−0.055	−0.040
	(0.100)	(0.148)	(0.145)
	−0.005	**−0.0014**	**−0.004**
Distance to nearest middle school	0.115***	0.083	0.150***
	(0.037)	(0.059)	(0.053)
	0.012	**0.002**	**0.031**
Distance to nearest secondary school	0.096***	0.067**	0.127***
	(0.023)	(0.032)	(0.035)
	0.011	**0.002**	**0.028**
Direct cost of primary schooling	1.529***	2.585***	0.641
	(0.541)	(0.832)	(0.752)
	0.193	**0.064**	**0.176**
Probability of school and work			
Distance to nearest primary school	−0.016	0.285	−0.475
	(0.176)	(0.221)	(0.351)
	−0.001	**0.001**	**−0.016**
Distance to nearest middle school	0.182***	0.202*	0.191**
	(0.068)	(0.115)	(0.090)
	0.006	**0.0007**	**0.005**
Distance to nearest secondary school	−0.012	−0.052	0.012
	(0.050)	(0.080)	(0.071)
	−0.001	**−0.0002**	**−0.001**
Direct cost of primary schooling	−0.426	0.569	−2.207
	(1.090)	(1.447)	(1.672)
	−0.022	**0.000**	**−0.084**
Probability of no school and no work			
Distance to nearest primary school	0.261**	0.175	0.477**
	(0.122)	(0.153)	(0.241)
	0.014	**0.000**	**0.003**
Distance to nearest middle school	0.039	−0.011	0.181
	(0.059)	(0.074)	(0.112)
	0.001	**−0.000**	**0.0006**
Distance to nearest secondary school	0.058	0.092**	−0.045
	(0.038)	(0.045)	(0.084)
	0.002	**0.000**	**−0.0005**

(*Continued Overleaf*)

Table 20.6 Continued

Variable	(1) Full sample	(2) Boys	(3) Girls
Direct cost of primary schooling	−0.979 (0.913) **−0.063**	−0.512 (1.257) **−0.000**	−0.998 (1.495) **−0.006**
N	1239	700	539
Log-likelihood	−885.37	−416.07	−423.61
Pseudo R²	0.223	0.207	0.229

Notes: The numbers in **bold** type are marginal effects. The numbers in parentheses are standard errors. Other regressors include those in tables 4 and 5. *, **, *** indicate significance at the 10%, 5%, and 1% levels respectively.

schooling would be more successful in drawing boys from the state of "no school and work" to that of "school and no work". On the other hand, a policy of improving proximity to middle and secondary schools via, for example, the construction of new schools, would be more successful in causing girls to attend school rather than work.

Since there may be heterogeneity in the effects of educational policy interventions upon different types of child work, child work is separated into that outside the ambit of the household and work within it. Column 1 of Table 20.7 presents probit estimates of the determinants of children's extra-household work. Of the four school cost measures, only distance from the nearest secondary school has a statistically significant positive effect upon children's extra-household work. In contrast, by the estimates in column 2 of Table 20.7, a child's propensity to work within the ambit of the household significantly increases in three of these four measures, namely, in distances to the nearest middle and secondary schools and in the monetary cost of primary schooling.[7] The estimates indicate that a kilometer decrease in distances to the nearest middle and secondary schools would cause a reduction of, respectively, 2.1 and 0.8 percentage points in the probability of intra-household work by the average child. It is also indicated that a one-standard deviation decrease in the village-average annual monetary cost of primary schooling would reduce this probability by 3.5 percentage points. By Table 20.1, intra-household work is the dominant form of child work in rural Northern India. Therefore, the strong positive relation between schooling costs and intra-household child work makes for the strong positive relation between schooling costs and child work as a whole reported in column 1 of Table 20.4.

Finally, given the Government of India's definition of work as participation economically productive activities, child work is also separated into economic work and household domestic work, the former consisting of all extra-household work besides intra-household work producing a marketable

Table 20.7 Determinants of extra-household and intra-household work probit marginal effects

Variable	(1) Extra-household work Full sample	(2) Intra-household work Full sample
Male	−0.003	−0.313***
	(0.010)	(0.025)
Age	0.011	0.033***
	(0.004)	(0.008)
Distance to nearest primary school	−0.004	−0.014
	(0.006)	(0.013)
Distance to nearest middle school	−0.002	0.021***
	(0.002)	(0.005)
Distance to nearest secondary school	0.003***	0.008**
	(0.001)	(0.003)
Direct cost of primary schooling	0.005	0.196***
	(0.033)	(0.072)
Household head is Illiterate	0.043***	0.095***
	(0.012)	(0.025)
Landholding	−0.002	−0.003
	(0.002)	(0.003)
Transfer	0.006	−0.142**
	(0.014)	(0.055)
Family size	−0.008***	−0.024***
	(0.003)	(0.005)
Number of children 0–4 age group	0.003	0.031**
	(0.007)	(0.015)
Number of children 5–9 age group	0.016***	0.018
	(0.006)	(0.014)
Female headed household	0.038	0.079
	(0.035)	(0.073)
Number of enterprises	−0.016	0.029
	(0.010)	(0.018)
Handicraft enterprise	*Dropped*	0.078
		(0.113)
Retail enterprise	0.009	−0.053
	(0.020)	(0.032)
Muslim	0.008	−0.025
	(0.018)	(0.035)
Hindu—upper caste	*Dropped*	−0.147***
		(0.023)
Hindu—middle caste	0.021	0.013
	(0.052)	(0.088)
Average male wage in agriculture	−0.0002	−0.002
	(0.001)	(0.002)
N	1027	1239
Log likelihood	−184.99	−521.61
Pseudo R²	0.149	0.239

Notes: The numbers in parentheses are standard errors. Other regressors include indicators of the presence of a paved road, the presence of irrigation, and a state-specific indicator for Bihar. *, **, *** indicate significance at the 10%, 5%, and 1% levels respectively. *Dropped* indicates the variable, and corresponding observations, were dropped since it predicted failure in the probit model perfectly.

output. Table 20.8 reports probit estimates of the determinants of these two types of child work. The estimates in column 1 indicate that the probability that a child shall engage in economic work is positively and significantly related to the direct cost of primary schooling and to the distance from the nearest secondary school, although, curiously, negatively related to the distance from the nearest public primary school. The probability that a child shall perform domestic chores significantly increases in the direct cost of primary schooling and in the distance from the nearest middle school. For example, a one-standard deviation reduction in the direct cost of primary school would reduce economic and domestic work by, respectively, 1.7 and 1.5 percentage points. Thus, both domestic and economic work are almost equally responsive to changes in the monetary costs of schooling.

6 Concluding remarks

This study aims to assess the extent of contemporaneous trade-off, between children's work and school attendance in rural Uttar Pradesh and Bihar, two Northern Indian states. Its empirical strategy consists of examination of the effect of a policy intervention, namely, reduction in schooling costs, upon children's school enrollment in a time period, and, separately, of its effect upon their participation in work in the same period. The finding that a reduction in schooling costs results in both an increase in school enrollment and a comparable decrease in child work would indicate that child work and school attendance are highly substitutable activities. A subsidiary strategy consists of examination of the effect of schooling costs upon the probability that a child shall work rather than enroll in school relative to the probability that she shall enroll in school rather than work. The finding that a reduction in schooling costs causes this relative probability to decrease shall also indicate that there is contemporaneous trade-off between children's work and school attendance.

Analyses of data from the 1997–8 Survey of Living Conditions in rural Uttar Pradesh and Bihar, two Northern Indian states, reveal a positive relation between child work and schooling costs, a negative relation between school enrollment and schooling costs, and that the increase in the probability of school enrollment from a decrease in schooling costs is comparable in magnitude to the corresponding decrease in the probability of child work, implying children's school attendance and work are highly substitutable activities. Specifically, a kilometer decrease in distances to the nearest middle and secondary schools would each increase the probability that the average child enrolls in school by 1.5 percentage points while reducing the probability that she shall work by, respectively, 1.9 and 1.2 percentage points. Further, a one-standard deviation reduction in the monetary cost of primary schooling would increase the probability of school enrollment by 3.3 percentage points while decreasing the probability of work by 3.7 percentage points. Strong substitutability is also implied by the finding of a significant positive relation

Table 20.8 Determinants of economic and domestic work probit marginal effects

Variable	(1) Economic work Full sample	(2) Domestic work Full sample
Male	−0.010 (0.015)	−0.319*** (0.023)
Age	0.026*** (0.005)	0.019*** (0.006)
Distance to nearest primary school	−0.015* (0.008)	−0.001 (0.009)
Distance to nearest middle school	0.001 (0.003)	0.014*** (0.003)
Distance to nearest secondary school	0.006*** (0.002)	0.004 (0.002)
Direct cost of primary schooling	0.093** (0.043)	0.087** (0.047)
Household head is Illiterate	0.054*** (0.016)	0.080*** (0.018)
Landholding	−0.0004 (0.002)	−0.001 (0.001)
Transfer	−0.0002 (0.0003)	−0.0008*** (0.0003)
Family size	−0.018*** (0.004)	−0.012*** (0.004)
Number of children 0–4 age group	0.023*** (0.009)	0.015 (0.011)
Number of children 5–9 age group	0.015* (0.008)	0.016 (0.010)
Female headed household	0.054 (0.047)	0.051 (0.051)
Number of enterprises	0.017 (0.013)	0.006 (0.013)
Handicraft enterprise	0.030 (0.087)	−0.017 (0.068)
Retail enterprise	−0.005 (0.024)	−0.034 (0.022)
Muslim	−0.022 (0.019)	0.020 (0.029)
Hindu—upper caste	−0.085*** (0.014)	−0.071*** (0.018)
Hindu—middle caste	0.030 (0.062)	0.0003 (0.060)
Average male wage in agriculture	0.0001 (0.001)	−0.0018 (0.0012)
N	1239	1239
Log likelihood	−384.72	−405.56
Pseudo R^2	0.136	0.307

Notes: The numbers in parentheses are standard errors. Other regressors include indicators of the presence of a paved road, the presence of irrigation, and a state-specific indicator for Bihar. *, **, *** indicate significance at the 10%, 5%, and 1% levels respectively.

424   G. Hazarika and A. S. Bedi

between schooling costs and the probability that a child shall work rather than enroll in school relative to the probability that she shall enroll in school rather than work. The data suggest that this strong substitutability results from significant trade-off between school enrollment and intra-household child work, the dominant form of child work in rural Northern India.

The study uncovers notable gender differences in the effect of schooling costs upon child work and school enrollment. This implies that policy measures would do well to be gender sensitive. The estimates suggest that a lowering of the monetary cost of schooling shall be the better approach to reducing work by, and increasing the school enrollment of, boys. On the other hand, reducing distances to schools appears to be the better approach to reducing work by, and increasing the school enrollment of, girls. Perhaps it is mainly poverty that causes boys to work rather than attend school, whereas it is mainly parents' concern for their daughters' security en route to school, and social and cultural norms, that impede girls' school enrollment.

In sum, this study finds that educational interventions shall be successful in both reducing child work and raising school attendance in rural Uttar Pradesh and Bihar, two of India's poorest and most populous states. Thus, the Government of India and various NGOs seem well-advised in their use of educational interventions to combat child work.

Notes

1 Increases in school enrollment from reduction in schooling costs must then result mainly from decreases in children's leisure, and so this second reason may be viewed as expanding upon the first.
2 It may, of course, be argued that weak trade-off between children's work and schooling makes child work less objectionable. On the other hand, child work is objectionable not merely because it reduces schooling.
3 For example, the Food-for-Education Program in Bangladesh (Ravallion and Wodon 2000), *Progresa* in Mexico (Skoufias and Parker 2001), and Bolsa Escola and PETI in Brazil (World Bank 2001) provide subsidies to households, conditional upon children attending school, in a bid to reduce the opportunity costs of children's school attendance.
4 It is noteworthy in this connection that India's Parliament passed the 86th amendment to the Nation's Constitution in 2002 by which free and compulsory education for all children in the age group 6–14 is a fundamental right.
5 Indeed, D. P. Chaudhri (1996) notes that children who neither work nor attend school make up a substantial fraction of children in India, although work, by his definition, includes only economic work or a sub-section thereof.
6 In 2000, the two states were subdivided. Uttaranchal was carved from Uttar Pradesh and Jharkhand from Bihar.
7 This is markedly different from Hazarika's and Bedi's (2003) finding that only extra-household child work is responsive to changes in schooling costs in rural Pakistan. Perhaps Pakistani parents consider intra-household child work to be essential training that may not be acquired in educational institutions whereas the view is less common or strongly held in rural UP and Bihar. Since the questionnaires do not elicit parents' views on different types of child work, this may not be verified. It is unlikely, however, that this study's disparate findings are

due to variation in data quality since both data sets are part of the World Bank's LSMS series and so use similar questionnaires and modes of data collection. While there are differences in sample characteristics, these are not remarkable. In fact, the average age of children, their gender composition, and average household land holding are similar. Thus, it is likely that the explanation lies not in dissimilar data but in divergent parental attitudes toward work and education.

References

Chaudhri, D. P. (1996) *Dynamic Profile of Child Labor in India 1951–1991*, Child Labor Action and Support Project. New Delhi: ILO.

Government of India (2006) Union Budget 2006–7. http://indiabudget.nic.in/ub2006–07/ubmain.htm.

Government of India, Planning Commission (2001) *National Human Development Report*. http://planningcommission.nic.in/reports/genrep/nhdrep/nhdreportf.htm.

Government of India, National Commission on Labor (2001) Report of the Study Group on Women and Child Labor.

Grootaert, C. (1999) "Child Labor in Cote d'Ivoire." In *The Policy Analysis of Child Labor: A comparative analysis*, edited by C. Grootaert and H. A. Patrinos. London: St Martin's Press.

Hazarika, G. and A. S. Bedi (2003) "Schooling Costs and Child Work in Rural Pakistan.", *Journal of Development Studies* 39(5): 29–64.

Human Rights News (2006) "Child Labor Law Welcomed, But Needs Enforcing." *Human Rights News*, October. New York: Human Rights Watch.

Human Rights Watch (1996) *The Small Hands of Slavery—Bonded Child Labor in India*, New York: Human Rights Watch.

ILO (1995) *World Labor Report*. Geneva: ILO.

——. (1998a) "Child Labor: Targeting the Intolerable." 86th Session, International Labor Conference, Geneva: ILO.

——. (1998b) "Child Labor in Africa: Targeting the intolerable." African Regional Tripartite Meeting on Child Labor. Geneva: International Labor Office.

Nieuwenhuys, O. (1994) *Children's Lifeworlds*. London and New York: Routledge Press.

Ravallion, M. and Q. Wodon (2000) "Does Child Labor Displace Schooling? Evidence on behavioural responses to an enrollment subsidy." *The Economic Journal* 110(462): C158–75.

Ray, R. and G. Lancaster (2005) "The Impact of Children's Work on Schooling: Multicountry evidence". *International Labor Review* 144(2): 189–210.

Skoufias, E. and S. Parker (2001) "Conditional Cash Transfers and Their Impact on Child Work and Schooling." Washington, DC: International Food Policy Research Institute. FCND Discussion Paper 123.

World Bank (2001) *Spectrum: The Global Fight Against Child Labor*. Publication of the Social Protection Unit of the World Bank, Winter 2001, Washington, DC: World Bank.

Wu, K. B., V. Kaul, and D. Sankar (2005) "The Quiet Revolution." *Finance and Development* 42(2).

21 Glass ceilings, sticky floors, or sticky doors? A quantile regression approach to exploring gender wage gaps in Sri Lanka[*]

Dileni Gunewardena, Darshi Abeyrathna, Amalie Ellagala, Kamani Rajakaruna, and Shobana Rajendran

1 Introduction

The extension of standard decompositions of mean wage gaps to the examination of conditional wage gaps across the distribution using counterfactual analysis based on quantile regression has led to a new approach to the examination of "glass ceilings" (Albrecht, Bjorkland, and Vroman 2003; Arulampalam et al. 2007). The term glass ceilings refers to the phenomenon that "women do quite well in the labor market up to a point, after which there is an effective limit on their prospects" (Albrecht, Bjorkland, and Vroman 2003). Thus, larger wage gaps, conditional on covariates, *at the top of the wage distribution* would be consistent with the existence of "glass ceilings".

Empirical studies revealed, however, that apart from the existence of glass ceilings, wage gaps were sometimes wider at the bottom of the conditional wage distribution, consistent with the term "sticky floor" (Arulampalam et al. 2007). This term is sometimes taken to refer to self-imposed limitation on employment, although sticky floors may occur because "only the more articulate and better educated are willing to take legal action against breaches of the law", because men are initially appointed at a higher starting salary (rung) within a particular scale, or because women at the bottom have less bargaining power compared to men owing to family commitments or social custom (Arulampalam, Booth, and Bryan 2007). Others argue that it is due to labor market segmentation with informal jobs occupying the lower end of the distribution (Tanuri-Pianto et al. 2004). A variant on this argument is that both glass ceilings and sticky floors are the manifestation of inequitable rationing of "good" jobs (Pendakur and Pendakur 2007). When there are two or more groups of unequal status in the labor market, the subordinate group will have earnings distributions which look similar to the dominant group over ordinary jobs, but are comparatively thin over high-paying jobs. Since "good jobs" will exist for all types of worker, including those with high ability, and those with low ability, glass ceilings may manifest themselves in any part of the distribution and "sticky floors" are really "glass ceilings at the ground floor" (de la Rica et al. 2007). In these latter arguments, sticky floors are really sticky doors, in the sense that they reflect the barriers against access to "good jobs" for disadvantaged groups.[1]

Much of the glass ceiling literature is on OECD countries. A small but growing number of studies on developing countries include Chile (Montenegro 2001; Nopo 2006), China (Bishop, Luo, and Wang 2005), Morocco (Nordman and Wolff 2007), the Philippines (Sakellariou 2004), and Vietnam (Pham and Reilly 2006).

This paper adds to that literature by examining if the Sri Lankan labor market is characterized by "sticky floors" and/or "glass ceilings," using a quantile regression approach to decompose wage gaps from Sri Lankan quarterly labor force data for the 1996–2004 period. The Sri Lankan case is instructive as an example of a developing country labor market where women have high productive characteristics, relative to males, reflecting perhaps the considerable advances Sri Lanka has made in gender equity in human capital outcomes. Standard analyses of the mean gender wage gap in Sri Lanka indicate that the gap is quite small, but that the entire gap is attributed to differences in returns to characteristics (Aturupane 1996; Gunewardena 2002; Ajwad and Kurukulasuriya 2002).

The aim of the paper is to determine whether wage gaps, conditional on covariates, vary across the distribution. Quantile regression techniques are used to control for individual characteristics, and the Machado-Mata (2005) counterfactual decomposition is used to derive conditional gaps over the entire wage distribution. The analysis is conducted separately for the public and private sectors. We are aware of only one other paper that uses this approach to study gender earnings gaps in a developing country (Pham and Reilly 2007). Their study for Vietnam does not conduct a disaggregated analysis for public and private sectors, and suffers from the lack of data on actual experience, using potential experience instead, which can lead to misleading results for females who have intermittent labor force participation.

The paper is structured as follows. Section 2 describes the data and discusses raw wage distributions, Section 3 describes the Machado Mata decomposition while section 4 presents and discusses decomposition results. Section 5 concludes with policy implications and suggestions for future research.

2 Methodology

The basic premise underlying wage gap decompositions is that in the absence of discrimination, the estimated effects of individuals' observed characteristics are identical for each group. These effects are usually evaluated at the mean by least squares methods. Thus, the standard Oaxaca (1973) and Blinder (1973) decomposition of the mean wage gap is:

$$\ln w^m - \ln w^f = X^{*f} (\beta^m - \beta^f) + (X^{*m} - X^{*f})\beta^m \tag{1}$$

where w is the hourly wage; X is a vector of covariates for the ith individual and β is a vector of coefficients; the asterisks on the X vectors denote *mean* covariates. The first term on the right-hand side is the unexplained component, i.e. differences in coefficients $(\beta^m - \beta^f)$, evaluated at the same set of average covariates (X^{*f}), in this case the female, and the second term the explained component attributed to differences in average endowments $(X^{*m} - X^{*f})$ weighted by the male wage structure.

The decomposition may also be expressed in terms of average male covariates (X^m) and female wage structure:

$$\ln w^m - \ln w^f = X^{*m} (\beta^m - \beta^f) + (X^{*m} - X^{*f})\beta^f \tag{2}$$

The two specifications derive from distinct theoretical assumptions about the underlying discriminatory behavior (Neumark 1988). Using the male wage structure as the underlying (discrimination-free) structure implies that women are actively discriminated *against*, while the assumption that the female wage structure is the "true" structure implies that all discrimination is "in *favour of* men".

While least squares constrains the effect of the covariates to be fixed along the wage distribution, quantile regression (QR) analysis, introduced by Koenker and Basset (1978), allows one to study the effects of a covariate on the whole conditional distribution of the dependent variable.

Quantile regressions are a natural extension of classical least squares estimation of conditional mean models to the estimation of an ensemble of models for conditional quantile functions—of which the central special case is the median regression estimator or least absolute deviations (LAD) estimator that minimizes a sum of absolute errors (Koenker and Hallock 2001). The θth quantile of y_i conditional on X_i is given by

$$Q_\theta (y_i | X_i) = X_i \beta_\theta, \, \theta \in (0,1) \tag{3}$$

where the coefficient β_θ is the slope of the quantile line giving the effects of changes in X on the θth conditional quantile of y.

As shown by Koenker and Basset (1978), the quantile regression estimator of β_θ solves the following minimization problem:

$$\beta_\theta = argmin \left[\sum_{i:y_i \geq X_i\beta} \theta|y_i - X_i\beta| + \sum_{i:y_i < X_i\beta} (1 - \theta)|y_i - X_i\beta| \right] \tag{4}$$

Coefficients of quantile regressions are interpreted in the usual way. Standard errors are bootstrap standard errors.

The extension of quantile regression to wage gap decomposition requires a decision as to where on the covariates distribution the gaps are evaluated.

Mueller (1998) and Garcia et al. (2001) use coefficients from the quantile regressions, but evaluate wage gaps by combining them with the means of the covariate distributions. This is problematic as mean covariates are unlikely to be representative of covariates at each θth conditional quantile of y. Other approaches include using the average characteristics around a symmetric neighborhood of every quantile (Bishop, Luo, and Wang 2005) or deriving covariates from an auxiliary regression-based framework (Gardeazabal and Ugidos 2005; Hyder and Reilly 2005).

The distinctiveness of the Machado and Mata (2005) approach is that it proposes a method whereby the entire conditional distribution of covariates is derived. Their method combines quantile regression with a bootstrap approach. Formally, it involves six steps.

1 Generate a random sample of size n from a $U[0, 1]$: $u_1 \ldots, u_n$.[2]
2 Estimate n male and female coefficients separately from male and female samples: $\beta_{ui}^m, \beta_{ui}^f; i = 1, \ldots n$.
3 Generate for each sample, a random sample of size n, with replacement, from the covariates X, denoted by $\{X_i^m\}_{i=1}^n$ and $\{X_i^f\}_{i=1}^n$
4 $\{X_i^m \beta^m\}_{i=1}^n$ and $\{X_i^f \beta^f\}_{i=1}^n$ are random samples of size n from the marginal wage distributions of y consistent with the linear model defined by (3).
5 Generate a random sample of the counterfactual distribution. $\{X_i^m \beta^f\}_{i=1}^n$ is a random sample from the wage distribution that would have prevailed among females if all covariates had been distributed as in the male distribution.

In order to simplify the comparison with the Blinder–Oaxaca decomposition, we present the decomposition of the quantiles of the simulated wage distribution as follows, where (5), analogous to (1) uses female covariates and the male earnings structure as the reference, while (6) analogous to (2) is based on male covariates and the female wage structure.

$$Q_\theta(y^m) - Q_\theta(y^f) = [Q_\theta(X_i^f \beta^m) - Q_\theta(X_i^f \beta^f)] + [Q_\theta(X_i^m \beta^m) - Q_\theta(X_i^f \beta^m)] + \text{residual} \tag{5}$$

$$Q_\theta(y^m) - Q_\theta(y^f) = [Q_\theta(X_i^m \beta^m) - Q_\theta(X_i^m \beta^f)] + [Q_\theta(X_i^m \beta^f) - Q_\theta(X_i^f \beta^f)] + \text{residual} \tag{6}$$

The first term on the right-hand side is the contribution of the coefficients, and the second term is the contribution of the covariates to the difference between the θth quantile of the male wage distribution and the θth quantile of the female wage distribution. The residual term comprises the simulation errors which disappear with more simulations, the sampling errors which disappear with more observations, and the specification error induced by estimating linear quantile regression (Melly 2005). We assume that the linear quantile model is correctly specified.

3 Data description and raw wage gaps

The study uses data from the Quarterly Labor Force Surveys (QLFS) conducted by the Department of Census and Statistics for the first and last six
quarters of the 1996–2004 period. The survey schedule is administered to
approximately 4,000 housing units per quarter. The sample is selected using a
two-step stratified random sampling procedure with no rotation, and a new
random sample is drawn each quarter. The survey excluded the Northern and
Eastern provinces which are the two most severely affected by the protracted
conflict between separatist guerillas and the Sri Lankan government.

The sample is selected to include all individuals between the ages of 18 and
58, who were employees in their main occupation of work, who were "usually
employed" (had worked for 26 weeks or more) in the previous 12 months,
and who were currently employed (had worked at least one hour in the week
prior to when the survey was administered). We exclude individuals who were
self-employed or worked with or without pay for a family-operated farm or
business, as well as agricultural workers and any individuals who were currently attending a school or educational institution. In addition, we exclude
individuals who claimed to work usually fewer than 20 or more than 70 hours
a week.[3] The sample includes formal and informal sector employees, but
the data does not permit us to identify formality, i.e. no sample separation
is possible. Finally, our sample contains only those individuals with non-
missing observations on all the regressors. The selected sample comprises a
total of 9,834 individuals in the first period and 10,594 individuals in the
second period.

The definition of earnings used throughout this paper is *the log of hourly
wages from the main occupation* where hourly wages is calculated as earnings
in the last month from the main occupation divided by the hours usually
worked (at the main occupation) in a month calculated as 30/7 multiplied by
hours usually worked in a given week. Nominal values are converted to real
terms using the Sri Lanka Consumer Price Index (SLCPI) with a base period
of 1995 to 1997 (Central Bank of Sri Lanka 2005).

Two specifications are used. The vector of regressors common to both
includes seven ISCED-based categories of schooling, experience in the current occupation and age (in years and in quadratic form), whether any (for-
mal/informal) training received, whether currently married, and ethnicity and
location dummies. The second specification also included part-time employment status, seven occupational (ISCO88) categories, and four ISIC industrial
groups.[4]

We conduct the analysis separately for public and private sectors. While
compliance with equal pay legislation is more likely in the public sector, and
wage structures and promotion schemes are less likely to leave room for
individual variation, the public sector is subject to political constraints and
not to profit constraints, and any tastes for discrimination are more likely to
persist. Alternatively, whether public sector wage premiums (if any) are

enjoyed by males or females may be determined by the respective strength of their voice within the public sector.

Selection bias is potentially a problem in our data, given that female labor force participation in Sri Lanka, at 31%, was less than half that of males, and female unemployment was over twice that of males in the period under study. Therefore, we explored selectivity within the mean regression framework (Gunewardena et al. 2007). We found no evidence of a selection effect into wage employment for males or females, but found some evidence for selection into public sector wage employment, although differences in magnitude between selectivity corrected and uncorrected mean wage gaps were relatively small, while evidence for selectivity bias in the private wage sector sample differed according to the method used.[5]

The techniques to correct for selectivity bias in quantile regression models are less well known and there is little consensus regarding the most appropriate correction procedure (Buchinsky 2001; Hyder and Reilly 2005). For this reason, and given the absence of selectivity bias in our pooled sample estimates, the ambiguous evidence for bias in private sector estimates and the relatively small difference in selectivity corrected public sector wage gap estimates in our mean regression models, as well as the lack of sufficiently good instruments to represent a labor market participation decision in our sample, and the trade-off in using potential instead of actual experience in the selectivity corrected model, we decide to proceed without a selection correction procedure in either the mean or quantile regression models. Other studies with similar constraints that make the same judgment call include de la Rica et al. (2007), Pham and Reilly (2007), Newell and Reilly (2001), Montenegro (2001) and Sakellariou (2004). We acknowledge therefore, that our public and private sector results should be interpreted as being *conditional on the selected samples* and that in the absence of selectivity correction, the coefficients in our regressions are biased estimates of *returns* to covariates and cannot be applied to the working age population in general.

The mean unconditional gender gap in log hourly wages in 1996/7 was insignificantly different from zero at the 5% level and was 0.044 (4.3% of male wages) in 2003/4 (Table 21.1 and Table 21.2). These results are unusual and have few parallels in the empirical literature.[6]

Figure 21.1 indicates that overall, male and female wage distributions are very different.[7] The male distribution lies "within" the female distribution, and is characterised by a higher density function around the mode, and a lower dispersion. At the lower quantiles of the distribution, males enjoy an earnings advantage over females, *while at the 75th and 90th percentiles, the advantage is enjoyed by females.*[8] The raw gaps range from 0.22 log hourly wages (20% of the male wage) in 2003/04 and 0.15 (14%) in 1996/97 at the 10th percentile, to a negative (female-favoring) gap of 0.15 (16%) in the 90th percentile in both periods (Table 21.1 and Table 21.2). These results are striking, although similar to those reported by Sakellariou (2004) for the Philippines in 1999.

Table 21.1 Raw and estimated wage gaps, 1996/7 and 2003/4

	1996/7						2003/4					
Raw gap	Mean	10th	25th	50th	75th	90th	Mean	10th	25th	50th	75th	90th
Pooled	0.026	0.152	0.102	0.122	-0.128	-0.145	0.044	0.221	0.167	0.074	-0.124	-0.149
	(0.014)	(0.019)	(0.015)	(0.016)	(0.006)	(0.019)	(0.013)	(0.020)	(0.014)	(0.014)	(0.018)	(0.024)
Public	-0.146	0	-0.127	-0.237	-0.223	-0.104	-0.125	-0.091	-0.172	-0.207	-0.188	-0.079
	(0.019)	(0.021)	(0.028)	(0.024)	(0.030)	(0.033)	(0.018)	(0.030)	(0.024)	(0.024)	(0.022)	(0.030)
Private	0.212	0.288	0.188	0.201	0.251	0.236	0.244	0.293	0.267	0.249	0.22	0.22
	(0.016)	(0.034)	(0.025)	(0.006)	(0.023)	(0.030)	(0.015)	(0.021)	(0.017)	(0.013)	(0.014)	(0.019)
Excluding controls for part-time employment status, occupation, and industry												
Male characteristics, female wage structure												
Pooled	0.105	0.219	0.151	0.088	0.032	*0.021*	0.151	0.25	0.197	0.147	0.084	0.049
	(0.012)	(0.024)	(0.014)	(0.014)	(0.016)	(0.021)	(0.012)	(0.021)	(0.015)	(0.013)	(0.015)	(0.021)
Public	*0.027*	0.175	0.087	-0.034	-0.059	*-0.03*	0.006	0.146	*0.016*	-0.056	-0.074	-0.042
	(0.019)	(0.022)	(0.016)	(0.014)	(0.016)	(0.018)	(0.018)	(0.019)	(0.015)	(0.012)	(0.013)	(0.017)
Private	0.201	0.328	0.24	0.198	0.176	0.121	0.244	0.293	0.268	0.249	0.22	0.222
	(0.018)	(0.024)	(0.016)	(0.012)	(0.014)	(0.017)	(0.016)	(0.021)	(0.016)	(0.013)	(0.014)	(0.019)
Female Characteristics, male wage structure												
Pooled	0.110	0.162	0.142	0.117	0.071	0.055	0.150	0.252	0.207	0.138	0.063	0.064
	(0.011)	(0.023)	(0.017)	(0.016)	(0.018)	(0.022)	(0.011)	(0.021)	(0.015)	(0.014)	(0.017)	(0.019)
Public	*-0.001*	0.081	*-0.002*	-0.042	-0.026	*0.001*	*0.008*	0.042	-0.029	-0.047	-0.026	*0.022*
	(0.016)	(0.021)	(0.015)	(0.013)	(0.012)	(0.015)	(0.016)	(0.020)	(0.014)	(0.011)	(0.012)	(0.015)
Private	0.182	0.178	0.152	0.183	0.223	0.238	0.248	0.257	0.251	0.252	0.242	0.249
	(0.015)	(0.023)	(0.014)	(0.010)	(0.014)	(0.022)	(0.014)	(0.022)	(0.013)	(0.011)	(0.014)	(0.021)
Including controls for part-time employment status, occupation, and industry												
Male characteristics, female wage structure												
Pooled	0.188	0.261	0.224	0.186	0.149	0.116	0.205	0.312	0.258	0.207	0.143	0.085
	(0.018)	(0.021)	(0.015)	(0.014)	(0.016)	(0.022)	(0.017)	(0.022)	(0.015)	(0.012)	(0.017)	(0.023)
Public	0.142	0.259	0.2	0.093	0.042	0.045	0.134	0.273	0.178	0.101	0.051	0.053
	(0.033)	(0.019)	(0.014)	(0.013)	(0.015)	(0.017)	(0.021)	(0.020)	(0.014)	(0.012)	(0.014)	(0.017)
Private	0.224	0.292	0.247	0.235	0.24	0.217	0.25	0.331	0.297	0.271	0.231	0.188
	(0.025)	(0.025)	(0.015)	(0.012)	(0.013)	(0.018)	(0.023)	(0.022)	(0.016)	(0.014)	(0.013)	(0.018)

Female characteristics, male wage structure

	Average	10%	25%	50%	75%	90%	Average	10%	25%	50%	75%	90%
Pooled	0.178	0.185	0.174	0.185	0.136	0.138	0.202	0.278	0.241	0.187	0.106	0.120
	(0.012)	(0.022)	(0.015)	(0.017)	(0.020)	(0.022)	(0.011)	(0.023)	(0.016)	(0.016)	(0.019)	(0.021)
Public	0.089	0.147	0.088	0.057	0.074	0.086	0.070	0.097	0.032	0.026	0.035	0.087
	(0.017)	(0.021)	(0.015)	(0.013)	(0.013)	(0.017)	(0.016)	(0.021)	(0.013)	(0.011)	(0.012)	(0.014)
Private	0.211	0.180	0.173	0.199	0.250	0.255	0.266	0.278	0.264	0.260	0.255	0.235
	(0.016)	(0.022)	(0.015)	(0.011)	(0.014)	(0.023)	(0.015)	(0.022)	(0.014)	(0.012)	(0.012)	(0.021)

Note: Standard errors are given in parentheses. Except for the coefficients in *italics*, all coefficients are significantly different from zero at the 5% level of significance.

Table 21.2 Raw wage gaps as % of male gap, 1996/97 & 2003/04

	1996/7						2003/4					
	Average	10%	25%	50%	75%	90%	Average	10%	25%	50%	75%	90%
Pooled	2.6	14.1	9.7	11.5	-13.7	-15.6	4.3	19.8	15.4	7.1	-13.2	-16.1
Public	-15.7	0.0	-13.5	-26.7	-25.0	-11.0	-13.3	-9.5	-18.8	-23.0	-20.7	-8.2
Private	19.1	25.0	17.1	18.2	22.2	21.0	21.9	26.7	22.7	23.0	22.1	20.1

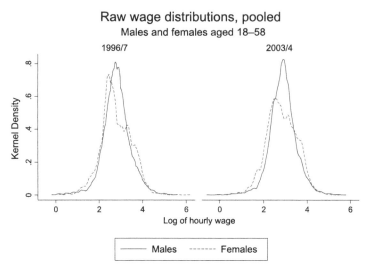

Figure 21.1 Kernel density functions, pooled sample 1996/7 and 2003/4.

Sectoral disaggregation indicates that the mean female private sector wage is approximately 80% of the mean male wage, while somewhat unusually, if not unexpectedly, the public sector mean female wage was 13–16% higher than the public sector mean male wage. The female public sector wage distribution lies almost entirely to the right of the corresponding male wage distribution, while the female private sector wage distribution lies to the left of the private sector male wage distribution (Figure 21.2). Table 21.1 indicates zero or negative (female-favoring) raw wage gaps in the public sector and positive (male favoring) raw wage gaps throughout the private sector in both periods. These differences are statistically significant at the 1% level, unless otherwise indicated.

We are not aware of any other studies/countries where higher female wages are indicated throughout the public sector distribution. We suspect this result may be due to the better endowments of women in the public sector relative to men, as well as the gender composition of occupations in the public sector, where women work mainly in the professional, technical, and clerical occupations. It is also consistent with the selection of "higher quality" women into public sector wage employment.

4 Decomposition results

The estimated wage gaps presented in the second and third panels of Table 21.1 and as the solid line in Figure 21.3 to Figure 21.6 is the unexplained wage gap. The 95% confidence interval for the point estimate and the raw gap are also presented in the figures for ease of comparison.

Table 21.1 indicates that once covariates are controlled for, the estimated

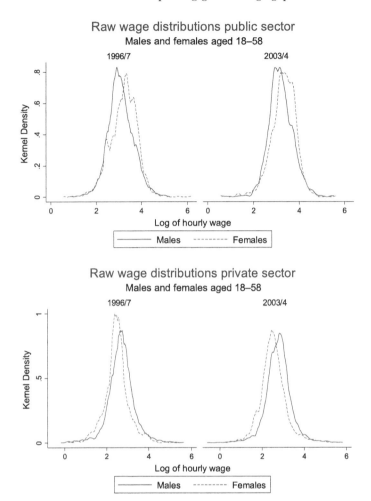

Figure 21.2 Kernel density functions, public, and private sectors, 1996/7 and 2003/4.

mean wage gap is positive, indicating that women are underpaid on average. These results are similar to Montenegro (2003) for Chile and Sakellariou (2004) for the Philippines. Furthermore, pooled sample estimates indicate that in the absence of "discrimination," females would earn up to four times more than males on average (Table 21.2). These results are consistent with and larger in magnitude than previous results for Sri Lanka (Ajwad and Kurukulasuriya 2002, Gunewardena 2002) and similar to results from a series of studies reported in World Bank (2001) using data from the mid-1980s to the mid-1990s for UK, New Zealand, Bulgaria, Israel, Poland, Slovenia, the Russian Federation, Brazil, Chile, Honduras, Jamaica, China, and the Philippines.

The estimated gap is smaller in the public sector than in the private sector. These results are similar to those found in Europe (Arulampalam, Booth, and

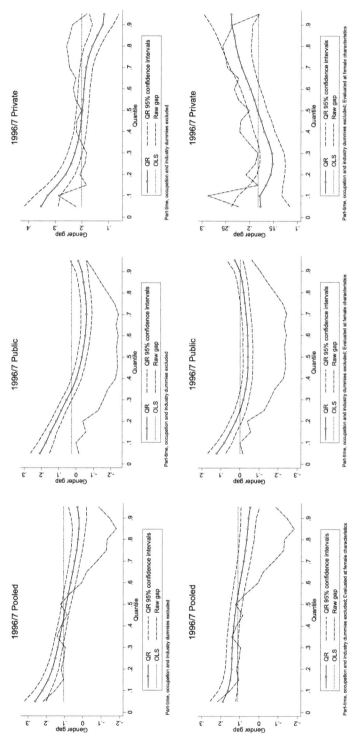

Figure 21.3 Gender wage gap due to differences in coefficients, part time, occupation and industry dummies excluded, 1996/7.

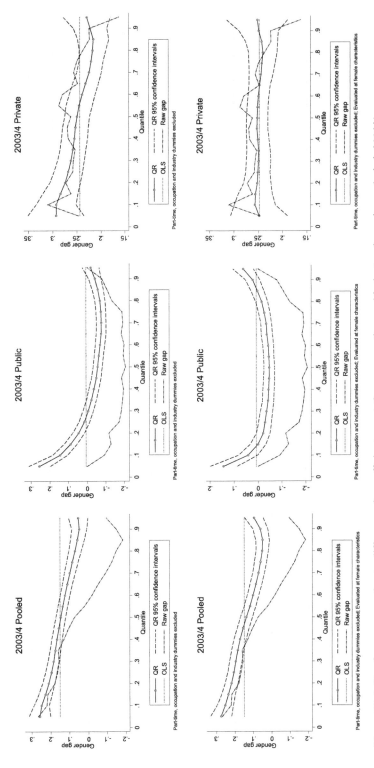

Figure 21.4 Gender wage gap due to differences in coefficients, part time, occupation and industry dummies excluded, 2003/4.

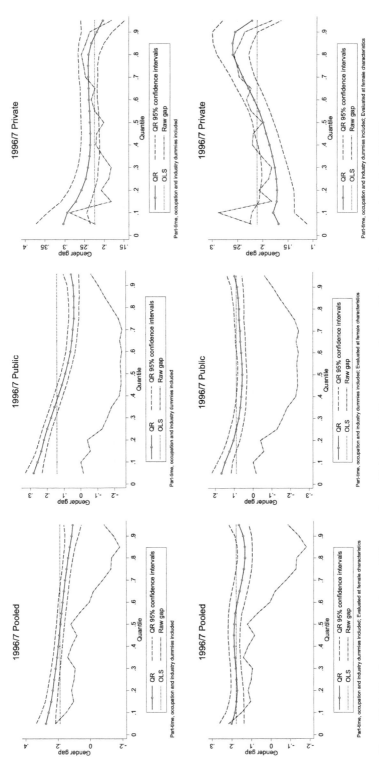

Figure 21.5 Gender wage gap due to differences in coefficients, part time, occupation, and industry dummies included, 1996/7.

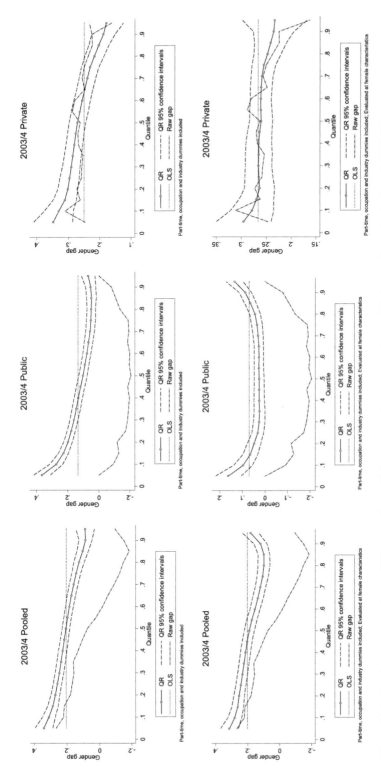

Figure 21.6 Gender wage gap due to differences in coefficients, part time, occupation and industry dummies included, 2003/2004.

Bryan 2007) and Australia (Kee 2006) though different from results for the Ukraine (Ganguli and Terrell 2005). In Sri Lanka, the female-favoring raw gap in the public sector, is more than entirely explained by the difference in covariates (i.e. females have more favorable characteristics at the mean than males). On the other hand, almost 100% of the private sector gap is due to the difference in coefficients, which is similar to results found for Ireland, the USA, the Czech Republic, the Democratic Republic of Germany, Hungary, the Russian Federation, and Venezuela (World Bank 2001).

Estimated wage gaps are positive at every quantile in the pooled distribution, for both years, indicating that females are underpaid (or males are overpaid) throughout the distribution.[9] Moreover, they are larger than raw wage gaps, lying clearly above the raw wage gap over a large part of the distribution (Table 21.1 and Figure 21.3 to Figure 21.6). Over 100% of the positive (male-favoring) raw wage gap (from the 10th percentile to the median) is unexplained, while the negative (female-favoring) raw wage gap in the upper part of the distribution is largely explained by better female endowments.[10] *This indicates that women have better characteristics throughout the earnings distribution and, in the absence of discrimination, would have earned more than men.* These results are similar to Arulampalam, Booth, and Bryan's (2006) results for Belgium, Finland, France, Italy and Spain, Montenegro's (2003) results for Chile and Sakellariou's (2004) results for the Philippines.[11]

While public sector results are similar in this last respect to pooled sample results,[12] in the private sector the estimated wage gap coincides almost entirely with the raw wage gap, indicating that close to 100% of the wage gap is unexplained. *This indicates that women in the private sector have similar characteristics to men, and in the absence of discrimination women would have earned the same as men.* These results are similar to Arulampalam et al.'s (2007) disaggregated results for Belgium, France, Ireland and Spain, where estimated public sector wage gaps are higher than raw wage gaps.

The results described above are robust to the choice of whether gaps are evaluated at male or female characteristics. However, magnitudes of estimated gaps differ between these sets of estimates. In both years, a slightly larger proportion of the gap (with some exceptions) is unexplained when we use the female structure (male characteristics) than the male structure (female characteristics) (Table 21.3). Breunig and Rospabe (2005) obtain a similar result in their analysis of wages in France and interpret it as indicating that there are likely to be more unobservable factors that influence women's choice of work than men's.

Finally, does the QR-based decomposition provide more information than mean decomposition? Table 21.1 and Figure 21.3 to Figure 21.6 indicate that OLS underestimates the conditional wage gap at the bottom of the pooled distribution and overestimates it at the top. There is clear evidence of a falling wage gap throughout the distribution, when the estimated wage gap is evaluated at male characteristics, and evidence of a falling gap up to the median when evaluated at female characteristics. Thus, there appear to be "sticky

Table 21.3 Unexplained gaps as a % of the wage gap

	1996/7						2003/4					
Excluding controls for part-time employment status, occupation, and industry												
Male characteristics, female wage structure												
Pooled	403.8	144.1	148.0	72.1	-25.0	-14.5	343.2	112.7	118.0	198.6	-68.5	-32.2
Public	-18.5	—	-68.5	14.3	26.5	28.8	-4.8	-160.4	-9.3	27.1	39.4	53.2
Private	94.8	113.9	127.7	98.5	70.1	51.3	98.8	94.2	103.9	95.0	88.0	98.7
Female characteristics, male wage structure												
Pooled	423.1	106.6	139.2	95.9	-55.5	-37.9	340.9	114.5	123.4	186.5	-49.2	-41.6
Public	0.7	—	1.6	17.7	11.7	-1.0	-6.4	-46.2	16.9	22.7	13.8	-27.8
Private	85.8	61.8	80.9	91.0	88.8	100.8	100.4	82.6	97.3	96.2	96.8	110.7
Including controls for part-time employment status, occupation, and industry												
Male characteristics, female wage structure												
Pooled	723.1	171.7	219.6	152.5	-116.4	-80.0	452.3	141.2	154.5	282.4	-116.1	-57.0
Public	-97.3	—	-157.5	-39.2	-18.8	-43.3	-61.6	-300.0	-103.5	-48.8	-27.1	-67.1
Private	105.7	101.4	131.4	116.9	95.6	91.9	104.0	106.4	115.1	103.4	92.4	82.7
Female characteristics, male wage structure												
Pooled	684.6	121.7	170.6	151.6	-106.3	-95.2	459.1	125.8	144.3	252.7	-85.5	-80.5
Public	-61.0	—	-69.3	-24.1	-33.2	-82.7	-56.0	-106.6	-18.6	-12.6	-18.6	-110.1
Private	99.5	62.5	92.0	99.0	99.6	108.1	107.7	89.4	102.3	99.2	102.0	104.4

floors" for women in the Sri Lankan wage employment market, i.e. the wage gap between otherwise identical men and women is greater at the bottom of the wage distribution.

However, is this "sticky floor" simply a manifestation of a "sticky door", i.e. is it completely explained by sectoral stratification, where the public sector wage distribution lies above the private sector wage distribution? If this were so, we would expect public and private sector-estimated wage gaps to be flat across their respective distributions. Rather, we find that in the public sector, the quantile regression-based decomposition clearly provides more information about the distribution of the conditional wage gap than the OLS-based decomposition, while in the private sector, the result differs between years. In 2003/4 (Figure 21.5) the quantile regression estimates of the conditional wage gap do not significantly differ from the conditional mean wage gap, except around the 10th percentile (when evaluated at male characteristics), whereas in 1996/7 (Figure 21.3) there is a difference between QR and OLS estimates of the unexplained gap below the 30th percentile and above the 80th percentile, when evaluated at male characteristics and between the 20th and 30th percentiles and above the 65th percentile, when evaluated at female characteristics.

Among developing country studies, the result of falling wage gaps in the conditional distribution is also reported for Vietnam in the 1993–2002 period (Pham and Reilly 2007) and over most of the distribution for the Philippines in 1999 (Sakellariou 2004) although not for Chile (Montenegro 2003, Nopo 2006), where conditional wage gaps rise throughout the distribution.

Many of these results do not change when we include controls for part-time status, occupation, and industry. However, unexplained (estimated) wage gaps *are larger when occupation, industry, and part-time status are controlled for, than when they are excluded*.[13] The magnitude of increase is sufficiently large that the negative estimated wage gaps in the upper part of the distribution in the public sector become positive. These results are consistent with the idea of females selecting into occupations and industries, and choosing hours of work that reward their characteristics better, and is not consistent with the more commonly observed explanation of occupational segregation where females are tracked into lower paying occupations and industries. These results contrast with those found in developed countries; for example, Arulampalam, et al. (2007) find that either the results do not change, or "glass ceilings" disappear, when controls for occupation and industry are included. Albrecht, Bjorklund, and Vroman (2003) find that controlling for occupation substantially reduces the gender gap throughout the wage distribution. On the other hand, in the Philippines, Sakellariou finds that "women are heavily favored in their returns to . . . occupation across the entire earnings distribution", which is consistent with a widening of the wage gap when occupational controls are included.

Among estimates that control for occupation, industry and part-time status, a larger proportion of the gap is unexplained when we use the female structure (male characteristics) than the male structure (female characteristics) *throughout all three distributions*, indicating that there are likely to be more unobservable factors that influence women's choice of work *within* broad occupational and industrial categories, than men's.

Table 21.4 provides a summary of the results in terms of sticky floors and glass ceilings. The table indicates that none of the distributions are monotonically increasing in the estimated wage gap, and only the pooled distribution—evaluated at male characteristics—is monotonically decreasing. However, by the other three definitions used, there is clear evidence for a "sticky floor" (in the pooled distribution) in the 2003/04 data, robust to either model specification and to whether male or female characteristics are used to evaluate the gap in the absence of discrimination. In the public sector too, there is evidence of a sticky floor in both years. In the private sector, a sticky floor is evident in 2003/4, only when the weakest definition (10th percentile greater than the median) is used, evaluated at male characteristics, but there is stronger evidence for a sticky floor in 1996/7. In both public and private sectors, there is also some evidence of a "glass ceiling," when estimated wage gaps are evaluated at female characteristics in 1996/7. Thus, it appears that sticky floors predominate in the Sri Lankan wage market for women, and are not simply a manifestation of occupational segregation or sectoral stratification (sticky doors).

5 Conclusions, policy implications, limitations of the study, and future work

We discuss some policy recommendations here, subject to the caveat that they are of general applicability only if our sample were representative of the general working age population.

First, we see that in all three samples, and for most of the distribution, conditional wage gaps are similar to or larger than unconditional wage gaps. This indicates that despite the better quality of women in the labor force, which resulted in smaller (and female-favoring) unconditional gaps, women are underpaid. Alternatively, one might suppose that our model suffers from omitted variable bias; i.e. women have less mobility and a greater responsibility for child-rearing (which restricts them from working late hours, traveling on the job, moving to towns where jobs are better paying, etc.) all of which would reduce productivity and bias estimates of their wage upward. They also lack the characteristics that enable a good "fit" into the workplace—in a society where "most formal organizations are masculine in nature" (Wickramasinghe and Jayatilaka 2006). These factors lead to women being paid less for a variety of reasons (they do not get hired into better paying jobs, they are overlooked for promotion, alternatively they self-select into convenient, but low paying jobs, etc.). If this explanation was accurate, it would support Wickramasinghe and Jayatilaka's (2006) assertion that public expenditure on education (a majority of beneficiaries of whom are women in Sri Lanka) is underutilized due to gender bias and stereotyping of women. Thus, to ensure

Table 21.4 Summary of results, sticky floors and glass ceilings

	Part time, occupation, and industry excluded							Part time, occupation and industry included						
	Glass ceiling measured by[1]		Sticky floor measured by[2]			Profile of estimated wage gap along distribution	Range of estimated wage gap (%)	Glass ceiling measured by[1]		Sticky floor measured by[2]			Profile of estimated wage gap along distribution	Range of estimated wage gap (%)
	90–75 diff	90–50 diff	10–all	10–25 diff	10–50 diff			90–75 diff	90–50 diff	10–all	10–25 diff	10–50 diff		
	[1]	[2]	[3]	[4]	[5]	[6]	[7]	[8]	[9]	[10]	[11]	[12]	[13]	[14]
Pooled														
1996/7														
Male			✓	✓	✓	Decreasing	2–22							12–26
Female			✓	✓	✓		6–16							4–26
2003/4														
Male			✓	✓	✓	Decreasing	5–25				✓	✓		9–31
Female			✓	✓	✓		6–25			✓	✓	✓		12–28
Public														
1996/7														
Male			✓	✓	✓		–3–18			✓	✓	✓		4–26
Female	✓		✓	✓	✓		–3–3			✓	✓	✓		6–15
2003/4														
Male			✓	✓	✓		–7–15			✓	✓	✓	Decreasing	5–27
Female			✓	✓	✓		–5–4			✓		✓		3–10
Private														
1996/7														
Male			✓	✓			12–33			✓	✓	✓		22–29
Female		✓			✓		15–24		✓					17–26
2003/4														
Male							22–29							19–33
Female					✓		25–26							24–28

1 A "glass ceiling" is defined to exist if the 90th percentile wage gap is higher than the reference wage gap by at least 4 percentage points.
2 A "sticky floor" is defined to exist if the 10th percentile wage gap is higher than the reference wage gap by at least 4 percentage points.

returns to the state from this expenditure, policies that promote gender equity in hiring, and in the workplace, are indicated (ILO/EFC 2005).

The second important finding of this study is that women are underpaid *more* at the bottom of the wage distribution. A directly applicable policy recommendation would be "to rectify existing gender-based anomalies in the wages of employees in manual labor and subcontracting" (ILO/EFC 2005). There are, however, less obvious but equally important policy applications of this result. For example, there is ample evidence that female wages among the lowest paying occupations (e.g. domestic workers) have risen in the last two decades in response to labor supply shortages arising from female migration overseas for employment. Any attempt, such as the cabinet-approved proposed ban on migration for work of mothers with young children (Government of Sri Lanka 2007) would only serve to worsen wage offers for such women in the local market. Similarly, any form of labor market restriction such as the controversial Termination of Workers Act (TEWA) is likely to exert a downward pressure on women's wages at the bottom of the distribution by encouraging firms that would potentially hire these women to remain informal.

Finally, our study finds evidence that is consistent with women selecting into "better paying" occupations. Our descriptive statistics revealed that most women in the private sector with slightly better educational qualifications were in the textile and garment trades, as opposed to being constrained to work in elementary occupations and most women in the public sector were clerks, teachers, and nurses. While these women are paid less than their male counterparts within these occupations and industries, they are nevertheless better paid than women in other occupations and industries. This has implications for the impact on the wage gap of intermittent public sector downsizing exercises and of contractions in the garment industry following its openness to competitive forces after the ending of the quota.

Notes

* This work was carried out through a grant from the Poverty and Economic Policy (PEP) Research Network (www.pep-net.org), which is financed by the Australian Aid Agency (AusAID) (http://www.ausaid.gov.au), the Canadian International Development Agency (www.acdi-cida.gc.ca), and the International Development Research Centre (IDRC) (www.idrc.ca). This paper was partially written while Gunewardena was a visitor at the Department of Economics, University of Warwick whose hospitality is gratefully acknowledged. We thank Wiji Arulampalam, O.G.Dayaratne Banda, Sami Bibi, Mark Bryan, Suresh de Mel, Evan Due, Miguel Jaramillo, Swarna Jayaweera, Nanak Kakwani, Ravi Kanbur, Thusitha Kumara, Swapna Mukhopadyay, Robin Naylor, Jeffrey Round, Fabio Soares, Upul Sonnadara, Jasmine Suministrado, Ian Walker and an anonymous referee for encouraging comments and help. Data from the Quarterly Labour Force Surveys are gratefully used by permission of the Department of Census and Statistics, Sri Lanka, which bears no responsibility for the analysis or interpretations presented here.

1 I am grateful to Robin Naylor for suggesting this line of investigation and the term "sticky doors".

2 In our case, $n = 5,000$.

3 These restrictions are imposed to limit the sample to workers with labor force attachment, and to address any potential problems of misreporting, especially of hours worked. As a result of the relatively high lower bound on hours worked, the sample may underrepresent part-time workers.

4 Our preferred model excludes controls for part-time status, occupation, and industry as they are choice variables that are arguably endogenous. If discrimination operates by tracking females into low-paying occupations and industries or part-time work, any estimates that control for these factors would underestimate discrimination and gender wage gaps.

5 For a detailed presentation of the selectivity correction, see Gunewardena et al. 2007.

6 In a survey of mean gender wage gaps for over 90 country/year observations, gaps of less than 5% were found only in Argentina in 1995, and Costa Rica in 1989, while in Chile in 1996 the gap was 1% in favour of females (World Bank 2001). More recently, Sakellariou (2004) reports an insignificant male–female gap in the log of monthly earnings in the Philippines in 1999. In Arulampalam, Booth, and Bryan's 2007 study of eleven European countries, mean log wage gaps ranged from 0.06 (Italy) to 0.25 (Britain). By way of comparison, the log wage gap in urban China in the 1990s was 0.22 (Bishop, Luo, and Wang 2005) while in Vietnam mean log wage gaps declined from 0.29 in 1993 to 0.15 in 2002 (Pham and Reilly 2006).

7 The density functions in Figure 21.1 were estimated using an Epanechnikov kernel estimator.

8 Wilcoxon rank-sum tests indicated that for all sectors and years, male and female distributions were significantly different from each other. Tests of differences between periods indicated that distributions were different except in the case of private sector females.

9 Except at the 90th percentile, when evaluated at male characteristics, in 1996/7.

10 Except in the case of the raw median wage gap in 1996/7 where only 72% and 96% are explained.

11 Note however that negative (female-favoring) raw gaps are observed only in the Philippines (Sakellariou 2004) and Chile (Montenegro 2003).

12 The estimated wage gap is larger than the raw wage gap up to the 85th percentile of the public sector distribution.

13 Except in the private sector, 10th percentile in 1996/7 and 90th percentile in 2003/4.

References

Ajwad, M. J. and P. Kurukulasuriya (2002) "Ethnic and Gender Wage Disparities in Sri Lanka." *Sri Lanka Economic Journal* 3 (1).

Albrecht, J., A. Bjorklund, and S. Vroman (2003) "Is There a Glass Ceiling in Sweden?", *Journal of Labour Economics* 21(1): 145–77.

Arulampalam, Wiji, A. L. Booth, and M. L. Bryan (2007) "Is there a Glass Ceiling over Europe? Exploring the gender pay gap across the wages distribution." *Industrial and Labor Relations Review* 60(2): 163–86

Aturupane, H. (1996) "Is Education More Profitable for Women? An economic analysis of the impact of schooling on the earnings of men and women in Sri Lanka." *Sri Lanka Journal of Social Sciences* 19(1 and 2): 27–45.

Bishop, J. A., F. Luo, and F. Wang (2005) "Economic Transition, Gender Bias, and the Distribution of Earnings in China." *Economics of Transition* 13(2): 239–59.

Blinder, A. (1973) "Wage Ddiscrimination: Reduced form and structural estimates." *Journal of Human Resources* 18 (Fall): 436–55.

Breunig, R. and S. Rospabe (2005) "Parametric vs. Semi-parametric Estimation of the Male–female Wage Gap: An application to France". Mimeo. Australian National University.

Buchinsky, M. (1994) "Changes in the US wage structure 1963–1987: An application of quantile regression." *Econometrica* 62: 405–58.

——. (1998) "Recent advances in quantile regression models." *Journal of Human Resources* 33: 88–126.

——. (2001) Quantile regression with sample selection: Estimating women's return to education in the U.S. Empirical Economics, 26(1): 87–113.

Central Bank of Sri Lanka (2005) *Annual Report 2004*. Colombo: Central Bank of Sri Lanka.

De la Rica, S., J. J. Dolado, and V. Llorens (2007) "Ceilings and Floors: Gender wage gaps by education in Spain." Forthcoming. *Journal of Population Economics* 21(3): 751–76.

Department of Census and Statistics (1996–2004) *Quarterly Reports of the Sri Lanka Labour Force Survey*. Colombo: Department of Census and Statistics.

Ganguli, I. and K. Terrell (2005) "Wage Ceilings and Floors: The gender gap in Ukraine's transition." IZA Discussion Paper 1776. Bonn: Institute for the Study of Labor.

García, J., P.J. Hernández, A. López-Nicolás (2001) "How wide is the gap? An investigation of gender wage differences using quantile regression" *Empirical Economics*, 26(1): 149–167.

Gardeazabal, J and A. Ugidos (2005) "Gender wage discrimination at Quantiles." *Journal of Population Economics*, 18(1): 165–79.

Government of Sri Lanka (2007) "Summary of the Cabinet Decisions, 3 March 2007: Restriction on migration of mothers." Government of Sri Lanka press release, March 8, 2007, http://www.news.lk/index.php?option=com_content& task= view&id=1916&Itemid=51.

Gunewardena, D. (2002) "Reducing the Gender Wage Gap in Sri Lanka: Is education enough?" *Sri Lanka Economic Journal* 3(2): 57–103.

——, S. Rajendran, D. Abeyrathna, K. Rajakaruna, and A. Ellagala (2007) "Glass Ceilings, Sticky Floors or Sticky Doors? A quantile regression approach to exploring gender wage gaps in Sri Lanka." Final Report, PMMA project pr-pmma-416. Pep Network, www.pep-net.org.

Hyder, A. and B. Reilly (2005) "The Public Sector Pay Gap in Pakistan: A quantile regression analysis." *Pakistan Development Review* 44(3): 271–306.

International Labour Organization and the Employers Federation of Ceylon (2005) "Guidelines for Company Policy on Gender Equity/Equality." Colombo.

Kee, H. J. (2006) "Glass Ceiling or Sticky Floor? Exploring the Australian gender pay gap." *The Economic Record* 82(259): 408–27.

Koenker, R. and G. Bassett (1978) "Regression Quantiles." *Econometrica* 46: 33–50.

——. and K. Hallock (2001) "Quantile Regression." *Journal of Economic Perspectives* 15(4): 143–56.

Machado, J. and J. Mata (2005) Counterfactual Decompositions of Changes in Wage Distributions using Quantile Regression. *Journal of Applied Econometrics* 20: 445–65.

Melly, B. (2005) "Public–Private Sector Wage Differentials in Germany: Evidence from quantile regressions." *Empirical Economics* 30: 505–20.

Montenegro, C. (2001) Wage Distribution in Chile: Does Gender Matter? A quantile regression approach. Policy Research Report on Gender and Development Working Paper Series 20.

Mueller, R. (1998) "Public–private Sector Wage Differentials in Canada: Evidence from quantile regressions." *Economics Letters* 60: 229–35.

Neumark, D. (1988) Employers' Discriminatory Behavior and the Estimation of Wage Discrimination. *The Journal of Human Resources* 23(3): 279–95.

Newell, A. and B. Reilly (2001) "The Gender Pay Gap in the Transition from Communism: Some empirical evidence. *Economic Systems* 25(4): 287–304.

Ñopo, H. (2006) "The Gender Wage Gap in Chile 1992–2003 from a Matching Comparisons Perspective." InterAmerican Development Bank Working Paper #562

Nordman, C. and F.-C. Wolff (2007) "Is There a Glass Ceiling in Morocco? Evidence from matched worker-firm data." DIAL working paper 2007–4.

Oaxaca, R. (1973) "Male–female Wage Differentials in Urban Labor Markets." *International Economic Review* 14 (October): 693–709.

Pendakur, K. and R. Pendakur (2007) "Minority Earnings Disparity Across the Distribution.". *Canadian Public Policy*, 33(1): 41–62.

Pham, T. H. and B. Reilly (2007) "The Gender Pay Gap in Vietnam, 1993–2002: A quantile regression approach." *Journal of Asian Economics* 18(5): 775–808.

Sakellariou, C. (2004) "The Use of Quantile Regressions in Estimating Gender Wage Differentials: A case study of the Philippines." *Applied Economics* 36, 1001–7.

Tannuri-Pianto, M., D. Pianto, and O. Arias (2004) "Informal Employment in Bolivia: A lost proposition?." In Econometric Society Series, Econometric Society, Latin American Meetings, 149.

Wickramasinghe, M. and W. Jayatilaka (2006) *Beyond Glass Ceilings and Brick Walls: Gender at the workplace*. Colombo: International Labour Organisation and the Employers Federation of Ceylon.

World Bank (2001) *Engendering Development through Gender Equality in Rights, Resources and Voice*. World Bank Policy Research Report. Washington, DC: Oxford University Press.

22 Skills, training, and enterprise performance

Survey evidence from transition countries in Central and Eastern Europe

Joe Emanuele Colombano and Libor Krkoska[*]

1 Introduction

The importance of human capital for economic performance has been widely acknowledged by the economic community for many decades. This paper contributes to the literature on the topic by analysing the microeconomic impact of country level human capital endowment as well as enterprise level skills transfers, using enterprise survey data from over 30 countries in both Europe and Asia. In particular it investigates whether enterprise-level training may compensate for inadequacies in the formal education system.

Particular attention has been paid to the impact of human capital on enterprise behaviour and performance in transition countries in central and eastern Europe. These countries are generally assumed to have highly skilled labour, compared with other countries at the same level of development (see, for example, Fischer, Sahay, and Végh 1998). However, surveys of the quality of current curricula indicate that many of today's pupils in former communist countries continue to be trained in obsolete ways (World Bank 2001). This may jeopardize the skill endowment of tomorrow's workforce and hamper the competitiveness of transition countries in the global market. The question of interactions between human capital endowment and enterprise behaviour, including the provision of employee training, is thus particularly important and may provide lessons not only for transition countries, but also for other developing as well as developed economies.

Since the pioneering work of Mankiw, Romer, and Weil (1992) on conditional convergence, most cross-country and panel data analyses have concluded that countries reach their own steady state due to differences in stocks of human capital, in addition to rates of investments and population growth. World Bank (1993) ascribed the East Asian high growth performance to the unusually rapid accumulation of physical and human capital in the region. Benhabib and Spiegel (1994) found that the growth rate of total factor productivity was a function of the average years of schooling in the labour force, among other things. By means of panel estimations for 100 countries over three decades, Barro (1997) found that secondary and higher education had a significantly positive effect on real GDP growth per capita. Gross primary school enrolment rates are also included in the GDP growth regressions for 1960–92 in Doppelhofer, Miller and Sala-i-Martin (2000).

Lately, data improvements have allowed for better specification of human capital variables. The literature discussed above concentrated on various measures of formal schooling as a proxy for human capital—mostly using enrolment rates and total years of formal education. Since the late 1990s different measures of human capital have been used by researchers. Barro (1991) and Barro and Lee (1996) questioned the comparability of years of education achieved across countries and considered country surveys and data on differences in school resources as a proxy for quality variation across countries. Similarly, the literature on the economics of education also considered the effects of increases in the quality of education. By comparing returns in the USA with education in the southern and the northern states of the country, Card and Krueger (1992), for example, showed that "quality inputs" into education, such as smaller classes and higher spending, positively affected wages.

However, it was not until the development of international student assessment tests and direct measures of cognitive abilities that cross-country comparisons of human capital quality became possible. By relying on the outcomes of six such tests of students' achievements in science and mathematics, Hanushek and Kimko (2000) constructed a composite labour force quality measure for 31 countries covering four decades since the 1960s.[1] Remarkably, the study found that a difference of one standard deviation in test performance was related to a 1% difference in annual growth rates of per capita GDP. (Initial levels of income, average years of education, and population growth rates were controlled in these regressions.) Further studies relied on similar proxies of human capital quality. By using the same sources as Hanushek and Kimko (2000) to measure school quality, Barro (2001) regressed real growth per capita on measures of both quality and quantity of education, controlling for fertility rate, government consumption, and rule of law indexes, among other things. While the coefficient on the quantity measure was positive but non-significant, the coefficient on the quality measure was a strong and significant predictor of real growth per capita.

A further development in the literature came with the emergence of yet more accurate ways to assess human capital relevance to economic development. Starting in the mid-1990s, the OECD in cooperation with several national statistical authorities developed international tests to measure a participant's master of key competencies required in adult settings, including the workplace, regardless of conformity to national curricula or formal educational qualifications. Given the almost-yearly regularity with which such tests were administered and the number of countries included, by the early 2000s a considerable amount of information was available to conduct panel data analysis. By using the results from the mid-1990s International Adult Literacy Survey of 16–65 year olds, Coulombe, Tremblay, and Marchand

(2004) estimated the quality of the labour force between 1960 and 1995. These results were included in a panel data analysis of cross-country growth in 14 OECD countries. The study found that direct measures of human capital based on literacy scores had a positive effect on growth. Specifically, a 1% difference in test performance was associated with a 2.5% relative increase in labour productivity. Including better data on the skill relevance of the labour force improves the growth regressions and emphasises the relevance of human capital to economic development.

An important subset of the literature on the impact of human capital on GDP growth covers the transition countries in central and eastern Europe (CEE) and the Commonwealth of Independent States (CIS). The time series are, however, short and the analyses of long-term relationships using these data give only indicative results. Nevertheless, the human capital endowment is expected to have a strong impact on long-run growth potential in transition economies (see Fischer, Sahay, and Végh 1998). Further papers relating GDP growth to human capital endowment in transition countries include Doppelhofer, Miller, and Sala-i-Martin 2000, and Doyle, Kuijs, and Jiang 2001.

While literature on the relationship between human capital and economic performance at the macroeconomic level is relatively rich, very little work has been done to date on the relationship between country-level human capital and enterprise performance and behaviour. A good overview of empirical literature analysing, among others, links between human capital and enterprise restructuring in transition countries is provided by Djankov and Murrell (2002).

Our paper contributes to the literature by focusing on the impact of human capital endowment and enterprise training on economic performance at the microeconomic levels. Economic development in general and transition from central planning to market economies in particular, involve major employment reallocation and significant changes in the skill content of jobs (Commander and Kollo 2004). As a result, demand for new skills has emerged. Knowledge-based jobs have increased as a percentage of total jobs and employers' hiring decisions are beginning to reflect applicants' actual skills and knowledge, not just their formal job experience and years of schooling. Meeting such demand and filling the gaps in skills through enterprise training is essential for increasing enterprise productivity and competitiveness.

The paper also considers differences in the provision of training by enterprise characteristics, such as size, location, and ownership. In order to be effective, government interventions to promote skills transfer at the enterprise level, particularly in transition and developing countries, need to be based on a deep knowledge of the existing skill gaps. This ensures that instruments are targeted at the right type of enterprises and activities.

2 Empirical analysis

In this paper, the effects of human capital on economic performance and enterprise conduct is analysed against three main measures: school enrolment rates, academic competency, and functional competency.

School enrolment rates are a standard measure of human capital endowment based on the share of population in a relevant age bracket enrolled in formal education. For the sake of this research, only secondary and tertiary levels are included as it is assumed that countries in the sample (advanced and middle-income countries) have universal primary enrolments. Enrolment rates are complemented by a combined measure of school enrolment estimating the average number of years of formal schooling.

As a measure of academic competence, we use the IEA's Trends in International Mathematics and Science Study (TIMSS).[2] TIMSS rates educational achievements in relation to their adherence to national curricula in mathematics and science. As such, this measure captures a qualitative outcome of the education system, that is, the mastery of academic subjects critical to economic development as per the national curriculum.[3]

The functional competency measure uses data from the OECD's Programme on International Student Assessment (PISA)[4], which focuses on young people's ability to use their knowledge and skills to meet real life challenges, rather than on the extent to which they have mastered a specific school curriculum. In terms of human capital quality, this indicator is superior to the previous two as it measures the relevance of human capital to the country's level of development.

It is important to recognize the issue of time lag between the acquisition of skills and their use in practice. The measures of academic and functional competency capture the achievement of young people who are in school at the time the test was given. However, these students will not affect economic outcomes until they join the workforce. The analysis in this and similar papers thus makes an important assumption of the rigidity of educational systems, i.e. there is a very high correlation between current test scores and the human capital of previous generations. This assumption thus introduces a further measurement error to the human capital variables.[5]

As shown in Table 22.1, the three types of human capital measure described above are highly correlated. An interesting pattern in correlation coefficients between different types of human capital measure can also be observed. The correlations between secondary enrolment and measures of either academic or functional competency are between 0.50 and 0.60. The correlations between tertiary enrolment and measures of either academic or functional competency are between 0.60 and 0.70. Finally, the correlations between academic and functional competency are above 0.76. This observation seems to suggest that when reviewing the functional competence of the population—that is, whether employees have the skills required in the workplace—academic competence or the efficiency of the school system is a

Table 22.1 Correlation between human capital measures

	Secondary enrolment	Tertiary enrolment	Years of schooling	Academic competency: mathematics	Academic competency: science	Academic competency: average	Functional competency: mathematics	Functional competency: reading	Functional competency: science	Functional competency: average
Tertiary enrolment	0.79**	—								
Years of schooling	0.86**	0.72**	—							
Academic competency: mathematics	0.53**	0.66**	0.58**	—						
Academic competency: science	0.57**	0.70**	0.57**	0.95**	—					
Academic competency: average	0.56**	0.68**	0.58**	0.99**	0.99**	—				
Functional competency: mathematics	0.54**	0.59**	0.35**	0.86**	0.88**	0.89**	—			
Functional competency: reading	0.60**	0.69**	0.45**	0.76**	0.83**	0.81**	0.95**	—		
Functional competency: science	0.50**	0.61**	0.33*	0.86**	0.90**	0.90**	0.98**	0.95**	—	
Functional competency: average	0.55**	0.64**	0.38**	0.85**	0.89**	0.89**	0.99**	0.98**	0.99**	—
Training: country average	0.30	0.26	0.41*	0.37	0.51*	0.45*	0.31	0.16	0.19	0.22

Sources: Authors' calculations are based on WDI, OECD, IEA, and BEEPS data. The data on enrolment and years of schooling are a simple arithmetic average of rates, in 1999—2004 as reported by WDI. The data on academic competence are from IEA and the data on functional competence are from the OECD for the latest available year (2003). The data on training are from the BEEPS 2004-5.

Notes: * denotes the 5% significance level; ** denotes the 1% significance level.

better proxy than tertiary enrolment which is in itself a better proxy than secondary enrolment.

The correlation between training provided by enterprises at the country level[6] and standard human capital measures is weak. Only formal schooling (the average number of years), academic competency in science, and average academic competency are positively correlated at a statistically significant level with the average share of enterprises with a training programme. One possible explanation for this finding is the specific measure of training used, that is, the share of companies with a training programme. This measure is similar to enrolment rates and does not reflect the quality of the training provided. However, the positive signs of all simple correlations between share of companies with a training programme and all human capital measures do not support the main hypothesis investigated in the paper that enterprises in countries with worse skills train their employees more often.

In the rest of the empirical analysis we look directly at the relevance of country-level human capital measures by relating them to enterprise decisions to develop training programmes, managers' perception of skills of the available workforce and enterprise performance (focusing on sales growth and change in employment), using enterprise level data. Reviewing these factors should address how employers, that is, enterprises, adapt to different human capital endowments in the countries where they operate. Do they try to correct shortcomings of formal education systems by providing extensive training for their employees? Or, alternatively, do they adopt the prevailing approaches to skills transfer in the countries where they operate and provide greater training for employees in countries with an already high level of average human capital? This point is particularly important for transition countries where education systems were previously geared for central planning requirements and significant enterprise efforts may be needed to ensure their employees have necessary skills for market economy requirements.

Table 22.2 shows the extent of training programmes set up by enterprises in 34 countries covered by the Business Environment and Enterprise Performance Survey (BEEPS) in 2004–5. The BEEPS was undertaken jointly by the EBRD and the World Bank in 13,500 firms in 26 transition countries[7] in 1999, 2002, and 2005, and eight non-transition countries[8] in 2004. In this paper, data on skills from the 2005 round for transition countries and the 2004 round for non-transition countries are used. The distribution of the sample between manufacturing and service sectors was determined according to the sector's relative contribution to the GDP in each country. Firms that operate in sectors subject to government price regulation and prudential supervision, such as banking, utilities, and railways, were excluded from the sample, as were farms and other types of agriculture enterprises. Companies that had 10,000 employees or more were also excluded from the sample, as were firms that started their operations in 2002–5. There are several questions on skills and the labour force in the BEEPS. Responses to the following questions were used in this paper⊗ i) did the surveyed firm offer

Table 22.2 Extent of training by firm ownership, size, and location

	New EU	SEE	CIS	Russia	EU	South Korea	Turkey	Vietnam
All enterprises	47.8	37.8	31.1	33.4	38.3	33.8	23.5	43.6
State-owned	67.5	44.1	41.8	49.2	52.6	0.0	61.8	68.6
Locally owned private	44.9	36.0	29.1	31.0	36.3	29.3	18.8	38.5
Foreign-owned	80.0	57.1	50.0	63.6	69.7	85.4	57.1	75.0
Capital city	50.8	44.0	33.4	27.4	39.4	52.1	29.3	64.2
Non-capital urban	44.5	36.7	32.7	40.1	39.1	26.3	20.6	48.1
Rural location	49.7	31.9	23.0	17.8	37.3	16.0	22.3	30.1
Large firm	80.3	60.4	52.0	53.5	79.4	90.8	58.3	74.6
Medium firm	73.4	49.1	46.3	47.1	63.7	64.0	35.7	61.25
Small firm	54.0	40.5	30.1	33.2	42.4	37.6	20.0	39.3
Micro firm	27.5	21.8	15.0	11.7	22.4	12.9	11.6	20.9

Source: BEEPS 2004–5.

Notes: The number presented in the table is the share of enterprises having a training programme for at least one category of employees with given characteristics and in a given country / region.

New EU refers to the Czech Republic, Estonia, Hungary, Latvia, Lithuania, Poland, the Slovak Republic and Slovenia. South-eastern Europe (SEE) includes Albania, Bosnia and Herzegovina, Bulgaria, Croatia, FYR Macedonia, Romania, Serbia, and Montenegro (the data were collected before the split of the country). The Commonwealth of Independent States (CIS) includes Armenia, Azerbaijan, Belarus, Georgia, Kazakhstan, the Kyrgyz Republic, Moldova, Russia, Tajikistan, Ukraine, and Uzbekistan. EU countries covered by BEEPS include Germany, Greece, Ireland, Portugal, and Spain.

Ownership refers to a majority stake; rural location is defined as a municipality with fewer than 50,000 inhabitants; large firms are those with more than 199 employees; medium firms are those with 50–199 employees; small firms are those with 10–49 employees and micro firms have fewer than 10 employees.

training to their employees, and (ii) how problematic are skills and education of available workers for the operation and growth of the surveyed firm.

The share of enterprises having a training programme for individual countries and major regions, as well as sub-categories of companies by ownership, location, and size are presented in Table 22.2. It is interesting to note that the highest share of companies with training programmes, at over 40% of all enterprises, is in the new EU member states and Vietnam, exceeding the average for the pre-2004 EU member states. A partial explanation for the high share of companies with training programmes in the new EU member states, particularly among foreign-owned companies, may lie in the existence of public subsidies for skills transfer in those countries. The lowest share of enterprises with training programmes is in Turkey, early transition countries in the CIS and Russia. This finding may also explain why there is no significant difference in provision of training by enterprises between all transition and non-transition countries. Enterprises in advanced transition countries train their employees more often than enterprises in non-transition countries, while enterprises in early transition countries train their employees less often.

The differences between companies by ownership, location, and size in Table 22.2 indicate that large, foreign-owned companies in the capital city are more likely to have a training programme while locally owned, micro enterprises are the least likely to engage in such activities. The results presented in Table 22.3 confirm these observations while controlling for various enterprise and country characteristics. A simple probit model is used:

$$training\_dummy_{i,j} = a_i + \omega_k + \beta \cdot ownership_{i,j} + \gamma \cdot location_{i,j} + \delta \cdot size_{i,j}$$
$$+ \phi \cdot performance_{i,j} + + \varphi \cdot human\_capital\_average_i + u_{i,j},$$

where *ownership* is a vector variable with dummies for local private ownership and foreign ownership, *location* is a vector variable with dummies for the location of the company in the capital and rural area, *size* is a vector variable with the dummies for medium, small, and micro-sized enterprises,[9] *performance* is a vector variable describing sales growth and employment growth, and *u* is a random term with a standard asymptotic multivariate normal distribution. Indexes *i*, *j*, and *k* describe country, company, and industry respectively. Note that the regression equation includes a constant multiplied by a country-level variable on human capital as well as country dummies to control for the impact of other potential country-level explanatory variables.

Given the strong correlation between country-level measures of human capital, separate results for four main measures of human capital endowment are presented: secondary enrolment, tertiary enrolment, academic competency and functional competency. It is noteworthy that country-level variables explain between 20–30% of data variability in the regressions. This leads to the conclusion that enterprise characteristics are more important for the existence of a training programme than country characteristics, including the country level of human capital endowment, although country-level variables do have a statistically significant impact.

When compared with state ownership, foreign ownership of a company significantly increases the likelihood of having a training programme, by about 15–16%, depending on the specification of a human capital measure. One possible explanation is that foreign-owned companies acquire enterprises that already have a training programme. Another potential reason is that foreign-owned enterprises train their employees more often because the available skills and work practices are different from those in their home countries. An interesting issue, going beyond the scope of this paper, is the dynamic of the training provision in newly acquired companies. Does it increase in first years following the acquisition above the level of training provided in the parent company and converge towards the same level later on, or is the provision of training different across subsidiaries in different countries regardless of the time since acquisition?

The size of the company is also important for the existence of a training programme. The probability of having a training programme decreases

Table 22.3 Training by firm type and human capital

	Training dummy			
Locally owned private	−0.00	−0.00	−0.02	−0.07*
	(0.04)	(0.04)	(0.04)	(0.03)
Foreign-owned	0.16**	0.16**	0.16*	0.15*
	(0.05)	(0.05)	(0.07)	(0.06)
Capital city dummy	0.05$^+$	0.05$^+$	0.02	0.02
	(0.03)	(0.03)	(0.03)	(0.03)
Rural location dummy	−0.01	−0.01	−0.02	0.01
	(0.03)	(0.03)	(0.03)	(0.05)
Medium firm dummy	−0.14**	−0.14**	−0.16**	−0.18**
	(0.04)	(0.04)	(0.05)	(0.05)
Small firm dummy	−0.30**	−0.29**	−0.32**	−0.32**
	(0.04)	(0.04)	(0.05)	(0.05)
Micro firm dummy	−0.45**	−0.45**	−0.46**	−0.51**
	(0.03)	(0.03)	(0.04)	(0.03)
Sales growth	0.10**	0.10**	0.15**	0.16**
	(0.03)	(0.03)	(0.05)	(0.05)
Employment growth	1.03	1.04	2.59**	2.67**
	(0.78)	(0.78)	(0.93)	(0.96)
Secondary enrolment	1.01**	—	—	—
	(0.07)			
Tertiary enrolment	—	−0.18*	—	—
		(0.08)		
Academic competency	—	—	1.03**	—
			(0.05)	
Functional competency	—	—	—	0.99**
				(0.03)
Number of observations	4,166	4,166	2,752	2,495
R^2	0.15	0.15	0.15	0.17
R^2 for country variables only as a percentage of R^2 for full model	28.5	28.5	24.0	19.5

Source: BEEPS 2004–5.

Notes: Statistically significant differences from 0 are denoted by + for the 10% significance level, * for the 5% significance level and ** for the 1% significance level. Robust standard errors are in brackets. The hypothesis of multicollinearity in the data has also been tested and rejected. The benchmark categories are state-owned for ownership, non-capital city urban for location and industry for sector. Country and industry dummies were used in all regressions. Probit was used to estimate the coefficients.

progressively with the size of the company. Medium-sized companies are 14–18% less likely to have a training programme compared with large companies, small companies are 29–32% less likely to have a training programme, and micro-sized companies are 45–51% less likely to have a training programme. This is not surprising as it is not very efficient for the smallest companies with fewer than 10 employees to conduct in-house training. However, this result also highlights the need for smaller companies to enrol their employees in outside training schemes in order to be competitive and ensure the same quality of skills as those of employees in larger companies. Another implication of this result is that the authorities need to adopt a different approach in encouraging enterprise-level skills transfer in small and medium-sized enterprises (SMEs) compared with larger companies.

Company performance is also shown to be related to the likelihood of having a training programme. Dynamic companies in terms of sales growth and—in some companies—higher employment growth[10] are more likely to have a training programme. However, the direction of the causality between sales growth and skills transfer is uncertain. More successful companies may feel the need to undertake a training programme as they expand. On the other hand, having a training programme may contribute to stronger sales compared with competitors without skills transfer mechanisms.

The country level of human capital endowment, common for all enterprises, is shown to be strongly related to the likelihood of having a training programme. However, only secondary enrolment and academic and functional competency are shown to increase the likelihood of having a training programme. Companies in countries with higher tertiary enrolment are actually less likely to have training programmes, possibly because they may interpret the higher share of tertiary education as a signal of labour quality. In addition, these companies may rely to a greater extent on the ability of their workforce to learn on the job than enterprises in countries with lower tertiary enrolment.[11]

The BEEPS database allows managers' perceptions of skills-related obstacles also to be investigated. Table 22.4 presents the analysis of the perception of workers' skills and education as a potential obstacle to enterprise operations and growth of business on a scale from 1 to 4, with 1 being the smallest obstacle (no obstacle) and 4 the largest obstacle. The following ordered probit regression has been estimated:

$$skills\_perception_{i,j} = a_i + \omega_k + \beta \cdot ownership_{i,j} + \gamma \cdot location_{i,j} + \delta \cdot size_{i,j}$$
$$+ \phi \cdot performance_{i,j} + + \varphi \cdot human\_capital\_average_i + u_{i,j}$$

where *ownership* is a vector variable with dummies for local private ownership and foreign ownership, *location* is a vector variable with dummies for the location of the company in the capital and rural area, *size* is a vector variable with the dummies for medium, small and micro-sized enterprises, *performance* is a vector variable describing sales growth and employment growth, and *u* is a random term with a standard asymptotic multivariate normal distribution. Indexes *i*, *j*, and *k* describe country, company, and industry respectively. The regression equation includes a constant multiplied by a country-level variable on human capital as well as country dummies to control for the impact of other potential country-level explanatory variables.

Table 22.4 Skill perception by firm type and human capital

	Skill perception			
Locally owned private	−0.04	−0.04	−0.08	−0.13
	(0.07)	(0.07)	(0.10)	(0.10)
Foreign-owned	−0.02	−0.02	−0.03	−0.08
	(0.08)	(0.08)	(0.10)	(0.11)
Capital city dummy	0.01	0.01	−0.01	0.03
	(0.06)	(0.06)	(0.07)	(0.08)
Rural location dummy	−0.05	−0.05	0.06	−0.02
	(0.06)	(0.06)	(0.07)	(0.09)
Medium firm dummy	0.05	0.05	0.05	0.03
	(0.06)	(0.06)	(0.08)	(0.09)
Small firm dummy	−0.10	−0.10	−0.13[+]	−0.04
	(0.07)	(0.07)	(0.07)	(0.09)
Micro firm dummy	−0.12	−0.12	−0.15[+]	−0.09
	(0.09)	(0.09)	(0.08)	(0.11)
Sales growth	0.18*	0.18*	0.20*	0.25*
	(0.07)	(0.07)	(0.09)	(0.12)
Employment growth	1.62	1.62	4.07**	3.44*
	(1.36)	(1.36)	(1.41)	(1.71)
Secondary enrolment	2.48**	—	—	—
	(0.13)			
Tertiary enrolment	—	−1.84**	—	—
		(0.14)		
Academic competency	—	—	−0.20*	—
			(0.09)	
Functional competency	—	—	—	−0.10
				(0.08)
Number of observations	4112	4112	2719	2471
R^2	0.03	0.03	0.02	0.02
R^2 for country dummies only as a percentage of R^2 for full model	88.5	88.5	78.4	77.1

Source: BEEPS 2004–5.

Notes: Statistically significant differences from 0 are denoted by + for the 10% significance level, * for the 5% significance level and ** for the 1% significance level. Robust standard errors are in brackets. The hypothesis of multicollinearity in the data has also been tested and rejected. The benchmark categories are state-owned for ownership, non-capital city urban for location and industry for sector. Country and industry dummies were used in all regressions. Probit was used for the training dummy as the dependent variable and ordered probit was used for the perception of skills as a business obstacle as the dependent variable.

The data show clearly that the importance of country-level variables is much higher in forming managers' perceptions than in explaining enterprise behaviour, that is, the existence of a training programme. Country characteristics explain more than three-quarters of data variability in the perception regressions, while coefficients for most of the enterprise characteristics are insignificant. Sales growth is the exception in all specifications, with managers in more dynamic companies being more concerned about the skills of the available workforce. Employment growth and company size are also significant in the formation of skills perception but only in some specifications.

Analysis of the relationship between the country level of human capital and the perception of skills of the available workforce as a business obstacle by company managers give some interesting results. Functional competency does not seem to be related to the perception of the skills at the enterprise level. Higher academic competency and tertiary enrolment, both of which are relatively easily observable by managers, lead to skills being perceived as a smaller business obstacle, as could be expected. Higher secondary enrolment, surprisingly, actually increases the perception of skills as a business obstacle. One potential explanation is that higher secondary school enrolment beyond a certain threshold is not related to requirements of enterprises and the pool of potential skilled blue collar workers is smaller in advanced and middle income countries with higher secondary school enrolment. The investigation of this interesting hypothesis is, however, beyond the scope of this paper.

The rest of this section focuses on the relationship between skills endowment, training of employees and enterprise performance. Table 22.5 presents the results of regressions of sales growth on enterprise and country characteristics, including training and the country level of human capital as per the following:

$$sales\_growth_{i,j} = a_i + \omega_k + \lambda \cdot training\_dummy_{i,j} + \beta \cdot ownership_{i,j}$$
$$+ \gamma \cdot location_{i,j} + \delta \cdot size_{i,j} + + \varphi \cdot human\_capital\_average_i + u_{i,j}.$$

In this equation, the training dummy describes whether a company j in country i has a training programme. *Ownership* is a vector variable with dummies for local private ownership and foreign ownership, *location* is a vector variable with dummies for the location of the company in the capital and rural area, *size* is a vector variable with the dummies for medium, small and microsized enterprises, and u is a random term with a standard asymptotic multivariate normal distribution. Indexes i, j and k describe country, company and industry, respectively. The regression equation includes a constant multiplied by a country-level variable on human capital as well as country dummies to control for the impact of other potential country-level explanatory variables.

As in the previous enterprise-level regressions, four different specifications are presented with the main four measures of the country level of skills. This section does not comment on the importance of non-skills related enterprise characteristics (such as ownership) for sales growth, but notes that the results for these are in line with the literature (see ERBD 2005, Chapter 4, for more detail).[12]

Training programmes are shown to have a strong positive relationship to sales growth, equivalent to 4.1–4.4 percentage point higher sales growth. All measures of the country level of human capital are also significantly related to sales growth. Tertiary enrolment, academic competency and functional

Table 22.5 Relationship between sales growth, enterprise training and human capital

	Sales growth			
Training	4.37**	4.37**	4.11**	4.40**
	(0.98)	(0.98)	(1.43)	(1.48)
Locally owned private	6.43**	6.43**	5.66**	4.24**
	(1.25)	(1.25)	(1.20)	(1.26)
Foreign-owned	9.00**	9.00**	6.85**	7.13**
	(2.07)	(2.07)	(1.82)	(1.71)
Capital city dummy	0.95	0.95	−0.26	−0.71
	(1.14)	(1.14)	(1.41)	(1.48)
Rural location dummy	−0.99	−0.99	−1.34	1.27
	(0.73)	(0.73)	(0.98)	(1.07)
Medium firm dummy	−0.07	−0.07	−0.07	0.42
	(1.00)	(1.00)	(0.98)	(0.85)
Small firm dummy	−0.31	−0.31	1.63	1.61*
	(1.17)	(1.17)	(1.00)	(0.71)
Micro firm dummy	0.36	0.36	1.84	3.83*
	(1.54)	(1.54)	(1.38)	(1.30)
Secondary enrolment	−0.13**	—	—	—
	(0.02)			
Tertiary enrolment	—	0.29**	—	—
		(0.01)		
Academic competency	—	—	0.36**	—
			(0.03)	
Functional competency	—	—	—	0.33**
				(0.03)
Number of observations	12408	12408	7885	7177
R^2	0.09	0.09	0.09	0.09
R^2 for country dummies only as a percentage of R^2 for full model	90.0	90.0	90.4	87.5

Source: BEEPS 2004–5.

Notes: Statistically significant differences from 0 are denoted by + for the 10% significance level, * for the 5% significance level and ** for the 1% significance level. Robust standard errors are in brackets. The hypothesis of multicollinearity in the data has also been tested and rejected. The benchmark categories are state-owned for ownership, non-capital city urban for location and industry for sector. Country and industry dummies were used in all regressions.

competency are positively related to sales growth, with a 10% increase in the respective measure of human capital associated with about a 2.9–3.6% increase in sales growth. Secondary enrolment, on the other hand, is negatively related to sales growth, with the possible explanation similar to the one provided above on the potential shortages of blue collar skilled labour in countries with high secondary enrolment. This result can be also seen as the basis for higher secondary enrolment leading to managers perceiving the skills of the available workforce as an obstacle to business performance.

Finally, the relationship between skills, training and employment growth is analysed as per the following:

$$employment \_ growth_{i,j} = a_i + \omega_k + \lambda \cdot training \_ dummy_{i,j} + \beta \cdot ownership_{i,j}$$
$$+ \gamma \cdot location_{i,j} + \delta \cdot size_{i,j} + + \eta \cdot sales \_ growth_{i,j}$$
$$+ \varphi \cdot human \_ capital \_ average_i + u_{i,j},$$

where the training dummy describes whether a company *j* in country *i* has a training programme, *ownership* is a vector variable with dummies for local, private ownership and foreign ownership, *location* is a vector variable with dummies for the location of the company in the capital and rural area, *size* is a vector variable with the dummies for medium, small and micro-sized enterprises, and *u* is a random term with a standard asymptotic multivariate normal distribution. Indexes *i*, *j*, and *k* describe country, company and industry, respectively. The regression equation includes a constant multiplied by a country-level variable on human capital as well as country dummies to control for the impact of other potential country-level explanatory variables.

It should be noted that contemporary values on size and sales on the right-hand side of the equation are used, which may create endogeneity problems. One way of addressing this issue is to use lagged variables. In this case, information on sales and employment 12 months prior to the survey is available, but no data on the change in training provision. Another approach is to estimate using a reduced form of the equation, eliminating all the potential endogenous variables. Such an approach leads to qualitatively the same results as estimates presented in this paper and are available on request.

Although enterprise level data explain about 50% of data variability in these regressions, the explanatory power of the regressions is low and there are no enterprise level characteristics consistently significant, unlike in the previous regressions. In some regressions, having a training programme is associated with higher employment growth but the coefficients are not very high. The most consistent relationship, not surprisingly, is positive association between sales growth and employment growth. One may therefore conclude that there is no empirical evidence identifying a direct relationship between enterprise-level skills transfer on the one hand and job creation on the other hand.

Looking more closely at the relationship between country-level human capital variables and employment growth, again a negative relationship between secondary enrolment and employment growth appears, consistent with previous regressions. The positive association between tertiary enrolment and employment growth is also in line with previous results. The negative relationship between employment growth and academic as well as functional competency is noteworthy, particularly when compared with the result on academic competency and sales growth. The data show that in countries with better academic and functional competency, enterprises grow faster but their employment growth is slower, highlighting the links between the quality of the human capital and labour productivity at the enterprise level. One may therefore conclude that better qualified employees are associated with stronger sales growth, but enterprises need fewer of them to achieve such a performance.

3 Summary and concluding remarks

This paper analysed the impact of various human capital measures at the microeconomic level. It found that qualitative measures of human capital— that is, academic and functional competency—are strongly associated with

Table 22.6 Relationship between employment growth, enterprise training and country-level human capital

	Employment growth			
Training	0.06	0.06	0.11*	0.10*
	(0.04)	(0.04)	(0.04)	(0.04)
Locally owned private	0.20**	0.20**	0.14	0.13
	(0.06)	(0.06)	(0.09)	(0.10)
Foreign-owned	0.30*	0.30*	0.29	0.22
	(0.14)	(0.14)	(0.17)	(0.16)
Capital city dummy	0.15**	0.15**	0.15*	0.10
	(0.05)	(0.05)	(0.07)	(0.08)
Rural location dummy	0.02	0.02	0.02	0.03
	(0.04)	(0.04)	(0.04)	(0.05)
Medium firm dummy	0.01	0.01	0.02	0.15
	(0.09)	(0.09)	(0.12)	(0.09)
Small firm dummy	−0.04	−0.04	0.00	0.03
	(0.07)	(0.07)	(0.09)	(0.08)
Micro firm dummy	−0.21**	−0.21**	−0.14	−0.13
	(0.07)	(0.07)	(0.08)	(0.07)
Sales growth	0.24**	0.24**	0.22**	0.24
	(0.07)	(0.07)	(0.11)	(0.14)
Secondary enrolment	−0.51**	—	—	—
	(0.12)			
Tertiary enrolment	—	0.51**	—	—
		(0.12)		
Academic competency	—	—	−0.79**	—
			(0.06)	
Functional competency	—	—	—	−0.80**
				(0.07)
Number of observations	4166	4166	2752	2495
R^2	0.04	0.04	0.04	0.05
R^2 for country dummies only as a percentage of R^2 for full model	54.4	54.4	50.3	51.0

Source: BEEPS 2004–5.

Notes: Statistically significant differences from 0 are denoted by + for the 10% significance level, * for the 5% significance level and ** for the 1% significance level. Robust standard errors are in brackets. The hypothesis of multicollinearity in the data has also been tested and rejected. The benchmark categories are state-owned for ownership, non-capital city urban for location and industry for sector. Country and industry dummies were used in all regressions.

sales growth at the enterprise level. It also found that enterprise decisions on within-company skills transfer are mostly driven by enterprise characteristics, with ownership and size the two key features determining the likelihood of having a training programme.

The key finding of the paper is that enterprise training is more common in countries where the available workforce has above average skills, further enlarging the skills gap between countries with different human capital endowments. In particular, the paper shows that the existence of a training programme is positively related to the level of skills in a country, controlling for other enterprise and country characteristics. This implies that skills transfer at the enterprise level on average does not compensate for poor levels of human capital at the country level. However, the data do not provide any robust evidence of a direct link between job creation and either better country-level skills or more frequent enterprise-level skills transfer.

Such findings lead to several policy implications:

- Policy makers should not rely on enterprises to rectify poor country-level skills. Furthermore, empirical evidence suggests that enterprises in countries where the overall level of human capital is higher train their employees more often than enterprises in countries with a less skilled workforce.
- Human capital endowment at the country level and training at the enterprise level are strongly associated with enterprise performance. The quality of skills attained in the formal education system rather than the number of students enrolled, however, is what impacts economic performance. The reform of the education system should therefore ensure that improvements in qualitative outcomes, that is, academic and functional competency, are among the key objectives.
- There are significant differences in the provision of enterprise training. Smaller, locally owned enterprises outside the capital are less likely to offer employee training programmes. While governments may be willing to provide funds for skills transfer at the enterprise level, these funds are usually taken by large foreign-owned companies which are more likely to have training programmes already in place. The implication is that policy makers should prioritise public support for training employees in locally owned SMEs rather than in large foreign-owned enterprises, subject to otherwise similar characteristics of these enterprises besides their size.

There are several potential extensions of this paper. One option is to look in more detail at training provided for different categories of employees, distinguishing between skilled, unskilled and non-production workers. Another potential extension could look at more detailed information on training, namely the share of employees trained in a given year. It should also be possible to measure more precisely the outcomes of enterprise training programmes, and devise quality measures of enterprise training similar to academic and functional competency. It would be also useful to analyse the ownership variables by the country of origin of the foreign owner. Unfortunately the available data do not contain this information.

Notes

* The authors are grateful to Randall Filer, Ravi Kanbur, Nevila Konica, Yulia Rodionova, Peter Sanfey and Utku Teksoz for helpful comments on an earlier draft.

1 Tests were administered by the International Association for the Evaluation of Educational Achievements (IEA) and the International Assessment of Educational Progress (IAEP).

2 The transition countries covered by TIMS are Armenia, Bulgaria, the Czech Republic, Estonia, FYR Macedonia, Hungary, Latvia, Lithuania, Moldova, Romania, Russia, Serbia and Montenegro (the data were collected before the country split into two separate entities), the Slovak Republic, and Slovenia. Non-transition countries include Argentina, Australia, Austria, Bahrain, Belgium, Botswana, Canada, Chile, Colombia, Cyprus, Denmark, Egypt, Finland, France, Ghana, Germany, Greece, Hong Kong, Iceland, Indonesia, Iran, Ireland, Israel, Italy, Japan, Jordan, South Korea, Kuwait, Lebanon, Malaysia, Mexico, Morocco, the Netherlands, New Zealand, Norway, Philippines, Portugal, Saudi Arabia, Singapore, South Africa, Spain, Sweden, Switzerland, Syria, Thailand, Tunisia, Turkey, the United Kingdom, the United States and Yemen.

3 It could also be seen as a proxy for the quality, or efficiency, of the public sector given that in most countries the provision of education is provided or regulated by the state.

4 The transition countries included in PISA are Albania, Bulgaria, the Czech Republic, FYR Macedonia, Hungary, Latvia, Poland, Romania, Russia, Serbia and Montenegro (the data were collected before the country split into two separate entities) and the Slovak Republic. Non-transition countries covered are Argentina, Australia, Austria, Belgium, Brazil, Canada, Chile, Denmark, Finland, France, Germany, Greece, Hong Kong, Iceland, Indonesia, Ireland, Israel, Italy, Japan, South Korea, Liechtenstein, Luxembourg, Mexico, the Netherlands, New Zealand, Norway, Peru, Portugal, Spain, Sweden, Switzerland, Thailand, Tunisia, Turkey, the United Kingdom, the United States, and Uruguay.

5 Data on academic and functional competency are available only from the mid/late 1990s onwards. As a result, data on enrolment, years of schooling, GDP per capita, and GDP growth are calculated as a simple average, 1999–2004.

6 Throughout the paper training is a dummy variable indicating whether an enterprise runs a formal training programme for at least one category of employees. On a country level, training refers to a simple arithmetic average of the enterprise-level training dummy; that is, it is an indicator describing the share of enterprises with a formal training programme for at least one category of employee.

7 The countries covered include Albania, Armenia, Azerbaijan, Belarus, Bosnia and Herzegovina, Bulgaria, Croatia, the Czech Republic, Estonia, FYR Macedonia, Georgia, Hungary, Kazakhstan, the Kyrgyz Republic, Latvia, Lithuania, Moldova, Montenegro, Poland, Romania, Russia, Serbia, the Slovak Republic, Slovenia, Tajikistan, Ukraine, and Uzbekistan. The survey was not conducted in Turkmenistan.

8 The countries covered include Germany (distinguishing between former East and West Germany), Greece, Ireland, Portugal, South Korea, Spain, Turkey, and Vietnam.

9 In line with the literature, micro companies are defined as those with fewer than 10 employees, small companies as those with between 10 and 49 employees, medium-sized companies as those with 50–199 employees, and large companies as those with 200 and more employees.
10 The share of employees trained in the past 12 months is, however, positively associated with employment growth in all specifications.
11 The share of employees trained in the past 12 months is positively related to the country level of human capital for all measures used. This implies that in countries with higher tertiary enrolment, companies are less likely to have a training programme, but when they have one they train a higher share of their employees.
12 The regressions show that locally owned companies grow by 4.2 to 6.4% faster than state-owned companies. Foreign-owned enterprises grow by 6.9 to 9.0% faster than state-owned companies, depending on specification. Other enterprise characteristics are not significantly related to sales growth, except for the size in one specification.

References

Barro, R. (1991) "Economic Work in a Cross-section of Countries." *Quarterly Journal of Economics* 106: 407–43.
——. (1997) *Determinant of Economic Growth: A cross-country empirical study.* Cambridge, MA: MIT Press.
——. (2001) "Education and Economic Growth." In *The Contribution of Human and Social Capital to Sustained Economic Growth and Well-Being*, edited by J. F. Helliwell. OECD: Paris. Ch. 3, pp. 14–41.
——. and J. W. Lee (1996) "International Measures of Schooling Years and Schooling Quality." *American Economic Review* 86: 218–23.
Benhabib, J. and M. M. Spiegel (1994) "The Role of Human Capital in Economic Development: Evidence from Aggregate Cross-Country Data." *Journal of Monetary Economics* 34: 143–73.
Card, D. and A. B. Krueger (1992) "School Quality and Black-White Relative Earnings: A direct assessment." *Quarterly Journal of Economics* 107(1): 151–200.
Commander, S. and J. Kollo (2004) "The Changing Demand for Skills: Evidence from the transition." IZA Working Paper 1073.
Coulombe, S., J.-F. Tremblay, and S. Marchand (2004) *Literacy Scores, Human Capital and Growth across Fourteen OECD Countries.* Ottawa: Statistics Canada.
Djankov, S. and P. Murrell (2002) "Enterprise Restructuring in Transition: A quantitative survey." *Journal of Economic Literature* 40: 739–92.
Doppelhofer, G., R. I. Miller, and X. Sala-i-Martin (2000) "Determinants of Long-term Growth: A Bayesian averaging of classical estimates (BACE) approach." OECD working paper 266.
Doyle, P., L. Kuijs, and G. Jiang (2001) "Real Convergence to EU Income Levels: Central Europe from 1990 to the long term." IMF working paper 01/146.
Fischer, S., R. Sahay, and C. A. Végh (1998) "How Far is Eastern Europe from Brussels?" IMF working paper 98/53.
Hanushek, E. A. and D. D. Kimko (2000) "Schooling, Labor-force Quality, and the Growth of Nations." *American Economic Review* 90: 1184–8.
Mankiw, N. G., D. Romer, and D. N. Weil (1992) "A Contribution to the Empirics of Economic Growth." *Quarterly Journal of Economics* 107: 407–37.

World Bank (1993) *The East Asian Miracle: Economic Growth and Public Policy*. Oxford University Press.

—— . (2001) "Hidden Challenges to Education Systems in Transition Economies." Education Sector Strategy Paper for Europe and Central Asia Region. Washington, DC: World Bank.

23 Exploring gender wage "discrimination" in South Africa, 1995–2004

A quantile regression approach

Miracle Ntuli[*]

1 Introduction

For a long time, African women were subjected to both legalized and informal social discrimination which has hampered their full integration into the South African labour market. Hence the post-Apartheid regime has since 1994, implemented fundamental constitutional changes to ensure fair access and treatment of women in the labour market. For example, there is the Employment Equity Act (1998) which abolishes discrimination in the work place (Maziya 2001). With these enabling policies one would expect to see a decline in labour market inequalities which is matched with progressive changes in the place of African women in the job market. Indeed, analyses of micro-data collected from the mid-1990s onwards attest to an improved assimilation of women into the labour market. However, this is associated with persistent inequity among the workforce. For instance, women still earn significantly less than men, see Figure 23.1. Despite the abolition of legalized discrimination and the introduction of Affirmative Action legislation, there is still wide acknowledgement that a significant portion of these wage differentials is due to gender "discrimination".[1] Quite worryingly, the latter has received less attention in the literature than it deserves as it has always stood on the shadow of institutionalized racism (Isemonger and Roberts 1999).

To be explicit, the few studies which were devoted to gender "discrimination" and especially its wage aspect include Casale (1998), Isemonger and Roberts (1999), Winter (1999), Hinks (2002), Rospabe (2001) and Gruen (2004) inter alia. These studies have exclusively investigated the gender pay gaps at the conditional mean of the wage distributions. As a result, they have neglected the distributional implications of standardizing the size of the wage gaps across the entire wage distribution. This caveat creates a huge potential for studies which seek to understand the South African gender wage gap conundrum by carrying out distributional analyses.

Also, to this point, there is still a dearth of information on whether the incidence of gender wage "discrimination" increased or decreased over time. This is because existing works have utilized different analytical methods, making comparative analyses of their results fraught with difficulties (although

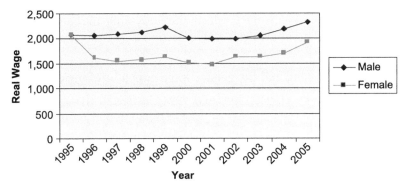

Figure 23.1 Real wages for Africans by gender (1995–2005).

their scope spreads over the period 1994 to 2004). Even so, most of these studies have suggested the presence of "discrimination" in one particular year. Hence, they have not provided us with any systematic analysis of whether "discrimination" is increasing or decreasing. Obviously, this limited focus fails to reveal long term trends of the gender wage gaps. Generally, such trends are important in assessing the effectiveness of counter legislation.

In light of the limitations in the existing works, this paper aims to contribute to the debate by applying quantile regression and counterfactual decomposition methods adjusted for the quantile regression framework to investigate whether a "glass ceiling"[2] exists or if instead a "sticky floor" is more prevalent among the African populace in the South African "formal" labour market. In addition, we aim to assess whether the incidence of gender wage "discrimination" has been increasing or decreasing across the entire wage distribution from 1995 to 2004. By addressing these issues, this research helps in taking stock of the achievements made in gender mainstreaming after 10 years of South Africa's democratic independence. In carrying out such an audit, it is critical that all decisions are underpinned by sound research that systematically explores the prevalence of labour market discrimination. This is critical because the existence of labour market discrimination inevitably negates any endeavours to close gender disparities regarding participation in economic activities.

Ten years after the abolition of legalized discrimination and the introduction of Affirmative Action legislation, one would have expected that the gaps between male and female wages attributable to "discrimination" might have decreased. However, we will show that on the contrary, they seem to be rising in the upper tails of the wage distribution from 1995 to 2004. It will also be revealed that the South African gender wage gap is wider at the bottom percentiles of the wage distribution "sticky floor" than at the top.

Turning to the organization of this study, section 2 reviews some empirical literature which employed the quantile regression approach. Thereafter, section 3 poses the human capital earnings functions and the specification of the empirical wage model while section 4 expounds on the methodology and data analyses. Section 5 presents the results of the study while the conclusions and policy recommendations are dealt with in section 6.

2   Quantile regression and the gender wage gap: a brief review

Generally, Buchinsky (1994, 1995, and 1998) instigated the application of quantile regression in the context of wage estimation and returns to education (Kee 2005). Although, his focus was on wage disparities among women, his work has been influential to studies on gender wage disparities, especially the sample selection correction procedure.[3]

Following Buchinsky's seminal work, a small but growing literature has adopted this methodology (Kee 2005). For example, Albrecht et al. (2004) used quantile regression decomposition methods based on Machado and Mata (2001, 2005) (MM)[4] to analyse the gender pay gap in the Netherlands. The outcomes from the decompositions revealed that the majority of the gender wage gap was due to differences between returns to labour market attributes rather than to disparities in characteristics. This result mainly occurred in the top half of the distribution (strong "glass ceiling" effect).

In contrast to the above study which pooled individuals with different levels of education, other studies stratified their samples by education groups. For example, de la Rica, Dolado, and Llorens (2005) discovered that in Spain for the more educated there is a "glass ceiling" while for the less educated there is a "sticky floor."

Besides, Kee (2005) conducted a sectoral analysis of the gender pay gap in both the public and private sectors of the Australian labour market. The study detected a strong glass ceiling effect in the private sector. Another conclusion was that the gender wage gap accelerated across the distribution even after extensive controls, suggesting that the observed pay gap was a result of differences in returns to gender.

As for the developing countries, most studies, which pursued the quantile regression approach, did not decompose the raw gender pay gap along the wage distribution. Instead, they estimated pooled quantile regressions and assessed the evolution of a gender dummy along the wage distribution. This approach may lead such studies to detect the gender wage premia but under identify its source. Typical studies include Hyder and Reilly (2005) and Ajwad and Kurukulasuriya (2002) who investigated Pakistani and Sri Lankan cases respectively. Specifically, the latter investigated ethnic and gender wage disparities in Sri Lanka's formal sector using the Sri Lanka Integrated Survey (1999–2000). They discovered that the premium paid to male workers in the labour force was more pronounced at the top of the wage distribution.

In a recent development, Gunawardena (2006) addressed the above limitation by applying quantile regression estimation and decomposition methods to explore gender wage gaps in Sri Lanka. More importantly, the study's findings contradict those reported in Ajwad and Kurukulasuriya (2002).

In particular, a "sticky floor" was detected in both the public and private sectors.

In the African context, Nielsen and Rosholm (2001) used quantile regression to investigate sectoral wage gaps in Zambia. In so doing, the study scrutinized the raw gender pay gap and concluded that between 1991 and 1993 the gender pay gap in the private sector was lower at the bottom of the distribution, but in 1996 it was similar across all quantiles. As in the Sri Lankan (2002) and Pakistan cases, the Zambia study did not conduct a decomposition analysis of the wage gap. As a result, the factors that drive the gender pay gaps in the three studies remained unknown. All the same, none of the South African studies carried out on this topic has made recourse to quantile regression techniques.

Overall, we conclude that the application of quantile regression in the context of gender wage gaps in developing countries is still in its infancy. Hence, by utilizing these new approaches, this study will not only make a significant methodological contribution but will also help in the formulation of target oriented labour market policy and intervention mechanisms. This is possible as the quantile regression decomposition methods provide different coefficients of gender wage "discrimination" for the distinct percentiles of the conditional wage distribution.

3 Earnings functions

The earnings functions utilized in the study are an extension of the "standard" Mincerian (1974) income function. A detailed derivation of the latter is given e.g. in Cahuc and Zylberberg (2004: 69–87). Based on this derivation a wage model of the following form results:

$$\ln y_i = \rho_0 + \rho_1 s_i + \rho_2 x_i - \rho_3 x_i^2 + u_i \tag{1}$$

Equation (1) expresses an individual's log hourly income ($\ln y_i$) as a function of his/her measured human capital stock which depends on years of education (s), years of experience (x) and its square (x^2). Notionally, earnings should increase with the accumulation of human capital as it enhances productivity, that is, ρ_1 and ρ_2 are > 0. The square of the years of experience captures the non-linear effect of experience, as it often follows a parabolic shape which peaks somewhere in midlife, thus ρ_3 is < 0. This study extends the Mincerian wage model to include other controls often included in analyses of gender pay gaps in South Africa. The variables are defined according to data availability and they can be categorized into controls for human capital (education, experience, and hours worked), individual characteristics (marital status, having young children), geographical location (provinces), sector and industry of employment, trade union membership, occupation, and controls for sample selection bias.[5] Controlling for selection bias entails estimating employment models which are modelled as follows.

Modelling employment

The process of selection into employment is often modelled as a binary choice model where individuals are confronted with the "choice" of being employed or remaining unemployed (Chamberlain and van der Berg 2002). The assumption underlying such an approach is that all unemployment is voluntary (Bhorat and Leibbrandt 2001: 113; Chamberlain and van der Berg 2002), which is clearly not the case in South Africa (Kingdon and Knight 2000). As a result, it is not appropriate to model selection into employment in this manner (Bhorat and Leibbrandt 2001). Instead, an individual can choose to participate in the labour market, but the individual's choice to participate does not guarantee employment (Chamberlain and van der Berg 2002). Thus, there is selection into employment. This means that controlling for sample selection bias involves estimating the earnings functions in three sequential phases; predicting participation, employment and eventual earnings separately by gender. Accordingly, we specify the log odds that an individual will participate in the labour market as a function of age, age-squared, education, presence of children aged below 15 years in the household, provinces, non-labour income, marital status, and urban residence. In contrast to the labour force participation models, household formation variables, to be exact, household size and the proportion of working age females in the household are also included in the employment equations.

4 Methodology

This section presents the study's estimation framework which consists of two stages. The first stage involves estimating separate human capital earnings functions for men and women at different percentiles of the wage distributions using quantile regression, (accounting for female sample selection bias). The process of controlling for selectivity entails fitting Heckprobit models of employment on the broadly defined sample of female participants (see STATA 2001: 31–47). The consistent estimates of the employment model will be utilized to compute sample selection correction terms (λs) and these are eventually included in the wage models. The second stage involves using quantile regression decomposition methods to analyse the size and components of the gender wage gaps over the entire conditional wage distribution. The aforesaid estimation techniques are described below.

A. Quantile regression (QR)

Following Koenker and Bassett (1978) and Buchinsky (1998), the model of QR in a (log) wage-equation setting can be described as follows. Let (w_i, x_i) be a random sample, where w_i denotes the (logged) monthly gross wage of an individual i and x_i is a vector $K \times 1$ of regressors, and let $Q_\theta(w_i|x_i)$ be θ^{th} order quantile of the conditional distribution of w_i given x_i. Then, under the assumption of a linear specification, the model can be defined as

$$\ln w_i = x_i' \beta_\theta + u_{\theta i} \qquad Q_\theta(w_i \mid x_i) = \ln x_i' \beta_\theta \qquad (2)$$

where the distribution of the error term $u_{\theta i}$, $Fu_\theta(\cdot)$, is left unspecified, just assuming that $u_{\theta i}$ satisfies $Q_\theta(u_{\theta i}|x_i) = 0$. Unlike in least squares where the parameter estimates minimize the sum of squared errors, in quantile regression the estimation procedure is to minimize the absolute sum of the errors from a particular quantile of the log earnings across workers. Hence, the θ_{th} regression quantile parameter $(0 < \theta < 1)$, is defined as the solution to the problem:

$$\min_{\beta \in R^k} \left\{ \sum_{i:\ln w_i \geq x_i\beta} \theta \mid \ln w_i - x_i\beta_\theta \mid + \sum_{i:\ln w_i \leq x_i\beta} (1 - \theta)|\ln w_i - x_i\beta_\theta| \right\} \qquad (3)$$

The solution to equation (3) is obtained by linear programming algorithms. To avoid understating the standard errors (since they are heteroscedastic), they are estimated by bootstrap methods[6] (Efron 1979; Buchinsky 1994; Deaton 1997). The estimated vector of QR coefficients (β_θ) is interpreted as the marginal change in the conditional quantile θ due to a marginal change in the corresponding element of the vector of coefficients on w_i.

B. Counterfactual wage decomposition

The study follows Albrecht, Vureen, and Vroman's (2003) adoption of the Machado and Mata (MM)'s (2000, 2005) bootstrap method which generalizes the Oaxaca–Blinder (1973) criterion to implement the decomposition directly at each quantile (see Kee 2005; de la Rica, Dolado, and Llorens 2005; Albrecht, Vureen, and Vroman 2004). The steps in (MM)'s procedure can be summarized as follows.

1   Using a standard uniform distribution, sample a quantile say the θth quantile.
2   With the male database, estimate the coefficient vectors β_θ^m at the θth quantile.
3   From the female database take a draw from women's data (x_f), and construct a predicted wage by multiplying the chosen x_f by the estimate of β_θ^m. Repeat steps one, two and three N times (e.g. $N = 5,000$) and construct a counterfactual male distribution, namely what women would have earned if they were "paid like men".
4   Then use the generated wage distribution to construct the counterfactual gap $(x_f'\beta_\theta^m - \beta_\theta^f)$ which yields that part of the raw gap explained by different rewards, that is $x_f'(\beta_\theta^m - \beta_\theta^f)$.

Data

The data utilized for the study are obtained from the September (2004) Labour Force Survey (LFS) and the (1995, 1999) October Household Surveys (OHSs) carried out by Statistics South Africa (Stats SA). The OHS are annual surveys. These surveys are independent cross-sections specifically, for each of them different samples were drawn from the population (Gruen 2004). A large but varying number of households across all provinces of South Africa were sampled allowing a detailed snapshot of labour market conditions and outcomes (Gruen 2004). For the years 1995 and 1999 in particular, similar sample designs have been applied. Three thousand enumeration areas (EAs) were sampled and 10 households within each of them have been interviewed, resulting in a sample size of 30,000 households. The total sample of labour force participants comprises of individuals aged between 15 and 65 and either reported to be employed or were categorized as unemployed using the broad definition.[7]

On the other hand, the LFS is a bi-annual rotating panel household survey. The rotating panel methodology is specifically designed to measure the dynamics of employment and unemployment in the country. The LFS captured information about the labour market situation of approximately 68,000 adults of working age (15–65 years) living in over 30,000 households across the country. Both the OHS, and the LFS have sampling weights and they were considered in the analyses. However, a drawback of both the OHS and the LFS is that the wage information is given in the form of either points or intervals. This compromises our analyses as it necessitates employing an indirect method to obtain a wage series compatible with quantile regressions.

Data analysis

First, we dwell on the sample delineation process before describing the variables used in this study. Accordingly, the selected sub-sample comprises of working age Africans (15–65 years) employed in the "formal" sector, provided they availed their wage information. Noteworthy is the fact that our definition of the "formal" sector encompasses the formal and domestic sectors, the latter is included as it employs most African women. Ultimately, the data cleaning exercise engendered the weighted sample statistics presented in Figure 23.2. The available information tallies with the economy's labour force participation rates since the numbers of employed males constantly outnumber those of women from 1995–2004. The figure also shows that the total sample of African employees who availed their wage information decreased by 7% between 1995 and 2004. Quite worryingly, the statistics suggest a wholesale collapse of employment between 1995 and 1999, which is clearly not the case. Probably, the smaller sample sizes for 1999 are due to a sample composition shift or it could be that odd things which we cannot explain happened that year. Nonetheless, the statistics accord with the feminization

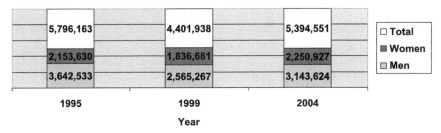

	1995	1999	2004
Total	5,796,163	4,401,938	5,394,551
Women	2,153,630	1,836,681	2,250,927
Men	3,642,533	2,565,267	3,143,624

Figure 23.2 Sample delimitation process.

of the labour market. While, the sub-sample of employed women increased by about 4% from 1995 to 2004 that for men decreased by 13%.

Second, analyses of empirical wage density functions for the years 1995, 1999, and 2004 were carried out by gender. Incidentally, log real gross monthly wages are used in this study. These real wage series' were obtained from deflating nominal monthly wages for the years 1995, 1999, and 2004 to the 1995 base (expressed in 2000 prices) using the South African Reserve Bank's Consumer Price Index (CPI) series (KBP7031J). The density functions were approximated using an Epanechnikov kernel estimator (see Johnston and DiNardo 1997: 370–5; StataCorp 2003). Figure 23.3 shows the resulting density plots.

The three panels in Figure 23.3 indicate that male and female wage distributions are clearly distinct. The female wage distributions mainly lie to the left of the male wage distributions, especially at the lower percentiles of the distributions. Also, the latter are characterized by a higher density function around the mode and a relatively lower dispersion. It is also apparent that the advantage that the males enjoy over females at the lower quantiles of the distributions is significantly reduced at the upper quantiles. Thus, if one considers only the raw wage distributions, it appears that there is a "sticky floor" and no "glass ceiling" for African women.

Thereafter, a summary of both the dependent and independent variables used by year and gender is provided. The descriptive statistics are presented in Table 23.1.

Considering the dependent variable, the statistics demonstrate that men's earnings are on average higher than women's. The disadvantaged position of women is further highlighted by a 3% decline in their real wages between 1995 and 1999. In contrast, those of men increased by close to 6% in the same period. Despite these differences, both sexes experienced an increase in their incomes between 1995 and 2004. In particular, the wages for men and women concomitantly increased by 12% and 7% respectively.

Turning to the covariates, the displayed information conveys some traits of patriarchy in trade union membership. Probably this is due to the relatively high concentration of women in non-unionized sectors such as the social services (includes domestic workers). Consequently, men's relatively high wages are partly attributable to the union wage premia.

Table 23.1 Descriptive statistics for African employees by gender (1995, 1999, and 2004)

Variable	1995				1999				2004			
	Females		Males		Females		Males		Females		Males	
	Mean/prop	Std dev.	Mean/prop	Std dev.	Mean/prop	Std dev.	Mean/prop	Std dev.	Mean/prop	Std dev.	Mean/prop	Std dev.
real monthly income	1200	27.4	1487	28.39	1164	51.04	1574	50.02	1284	48.2	1667	47.9
Demographic variables												
Children <15 years	0.755	0.009	0.621	0.012	0.678	0.008	0.51	0.008	0.681	0.009	0.487	0.011
Children <6 years	0.452	0.01	0.385	0.01	0.433	0.009	0.35	0.007	0.418	0.009	0.335	0.009
Married	0.453	0.01	0.595	0.007	0.392	0.01	0.54	0.009	0.32	0.009	0.45	0.011
Human capital												
Age	37.33	0.165	37.52	0.16	37.2	0.19	36.9	0.144	38.2	0.21	37.1	0.21
Age-Squared	1493	12.8	1516	10.5	1484	14.9	1461	11.2	1565	16.5	1486	17.23
Log hours	3.68	0.007	3.76	0.005	3.75	0.007	3.83	0.005	3.7	0.08	3.83	0.005
None	0.078	0.005	0.118	0.005	0.06	0.004	0.09	0.005	0.074	0.004	0.065	0.004
Elementary	0.04	0.003	0.048	0.003	0.024	0.003	0.03	0.003	0.015	0.002	0.019	0.003
Primary	0.24	0.008	0.263	0.007	0.27	0.008	0.28	0.007	0.2	0.008	0.226	0.007
Secondary	0.45	0.011	0.479	0.009	0.45	0.01	0.49	0.008	0.538	0.002	0.57	0.009
College	—	—	—	—	0.026	0.003	0.01	0.002	0.013	0.002	0.014	0.002
Diploma	0.11	0.008	0.061	0.005	0.09	0.004	0.05	0.003	0.114	0.006	0.067	0.004
Degree	0.027	0.004	0.023	0.003	0.04	0.005	0.03	0.003	0.053	0.006	0.038	0.004
Occupations												
Manager	0.006	0.001	0.019	0.002	0.009	0.002	0.03	0.003	0.016	0.002	0.032	0.004
Professional	0.026	0.003	0.018	0.002	0.040	0.005	0.33	0.002	0.039	0.005	0.026	0.003
Technician	0.16	0.009	0.066	0.004	0.124	0.008	0.07	0.003	0.12	0.006	0.063	0.004
Clerk	0.11	0.007	0.071	0.004	0.100	0.006	0.07	0.004	0.123	0.007	0.059	0.004
Skilled	0.12	0.006	0.117	0.005	0.086	0.005	0.13	0.006	0.104	0.006	0.157	0.007

Agriculturalist	0.002	0.001	0.007	0.001	0.010	0.003	0.03	0.003	0.003	0.001	0.006	0.001
Artisan	0.024	0.003	0.133	0.005	0.040	0.005	0.18	0.006	0.035	0.004	0.18	0.008
Operator	0.05	0.005	0.211	0.005	0.035	0.005	0.23	0.007	0.04	0.004	0.178	0.007
Elementary	0.52	0.011	0.361	0.01	0.550	0.008	0.22	0.007	0.513	0.011	0.26	0.009
Industries												
Agriculture	0.08	0.009	0.211	0.011	0.084	0.084	0.13	0.008	0.049	0.004	0.095	0.006
Mining	0.005	0.002	0.094	0.009	0.004	0.002	0.14	0.011	0.002	0.001	0.106	0.012
Manufacturing	0.11	0.009	0.165	0.009	0.096	0.008	0.17	0.007	0.112	0.006	0.174	0.007
Electricity	0.002	0.001	0.013	0.001	0.002	0.001	0.02	0.002	0.005	0.001	0.013	0.002
Construction	0.005	0.001	0.063	0.004	0.008	0.002	0.06	0.005	0.013	0.002	0.097	0.007
Trade	0.16	0.008	0.124	0.005	0.14	0.007	0.13	0.006	0.16	0.008	0.156	0.007
Transport	0.01	0.002	0.063	0.004	0.01	0.001	0.06	0.004	0.02	0.003	0.061	0.004
Finance	0.03	0.003	0.039	0.003	0.049	0.006	0.07	0.004	0.05	0.004	0.107	0.006
Social Services	0.61	0.013	0.232	0.012	0.598	0.01	0.21	0.008	0.59	0.01	0.195	0.008
Provinces												
Western Cape	0.03	0.005	0.045	0.006	0.050	0.006	0.06	0.006	0.054	0.005	0.049	0.005
Eastern Cape	0.146	0.008	0.095	0.004	0.120	0.009	0.07	0.006	0.12	0.006	0.081	0.006
Northern Cape	0.007	0.002	0.012	0.002	0.012	0.002	0.01	0.002	0.01	0.009	0.017	0.002
Free State	0.103	0.005	0.099	0.004	0.098	0.008	0.11	0.008	0.078	0.003	0.182	0.008
Kwazulu/Natal	0.215	0.011	0.185	0.008	0.200	0.014	0.16	0.01	0.223	0.01	0.181	0.013
North West	0.091	0.008	0.111	0.006	0.095	0.007	0.12	0.008	0.085	0.005	0.098	0.008
Gauteng	0.242	0.014	0.282	0.012	0.245	0.011	0.3	0.005	0.26	0.009	0.305	0.011
Mpumalanga	0.068	0.006	0.093	0.004	0.077	0.007	0.09	0.007	0.076	0.004	0.086	0.006
Northern Province	0.098	0.007	0.077	0.004	0.096	0.007	0.08	0.005	0.097	0.001	0.095	0.009
Trade Unionism	0.26	0.011	0.38	0.012	0.32	0.009	0.48	0.01	0.28	0.01	0.382	0.012
N	6,734		9,964		4,949		6,470		5,121		5,918	

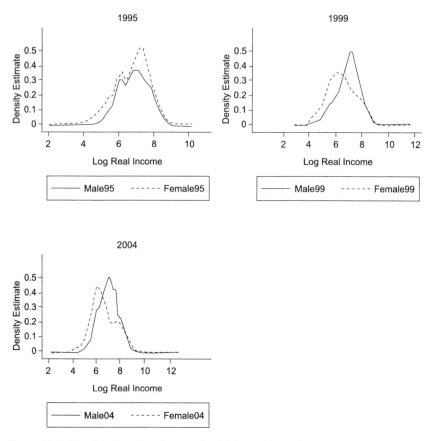

Figure 23.3 Distribution of real wages for Africans by gender.

Furthermore, the data reveals that the distribution of participants among the provinces (by gender) does not significantly differ across the data sets. Perhaps this is attributable to the similarity of the sample designs.

In the case of education, the statistics exhibit that there is a slightly higher proportion of male participants who attained primary level and below than women. Interestingly, both sexes have a higher proportion of participants who attained secondary school than the other levels. In this vein, for both sexes, the ratio of secondary school graduates increased by around 9% from 1995 to 2004. The data also shows that there are slightly more women with diplomas and degrees than males.

The statistics also portray some aspects of industrial concentration. Both genders are concentrated in social services, trade, manufacturing, and agriculture. Despite these obvious similarities there are gender disparities in the proportions of participants across these industries. For instance, there is a relatively higher percentage of women in the social services, for example; in 1995 the industry accommodated 61% of the female participants and the corresponding proportion of men was 23%. In contrast, men appear to dominate women in sectors such as agriculture, mining, and construction.

Furthermore, the figures expose that there is a higher ratio of participants in elementary and skilled occupational categories irrespective of sex. It is also evident that there is gender-based occupational concentration. As such, there are more male artisans and operators than women. Inversely, women outnumber men in occupations such as technicians and clerks.

Lastly, the information given for marriage and fertility harmonizes with the stylized facts as both variables are generally declining with time. Subsequent to this data description process, we proceed to analyse the study's estimation results.

5 Estimation results

The outcomes of the quantile regression equations reported at the 10th, 25th, 50th, 75th, and 90th percentiles of the wage distributions form the starting point for discussion in this section[8]. The results are presented in Tables 23.2a (for 1995), 23.2b (for 1999) and 23.2c (for 2004). For these regressions the omitted (base) variables correspond to an unmarried, non-unionized worker with elementary education, residing in Gauteng province, employed as an operator in the manufacturing industry. The distinct wage models are analysed together and their coefficients provide an indication of whether or not the returns to observable characteristics differ by gender and how these differences change as we move across the wage distributions.

The following findings stand out. The coefficients on age/experience for men are always significant. This means having more experience increases wages up to a certain point of the life cycle but after this peak, an additional year of experience decreases earnings. This effect slightly decreases as we move up the quantiles of the wage distributions. In contrast to the male equations, these variables do not always feature significantly in the female regressions, although most of the cases conform to the theoretical predictions. Probably, this irregularity in women's returns is due to family related career interruptions.

We also discover that earnings increase with the number of hours worked (if significant). Despite this commonality, some sex disparities in the effects of the variables are perceived. Accordingly, the discrepancies are skewed in favour of women since the coefficients are generally higher in the female regressions. Even so, the returns are higher at the bottom than at the top of the wage distributions.

Besides, being married (proxy for factors such as stability, discipline and motivation) confers some relatively higher returns for men than women. The advantages conferred to workers by this status indicate that it acts as a motivational/productivity signal to employers. Incidentally, the sizes of the 2004 coefficients increase with the percentiles of both sexes' wage distributions, whereas the pattern is not as obvious for females. Conversely, the outcomes

Table 23.2a Quantile regressions for African men and women's log real wages (1995)

Quantile	Males					Females				
	θ = 10	θ = 25	θ = 50	θ = 75	θ = 90	θ = 10	θ = 25	θ = 50	θ = 75	θ = 90
Age	0.052*	0.038*	0.034*	0.026*	0.030*	0.029**	0.016	0.019**	0.024**	0.027**
	(0.008)	(0.006)	(0.005)	(0.005)	(0.007)	(0.015)	(0.012)	(0.008)	(0.010)	(0.011)
Age-squared	−0.001*	−0.0004*	−0.0003*	−0.0003*	−0.0003*	−0.0035*	−0.0013*	−0.0002***	−0.0002**	−0.0003**
	(0.000)	(0.000)	(0.000)	(0.000)	(0.000)	(0.0002)	(0.0001)	(0.0001)	(0.0001)	(0.0001)
Log hours	0.112**	0.041	0.005	0.013	−0.003	0.202*	0.136*	0.064***	0.030	−0.044
	(0.052)	(0.033)	(0.028)	(0.029)	(0.037)	(0.047)	(0.041)	(0.034)	(0.032)	(0.037)
Married	0.212*	0.170*	0.132*	0.122*	0.151*	−0.106*	−0.114*	−0.051**	−0.054**	−0.002
	(0.029)	(0.024)	(0.018)	(0.018)	(0.025)	(0.033)	(0.028)	(0.023)	(0.022)	(0.025)
Education levels										
Primary	0.137*	0.100*	0.063*	0.072*	0.008	0.1758*	0.200*	0.109**	0.064***	0.044
	(0.036)	(0.029)	(0.021)	(0.021)	(0.032)	(0.056)	(0.043)	(0.040)	(0.038)	(0.042)
Secondary	0.358*	0.299*	0.245*	0.263*	0.207*	0.580*	0.543*	0.403*	0.310*	0.278*
	(0.043)	(0.031)	(0.024)	(0.024)	(0.038)	(0.059)	(0.047)	(0.044)	(0.037)	(0.041)
Diploma	0.669*	0.546*	0.465*	0.518*	0.498*	0.716*	0.727*	0.493*	0.437*	0.407*
	(0.088)	(0.050)	(0.050)	(0.043)	(0.055)	(0.102)	(0.085)	(0.066)	(0.070)	(0.081)
Degree	1.152*	0.999*	0.906*	0.922*	0.842*	0.900*	0.943*	0.742*	0.640*	0.644*
	(0.116)	(0.096)	(0.104)	(0.095)	(0.126)	(0.177)	(0.126)	(0.108)	(0.136)	(0.130)
Occupations										
Manager	0.375*	0.389*	0.527*	0.648*	0.844*	0.841**	0.693*	0.845*	1.007*	0.818*
	(0.118)	(0.080)	(0.079)	(0.081)	(0.131)	(0.329)	(0.137)	(0.212)	(0.182)	(0.126)
Professional	0.300*	0.306*	0.377*	0.453*	0.459*	0.827*	0.859*	0.840*	0.808*	0.584*
	(0.113)	(0.115)	(0.112)	(0.092)	(0.096)	(0.200)	(0.113)	(0.134)	(0.128)	(0.109)
Technician	0.511*	0.476*	0.527*	0.486*	0.384*	1.000*	0.968*	0.991*	0.957*	0.697*
	(0.090)	(0.054)	(0.043)	(0.039)	(0.048)	(0.145)	(0.085)	(0.098)	(0.081)	(0.084)
Clerk	0.101	0.211*	0.219*	0.265*	0.209*	0.389*	0.453*	0.471*	0.527*	0.336*
	(0.071)	(0.041)	(0.036)	(0.042)	(0.061)	(0.124)	(0.076)	(0.088)	(0.077)	(0.077)

Skilled	0.014	0.014	0.133*	0.180*	0.166*	0.027	0.131***	0.233*	0.313*	0.223**
	(0.052)	(0.038)	(0.033)	(0.031)	(0.048)	(0.130)	(0.076)	(0.099)	(0.080)	(0.090)
Agric worker	−0.403**	−0.386**	0.034	0.242**	0.153	−0.206	−0.197	−0.139	0.113	−0.314
	(0.172)	(0.164)	(0.169)	(0.095)	(0.170)	(0.231)	(0.261)	(0.337)	(0.279)	(0.277)
Artisan	−0.021	−0.008	0.047***	0.113*	0.138**	−0.234	−0.152	−0.041	−0.036	−0.020
	(0.047)	(0.037)	(0.026)	(0.027)	(0.045)	(0.208)	(0.127)	(0.067)	(0.085)	(0.122)
Elementary jobs	−0.259*	−0.274*	−0.191*	−0.205*	−0.280*	−0.292**	−0.295*	−0.234**	−0.174**	−0.296*
	(0.039)	(0.031)	(0.023)	(0.023)	(0.036)	(0.123)	(0.064)	(0.093)	(0.068)	(0.077)
Industries										
Agriculture	−0.513*	−0.586*	−0.720*	−0.716*	−0.712*	−0.326*	−0.359*	−0.430*	−0.473*	−0.345*
	(0.060)	(0.047)	(0.046)	(0.041)	(0.057)	(0.086)	(0.067)	(0.107)	(0.076)	(0.084)
Mining	−0.128***	−0.115**	−0.079***	−0.071**	−0.111**	−0.105	−0.211	−0.152	0.076	0.178
	(0.078)	(0.051)	(0.045)	(0.036)	(0.050)	(0.183)	(0.201)	(0.283)	(0.199)	(0.188)
Electricity	0.347*	0.232*	0.273*	0.169**	0.164***	0.455	0.626*	0.280	0.045	0.102
	(0.116)	(0.071)	(0.072)	(0.072)	(0.091)	(0.308)	(0.223)	(0.199)	(0.273)	(0.199)
Construction	−0.184*	−0.149*	−0.205*	−0.209*	−0.215*	0.192	0.128	0.048	0.106	0.121
	(0.064)	(0.053)	(0.044)	(0.040)	(0.060)	(0.248)	(0.278)	(0.211)	(0.170)	(0.230)
Trade	−0.163**	−0.181*	−0.227*	−0.219*	−0.204*	−0.086	−0.155**	−0.152***	−0.240*	−0.118**
	(0.066)	(0.043)	(0.039)	(0.034)	(0.044)	(0.078)	(0.061)	(0.086)	(0.064)	(0.058)
Transport	0.140**	0.099**	0.018	−0.017	0.032	−0.005	0.039	0.002	0.112	0.306***
	(0.057)	(0.047)	(0.035)	(0.036)	(0.050)	(0.162)	(0.105)	(0.140)	(0.104)	(0.160)
Finance	0.083	0.024	−0.051	−0.045	−0.076	0.101	0.130	0.043	−0.028	0.096
	(0.089)	(0.052)	(0.062)	(0.058)	(0.067)	(0.122)	(0.089)	(0.101)	(0.085)	(0.094)
Social Service	−0.089	−0.016	−0.023	−0.040	−0.038	−0.191**	−0.175**	−0.171***	−0.186*	−0.089
	(0.057)	(0.047)	(0.040)	(0.029)	(0.049)	(0.078)	(0.059)	(0.095)	(0.055)	(0.060)
Unionism	0.346*	0.298*	0.204*	0.168*	0.123*	0.366*	0.331*	0.292*	0.268*	0.206*
	(0.037)	(0.023)	(0.020)	(0.018)	(0.024)	(0.044)	(0.035)	(0.029)	(0.027)	(0.025)
Provinces										
Western Cape	−0.022	−0.035	−0.081	−0.131**	−0.055	−0.005	−0.097	−0.192*	−0.218**	−0.080
	(0.087)	(0.059)	(0.056)	(0.059)	(0.091)	(0.070)	(0.066)	(0.054)	(0.083)	(0.134)
Eastern Cape	−0.377*	−0.275*	−0.229*	−0.159*	−0.087***	−0.472*	−0.398*	−0.368*	−0.279*	−0.179*
	(0.063)	(0.050)	(0.044)	(0.036)	(0.049)	(0.076)	(0.050)	(0.041)	(0.042)	(0.042)

(*Continued overleaf*)

Table 23.2a Continued

Quantile	Males					Females				
	θ = 10	θ = 25	θ = 50	θ = 75	θ = 90	θ = 10	θ = 25	θ = 50	θ = 75	θ = 90
Northern Cape	-0.187**	-0.209**	-0.183**	-0.238**	-0.257**	-0.537*	-0.395**	-0.367*	-0.329*	-0.375*
	(0.079)	(0.076)	(0.070)	(0.065)	(0.107)	(0.137)	(0.150)	(0.110)	(0.061)	(0.088)
Free State	-0.423*	-0.381*	-0.365*	-0.372*	-0.351*	-1.124*	-0.980*	-0.848*	-0.661*	-0.488*
	(0.061)	(0.048)	(0.037)	(0.035)	(0.043)	(0.095)	(0.070)	(0.049)	(0.053)	(0.049)
Kwazulu/Natal	-0.141**	-0.093**	-0.059***	-0.027	0.023	-0.265*	-0.226*	-0.210*	-0.158*	-0.079**
	(0.055)	(0.045)	(0.032)	(0.034)	(0.052)	(0.061)	(0.044)	(0.037)	(0.038)	(0.039)
North West	-0.134**	-0.107**	-0.147*	-0.138*	-0.064	-0.584*	-0.440*	-0.362*	-0.261*	-0.153*
	(0.063)	(0.052)	(0.040)	(0.037)	(0.063)	(0.076)	(0.078)	(0.057)	(0.053)	(0.042)
Mpumalanga	-0.282*	-0.277*	-0.193*	-0.100**	0.007	-0.379*	-0.361*	-0.254*	-0.207*	-0.025
	(0.065)	(0.053)	(0.048)	(0.046)	(0.064)	(0.076)	(0.057)	(0.065)	(0.058)	(0.080)
Northern Province	-0.237*	-0.099	-0.074	0.037	0.096**	-0.232*	-0.245*	-0.107**	-0.038	-0.009
	(0.081)	(0.061)	(0.053)	(0.042)	(0.049)	(0.058)	(0.067)	(0.047)	(0.046)	(0.048)
Sample Selection Correction Terms										
Lambda1	—	—	—	—	—	1.103	2.069	3.427	5.556***	0.549
						(4.139)	(3.389)	(2.455)	(3.078)	(4.282)
Lambda2	—	—	—	—	—	-2.455	-2.851	-4.719	-7.356***	-0.637
						(5.608)	(4.685)	(3.337)	(4.169)	(5.816)
Lambda3	—	—	—	—	—	-0.004	-0.362	-0.408***	-0.666***	-0.175
						(0.368)	(0.272)	(0.215)	(0.284)	(0.372)
Lambda4	—	—	—	—	—	0.031	0.060	0.092**	0.122**	0.050
						(0.060)	(0.042)	(0.032)	(0.043)	(0.063)
Constant	4.609*	5.563*	6.174*	6.595*	6.936*	4.618*	5.092*	5.663*	5.818*	6.737*
	(0.268)	(0.187)	(0.160)	(0.143)	(0.207)	(0.484)	(0.361)	(0.320)	(0.335)	(0.449)
Observations	9,964	9,964	9,964	9,964	9,964	6,734	6,734	6,734	6,734	6,734

Note: Bootstrapped Standard errors (200, replications accounting for clustering) in parentheses* significant at 1%; ** significant at 5% *; ** *significant at 10%

Table 23.2b Quantile regressions for African men and women's log real wages (1999)

Quantile	Males					Females				
	θ = 10	θ = 25	θ = 50	θ = 75	θ = 90	θ = 10	θ = 25	θ = 50	θ = 75	θ = 90
Age	0.076*	0.050*	0.044*	0.044*	0.062*	0.059*	0.036*	0.034*	0.035*	0.043*
	(0.012)	(0.009)	(0.007)	(0.008)	(0.011)	(0.015)	(0.009)	(0.010)	(0.010)	(0.013)
Age-squared	-0.001*	-0.001*	-0.0005*	-0.0004*	-0.001*	-0.007*	-0.0004*	-0.0003*	-0.0004*	-0.0004*
	(0.0002)	(0.0001)	(0.0001)	(0.0001)	(0.0001)	(0.0001)	(0.0001)	(0.0001)	(0.0001)	(0.0001)
Log Hours	0.232*	0.103**	0.058	0.064***	0.073	0.425*	0.335*	0.286*	0.254*	0.229*
	(0.058)	(0.051)	(0.036)	(0.035)	(0.055)	(0.045)	(0.035)	(0.037)	(0.039)	(0.056)
Married	0.152*	0.144*	0.125*	0.128*	0.123*	-0.005	0.013	0.020	0.056***	0.113*
	(0.043)	(0.028)	(0.022)	(0.026)	(0.036)	(0.044)	(0.027)	(0.028)	(0.030)	(0.042)
Education Levels										
Primary	0.111***	0.020	0.068*	0.013	-0.034	0.167**	0.139*	0.095*	-0.019	0.035
	(0.057)	(0.034)	(0.026)	(0.033)	(0.042)	(0.066)	(0.042)	(0.036)	(0.042)	(0.055)
Secondary	0.291*	0.203*	0.248*	0.240*	0.247*	0.387*	0.320*	0.324*	0.229*	0.267*
	(0.058)	(0.040)	(0.030)	(0.034)	(0.050)	(0.067)	(0.042)	(0.043)	(0.049)	(0.056)
Diploma	0.820*	0.763*	0.716*	0.667*	0.770*	0.971*	0.912*	0.746*	0.589*	0.545*
	(0.091)	(0.084)	(0.071)	(0.068)	(0.110)	(0.112)	(0.083)	(0.069)	(0.071)	(0.102)
Degree	0.897*	0.808*	0.832*	0.883*	0.690*	1.061*	1.013*	0.944*	0.781*	0.818*
	(0.118)	(0.090)	(0.085)	(0.124)	(0.134)	(0.204)	(0.093)	(0.100)	(0.094)	(0.161)
Occupations										
Manager	0.445*	0.484*	0.512*	0.654*	0.857*	-0.079	0.794*	0.733*	0.648*	0.565**
	(0.141)	(0.088)	(0.104)	(0.088)	(0.186)	(0.474)	(0.235)	(0.150)	(0.159)	(0.285)
Professional	0.463*	0.349*	0.381*	0.356*	0.535*	0.613*	0.870*	1.002*	0.927*	0.789*
	(0.096)	(0.092)	(0.081)	(0.103)	(0.119)	(0.210)	(0.126)	(0.130)	(0.132)	(0.141)
Technician	0.274*	0.320*	0.377*	0.368*	0.470	0.577*	0.795*	0.958*	0.861*	0.868*
	(0.084)	(0.063)	(0.055)	(0.069)	(0.073)	(0.125)	(0.105)	(0.108)	(0.117)	(0.113)
Clerk	0.162***	0.219*	0.231*	0.187*	0.332*	0.095	0.306*	0.422*	0.495*	0.447*
	(0.087)	(0.057)	(0.043)	(0.039)	(0.078)	(0.124)	(0.096)	(0.102)	(0.116)	(0.108)

(Continued overleaf)

Table 23.2b Continued

Quantile	Males					Females				
	θ = 10	θ = 25	θ = 50	θ = 75	θ = 90	θ = 10	θ = 25	θ = 50	θ = 75	θ = 90
Skilled	0.032	0.030	0.044	0.109*	0.225*	-0.050	0.114	0.153**	0.160	0.288**
	(0.062)	(0.046)	(0.033)	(0.034)	(0.060)	(0.128)	(0.095)	(0.091)	(0.128)	(0.123)
Agric worker	-0.292*	-0.281*	-0.177**	-0.061	-0.017	-0.513**	-0.226	-0.062	-0.295	0.055
	(0.100)	(0.082)	(0.053)	(0.077)	(0.082)	(0.233)	(0.168)	(0.127)	(0.186)	(0.361)
Artisan	0.087	0.034	-0.004	0.011	0.039	-0.056	0.118	0.147	0.032	-0.004
	(0.065)	(0.037)	(0.027)	(0.032)	(0.052)	(0.144)	(0.101)	(0.091)	(0.116)	(0.115)
Elementary Jobs	-0.198*	-0.184*	-0.194*	-0.188*	-0.148*	-0.408*	-0.277*	-0.242*	-0.326*	-0.270*
	(0.054)	(0.037)	(0.028)	(0.031)	(0.047)	(0.101)	(0.088)	(0.087)	(0.109)	(0.080)
Industries										
Agriculture	-0.563*	-0.731*	-0.806*	-0.792*	-0.72*	-0.183	-0.294*	-0.327*	-0.433*	-0.460*
	(0.081)	(0.057)	(0.045)	(0.052)	(0.074)	(0.131)	(0.074)	(0.075)	(0.078)	(0.092)
Mining	0.185**	0.031	-0.070**	-0.134*	-0.133**	0.083	0.396	0.230	-0.001	0.568
	(0.080)	(0.046)	(0.036)	(0.043)	(0.069)	(0.447)	(0.241)	(0.159)	(0.135)	(0.390)
Electricity	0.171	0.278*	0.339*	0.285*	0.382**	0.723*	0.440***	0.417	0.755**	1.236**
	(0.155)	(0.092)	(0.089)	(0.111)	(0.156)	(0.247)	(0.236)	(0.315)	(0.377)	(0.549)
Construction	-0.153	-0.195*	-0.144*	-0.202*	-0.178**	0.033	0.166	0.299***	0.197	-0.092
	(0.100)	(0.056)	(0.050)	(0.057)	(0.074)	(0.655)	(0.312)	(0.161)	(0.169)	(0.348)
Trade	-0.125	-0.193*	-0.229*	-0.252*	-0.274*	-0.178	-0.141***	-0.122***	-0.276*	-0.183**
	(0.085)	(0.053)	(0.036)	(0.040)	(0.062)	(0.125)	(0.078)	(0.063)	(0.081)	(0.084)
Transport	-0.002	0.064	0.058	0.038	0.034	0.352	0.234***	0.092	-0.051	0.423**
	(0.134)	(0.061)	(0.038)	(0.050)	(0.082)	(0.355)	(0.140)	(0.150)	(0.167)	(0.169)
Finance	0.129	-0.004	-0.110**	-0.116**	-0.154**	0.339*	0.260*	0.229*	0.023	0.213
	(0.078)	(0.064)	(0.042)	(0.055)	(0.078)	(0.121)	(0.095)	(0.078)	(0.080)	(0.134)
Social Service	0.056	0.090***	0.108*	0.079***	0.040	-0.116	-0.174**	-0.179*	-0.257*	-0.179*
	(0.075)	(0.051)	(0.036)	(0.046)	(0.063)	(0.107)	(0.071)	(0.063)	(0.064)	(0.071)
Unionism	0.441*	0.348*	0.266*	0.216*	0.181*	0.525**	0.483*	0.486*	0.534*	0.536*
	(0.041)	(0.030)	(0.026)	(0.027)	(0.035)	(0.051)	(0.040)	(0.035)	(0.041)	(0.048)

Provinces										
Western Cape	0.104	0.090***	-0.017	-0.032	-0.067	0.306*	0.181*	0.090***	0.070	0.012
	(0.086)	(0.050)	(0.055)	(0.052)	(0.068)	(0.084)	(0.055)	(0.049)	(0.051)	(0.068)
Eastern Cape	-0.520*	-0.447*	-0.386*	-0.281*	-0.326*	-0.780*	-0.633*	-0.662*	-0.580*	-0.439*
	(0.081)	(0.070)	(0.048)	(0.061)	(0.070)	(0.089)	(0.058)	(0.048)	(0.055)	(0.071)
Northern Cape	-0.217	-0.117	-0.081	-0.018	0.040	-0.477*	-0.416*	-0.408*	-0.399*	-0.413*
	(0.149)	(0.115)	(0.072)	(0.084)	(0.133)	(0.138)	(0.112)	(0.083)	(0.078)	(0.076)
Free State	-0.412*	-0.357*	-0.355*	-0.361*	-0.357*	-0.888*	-0.867*	-0.687*	-0.541*	-0.394*
	(0.064)	(0.048)	(0.042)	(0.039)	(0.063)	(0.084)	(0.053)	(0.060)	(0.065)	(0.075)
Kwazulu/Natal	-0.140**	-0.130*	-0.112*	-0.103**	-0.083	-0.364*	-0.328*	-0.355*	-0.248*	-0.168**
	(0.066)	(0.046)	(0.041)	(0.047)	(0.065)	(0.078)	(0.044)	(0.048)	(0.052)	(0.069)
North West	-0.255*	-0.147*	-0.154*	-0.114*	-0.121*	-0.348*	-0.325*	-0.332*	-0.239*	-0.197*
	(0.077)	(0.049)	(0.037)	(0.039)	(0.048)	(0.079)	(0.056)	(0.050)	(0.046)	(0.057)
Mpumalanga	-0.220*	-0.141*	-0.126*	-0.123*	-0.105***	-0.379*	-0.341*	-0.350*	-0.268*	-0.197*
	(0.076)	(0.040)	(0.042)	(0.042)	(0.062)	(0.080)	(0.049)	(0.047)	(0.049)	(0.074)
Northern Province	-0.181*	-0.233*	-0.276*	-0.231*	-0.205*	-0.357*	-0.349*	-0.388*	-0.360*	-0.211*
	(0.080)	(0.047)	(0.046)	(0.059)	(0.087)	(0.076)	(0.050)	(0.042)	(0.053)	(0.077)
Sample Selection Correction Terms										
lambda1	—	—	—	—	—	-6.141	-5.225	-7.569**	-3.387	1.863
						(6.134)	(3.592)	(3.697)	(5.392)	(6.230)
lambda2	—	—	—	—	—	8.253	6.896	9.894**	4.294	-2.295
						(8.258)	(4.833)	(4.968)	(7.103)	(8.326)
lambda3	—	—	—	—	—	0.406	0.427	0.671**	0.297	-0.272
						(0.540)	(0.327)	(0.327)	(0.520)	(0.579)
lambda4	—	—	—	—	—	-0.052	-0.089	-0.153**	-0.101	0.019
						(0.097)	(0.055)	(0.061)	(0.098)	(0.106)
Constant	3.301*	4.857*	5.598*	5.930*	5.838*	3.409*	4.384*	5.217	5.542*	5.052*
	(0.314)	(0.269)	(0.195)	(0.203)	(0.303)	(0.685)	(0.417)	(0.407)	(0.559)	(0.598)
Observations	6,470	6,470	6,470	6,470	6,470	4,949	4,949	4,949	4,949	4,949

Note: Bootstrapped Standard errors (200, replications accounting for clustering) in parentheses* significant at 1%; ** significant at 5%*; ***significant at 10%

Table 23.2c Quantile regressions for African men and women's log real wages (2004)

Quantile	Males					Females				
	0 = 10	0 = 25	0 = 50	0 = 75	0 = 90	0 = 10	0 = 25	0 = 50	0 = 75	0 = 90
Age	0.047*	0.03*	0.032*	0.035*	0.036*	0.026**	0.041*	0.031	0.013	0.018***
	(0.010)	(0.006)	(0.006)	(0.006)	(0.011)	(0.012)	(0.009)	(0.008)	(0.009)	(0.011)
Age2	-0.0005*	-0.0003*	-0.0003*	-0.0003*	-0.0003**	-0.0003**	-0.0004***	-0.0003*	-0.0003*	-7E-05
	(0.000)	(0.000)	(0.000)	(0.000)	(0.000)	(0.000)	(0.000)	(0.000)	(0.000)	(0.000)
Log hours	0.362*	0.192*	0.1**	0.028	-0.054	0.432*	0.4*	0.427*	0.337*	0.287*
	(0.068)	(0.044)	(0.048)	(0.044)	(0.071)	(0.034)	(0.028)	(0.030)	(0.040)	(0.042)
Married	0.147*	0.117*	0.11*	0.126*	0.178*	0.07***	0.097*	0.094*	0.126*	0.084*
	(0.034)	(0.023)	(0.020)	(0.024)	(0.031)	(0.037)	(0.025)	(0.022)	(0.023)	(0.025)
Education levels										
Primary	-0.027	0.004	-0.039	-0.074**	-0.116**	0.247*	0.176*	0.088***	-0.003	0.001
	(0.054)	(0.030)	(0.028)	(0.031)	(0.046)	(0.072)	(0.038)	(0.041)	(0.034)	(0.035)
Secondary	0.154*	0.178*	0.177*	0.17*	0.178*	0.422*	0.422*	0.251*	0.176*	0.276*
	(0.059)	(0.032)	(0.032)	(0.030)	(0.047)	(0.065)	(0.041)	(0.043)	(0.038)	(0.036)
Diploma	0.716*	0.769*	0.734*	0.637*	0.675*	0.683*	0.861*	0.684*	0.502*	0.493*
	(0.094)	(0.062)	(0.067)	(0.056)	(0.079)	(0.100)	(0.082)	(0.069)	(0.066)	(0.063)
Degree	0.943*	1.01*	1.067*	1.122*	1.104*	0.742*	0.944*	0.611*	0.667*	0.792*
	(0.173)	(0.110)	(0.121)	(0.130)	(0.157)	(0.166)	(0.123)	(0.094)	(0.117)	(0.124)
Occupations										
Manager	0.572*	0.771*	0.754*	0.83*	0.955*	0.903*	1.053*	1.453*	1.463*	1.526*
	(0.139)	(0.141)	(0.096)	(0.082)	(0.198)	(0.239)	(0.157)	(0.146)	(0.166)	(0.159)
Professional	0.451*	0.416*	0.251**	0.259**	0.563**	0.781*	1.027*	1.239*	1.051*	0.984*
	(0.173)	(0.092)	(0.120)	(0.124)	(0.220)	(0.187)	(0.136)	(0.110)	(0.144)	(0.144)
Technician	0.341*	0.252*	0.207*	0.323*	0.504*	0.7*	0.842*	0.957*	0.963*	0.831*
	(0.077)	(0.055)	(0.068)	(0.068)	(0.067)	(0.139)	(0.086)	(0.080)	(0.102)	(0.099)
Clerk	0.15	0.176*	0.162*	0.37*	0.52*	0.256***	0.393*	0.65*	0.635*	0.602*
	(0.092)	(0.054)	(0.056)	(0.061)	(0.088)	(0.135)	(0.083)	(0.080)	(0.092)	(0.090)

	(1)	(2)	(3)	(4)	(5)	(6)	(7)	(8)	(9)	(10)
Skilled	−0.05	−0.011	−0.047	0.001	0.165*	−0.02	0.158***	0.329*	0.357*	0.353*
	(0.059)	(0.048)	(0.040)	(0.046)	(0.057)	(0.127)	(0.083)	(0.078)	(0.102)	(0.094)
Agricwkr	−0.052	−0.223*	−0.327*	−0.334*	−0.195*	0.168	0.149	0.04	−0.013	−0.438
	(0.234)	(0.074)	(0.077)	(0.132)	(0.093)	(0.549)	(0.182)	(0.137)	(0.325)	(0.361)
Artisan	−0.013	0.018	−0.029	0.043	0.093***	−0.167	0.005	0.121***	0.106	−0.045
	(0.042)	(0.034)	(0.031)	(0.032)	(0.051)	(0.147)	(0.078)	(0.067)	(0.096)	(0.104)
Elementary	−0.227*	−0.194*	−0.233*	−0.2*	−0.15*	−0.24**	−0.096	−0.095	−0.145***	−0.24*
	(0.044)	(0.027)	(0.027)	(0.027)	(0.044)	(0.105)	(0.070)	(0.065)	(0.085)	(0.085)
Industries										
Agriculture	−0.272*	−0.378*	−0.504*	−0.6*	−0.605*	0.016	−0.079	−0.191*	−0.313*	−0.328*
	(0.059)	(0.040)	(0.032)	(0.038)	(0.064)	(0.096)	(0.063)	(0.048)	(0.070)	(0.069)
Mining	0.281*	0.248*	0.201*	0.113**	0.144***	−0.117	0.066	0.044	0.133	1.006*
	(0.060)	(0.040)	(0.040)	(0.052)	(0.074)	(0.358)	(0.288)	(0.245)	(0.350)	(0.288)
Electricity	0.202	0.028	0.158**	−0.039	−0.099	0.632*	0.683*	0.65*	0.386*	0.452*
	(0.147)	(0.087)	(0.061)	(0.066)	(0.177)	(0.250)	(0.208)	(0.162)	(0.164)	(0.160)
Construction	−0.12	−0.143*	−0.146*	−0.188*	−0.189*	0.015	0.051	−0.003	0.246	0.278
	(0.075)	(0.053)	(0.041)	(0.043)	(0.074)	(0.131)	(0.110)	(0.083)	(0.158)	(0.175)
Trade	−0.255*	−0.263*	−0.209*	−0.198*	−0.22*	−0.089	−0.179*	−0.268*	−0.269*	−0.213*
	(0.056)	(0.041)	(0.037)	(0.040)	(0.070)	(0.107)	(0.068)	(0.058)	(0.073)	(0.072)
Transport	−0.008	0.049	0.104***	0.11**	0.126***	0.332*	0.252*	0.258*	0.414*	0.649*
	(0.091)	(0.057)	(0.053)	(0.053)	(0.073)	(0.127)	(0.103)	(0.117)	(0.127)	(0.113)
Finance	−0.055	−0.065	−0.114**	−0.083	−0.133***	0.251***	0.137***	0.051	0.092	0.073
	(0.079)	(0.056)	(0.048)	(0.057)	(0.069)	(0.131)	(0.076)	(0.063)	(0.077)	(0.078)
Social services	−0.075	0.027	0.111**	0.108**	0.087	−0.057	−0.146*	−0.162*	−0.193*	−0.118***
	(0.072)	(0.049)	(0.041)	(0.039)	(0.062)	(0.092)	(0.059)	(0.044)	(0.069)	(0.067)
Unionism	0.513*	0.483*	0.385*	0.344*	0.253*	0.71*	0.654*	0.606*	0.584*	0.603*
	(0.035)	(0.027)	(0.026)	(0.026)	(0.034)	(0.053)	(0.038)	(0.036)	(0.038)	(0.037)
Provinces										
Western Cape	−0.109***	−0.085	−0.131*	−0.115*	−0.213*	0.164	0.016	−0.034	0.01	0.01
	(0.062)	(0.061)	(0.037)	(0.042)	(0.055)	(0.115)	(0.049)	(0.043)	(0.051)	(0.051)
Eastern Cape	−0.354*	−0.293*	−0.213*	−0.129*	−0.152*	−0.615*	−0.57*	−0.507*	−0.352*	−0.4*
	(0.073)	(0.052)	(0.044)	(0.043)	(0.057)	(0.065)	(0.046)	(0.042)	(0.048)	(0.042)

(Continued overleaf)

Table 23.2c Continued

Quantile	Males					Females				
	θ = 10	θ = 25	θ = 50	θ = 75	θ = 90	θ = 10	θ = 25	θ = 50	θ = 75	θ = 90
Northern Cape	-0.438*	-0.289*	-0.201*	-0.049	0.019	-0.253	-0.281*	-0.21*	-0.191*	-0.262*
	(0.097)	(0.050)	(0.052)	(0.071)	(0.104)	(0.178)	(0.071)	(0.060)	(0.069)	(0.076)
Free State	-0.427*	-0.356*	-0.351*	-0.328*	-0.334*	-0.669*	-0.583*	-0.509*	-0.458*	-0.514*
	(0.061)	(0.040)	(0.034)	(0.046)	(0.055)	(0.072)	(0.058)	(0.038)	(0.046)	(0.042)
KwaZulu/Natal	-0.171*	-0.114*	-0.055	0.038	0.005	-0.333*	-0.3*	-0.277*	-0.266*	-0.3*
	(0.048)	(0.034)	(0.034)	(0.034)	(0.045)	(0.055)	(0.040)	(0.034)	(0.037)	(0.033)
North West	-0.193*	-0.206*	-0.207*	-0.183*	-0.205*	-0.333*	-0.323*	-0.28*	-0.244*	-0.287*
	(0.059)	(0.038)	(0.040)	(0.040)	(0.060)	(0.072)	(0.050)	(0.046)	(0.042)	(0.040)
Mpumalanga	-0.309*	-0.254*	-0.259*	-0.167*	-0.051	-0.532*	-0.433*	-0.404*	-0.339*	-0.296*
	(0.063)	(0.042)	(0.037)	(0.051)	(0.080)	(0.084)	(0.057)	(0.043)	(0.045)	(0.047)
Northern Province	-0.315*	-0.226*	-0.216*	-0.149*	-0.185*	-0.517*	-0.545*	-0.435*	-0.337*	-0.311
	(0.080)	(0.042)	(0.044)	(0.050)	(0.056)	(0.070)	(0.051)	(0.040)	(0.047)	(0.043)
Sample Selection Correction Terms										
lambda1	—	—	—	—	—	-3.029	-8.249**	1.175	3.254	0.977
						(3.305)	(3.021)	(2.125)	(2.836)	(2.734)
lambda2	—	—	—	—	—	3.897	11.25**	-1.349	-4.657	-1.632
						(4.460)	(4.047)	(2.903)	(3.803)	(3.676)
lambda3	—	—	—	—	—	0.248	0.73**	-0.215	-0.248	0.028
						(0.303)	(0.278)	(0.186)	(0.262)	(0.254)
lambda4	—	—	—	—	—	0.044	-0.077***	0.042	0.033	-0.001
						(0.046)	(0.047)	(0.028)	(0.043)	(0.041)
Constant	3.755*	4.997*	5.733*	6.188*	6.739*	3.756*	4.029*	3.811*	4.863*	5.405*
	(0.333)	(0.225)	(0.210)	(0.222)	(0.379)	(0.436)	(0.340)	(0.283)	(0.335)	(0.341)
Observations	5918	5918	5918	5918	5918	5121	5121	5121	5121	5121

Note: Bootstrapped Standard errors (200, replications accounting for clustering) in parentheses* significant at 1%; ** significant at 5%*; ***significant at 10%

for 1999 and 2004 portray returns that are lower at the upper tails of the male wage distribution, while they are mostly insignificant in the case of females. Interestingly, the findings for 1995 diverge from the above as marriage lowers women's returns. Most likely, the relatively higher fertility rates observed in 1995 made marriage serve as a signal of potential career interruptions to the employers who may have discriminated against married women.

The study also establishes that educational attainment yields higher returns as compared to the base level. The returns tend to increase with the education levels. This upshot contradicts the law of diminishing returns to the formation of human capital (Mwabu and Schultz 1998). Another observation is that there are gender gaps in these returns. Accordingly, the period from 1995 to 2004 is distinguished by women who enjoy higher returns at the secondary school echelon and below than men. The gender gap in returns to secondary education declines as we approach the top end of the wage distributions. Also, in contrast to the case for secondary school, men have higher coefficients for degrees than women, except in 1999. Nevertheless, the gender gap in returns to a degree fluctuates along the wage distributions.

In likeness with inter alia Butcher and Rouse (2001) and Mwabu and Schultz (1998) union members are found to earn significantly more than non-union members. This outcome highlights the strong bargaining power of South African unions. The union wage premia are higher at the bottom of both male and female wage distributions, except for women in 1999 where the picture is not clear. The lower returns in the upper quantiles are explainable by the consideration that most wages in the upper market are set by direct contracts as compared to collective bargaining (Bhorat, Lundall, and Rospabe 2002). Apparently, some gender disparities in favour of women are evident in the premia. At most the gender gaps tend to increase with the quantiles of the wage distributions.

Furthermore, the outcomes for the industrial sectors showcase that few industries significantly offer higher wages than the manufacturing sector. Overall, this is exemplified by the transport and electricity sectors. Alternatively, industries such as agriculture and trade pay less than manufacturing. Nonetheless, the progression of the returns along the wage distributions differs by sector and time period. For example, in 2004 there is a decline in men's mining coefficients as we approach the upper tails of the wage distributions, while the opposite applies to transport. All the same, gender gaps in industrial returns are difficult to analyse due to perceived inconsistencies in the significance of the variables.

Additionally, the outcomes for the occupational dummies display a wage hierarchy relative to the base category (operator). Accordingly, managers, professionals, technicians, and clerks earn significantly more than operators, whereas the opposite applies to employees of the agriculture sector and those in elementary occupations. It is also highlighted that women in higher paying jobs (relative to operators) get larger rewards than men. In most cases, the gender differential in returns to the variable of interest increase with the percentiles of the wage distribution.

Lastly, the female selection bias correction terms featured to be insignificant in most cases. Nevertheless, this finding is not unique as it tallies with that of Winter (1999). Probably, it indicates that selection bias does not generally bind in the formal sector which is the domain of both studies.

In sum, the evidence presented so far points out that returns to observable characteristics differ by gender and that these differences change as we move throughout the distribution. Therefore, the next step is to investigate the sources of the gender gap.

Table 23.3 presents the raw/observed and the counterfactual gender wage gaps for 1995, 1999, and 2004. The raw wage gaps are defined as the difference between male and female unconditional log wages at the different quantiles of the wage distributions (Albrecht, Vureen, and Vroman 2004). The counterfactual gap shows the disparities between the quantiles of women's log wage distributions and the corresponding quantiles of a counterfactual distribution that arises if women maintained their characteristics but were paid like men.[9]

First, we explore the raw gender wage gaps. Table 23.3 exhibits a monotonically declining gap as we move towards the upper quantiles of the 1995 wage distribution. However, this pattern is not robust across the time periods. For instance, the 1999 gap increases dramatically from the 10th to the 25th percentile and declines thereafter. The evolution of the 1999 gap identifies females whose wages lie in the 25th percentile as the most disadvantaged.[10] Besides, Table 23.3 displays a gender gap that is generally decreasing as we approach the upper tails of the 2004 wage distribution although the evolution of the gap from the 10th to the 50th percentiles is relatively flat. This tendency for a deceleration of the gap as we move up the quantiles of the wage distributions possibly indicates a "sticky floor." Hence, by focusing only on

Table 23.3 Gender gaps (observed and counterfactual) 1995, 1999, and 2004

		$\theta = 10$	$\theta = 25$	$\theta = 50$	$\theta = 75$	$\theta = 90$
1995	Observed	0.56	0.41	0.36	0.16	0.11
	Counterfactual	0.60	0.46	0.29	0.14	0.17
	% of observed gap due to different returns	107	112	81	88	154
1999	Observed	0.56	0.76	0.55	0.11	0.13
	Counterfactual	0.59	0.69	0.51	0.18	0.15
	% of observed gap due to different returns	105	91	93	164	115
2004	Observed	0.66	0.61	0.60	0.15	0.05
	Counterfactual	0.52	0.44	0.44	0.15	0.13
	% of observed gap due to different returns	79	72	73	100	260

the mean raw gender wage gap, substantial variations of the gap will be hidden.

Second, we investigate the counterfactual wage gaps. A striking feature of these gaps is that they are positive across the data sets. This positive gap implies that men's returns are greater than women's. Thus, even if women had the same distribution of characteristics as men, they would still receive lower pay across the wage distribution. The percentage contribution of the counterfactual wage gaps to the raw wage gaps are also presented in Table 23.3. A percentage value greater than 100 potentially means that women have characteristics that compensate them for any unobservables which may include "discrimination." In other words, it implies that women have better characteristics than men. However, the very large percentage values found for instance, in the upper quantiles of the 2004 wage distribution merit comment. Possibly, they emerged because the raw wage gap is relatively small.

More importantly, Table 23.3 shows that the counterfactual wage gap for 1995 decreases from the bottom to the upper tails of the conditional wage distributions. In addition, it exhibits that the 1999 gap strictly declines monotonically from the 25th percentile towards the upper quantiles of the wage distribution. Lastly, Table 23.3 reveals that the 2004 gap is somewhat flat from the bottom to the middle of the distribution and declines thereafter. In sum, the evidence presented so far unequivocally supports the existence of a "sticky floor" in the "formal" sector of the South African labour market. Thus, low income females are more likely to be disadvantaged, although it is not clear whether the disadvantage is mainly due to "discrimination" or to other unobserved heterogeneity that the model does not control for.

Finally, we probe into the issue of whether the component of the raw gender wage gap attributable to different returns has been increasing or decreasing along the wage distribution over the period 1995–2004. In this case, it is perceptible that the portion of the wage distribution that ranges from the 10th to the 25th percentiles experienced a decline in the returns component of the gap over the period in question (although the case for 1999 merits comment). The decline observed at the bottom tails of the wage distributions could be due to the strengthening of minimum wage policies with time. All the same, the effect of different pay structures on gender wage differentials is still substantial despite the observed decline. On the other hand, the 50th and 75th percentiles saw an increase in the component from 1995 to 2004; so, we conclude that highly paid women are facing more and more gender based wage inequalities with time.

6 Conclusion and policy recommendations

This paper explored gender wage gaps throughout the wage distribution for African "formal" sector employees in South Africa over the period 1995–2004. The analyses utilized individual data from the 1995 and 1999 October Household Surveys and the 2004 September Labour Force Survey.

Quantile regression techniques were used to control for various character-istics at different points of the wage distributions. In addition, the Machado Mata (2005) decomposition method was utilized to estimate the component of the wage gaps not explained by different characteristics (counterfactual gap).

Based on this methodology, our findings on unconditional wage gaps indi-cate that the mean gender wage gap conceals some variations in the gap across the wage distribution. In fact, the magnitudes of these gaps slide as we approach the upper tails of the wage distributions. Analogously, the absolute sizes of the counterfactual wage gaps generally decline as we proceed from the bottom to the upper tails of the wage distributions. As it is, both the raw and counterfactual gaps align us towards an existence of a "sticky floor" in the South African labour market.

Additionally, the study revealed that the counterfactual wage gaps did not generally show a declining tendency along the whole wage distribution between 1995 and 2004. Instead, a slight decline was evident only in the 10th, 25th, and 90th percentiles of the wage distribution. If discrimination is the main factor that drove these pay gaps, then female workers in the upper quantiles became more disadvantaged with time, even under the existence of equal opportunity legislation.

On the basis of our findings, it is suggested that if the labour market outcomes for African men and women are to be leveled, considerable efforts should be invested in strengthening the implementation of countervailing clauses on the violation of the gender neutral labour market institutions embedded in new the labour legislation. Quite significantly, it is recom-mended that mitigatory measures should focus more on women at the bottom end of the wage distribution because they are the most likely to be "dis-criminated" against. Also, the policy makers should design strategies to curb the widening of the wage gaps in top paying jobs. Furthermore, because discrimination and the subordinate role of women seem to be entrenched at various stages it is essential to reach an understanding of the barriers that exist in the labour market and also in the greater society and how they affect African women.

Notes

* I am greatly indebted to Martin Wittenberg and the IZA Research Associates and visitors, for helpful comments on earlier drafts of this paper. I also thank the Data First Resource Unit, the AERC, and the Mellon Foundation for providing the data and the funding utilized for the study. The usual disclaimer applies.
1 Sex wage discrimination is as a situation whereby persons who are equally pro-ductive in a physical or material sense, receive different wages solely because of their gender (Altonji and Blank 1999: 3168). Discrimination here is in quotes because it is difficult to get its exact measure.
2 A glass ceiling is a situation where the gender gaps are wider at the top than at the bottom of the wage distribution. The opposite case is called a sticky floor.
3 The method entails estimating a labour force participation model and obtaining an index of labour force participation, which is transformed into several power

series expansions. The power series expansions are then included in the wage equation as controls for selection bias. This formulation is adopted since the form of selection bias over the different percentiles of the wage distribution is unknown.

4 MM's bootstrap procedure entails constructing a counterfactual male distribution, namely what women would have been paid if they were paid like men given their characteristics. The generated wage distribution will be used together with the actual female wage distribution, to construct the counterfactual wage gap which yields part of the raw wage gap explained by different rewards.

5 While we are aware of the possible endogeneity of some of the covariates, data limitations limit us in controlling for the problems; hence the reader should be aware of this.

6 With 200 replications and accounting for clustering.

7 Includes people who although not actively looking for a job would nevertheless like to work.

8 Despite being necessary, the discussion of participation and employment models has been omitted in this paper. However, the outcomes are available on request.

9 We are unable to compute standard errors for the decomposition due to low computational power as we are using a large sample size.

10 Probably, the sharp increase from the 10th to the 25th percentiles of the 1999 wage distribution is due to a selection effect as the 1999 sample suggested a wholesale collapse of employment, which is clearly not the case when the overall sample of workers is considered.

References

Ajwad, M. I and Kurukulasuriya (2002) "Ethnic and Gender Wage Disparities in Sri lanka." World Bank Research working paper 2859.

Albrecht, J., A. Bjorkland, and S. Vroman (2003) "Is there a Glass Ceiling in Sweden?" *Journal of Labour Economics* 21(1): 145–77.

——, A. Vureen, and S. Vroman (2004) "Decomposing the Gender Wage Gap in the Netherlands with Sample Selection Adjustments." IZA discussion paper 1400.

Altonji, J. G and R. M. Blank (1999) *Race and Gender in the Labour Market.* In *Handbook of Labour Economics*, edited by O. Ashenfelter and D. Card. Amsterdam: North Holland, Vol. 3, ch. 48, pp. 3143–259.

Bhorat, H. and M. Leibbrandt (2001) *Modelling Vulnerability and Low Earnings in the South African Labour Market.* In *Fighting poverty: Labour Markets and Inequality in South Africa*, edited by H Bhorat, M. Leibbrandt, M. Maziya, S. van der Berg, and I. Woolard. Lansdowne: UCT Press, ch. 3, pp. 107–29.

——, P. Lundall, and S. Rospabe (2002) "The South African Labour Market in a Globalising World: Economic and legislative considerations." ILO Publication: Employment Paper: 2002/32.

Blinder, S. (1973) "Wage Discrimination; Reduced Form and Structural Estimate." *Journal of Human Resources* 8(4): 436–55.

Buchinsky, M. (1994) "Changes in the US Wage Structure 1963–1987: An application of quantile regression." *Econometrica* 62: 405–58.

——. (1995) "Quantile regression Box Cox Transformation Model and Changes in the Returns to Schooling and Experience." *Journal of Econometrics* 65: 109–54.

——. (1998) "The Dynamics of Changes in the Female Wage Distribution in the USA: A quantile regression approach." *Journal of Applied Econometrics* 13: 1–30.

Butcher, K-F and C. E. Rouse (2001) "Wage Effects of Unions and Industrial Councils." In South Africa World Bank Policy Research working paper 2520.

Cahuc, P. and A. Zylberberg (2004) *Labour Economics*. Cambridge, MA; London: Massachusetts Institute of technology Press.

Casale, D. (1998) "Gender Discrimination and the Determination of Wages in the South African Labour Market." Honours thesis. Durban: University of Natal.

Chamberlain, D. and van der Berg (2002) "Earning Functions Labour Market Discrimination and Quality of Education in South Africa." Stellen Bosch University Economic working papers 2/2002.

Deaton, A. (1997) *The Analysis of Household Surveys: A Micro econometric approach to development policy*. Baltimore; London: Johns Hopkins Press.

de la Rica, S., J. J. Dolado, and V. Llorens (2005) *Ceilings and Floors, Gender Wage Gaps by Education in Spain*. IZA discussion paper 1483.

Efron, B. (1979) "Bootstrap Methods: Another look at the jacknife." *The Annals of Statistics* 7: 1–26.

Gruen, C. (2004) "Direct and Indirect Gender Wage Discrimination in the South Africa Labour Market." *International Journal of Manpower* 25(3–4): 321–42.

Gunawardena, D. (2006) "Exploring Gender Wage Gaps in Sri Lanka: A quantile regression approach." Paper presented during the 5th PEP Research Network General Meeting, June 18–22, Addis Ababa, Ethiopia.

Hinks, T. (2002) "Gender, Wage Differentials and Discrimination in the New South Africa." *Applied Economics* 34(16): 2043–205.

Hyder, A. and B. Reilly (2005) *The Public Sector Pay Gap in Pakistan; A quantile Regression Analysis*. PRUS working paper: 33.

Isemonger, A. G and N. J. Roberts (1999) "Post Entry Gender Discrimination in the South African Labor Market." *Journal of Studies in Economics and Econometrics* 23 (2).

Johnston, J. and J. Dinardo (1997) *Econometric Methods*, fourth edition. Singapore: McGraw Hill.

Kee, H. J. (2005) "Glass Ceiling or Sticky Floor? Exploring the Australian gender pay gap using quantile regression and counterfactual decomposition methods." The Australian National University Discussion Paper 487.

Kingdon, G. and J. Knight (2000) "Are Searching and Non Searching Unemployment Distinct States when Unemployment is high? The Case of South Africa." Working paper. University of Oxford: Centre for the Study of African Economies.

Koenker, R. and G. Basset (1978) "Regression Quantiles." *Econometrica* 46: 33–50.

Machado, J. A. F. and J. Mata (2001) "Earning Functions in Portugal 1982–1994: Evidence from quantile regressions." *Empirical Economics* 26: 115–34.

—— and —— . (2005) "Counterfactual Decomposition of Changes in Wage Distributions using Quantile Regression." *Journal of Applied Econometrics* (20): 445–65.

Maziya, M. (2001) "Contemporary Labour Market Policy and Poverty in South Africa." Chapter 8 In H. Bhorat, M. Leibbrandt, M. Maziya, S. Van Der Berg, and I. Woolard, *Fighting Poverty: Labour Markets and Inequality in South Africa*. Cape Town: UCT Press.

Mincer, J. (1974) "*Schooling Experience and Earnings*." New York: Colombia University Press for the National Bureau of Economic Research.

Mwabu, G. and P. Schultz (1998) "Labour Unions and the Distribution of Wages and Employment in South Africa." *Industrial Labour Relation Review* 51(4): 680–703.

Nielsen, H. S and M. Rosholm (2001) "The Public–Private Wage Gap in Zambia in the 1990s, A quantile regression approach." *Empirical Economics* 26(1): 169–82.

Oaxaca, R. L (1973) "Male Female Wage Differentials in Urban Labour Markets." *International Economic Review*, Philadelphia, 14(3): 693–709.

Rospabe, S. (2001) "An Empirical Evaluation of Gender Discrimination in Employment Occupation and Wage in South Africa in the late 1990s." Mimeo. University of Cape Town.

StataCorp (2003) Stata Statistical Software: Release 8.0. College Station, TX: Stata Corporation.

Winter, C. (1999) "Women Workers in South Africa: Participation, pay and prejudice in the formal labour market." World Bank Informal Discussion Paper series.

24 The determinants of female labor supply in Belarus

*Francesco Pastore and Alina Verashchagina**

Introduction

In their study of female labor market participation during transition, Paci and Reilly (2004: 130) notice that much attention has been lent in the literature to women' wages and the gender wage gap (GWG since now), whereas little systematic work has been undertaken on the determinants of female labor supply. However, as well known, these two issues are closely related to each other and should therefore be treated jointly.

Although with some exceptions,[1] a general finding of the literature on the gender pay gap during transition is that it is stable or slightly declining as compared to the pre-transition period. In principle, labor supply considerations would suggest that lower gender pay gap be accompanied by increasing female as compared to male labor market participation. However, this was not the case and, in fact, the former has been declining for a long time all over Central and Eastern European Countries (CEECs) as well as in the Commonwealth of Independent States (CIS), although from a high of over 80%, which has rarely been reached in market economies. As, among others, Hunt (2002) argues, a general cause of declining gender pay gap in East Germany was indeed the reduction in female participation rates, through sample selection mechanisms. In other words, the causality chain would run in the opposite direction of that commonly hypothesized. It was not the reduced gender pay gap that caused reduced female participation, but rather reduced female participation to yield an *apparent* reduction in the gender pay gap.

Privatization of state-owned enterprises (Paci and Reilly 2004) or also the simple process of liberalization of wage-setting mechanisms and a general weakening of employment protection legislation (Munich, Svejnar, and Terrell 2005) would be the *causa causarum*. They would have caused increasingly hard budget constraints for firms (and consequently for households), forcing the least motivated and skilled women from low-wage employment into inactivity (or informal economic activities). This would give the false impression of an increase in female wages and a reduction in the unexplained gender wage gap: in fact, women's average wages were declining when taking into account those who had become unemployed or inactive. The ensuing literature has confirmed this finding in the case of several transition countries using different methods to control for sample selection (Orazem and Vodopivec 1997, for Slovenia; Oglobin 1999, for Russia; Paci and Reilly 2004, for Albania, Bosnia-Herzegovina, Bulgaria, Poland, Serbia, Tajikistan, Uzbekistan).

This paper aims to investigate the issue now outlined in more depth for the specific case of Belarus, where female labor force participation has been remarkably high at over 80% and quite stable during transition. The obvious question is, why did participation not decline in Belarus? Is this an achievement or a sign of increasing hardship for households? What types of difficulty do women experience? Are such difficulties evenly distributed or do they concentrate in particular categories of women? In the latter case, which are the weakest segments?

The high participation rate of women in Belarus mirrors the permanence of the two-bread-winner family scheme, which prevailed in all socialist countries. During the course of reform, household income experienced increasingly hard budget constraints due to the contraction, especially at the eve of transition, of real wages, public and firms' expenditure in the care of children and elderly people. Such economic tensions are expected to change the way women reconcile working and reproductive activities. Having children meant for many women to segregate themselves in occupations with a low level of commitment in terms of working time, but often with low pay and low career perspectives. This happened also through the typical pre-market mechanisms of gender differentiation, such as the tendency to choose educational types, which can be used in low-wage sectors only. Here we mention only few of the mechanisms that form the working profiles of women. In what follows we investigate the issue in more detail, aiming to understand which are the determinants of female labor supply in Belarus.

The paper is structured as follows. Section 1 intends to reinforce the motivation. Section 2 illustrates the methodology and the data used. Section 3 discusses the results. The final section concludes on the main findings of the paper.

1 Motivation and aims of the research

Gender analysis is given little importance in the current policy agenda in Belarus, mainly due to the high degree of protection of female employment inherited from the past. However, as Pastore and Verashchagina (2007) note, the gender pay gap has doubled during the last decade. Neglecting the underlying changes in the role that women play both at the labor market and within households can be detrimental for revitalizing the economy, while more careful investigation of gender-related issues can provide additional tools to combat poverty and can contribute to forming a stable and socially acceptable long-term growth path.

The case of Belarus, a country known as a gradual reformer, is somehow different from that of its neighbours such as Poland. The latter experienced high, sometimes double-digit unemployment rates, accompanied by drastic reduction of female participation since the beginning of transition. Conversely, the unemployment rate in Belarus has been quite stable over the last decade at about 2–4%[2]. Also, the participation rate of women remains high, in the range of 80%, and women represent about 53% of total employment. In addition, as documented in Pastore and Verashchagina (2007), until the mid-1990s, employment shares by gender were even across sectors. In later years, however, there has been a sudden reallocation of women towards such sectors as food, textile and clothing industries, trade and catering, public health, social services, education, and culture. The feminization of low productivity sectors caused an increase in the GWG.[3]

Furthermore, the labor market position of women in Belarus might worsen in the future for several reasons. Above all, with time passing, the inherited system of labor market regulation might become unable to continue to grant women the same rights as men. One of the reasons for that is the emergence of a small, but buoyant private sector. The existing benefits that the current labor legislation recognizes make female labor more expensive, therefore discouraging firms from employing women. When losing jobs, less motivated women tend to be relegated to their home duties or to be segregated in low-pay sectors.

All this is slowly changing gender roles within the household and, in general, in society. Figure 24.1 documents how differently Belarusian people look at the role of men and women in the society as compared to other neighbouring countries (see also Kungurova 2004). The prevailing idea that women should dedicate their life to the household does not fit nowadays with the very high female labor force participation in Belarus.

A possible acceleration of unemployment and inactivity rates might challenge the traditional two-bread-winner household model. It can be the result of the rational choice made by households to switch to a one-bread-winner model if the state will not be able in future to provide good quality and affordable kindergartens and schools, encourage part-time or temporary employment, and sustain a well-functioning pension system able to support the shift of generations of workers.

This paper aims to address these issues by studying the determinants of female labor supply. In particular, we aim to provide an in-depth investigation of the impact of several demand and supply side factors of female participation, which should warrant important information to design a long-sighted policy response.

2 Methodology and data

In the transition literature, the determinants of female labor supply have been typically studied following two main approaches. The first approach consists of estimating the reduced form selection equation and the selectivity

Men should do a living and women should take care of the household*

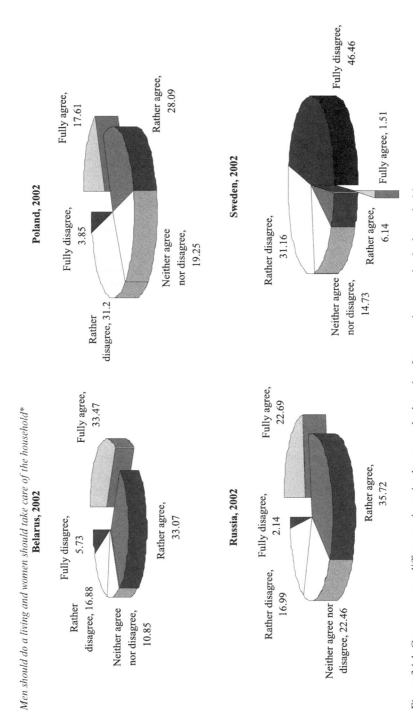

Figure 24.1 Cross-country differences in attitudes towards the role of men and women in the household.

Source: Own elaboration on the basis of ISSP data* (http://www.issp.org/).

corrected wage equation. As observed in the Introduction, this is the typical exercise that previous studies have carried out mainly to assess the impact of reduced female participation on wages during the process of economic transition.

The second approach consists of using the expected wage that women can obtain, as estimated based on their characteristics, as a proxy for their reservation wage at the second stage of the analysis. The structural female labor force participation equation is used to test for the impact of the reservation wage on female participation. It is estimated by probit and includes as independent variable the reservation wage as computed, based on the selectivity corrected wage equation. The use of a sample selection procedure in the first stage allows us to compute the expected wage also for non-employed women. Only a few previous studies in the transition literature have adopted this approach; namely Saget (1999) for Hungary and Paci and Reilly (2004) for a group of transition countries.[4]

The analysis begins with the Heckman procedure (Heckman 1979). It is used, first, to verify whether there is sample selection bias in wage equation estimates in the case of Belarus, and, second, to predict the wage offer for each individual, controlling for sample selection into employment. Together with a set of other variables, the reservation wage attained using the Heckman procedure is used then to estimate the probability of female participation in the labor market. The structural participation equation is as follows:

$$\text{Prob } [p_i] = f(Z_i, w_i), \qquad I = 1, \ldots, N$$

where $p_i = 1$ if the woman participates into the labor market; Z_i is a vector of characteristics that are assumed to affect female participation; w_i is predicted wages.

Although used more frequently, the correct specification of the Heckman model is subject to several contrasting interpretations. According to Wooldridge (2001), for instance, as a rule, all of, and only, the variables included in the main equation should also be included in the selection equation to identify the model. This rule has, however, been interpreted in different ways. Similar to Paci and Reilly (2004, § 5.17, 124), this study excludes from the selection equation such variables as sectors and branches of industry that are not defined for unemployed or inactive women.

The econometric analysis is based on the Belarusian Household Survey of Incomes and Expenditures (BHSIE), elicited quarterly by the Ministry of Statistics and Analysis. Table 24.A1 of the Appendix provides the definition of all the variables used in the econometric analysis, while Table 24.A2 gives descriptive statistics for the dependent and independent variables.

Additional regressors have been introduced as compared to Pastore and Verashchagina (2005). Also, the dependent variable is defined in a different way. Two types of information on wages are available. The first is the wage declared by respondents at the fourth quarter interview. The second is the average wage computed by the National Statistical Office, considering answers to the four quarters of the survey. Due to the lack of information on the way this average value is computed, we opted for using the respondent's answer at the end of the year.

The log of hourly wages,[5] obtained as usual by dividing the net monthly wage by the declared weekly hours times 4.3, is used as the dependent variable, despite the fact that hourly wage rates are not widely used in Belarus. The alternative way to account for differences in hours worked between men and women is by incorporating working hours as an explanatory variable. In fact, the hours of work cannot be used as a regressor in sample selection procedures, because it is in contrast with Wooldridge's rule.

Taking into account this last, overall, three types of determinant of female participation are considered; first, the individual characteristics, such as the level and type of educational qualification attained, age, marital status and, finally, regional dummies. Apart from using age and age groups, we try different definitions of work experience, starting with values declared by the respondents (actual work experience). However, this last measure has several drawbacks: (i) only employed women declare it; (ii) many observations are missing. Therefore, we prefer potential work experience (PWE), computed in the usual way: age minus years of education minus six, which is the age, when schooling starts in Belarus. In addition, we correct PWE using a non-traditional definition of work experience. Following Munich, Svejnar, and Terrell (2005), this is obtained by subtracting the number of children multiplied by three from PWE. This definition aims to account for the child leave as defined in the Labour Code of the Republic of Belarus, which is provided until the child is 3 years old.[6] Note also that sometimes age groups substitute PWE in the selection equation.

In order to correctly perform the sample selection procedure one needs to find proper instruments for the participation equation. As is well known, given the interrelation between wages and participation, it is difficult to find variables that affect participation without affecting wages.[7] Data limitations are often impossible to overcome. Also the data set available for this study is unfortunately limited. The focus has been placed, therefore, on two groups of factors, household and region-specific, that should affect the opportunity cost of working.

The former are drawn from the BHSIE itself and have been obtained merging the data relative to individuals and those relative to households. They include "*age when the first child was born,*" which presumably affects the early stages of a woman's career. In almost all transition countries, the age of the first marriage, and child, is dramatically increasing, a sign of the increasing importance of maternity as a factor able to affect women participation to the labor market. In Belarus, age at first birth is increasing very slowly, from 22.9 in 1990 to 23.3 in 2000.[8] One problem with this variable is that it affects wages too: having children early in a woman's life means putting less effort in the development of her human capital and therefore having lower productivity. In addition, the age at first child is itself affected by numerous economic and cultural factors, specific for the period of reforms. Nonetheless, our reasoning is that deciding to have children represents a sufficiently independent factor in a country where the fertility rate remains stable over the recent decade,[9] suggesting that social norms play an important role in fertility decisions. Furthermore, we distinguish between those who are under 30 from the rest of the sample, since the effect of birth of the first child may reduce with age.

Second, we test also whether *the number of children* and specifically *the number of dependent children (under the age of 5)* in the family reduces the probability for a woman to be employed, unless there is help provided at the household level. This is a sensitive issue considering its possible impact on fertility.

A third factor, which may affect women participation in the labor market, is the *presence of elderly people* (over-60) in the family. The effect may be twofold. On the one hand, old people may need special care, forcing women to provide constant care and therefore possibly reduce participation into paid work. On the other hand, grandparents tend to take care of small children and thus, conversely, they make it easier for young mothers to work.

The household consumption, considered as a proxy for family wealth (see Paci and Reilly, 2004) is another potential instrument. The hypothesis to be tested is whether the members of poorer families tend to be more engaged in the working process out of necessity rather than choice. This variable is expected to shed light on the discussed linkage between female participation and poverty. To test for the presence of non-linearity in the effect of this variable on participation, we use a set of dummies for the 10th, 25th, 50th, 75th, and 90th percentile of the log of total household expenditure. We also check for the effect of moving alongside the expenditure distribution by constructing a splined function.

Another instrument used in the estimates is the logged difference between the total household income and the respondents' total monthly income, which tends to account for the person's contribution to the household income which would also determine gender roles within the family. Cagatay (1998) and Valenzuela (2003) discuss the determinants of poverty, linking it with the female dominance in the family. The BHSIE data suggests that it may be relevant for our case study, since about half of the households are reported to have a woman as household head.

The second set of variables is based on (scant) official statistics, at the regional level, and was meant to provide exogenous determinants of women participation (see Table 24.A1 of the Appendix). They include: the percentage of the total population younger than 16; the percentage of the population older than the working age; the percentage of children attending preschool establishments; and the number of hospital beds per 1,000 of population. All these variables were intended to control for the demand and supply factors of female participation.

3 Results

Tables 24.1–24.3 present the results of different Heckman selection procedures. The maximum likelihood estimator has been preferred to the two-step procedure based on testing of the assumption of normality of residuals and of absence of collinearity between the inverse Mills ratio and the regressors in the main equation (for a discussion of these tests, see, for instance, Vella 1998; and Puhani 2000). For the sake of brevity, we report only the results of those tests with reference to the specification using as instrumental variables household expenditure and the difference between the household and the woman's income.[10] In the case of estimates in Table 24.2 the normality assumption is not violated (by using normal probability plot of the residuals). Moreover, the mean value for the *variable inflation factor* (VIF) test in an OLS specification of the wage equation including the inverse Mills ratio is 3.12. This is far below the critical value of 10 used to reject the hypothesis of absence of multicollinearity.

The estimates essentially differ in terms of the instruments used, whereas the coefficients of all other variables in the main and selection equation are similar. In Tables 24.1 and 24.2 we use household specific effects as instruments. The former uses the number of dependent people in the household, namely children under the age of 5 and the elderly over 60. The estimates in Table 24.2 are exactly the same as those in Table 24.1, the only difference being that the former includes measures of household income and expenditure. Table 24.3 uses indices intended to catch region-specific effects, such as the local supply of childcare and care for elderly people. The instruments in Tables 24.1 and 24.2 aim to catch demand-side factors, whereas the instruments used in Table 24.3 aim to catch supply-side factors.

This sensitivity analysis is informative on such matters as the specific supply and/or demand side factors that might cause sample selection mechanisms as well as the stability of the sample selection procedure itself. In fact, as shown below, the results of the tests for sample selection bias markedly differ from one estimate to the other.

More specifically, the instruments used in Table 24.1 include: children under the age of 5 present in the household, the woman's age when the first child was born, the number of dependent children and the presence of elderly people in the household. As expected, the presence of dependent children under the age of 5 and of the over-60s in the household reduces female participation in a statistically significant way. This confirms that women' participation to the labor market is influenced by opportunity cost considerations. The impact of elderly people in the household was greater in 2001 than in 1996, which might be due to some kind of reduction in the state expenditure in the care of elderly people.

Other household-specific instruments are not highly significant. In other words, the fact that a woman has children very early in her life, say between a 15–17 or a 18–22 age range, does not seem to cause any stigma or problem able to reduce her employment opportunities. In addition, the number of children itself does not seem to matter. Only in 1996, does the model seems to detect a statistically significant effect of the number of children, although none with a high level of significance. What matters, then, is only the young age of children. Once children have grown up sufficiently, they do not represent any impediment to women's participation in the labor market. This is interesting, as it suggests that the Belarusian welfare system does help women to reconcile work with child bearing.

Overall, in neither of the two years was any selection mechanism detected, although σ and λ are both statistically significant. The statistical significance of these variables might explain why the returns to education based on reduced form estimates are different from (lower than) those estimated by (unreported) OLS-augmented earnings equations (see also, for comparison, Pastore and Verashchagina 2006a). This confirms expectations, since, taking into consideration the non-employed, returns to education should be lower if the non-employed have lower human capital endowment and motivation. Also, because of this, the predicted hourly wage offers for women have been computed using the sample selection corrections contained in Table 24.1. In addition, as already noted, this allows us to compute expected wages for non-employed women also and for those who do not report their wages or hours worked, for whatever reasons.

Table 24.1 Maximum likelihood estimates for the selectivity corrected female wage equation. The role of household characteristics

Regressors[a]	1996		2001	
	Selection equation	*Wage equation*	*Selection equation*	*Wage equation*
Constant	0.477***	1.534***	0.22	6.059***
	0.143	0.103	0.134	0.098
University	0.856***	0.606***	0.998***	0.670***
	0.101	0.057	0.109	0.063
Technical school	0.673***	0.248***	0.834***	0.315***
	0.09	0.051	0.097	0.058
Vocational school	0.529***	0.057	0.694***	0.114
	0.089	0.05	0.104	0.059
General secondary school	0.509***	0.074	0.713***	0.101
	0.089	0.049	0.097	0.057
PWE	—	0.016**	—	0.026***
		0.005		0.005
PWE2	—	−0.000**	—	−0.001***
		0		0
$16 \leq Age \leq 20$	−1.497***	—	−1.445***	—
	0.144		0.119	
$21 \leq Age \leq 30$	−0.650***	—	−0.553***	—
	0.11		0.093	

31≤Age≤40	0.007	—	0.051	—
	0.09		0.084	
41≤Age≤50	0.288**	—	0.342***	—
	0.093		0.086	
Married	−0.054	−0.018	0.021	−0.039
	0.097	0.036	0.066	0.026
Divorced/Widowed	0.047	−0.013	0.15	−0.047
	0.116	0.044	0.086	0.033
Disabled	−1.965***	−0.216	−2.077***	−0.700**
	0.261	0.237	0.278	0.264
Chernobyl affected	−0.036	0.071	−0.072	−0.054
	0.1	0.039	0.097	0.036
Children under 5 present in the HH	−0.530***	—	−0.680***	—
	0.06		0.063	
15≤Age the first child was born≤17	−0.234	—	0.515*	—
	0.293		0.255	
18≤Age the first child was born≤22	0.224*	—	0.207*	—
	0.094		0.092	
More than 3 dependent children	−0.202*	—	0.004	—
	0.079		0.087	
Presence of old persons over 60	−0.151*	—	−0.285***	—
	0.073		0.071	
rho		−0.1481		0.0020
		0.1287		0.1126
sigma		0.4978		0.4964
		0.0078		0.0066
lambda		−0.0737		0.0010
		0.0647		0.0010
Sample size		3,818		3,878
Log likelihood		−3764.336		−3729.716
LR test of indep. eqns. (rho=0):		chi2(1)=1.33		chi2(1)=0.00
		Prob>chi2=0.2489		Prob>chi2=0.9859

Source: Own elaboration on the BHSIE.

Note: *significant at 10%; ** significant at 5%; ***significant at 1%. The figures under the coefficients represent standard errors.

a The list of variables incorporated into both wage and selectivity equations includes as well 18 regional dummies as described in Table 24.A1 of the Appendix I, not reported for lack of space.

For comparison, we also provide the results of estimates based on a slightly different set of instruments. The model presented in Table 24.2 is similar to that in Table 24.1, the only difference being that other two instruments were added: household expenditure (taken as a proxy of the household income) and the difference between the individual woman's personal income and the household income. As noted in the methodological section, these last two instruments have an important drawback, being potentially endogenous: on the one hand, in fact, increasing household income might cause higher female participation, but, on the other hand, a higher female employment might cause higher household income (on this issue see also Paci and Reilly 2004:

124). This suggests taking the estimates of Table 24.2 with the due caveats. Nonetheless, it is interesting to note that the two variables are statistically highly significant and reveal sample selection mechanisms. In turn, this causes a reduction in the returns to education of women by 20% as compared to those obtained by OLS-augmented earnings equations. This result echoes that obtained by Pastore and Verashchagina (2005 and 2006b).

Table 24.2 reports the results of experiments on the hypothesis of non-linearity of the effect of household income on female participation. The hypothesis is that female participation is low for women belonging to low-income households, but increases with the household income, up to a certain level of income, when it starts to decline. In fact, women belonging to poor households would be less prone to work, since they are forced to take care of children. Also, women belonging to wealthy households have a lower-than-average probability of participating in the labor market, since they have a higher opportunity cost of working. Taking care of the household produces a higher income than that obtained by working.

This was done first by including in the participation equation, instead of logged household expenditure, a set of dummies identifying different percentiles of the consumption distribution.[11] Contrary to a-priori expectations, the hypothesis of a non-linear effect of household income on female participation was rejected. Female participation is lower for the poorest households and increases steadily when moving to the upper percentiles (see the estimated coefficients for Selection equation (2) in Table 24.2). This result is confirmed by the coefficients of a splined function of household expenditure with nodes determined by a certain percentile value of the household expenditure. These coefficients show up as statistically insignificant, meaning that a simple move among the percentile groups does not change the effect on female participation. The only exception is the borderline of the 10th percentile, which is highly significant (see the estimated coefficients for Selection equation (3) in Table 24.2). This finding is hardly surprising in the case of Belarus, considering that the income distribution is very flat, and is suggestive of the existence of poverty trap mechanisms for the poorest households: in fact, belonging to the poor households seems to create strong obstacles for women's participation in the labor force. In turn, a one-bread-winner model of household is likely further to reduce income and welfare levels. At the same time, once in the labor force women are found to work more intensively in case they belong to wealthier families. The interpretation would be that the rising standards of living still do not match families' expectations, thus sustaining the two-bread-winner family model.

In Table 24.3, regional characteristics of the demand for and supply of social services are taken into account instead of household characteristics. The regional variables include the number of pre-school institutions, the share of young and elderly population, and the number of hospital beds. Again, the coefficients of the instrumental variables used suggest that they do not affect female participation, with the only exception being the share of

Table 24.2† Maximum likelihood estimates for the selectivity corrected female wage equation. The role of the household's income

Additional instruments	1996 Selection equation[1]	1996 Selection equation[2]	1996 Selection equation[3]	2001 Selection equation[1]	2001 Selection equation[2]	2001 Selection equation[3]
Difference between personal and household income	-0.249*** (0.03)	-0.2122*** (0.0288)	-0.2340*** (0.0298)	-0.208*** (0.027)	-0.2046*** (0.0270)	-0.2018*** (0.0271)
Household expenditure	0.596*** (0.044)	—	—	0.630*** (0.041)	—	—
p10	—	-0.6455*** (0.1024)	1.0666*** (0.2524)	—	-0.9123*** (0.0927)	1.3851*** (0.2333)
P25	—	-0.4302*** (0.0762)	-0.0602 (0.4185)	—	-0.4039*** (0.0727)	-0.9209* (0.4038)
P50	—	—	-0.5778 (0.3960)	—	—	0.2098 (0.3936)
P75	—	0.3514*** (0.0628)	-0.3822 (0.4849)	—	0.1970*** (0.0590)	0.0753 (0.4511)
P90	—	0.3531*** (0.0726)	0.3857 (0.3975)	—	0.4102*** (0.0686)	-0.6355 (0.3780)
P100	—	0.5750*** (0.0879)	—	—	0.6753*** (0.0815)	—
rho	-0.7156 (0.0358)	-0.6867 (0.0403)	-0.7027 (0.0379)	-0.8504 (0.0201)	-0.8502 (0.0202)	-0.8404 (0.0215)
sigma	0.5492 (0.0106)	0.5439 (0.0107)	0.5464 (0.0106)	0.5657 (0.0095)	0.5645 (0.0095)	0.5629 (0.0096)
lambda	-0.3930 (0.0256)	-0.3735 (0.0277)	-0.3840 (0.026492)	-0.4811 (0.0175)	-0.4800 (0.0175)	-0.4730 (0.0181)
Sample size	3,818	3,818	3,818	3,858	3,858	3,858
Log likelihood	-3681.478	-3680.5190	-3674.347	-3577.585	-3567.541	-3575.748
LR test of indep. eqns (rho=0):	chi2(1)=87.2 Prob>chi2=0.0	chi2(1)=73.57 Prob>chi2=0.0	chi2(1)=81.58 Prob>chi2=0.0	chi2(1)=138.36 Prob>chi2=0.0	chi2(1)=140.27 Prob>chi2=0.0	chi2(1)=128.87 Prob>chi2=0.0

Source: Own elaboration on the BHSIE.

Note: * significant at 10%; ** significant at 5%; *** significant at 1%. The figures under the coefficients represent standard errors.

† The estimates include all the variables in Table 24.1, plus the two extra instruments reported here. Both household expenditure as well as the difference between household and personal income enter the specification in logged form in the Selection equation. [1] The household income enters Selection equation[2] in the form of dummies representing different percentiles of the personal income distribution and Selection equation[3] in the form of a spline function.

Table 24.3† Maximum likelihood estimates for the selectivity corrected female wage equation. The role of regional characteristics

Regressors	1996		2001	
	Selection equation	*Wage equation*	*Selection equation*	*Wage equation*
Constant	4.644	0.983***	0.299	5.553***
	4.532	0.111	2.786	0.079
University	0.927***	0.833***	1.043***	0.916***
	0.101	0.062	0.107	0.058
Technical school	0.766***	0.424***	0.881***	0.497***
	0.09	0.055	0.095	0.055
Vocational school	0.597***	0.228***	0.753***	0.315***
	0.09	0.052	0.102	0.057
General secondary school	0.556***	0.219***	0.772***	0.266***
	0.088	0.051	0.095	0.055
PWE	—	0.030***	—	0.031***
		0.006		0.005
PWE2	—	−0.001***	—	−0.001***
		0		0
16≤Age≤20	−1.554***	—	−1.378***	—
	0.134		0.114	
21≤Age≤30	−0.786***	—	−0.676***	—
	0.091		0.079	
31≤Age≤40	−0.056	—	0.006	—
	0.088		0.081	
41≤Age≤50	0.255**	—	0.355***	—
	0.093		0.084	
Married	−0.199*	−0.05	0.018	−0.085**
	0.086	0.038	0.064	0.026
Divorced/Widowed	−0.07	−0.026	0.146	−0.044
	0.107	0.045	0.083	0.034
Disabled	−1.918***	−0.37	−2.094***	−1.038***
	0.26	0.249	0.281	0.264
Chernobyl affected	−0.004	0.092*	−0.052	−0.019
	0.098	0.04	0.094	0.038
Preschool institutions[a]	−0.041	—	−0.173	—
	0.092		0.113	
Younger WAP[a]	−0.334	—	−0.919	—
	0.966		0.633	
Older WAP[a]	0.022	—	0.677**	—
	0.183		0.257	
Hospital beds[a]	−0.632	—	0.248	—
	0.394		0.346	
rho	0.2232		0.2676	
	0.1419		0.0752	
sigma	0.5217		0.5257	
	0.0099		0.0082	
lambda	0.1165		0.1407	
	0.0756		0.0407	

Sample size	3,818	3,878
Log likelihood value	−3931.606	−3925.177
LR test of indep. eqns	chi2(1)=1.65	chi2(1)=8.06
(rho=0):	Prob>chi2=0.1996	Prob>chi2=0.0045

Source: Own elaboration on the BHSIE.

Note: * significant at 10%; ** significant at 5%; *** significant at 1%. The figures under the coefficients represent standard errors. † Different from Table 24.1, instead of household level variables, the instruments in the selection equation here are built on the basis of the regional level data. The set of regional dummies has been dropped.

a For the definition of these instruments see Table 24.A1 of Appendix I, as well as the section on data and methodology. WAP stands for the working age population (16 through 60 for men, and 16 through 55 for women)

people older than the working-age population. The coefficient is positive, suggesting that elderly people help the young generation to cope with the care of dependent people in the household. There appears to be no sample selection at work.

Overall, Tables 24.1–24.3 confirm that the Heckman procedure is very sensitive to the types of instrument used in the selection equation. For this reason, it is difficult to choose the right model on which to compute the expected wages to include in the estimates of the so-called structural female labor force participation model. Two alternative probit estimates are hence presented. Table 24.4 is based on predicted hourly wage offers for women from the baseline model in Table 24.1, whereas Table 24.5 is based on predicted hourly wage offers for women from the baseline model in Table 24.2. Note that in both cases the other variables in the reduced form model have been included. The tables present estimated coefficients and marginal effects.

Table 24.4 confirms the results of Table 24.1 regarding the significance level of household-specific factors, such as having dependent children, the age when the first child was born, the number of children, and the presence of over-60s in the household. The impact of age on labor market participation is non-linear, with younger women working significantly less than older ones. Those aged over 40 are the most active. Disabled women also have a much lower degree of participation. These results are stable across the two specifications.

The aim of this exercise is to see the *ceteris paribus* impact of the individual expected hourly wage on the probability of labor market participation together with the other variables included in the selection equation of the reduced form model. The results confirm that the expected wage does affect female participation. The estimated marginal effects for the predicted hourly wage offer are slightly decreasing between 1996 and 2001. The higher pseudo-R^2 in Table 24.4 suggests that the model with individual characteristics only is to be preferred to that including regional characteristics.

Note that the attained coefficients for the expected wages in the estimated labor supply model of both Table 24.4 and 24.5 are almost half those that Saget (1999) obtains for Hungary. We further calculate the elasticity of female labor force participation with respect to wages, at the sample

Table 24.4 Structural female labor force participation model as based on Table 24.1

Regressors[a]	1996		2001	
	Probit estimates	*Marginal effects*	*Probit estimates*	*Marginal effects*
Constant	−0.883**	—	−5.815***	—
	0.2770		0.857	
16≤Age≤20	−1.531***	−0.5560***	−1.530***	−0.5534***
	0.1510	0.0448	0.118	0.0373
21≤Age≤30	−0.572***	−0.2004***	−0.525***	−0.1746***
	0.1100	0.0404	0.093	0.0331
31≤Age≤40	0.0820	0.0265	0.063	0.0190
	0.0890	0.0282	0.082	0.0246
41≤Age≤50	0.304**	0.0938**	0.318***	0.0917***
	0.0930	0.0271	0.086	0.0233
Married	−0.0560	−0.0181	0.067	0.0205
	0.0990	0.0317	0.066	0.0204
Divorced/Widowed	0.0350	0.0113	0.214*	0.0617*
	0.1180	0.0376	0.088	0.0239
Disabled	−1.786***	−0.6155***	−1.386***	−0.5110***
	0.2650	0.0565	0.323	0.1052
Chernobyl affected	−0.0870	−0.0289	−0.007	−0.0023
	0.1060	0.0361	0.096	0.0294
Children under 5 present in the HH	−0.507***	−0.1766***	−0.671***	−0.2300***
	0.0610	0.0222	0.065	0.0239
15≤Age the first child was born≤17	−0.2530	−0.0883	0.668*	0.1518
	0.3100	0.1144	0.29	0.0441
18≤Age the first child was born≤22	0.285**	0.0856**	0.340***	0.0929***
	0.0940	0.0261	0.092	0.0224
More than 3 dependent children	−0.193**	−0.0653**	0.006	0.0019
	0.0750	0.0263	0.083	0.0251
Presence of old persons over 60	−0.161*	−0.0541*	−0.308***	−0.1010***
	0.0740	0.0256	0.073	0.0257
Predicted log hourly wage offer[b]	1.023***	0.3323***	1.042***	0.3174***
	0.1390	0.0445	0.131	0.0391
Sample size	3,818		3,878	
Log likelihood value	−1834.9583		−1708.7396	
Pseudo R2	0.2036		0.2449	

Source: Own elaboration on the BHSIE.

Note: * significant at 10%; ** significant at 5%; *** significant at 1%. The figures under the coefficients represent standard errors.
a Both the wage and the selectivity equations include 18 regional dummies as described in Table 24.A1 of the Appendix. The coefficients of these variables are omitted.
b The predicted hourly wage is calculated on the basis of specification as reported in Table 24.1.

means.[12] The attained levels of 0.45 for 1996 and of 0.41 for 2001 are based on the estimates reported in Table 24.4. They suggest that a 10% increase/decrease in wages would cause less than 5% increase/decrease in female labor supply.

Table 24.5 Structural female labor force participation model as based on Table 24.2

Regressors	1996		2001	
	Probit estimates	*Marginal effects*	*Probit estimates*	*Marginal effects*
Constant	2.466	—	−2.966	—
	4.513		2.878	
16≤Age≤20	−1.295***	−0.4812***	−1.301***	−0.4785***
	0.142	0.0479	0.119	0.0419
21≤Age≤30	−0.521***	−0.1825***	−0.497***	−0.1671***
	0.087	0.0320	0.08	0.0285
31≤Age≤40	0.058	0.0189	0.06	0.0185
	0.086	0.0278	0.081	0.0246
41≤Age≤50	0.289**	0.0902***	0.353***	0.1035***
	0.092	0.0272	0.084	0.0229
Married	−0.112	−0.0359	0.106	0.0332
	0.088	0.0277	0.065	0.0207
Divorced/Widowed	−0.022	−0.0073	0.190*	0.0561
	0.108	0.0357	0.085	0.0239
Disabled	−1.521***	−0.5501***	−1.100***	−0.4122***
	0.263	0.0716	0.32	0.1188
Chernobyl affected	−0.094	−0.0317	−0.052	−0.0165
	0.103	0.0354	0.095	0.0303
Preschool institutions[a]	0.049	0.0159	0.007	0.0023
	0.072	0.0237	0.102	0.0316
Younger WAP[a]	−0.253	−0.0828	−1.191	−0.3697
	0.965	0.3161	0.633	0.1965
Older WAP[a]	−0.014	−0.0044	0.564*	0.1753*
	0.178	0.0583	0.257	0.0798
Hospital beds[a]	−0.542	−0.1776	−0.101	−0.0315
	0.389	0.1273	0.345	0.1073
Predicted log hourly wage offer[b]	1.092***	0.3576***	0.976***	0.3031***
	0.116	0.0370	0.108	0.0327
Sample size	3,818		3,878	
Log likelihood value	−1877.2529		−1775.7394	
Pseudo R2	0.1853		0.2153	

Source: Own elaboration on the BHSIE.

Note: * significant at 10%; ** significant at 5%; *** significant at 1%. The figures under the coefficients represent standard errors.

a   For the definition of these instruments see Table 24.A1 of Appendix I, as well as the section on data and methodology. WAP stand for the working-age population (under 60 for men, and under 55 for women)

b   The predicted hourly wage is calculated on the basis of specification as reported in Table 24.3.

The results for Belarus are again much lower than those that Saget (1999: 589) finds in the Hungarian case (1.81), but are similar to some of the findings of Paci and Reilly (2004: Table 5.5). They find low elasticity values in the case of Bulgaria (0.275 in 1995 and 0.160 in 2001), Albania (0.522 in 2002), and Tajikistan (0.720 in 1999), but higher than unity in the case of Bosnia and Herzegovina (1.239 in 2001), Serbia (1.904 in 2001), and Uzbekistan (1.941 in 2001).

Table 24.6 provides wage elasticities of labor supply for different groups of women. The values are quite stable with a few exceptions. Confirming previous findings, for instance, the youngest group have higher than average elasticity. The same is true for women having more than three children.

Interestingly, when calculating the wage elasticity at different deciles of the log hourly wage distribution (Figure 24.2), although being still lower than unity, the measures are much higher for lower deciles. This suggests that a reduction/increase in wages might have a more important impact on female participation if implemented for jobs with the lowest content in terms of skills. In turn, this finding might be taken as an argument in favour of the aforementioned hypothesis that the least skilled women are the most vulnerable to changes in the economic conditions of the country.

Overall, the latter findings are indicative of a low responsiveness of female labor supply to economic incentives in Belarus, which is to be expected considering the high participation rate of women and the two-bread-winner family model prevailing in the country. In addition, the evidence provided here is in line with the theoretical considerations brought to the fore in Malysheva and Verashchagina (2008) and supports the revealed differences in transition path between the CEE and the CIS. It is clear that the documented low elasticity measures of female labor supply found in this paper are related to the current economic situation. It cannot be used as an argument to exclude the possibility of a contraction of female activity rates in the years to come if the state reduces support to women' employment and to female-

Table 24.6 Wage elasticity of labor supply for different groups of women

Target population	1996		2001	
	Nobs.	*Wage elasticity*	*Nobs.*	*Wage elasticity*
All women	3818	0.449 (0.060)	3878	0.413 (0.051)
Specific groups of women:				
21≤Age≤30	903	0.688 (0.581)	882	0.626 (0.086)
31≤Age≤40	1233	0.423 (0.067)	1052	0.392 (0.058)
41≤Age≤50	981	0.347 (0.059)	1101	0.315 (0.048)
Single	541	0.449 (0.060)	725	0.413 (0.051)
Married	2763	0.457 (0.063)	2555	0.403 (0.050)
Divorced/Widowed	514	0.435 (0.077)	598	0.333 (0.050)
18≤Age the first child was born≤22	461	0.337 (0.053)	419	0.286 (0.045)
More than 3 dependent children	468	0.536 (0.076)	437	0.410 (0.057)

Source: Own elaboration on the BHSIE.

Note: all coefficients reported in the table are significant at 1%. The estimates are based on the marginal effects reported in Table 24.4.

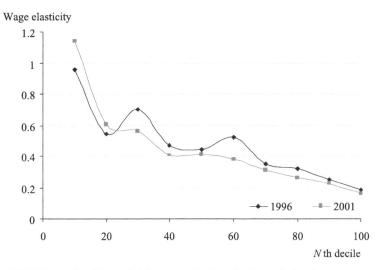

Wage elasticity

Figure 24.2 Wage elasticity of labor supply by deciles of the log hourly wage distribution.
Source: Own elaboration on the BHSIE.

dominated sectors. This may, in fact, exacerbate the poverty trap mechanisms found in the data: as noted above, female labor supply might respond to increasing disincentives, especially for the poorest households.

Concluding remarks

The gender literature on economic transition has asked the question whether women fare better (or worse) in a market economy as compared to a centrally planned economy. Previous studies have observed a reduction in (or sometimes stable) gender pay gap, suggesting that women receive higher wages in a market economy. However, a stream of literature has contended that the reduction in the gender pay gap is not necessarily a consequence of improved welfare: in fact, it was related to a reduction, not to an increase in female participation. Numerous reasons have been raised to explain reduced female participation in studies relative to CEE and CIS countries. First is the increased hardship of finding (or keeping) a job and the increasing uncertainty of the entire economic system due, in turn, to price and wage liberalization as well as privatization of state-owned enterprises. Second is the increasingly hard budget constraint of (state or private) firms. This has caused a reduction in the state and corporate expenditure for providing child-care facilities and services for elderly people, which has translated into a dramatically increased opportunity cost of supplying labor for many women. The consequent reduction in female labor supply can actually also explain the increased average wages of the most motivated working women.

The question asked in this study is whether the mechanisms at work in other transition countries were also at place in Belarus, despite the slow transition process. The main conclusion of our enquiry is that unlike in other transition countries, in Belarus female labor force participation remains very high, despite the now documented increase in the GWG (Pastore and Verashchagina, 2007). The latter is still lower than in the neighbouring countries, but if the outlined trend of rising pay gap continues, there is a high probability of women withdrawing from the labor market. It is worth investigating the evolution of the GWG and participation in the future.

This paper adds to the literature by providing a systematic study of the determinants of female labor supply in 1996 and 2001 (data from the Belarusian Household Survey). A selectivity corrected wage equation is estimated to compute the expected wage offer for women. The latter enters as regressor in the structural female labor force participation equation, estimated by probit. The results provide interesting insights into several aspects of the link between female participation and their wages in Belarus. The opportunity cost of working—as measured by demand and supply side measures of facilities for the care of children and elderly people—does affect female participation, but without generating sample selection mechanisms. In other words, having dependent children, under the age of 5, or elderly people, aged more than 60, reduces the probability of a woman participating in the labor market, but this reduction seems to be randomly distributed across the sample of women. This suggests that welfare state answers to women's needs do not generate discrimination against specific groups of women. However, sample selection procedures prove to be very sensitive to the type if instruments used in the selectivity equation. In fact, sample selection is detected when a measure of household income, as proxied by the household expenditure, is used as a determinant of female participation. Female participation is found to be lower for the poorest households, which might generate poverty trap mechanisms. The low estimated elasticity (about 0.45 in 1996 and 0.41 in 2001) of female labor supply to wages confirms that for a woman, rather than being a choice, working is a need consistent with the prevailing two-bread-winner strategy of Belarusian households.

Notes

* The authors gratefully acknowledge support from the Economics Education and Research Consortium—Russia (research grant # 04–133) within the GDN regional competition framework. We would like to thank for comments the participants of seminars held at the EERC in Moscow, Russia (December 2004) and Kiev, Ukraine (July 2005 and July 2006) and especially Michael Beenstock, Irina Denisova, John Earle, Randall Filer, Eric Livny. Our gratitude goes to Francesca Bettio for always useful discussions on the topic and to the editors of the volume for their guidance at the final stage. The usual disclaimer applies.

1 In fact, as Paci and Reilly (2004) also noted, there is not full consensus on this issue. For instance, Joliffe and Campos (2005) find that the gender pay gap dramatically reduced in Hungary over the period 1986 to 1998. In a similar vein, Brainerd (2000) finds that the gender pay gap has dramatically reduced in CEECs, but has increased in Russia and Ukraine. The interpretation she provides is that in these latter countries, women have been penalized by the tremendous widening of the wage distribution. Pastore and Verashchagina (2007) also find an increase in the GWG in neighbouring Belarus over the years 1996–2004, despite there being practically no change in wage inequality over the period considered.
2 Here we refer to registered unemployment rates.
3 In addition, according to the official statistics, in Belarus the share of men having per capita incomes below the minimum standard rose from 39.4 per cent in 1995 to 42.9 per cent in 2000, while the corresponding figures for women rose from 37.4 to 41 per cent. Women generally tend to be overrepresented among the poor; even though, as Quisumbing, Haddad, and Pena (2001) note in their study of 10 developing countries, this might not be so straightforward and needs further investigation in order to understand which are the ways to combat poverty.
4 These include Albania, Bulgaria, Bosnia and Herzegovina, Serbia, Tajikistan, and Uzbekistan.
5 The calculation of hourly wages forces us to lose some information as compared to using monthly wages, since some individuals refuse to give this information. Additionally, since in some cases people declare unusually low wages and unusually high working hours, the variable has been truncated to exclude outliers, defined as those with wages higher or lower than the mean by three times the standard deviation of the distribution.
6 This measure can understate the real values in the case of overlapping three-year periods taken for two children born one after another.
7 Angrist and Evans (1998) propose to use parental preferences for a mixed sibling-sex composition to construct instrumental variables in estimates of the effect of childbearing on labor supply to control for endogeneity of fertility. In the BHSIE data, there is no way to identify the sex of siblings.
8 The age of the first birth in Belarus remains one of the lowest in the region. Source: UNECE Gender Statistics Database [http://www.unece.org/stats/gender/].
9 After a dramatic decline in the first half of the 1990s from 1.9 down to 1.3 the fertility rate in Belarus has remained low and pretty stable, in the range 1.2–1.3.
10 Similar results of such tests relative to the other specifications are available on request from the authors.
11 We deliberately excluded the 50th percentile in order to see how the border groups tend to behave. We had different expectations regarding the tails of the household consumption distribution. Female participation could be high at the bottom end of the distribution, since in this case the decision is driven by necessity. Vice versa, female participation could be lower with the rise of family wealth.
12 The marginal effects in probit is at the means of other covariates: $ME = \partial P(y = 1 \mid x) / \partial x' = \phi(x'\beta)\beta$, where $\phi(.)$ is the density function. The elasticity for each variable is obtained dividing marginal effects by the average probability of participation, which is estimated to be equal to 0.74 in 1996 and 0.77 in 2001.

References

Angrist, J. D. and W. N. Evans (1998) "Children and Their Parents' Labour Supply: Evidence form Exogenous Variation in Family Size." *The American Economic Review* 88(3): 450–77.

Brainerd, E. (2000) "Women in Transition: Change in Gender Wage Differentials in Eastern Europe and FSU." *Industrial and Labour Relations Review* 54(1): 139–62.

Cagatay, N. (1998) "Gender and Poverty." WP 5, UNDP, Social Development and Poverty Elimination Division.

Heckman, J. J. (1979) "Sample Selection Bias as a Specification Error." *Econometrica* 47(1): 153–62

Hunt, J. (2002) "The Transition in East Germany: When is a ten-point fall in the gender pay gap bad news?" *Journal of Labor Economics* 20(1): 148–69.

Jolliffe, D. and H. F. Campos (2005) "Does Market Liberalisation Reduce Gender Discrimination? Econometric evidence from Hungary, 1986–1998." *Labour Economics* 12(1): 1–22.

Kungurova, N. I. (2004) "Where Does Gender Equality Lead?" *Belarus Economic Journal* 1(26): 95–8. [Кунгурова Н.И., "Куда ведет гендерное равенство?", *Белорусский экономический журнал*, № 1, 2004, cc. 95–8].

Malysheva, M. and A. Verashchagina (2008) "The Transition from a Planned to a Market Economy: How are women faring?" In *Frontiers in the Economics of Gender*, edited by F. Bettio and A. Verashchagina. Routledge Siena Studies in Political Economy.

Munich, D., J. Svejnar, and K. Terrell (2005) "Is Women's Human Capital Valued More by Markets than by Planners?" *Journal of Comparative Economics* 33(2): 278–99.

Ogloblin, C. (1999) "The Gender Earnings Differentials in the Russian Transition Economy." *Industrial and Labour Relations Review* 52(4): 602–27.

Orazem, P. F. and Vodopivec, M. (1997) "Value of Human Capital in Transition to Market: Evidence from Slovenia." *European Economic Review* 41(3–5): 893–903.

Paci, P. and B. Reilly (2004) "Does Economic Liberalisation Reduce Gender Inequality in the Labour Market? The experience of the transitional economies of Europe and Central Asia." Washington DC: World Bank.

Pastore, F. and A. Verashchagina (2005) "The Gender Wage Gap in Belarus." *Transition Studies Review* 12(3): 497–511.

—— and —— . (2006a), "The Distribution of Wages in Belarus." *Comparative Economic Studies* 48(2): 351–76.

—— and —— . (2006b) "Private Returns to Human Capital over Transition. A case study of Belarus." *Economics of Education Review* 25(1): 91–107.

—— and —— . (2007) "When Does Transition Increase the Gender Wage Gap? An application to Belarus." IZA discussion paper 2796.

Puhani, P. A. (2000) "The Heckman Correction for Sample Selection and its Critique." *Journal of Economic Surveys* 14(1): 53–68.

Quisumbing, A. R., L. Haddadand, and C. Pena (2001) "Are Women Overrepresented Among the Poor? An analysis of poverty in 10 developing countries." *Journal of Development Economics* 66(1): 225–69.

Saget, C. (1999) "The Determinants of Female Labour Supply in Hungary." *Economics of Transition* 7(3): 575–91.

Valenzuela, M. E. (2003) *The Incorporation of Gender in Employment and Anti-poverty Policies: Challenges for the future*. Geneva: DP, ILO.

Vella, F. (1998) "Estimating Models with Sample Selection Bias. A survey." *Journal of Human Resources* 33(1): 127–69.

Wooldridge, J. M. (2001) *Econometric Analysis of Cross Section and Panel Data*, Cambridge, MA: MIT Press.

Appendix I

Table 24.A1 Definition of variables

Variable name	Definition
lhwage	natural log of hourly wage from the main job
university	= 1, if university degree; = 0, otherwise (including those with PhD)
technical school	= 1, if diploma of technical secondary school; = 0, otherwise
vocational school	= 1, if diploma of vocational secondary school; = 0, otherwise
general secondary school	= 1, if diploma of general secondary school; = 0, otherwise
compulsory education (low secondary school, baseline)	= 1, if diploma of basic school; = 0, otherwise
age	age of a person
age groups: 16≤Age≤20, 21≤Age≤30, 31≤Age≤40, 41≤Age≤50, 51≤Age≤60, Age>60	age groups divide the sample into 6 categories: aged 16 to 20, 21 to 30, 31 to 40, 41 to 50, 51 to 60 and over 60
awe	actual (declared) work experience (in years)
pwe	potential work experience =(age − education − 6) − no.children*3
pwe2	potential work experience squared
marital	marital status is represented by three dummy variables: married, single and divorced/widowed
disabled	dummy for disabled persons
chernob	dummy for persons who report to be Chernobyl influenced
Brest_ru, Brest_sm, Brest_lar, Gomel_ru, Gomel_sm, Gomel_lar, Grodno_ru, Grodno_sm, Grodno_lar, Minsk_ru, Minsk_sm, Minsk_lar, Minsk_city, Vitebsk_ru, Vitebsk_sm, Vitebsk_lar, Mogilev_ru, Mogilev_sm, Mogilev_lar	nineteen regional dummies are constructed by dividing each of the six existing oblasts/regions (Brest, Gomel, Grodno, Minsk, Vitebsk, Mogilev) into three sub-regions, relative to areas with large cities, small cities and rural areas. Minsk city is kept separately and represents a baseline

(*Continued Overleaf*)

Table 24.A1 Continued

Variable name	Definition
Instruments	
Household level data	
15/18/23≤Age the first child was born≤17/22/28	Dummy for the age when the first child was born, three groups are considered: 15–17, 18–22, 23–28 (only for women with age≤30 at the time of the interview)
children under 5 in the HH	=1 if there are children in the household under 5 years old
more than 3 children	=1 if the number of dependent is greater than 3
old60 in the HH	=1, if in the household there are elderly over 60
ltotalexp	total household expenditures, in natural log terms
ldifer	difference between the total household income and the respondent's total monthly income
Aggregate level data (by regions)	
preschool	% of children attending pre-school establishments, in log terms
younger_wap	percentage of the population younger than the working age (<16), in log terms
older_wap	percentage of the population older than the working age (>55 for women, >60 for men), in log terms
hospital beds	number of hospital beds per 10,000 of population, in log terms

Table 24.A2 Descriptive statistics

Variable	1996					2001				
	Obs	Mean	Std dev.	Min	Max	Obs	Mean	Std dev.	Min	Max
lhwage	2705	1.631	0.571	0.006	3.606	2830	6.276	0.579	3.57	7.906
university	3818	0.167	0.373	0	1	3878	0.186	0.389	0	1
technical	3818	0.258	0.437	0	1	3878	0.312	0.463	0	1
vocational	3818	0.235	0.424	0	1	3878	0.163	0.370	0	1
gen. secondary	3818	0.212	0.409	0	1	3878	0.225	0.417	0	1
pwe	3818	13.840	9.511	0	50	3878	14.576	9.635	0	50
pwe2	3818	281.991	329.329	0	2500	3878	305.278	325.252	0	2500
single	3818	0.142	0.349	0	1	3878	0.189	0.390	0	1
married	3818	0.724	0.447	0	1	3878	0.659	0.474	0	1
div/widow	3818	0.135	0.341	0	1	3878	0.154	0.361	0	1
disabled	3818	0.012	0.107	0	1	3878	0.011	0.102	0	1
chernob	3818	0.065	0.247	0	1	3878	0.073	0.261	0	1
student	3818	0.000	0.000	0	0	3878	0.000	0.000	0	0
pensioner	3818	0.000	0.000	0	0	3878	0.000	0.000	0	0
self-employed	3818	0.000	0.000	0	0	3878	0.000	0.000	0	0
age	3818	36.271	10.760	16	60	3878	37.049	11.212	16	60
16≤Age≤20	3818	0.081	0.273	0	1	3878	0.086	0.280	0	1
21≤Age≤30	3818	0.237	0.425	0	1	3878	0.227	0.419	0	1
31≤Age≤40	3818	0.323	0.468	0	1	3878	0.271	0.445	0	1
41≤Age≤50	3818	0.257	0.437	0	1	3878	0.284	0.451	0	1
51≤Age≤60	3818	0.102	0.303	0	1	3878	0.132	0.338	0	1
15≤Age first child ≤17	3818	0.007	0.084	0	1	3878	0.008	0.078	0	1
18≤Age first child ≤22	3818	0.121	0.326	0	1	3878	0.108	0.310	0	1
children under 5 in the HH	3818	0.235	0.424	0	1	3878	0.191	0.393	0	1
more than 3 children	3818	0.123	0.328	0	1	3878	0.113	0.316	0	1
old60 in the HH	3818	0.120	0.325	0	1	3878	0.130	0.337	0	1

(Conntinued overleaf)

Table 24.A2 Continued.

Variable	1996					2001				
	Obs	Mean	Std dev.	Min	Max	Obs	Mean	Std dev.	Min	Max
ltotalexp	3818	7.712	0.623	4.605	11.044	3878	12.211	0.607	9.507	15.805
ldifer	3818	7.425	1.097	0	11.049	3858	11.912	1.452	0	15.694
pre-school	3818	4.054	0.337	3.578	4.292	3878	4.209	0.250	3.842	4.378
younger_wap	3818	3.139	0.031	3.086	3.19	3878	2.993	0.052	2.901	3.068
older_wap	3818	3.045	0.147	2.708	3.14	3878	3.055	0.122	2.779	3.144
hospital beds	3818	4.827	0.079	4.665	4.903	3878	4.840	0.079	4.672	4.922

Note: We exclude respondents over 60 years old, students, pensioners, self-employed, and outliers on the basis of declared wages.

25 Islands through the glass ceiling?

Evidence of gender wage gaps in Madagascar and Mauritius[*]

Christophe J. Nordman and
François-Charles Wolff

1 Introduction

Many empirical studies have shown that women and men face unequal treatment in the work place, especially in terms of wages. Almost all developed countries' labor markets are characterized by a significant gender wage gap, whose explanation may be related to differences in the level of human capital between male and female employees or to discrimination from employers against the female workforce (Blau and Kahn 2000). Furthermore, this gender wage gap is unlikely to remain constant throughout the wage distribution as revealed for Sweden, Spain, or France (Albrecht, Björklund, and Vroman 2003; de la Rica, Dolado, and Llorens 2008; Jellal, Nordman, and Wolff 2008). This is the so-called glass ceiling hypothesis according to which women face more difficulties than men in reaching top positions within the firm and thus benefiting from high wages.[1]

Contrary to the case of developed countries, less is known about gender wage differences in developing countries, especially with respect to the possible varying magnitude of the gender gap across the wage distribution. In particular, gender-specific studies on Africa remain particularly scarce as can be inferred from the meta-analysis of Weichselbaumer and Winter-Ebmer (2005). A few recent contributions are those of Mwabu and Schultz (1996) on South Africa, Said (2003) on Egypt, Nordman and Roubaud (2009) on Madagascar, Nordman and Wolff (2009) on Morocco, and Fafchamps, Söderbom, and Benhassine (2006) using data on the manufacturing sector among several African countries. This is somewhat puzzling as reducing gender inequality is usually recommended as an efficient tool in the combat against poverty in poor countries.[2]

The purpose of this contribution is then to add new evidence on the magnitude of the gender wage gap in African countries and on the relevance of the glass ceiling hypothesis. In a context where wages and productivity remain usually low, it may be that employers tend to limit the use of discrimination against women. To investigate more closely the gender wage differences, we rely on a comparison between the Mauritius and Madagascar islands using recent Investment Climate Assessment (ICA) surveys carried out in 2005. The use of matched employer–employee data allows us to control accurately for firm unobserved heterogeneity in wage regressions through the inclusion of fixed effects and to study the role of the firm characteristics in the gender wage gap.

The selected islands are particularly interesting in a comparative perspective. First, beyond the fact that they are close neighbors in the Indian Ocean, Mauritius is perhaps the most interesting economic development success story of the decade of the 1980s. Its GDP per capita ($13,240 in 2005 in PPP) places it in the category of newly industrialized country. By contrast, Madagascar, in spite of the dynamism of its Export Processing Zones (EPZs) since the 1990s, remains one of the poorest countries in the world. According to the 2006 Human Development Indicator (HDI) ranking of the UNDP, Mauritius stands at the 63rd position while Madagascar appears far below in the ranking, at only the 143rd place (out of 177 countries).

A comparative case study of both countries is then worthwhile to assess whether gender inequalities in pay are somehow linked to the level of economic development. The fact that these two close islands have quite distinct economic performance and labor market features may be helpful in the understanding of the roots of gender wage differences. In our empirical analysis, we focus more closely on the role of firm characteristics and job segregation across firms as potential factors explaining the gender wage gap (Meng 2004). Do firms' characteristics matter when explaining wage differences between male and female employees? We also investigate the relevance of the glass ceiling hypothesis and measure the gender wage gap across the whole wage distribution using quantile regressions.

The remainder of this contribution is organized as follows. In section 2, we briefly describe the functioning of the labor market in Mauritius and Madagascar. We describe the ICA surveys in section 3 and present descriptive statistics on workers, firms, and wages. Our different econometric results based on both fixed-effect models, decomposition techniques, and quantile regressions are presented in section 4. Finally, concluding comments are in section 5.

2 Labor markets in Mauritius and Madagascar Islands

Several characteristics of the labor markets are helpful to understand the pattern of wages in Mauritius and Madagascar. In fact, both countries face very different contexts. For instance, unit production costs in Madagascar are among the lowest in the world, much lower than levels in China, India, or Mauritius (Cling, Razafindrakoto, and Roubaud 2005). In the meantime, work productivity is much lower in Madagascar than in Mauritius. Let us further describe the situation of both islands.

In Mauritius, the labor market has greatly evolved due to the fundamental structural changes of the economy over the last 30 years (English 2002; World

Bank 2006). The rapid development of the manufacturing sector in the 1970s and 1980s led to the rapid expansion of relatively low-skilled jobs to meet the need of the fast-growing EPZ sector. However, by the end of the 1980s and early 1990s, the emergence of new sectors, particularly in the fields of tourism and financial services, required higher skilled manpower. Following the new millennium, the demand for high-skilled labor was further accentuated as the Mauritian government moved forward to promoting new poles of growth in high value-added services such as the ICT sector.

This economic transformation inevitably entailed some adjustment costs. Nowadays, the new sectors are service-oriented and therefore necessitate a different input mix, generally more capital than labor intensive. However, these new emerging sectors have some potential to absorb labor, in particular, skilled workers. Unfortunately, those workers who are being laid off from the traditional sectors are not technically prepared to be absorbed in the new sectors, which require not only additional academic qualifications, but also generic skills such as language skills. This explains the steady rise of the unemployment rate since 1991, about 10.4% in June 2005 which is the period covered by the ICA survey in this study.

In 2006, Mauritius had a total labor force of 546,200 individuals, 60.4% being males. Total employment represented 90% of the workforce, including 3.4% of foreign workers. The government of Mauritius administratively establishes minimum wages (through the National Remuneration Board, NRB hereafter), which vary according to the sector of employment. While the minimum wage increases annually, based on inflation, most trade unions negotiate wages higher than those set by the NRB.[3]

The Malagasy labor market is very different in nature. During the 2001–5 period covered by the household EPM surveys in Madagascar,[4] the Malagasy economy was in instability as a result of experiencing several large-scale shocks. Between 2001 and 2005, poverty declined more rapidly in rural areas than in urban areas[5]. According to the EPM 2001–5, the workforce participation in Madagascar is high, more than 80% of 9.17 million individuals of working age 15–64, especially in rural areas. Employment growth was driven by greater participation among women who currently make up half the workforce.

The primary sector accounts for over 88% of rural employment and 45% of urban employment. However, over 85% of workers in Madagascar are employed in non-wage activities, predominantly agricultural. Therefore, the informal sector largely dominates the labor market. Although a high proportion of the working-age population was gainfully employed in 2005, 65.4% of them live in poverty. Nevertheless, open unemployment is structurally low in Madagascar, though underemployment is problematic in urban areas.

It is important to note that wage workers in the private formal sector (the survey coverage in this paper) have median earnings that are 60% higher than for informal wage workers (Stifel, Rakotomanana, and Celada 2007). Median earnings among employees in registered non-farm enterprises earn more than two-and-a-half times more than those working in unregistered firms. Also, most workers in Madagascar have no formal education and uneducated workers are more likely to be employed in agriculture. This is because "good" jobs, i.e. non-agricultural waged employment, are found in the formal sector of the economy and access to these jobs depends crucially on educational attainment. In spite of equal access to the general workforce across gender, men have greater access to "good" jobs than women. However, Stifel, Rakotomanana, and Celada (2007) found no evidence of labor market segmentation between the private formal and informal wage sectors.

This brief description shows that the labor markets in Mauritius and Madagascar are really different. In a context where gender differences may be highly sensitive to the level of wages paid to workers, our surveys of both countries offer a unique opportunity to understand how the economic context affects the magnitude of the gender wage gap.

3 Data and descriptive statistics

3.1 The ICA surveys

The matched employer–employee data for Mauritius and Madagascar stem from the Investment Climate Assessment (ICA) surveys conducted by the World Bank in 2005 in the framework of the African RPED program. The Africa Regional Program on Enterprise Development is an ongoing research project with the overall purpose of generating business knowledge and policy advice useful to private sector manufacturing development in Sub-Saharan Africa.

These surveys are based on the notion that the workplace is the micro-data unit where labor supply and labor demand meet. In that spirit, the ICAs collect data both on the firm characteristics and on a sample of employees in each workplace. The questionnaires addressed to both employers and employees are specifically adapted for each country, but they enable cross-country comparisons as they are made up of very similar questions. In the cases of Madagascar and Mauritius, the 32 questions of the "employee" questionnaires are identical.

In Mauritius and Madagascar, the firms have been randomly selected among the population of formal establishments, with no constraint on the size of the firms. These firms belong to the manufacturing sector in Mauritius[6] and to the following 14 sectors of production in Madagascar: mining, food and beverage, tobacco, textiles, apparel, leather, wood, paper and plastics, publishing, chemicals, metals, machinery and equipment, furniture, and construction. The firm samples comprise 198 and 290 enterprises for Mauritius and Madagascar respectively. These firms have been randomly selected using a stratification based on sector, size, and localization.

In each firm, up to 10 employees have been randomly sampled following the idea advocated by Mairesse and Greenan (1999). Note that all the employees of small firms have been interviewed, while the sampling rate decreases with the size of the firms. In the Malagasy sample, there is no firm with fewer than 10 employees, while there are four in the Mauritian sample. The number of workers interviewed in Mauritius and Madagascar are respectively equal to 1,474 and 1,821. After deleting missing values, the sizes of the samples reduce to respectively 1,363 and 1,734 workers.

3.2 Description of the samples

Descriptive statistics concerning employees are in Table 25.1. The question-naires of the surveys allow us to construct identical human capital indicators for the workers in both countries. For each respondent, we compute the number of years of completed schooling, the number of years of actual experience off the current firm, and the number of years of tenure in the incumbent firm. These different covariates are then introduced into the wage regressions. We also add two demographic variables, i.e. a dummy for gender and a dummy indicating whether the individual is married or not.

The female proportion in each sample is 44 and 37% for Mauritius and Madagascar respectively. A first point worth mentioning is that the Malagasy workers are the most educated, 11.9 years on average versus 10 years. Given Madagascar's level of economic development with regard to that of Mauritius, this result could be surprising. However, Madagascar has been one of the few low-income countries to recognize early the importance of developing its educational system, and this country has made rapid progress in the devel-opment of public primary schools. Madagascar is also one of the few African countries to have achieved equal access in schooling between boys and girls, at least at low levels of the education system (World Bank 2001). This situation is clearly reflected in our data as women exhibit a higher level of education than men in Madagascar (12.3 years versus 11.6 years).[7]

Mauritian workers offset the gap in education as compared to their Malagasy counterparts against higher levels of labor market experience, both in terms of years of experience off the firm (6.2 years against 5 years) and tenure in the incumbent firm (8.8 versus 6 years). These gaps are partly explained by age difference of the workers in the two samples (36.5 against 34.6 years). For both countries, the gender experience gap is in favor of males, often reaching two years as for tenure and experience off the firm in Mauritius and for experience in Madagascar.

According to Table 25.1, the proportions of workers on top of the occu-pational distribution (owners, managers, professionals) are roughly similar across the two islands. The noticeable difference stems from a higher share of women in the category of professionals in Madagascar (with university degree or equivalent), which conforms to the previous finding of a greater education level for females in the Malagasy sample. Similarly, a higher pro-portion of male Malagasy managers is observed. In the middle of the occupational distribution, there is a higher share of skilled workers in the

Table 25.1 Descriptive statistics of the workers

Variables	Mauritius			Madagascar		
	Men	Women	All	Men	Women	All
Dependent variable: log hourly wage						
Mean	4.46	3.96	4.24	8.03	7.98	8.01
	(0.79)	(0.73)	(0.81)	(0.76)	(0.80)	(0.77)
Quartile 1	3.98	3.45	3.71	7.54	7.50	7.52
Quartile 2	4.37	3.89	4.19	7.96	7.90	7.94
Quartile 3	4.80	4.36	4.64	8.42	8.44	8.42
Individual characteristics						
Female	0.00	1.00	0.44	0.00	1.00	0.37
			(0.50)			(0.48)
Married	0.70	0.70	0.70	0.79	0.65	0.74
	(0.46)	(0.46)	(.46)	(0.41)	(0.48)	(0.44)
Years of completed education	10.15	9.85	10.02	11.63	12.34	11.89
	(3.93)	(3.45)	(3.73)	(4.63)	(4.54)	(4.61)
Years of experience off the firm	7.12	5.17	6.26	5.75	3.70	4.99
	(7.62)	(6.32)	(7.14)	(6.36)	(4.95)	(5.96)
Years of tenure in the current firm	9.99	7.39	8.85	6.26	5.70	6.05
	(9.13)	(6.58)	(8.21)	(6.36)	(6.07)	(6.26)
Occupations						
Owners (as managers)	0.02	0.01	0.01	0.01	0.01	0.01
	(0.12)	(0.09)	(0.11)	(0.08)	(0.09)	(0.08)
Employed managers	0.05	0.01	0.04	0.02	0.02	0.02
	(0.23)	(0.11)	(0.19)	(0.13)	(0.13)	(0.13)
Professionals (University Degree)	0.07	0.06	0.06	0.07	0.09	0.08
	(0.25)	(0.23)	(0.24)	(0.26)	(0.28)	(0.27)
Technicians (with diploma or other formal qualification)	0.10	0.02	0.06	0.07	0.04	0.06
	(0.30)	(0.15)	(0.25)	(0.26)	0.20	(0.24)
Skilled foremen and supervisors	0.14	0.08	0.11	0.08	0.08	0.08
	(0.35)	(0.27)	(0.32)	(0.27)	(0.27)	(0.27)
Skilled machine maintenance and repair workers	0.15	0.07	0.11	0.07	0.02	0.05
	(0.36)	(0.25)	(0.32)	(0.26)	(0.14)	(0.23)
Unskilled production workers	0.24	0.29	0.26	0.47	0.40	0.44
	(0.43)	(0.45)	(0.44)	(0.50)	(0.49)	(0.50)
Health worker, office, and sales workers	0.12	0.33	0.21	0.06	0.22	0.12
	(0.32)	(0.47)	(0.41)	(0.24)	(0.42)	(0.33)
Service workers (cleaners, guards)	0.12	0.14	0.13	0.15	0.13	0.14
	(0.32)	(0.35)	(0.33)	(0.36)	(0.34)	(0.35)
Number of observations	764	599	1,363	1,093	641	1,734

Source: ICA Madagascar and Mauritius 2005.

Note: standard deviations are in parentheses

Mauritian sample (such as technicians, foremen, and supervisors, machine maintenance and repair workers). Interestingly, men exceed women in these categories of skilled workers for both countries. Finally, unskilled production workers are prevalent in Madagascar (44% against 26%) and almost equally distributed across gender in the two islands.

We describe in Table 25.2 the main characteristics of the selected firms for Mauritius and Madagascar. The average numbers of total employees in the Malagasy and Mauritian firms amount respectively to 174 and 192 salaried workers. Similar average proportions of females in each firm are found for both countries, about 35%. More firms are owned by a woman in Madagascar, 19 versus 10%. This may affect the measure of the gender wage gap if female owners are less likely to offer lower wages to women than male ones.

While Mauritian firms display a higher share of managers and executives (10 versus 6%), the reverse pattern holds for executives (only 6% for Madagascar, 3% for Mauritius). More generally, these proportions are low as compared to those observed in developed countries. The ratio of labor costs to total costs exceeds 50% in both firm samples and is slightly higher in Madagascar (63 versus 56%), but the proportions of highly labor-intensive firms look alike (22 and 25%). Also, the share of unionized employees is similar in both firm samples (about 10%). The proportion of firms providing workers with formal training schemes is found to be higher in the Mauritian sample (58 versus 48%) and the share of exporting firms is more than twice as high in Mauritius (64%). Mauritian firms are thus more concerned with international competition on their product market.

To summarize, the firm samples are somewhat different, with particularly distinct vocation to export and sectors of activity. The Malagasy firm sample seems notably more heterogeneous. On the contrary, the two firm samples look alike regarding the personnel used, especially the firms' average number of employees and their proportion of females. It thus matters to account for firm heterogeneity in the empirical analysis.[8] As we have matched employer–employee data, we are able to control for both the characteristics of the workers and the firms. There are several ways to proceed.

A first possibility would be to include in the regressions a large set of explanatory variables related to the firm in wage equations. Another way is to control for both observed and unobserved heterogeneity at the firm level using fixed effect models, which is easy to implement with linear wage regression. This implementation is more difficult in the context of quantile regressions. We then turn to an alternative, more parsimonious approach following Muller and Nordman (2004) and Jellal, Nordman, and Wolff (2008). It consists in summarizing the main statistical information of the firms using a principal component analysis, and the different factors are then introduced as additional covariates in the quantile regressions.[9]

Table 25.2 Descriptive statistics of the firms

Variables	Mauritius			Madagascar		
	Number of observed firms for the variable	Mean	Standard deviation	Number of observed firms for the variable	Mean	Standard deviation
Total number of employees	183	174.191	424.886	281	191.911	446.067
Share of female employees	182	0.375	0.299	281	0.332	0.310
Principal owner is female (1 if yes)	189	0.101	0.302	281	0.196	0.397
Share of managers/executives in the permanent employees	173	0.099	0.169	270	0.057	0.054
Share of executives in the permanent employees	170	0.029	0.054	269	0.059	0.068
Share of unionized employees	180	0.114	0.242	263	0.095	0.226
Labor intensity (labor costs/total costs)	149	0.560	3.767	228	0.629	6.617
Highly labor intensive firms (1 if labor costs > 75% total costs)	189	0.254	0.436	281	0.217	0.413
Firm provided (on- or off-the-job) formal training (1 if yes)	189	0.587	0.494	281	0.484	0.501
Exporting firm (1 if yes)	189	0.640	0.481	281	0.302	0.460
Sector dummies						
Mining				281	0.007	0.084
Food and beverages				281	0.157	0.364
Tobacco				281	0.014	0.119
Textiles				281	0.103	0.305
Apparel				281	0.174	0.380
Leather				281	0.021	0.145
Wood				281	0.132	0.339
Paper and plastics				281	0.064	0.245
Publishing				281	0.110	0.314
Chemicals				281	0.060	0.239
Metals				281	0.043	0.203
Machinery and equipment				281	0.025	0.156
Furniture				281	0.085	0.280
Construction				281	0.004	0.060

Source: ICA Madagascar and Mauritius 2005.

3.3 How large are gender wage differences?

Before turning to the econometric analysis, we begin with a descriptive analysis of the wage distributions by gender in both countries. As shown in Table 25.1, we evidence higher wages for men in the two countries. Our measure of earnings is based on hourly wage. While the gap is important in Mauritius at the mean point of the worker sample (the difference in log wages between men and women reaches 50 percentage points of log), the gender gap seems rather insignificant in the case of Madagascar. This result holds true for that country across the three different wage quartiles considered, while the gap diminishes as we move up from the first to the third quartile in Mauritius (0.53 log points at the first quartile, 0.48 at the second quartile, and 0.44 at the third quartile).

In Figure 25.1, we plot the value of the gender wage gap throughout the wage distribution. The gap is obtained by estimating quantile regressions at each percentile with only the female dummy as covariate. The different coefficient estimates for the gender dummy are then identical to the statistical log wage gaps.

Clearly, we obtain very different profiles for the two countries and the corresponding confidence intervals do not overlap. In Madagascar, the gap remains almost constant along the wage distribution and its magnitude is very low. We even observe that women slightly outdo men in earnings in the upper part of the distribution (at least around the third quartile). By contrast, for Mauritius, we find that the gender gap is much higher, comprised of between 40 and 50% along the wage distribution. Nevertheless, the gender profile is somewhat striking. In particular, the gender wage gap is slightly

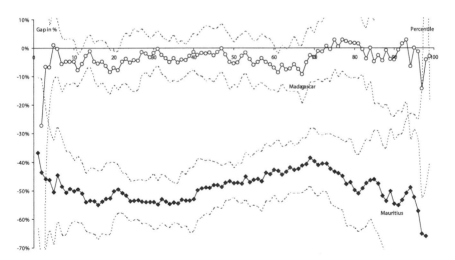

Figure 25.1 The gender gap in Mauritius and Madagascar Islands.

Source: ICA Madagascar and Mauritius 2005.

Note: The dotted lines correspond to confidence intervals at 95%.

decreasing from the 30th to the 70th percentile and then strongly increasing, especially above the 90th percentile.

Albeit preliminary, these findings suggest that the gender wage gap observed in the formal sectors of Mauritius and Madagascar is very different. To further understand the factors that influence the magnitude of this gender gap, we turn in the next section to an econometric analysis using OLS, fixed effects, and quantile regression models. We also rely on decomposition methods to examine whether the gender wage gap stems from differences in endowments between men and women or from differences in the returns to these characteristics.

4 Econometric results

4.1 The magnitude of the gender wage gap

We begin our empirical analysis by assessing the magnitude of the gender wage gap in both countries at the mean wage level. For that purpose, we turn to basic OLS regressions with the log hourly wage as dependent variable. The different covariates introduced into the regressions are respectively marital status, the completed years of education, years of experience off the firm, and years of tenure in the firm.[10] For the three last explanatory variables, we rely on quadratic profiles. To account for gender differences, we add a gender dummy variable, so that the model we estimate is (i and j as subscripts standing respectively for the employee and the firm):

$$\ln w_{ji} = \beta X_{ji} + \gamma F_{ji} + \varepsilon_{ji} \tag{1}$$

where $\ln w_{ji}$ the log hourly wage, X_{ji} the set of covariates, F_{ji} the gender dummy variable, β and γ are parameters to be estimated, and ε_{ji} is a residual. Since we have several employees per firm in many cases, we obtain robust standard errors using a clustering correction at the firm level. As we account for both male and female workers when estimating model (1), this means that the returns to the different explanatory variables are supposed not to be gender-specific. The relevance of this assumption is tested later on.

The OLS estimates are respectively reported in columns (1) for Mauritius and (5) for Madagascar of Table 25.3. In Mauritius, we find a negative coefficient for the gender dummy variable, significant at the 1% level. On average, wages received by women in Mauritian firms are 35.3% lower than wages earned by men. The gender gap is then large and may stem from discrimination between male and female employees. The gender pattern is really different in Madagascar. Although the coefficient associated to the gender dummy is negative, its magnitude is much lower and insignificant. Thus, male workers do not outdo female workers in earnings in these Malagasy firms.

This difference between both Islands may lie in the composition of occupations, which are not controlled for in columns (1) and (5). A difficulty with

Table 25.3 Linear regressions of the log hourly wage rate

Variables	Mauritius				Madagascar			
	(1)	(2)	(3)	(4)	(5)	(6)	(7)	(8)
Constant	3.461***	3.692***	3.319***	3.480***	7.065***	7.033***	7.158***	7.240***
	(32.29)	(35.52)	(33.95)	(36.56)	(52.47)	(52.95)	(82.10)	(86.19)
Female	-0.353***	-0.397***	-0.227***	-0.223***	-0.056	-0.098**	0.011	-0.047
	(7.98)	(9.26)	(7.04)	(7.08)	(1.29)	(2.19)	(0.36)	(1.59)
Married	0.084**	0.070*	0.125***	0.107***	0.094**	0.118***	0.040	0.052*
	(1.98)	(1.74)	(3.67)	(3.43)	(2.21)	(2.82)	(1.26)	(1.79)
Years of completed schooling	-0.033*	-0.054***	-0.009	-00.027*	0.047***	0.028*	0.041***	0.015
	(1.72)	(3.28)	(0.57)	(1.71)	(2.18)	(1.67)	(3.35)	(1.33)
(Years of completed schooling)^2/100	0.620***	0.494***	0.501***	0.359***	0.096	0.050	0.087*	0.063
	(6.03)	(5.67)	(6.62)	(4.95)	(1.12)	(0.73)	(1.94)	(1.53)
Years of experience off the firm	0.028***	0.020**	0.017***	0.010**	0.003	0.005	0.004	0.004
	(3.26)	(2.46)	(3.06)	(2.04)	(0.36)	(0.76)	(0.68)	(0.68)
(Years of experience off the firm)^2/100	-0.052	-0.038	-0.005	0.002	0.030	0.010	0.028	0.017
	(1.46)	(1.10)	(0.25)	(0.09)	(0.93)	(0.34)	(1.17)	(0.76)
Years of tenure in the current firm	0.056***	0.050***	0.056***	0.048***	0.034***	0.031***	0.033***	0.027***
	(7.25)	(6.90)	(10.68)	(9.80)	(3.11)	(2.87)	(4.63)	(4.17)
(Years of tenure in the current firm)^2/100	-0.091***	-0.084***	-0.098***	-0.089***	-0.064	-0.072**	-0.056**	-0.059**
	(3.72)	(3.72)	(6.49)	(6.36)	(1.62)	(1.98)	(2.20)	(2.57)
Dummies for occupation	NO	YES	NO	YES	NO	YES	NO	YES
Firm fixed effects	NO	NO	YES	YES	NO	NO	YES	YES
Observations	1363	1363	1363	1363	1734	1734	1734	1734
R-squared	0.36	0.43	0.38	0.48	0.21	0.32	0.22	0.38

Source: ICA Madagascar and Mauritius 2005.

Note: Significance levels are respectively equal to 1% (***), 5% (**) and 10% (*).

occupations is that they may be endogenous if employers discriminate between male and female workers on the basis of the type of job they do. Despite this shortcoming, we add in columns (2) and (6) a set of nine dummy variables related to occupations. Both in Mauritius and Madagascar, we note a slight increase (in absolute value) of the gender estimate. The gender wage gap is now around 40% in the former island, while it is around 10% in the latter. The point of interest here is that the gender term is now significant in Madagascar. An interpretation of this finding is that gender discrimination does not necessarily lead to differences in wage in Madagascar, but it seems more closely related to the type of job held by male and female workers.

In the above linear models, we only include individual characteristics. In so doing, we neglect the role of heterogeneity at the firm level. This is problematic as there may exist some factors that influence the wages of men and women in a different way. A female manager may, for instance, be more reluctant to give lower wages to women than a male boss. Similarly, it may be that the gender wage gap arises as a result of gender-specific sorting of workers across firms that pay different wages. As we have matched employer–employee data, we can easily control for such observed and unobserved heterogeneity by estimating fixed effect models. The corresponding specification becomes:

$$\ln w_{ji} = \beta X_{ji} + \gamma F_{ji} + \delta_j + \varepsilon_{ji} \tag{2}$$

where δ_j is a firm fixed effect. In the fixed effect formulation, the firms' residuals are supposed to be correlated with the exogenous explanatory variables X_{ji}.[11] By definition, the work place is the same for all the workers belonging to a given firm. All the firm characteristics, which are by definition constant for all the workers in a same place, are picked up by the fixed effect.

The fixed effect estimates are in columns (3) and (7) of Table 25.3. Interestingly, accounting for firm heterogeneity strongly reduces the magnitude of the gender wage gap. In Mauritius, it now amounts to 22.7%, while it was around 35% with a regression based on employees' characteristics only. That the gap is divided by almost two suggests that working with individual data would lead to a significant over-estimation of the adjusted gender wage gap. In Madagascar, the gender gap is no longer negative but, again, it turns out to be insignificant. Finally, these results are fairly robust to the inclusion of occupational dummies (columns (4) and (8) of Table 25.3). Such controls do not affect the gender gap in Mauritius (around 22%), while the fixed effect specification with occupations leads to a gender gap of around 5%, hardly significant. For Mauritius, and to a lesser extent for Madagascar, this suggests that most occupational heterogeneity across gender may be captured at the firm level since adding dummies for occupation does not affect the gender dummy coefficient in a firm fixed effect model.

Let us briefly discuss the role of the other covariates. As shown in Table 25.3, married employees tend to receive slightly higher hourly wages. The most important factor is undoubtedly education. As evidenced in other studies related to the determinants of wages in Africa (see Schultz 2004; Söderbom et al. 2006; Kuepie, Nordman, and Roubaud 2009), we find a convex profile for the years of completed schooling. Years of experience off the firm have a positive influence on the hourly wage rate, but this effect is only significant in Mauritius. Finally, years of tenure in the current firm follow an expected concave profile.

4.2 The role of the firm in the gender earnings gap

Our results suggest that gender matters to understand differences in wages (at least in Mauritius), but that firm effects are also important. To assess the relative impact of these various explanatory factors, we first follow the regression-based decomposition approach proposed in Fields (2004). The explained portion of the regression is decomposed into weights for each of the regressors. From the regression $\ln w = \beta X + \gamma F + \varepsilon$, and assuming that there are K regressors in X indexed by indexed by k (with $k = 1, \ldots, K$), then the variance of w can be decomposed such as:

$$\operatorname{var}(\ln w) = \sum_k \operatorname{cov}(\beta_k X_k, \ln w) + \operatorname{cov}(\gamma F, \ln w) + \operatorname{cov}(\varepsilon, \ln w). \qquad (3)$$

Let us define $s(X_k) = \operatorname{cov}(\beta_k X_k, \ln w)/\operatorname{var}(\ln w)$, $s(F) = \operatorname{cov}(\gamma F, \ln w)/\operatorname{var}(\ln w)$ and $s(\varepsilon) = \operatorname{cov}(\varepsilon, \ln w)/\operatorname{var}(\ln w)$. It follows that:

$$\sum_k s(X_k) + s(F) + s(\varepsilon) = 100\% \qquad (4)$$

The first two terms on the left-hand side of (4) will sum exactly to the R-squared, meaning that the s terms give the weights of each of the regressor.

Table 25.4 presents the corresponding decomposition results. In columns (1) and (3), the weights are obtained from coefficients of OLS regressions without controls for firm characteristics. In Mauritius, we learn that 18.5% of the variation in the log wages is explained by gender while the contribution of gender only amounts to 0.5% in Madagascar. The other covariates indicate that marital status and years of experience off the firm account for a very low proportion of what is explained, less than 5%. In Mauritius, the largest percentage contribution to hourly wages is made by education (51.8%). This influential role of education is even more pronounced in Madagascar, where it amounts to 84%.

Decomposition results are different once firm heterogeneity is controlled for. To obtain the results reported in columns (2) and (4), we have estimated OLS regressions with firm dummy variables, which is equivalent to the fixed

Table 25.4 Decomposition analysis of the factors contributing to the log wage (in %)

Variables	Mauritius		Madagascar	
	(1) No firm effects	*(2) Fixed effects*	*(3) No firm effects*	*(4) Fixed effects*
Female	18.52	6.18	0.52	0.00
Married	1.71	1.32	2.32	0.32
Years of completed education	51.84	25.91	83.98	23.61
Years of experience off the firm	3.40	1.59	1.33	0.45
Years of tenure in the current firm	24.52	11.95	11.85	3.92
Fixed effects		53.05		71.70
Total	100.0	100.0	100.0	100.0

Source: ICA Madagascar and Mauritius 2005.

effects regressions. We find that these firm fixed effects account for a large proportion of what is explained. Their weight is 53% in Mauritius, and even 71.7% in Madagascar. At the same time, inclusion of fixed effects strongly reduces the importance of gender in explaining variation in wages. The weight of the gender dummy is now three times lower in Mauritius, 6.2% instead of 18.5%, and is null in Madagascar. The contribution of education in both countries is also strongly reduced with fixed effects.

How, then, can we explain these results? An explanation could be related to the presence of gender segregation across firms. If there exist in a country high-paying firms that hire more men than women and at the same time low-paying firms hiring more women than men, then firms' characteristics would deeply influence the gender differences in wage. One thus would expect a lower wage gap once firm heterogeneity is controlled for. The results reported in Table 3 and 4 suggest that gender segregation is likely to be at work, as the magnitude of the gender effect is significantly reduced in the fixed effects regressions.

It thus matters to know whether the role of the firm is still so important once the issue of gender segregation is taken into account. To answer this question properly, we choose to rely on Oaxaca–Blinder decompositions. Let us first neglect the role of firm characteristics. Let $\ln w^H$ and $\ln w^F$ be the log hourly wage of men and women respectively. From separate regressions $\ln w^H = \beta^H X^H + \varepsilon^H$ and $\ln w^F = \beta^F X^F + \varepsilon^F$ performed on the male and female samples, we deduce that the gender wage gap is $\ln w^H - \ln w^F = \beta^H X^H - \beta^F X^F + \varepsilon^H - \varepsilon^F$. This gap can be decomposed in the following way (Oaxaca and Ramson 1994)[12]:

$$\ln w^H - \ln w^F = \beta^H (X^H - X^F) + (\beta^H - \beta^F)X^F + (\varepsilon^H - \varepsilon^F) \tag{5}$$

In (5), the first term on the right-hand side $\beta^H (X^H - X^F)$ is due to differences in labor market characteristics between men and women. It is usually called endowment effects or the explained part of the gender wage gap. The second term $(\beta^H - \beta^F)X^F$ is due to the difference in the price that the market pays to male and female workers for their personal characteristics, i.e. price effects. This basic Oaxaca–Blinder decomposition can easily be extended to account for firm fixed effects. Following Meng (2004), we deduce from $\ln w^H = \beta^H X^H + \delta^H + \varepsilon^H$ and $\ln w^F = \beta^F X^F + \delta^F + \varepsilon^F$ that:

$$\ln w^H - \ln w^F = \beta^H (X^H - X^F) + (\beta^H - \beta^F) X^F + (\delta^H - \delta^F) + (\varepsilon^H - \varepsilon^F) \quad (6)$$

On the right-hand side of (6), the first two terms are respectively the endowment and price effects. The third term $(\delta^H - \delta^F)$ is the portion of the gender gap that is due to firms paying different premia to the male and female employees.[13] Although (6) is informative about firm effects, it does not account for the possibility of gender segregation across firms. To control for gender segregation, we estimate gender-specific earnings equations with both individual and firm covariates, along with the proportion of female workers measured at the firm level. In so doing, we then purge the effect of the gender employment ratio and obtain estimated wages net of gender segregation across firms. These adjusted wages are subsequently used for the decomposition (6).

Results from various decompositions using linear regressions are in Table 25.5. As a benchmark, we indicate in columns (1) and (4) the standard Oaxaca–Blinder decompositions using OLS regressions. We again find a large gender wage gap in Mauritius, as it amounts to 36.9%. Interestingly, the gender gap in this country is mainly due to differences in the returns to the labor market characteristics. Endowments effects account for about 11.8 points of percentage of the total gender gap, the rest being due to discrimination. Endowed with the same characteristics, female employees would earn on average 25.1% less than male employees. The gender gap is strongly reduced in Madagascar. With the adjusted wages and estimates of

Table 25.5 Decomposition of the gender wage gap using OLS and fixed effects regression

Effects	Mauritius			Madagascar		
	OLS	Fixed effects		OLS	Fixed effects	
	(1)	(2)	(3)	(4)	(5)	(6)
Endowments effects	0.118	0.157	0.200	0.032	0.013	0.013
Price effects	0.252	0.254	0.276	−0.106	−0.101	0.042
Firm effects		−0.010	−0.061		0.018	−0.009
Total difference	0.369	0.369	0.415	−0.074	−0.074	0.066

Source: ICA Madagascar and Mauritius 2005.

Note: Gender segregation across firms is corrected only in models (1), (2), (4), and (5).

gender-specific regressions, we now find that women earn slightly more than men (7.4%).

Both in Mauritius and in Madagascar, we find little impact of the characteristics of the firm. As shown in columns (2) and (5) of Table 25.5, the weights attached to the firm effects are very low. Results from a decomposition based on fixed effect regressions indicate for instance that the endowment effects account for 15.7 points, the price effects for 25.4 points and the firm effects for 1 point in Mauritius. Then, the decomposition of the fixed effects model shows that Mauritian firms tend to narrow the gender earnings gap. Indeed, the negative sign on the firm effects component indicates that firms pay, on average, a higher premium to their female employees than they do to their male workers. The gender gap would then have been higher without this narrowing influence of the firm. In Madagascar, the pattern is reversed as firms seem to increase the gender earnings gap. Nevertheless, the role of the firms remains extremely low in comparison with the role of individual characteristics.

A last finding is about gender segregation across firms. In columns (3) and (6), we perform the same decomposition using fixed effect regressions, but do not adjust the hourly wage. As expected, the gender gap is now higher in Mauritius, around 41.5% instead of 36.9% (and also in Madagascar). This finding indicates that gender segregation across firms is an explanation of the wage gap observed in the two countries, such that high-paying and low-paying firms tend to hire gender-specific employees disproportionately.

4.3 Does the gender wage gap vary along the wage distribution?

The ICA surveys indicate that wages are significantly different for men and women, at least in Mauritius. That we do not observe any gender wage gap for Madagascar using OLS regressions does not necessarily mean that there is no discrimination against women on the labor market. Indeed, as evidenced by Albrecht, Björklund, and Vroman (2003), the gender gap is unlikely to remain constant throughout the log wage distribution. Then, we now turn to quantile regressions that allow us to investigate the magnitude of the gender wage gap along the wage distribution.

Quantile wage regressions consider specific parts of the conditional distribution of the hourly wage and indicate the influence of the different explanatory variables on wages respectively at the bottom, at the median and at the top of the log hourly wage distribution (Koenker and Hallock, 2001). Using our previous notation, the model that we seek to estimate is:

$$q_\theta(\ln w_{ji}) = \beta(\theta)\, X_{ji} + \gamma(\theta)\, F_{ji} \qquad (7)$$

where $q_\theta(\ln w_{ji})$ is the θth conditional quantile of the log hourly wage.[14] The set of coefficients $\beta(\theta)$ provides the estimated rates of return to the different covariates (gender being excluded) at the θth quantile of the log wage distribution and the coefficient $\gamma(\theta)$ measures the intercept shift due to gender differences. If there is a glass ceiling in a given country, then a huge rise in the estimate associated with the gender dummy is expected as higher percentiles of the log hourly wage are considered. Results from these different quantile regressions based on the male-female pooled samples are in Table 25.6.

Let us first focus on the results for Mauritius. In panel (1), we only control for gender, marital status, education, experience off the firm, and years of tenure in the firm. We find that the magnitude of the gender wage gap does not remain constant along the wage distribution. For instance, the gender wage gap amounts to 32% at the first decile, around 35% at the median, 37% at the third quartile, and 38% at the ninth decile. Hence, the gap is increasing throughout the conditional wage distribution, but the acceleration is not so sharp in the upper part of the distribution. In comparison, the mean gap was around 35%. With a rise of only three points when moving from the median to the ninth decile, it seems hazardous to interpret these findings as evidence of a glass ceiling effect.[15]

We run several additional specifications to further investigate the magnitude of the gender wage gap. First, as firm characteristics may play a role, we add a set of firm factors obtained through a Principal Component Analysis (PCA) into the quantile regressions. According to the estimates reported in panel (2) of Table 25.6, the role of these firm factors varies across the distribution. Adding firm factors leads to a slight increase in the magnitude of the gender gap, but only in the lower and the upper parts of the wage distribution. In panels (3) and (4), we perform the same regressions, but with controls for occupations in the firm. In that case, we observe much more differences in the magnitude of the gender wage gap. For instance, it is equal to 34.2% at the first decile, and 47.8% at the ninth decile. But again, the difficulty is to know whether occupations within the firm are not subject to gender discrimination themselves.

We then estimate the same regressions using the data from Madagascar. Two comments are in order. First, when the regression only includes the basic control variables, there is no evidence of gender differences in wage. The estimate associated to the gender dummy remains insignificantly different from zero along the different percentiles of the conditional wage distribution. Second, accounting for occupational dummies and firm factors matters when measuring the gender gap. As shown in panels (7), (8), and (9), the gender gap appears to be larger and significant in the upper part of the distribution. For instance, once occupations and firm factors are controlled for, the gender gap amounts to 9% at the median, but it is around 16% at the third quartile and ninth decile.

It is also interesting to consider the issue of gender segregation across firms. In panels (5) and (10), we re-estimate the quantile wage regressions with the adjusted log hourly wage as the dependent variable (see Section 4.2). If women are more likely to work in low-paying jobs, then controlling for gender segregation should reduce the magnitude of the gender gap especially

Table 25.6 Quantile regressions of the log hourly wage rate

Percentile	10th	25th	50th	75th	90th	Mean (OLS)
Mauritius Island						
(1): Basic control variable	-0.320***	-0.359***	-0.346***	-0.368***	-0.381***	-0.353***
	(5.97)	(8.47)	(10.15)	(7.24)	(4.80)	(7.98)
(2): (1) + firm factors	-0.347***	-0.299***	-0.312***	-0.350***	-0.428***	-0.349***
	(5.48)	(6.63)	(6.98)	(6.55)	(5.70)	(7.54)
(3): (1) + occupation	-0.342***	-0.365***	-0.406***	-0.430***	-0.478***	-0.397***
	(5.48)	(7.79)	(9.31)	(8.88)	(5.64)	(9.26)
(4): (3) + firm factors	-0.324***	-0.332***	-0.399***	-0.409***	-0.454***	-0.393***
	(4.65)	(5.85)	(10.77)	(7.23)	(5.82)	(8.29)
(5): (1) + control for gender segregation across firms	-0.245***	-0.251***	-0.238***	-0.209***	-0.181***	-0.266***
	(10.34)	(19.12)	(11.84)	(10.51)	(6.33)	(14.90)
Madagascar Island						
(6): Basic control variable	-0.048	-0.036	-0.004	-0.061	0.014	-0.056
	(1.43)	(0.96)	(0.09)	(1.19)	(0.17)	(1.29)
(7): (6) + firm factors	-0.026	-0.013	-0.078*	-0.093**	-0.015	-0.078*
	(0.59)	(0.34)	(1.86)	(1.98)	(0.22)	(1.85)
(8): (6) + occupation	-0.049	-0.080**	-0.054	-0.124***	-0.130*	-0.098**
	(1.40)	(2.11)	(1.22)	(2.99)	(1.77)	(2.19)
(9): (8) + firm factors	-0.043	-0.045	-0.088**	-0.168***	-0.154**	-0.115***
	(1.21)	(1.07)	(2.46)	(3.57)	(2.57)	(2.64)
(10): (1) + control for gender segregation across firms	0.032*	0.062***	0.097***	0.122***	0.136***	0.097***
	(1.77)	(4.55)	(4.65)	(3.62)	(6.30)	(5.63)

Source: ICA Madagascar and Mauritius 2005.

Note: Gender segregation across firms is corrected in models (5) and (10). Significance levels are respectively equal to 1% (***), 5% (**) and 10% (*).

in the upper part of the distribution. Our findings for Mauritius show that gender segregation really matters for high-paid occupations since the gender gap obtained with the adjusted wage is now slightly lower at the top than at the bottom of the wage distribution. While the gap is equal to 25 points at the first decile, it is around 21 points at the third quartile and 18% at the ninth decile. The situation is even "worse" in Madagascar. We now evidence a positive gender gap in the Malagasy firms, meaning that women tend to earn slightly more than men once we control for the fact that women are more likely to be over-represented in low-pay firms.[16]

Finally, we perform a quantile decomposition to know whether differentiated returns to labor market characteristics matter more on top of the wage distribution. We follow the method described in Machado and Mata (2005) and estimate a set of 300 randomly chosen quantile regressions. We perform the decomposition twice, once with the log hourly wage measured from the survey and once with the adjusted wage. These decompositions are reported in Table 25.7. Our results are twofold.

First, we find that when gender segregation across firms is not taken into account, the gender wage gap is mainly due to differences in coefficients rather than differences in characteristics. In Mauritius, the discrimination effect amounts to around 40% above the third quartile, differences in characteristics being much lower (as is the case in Madagascar). Second, the role of individual labor market characteristics becomes more important in the decomposition once we pick up the effect of gender segregation across firms. In Mauritius, the weight of differences in characteristics in the explanation of the gender gap at the first decile is more than one quarter, while it was less than 10% without control for gender segregation. Nevertheless, in Madagascar, the gap remains mainly explained by differences in the returns to labor market characteristics.

5 Concluding comments

Based on the matched employer–employee ICA surveys, our comparative analysis of the gender wage gap clearly highlights contrasted situations in Mauritius and Madagascar. Before turning to an explanation of these differences, let us briefly summarize our main findings.

First, wages received by women in Mauritian firms are on average 35% lower than wages earned by men. Conversely, in Madagascar, the effect of the gender dummy in OLS regressions is very low and insignificant. Adding controls for occupations in the regressions leads to an increase in the gender dummy coefficients in both countries. This suggests that gender discrimination practices will not necessarily be reflected in differences in wages, but they may also arise as a result of the existence of gender-specific occupations. This is what Bourdieu (1998) called "male domination", a phenomenon which prevents women from having access to certain well-paid segments or professions.

Table 25.7 Quantile decomposition of the gender wage gap

Decomposition		Mauritius		Madagascar	
		No gender segregation accounted for	With gender segregation accounted for	No gender segregation accounted for	With gender segregation accounted for
Machado-Mata decomposition					
Percentile 10th	Difference in characteristics	−0.048	−0.113	−0.008	−0.014
	Difference in coefficients	−0.382	−0.282	−0.050	0.043
	Total difference	−0.430	−0.395	−0.058	0.029
Percentile 25th	Difference in characteristics	−0.089	−0.113	0.012	−0.018
	Difference in coefficients	−0.326	−0.280	−0.049	0.061
	Total difference	−0.416	−0.393	−0.037	0.044
Percentile 50th	Difference in characteristics	−0.466	−0.125	0.001	−0.026
	Difference in coefficients	−0.333	−0.283	−0.019	0.103
	Total difference	−0.467	−0.408	−0.018	0.077
Percentile 75th	Difference in characteristics	−0.150	−0.130	0.005	−0.017
	Difference in coefficients	−0.386	−0.271	−0.048	0.130
	Total difference	−0.536	−0.391	−0.043	0.113
Percentile 90th	Difference in characteristics	−0.160	−0.114	0.017	−0.011
	Difference in coefficients	−0.462	−0.264	−0.035	0.142
	Total difference	−0.622	−0.378	−0.018	0.131

Source: ICA Madagascar and Mauritius 2005.

Second, accounting for firm heterogeneity in the wage regressions through the use of firm fixed effects strongly reduces the magnitude of the gender wage gap, a finding also observed in developed countries (Meng 2004). In fact, insights from regression-based decompositions of wages indicate that firm effects account for a large proportion of what is explained in wage differentials across workers. This may be the result of gender-specific sorting of workers across firms that pay different wages, i.e. the existence of high–paying firms for men and low–paying firms for women. Interestingly, gender segregation across firms is indeed at work in Mauritius and Madagascar. The use of adjusted wages, net of the effect of the firm-specific gender employment ratio, reveals that the role of the firms is weak in comparison with that of individual characteristics.

Third, it is difficult to evidence a gender wage pattern consistent with the glass ceiling phenomenon recently observed in developed countries. The gender gap remains almost flat in both islands across the wage distribution, at least when occupations or firms characteristics are not controlled for in the quantile regressions. Furthermore, results from wage decompositions at different quantiles show that, at the top of the distribution, the gender wage gap is mainly explained by differences in returns to endowments rather than by differences in these mean characteristics.

This comparative study leads to two main conclusions with respect to the measurement of the gender gap in African countries. A first point is that there seems to be much more heterogeneity with regard to the situation of women in African labor markets than in developed countries. For instance, the gender gap is significant in Mauritius and is not in Madagascar, and there is no clear glass ceiling effect in these islands contrary to what is observed in Morocco (Nordman and Wolff 2009). How can we explain the difference between the two selected islands? From our perspective, it seems that the gender differences in wages may stem from the differentiated level of economic development of these countries. In Madagascar, wages remain much lower than in Mauritius and this certainly prevents employers from paying some kind of discriminating premium according to gender. At the same time, the higher gender wage gap observed in Mauritius may be the result of the emergence of more capital-intensive sectors that offer higher wages, in particular if these sectors mainly turn to a male workforce.

This possibility is clearly linked to our second result, which concerns the role of gender segregation across firms when explaining the gender wage gap. According to our regressions, firms' characteristics are important, but this is mainly due to the fact that men are more likely to be hired in firms paying high wages and women in firms paying low wages. This means that a close look at the hiring process in African firms is needed. Unfortunately, such empirical analysis cannot be conducted with cross-sectional matched employer–employee data.[17] It would then be useful to estimate the magnitude of the gender wage gap using OLS and quantile regressions in a setting where selectivity issues of employees would be controlled for. Detailed surveys on the labor force in African countries may undoubtedly help towards a better understanding of the selection of female employees in paid jobs, a topic that we leave for future research.

Notes

* We would like to thank the participants at the University of Michigan—Cornell University Labor Conference 2007 in Ann Arbor for helpful suggestions on a related paper that stimulated the preparation of this research. The usual disclaimer applies.
1 For a review of the literature on the glass ceiling effect, see Barnet-Verzat and Wolff (2008).
2 Note also that the decrease in gender inequalities is one of the Millennium Development Goals.
3 The NRB issues remuneration orders for more than 90% of the workforce in the private sector.
4 *Enquêtes Périodiques auprès des Ménages* (see Stifel, Rakotomanana, and Celada 2007; Nordman Rakotomanana, and Robilliard 2009).
5 This is in contrast to the period 1997–2001 where the small poverty decline was mainly driven by economic improvement in towns.
6 At the time we write this paper, the ICA reports for these two countries have not been made available by the World Bank yet (except World Bank, 2006). Unfortunately, for Mauritius, we could not obtain more precise branch identification in the data set we have at hand. This is not an important drawback in our study as we can control for the firms' characteristics in a very precise way thanks to the availability of the firm level data.
7 In Mauritius, the education gap is hardly in favor of men (10.1 against 9.8 years).
8 However, as we only have cross-sectional data, controlling for unobserved heterogeneity at the worker level is impossible.
9 More specifically, we use a PCA including a wide range of firm characteristics to summarize the information about the surveyed firms. In a PCA, a set of variables is transformed into orthogonal components, which are linear combinations of the variables and have maximum variance subject to being uncorrelated with one another. We use 15 components (called firm factors) as they account for a large proportion of the total variance of the original variables. These factors are then used to summarize the original data. As long as the computed factors account for most of the firm heterogeneity bias, this approach allows us to obtain consistent estimates close to those of the fixed effect estimates.
10 We choose to use actual experience off the firm instead of the years of potential experience as the measurement of potential experience may lead to gender-specific measurement errors (the latter being more likely for women). See the results of using potential versus actual experience in Nordman and Roubaud (2009) for the case of Madagascar.
11 Nevertheless, it could be argued that the firm effects are not correlated to the explanatory variables (exogeneity assumption). We have then estimated random effect models and performed Hausman tests. For both countries, we find that the fixed effect specification (endogeneity assumption) is the most appropriate one.
12 In (5), the chosen counterfactual distribution is female workers paid as men.
13 The firm specific premium paid to the employee is given by the corresponding firm fixed effect (Meng 2004).
14 In a quantile regression, the distribution of the error term is left unspecified. The quantile regression method provides robust estimates, particularly for mis-specification errors related to non-normality and heteroskedasticity.

15 We also have a look at the confidence intervals associated to the gender dummy variable and find that these intervals overlap when considering two succeeding deciles.
16 All these results remain valid when we add firm factors and occupational dummies in the regression. In Madagascar, the gender wage gap is positive and comprised between 9 and 12 points of percentage. In Mauritius, the gap is again slightly lower in the upper part of the wage distribution.
17 By definition, we only have information on the workers currently employed in the firms.

References

Albrecht, J., A. Björklund, and S. Vroman (2003) "Is there a Glass Ceiling in Sweden?" *Journal of Labor Economics* 21: 145–77.

Barnet-Verzat, C. and F. C. Wolff (2008) "Gender Wage Gap and the Glass Ceiling Effect: A firm-level investigation", *International Journal of Manpower*, 29: 486–502.

Blau, F. and L. Kahn (2000) "Gender Differences in Pay." *Journal of Economic Perspectives* 14: 75–99.

Bourdieu, P. (1998) *La domination masculine*. Paris: Seuil.

Cling, J.-P., M. Razafindrakoto, and F. Roubaud (2005) "Export Processing Zones in Madagascar: a success story under threat?" *World Development* 33: 785–803.

De la Rica, S., J. J. Dolado, and V. Llorens (2008) "Ceilings or Floors? Gender wage gaps by education in Spain." *Journal of Population Economics*. 21: 751–776.

English, P. (2002) "Mauritius—Reigniting the Engines of Growth: a teaching case study. Vol I and II." Working Paper 28619. Washington: The World Bank Institute.

Fafchamps, M., M. Söderbom, and N. Benhassine (2006) "Job Sorting in African Labor Markets." CSAE working paper, WPS/2006-02. University of Oxford.

Fields, G. (2004) "Regression-Based Decompositions: A new tool for managerial decision-making." Mimeo. Cornell University.

Jellal, M., C. J. Nordman, and F. C. Wolff (2008) "Evidence on the Glass Ceiling in France using Matched Worker-firm Data." *Applied Economics*. 40: 3233–3250.

Koenker, R. and K. Hallock (2001) "Quantile Regression." *Journal of Economic Perspectives* 15: 143–56.

Kuepie, M., C. J. Nordman, and F. Roubaud (2009) "Education and Earnings in Urban West Africa." *Journal of Comparative Economics.* Forthcoming.

Machado, J. A. and J. Mata (2005) "Counterfactual Decomposition of Changes in Wage Distributions Using Quantile Regression." *Journal of Applied Econometrics*. 20: 445–65.

Mairesse, J. and N. Greenan (1999) "Using Employee Level Data in a Firm Level Econometric Study." NBER working paper 7028.

Meng, X. (2004) "Gender Earnings Gap: The role of firm specific effects." *Labour Economics* 11: 555–73.

Muller, C. and C. J. Nordman (2004) "Which Human Capital Matters for Rich and Poor's Wages? Evidence from matched worker-firm data from Tunisia. CREDIT research paper 04/08, University of Nottingham.

Mwabu, G. and T. P. Schultz (1996) "Education Returns across Quantiles of the Wage Function." *American Economic Review* 86: 335–9.

Nordman, C. J. and F. Roubaud (2009) "Reassessing the Gender Wage Gap in Madagascar: Does Labor Force Attachment Really Matter?" Economic Development and Cultural Change, 57(4), July, forthcoming.

—— and F.C. Wolff (2009) Forthcoming in "Journal of African Economies".

—— , F. H. Rakotomanana, and A. S. Robilliard (2009) "Gender Disparities in the Malagasy Labor Market." In *Gender Disparities in Africa's Labor Markets*. World Bank, forthcoming.

Oaxaca, R. L. and M. R. Ramson (1994) "Identification and the Decomposition of Wage Differentials." *Journal of Econometrics* 61: 5–21.

Said, M. (2003) "The Distribution of Gender and Public Pay Sector Premia: Evidence from the Egyptian organized sector." School of Oriental and African Studies working paper 132. London: University of London.

Schultz, T. P. (2004) "Evidence of Returns to Schooling in Africa from Household Surveys: Monitoring and restructuring the market for education." *Journal of African Economies*. 13: 95–148.

Söderbom, M., F. Teal, A. Wambugu, and G. Kahyarara (2006) "Dynamics of Returns to Education in Kenyan and Tanzanian Manufacturing." *Oxford Bulletin of Economics and Statistics*. 68: 261–88.

Stifel D., F. H. Rakotomanana, and E. Celada (2007) "Assessing Labor Market Conditions in Madagascar, 2001–2005." Mimeo. Antananarivo: World Bank.

Weichselbaumer, D. and R. Winter-Ebmer (2005) "A Meta-Analysis of the International Gender Wage Gap." *Journal of Economic Surveys*. 19(3): 479–511.

World Bank (2001) "Education and Training in Madagascar: Towards a policy agenda for economic growth and poverty reduction." Volume 2: Main report. Report 22389-MAG. Washington, DC: World Bank, Africa Region, Human Development IV, June.

—— . (2006) "Summary of Mauritius Investment Climate Assessment." Newsletter note 28, Africa Region, Private Sector Unit, August.

Index

Abowd, J., F. Kramarz, and D. Margolis 140
academic competence 460–1; and employment growth 462; measuring 452
access to credit, and child labor 312
accountants, higher education 73
adult literacy programs 374, 376, 381; vs. formal schooling 372; Ghana 369; and wages 378
advanced cognitive skills 380
Affirmative Action legislation 468–9
Africa Regional Program on Enterprise Development (RPED) 524
age and minimum wages *250*, 260
Agenor, R. and P. Montiel 287
agricultural sector 265; and female workers 344; growth and poverty 16–17; minimum wages *240*, *253*, 254, *255*; productivity intensive growth 32; profile of growth 29–31
Agricultural Wages Advisory Board (AWAB) 238
Ahluwalia, I. J. 271–2
Ahmedabad, India 277
Aitken, B., A. Harrison, and R. Lipsey 319
Ajwad, M. I. and Kurukulasuriya 470
Alam, A. 302
Albrecht, J., A. Björklund, and S. Vroman 426, 442, 470, 536; A. Vureen, and S. Vroman 473, 490
All-India unions 54
Anderson, K. G., A. Case, and D. Lam 96, 99
Anderson, S., A. de Palma, and J.-F. Thisse 142
Annual Survey of Industries (ASI) 40, 343

antisweatshop movement 338
apartheid 91, 99; and youth 95
Arellano, M. and S. Bond 275
Arulampalam, W. et al. 426, 440, 442
Athukorala, P. and K. Sen 275
attitudinal shift in India 42
attrition; definition 110; and education 120–1; and labor force status 120; and labor market status 115–16, 125; and location 122; and migration 118, 121; non-ignorable 112, 116–18; probability 111, *130–4*; and substitute households 114–15; and unemployment 124, *135–6*; variables influencing 119
Australian labor market 470
average wages and minimum wages *243*

'bad jobs' sector 17
Bailey, M. and H. Gersbach 319
Barro, R. 449, 450; and J. W. Lee 450
basic cognitive skills *see* cognitive skills
Basu, A. K., N. H. Chau, and R. Kanbur 237
Basu, K. 279; G. S. Fields and S. Debgupta 279
Becker, G. S. 311, 355
Becketti, S. et al 118, 122
BEEPS 454–5, 458, *459*
Belarusian Household Survey of Incomes and Expenditures (BHSIE) 500–2
Bell, L. A. 237
benefits in Mexico 219–20
Benhabib, J. and M. M. Spiegel 449
benign growth 50; period of 52
Bennett, J. and S. Estrin 158, 169
Berik, G., Y. Rodgers, and J. Zveglich 341
Berlin Wall *see* reunification
Besley, T. and R. Burgess 273–7

BGLW test 118, 119, 122–4
Bhagwati, J. 310
Bhalrotra, S. 271–2, 277
Bhaskar, V. and T. To 140;
    A. Manning and T. To 140
Bhattacharya, B. B. and S. Sakthivel 274,
    276
Bhaumik, S. K. 344
Bhorat, H. 237; P. Lundall, and
    S. Rospabe 489
Bhowmik, S. K. 277
Bihar, India 412, 422, 424
birth and employment 501–4, 514
Bishop, J. A., F. Luo, and F. Wang 429
Black, S. and E. Brainerd 341
Blanchard, O. 236
Blinder, A. S. 350
Blinder-Oaxaca decomposition *see*
    Oaxaca-Blinder decomposition
Blunch, N.-H. 368, 378, 381; and
    C. Pörtner 369
Boissiere, M., J. Knight, and R. Sabot
    371, 378
bonus payments 66–7, 83–4
Bosch, M. and W. Maloney 139
Bourdieu, P. 539
BPS (Badan Pusat Statistik) 321
Brainerd, E. 63
Brecher, R. A. 302
Breunig, R. and S. Rospabe 440
Brown, D. K., A. V. Deardoff, and
    R. M. Stern 302–3
Brücker, H. and P. Trübswetter 390
Buchinsky, M. 470, 472
budget constraints 178, 183
bundling of benefits 219, 223
Business Environment and Enterprise
    Performance Survey (BEEPS)
    see BEEPS
business, starting costs 197
Busse, M. 306
Butcher, K.-F. and C. E. Rouse 489

Cagatay, N. 502
Calderon-Madrid, A. 220
Cape Area Panel Study (CAPS)
    see CAPS
Cape Town, youth data 92
capital 172; accumulation 272–3, 275,
    283; buying 170; mobility 287–90, *293*;
    variables, human 368
CAPS 92, 95, 108
Card, D. and A. B. Krueger 152, 325, 450
Carruth, A. and A. Oswald 287

Casella, A. 310
Census of India, on child labor 406–7
Central and Eastern European Countries
    (CEECs) 451, 496
child-care 358
child labor 308, 310–13, 344, 406–7;
    India 415–17, 420; and schooling 405,
    410–11; and trade openness *315*
Child Labor Act (1986) 407
churning 170–1
civil liberties and trade openness *315*
Clarke, S. 62
classification of occupations, Kenya 265
clothing sector; average wages *336–7*; and
    foreign owned firms 333
Cobb Douglas function 211
cognitive skills 370, 373, 380; and
    employment 379; and employment
    status *375*; and wages 371
Colombia, minimum wage 252
Commander, S. and J. Kollo 451; S. Dhar
    and R. Yemstov 63
commissions for informal workers 220–1
Commonwealth of Independent States
    (CIS) 451, 496
commuting 398; in Germany 392
company performance and training
    programmes 458
comparative advantage 302, 307, 309;
    and labor standards 303–4, 306
Competitive Condition 288–9
competitive price conditions *293*
compressed wage structure 188
Computable General Equilibrium (CGE)
    16
Computer Assisted Personal Interviews
    (CAPI) 113
Consumer Price Index (CPI) 44;
    S. Africa 475
contract workers, formal and informal
    277, *278*
contracts 280–1; composition of 275–6;
    free 279
Conway, K. S. and J. Kimmel 180, 184,
    186, 193
core labor standards (CLSs) 301
core of workers 48
cost-effectiveness of adult literacy
    programs 381
cost of labor 277
Cote d'Ivoire, schooling and child labor
    405
Coulombe, S., J.-F. Tremblay, and
    S. Marchand 450–1

counterfactual wage decomposition 473
Cowan, K., A. Micco and C. Pagés 237
Cramer's rule 149, 152
Currie, J. and A. Harrison 321

Dar es Salaam 188, 190–1, 193
Dasgupta, I. and S. Marjit 277
data collection in Tanzanian study 184–5
Datt, G. and M. Ravallion 16
Datta-Chaudhuri, M. 279, 282
De la Rica, S. et al 427, 470
De Soto, H. 197, 199
Deaton, A. 176, 182
deferred payments 280–1
Dehejia, R. and R. Gatti 311–13
Dehejia, V. and Y. Samy 303–4, 305–6
demographic structure 20
dependency ratio 20
dependent children 514
Deshpande, L. K. et al 276
developing countries 173, 191, *309*;
   export performance 305
development expenditure 275
Deveraux, S. 236
dichotomous school enrollment status
   410–11
Dinkelman, T. 90
discrimination 428, 492; neoclassical
   theory 355; in private sector 440
dismissal; employer opportunism vs.
   worker shirking 280–1; notice of 282;
   restrictions on 278
distance to school and enrollment
   417–22
Dixit, A. K. and J. E. Stiglitz 142
Djankov, S. and P. Murrell 451; et al 197
Doing Business project 197
Dollar, D., G. Iarossi, and T. Mengistae
   273
domestic firms vs. foreign owned firms
   322–3
domestic industries 56
domestic work and child labor 412–13,
   423
dominant strategy equilibrium 168
Doppelhofer, G., R. I. Miller, and
   X. Sala-i-Martin 450, 451
Doyle, P., L. Kuijs, and G. Jiang 451
DRER 43–4, 52, 57; cyclicity 49; effect
   53
dualism 16
Durbin-McFadden procedure 373, 379
Dutta Roy, S. 270–1

econometric analysis of India 274
econometric model 181, 184
economic crisis *see* financial crisis
economic transformation 523
Edmonds, E. and N. Pavcnik 311, 312;
   N. Pavcnik, and P. Topalova 343–4
education attainment in 373–4; and
   attrition 120–1; Cape Town 96, *97–8*,
   99; and child labor 313; and
   employment 381; and employment
   status 368–70, *375*; and foreign owned
   firms 333; and gender 478, 489; and
   gender wage gaps 345–8, 533; and
   human capital 450; India 407–8;
   Madagascar 525; and minimum wages
   249; returns to 371; and self-
   employment 379; in S. Africa 91;
   see also schooling
efficiency units 46, 47
efficiency wage models 236, 280–1
elderly people 502
Elias, P. and M. Birch 244
employment 101, *102*; and attrition 120;
   Cape Town *100*; as a choice 472;
   decline 271–3, 275; and education 381;
   effect 145; elasticity 41–2, 49–51, 53,
   57; figures, Russian firm 67–8; formal
   and informal 153, 160, 210; growth
   51–2, 275, 278, 462, 523; growth and
   poverty *26*; intensity 20; intensity of
   growth 17, *28*; intensity vs.
   productivity intensity 29–30; Kenya
   244, *245*; and minimum wages 260;
   permanent and non-permanent 275–6;
   probability 106–7; rate, definition 19;
   rigidity in India 270–1; seeking *104*;
   see also unemployment
Employment Equity Act (1998) 468
employment protection legislation
   see job security legislation
employment status 368, 373, 374–6,
   385–386; and education 369–70;
   S. Africa youth *94;* and wage structure
   369
enforcement of child labor laws 407
enforcement of labor regulations 276–7
English skills 105; Ghana 371
enhanced wage effect 320
enterprise performance and human
   capital 464
enterprises and training programmes 455
entrepreneurial decision 200–3
entrepreneurs 159, 173; formal and
   informal 198–9, 202–3

equality of returns (ER) condition 207, 210
equilibrium 45–6, *47*; conditions 44, 222; number of employers 148–9; wages 143, 144–5
evasion of social security laws 221, 225–6; size of firms 227
evolution of employment 206
expectations 47–8
export performance 304–5; and labor standards 307–9
exposure ratio 56

factor endowments 306
factor-price ratio 47
factories, employment in India 275–6
Fallon, P. R. and R. E. B. Lucas 270
Female-coefficient, Tanzania 188
female dominance 502
female labor force participation 506, 509, *510–11*, 512, 513–14
female migration 445
female selection bias 490
female workers and agriculture 344
fertility rate 355
FGM test 116–18, 119–22
Fields, G. 533; and R. Kanbur 236
Fields, G. S. 139, 157, 192
finance constraints 172–3
financial crisis: India 343; Russia 63–4, 68, 79; Turkey 111, 122
firing *see* dismissal
firm owners 527
firms' characteristics and gender wage gaps 534
Fischer, S., R. Sahay, C. A. Végh 451
Fitzgerald, J., P. Gottchalk, and R. Moffit 118, 119
Flanagan, R. 306
flexibility 271–2, 276
Fonseca, R., P. Lopez-Garcia, and C. Pissarides 198, 211
food, price of 52–3
foreign-owned firms 333; changes in 332–3; vs. domestic firms 322–3; reasons for wage decisions 325; and training programmes 456; and wages 319–24, 338–9
formal and informal sectors 139–41; choice between 165–7; employment 144, 210; and minimum wages 255; productivity growth 291
formal employment, Tanzania 183

formal entrepreneurship (FE) curve 207, 210
formal market employers 147
formal sector: entry into 147–54, 162–3, 198; Mexico 218–19; and minimum wages *256*; wages 180
Foster, A. and M. R. Rosenzweig 287
free contracts 279
Freedom House 307
freedom of association and collective bargaining (FACB) rights 308
Friedman, E. et al 197
Full-Employment Condition 288–9, *293*
functional competence 460–1; and employment growth 462; measuring 452
functional literacy measure 373
Funkhauser, E. 177, 183, 192

Galiani, S. and F. Weinschelbaum 141
Gandhi, Indira 42
Gandhi, Rajiv 42
Garcia, J. et al 429
Gardeazabal, J. and A. Ugidos 429
GDP: Germany 389; growth 18; and human capital 450
gearing ratio 44–5, 47
gender; attitudes *499*; discrimination 468; and education 108 370, 478, 489; and migration 394; and minimum wages *248*; and public and private sectors 434, 440; and wage distributions 431
gender wage gaps 73, 79, 342–58, *436–9*, *441*, 442–3, 490–1, 497, *540*; decompositions 470; difficulty measuring 468–9; and education 533; and firms' characteristics 534; Mauritius and Madagascar 529–42; and trade competition *357*; and unobserved characteristics 354–6; *see also* wage inequality
General Entropy Index (GEI) *85*
General Wages Advisory Board (GWAB) 238, 246
German Socioeconomic Panel (SOEP) 387
Gernandt, J. and F. Pfeiffer 388, 400
Ghana Living Standards Survey 373
Ghose, A. K. 52
Gindling, T. H. 177, 183, 192; and K. Terrel 154, 237
glass ceilings 426–7, 443, *444*, 470, 537, 541
Glewwe, P. 371, 378, 381

Glick, P. 176, 182, 188, 192
Global Exchange 319
globalization 309–10; *see also* trade
  openness
Goldberg, P. K. and N. Pavcnik 286
'good jobs' sector 17, 524
goods constraint 178
grade repetition, Cape Town 96
Green, W. H. 183
Gronau, R. 177, 178
Grootaert, C. 405
gross value added (GVA) 291
growth and poverty *23*, 29, 32–3;
  causality 31–2; changes 24–5
growth, profiling 20
growth rates 48–9, *54*, 56
growth spells 21, 36–8
Guha-Khasnobis, B. and R. Kanbur
  286
Gujarat, India 273
Gunawardena, D. 470; et al 431
GVA per worker *297*

Hanushek, E. A. and D. D. Kimko 450
Harris, J. R. and M. P. Todaro 139, 157
Harris-Todaro framework 154
Harriss-White, B. 276
Hausmann, R. and D. Rodrik 158
Hazarika, G. and A. S. Bedi 405; and
  R. Otero 341
health, S. Africa 105–7
Heckman, J. J., J. Stixrud, and S. Urzua
  368, 380
Heckman procedure 500, 509
Heckscher-Ohlin trade model 302
Henderson, D. 319
heterogeneous preferences between jobs
  142
Hicksian aggregate good 177
higher education, effect of wages 73
high-skilled labor, Mauritius 523
HIV/AIDS 106–7
HLFS *128*; new 124–5
home production 178–80, 182; choice of
  activity 185
Hoover Institute, The 319
horizontal heterogeneity in worker
  preferences 141
hours-variable 188
Household Labor Force Surveys
  (HLFSs) 110, 113
households: attrition rate 115–16;
  domestic work and child labor 412–13;
  income 504, 506, *507*; multiperson 180

human capital 395, 451; country-level
  measures of 456; and employment
  growth 462; and enterprise
  performance 464; explanatio 378
Human Development Indicator (HDI)
  522
Human Rights Watch 407
Hunt, J. 496
Hutter, B. 276
Hyder, A. and B. Reilly 429, 470

ICOR *see* incremental capital-output
  ratio
IDA *see* Industrial Disputes Act (1947)
IDB 220
Idson, T. and W. Oi 324
ignorable attrition, null hypothesis 118;
  see also non-ignorable attrition
ILO 301–2; conventions 308; Report on
  Kenya 157
import penetration ratio 55–6
IMSS 219, 225, 227
income-generating activities 369
incremental capital-output ratio (ICOR)
  229, 231
Indian economic politics 42
Indonesia, manufacturing 321
Industrial Disputes Act (IDA) (1947)
  269–71, 273, 279, 282
industrial relations approach to Russian
  wage formation 63
inequality in wages 82–6
inflation: Kenya 239; Russia 62, 66–7;
  and wages 79, 86
informal entrepreneurship (IE) curve 207
informal firms: comparative size 229;
  labor costs 231; visibility 199
informal labor, demand for 222
informal market employers 147
informal production 180–1, 183, 185,
  192, 193; *see also* home production
informal sector 157–8; benefits for
  workers 223; commissions for workers
  220–1; entry into 163–4; increasing
  198; Mexico 219–20; and minimum
  wages *257*; *see also* formal and
  informal sector
informality: as a consolation prize 174;
  likely industries 230–1; as a stepping
  stone 167, 173–4
Instrumental Variables (IV) 31, 311, 313
Integrated Labor Force Survey (ILFS)
  239
intermediate social costs 165–6

International Adult Literacy Survey 450–1
International Monetary Fund 343
investment 231
Investment Climate Assessment (ICA) surveys 522, 524
investment ratio, cyclic 48–9
Isemonger, A. G. and N. J. Roberts 468
Islam 16

Janata Party 42
Jellal, M., C. J. Nordman, and F. C. Wolff 527
Jhabvala, R. and R. Kanbur 277
job security 279
job security legislation 51, 270–1, 273, 278, 281–2; negative impact on workers 279
jobless growth 41, 50; India 283; period of 51
Johnson, H. G. 302
Johnson, S., D. Kaufmann, and A. Zoido-Lobaton 197
Jolliffe, D. 176, 182, 192, 371
Jones, P. 237
Jones, R. W. 287
Juhn, C., K. M. Murphy, and B. Pierce 400
Juhn-Murphy-Pierce technique 351, *353*

Kaitz ratio 252, *263–4*
Kakwani, N., M. Neri, and H. H. Son 16
Kapeliushnikov, R. 62
Kee, H. J. 470
Kennedy, P. E. 376
Kenya, minimum age policy 237
Kerala, India 273, 276
Kijima, Y. 348
Killingsworth, M. R. 179
KILM 21–2
Kingdon, Ge. and J. Knight 90
Knight, J. B. and R. H. Sabot 188
Koenker, R. and G. Basset 428, 472; and K. Hallock 428, 536
Krishna, P. and D. Mitra 343–4
Krugman, P. 388
Kucera, D. and R. Sarna 306
Kulundu Manda, D. 239

labor, core of workers 48
labor costs: in informal firms 231; probability of fines 227–9
labor demand, changes in India 270

labor force: participation (LFP) 118; status and attrition 120; transitions for women 103
Labor Force Survey (LFS) 474
labor legislation 273, 275, 283; enforcement 276–7
labor market: and attrition 125; Australia 470; conditions, local 81–2; formal and informal 139–41; local 81–2, 86–7; status and attrition 115–16; variables 57
labor protection laws *see* job security legislation
labor standards 302; and comparative advantage 303–4, 306; and developing countries 301; and export performance 307–9; in OECD countries 305; and trade 304–5; and trade openness 309–13
labor supply 142; elasticity 143
Laffer effect 146
Lam, D., C. Ardington, and M. Leibbrandt 96, 105
Lambert, P. J. 82
Lassibille, G. and J-P. Tan 183
Latin American and Caribbean (LAC) countries 29
Lazear, E. 281
leakage 50
least absolute deviations (LAD) estimator 428
least-cost point 46
Lee, L-F. 183
Lehmann, H., J. Wadsworth and A. Acquisti 63
Leibbrand, M., C. Woolard, and I. Woolard 176
leisure 142, 184; as a normal good 189, 192; value of 203
Lemos, S. 237
levels 381–2; measures of 450, 452–4; and skill perception *459*
Levin-Waldman, O. M. 252
Levy, S. 219
Lewis, W. A. 157
Likelihood Ratio test statistics 119
Lipsey, R. and F. Sjoholm 320
literacy and numeracy evaluation (LNE) 105
literacy skills, Ghana 371
Living Standards Measurement Survey (LSMS) 412
Loayza, N. V. 157, 160, 173; and C. Raddatz 16

local labor markets 81–2, 86–7
location: and attrition 122; and
 minimum wages *251*
longevity in S. Africa 91
low-educated workers 244
low social costs 165
Luke, P. and M. E. Schaffer 63
Lustig, N. C. and D. McLeod 236

Machado, J. A. F. and J. Mata 429, 470,
 473, 539
Machado-Mata counterfactual
 decomposition 427
machine building sector, Russia 64–5
Madagascar 522, 523–4, 537; descriptive
 statistics *526*, *528*; hourly wage rate
 531
Maddala, G. S. 191
Mah, J. S. 305
Maharashtra, India 273
Mairesse, J. and N. Greenan 524
male domination 539
Maloney, W. F. 139, 154, 157; and
 J. N. Mendez 237, 252
Malysheva, M. and A. Verashchagina
 512
managerial skill 198, 199, 200–1
Mankiw, N. G., D. Romer, and
 D. N. Weil 449
manufacturing: India 50; Indonesia 321;
 output *274*, 275; women in 355
Marcouiller, D., V. R. De Castilla, and
 C. Woodruff 139
marginal cost of labor (MCL) 227
marginal revenue product of labor 324
marital status 373
Marjit, S. 286–7, 295; and D. S. Maiti
 286; S. Ghosh, and A. K. Biswas 286;
 and S. Kar 286; S. Kar, and H. Beladi
 286
market clearing condition 206
market failures 303
marriage and wages 479, 489
matching procedures 396–7
matric education, S. Africa 91
Mauritius 522–3, 537; descriptive
 statistics *526*, *528*; hourly wage rate
 531
Maziya, M. 468
Mazumdar, D. 58
McCue, K. and W. R. Reed 141
median wage vs. minimum wages 252,
 253
Melly, B. 429

Meng, X. 522, 535, 541
metal working sector, Russia 64–5
Mexico, workers *228*, 232
migration: and attrition 118, 121; female
 445; and gender 394; within Germany
 389, 392
Mincer equation 372
Mincerian income function 471
minimum wage 31, 144, 151–4, 160,
 165–6; and age *250*, 260; agricultural
 sector *240*, *253*, 254, *255*; and average
 wages *243*; compliance 244–6; and
 education *249*; and employment 260;
 and formal and informal sectors 255;
 and formal sector *256*; fraction *247*,
 252; and gender *248*; increases 146–7;
 Indonesia 321–2; and informal sector
 257; justification 265; Kenya 238–9;
 laws 325; and location *251*; Mauritius
 523; vs. median wage 252, *253*;
 negative impact 237; rationale 236;
 removal 167; and self-employment
 262, 265; and structure of employment
 261, *263*; urban areas *241–2*; variable
 328; and wage distribution 253–60
Ministry of Labor, Kenya 238
Mishra, P. and U. Kumar 344
mixed-strategy equilibrium 170
mobility 17
mobility of capital 288–90, *293*
Moll, P. G. 371, 378
monitoring parameter 199
monopsonistic competition 140, 147, 154
Montenegro, C. 435; and C. Pagés 237
Morawetz, D. 40
Morley, S. A. 236
Morocco 541
Mother-coefficient, Tanzania 188
Mueller, R. 429
Muller, C. and C. J. Nordman 527
multiperson households 180
multiple-job-holding 192; Tanzania
 184–5
Mumbai, India 278–9
Munich, D., J. Svejnar, and K. Terrell
 496, 501
Muslims in India 413–15
Mwabu, G. and P. Schultz 489

Nash bargaining solution 200
Nash equilibrium 158–9, 161, 168–9
Nash sharing rule 204
National Child Labor Projects (NCLP)
 407

National Industrial Classification (NIC) system, India 343
National Remuneration Board (NRB) 523
National Sample Survey of India (NSS) 290–1
Neumark, D. 428; and W. Washer 237
Neumayer, E. and I. Soysa 308
new industry 173; setting up 159
NIC groups 55
Nicita, A. and M. Olarreaga 343
Nielsen, H. S. and M. Rosholm 471
Nieuwenhuys, O. 412
non-ignorable attrition 112, 116–18, 124
non-wage characteristics 141
Nordman, C. J. and F. C. Wolff 541

Oaxaca-Blinder decomposition 351, *352*, 355, 427–9, 473, 534–5
Oaxaca, R. L. 350; and M. R. Ramson 534
occupations, classification, Kenya 265
October Household Surveys (OHSs) 474
OECD countries, labor standards 305
oligopsony 154
Olofin, S. O. and A. O. Folawewo 286
Omolo, J. O. and J. M. Omitti 237, 244, 260
one-bread-winner households 506
Oostendorp, R. 342
operators 489
opportunistic behavior 280–2, 283
optimum labor supply, increasing 45–6
Orszag, M. and D. J. Snower 198
Other Path, The (De Soto) 197
output effect 44
output per worker *see* productivity
over-employment 180

Paci, P. and B. Reilly 496, 500, 511
panel data 306
parastatal sector workers 188
parental employment status 376
parental occupation 369
participation condition 178
participation model 181
participation rate, women 497
part-time jobs 178
Pastore, F. and A. Verashchagina 497–8, 500, 506
Paula, A. de, and J. Scheinkman 158, 160
payroll taxation 145–6, 149–51
Pendakur, K. and R. Pendakur 426
pensions 192–3

permanent employment 51
Pham, T. H. and B. Reilly 427
Philippines 442
Pissarides, C. 198
post-reform recession, India 43
potential work experience (PWE) 501
poverty: and employment growth *26*; and growth 20–1, *23*, 29, 31–3; Madagascar 523; and productivity *25*
poverty changes: and growth 24–5; and productivity *28*
poverty reduction 16–17; and value added 27
poverty trap mechanisms 506
Pradhan, M. and A. van Soest 177, 192
Prasada R. et al 16
price effect 44, 52, 53; negative 50
price flexibility 388
Principal Component Analysis (PCA) 527, 537
private sector *54*; Belarus 498; workers 187
privileged shares 64
producer price index 44
productive assets 220, 221, 223
productivity 19–20, 232, 324–5; benefit of formal firms 160; effect of social protection 224; formal vs. informal workers 223; increasing 280; informal firms 231; loss 225; and poverty *25*; and poverty changes *28*; and wages 320, 339
productivity growth 39, 272, 287, 291; India 286; source 292; unskilled sector 290
productivity intensity vs. employment intensity 29–30
profit-maximizing conditions 222
profit stream 167
profitability: of Russian firm 64; and social programs 230
profits, informal firms 229
Programme on International Student Assessment (PISA) 452
Psacharopoulos, G. and H. A. Patrinos 371
public and private sector 430–1, *435*, 443; gender differences 434, 440
public sector 54
pure-strategy equilibrium 169–70

quantile regression (QR) analysis 428–9, 431, 470–3, *480–8*, 536–7, *538*, 539, *540*; decomposition 440

Quarterly Labor Force Surveys (QLFS),
Sri Lanka 430

race distribution, S. Africa 92–3
'race to the bottom' 301–2, 319
racial differences in education, Cape
Town 96, 99, 108
Rama, M. 237
Ramaswamy, K. V. 277
Ramstetter, E. D. 320
Rauch, J. E. 157, 160
Ravallion, M. and G. Datt 16; and
Q. Wodon 405, 408, 410
Ray, R. and G. Lancaster 410
real effect exchange rate (REER) 53
real wage growth *80–1*
Reardon, T. 176
Rebitzer, J. and L. Taylor 152
recession, post-reform, India 43
Reddy, S. G. and C. Barry 313–14
reform period 54; India 43, 344
regional characteristics *508*
Regulation of Wages and Conditions of
Employment Act (CAP229) 238, 246
resource constraints on education in
S. Africa 91
retirement *see* pensions
retrenchment 270; legislation against 279
reunification, Germany 388–90, 394, 401
rigidity 271; *see also* flexibility
Riordan 91
risk sets 119, *129*; of attrition 115–16
Rodrick, D. 305; and A. Subramanian 42
Rodriguez, G. and Y. Samy 306
rotation number 113–14
rotation plan 113, 115, *128*
rural employment and cognitive skills
379
rural industrialization 287

Saget, C. 500, 509, 511
Sakellariou, C. 431, 435, 442
salaried employment: informal 225–6;
Mexico 219
salaries 239; for informal workers 226
Salop, S. C. 82
SARE, Mexican reform 197
Sarva Shiksha Abhiyan (SSA) program
407–8
Satchi, M. and J. Temple 16
school enrollment *418*, 452
schooling: and child labor 405, 410–11,
415–17, 420; costs 412–13; formal vs.
adult literacy programs 372; S. Africa

93; and wages 376–80; and work 96,
98, 99, 101, 108; *see also* education
search frictions 197
searching 203–06
secondary enrollment 461
sectoral growth pattern 16–18
sectoral productivity, profiling 21
sectors 21
segmentation 17
selection models 472
selective attrition *see* non-ignorable
attrition
selectivity bias 431; female 490
self-employment 221–2, 239–44, 246,
369; and education 379, 381; and home
production 180; Mexico 220; and
minimum wages 262, 265
sensitivity analyses 380
severance payments 281
Shapiro, C. and J. E. Stiglitz 280
Shapley decomposition 19
shareowners 64
Sherlock, S. 279
Shishko, R. and B. Rostker 176–7, 180,
182, 184, 193
signaling effects 378
Sinha, A. and C. Adam 286
Sivadasan, J. and J. Slemrod 343
size of companies and training
programmes 456–8
skill concentration 290–1
skill levels and foreign owned firms 320
skill perception 460; and human capital
459
skilled workers 333; average wages *328*,
331–2, *335*, *337*; productivity 287, 292
skills: achieving 368; and wages 378
skills-related obstacles 458–60
Slichter, S. 139
social clause 303
social programs 229, 231–2; and
profitability 230
social protection 219, 223–4, 225, 230;
for evading salaried workers 226
social security 221–5; evading 225–6;
Mexico 218–19
Spence, M. A. 368, 378, 380
spillover wage effects 154
standard economic theory 324
Standing, G., J. Sender and J. Weeks 90
start-up costs 209–10, *213–14*, 215;
effects of increase 212
State Institute of Statistics (SIS)
see TURKSTAT

statistical twins 397, *399*, 400, 402
Statistics South Africa (Stats SA) 474
steady state (SS) condition 207, 209
sticky doors 442
sticky floors 426–7, 440–443, *444*, 470, 471, 475, 490–1
Stifel, D., F. H. Rakotomanana, and E. Celada 523–4
strategic interaction 168
Straub, S. 160
structure of employment and minimum wages *261*, *263*
subcontracting 51
surveys 113

Tanuri-Pianto, M. et al 426
tax receipts 145, 154
Teal, F. 371
tenure 395
termination *see* dismissal
Termination of Workers Act (TEWA) 445
tertiary enrollment 460–1; and employment growth 462
Theisen, T. 176–7, 182, 183, 185, 191, 192
three sector economy 288
time constraint 178
time-series analysis 306
Topalova, P. 343–4
total factor productivity (TFP) 19
trade agreements, future 313
trade competition and gender wage gaps *357*
Trade Disputes Conciliation Act (1934) 278
trade flows 305
trade and labor standards 304–5
trade liberalization *see* trade openness
trade model 306
trade openness *315*, 341, 343, 344, 356; and labor standards 309–13
trade unions 278–9; members and wages 489
training programmes 455, 464; and company performance 458; and company size 456–8; and foreign owned firms 456
transition countries 451
transition, formal to informal, Mexico 220
Trends in International Mathematics and Science Study (TIMSS) 452
Trost, R. P. and L-F. Lee 183

Tunalı, İ: and C. Başlevent 122; and R. Baltacı 111, 112
Turkish Statistical Institute (TURKSTAT) *see* TURKSTAT
TURKSTAT 110, 111, 118, 125
turnover 82
turnover of staff: Cape Town 101; Russian firm *69–70*
turnover rates, Russian firm 68
two-bread-winner households 497–8, 506, 512, 514

Udomsaph, C. C. 320
underemployment 186
unemployment 207; and attrition 124, *135–6*; Belarus 498; benefits 212, *214*, 215; duration, S. Africa 90; Mexico 220; rate 68, 209, 210, *213*; value of 203–5; *see also* employment
unions *see* trade unions
unobserved characteristics and gender wage gap 354–6
unskilled workers 244, 333; average wages *327*, *329–30*, *334*, *336*; productivity 287, 290, 292
urban areas: employment and cognitive skills 379; Kenya, wage analysis 260; minimum wages *241–2*; wages 256
utility maximizing 178, 222
Uttar Pradesh, India 412, 422, 424

Valenzuela, M. E. 502
value added and poverty reduction 27
Van Beers, C. 305, 306
variable inflation factor (VIF) test 503
Velde, D. W. te and O. Morrissey 320
Vijverberg, W. P. M. 371
virtual income 190
virtual wage rate 179–80, 182, 183, *186*, 187–8, 191

wage bill 43–5
wage decisions, reasons 325
wage dispersion between formal and informal sectors 139–40
wage distribution 348–50; gender differences 431; and minimum wages 253–60; Russian firm *67*
wage-efficiency relationship *46*
wage elasticity 512
wage-employment trade-off 48–9, 51–2, 53, 56–8
wage-equalization 183
wage growth, continuous workers 75–9

wage index 142–3
wage inequality 82–6; Germany 388, 397, *398*, 400, 402; Zambia 471; *see also* gender wage gaps
wage rates 501, *531*
wage structure: and employment status 369; Russian firm 71–3
wages 504; and adult literacy programs 378; and foreign owned firms 319–24, 338–9; Germany *391*, *393*; and inflation 86; and marriage 479, 489; mobility 74–5; nominal and real 73–4; and productivity 320; and schooling 376–80; setting 82; and skills 378; S. Africa 475; and trade union members 489; and worker characteristics 326
Weichselbaumer, D. and R. Winter-Ebmer 521

Wickramasinghe, M. and W. Jayatilaka 443
Winter, C. 490
women: in manufacturing 355; responsibilities 443, 497
Woolridge, J. M. 500
work and schooling: Cape Town 96, *98*, 99; transition 101, 108
worker characteristics and wages 326
workforce composition, Russian firm 68
World Bank 16, 271, 355, 435, 449, 525
World Development Indicators (WDI) 239
WTO conferences 301–2
Wu, K. B., V. Kaul, and D. Sankar 408

youth employment, global 90

Zambia 471

For Product Safety Concerns and Information please contact our EU representative GPSR@taylorandfrancis.com Taylor & Francis Verlag GmbH, Kaufingerstraße 24, 80331 München, Germany

T - #0048 - 230425 - C0 - 234/156/32 - PB - 9780415743570 - Gloss Lamination